The P...
Treasure...

A Discerning Traveller's Companion

David Kemp

Dundurn Press
Toronto & Oxford
1992

Editing: Doris Cowan
Design and Production: Green Graphics
Cover design: Andy Tong
Printing and Binding: Gagné Printing Ltd., Louiseville, Quebec, Canada

The publisher wishes to acknowledge the generous assistance and ongoing support of **The Canada Council, The Book Publishing Industry Development Program** of the **Department of Communications, The Ontario Arts Council,** and **The Ontario Publishing Centre** of the **Ministry of Culture and Communications**.

J. Kirk Howard, Publisher

Canadian Cataloguing in Publication Data

Kemp, David, 1936 –
          The pleasures and treasures of Britain :
a discerning traveller's companion

ISBN 1-55002-159-1

1. Great Britain – Guidebooks.   I. Title.

DA650.K45 1992   914.104'859   C92-095294-1

Dundurn Press Limited   **Dundurn Distribution Limited**
2181 Queen Street East   73 Lime Walk
Suite 301   Headington, Oxford
Toronto, Canada   England
M4E 1E5   OX3 7AD

The Pleasures and Treasures of Britain

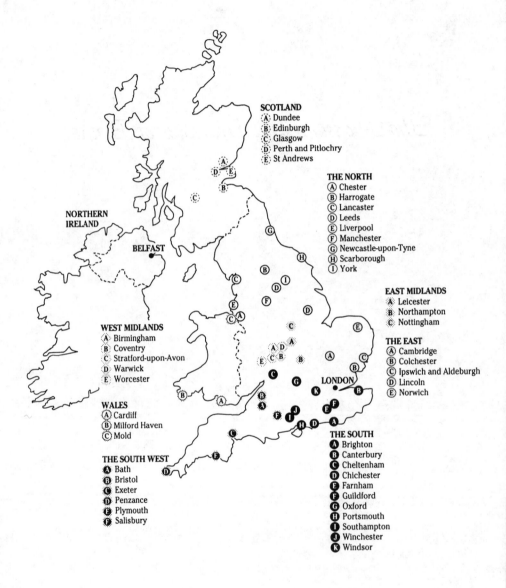

SCOTLAND
- (A) Dundee
- (B) Edinburgh
- (C) Glasgow
- (D) Perth and Pitlochry
- (E) St Andrews

THE NORTH
- (A) Chester
- (B) Harrogate
- (C) Lancaster
- (D) Leeds
- (E) Liverpool
- (F) Manchester
- (G) Newcastle-upon-Tyne
- (H) Scarborough
- (I) York

NORTHERN IRELAND

BELFAST

EAST MIDLANDS
- (A) Leicester
- (B) Northampton
- (C) Nottingham

WEST MIDLANDS
- (A) Birmingham
- (B) Coventry
- (C) Stratford-upon-Avon
- (D) Warwick
- (E) Worcester

THE EAST
- (A) Cambridge
- (B) Colchester
- (C) Ipswich and Aldeburgh
- (D) Lincoln
- (E) Norwich

WALES
- (A) Cardiff
- (B) Milford Haven
- (C) Mold

LONDON

THE SOUTH WEST
- (A) Bath
- (B) Bristol
- (C) Exeter
- (D) Penzance
- (E) Plymouth
- (F) Salisbury

THE SOUTH
- (A) Brighton
- (B) Canterbury
- (C) Cheltenham
- (D) Chichester
- (E) Farnham
- (F) Guildford
- (G) Oxford
- (H) Portsmouth
- (I) Southampton
- (J) Winchester
- (K) Windsor

CONTENTS

7. EAST MIDLANDS

8. THE NORTH

9. SCOTLAND

10. NORTHERN IRELAND

PREFACE

A long time ago, I toured the British Isles with a children's theatre company, and I vividly remember the lost feeling of arriving in a strange town on a Sunday afternoon and setting out to find a place to stay for a week. This was in the early sixties and the era of the theatrical landlady was as good as over. Impoverished thespians, of which happy band I was one, were forced to seek for shelter among the many Victorian-fronted bed-and-breakfast establishments that were (and are still) an inexpensive alternative to hotels in Britain. They are frequented by the ubiquitous commercial traveller, whose nose for cheap digs is legendary. However, if I never shared a breakfast table with anyone remotely resembling Willy Loman , it is certainly because most commercial travellers would not have been seen dead in the distinctly low-end establishments we lodged in. We had, I remember, the equivalent of $1.50 a night to splash out on accommodation, and even converted into 1990s dollars, it wasn't very much.

Another curious, or perhaps understandable, subterfuge we resorted to after learning from bitter experience, was never to mention to any landlady that we were actors. Children's Theatre gave us an easy out here. We became "visiting educational specialists," employees of the "local education authority" and even "scholastic literary representatives." What we got for our $1.50 was never much – three in a room, share the washroom and pay for a bath once a week – but I was young and the work was exciting, and I saw parts of Britain I would never have normally visited.

Looking back, I remember wishing that I didn't have to look at menu prices before entering a restaurant, and I longed for enough money to go to the theatre or the cinema and wished that I had a book that would let me know all about the places I would be interested in and not what the local information office thought I ought to be interested in.

In a perverse and odd kind of way, this is that longed-for book. Not that it's written with the pauper in mind. I've paid my dues with respect to sleeping on rubber sheets in Gloucester or under a leaky roof in Ipswich, and the combination of three-in-a-room and a weekly bath has lost its enchantment. But this book does give an extremely broad and informative overview of what you can do in a British town – a lot of the information cannot be found in the local newspaper or tourist information centre, good as some of them are. If you have any interest in culture or the arts, this book should be a valuable travelling companion.

The book is divided into ten geographic areas – the South West, the South, London, the East, the East Midlands, the West Midlands, Wales, Northern Ireland, the North and Scotland. Each town section begins with a brief and accessible historical introduction with mention made of the main places of interest. This is followed by a guided walk around the town, beginning and ending at a central parking place. The walk describes in detail how to get to most of the places mentioned previously. This is followed by a listing, with pertinent details, of museums, art galleries and public buildings.

The book also gives full details of the local professional theatre scene, while the section on cinema focuses on alternative programming as well as commercial films. Music is also well covered, with concert halls and festivals mentioned, as well as details of opera, ballet and dance. Every really good bookshop is mentioned, including secondhand and antiquarian establishments. Commerical art galleries are listed, together with their specialization, as are antique shops and markets. The restaurants listed cover a wide range of good cooking, from a budget lunch or supper to that "special occasion" meal; public houses are chosen for their ambiance and culinary value. Areas that have connections with particular writers and artists are mentioned, and a special section explores legends, fables, ghosts, characters, tall tales and unusual events of an area.

Every recommendation in every section is made without any favour being bestowed on the author. For future editions of the book, I would be grateful if readers would send their own particular recommendations with respect to any aspect of the book. A form for this purpose is included at the back of the book. Likewise, if you find that an establishment does not live up to its reputation, please let me know.

ACKNOWLEDGMENTS

To my wife, Susan, who not only managed to read my writing and
type the transcript, but who essentially edited the book,
and without whom it could not have been written.

To my father, William Kemp, who accompanied me on many of my journeys and did a
large number of "joe jobs" and lots of carrying and fetching
with supreme good humour.

To Mrs S.A. Bane and the staff of the Somerset County Library,
Frome, Somerset, England.

To the directors of tourism around the country,
especially Ron Sands of Lancaster Tourism.

To Waterstone's, Bath, for help with the bibliography.

To the Faculty of Arts and Science and the Faculty of Education,
Queen's University, for their support and help, and to the
Douglas and Art Libraries, Queen's University.

To Michael Dicketts and the staff of the Kingston Public Library,
Kingston, Ontario.

1

THE SOUTH WEST

BATH	PENZANCE
BRISTOL	PLYMOUTH
EXETER	SALISBURY

BATH

County of Avon
*Hourly train service from London (Paddington), approximately 75 minutes
104 miles (166 km) by road from London by M4*

This city on the River Avon (the Roman Aquae Sulis) was built in Palladian style in the 18th century and frequented by the fashionable and the ailing, who came to drink the waters. Bath stands on the site of Britain's only hot springs, where every day a quarter of a million gallons of water gushes out of the earth at a constant temperature of 46.5 degrees Centigrade. Legend has it that Bladud, father of Shakespeare's King Lear, discovered these springs in about 500 BC. The Romans also appreciated the bathing and curative uses of the springs, and it was they who put Bath on the map when, in honour of their goddess Minerva, they built one of the finest temples in Britain. Since 1878, when excavations began, some of the most important Roman artefacts in Europe have been recovered, and the Roman Baths remain one of the most fascinating museums in Britain.

The city continued to flourish after the Romans had gone. In the 18th century, Master of Ceremonies Richard "Beau" Nash (see Popjoy's Restaurant), dictated the rules of polite society, and architect John Wood created buildings of matching elegance in a classical style, using the local stone favoured also by the Romans: the result was basically the city we see today. Its heart was the restored 15th-century Abbey, and next to it was the social centre of the Pump Room. The 20th century has made some embellishments of its own. Bath has won many awards for floral design, and the Bath Festival (see below) has become one of the most important festivals of music in the country. There is a fascinating shopping centre where paved passages and narrow streets house small shops full of character.

WALKS

Bath is an easy city to walk, and to stroll its elegant streets is to allow its many flavours, matured over a millennium or so, to permeate. It is a city that has been much loved, and has given great pleasure in return, a city of grace, whose inhabitants seem more reluctant to leave than those of other places.

My **Bath Walk** is split into two parts. Part one takes in the Abbey, Abbey Green and Pulteney Bridge and Street. Part two takes in Milsom Street, the Assembly Rooms, the Circle and the Royal Crescent. Both start and finish at Walcot Street car park by the Hilton Hotel. You can do the both in a day, but you'll need to put your feet up in the evening.

Walk One – Turn left down Walcot Street and note the **Saracen's Head** pub on the right where Charles Dickens conceived the idea of the *Pickwick Papers*. Continue along the colonnade-fronted shops of Northgate Street to High Street. At the end of High Street by the quaint "Water is Best" statue, turn into **Bath Abbey**. The soaring west front is decorated with stone angels climbing up and tumbling down stone ladders. On one side of the churchyard is the National Trust shop and opposite are the **Roman Baths** and the **Pump Room**. Turn left into Stall Street, past the splendidly colonnaded front of the **King's and Queen's Baths** and left again into York Street. Second right is Abbey Street leading to **Abbey Green** with its great plane tree and the **Crystal Palace** pub, and then turn left through North Parade Passage to **Sally Lunn's House**. Continue into North Parade and cross the bridge. Look left at **Pulteney Bridge**, the only Florentine bridge in England with its Georgian shops and restaurants. Descend the steps to the footpath and walk towards Pulteney Bridge. Just before you get there note the **Garden Maze** laid out on the ground. Climb Pulteney Bridge steps into Argyle Street and continue across Laura Place into Great Pulteney Street, whose tall handsome houses bear plaques telling of former tenants – Napoleon III, William Wilberforce and Lord Lytton. At the end of the street is the **Holburne of Menstrie Museum**. Come back down Great Pulteney Street and note the chemist's window filled with opulent flasks and jars in Argyle Street. Cross Pulteney Bridge, walk up Bridge Street and turn right into the car park.

Walk Two – Turn left down Walcot Street, then take first right to cross Broad Street into Green Street. A medallion on the **Oliver Pub** commemorates Dr William Oliver of biscuit fame. Just around the corner, in Milsom Street, is the **National Centre for Photography** and across the road is Waterstone's Bookshop. Cross Milsom Street by Waterstone's, come back down to the junction of Green Street and turn right into Quiet Street which leads to Wood Street and Queen Square. The **Obelisk** was erected by Beau Nash in 1738 in memory of Frederick, Prince of Wales. Turn right up Gay Street beside the square to the **Circus** designed by John Wood the Elder in the 1750s: dark honey-coloured houses look inward upon a clump of ancient plane trees. Many famous people have lived here: William Pitt at No 7, David Livingstone at No 13, Clive of India at No 14 and Thomas Gainsborough at No 17. Turn left off the Circus and walk between Brock Street's smaller Georgian houses to the **Royal Crescent** – the most elegant sweep of houses in Europe. Number One Royal Crescent is beautifully restored and open to view. Return along Brock Street to the Circus and turn left along Bennett Street. On your right are the **Assembly Rooms**, once thought the most elegant in Europe, and the superb **Museum of Costume**. Turn left up Russell Street; at the top go right across Rivers Street and Julian Road (labelled Brunswick Place) and turn right down Landsdown Road. Continue over George Street and down into Broad Street. Bath Compact Discs is on your right and, a little further down, the **Bath Postal Museum** opposite the **Bath Book Exchange**, about which Dickens would have written had he seen it. At the end of Broad Street turn left into Walcot Street and the car park.

MUSEUMS AND GALLERIES

Assembly Rooms – Bennett Street, Tel 61111. Suite of 18th-century rooms designed by John Wood in 1771. Houses the **Museum of Costume** which, with period room setting and dioramas, illustrates the history of fashionable dress for men and women from the late 16th century to the present day. Recently refurbished to their original splendour. Open all week 10–5pm. There is also a fashion research centre at 4 the Circus.

Pump Room – Stall Street, Tel 444488. Overlooking the Baths. Hot spa water available. (Adjacent to the Roman Baths Museum.) One of the most elegant Georgian rooms in Europe. Open for morning coffee, lunch or afternoon tea.

Guildhall – 18th-century banqueting room. Open Mon–Fri 9–4:30.

Pulteney Bridge – circa 1771. Only Florentine bridge in England.

Bath Abbey – 15th century, built on site of Saxon abbey. Perpendicular with Norman arches. Superb stone fan-vaulting in Victorian nave.

Roman Baths Museum – Stall Street, Tel 61111. Most impressive Roman remains and artefacts in England. Not to be missed. Open daily 9–5pm.

No 1 Royal Crescent – Tel 428126. Restored Georgian residence. Among its distinguished occupants in its early years was the Duke of York who rented it in 1776. A kitchen museum in the basement has a fine collection of utensils that could have been used in any house in Bath in the 18th century. Open Tues–Sat 11–5pm (3pm in winter) Sun 2–5pm (1–3 in winter).

Herschel House and Museum – 19 New King Street, Tel 336228. Sir William Herschel's house, built in 1766. From its garden he discovered the planet Uranus in 1781. The museum houses his musical and astronomy collections as well as contemporary furniture and instruments. Sir William later became George III's personal astronomer and was knighted in 1816. Open daily 2–5pm (Sat and Sun only in winter).

Victorian Art Gallery – Bridge Street, Tel 61111. Houses the city's collection of paintings and ceramics. Of particular interest are the works of the Bakers of Bath and the famous topographical views of Thomas Malton. Open Mon–Fri 10–6pm, Sat 10–5pm.

Royal Photographic Society National Centre of Photography – The Octagon, Milsom Street, Tel 62841. Permanent collection and visiting exhibition. Housed in what was originally an 18th-century chapel. Open daily 10–5pm. Tel 460503.

American Museum - Claverton Down (4 miles–6 1/2 km), Tel 46053. The museum occupies an early 19th-century house which has the added distinction of being the place where Sir Winston Churchill made his first speech. Its aim is to show, by means of completely furnished rooms, how Americans lived in the 17th, 18th and 19th centuries. Open daily 2–5pm (Winter Sat/Sun only).

Holburne of Menstrie Museum – Great Pulteney Street, Tel 466669. Paintings by Thomas Gainsborough, Sir Joshua Reynolds and George Stubbs. Twentieth-century Craft Study Centre. The building, circa 1796, was originally designed to serve as a hotel. Open Easter–Sept: Mon–Sat 10–4, Sun 2–4 (Winter: Tues–Sat and Sun pm).

Bath Postal Museum - 8 Broad Street, Tel 460333. The museum building, parts of which date back to the 16th century, was Bath's main post office in the first half of the 19th century. The museum presents a comprehensive history of postal service including a full-scale replica of a 19th-century post office. Open Mon–Sat 11–5pm (April–Oct: Sun 2–5pm).

Beckford's Tower and Museum – Landsdown Road, Tel 336228. The tower was built in 1827 for the wealthy traveller, author and eccentric, Sir William Beckford, who had moved to Bath from Fonthill in Wiltshire. There is a large model of Beckford's Gothic Abbey at Fonthill and details of his life there, together with books by and about Beckford himself. There is a splendid view from the observation platform at the tower's summit (154 steps). Open Easter–Oct: Sat and Sun 2–5pm.

Bath Industrial Heritage Centre – Julian Road, Tel 318348. The museum building was constructed in 1777 as a real tennis court. It houses a reconstruction of the works of J B Bowler, a Victorian brass founder, general engineer and aerated water manufacturer. During 97 years of trading in Bath, the firm threw practically nothing away, and as a result visitors can see a remarkable collection of working machinery, hand tools, brasswork, patterns and documents of all kinds, displayed to convey an impression of the working life of a small provincial family business in Victorian England. Open daily 10–6pm (Winter 10–5pm).

Museum of Bookbinding – Manvers Street, Tel 466000. Bath is an important centre of craft bookbinding. Three internationally famous binding firms, those of Robert Riviere, Cedric Chivers and George Bayntum have flourished here during the last 150 years. The museum is in part of the postal sorting office and shows the history and contemporary practice of hand bookbinding. Open weekdays.

Police Museum – Bath Police Station, Manvers Street, Tel 463451. The museum tells the story of policing in Bath over a period of 150 years.

The Museum of English Native Art – The Old Schoolroom adjoining the Countess of Huntingdon's Chapel in The Vineyards, The Paragon, Tel 446020. This, the first museum of English folk painting, houses the Crane Kalman collection – a wonderful selection of 18th- and 19th-century paintings, depicting ordinary people, pursuits and incidents with a direct simplicity. Also on view are shop signs, weathervanes and country furniture. Open April-Oct 10:30-5:30 (Sun 2-6pm). Also at the same location is the **Huntingdon Centre**, Tel 333895, which is a centre for the appreciation of the history and architecture of Bath. Open

Mon–Fri 10:30–4pm.

Sally Lunn's Kitchen Museum – North Parade Passage, Tel 461634. Here in the oldest house in Bath, which is now a charming tea room, you can see in the basement how the legendary Sally Lunn created and baked her famous buns. The kitchen has some original medieval features, but mostly shows how a 17th-century cook would operate.

Geology Museum – 8 Broad Street, Tel 428144. The Bath area has been called the "birthplace of English geology," and on display are some very fine examples of the wealth of minerals, rocks and fossils that have been found in the area. Open Mon–Fri 9:30–6pm:Sat 9:30–5pm.

SALLY LUNN'S, BATH

THEATRE

Theatre Royal Bath - Tel 448844. Magnificently restored 19th-century playhouse (1805). No resident company, but it presents a year-round programme of varied theatrical entertainment which includes prior-to-London plays and musicals, touring theatre, ballet and opera and productions mounted by other regional theatre companies. Fully professional productions. A recent summer programme included Paul Scofield in a Jeffrey Archer play prior to the West End, the touring version of Willy Russell's *Shirley Valentine* and a special production of the musical *Hair*. Guided tours of the theatre available at 12 noon most Wednesdays and Saturdays. Contact Box Office.

MUSIC AND ART

The Bath Festival – Tel 463362/466411. This is one of the major musical events in the country – a celebration of classical music, jazz and visual arts, held the last week of May and first two weeks of June. Recent festivals have included Peter Donohue, Nina Simone, City of Birmingham Symphony, the Royal Philharmonic Orchestra, Marcel Marceau, Dizzy Gillespie, and the Tallis Scholars. Events are held in Bath and Bristol (see below). The **Bath Symphony Orchestra** (community based) and the **Bath University Concert Society** give regular recitals during the year, and visiting symphony orchestras play in the Abbey (see *Bath Events* leaflet from the Tourist Information Centre in the Abbey Churchyard – Bath 462831). During the period of the festival there are also many art exhibitions and especially, the **Contemporary Art Fair** with 40 major British galleries representing over 800 leading artists. Also, the **Bath Fringe** – a festival of alternative theatre, dance, jazz, poetry reading and one-person shows runs at the same time as the Bath Festival. Fringe Box Office – Tel 448243.

CINEMA

Commercial cinema at the **Beau Nash** (Tel 462959) in Westgate Street, but two more interesting cinemas – the **Little Theatre** (2 screens, Tel 66822) in St Michael's Place and **Robins** (3 screens, Tel 61506) on Monmouth Street offer programmes of interest. The Little Theatre is of special interest with many foreign-language and art films.

BOOKSTORES

Waterstone's – Milsom Street, Tel 448515. Superb, well-organized and very comprehensive. Children's store in the back.

County Bookshops – 2 The Mall, Southgate Shopping Centre, Tel 469659. Cut-price books, remainders and publishers' oddments, all at reduced price. They have another outlet at 3 Burton Street, Tel 310012, which has a similar wide-ranging selection of book bargains.

Sherratt and Hughes – University of Bath, Tel 465565. The university's bookshop.

Bilbo's – 3 New Bond Street Buildings, Tel 460829. Nicely crowded on three floors with friendly staff and a good bookshoppy feel.

One of my favourite shops is **Pennies From Heaven** just off Kingsmead Square close to the Theatre Royal. (Look for doll's house in window.) Friendly staff, nice music and excellent bargains.

For comics try **Four-Five-One Comics** at 1 Sussex Place, Claverton Street, Tel 442711.

Religious books can be found at the **Pastoral Book Centre** at 33/34 Pulteney Street, Tel 462736, New Age at **Arcania's**, 17 Union Passage, Tel 461687 and although it's hard to classify, the **Alternative Bookshop** at 15 Margaret Building Tel 334299 has much of interest.

ANTIQUARIAN AND SECONDHAND BOOKS

Bath Book Exchange – Broad Street. No telephone. Just like a secondhand bookshop from another century. Not to be missed.

Camden Books – 146 Walcot Street, Tel 461606. Old-fashioned secondhand bookshop. There aren't many left.

Derek and Glenda Wallis Antiquarian Bookshop – 6 Chapel Row, Queen Square, Tel 424677. Specializing in children's and illustrated books.

George Bayntum – Manvers Street. Rare books, first editions, beautiful bindings. Tel 466000. Also has a museum of bookbinding.

Bankes Books – 10 Brock Street, Tel 338109. Good antiquarian selection. Open by appointment only.

George Gregory – Manvers Street, Tel 466000. Large secondhand stock, good old prints.

Also in Manvers Street at No 23 is **PR Rainsford**, open usually from 10–1pm but telephone 445107 to be sure.

Robert and Susan Pyke in Claremont Road, Tel 311710, specialize in maritime subjects. Open by appointment.

Sulis Books – 2A St James Street, has a general stock and specializes in travel, topography, military, scientific, biography, literary and classic fiction.

Tyson's Books at 15 Lyme Gardens, Newbridge, Tel 20845, has a comprehensive secondhand stock plus prints, maps and engraving. Telephone first.

ANTIQUE DEALERS

Bartlett Street is your best bet. It's almost a continuation of Milsom Street at its top end and is just below Woods, my favourite restaurant. The **Great Western Antique Centre**, Tel 428731, is situated in an old department store and in its many small shops you can buy Victorian clothing, prints, buttons, pine furniture, fireplaces and railway memorabilia. The **Bartlett Street Antiques Centre**, Tel 423038, is more traditional with a wide range of less eclectic curiosities and treasure.

If you turn right at the top of Milsom Street and then turn left at the lights up Landsdown Hill and then first right down Guinea Lane you will find the **Bath Antiques Market**. Open on Wednesday only from 6:30–2:30pm, they have a wide range of over 50 dealers. If you walk east along Walcot Street past the Hilton Hotel on your right with the Abbey directly behind you, you will find the **Bath Saturday Antique Market** on your right. Open Saturday only, 7–5pm with over 100 stalls. Finally, the **Paragon Antique and**

Collectors Market is at 3 Bladud Buildings – Milsom Street and Broad Street – open Wednesday 6:30–3:30pm.

After you've looked at the antique markets, the next best accumulation of shops is Walcot Street (see Saturday Morning Antiques Market).

Illuminated Objects is at No 78, Tel 46241, specializing in 19th- to early 20th-century light fittings. **Laurence Brass** is at Nos 93-95, 16th–19th-century furniture, Tel 464057 and **Haliden** is at No 98, Tel 469240, specializing in Oriental carpets, embroideries, wall hangings and Chinese and Oriental porcelain.

Walcot Reclamation is a fascinating browse at No 108, Tel 444404, with chimney pieces statuary, Victorian baths and traditional building materials, while **Josephine** at No 142/144, Tel 445069 has decorative objects and furniture. If you continue out Walcot Street you will find London Road with **Robin and Jan Coleman** (decorative items), Tel 313791 at Pennard House, 3/4 Piccadilly London Road, **Simon Freeman Antiques**, Tel 311547, at 25 Walcot Buildings, London Road (general antiques), **David Gibson Antiques**, Tel 446646, at 2 Beaufort West, London Road East (superb long case clocks), **Jadis**, Tel 338797, at The Old Bank, 12 Walcot Buildings, London Road (18th–19th-century European and English furniture and decorative items), **Stuart King - Piccadilly Antiques** Tel 332779 at 1/2 Piccadilly, London Road East (general country, period painted pine, decorative and humorous items), **Carr Linford** Tel 317516, 10-11 Walcot Buildings, London Road (period and decorative furniture, 18th- and 19th-century and decorative items), **Pennard House Antiques** 3/4 Piccadilly, London Road, Tel 313791 (18th–19th-century pine 17th–19th-century French provincial furniture and decorative items) and **Scott Antiques**, Tel 462423 at 11 London Street (general antiques).

If you come back to the junction of Landsdown Hill and George Street and go up the hill to the Bath Saturday Morning Antique Market, you will find the Belvedere, Landsdown Road, 100 yards past Guinea Lane on the right. **Landsdown Antiques**, Tel 313417 is at No 23 (painted pine and country furniture 17th–19th century, metalware and decorative items), **Rosemary and David White**, Tel 428256 at No 27A (decorative items, 18th-early 20th century furniture and mirrors), **Gene and Sally Foster**, Tel 316216 at No 27B (patchwork quilts, decorative items 17th-19th century, Continental and English painted furniture, needlework, prints and metalware), **Frank Dux Antiques**, Tel 312367 at No 33 (Georgian oak furniture, silk pictures and glass, pottery and decorative items) and **Ann King**, Tel 336245 at No 38 (period clothes, shawls, bead dresses, linen, quilts and textiles).

As Bath is an easy city to walk around, the rest of the antique shops are listed under their respective streets. All are centrally located.

On Brock Street (between the Circus and Royal Crescent):
Alderson – No 23, Tel 421652. 17th–18th-century furniture, metalwork, glass and silver.
Helena Hood – 3 St Margaret's Building, Tel 424438. 18th–19th-century decorative items, prints, paintings, furniture, carpets and porcelain. (Located in pedestrian walkway north of Brock Street.)
Brian and Caroline Craik – 8 Margaret's Building, Tel 337161. Decorative items, metalwork, 18th and 19th century furniture.

Broad Street (parallel to Milsom Street running uphill from General Post Office):
Brian and Angela Downes Antiques – No 9, Tel 465352. Mahogany, rosewood and walnut furniture 1760–1900, porcelain clocks, boxes, brass and decorative items.
Martin Dodge Interiors – Nos 15-16, Tel 858000. 18th- and 19th-century furniture, decorative items especially papier mâché, watercolours and oils.
August and Read – No 21, Tel 448369. Regency to Victorian furniture, mirrors, oils, prints, engravings, bronzes, textiles and decorative items.
Bath Galleries – No 33, Tel 462946. Furniture, paintings, porcelain, jewellery, clocks, barometers and silver.
George Street (at the top of Milsom Street):
John Croft Antiques – No 3, Tel 466211. 17th- to early 19th-century furniture, clocks, barometers and decorative items.
Graylow and Company – 7 Princess Buildings, Tel 469859. Furniture and decorative accessories, mainly George III.
Heirloom and Howard – 12 Miles Buildings, Tel 442544. Chinese armorial porcelain, heraldic items, portrait engravings.

Quiet Street (at the bottom of Milsom Street):
Quiet Street Antiques – No 3, Tel 315727. Furniture 1750–1870, porcelain, decorative objects, caddies,

mirrors, boxes and long case, wall, bracket and carriage clocks.

Gay Street (parallel to Milsom Street off George Street):
M Sainsbury – No 35, Tel 424808. Pre-1800 antiquities. Open by appointment. **Queen's Parade Antiques** – No 35, Tel 420337. 18th- and 19th-century furniture, decorative items and period lamps.

Queen Street and Queen Square (off Gay Street):
No 12 Queen Street – 12 Queen Street, Tel 462363. Oak and country furniture, textiles, needlework and samplers.
Andrew Dando – 4 Wood Street, Queen Square, Tel 422702. English, Oriental and Continental porcelain, pottery and furniture. 17th to mid-19th century.

City Centre:
Abbey Galleries – 9 Abbey Churchyard, Tel 460565. Jewellery and silver.
Arkea Antiques – 10A Monmouth Street, Tel 429413. Just below Theatre Royal. Furniture, china, silver and clocks.
Arts of Living – 18 Green Street, Tel 464270. Persian, Afghan, Turkish, Caucasian and Turcoman rugs and carpets (off bottom of Milsom Street).
Aspidistra – 46 St James Parade, Tel 461948. Opposite Technical College. Books, prints, music, musical instruments and curiosities.
G A Baines of Bath – 14/15 John Street, Tel 332566. Parallel to and between Milsom and Gay Streets. English furniture, 18th and early 19th century.
Bath Stamp and Coin Shop - 12 Pulteney Bridge, Tel 463073. Coins, notes, medals, stamps and postal history.
The **Corridor Stamp Shop** – 7A The Corridor (just north of Roman Baths). Stamps, postcards, cigarette cards.

Good silver can be found at **M A Hughes** – 11 Pulteney Street by the bridge. Tel 465782, **Bryer's Antiques** at the entrance to the Guildhall Market, Tel 466352 and especially at **E P Mallory and Son**, 1-4 Bridge Street and 5 Old Bond Street. They also have jewellery, clocks and objets de vertu. **Beau Nash House**, Union Passage, Tel 447806 (close to Abbey) and **Anthony Em** in York Street have a very high quality stock of furniture and works of art.

ART GALLERIES

Lantern Gallery – 9 George Street, Tel 463727. Botanical, natural history and decorative old prints.
Adam Gallery – 13 John Street, Tel 480406. Specializing in 19th- and early 20th-century water colours and oils.
C.C.A. Galleries – (formerly Christie's Modern Art), 5 George Street, Tel 448121. Excellent range of contemporary paintings, prints and lithographs.
Peter Hayes Contemporary Ceramics - 2 Cleveland Bridge, Tel 466215.
Porter Design - 19 Circus Place, Tel 424910. Fine art publishers. Contemporary lithographs.
Trimbridge Galleries – 2 Trimbridge, Tel 466390. Watercolours, drawings, prints and oils, 18th to 20th century.
Nick Woodbridge – 15A George Street, Tel 338477. 18th- and 19th-century paintings and works of art especially topographical works, marine paintings and naive and primitive artefacts.
Artsite Gallery – 1 Pierrepont Place, Tel 61659. Contemporary art by national and international artists. Off Manvers Street by Railway Station.
Beaux Arts Gallery – York Street, Tel 464850. Contemporary art, sculpture and pottery.
Cleveland Bridge Gallery – 8 Cleveland Place East, Tel 447885. Major 20th-century artists in exhibition.
F-Stop Photography – 2 Longacre, London Road, Tel 316922. Exhibition of the work of young unknown photographers.
Rooksmoor Gallery – 31 Brock Street, Tel 420495. Contemporary paintings, ceramics, original prints and sculpture.
St James Gallery – 9 Margarets Buildings (near Royal Crescent) Tel 319917. Contemporary art, crafts and jewellery and ceramics.
Thursday Gallery – 2A York Street, Tel 66904. Paintings, prints and ceramics by new and established contemporary artists.
Underground Gallery – 72-74 Walcot Street, Tel 462546. Contemporary paintings, sculpture and ceramics

by established, up-and-coming and unknown artists particularly from Scotland and Cornwall.
York Street Gallery–12 York Street, Tel 447399. Contemporary paintings and ceramics.

RESTAURANTS

Popjoy's – Tel 460494. Next door to the Theatre Royal – used to be Beau Nash's house. Very elegant surroundings. The ghost of Nash's mistress, Julianna Popjoy, is said to visit sometimes. Interesting English cuisine. Good reports on the duck and the fruit tarts for dessert. Open Tues–Sat 12–2 and 6–10:30 (No Sat lunch).

Theatre Vaults – Tel 442465. French-style bistro in the vaults of the Theatre Royal. Good for pre-theatre supper. Excellent table d'hôte menu. Open 12–2 and 5:30–10.

Moon and Sixpence – 6A Broad Street, Tel 460962. Bistro – English/French cuisine. Reasonably priced. More formal in the evening. Good for lunch. Open 12–2:30 and 5:30–10:30.

Woods – 9-13 Alfred Street, Tel 314812. Excellent brasserie. French cuisine with divine desserts. Try their brown bread ice cream. Open 12:30–2 and 6:45–10:15.

Priory Hotel – Weston Road, Tel 331922. Very elegant, very good. Nouvelle French cuisine, expensive. Beautiful surroundings. Accommodations. Open 12:30–2 and 7–9:15 all week.

Dover House Restaurant - Royal Crescent Hotel, Bath, Tel 319090. You wouldn't expect a discreet restaurant/hotel in the centre of one of the most famous crescents in Europe to be inexpensive, now would you? For the very special occasion. However, the cuisine will never match the architectural setting, however good it may be.

Garlands – 7 Edgar Buildings, George Street, Tel 442283. Operates in premises recently vacated by the Clos du Roy (see below). Early days, but has great promise. Open Tues–Sat 12:15–2:15 and 7–10:30.

Clos du Roy-at Box House, Tel 744447. The village of Box is 3 miles east of Bath on the A4. Very elegant, very chic and very expensive. For the special occasion perhaps. Open 12–2:30 and 7–10.

PUBS

Garrick's Head – Tel 44819. Next door to Theatre Royal, beautifully restored by theatre designer Carl Toms. Meals, bar snacks and drinks.

Crystal Palace – Tel 423944, Abbey Green. A nice sheltered courtyard for the summer. Modernized Georgian. Good bar food.

Saracen's Head – 42 Broad Street, Tel 426518. Beamed bars with lots of atmosphere. Excellent value cold buffet lunches.

Claret's – Kingsmead Square, Tel 466688, is a wine bar with excellent food at moderate prices.

ARTISTIC ASSOCIATIONS

Chaucer's Wife of Bath would have lived in Northgate Street in medieval Bath; Oliver Goldsmith, author of *She Stoops to Conquer* (1773), William Congreve, who wrote *The Way of the World*, in 1700 and John Gay of *Beggar's Opera* fame (1728) all spent time writing in Bath while Richard Brinsley Sheridan often stayed with his father at New King Street, and *The Rivals* is set in the city. Jane Austen lived at 4 Sidney Place and The Paragon; *Northanger Abbey* (1818) satirizes Bath society. Sarah Siddons, the great actress, also lived in The Paragon around 1800. Charles Dickens created the character of "Little Nell" while visiting Walter Savage Landor in 1838. Landor lived in St James Square.

At Widcombe (formerly a village but now a part of the city) Henry Fielding wrote *Tom Jones* (1749) and based the character of "Squire Western" on his neighbour who lived at Widcombe Manor.

During its heyday as an artistic resort in the 18th century, Bath was a centre for portrait painting. The most celebrated artist actually to settle here was Thomas Gainsborough, who arrived from his native Suffolk in 1759 and stayed for 15 years. It is not known exactly where he lived, but Landsdown Road and the Circus are areas in which he probably had homes. Joseph Wright of Derby arrived in 1775 hoping to build a clientele to rival Gainsborough's, but he was unsuccessful and returned to Derby after two frustrating years. Thomas Barker was a landscape painter greatly influenced by Gainsborough. Though little known today, Barker was rich and successful during his 47-year sojourn in Bath. He lived at Doric House on Sion Hill, and there is a landscape mural by him on the ground floor. Walter Sickert, the leading British Impressionist, loved Bath and often visited the city. He spent the last five years of his life at St George's Hill House in Bathampton and he died there in 1942. When in the city, he loved to paint Pulteney Bridge; the combination of water and architecture reminded him of his beloved Venice.

EPHEMERA

Three culinary delights to try are a chocolate "Bath Oliver biscuit," available from gift shops in Milsom Street, a "Bath bun," best taken with morning coffee in the Pump Room (they have a string trio playing which is very "Palm Court"), and a "Sally Lunn," a cross between an English muffin and a scone (Bath's answer to the French brioche), which is best sampled with afternoon tea at – where else? – Sally Lunn's house, the oldest house in Bath (circa 1482), situated at 4 North Parade Passage. There's even a museum in the basement in which can be seen the remains of a Roman inn (circa 200 AD), a medieval abbey kitchen (circa 1150) and the original Georgian kitchen, all of which existed at one time on this site.

Halfway down Milsom Street, as you pass the Museum of Photography, look up at the façade on the second floor and you'll see the words Circulating Library and Bookshop – one of the interesting reminders of the days of Sheridan, Goldsmith and Jane Austen.

Bath Green Park Station, Green Park, opened in 1870, is architecturally the finest provincial station in Great Britain. The buildings are of Bath stone with a single-span glass-roofed train shed. The station ceased to operate in 1966 and, after becoming semi-derelict, it was bought and restored by Sainsbury's; the train shed is now used as a car park for their supermarket built over the original track area. The entrance block accommodates public meeting rooms, craft stalls and a restaurant.

The Theatre Royal was a popular venue in the 19th century for touring productions of Shakespeare. The actors were paid on Saturday afternoon so that they could settle up with their landladies before moving on to the next town. One Saturday, with *Richard III* due to be presented at the evening performance, the actor playing the Duke of Gloucester devoted his money to a more gratifying cause than paying for his lodging, and made his entrance in *Richard* in a visibly inebriated state. The gallery took one long look at him and with one voice started yelling, "Get off, you're drunk!" Gloucester steadied himself, pulled himself erect to his full height, and in a voice that rang through every corner of the house replied, "What? Drunk? Me? If you think I'm drunk, you just wait until you see the Duke of Buckingham." As a footnote, it must be stated that this story has been attributed to practically every 100-year-old theatre in the British Isles.

The legend of the discovery of Bath's curative springs is a fascinating one. Prince Bladud contracted leprosy and was banished from court by his father. Before he left his mother gave him a ring to remind him that he could return home should he ever be cured. Shunned by everyone, Bladud became a swineherd, but the animals entrusted to his care also caught the disease. To prevent their owner's finding out he drove the animals over the Avon, crossing it at a place which is still called Swineford. One day Bladud left the swine unattended. Maddened by the disease the beasts panicked and rushed up the valley, plunging at last into a black evil-smelling bog. With great difficulty, Bladud managed to haul them out and discovered that they were no longer leprous. Wherever the muddy water had touched his own skin, he too was clean. He immersed himself and emerged cured. Joyfully the Prince returned home where, even though he was ragged and unkempt, his mother's ring quickly identified him. Wells were sunk into the bog and the curative properties of the waters of Bath are still famous.

TOURIST INFORMATION BUREAU: The Colonnades, 11-13 Bath Street, Bath, Avon, BA1 1SW. Tel (0225) 462831

BRISTOL

County of Avon
120 miles (192 km) from London on the M4 and M32
Train from London (Paddington) approximately 60 minutes

Bristol's origins and development differ greatly from those of England's other major historic cities. There was no Roman settlement here, and it was neither an ancient cathedral city nor a county town. Bristol owed its existence entirely to its geographical position and to trade and manufacture, and this remains true today.

In Saxon times, lying as it did at the junction of the River Avon and its tributary the Frome, the town was easily defensible, as the river's meandering course acted as a moat. Later the Normans recognized this and built a castle at Bristol, but it was adventurous voyages overseas to capture trade that had by 1337 established Bristol as the wealthiest provincial town in England. In 1216 Bristol was prosperous enough to have its own mayor and by 1373 was granted county status, the first English borough to receive such a distinction.

By the 15th century, Bristol merchants were trading with Ireland, France, Spain, Portugal and Iceland: cloth was the principal export and wine the principal import. Through their trade with Iceland for fish, Bristol merchants heard the legends of the uncharted lands to the west and, stimulated by the thought of new fishing grounds and markets, they began to promote voyages of discovery. In 1497, John Cabot sailed west from Bristol and actually touched the North American coast at Newfoundland. His second expedition a year later disappeared, but English claims to North America were based on his initial voyage. The famous painting "Cabot's Departure" can be seen at the Council House on College Green.

Henry VIII's dissolution of the numerous religious houses ensured that Bristol, elevated by Henry to the status of a city in 1542, gained a cathedral (the former medieval abbey of St Augustine) and also meant that a great deal of land, formerly religious estates, became available for development. Further expansion took place when Oliver Cromwell demolished the castle and many new streets and squares were laid out. From the site of the castle, the city pushed out towards Clifton, and many buildings – the Infirmary, John Wesley's New Room (the first Methodist Chapel), John Wood's Exchange and the Theatre Royal – date from this period.

The driving force behind all this development was the growth of trade, notably from the mid-17th century with Virginia, the Carolinas and the West Indies. So excellent was the seamanship of Bristol vessels that a new phrase, "all ship shape and Bristol fashion," passed into the language. Thousands emigrated through the port of Bristol during the 17th century. Some sought religious freedom - Bristol was a prominent centre for nonconformity. In 1665 the first Quaker meeting house was established followed in 1681 by the founding of a Quaker colony in Pennsylvania by William Penn of Bristol.

Bristol grew rich on rum, slaves, sugar and tobacco – the staples of transatlantic commerce – and by the 18th century was the leading English city and port outside London. New industries were founded. In 1730 Walter Churchman of Bristol was granted the first patent to make chocolate. This was later taken over by Joseph Fry, and later the Rowntree family also established a chocolate factory in the area. In 1786 the Wills family began its connection with the tobacco industry and the family's philanthropy was to finance the building of the university tower – the Wills Memorial Building.

It was inevitable that Bristol's domination of trade and commerce would decline after the Industrial Revolution bypassed the southwest of England. The West Indian trade receded, the North American trade never recovered from the War of Independence and Bristol merchants found they could not compete with rivals in other ports (such as Liverpool). The long-awaited improvement of the Port of Bristol did very little to alter the downward trend.

It became very clear that new initiatives were needed, and they were forthcoming. From Bristol, John Loudon McAdam spread his ideas of road surfacing throughout the country at the end of the 18th century. Isambard Kingdom Brunel designed the *Great Western*, the first wooden steamship to cross the Atlantic, in 1838. He followed this in 1845 with the *Great Britain*, the first large iron-hulled screw-driven steamship. In 1853 he began the construction of the *Great Eastern*, the largest ship of its day. Although not a success as a passage ship, it was used in 1866 to lay the first transatlantic telegraph cable. Brunel was also the chief engineer of the Great Western Railway, which soon extended east to London and west to Penzance. He constructed all its viaducts, bridges and tunnels, including the Royal Albert Bridge across the River Tamar in Cornwall. In his spare time he designed the Clifton Suspension Bridge in 1829, perhaps the most widely known Bristol landmark.

Today the focus for the port's activities has moved to Avonmouth on the city's outskirts. The Royal Edward Dock was opened in 1908 and the £37-million Royal Portbury Dock was opened by the Queen in 1977.

Engineering is now Bristol's main industry, with aerospace predominating. There are many other important manufacturing interests including food, drink, tobacco, paper, printing and packaging, chemicals, paints, plastics, clothes, footwear and furniture. With the expansion of the old Bristol Dock as a focus for leisure activity, tourism has increased rapidly. In spite of its position as the largest financial centre outside of London, the old, the quaint, the peaceful and the historic still exist and can be sought out by the discriminating visitor.

WALKS

Because of its size and the number and variety of its attractions, I have not designated one walk for Bristol. I have instead divided the city into six areas, each quite easy to find one's way around in without specific directions. If you start at **Temple Meads and Redcliffe** (1), move into **Castle Park and Broadwood** (2) and then into **City Centre** (3) you will, at the very least, have taken half a day. **College Green, Park Street, Brandon Hill** and the **University** (4) will take up another half day (if you don't stay too long at any one spot) and the **Harbour** (5) and **Clifton** (6) are included as separate sections.

Walk Area 1 – *Temple Meads and Redcliffe*
Alongside **Temple Mead Station** is **Bristol Old Station**, built by Brunel in 1839. The original terminus of the Great Western Railway was 80 feet (24.3 m) longer than Bristol Cathedral and is the oldest surviving major railway terminus in the world. If you arrive in Bristol by train, a good idea is to go to the new ferry landing stage nearby and use the regular boat service to the harbour and city centre. The **Great Train Shed** with its mock hammerbeam roof, the widest single span of the age, is the home of the **Exploratory**, a hands-on science centre, with experiments, games and puzzles.

Chatterton House – Once the home of poet Thomas Chatterton (1752–1770). The house is maintained as a museum and is open by appointment (see Artistic Associations). Call the City Museum at (0272)223571 for details.

Redcliffe Parade – A row of beautifully restored 18th- and 19th-century houses. This clifftop promenade offers one of the best views of the harbour and the distinctive sandstone cliffs on which the parade stands give the area its name.

Temple Church – Just off Victoria Street, founded in 1145 by the Knights Templar. Virtually destroyed by enemy attack, the tower leans four feet (1.2 m) out of the perpendicular and has done so since circa 1400. Nearby is **St Thomas**, a fine 18th-century church built on Norman foundations. The Organ Galley, built in 1728, is one of the finest in the country.

Church of St Mary Redcliffe – Described by Queen Elizabeth I in 1574 as "the fairest, goodliest and most famous parish church in England," it was begun in 1280. The church was greatly enriched when William

Canynge, who was twice Member of Parliament for Bristol and mayor no fewer than five times, gave up all his worldly possessions to become a priest, singing his first mass in St Mary Redcliffe in 1467. This event is commemorated every Whit Sunday by the Rush Sunday service, when the lord Mayor and city councillors attend the service in full civic dress and walk over a chancel strewn with rushes, medieval style. Canynge's tomb is in the church, as is the tomb of Sir William Penn, whose son founded the Quaker colony of Pennsylvania. Look for the magnificent hexagonal outer porch and the **Handel Window**, where eight passages from *The Messiah* commemorate the great composer's ties with the church.

Walk Area 2 – *Castle Park and Broadmead*
Broadmead, like the adjoining Castle Park, was largely destroyed during the last war and was redeveloped as the city's largest shopping area. Apart from Marks and Spencers, however, I think the best shopping is to be found in Park Street and Queen Street.

Quaker's Friars – In the centre of the shopping precinct, in one of the service courts at the rear of the shops, are the cloisters of an old Dominican friary founded in 1227. In the 17th century, the Society of Friends (Quakers) acquired the buildings as a meeting house and used them until 1956. William Penn, founder of Pennsylvania, was married here in 1696, as was George Fox, the founder of the Quaker sect in 1669. Today, the **Bristol Tapestry**, which depicts the city's history over the last 1000 years, can be seen here. Open Mon–Fri 1–4:30pm, Sat 9:30–12:30am.

The New Room is John Wesley's Chapel, Tel 264740. The first Methodist church in the world opened here in 1739. Look especially for the double-decked pulpit, from which John Wesley preached, and the old Galleries. Open Mon–Sat 10–4:30pm.

A walk through the Arcade takes us to the Horsefair. In ancient times this was the scene of the world famous eight-day St James Fair, which was held annually for 500 years and only discontinued in 1838. **St James Church**, nearby, is claimed to be the oldest in Bristol, having been founded as a Benedictine priory in 1088 and systematically dismantled by Cromwell in 1656. The area was developed as the business and shopping centre of the city until devastated in the Second World War. The remains of the 14th century **St Peter's Church** are preserved as a reminder of this destruction. It is now a pleasant park.

Walk Area 3 – *City Centre*
The **Statue of Neptune** underlines Bristol's links to the sea, as do plaques commemorating such Bristol luminaries as John Cabot, and Samuel Plimsoll (see below). There are statues at the quayhead of Edward Colston, the benefactor, and Edmund Burke, the statesman, who was MP for Bristol in 1775.

The **Hippodrome** and **Colston Hall** (see below) should be noted.

St Stephen's Church was built at the expense of John Shepward, merchant and mayor of Bristol, in the 15th century. There is also a monument to commemorate Martin Pring, who discovered Plymouth Harbour in the USA, where the *Mayflower* anchored. Earlier, Pring had sailed with Sir Walter Raleigh.

All Saints Church is a Norman foundation with an 18th-century tower and a cupola dating from 1807. It was a meeting place for the medieval Guild of Kalendars. John Michael Rysbrack, the Antwerp sculptor, fashioned the fine effigy on Colston's tomb in 1725. All Saints is now an urban studies centre. Open Mon–Sat 8am–7pm. Tel 277977.

St Mary-on-the-Quay – Colston Street, was originally built in 1840 as a chapel for the followers of the evangelist Henry Irving, but is now a Roman Catholic Church.

St Nicholas Church Museum – St Nicholas Street (see Museums)

Christ Church – Close to St Nicholas, the church is easily recognizable by its colourful 18th-century quarterjacks (mechanical figures striking the bell on either side of the clock), loaned to the church by the Corporation at a nominal twelve and a half pence a year. The poet Robert Southey was born in nearby Wine Street and baptized here before the church was rebuilt in 1791.

St John's Church in Broad Street is built over the sole surviving remains of the city's medieval gateway. The church dates from the 14th century and its narrow nave is the original thickness of the medieval wall.

St Nicholas Market – Originally built in 1745 as a fruit and vegetable market, it has now expanded to include flowers, meat, fish, antiques, crafts, bric-à-brac, jewellery and ephemera. Bounded by Corn Street, High Street and St Nicholas Street. Open Mon–Sat 9–4pm.

Corn Street – The banking centre of Bristol for over 200 years. At the top of the street was the centre of the medieval city. At the junction of Corn Street, Broad Street and Wine Street, three of King Richard II's supporters were executed on the orders of Bolingbroke, soon to become Henry IV. (See Shakespeare's

Richard II, Act 3, Scene 1.)
Corn Exchange - Built by John Wood the Elder (see Bath), in 1743, it now forms part of St Nicholas' Market. The **Nails** stand on the pavement outside of the Exchange. These four bronze pillars, dating from the late 16th century, served as trading tables on which merchant completed their money transactions; hence the saying "to pay on the nail."
Old Council House – Built in 1827 by Robert Smirke; stands on the opposite corner to All Saints Church. A council house has stood here since 1552.

Walk Area 4 – *College Green, Park Street, the University and Brandon Hill*
The **Lord Mayor's Chapel** – at the bottom on Park Street, is all that remains above ground of the medieval Hospital of the Gaunts, founded in 1220. Since 1722 the chapel has been the Bristol Corporation's official place of worship - the only civic church in England. There is fine 16th-century stained glass and a beautiful fan-vaulted ceiling.
The Council House – built between 1935 and 1956 (the Second World War and its aftermath delayed its construction), is neo-Georgian and not to everyone's taste, but it does have a nice sweep.
Bristol Cathedral – A mixture of architectural styles, it was founded in 1140 as an Augustinian priory and is one of Britain's lesser-known cathedrals. The chapter house, in my opinion, has the finest Norman ceiling in the country. The candlesticks of 1712 were a thanksgiving donation by the privateers who rescued Thomas Selkirk (see Ephemera – the Llandoger Trow).
Bristol Cathedral School – Refounded in 1542 by Henry VIII, this is Bristol's only royal education foundation. Its origin lies in the grammar school of the original priory. A school has existed on this site for over 850 years.
Park Street and its extension **Queen's Road** offer the best shopping in Bristol with Park Street probably being the city's most famous street.
Wills Memorial Building, University of Bristol, was completed in 1925. It was financed by G A and H H Wills, the tobacco magnates, as a memorial to their father. The university refectory, which is housed in the building, is closely modelled on the Doge's Palace in Venice.
Berkeley Square – Tranquil 18th-century square. John Loudon McAdam (see introduction) lived in No 23.
Victoria Rooms – Fronted by fountains, the building boasts both assembly rooms and a theatre and was built in 1841.
Royal West of England Academy – Queen's Road. The magnificent interior is frequently used for art exhibitions.
Brandon Hill – A hill fort existed here during the Civil War (1642–52) and traces of it remain. Today the hill is dominated by the Cabot Tower, a monument built to commemorate the fourth centenary of John Cabot's voyage to North America.
Church of St George – Built in 1823 by Robert Smirke, this was the last church in Bristol to be designed on a classical model. William Friese Green, inventor of cinematography, was married there in 1874 and owned a studio in nearby Queen's Road.
Bristol University – Formerly the 19th-century University College, attained university status in 1909 and was the first university in England to offer drama as a discipline.

Walk Area 5 – *The Harbour*
Historic Harbour of Hotwells is bounded by Hotwell Road and Cumberland Road.
Dock Cottages – Dating from 1831, they form one of the most picturesque parts of the harbour.
Bristol Packet – A narrowboat or barge. Offers tours around the historic harbour. There are numerous small public houses (see Pubs).
Port of Bristol Workshops offers a treasure house of industrial archaeology. Much of the area is now a leisure centre for sailing, water skiing and boating of all kinds.
Historic Harbour of St Augustine's Beach is the part of the harbour extending right up to the city centre. The **Youth Hostel** is here, also the **Watershed** and **Arnolfini Arts Centres** (see Cinema) and the **Bristol Industrial Museum** (see Museums).
Historic Harbour at King Street and Welsh Back – During the reign of Queen Anne (1702-1714), **Queen's Square** was the largest square in Europe. Many of the original buildings were destroyed in the Reform Riots of 1831, but the rebuilt houses are also beautiful. No 37, an original building, was where one of the first American Consulates was established in 1792, while No 29 was the birthplace of Dr Richard Bright,

pioneer of kidney medicine. There is a splendid equestrian statue of King William III by John Michael Rysbrack.

King Street – one of Bristol's finest historical streets, laid out in 1663. The pink coloured building at the end of King Street is the **Merchant Venturer's Almshouses,** founded in the 15th century and restored in 1699 by the great Bristol benefactor, Edward Colston. Next door is the **Old Library** (now a restaurant), formerly used by Coleridge and Southey. The Palladian style **Hall of the Guild of Coopers** is the façade and entrance to the **Theatre Royal.**

On the corner of the harbour end of King Street is the **St Nicholas Almshouse,** whose courtyard contains a surviving bastion of the 13th-century town wall. The **Llandoger Trow** is worth a visit (see Ephemera) and behind it is the **Granary,** an old grain warehouse, now a disco, whose exuberant brick style was known as "Bristol Byzantine." **Welsh Back** is an old mooring area and its warehouses are now being converted into studios and apartments. **Bristol Bridge** is the oldest bridging point into the city, dating from Saxon times. The present bridge was built in 1768, although the Victorian iron superstructure, added to support the widened road, obscures the original lines. Adjacent to the bridge is the **Bristol Bridge Tavern,** which is noted for jazz, the **Lightship,** a pub built on a converted lightship and a centre for hiring rowing boats, which is a nice way to view the harbour.

Walk Area 6 – *Clifton*
As the prosperity of Bristol increased in the late 18th century, the wealthy began to move out to Clifton. The elegant Windsor Terrace and Cornwallis Crescent date from this time. Royal York Crescent and the Paragon were built a few years later.

The Roman Catholic **Cathedral of Saints Peter and Paul,** consecrated in 1973, has a spacious, open-plan interior.

Clifton College – A famous public school, founded in 1862. Its former pupils include Sir Henry Newbolt, Sir Michael Redgrave and John Cleese, who first conceived his "silly walks" at school (my speculation). The school still flies the Stars and Stripes on Independence Day in memory of its wartime service as General Omar Bradley's headquarters. (See Ephemera.)

Bristol Zoo – Just down the road from the college and one of the finest and most popular in the country.

Clifton Suspension Bridge – Probably Bristol's most distinctive landmark. Two hundred and forty-five feet (73.5 m) above water and with a 702-foot (210 m) span, the bridge was designed by Isambard Kingdom Brunel. Work began on it in 1836 but it was not officially opened until December 8, 1864, five years after Brunel's death. (See Ephemera.)

Near the bridge, on the Downs, is the **Observatory.** Originally a snuff mill, the present building was rebuilt after a fire in 1829 as a tower and observatory. There is a camera obscura in the tower and a giant's cave beneath, which was used as a hermitage.

MUSEUMS AND GALLERIES

City of Bristol Museum and Art Gallery – Adjacent to the University, Tel 223571. Open all week 10–5pm. Applied art: European ceramics, glass, textiles, metalwork and furniture dating from the 17th century to the present. Glass includes a number of important items of Bristol glass. Excellent ceramics. Furniture displayed in the **Red Lodge** and **Georgian House** (see below). Archaeology and history: good collection of antiquities from Egypt. Also a Polynesian collection and local Roman artefacts. Geology: The Bristol district is of special geological interest and there are good collections of fossils and an excellent minerals gallery. Oriental art: internationally significant collection of Oriental art with the largest collection of Chinese glass in the world. Natural history: excellent gallery of the natural history of southwest England. Be sure to see "Alfred," a magnificent gorilla who lived for many years at the Bristol Zoo. Fine art: good collection of 16th- to 20th-century French painting. Delacroix, Renoir and Seurat are all represented. An altarpiece by the 16th-century Venetian artist Antonio da Solario is especially fine. There is a magnificent collection of paintings by members of the Bristol School of Artists.

St Nicholas Church and City Museum – St Nicholas Street (Broadmead). Open Mon–Sat 10–5pm. Of special interest is the altarpiece by William Hogarth (1697–1764), painted for St Mary's Redcliffe. The church was constructed in 1762–69 and houses the **Bristol Brass Rubbing Centre.**

The **Georgian House** – 7 Great George Street (off Park Street). Built for a wealthy sugar merchant circa 1790, the house contains many original features. Beautifully furnished in Georgian style. Open Mon–Sat 10–1 and 2–5pm.

SS GREAT BRITAIN

BRISTOL

The **Red Lodge** – Park Row (University). Built circa 1590 as one of two lodges to the Great House, which stood on the site of the Colston Hall. Extensively altered in 1720, the Great Oak Room, with its original plasterwork, panelling and stone chimneypiece, is superb. Furnished in 17th-century oak upstairs and early 18th-century walnut and gilded pieces in the later rooms. From 1854 to 1919, the house served as the first girls' reform school in Britain and one room is maintained in memory of its founder, Miss Mary Carpenter. The school was financed originally by Lord Byron's widow. Open the same hours as the Georgian House.

Bristol Industrial Museum – Historic Harbour, St Augustine's Reach, Princess Wharf. Open Sat–Wed 10–1 and 2–5pm. Closed Thurs and Fri. Contains a wide range of transport, maritime and industrial exhibits of local interest including the Rolls-Royce collection of Bristol aero-engines and a full-size engineering model of a Concorde supersonic airliner.

Maritime Heritage Centre – Wapping Wharf, Gas Ferry Road (Historic Harbour, Hotwells). A collection of ship-building memorabilia from medieval times to the present day. Centrepiece is the SS *Great Britain*, Isambard Kingdom Brunel's magnificent ship, the first ocean-going ship to be built of iron and driven by a screw propeller. Open daily 10am–6pm.

Bristol Harbour Railway – The new Wapping Station and a refurbished stretch of track links the **Maritime Heritage Centre** to the **Industrial Museum**. The locomotive "Henry" (1937 Peckett 0-6-0) is steamed on occasion.

Harvey's Wine Museum – Denmark Street (College Green), Tel 277655. The 13th-century cellars of Gaunt's Hospital now house Harvey's Wine Museum. Displays of ancient corkscrews, bottles, decanters and a fine collection of 18th-century glass. Complimentary glass of sherry at the end. Open by appointment; Friday without prior appointment.

The Exploratory – The Great Train Shed, adjacent Temple Meads Station, Tel 252008. Hands-on science centre. Experiments, games and puzzles. Open Wed–Sat 10–5pm, Sun and Bank Hols 11–5pm.

Chatterton House – Redcliffe Way (close to Temple Meads). Once the home of Thomas Chatterton, the boy poet, who was born in 1752 at the school house in Redcliffe. Open by appointment. Phone Bristol Museum at 223571.

National Lifeboat Museum – St Augustine's Reach (off Wapping Road). The only one of its kind, the museum contains examples of different types of lifeboats, engines, photographs and models depicting the history of lifeboats and lifeboatmen. Open daily 10:30–4:30pm year round.

THEATRE

Theatre Royal – King Street. Tel (0272)250250 for 24-hour booking service. The home of the renowned Bristol Old Vic Company, one of England's top professional repertory theatres. It is the only surviving example of the large town theatre of the 18th century. The original Georgian auditorium is nothing short of breathtaking. For those interested, backstage tours are available every Friday and Saturday at noon. Most of the great actors of the 18th and 19th centuries played at the Theatre Royal – Mrs Siddons, Kean, Kemble, Macready, Hepry Irving and Ellen Terry - the only notable exception was David Garrick who did, however, tour the building before its opening and pronounced himself much pleased.

The Bristol Old Vic was founded in 1946 and has become internationally famous for the high quality of its productions. The company has toured to many parts of the world – from India and Sri Lanka to North and South America and the Middle East – and has appeared three times at the Edinburgh Festival. A number of its major successes have transferred to London, including the record-breaking *Salad Days,* Iris Murdoch's *A Severed Head, The Killing of Sister George* by Frank Marcus, *Conduct Unbecoming* by Barry England and *Born in the Gardens* by Bristol-born Peter Nichols. The company's classical productions have also been seen many times in London's West End.

Many of today's leading actors have been members of the Bristol Old Vic Company, including Sir Michael Hordern, Barbara Leigh-Hunt, Peter O'Toole, Beryl Reid, Dorothy Tutin, Susannah York, Donald Sinden, Donald Pleasance, John Neville, Felicity Kendall, Jeremy Irons, Timothy West, Prunella Scales and Paul Eddington.

The Bristol Old Vic Company also runs the New Vic, a small studio theatre which is one of the most exciting small performance venues in the country. Productions are often mounted here jointly with other touring or provincial repertory theatres and have included works by Athol Fugard, Nick Dear and Claire Luckham. Main-stage productions are generally a mixture of classical and modern works. Recent seasons have included productions of Shakespeare, Oscar Wilde, Arthur Miller, George Farquhar and Lanford Wilson. There is also a very useful restaurant (see Restaurants).

The Bristol Old Vic Trust also runs the Bristol Old Vic Theatre School, which opened in 1946 and is situated on the edge of Clifton Downs in premises bought with profits from one of the company's biggest successes, Julian Slade's *Salad Days.* Student performances are given in the Theatre Royal and the New Vic (generally at the end of June) and in the school`s own theatre, the **Redgrave Theatre** in Percival Road, Clifton, Tel 743384. Distinguished graduates of the school include Annette Crosbie, Robert Lang and Jane Lapotaire.

Bristol Hippodrome – The Centre, Tel 299444. The largest of Bristol's theatres, the Hippodrome is an Edwardian theatre with a seating capacity of 2000. Pantomime has always been a popular feature here, as well as seasons of ballet, opera, West End productions and first-class touring companies. Recent seasons have included regular visits from the Welsh National Opera, the London Festival Ballet and the musicals *42nd Street* and *Evita.*

The **Hope Centre** – Hope Chapel Hill, Hotwells, Tel 215271, is a community arts centre as is the **Albany Centre**, Shaftesbury Avenue, Montpelier, Tel 542154. These centres offer regular performances by small-scale touring companies. A sampling of recent programming found plays by Caryl Churchill and Vladimir Mayakovsky, and Tony Harrison's *The Passion.* Visiting companies included Spare Tyre Theatre, Cog Theatre and Medieval Players. Performances are usually on the weekends, as Monday to Thursday is taken up with a wide range of community leisure activity. There are also occasional performances of blues, jazz and folk.

Bristol University Drama Department – also gives occasional performances in its Studio Theatre in Park Row. For information call Bristol University at Tel 303030.

MUSIC

Colston Hall – City Centre, Tel 223682. Colston Hall is the major concert hall in the region and offers the widest variety of music entertainment from symphony concerts, light entertainment, jazz and rock to wrestling tournaments. The BBC makes frequent broadcasts from the hall and visiting orchestras generally include a series by the Bournemouth Symphony Orchestra, the London Philharmonic, the Royal Philharmonic and international ensembles such as the Leningrad Symphony Orchestra. Bristol's own orchestra, the Philharmonia of Bristol, also plays five or six concert series at the hall. Rounding out the rich musical tradition of the hall are concerts by the Bristol Bach Choir and the Bristol Choral Society and Orchestra, among others. Bristol Opera, an amateur company performing Grand Opera, can be seen at the Victoria Rooms Theatre, Queen's Road.

St George's, Brandon Hill, is the southwest's finest new concert hall. This Waterloo Church dates from 1823 and was designed by Sir Robert Smirke. The best known concerts are on Thursday lunchtimes which are regularly broadcast by the BBC. St George's mostly caters for solo instrumental and chamber ensembles but there is the occasional jazz concert. Recent visitors have been the London Mozart Players, the Fine Arts Brass Ensemble and the Alberni String Quartet.

Bristol University – Also offers a varied programme of concerts at various locations around the university. Evening concerts are given by the University Choral Society, the University Symphony Orchestra and the University Wind Band. There are also solo recitals and an attractive series of lunchtime concerts in the Wills Memorial Building which are free. Call the university at 303030 or pick up a brochure at the Tourist Information Office.

CINEMA

Commercial Cinema:

Odeon – Union Street, Broadmead. Three screens. Tel 290882.

Cannon – Frogmore Street, City Centre. Two screens. Tel 262849.

Cannon – Whiteladies Road (continuation of Queen's Road). Three screens. Tel 733640.

Cannon – Henleaze. Three screens. Tel 621644.

Gaiety Cinema – Wells Road. Tel 776224.

Concorde – Stapleton Road. Tel 510377.

Alternative Cinema:

Watershed Media Centre – 1 Canons Road (on Historic Harbour just off City Centre). Tel 253845. Britain's first media and communications centre featuring two cinemas, a gallery, a bar and a restaurant. Screenings are generally twice nightly at 6/6:30 and 8/8:15. Excellent programme of modern and classical films from Britain and around the world. Very good talks and courses on photography, video and television. There are also films for children and late-night screenings. Two galleries which mount exhibitions of (mostly) photography. One of the most exciting arts experiences in the south of England.

Arnolfini – 16 Narrow Quay (just across the harbour from the Watershed and next door to the Tourist Information Centre). As exciting and challenging as the Watershed in a different way. A cinema shows excellent films at 6/8:30pm. Arnolfini Live focuses on the fascinating genre of performance art. There are monthly talks by architects, arts workshops, a bookshop and three galleries with constantly changing and fascinating exhibitions.

BOOKSTORES

George's of Bristol – 89 Park Street, Tel 276602. A Blackwell Bookshop, probably the best and most comprehensive. It has four branches grouped at the top of Park Street: **Computer Bookshop** at 87, **Academic Bookshop** at 81, **Arts Bookshop** at 75 and the **Antiquarian Bookshop** at 52. The main branch is at 89 Park Street.

Chapter and Verse – 86 Park Street, Tel 293042. Crowded but incredibly friendly. I've often found books here that have been sold out in George's. Excellent service and a delight to browse in. A favourite of mine.

Sherratt and Hughes – 111/114 The Horsefair (Broadmead). Tel 272614. Serves both the High Street trade and University campuses. Well organized and comprehensive.

Waterstone's – 27–29 College Green (bottom of Park Street), Tel 250511. Excellent stock, knowledgeable service. A comparatively new arrival on the scene. The firm is excellent overall.

Claude Gill – 47–49 Union Street (Broadmead), Tel 299512. Good for technical books and a good general stock on two floors in spacious surroundings.

1/2 Price Books - 71 Park Street, Tel 265565. Excellent for browsing. Often wonderful bargains, especially if your taste is eclectic.

ANTIQUARIAN AND SECONDHAND BOOKS

Wise Owl Bookshop – 26 Upper Maudlin Street, Tel 262738. Books on all subjects and a fine specialized stock of music, books on music and the performing arts.

John Roberts Bookshop – 43 Triangle West, Clifton, Tel 268568. Secondhand and antiquarian. Topographical prints and maps.

Patterson and Liddle – 2C Chandos Road, Redland, Tel 731205. Carefully selected stock of books on many subjects, especially railway and aviation. Good stock of local prints and maps.

Bristol Books – 5 North Street, Bedminster, Tel 634716. Large stock of antiquarian and secondhand books. Special interest in literary criticism, language, linguistics and philosophy.

Ut's Bookshop – 68 Park Row, Tel 272996. Secondhand books. Foreign language books a specialty.

ART GALLERIES

Ginger Gallery – 84 Hotwell Road (in Floating Harbour). Paintings, prints, jewellery, ceramics, enamels, sculpture and photography. A very eclectic collection of modern works. Open Tues–Fri 10–4:45pm and Sat 10–5pm. Closed Mondays.

Pelter/Sands Art Gallery – 43–45 Park Street, Tel 293988. A large-scale commercial contemporary gallery on two floors in Park Street. Work shown includes 18th, 19th and 20th century. A stock of fine quality period oil paintings is always on hand, as well as regular exhibitions of contemporary painting and sculpture. Excellent quality.

The Eye Gallery – 36 Frogmore Street (near Colston Hall), Tel 221515. Contemporary art, ceramics and sculpture.

Bristol Guild - 66/70 Park Street, Tel 265548. In some ways, Bristol's most fascinating shop. Designer modern furniture, china, glass, fine crafts, regular art exhibitions. The Bristol Guild of Applied Arts was founded in 1908 and was born out of the Arts and Crafts movement led by William Morris (1834-1896). Not to be missed.

ANTIQUE DEALERS

Abbascombe Pine – 4 Upper Maudlin Street, Tel 299023. Refinished pine furniture. Some reproductions.

The Barometer Shop – 3 lower Park Row, Tel 272565. Self-explanatory.

Bizarre Antiques – 208 Gloucester Road, Bishopston, Tel 427888 (day) or 503498 (evening). Lots of general antiques. Seven day service.

Robin Butler – 20 Clifton Road, Tel 733017. Specializing in Georgian antiques.

Clifton Antiques Market – 26/28 The Mall, Clifton, Tel 734531. Forty dealers selling a wide range of antiques and bric-à-brac. Restoration workshops, buying, plus a coffee shop.

J Anthony – Felton, Tel (027587)2792. Timepieces of all kinds from all periods. Clocks, barometers, watches. Near airport.

Victoria's Emporium – 9 Perry Road, Tel 265982. Great for browsing. Bric-à-brac of all kinds.

Pastimes - 22 Lower Park Road, Tel 299330. All types of militaria.

RESTAURANTS

Bistro Twenty One – 21 Cotham Road South, Kingsdown, Tel 421744. At one time was one of the best bistros in England, but recently under new management which is stamping its own authority on the menu. Crowded and sometimes a bit uncomfortable, but the food is still excellent. Fresh fish from Cornwall – Squid Provencale is wonderful and the best end of lamb with honey and ginger could hardly be better. Open Mon–Sat: Lunch 12–2:30, Dinner 6:30–11:30. No Saturday lunch.

China Palace – 18A Baldwin Street, Tel 262719. Long menu of Cantonese and Szechuan dishes. Does not compromise to western taste I'm glad to say. Large and traditional. Open Mon–Sat noon–2:30 and 6–11:30pm. Sun noon–11:30pm.

Edwards - 24 Alma Vale Road, Clifton, Tel 741533. An oak-panelled restaurant tucked away in a narrow street. French cooking with English variations. The 17th-century pea soup with mace and spinach is well spoken of, as is the Irish stew. Open 12–2:30 and 7–10:30 Tues to Sat. No Saturday lunch.

Ganges – 368 Gloucester Road, Horfield, Tel 428505. Vividly decorated Indian restaurant with an interesting cuisine conceit. The restaurant tries to offer dishes from the regions through which the sacred river flows. Chicken tikka and lamb passanda are good. Open all week noon–2:15 and 6–11:30.

Harvey's – 12A Denmark Street, Tel 277665. As one would expect, the wine list is exemplary. There is a large bill of fare. The ambience is discreet and formal, very business-oriented but not stuffy. The set lunch is good value. (See Harvey's Wine Museum, above.) Open Mon–Sat (no Sat lunch) noon–12:15 and 7–11:15 (open 6:30 Sat).

Jameson's – 30 Upper Maudlin Street, Tel 276565. A friendly local bistro opposite Bristol Royal Infirmary. Salads are strong and good value. Open Tues–Sat for dinner only 7–11pm (Fri and Sat 11:30pm).

Trattoria Da Renato – 19 King Street, Tel 298291. Lunch and dinner. Italian cuisine, convenient for Theatre Royal.

TSMV Lochiel - Along from the Watershed Arts Centre. A former Scottish mail packet now converted to a floating restaurant and inn.

Malacca Restaurant – 89 Whiteladies Road (opposite Cannon Cinema), Tel 738930 and **Malaysian Satay House** – 13A Small Street, Tel 290051. I happen to be fond of Malaysian cuisine; here are two good places for those with similar tastes.

Bloomers Restaurant – King Street, Tel 291111. Useful for an after-theatre supper as the restaurant is a stone's throw from the Theatre Royal. Housed in the **Old Library**, which was once used by Coleridge and Wordsworth.

The **Siddons Buttery** – Theatre Royal, King Street. If you can't wait till after the show, the Buttery is good value for a pre-theatre supper. Excellent value and a nice roof garden in the summer. Open for lunch as well.

Glass Boat Restaurant – Welsh Back, Tel 290704. Elegant Continental dining in a converted boat.

PUBS

Ye Shakespeare – Victoria Street (Temple Meads). One of Britain's oldest inns dating from circa 1400.

Le Chateau Wine Bar – 32 Park Street, Tel 268654. Has the ambience of a 19th-century drinking parlour or salon. Very good food. Wide variety of wine by the glass and continental beers. Very handy for exhausted shoppers.

The Pump House – Merchant's Road (Historic Harbour, Hotwells). Once the main pumping station for the harbour, now beautifully restored. Outside tables in the summer especially attractive. Lunch time bar food.

Naval Volunteer – 17–18 King Street. Simple but with considerable character.

Nova Scotia – Merchant's Road (across the harbour from the Pump House). A traditional harbourside pub with outside tables in the summer.

The Lightship – Welsh Back. Converted lightship with cocktail bar, pub and disco.

Old Duke – King Street (across from the Llandoger Trow). Superb live traditional jazz every evening and Sunday lunchtime. Good value pub food.

Assize Courts – 15 Small Street. Close to City Centre. One the site of a merchant's house with upstairs assembly room where Elizabeth the First is said to have dined in 1574.

Bristol Clipper – Prince Street (close to Arnolfini Arts Centre). Old beamed pub in harbour. Bar food very good, if a bit pricey.

ARTISTIC ASSOCIATIONS

Joseph Cottle was a poet and publisher who had a bookshop on the corner of High Street and Corn Street. He was a friend of Wordsworth, Southey and Coleridge. He published *Lyrical Ballads* in 1798, and gave advances on their poetry to both Coleridge and Southey, which enabled each of them to marry. When Wordsworth arrived at Cottle's shop with his sister, Dorothy, in 1796, he finished his famous poem, "Tintern Abbey" in Cottle's parlour. The Wordsworths had been on a walking tour of the Wye Valley.

Charles Dickens acted in the Victoria Rooms in the mid-19th century while Peter Mark Roget, of Roget's *Thesaurus* fame, worked as a doctor in the city around the same time. Thomas Chatterton, the English poet, was born in 1752 in the School House in Redcliffe, where his father was a teacher (see Museums). While still a boy and living in Bristol, he wrote a number of poems, couched in elaborately archaic spelling, that he declared to be the work of one Thomas Rowley, a non-existent monk, poet and antiquarian of the 15th century. These literary fabrications are distinguished by their poetic genius. His clever deception was successful for a while, though finally exposed by Thomas Tyrwhitt and

Thomas Warton in 1797. In despair at his poverty after moving to London, he killed himself at the age of 17 by taking poison. Chatterton was a favourite figure of the English Romantic poets, becoming for them the prototype of neglected genius. The Pre-Raphaelite painter, Henry Wallace, is best known for his painting, *The Death of Chatterton,* which can be seen in the Tate Gallery, London.

The Bristol School of painters established itself about 1815 and centred around the artists Edward Bird and the Irish-born Francis Danby. The group produced imaginary landscapes in monochrome wash, often with fantastic architecture and exotically dressed figures. Their paintings of sites along the Frome and Avon rivers and of local beauty spots such as the Nightingale Valley and Leigh Woods were highly imaginative, as befitted a group who believed that landscape should be "a poetical shelter from the world." The areas mentioned, together with Wickham Bridge in Stapleton and the now ruined Snuff Mills, are still visited as local beauty spots. After the death of Bird in 1819, Danby became the Bristol School's dominant artist. In spite of this, he never quite settled down in the city; he moved house frequently and left Bristol altogether in 1824, heavily in debt. Danby had a taste for the epic as well as the idyllic and tackled spectacular subjects such as *The Opening of the Sixth Seal* and *The Delivery of Israel out of Egypt.* Samuel Colman, a painter with an extraordinary, apocalyptic imagination was a Bristolian who also painted extravagant subjects, but Danby's most gifted follower was Samuel Jackson, who, unlike his mentor, stayed in Bristol and earned a good living as a drawing-master and painter of topographical watercolours. He lived at No 3 Cotham Vale. William James Miller was born in Hillsbridge Parade in 1812. As a painter he was noted for his fresh and direct style and his Oriental scenes are especially well thought of. He lived on College Green and in what is now the White Hart Pub in Park Row. He was only 33 when he died. Perhaps the most interesting artist living in Bristol today is the land artist, Richard Long. Long's *River Avon Driftwood* in London's Tate Gallery is composed of pieces of driftwood laid in concentric circles on the floor. His work has been inspired by such West Country landmarks as the Avon Gorge, the ithyphallic Cerne Abbas Giant in Dorset and the wilder expanses of Dartmoor. He has a romantic fascination with the primeval elements of the environment.

EPHEMERA

Clifton Suspension Bridge (see under Clifton) spans the Avon Gorge. On the Bristol side of the gorge, and nowhere else in England, grows the scarlet lychinis known as the Flower of Bristowe. Bristowe was the earlier form of the city's name. The present "l" is a quirk of the Bristol dialect that also turns "ideas" into "ideals" and "bananas" into "bananals." Daredevil pilots have flown beneath the span of the bridge and suicides have jumped from it. The bridge's most famous story concerns Sarah Ann Henley who, in 1855, jumped off the bridge after a lover's quarrel but was gently parachuted down by her voluminous petticoats to the mud below – she lived to be 85.

At Clifton College there is a plaque commemorating the highest individual cricket score ever made. On the college grounds in 1899, A E J Collins made 628 not out. To give that score some context, 100 runs is considered an achievement, 200 is a rare score, while in the last 50 years only a handful of players have scored 300 runs or more.

The Llandoger Trow, Historic Harbour, King Street and Welsh Back, is an inn with a series of romantic associations to match its appearance. Its name derives from the sailing barges which once plied between Bristol and the Welsh coast. The inn is said to have been the haunt of pirates and was suspected of being R L Stevenson's model for the Admiral Benbow in *Treasure Island.* Moreover, it is also thought to have been the scene of interviews between Daniel Defoe and Alexander Selkirk. Selkirk was put ashore on the Juan Fernandez Islands in 1705 and remained there for four years. His adventures suggested to Defoe the story of Robinson Crusoe.

Christmas Steps (far end of City Centre) is one of my favourite Bristol locations. Built in 1669 at the personal expense of Jonathan Blackwell, a wealthy wine merchant, the area exudes an almost medieval air. The steps are flanked by old houses which accommodate stores selling prints, antiques, bric-à-brac, antique jewellery, stamps and two shops which sell brass instruments. At the top of the Steps is the Chapel of the Three Kings of Cologne, built in the 1480s by John Foster, the founder of the adjacent Foster's Almshouses and mayor of Bristol in 1481. The warden of the Almshouses has the key of the tiny chapel, measuring just 18 feet by 22 feet (5.4 m by 6.6 m). The Three Kings are the wise men of the nativity, and their original shrines are in Cologne Cathedral. The Almshouses, though a 15th-century foundation, were rebuilt in the 19th century in a style best described as Burgundian Gothic, and would make a wonderful setting for *Romeo and Juliet.*

In St Stephen's Church (off City Centre) there is a monument to Edward Blanket, a Bristol wool merchant who is said to have given his name to the bed coverings. At the quayhead in the city centre, next to Neptune's statue, there is a plaque to commemorate Samuel Plimsoll, a politician and social reformer, best remembered for his strenuous campaign to prevent shipowners from sailing undermanned, unsafe and over-insured ships. His Parliamentary Bill of 1876 gave government powers of inspection and obliged all ships to carry a mark (the Plimsoll line), showing the waterline at maximum loading. A plimsoll is also a rubber-soled canvas shoe beloved of yachtsmen and English schoolchildren. I'd like to think Samuel gave his name to that as well.

Finally, in Broad Street (city centre), one should note the striking art nouveau façade of the former Edward Everard printing house, built in 1900. It is decorated with Carrara marble-ware tiles and includes figures representing literary symbols as well as William Morris, the 19th-century arts and crafts revivalist, and Johannes Gutenberg at his printing press in the 15th century.

TOURIST INFORMATION BUREAU: 14 Narrow Quay, Bristol, Avon, BS1 4QA. Tel (0272) 260767

EXETER

London 172 miles (275.2 km) by M4 and M5
Regular train service from London (Paddington) approximately 2 hours 30 minutes

Exeter has been inhabited for over 2000 years. Tradition has it that the Celtic settlement of Exeter was besieged by the Roman general Vespasian in the year 49. Roman occupation certainly began in the year 50 and Exeter, or Isca Dumnorium, became the administrative centre for Devon and Cornwall. The name Isca is still used by a number of businesses in Exeter today. The Romans built massive walls around the city, but when they withdrew from Britain in the 5th century the walls fell into disrepair, allowing the Danes to capture the city with ease in 876. King Alfred got rid of the Danes the following year, and fortified the walls. When the Danes attacked again in 1003 it was only through the treachery of the city reeve (he actually opened the gates for them) that the city again fell.

After the Norman invasion, Exeter became a dangerous centre of Saxon resistance, which forced William the Conqueror to lay siege to the city in 1068. An honourable surrender was agreed but William was taking no chances and work was begun immediately on Rougemont Castle. The Gatehouse still stands at the top of Castle Street and is one of the finest examples of Norman military architecture in existence.

In medieval times a stone bridge was built across the River Exe, replacing the wooden one which the Romans almost certainly constructed. You can see the old stone bridge in a park by the river.

Exeter proclaimed a mayor in 1200 – one of only three English cities to do so, and indeed the city's allegiance to the Crown was twice marked by the gift of a sword, one from Edward IV in the 15th century and another from Henry II in the 16th century. Work was begun on Exeter's canal in 1564 and when it opened in 1566 it once again brought maritime trade to Exeter (the river had been impassable to ships since the end of the 13th century).

Devon's wool industry flourished in Tudor times and Exeter became a rich trading city and a major port. The famous sea captains of Devon – Sir Francis Drake, Sir Walter Raleigh, Sir Martin Frobisher, Sir John Hawkins and Sir Humphrey Gilbert – were often seen at Mol's Coffee House in Cathedral Yard and the nearby Ship Inn was a favourite haunt of Sir Francis Drake. "Next to my own ship I do most love that old Ship in Exon," he wrote. Loyalty to the Crown was again evident when England was threatened by invasion in 1588 and Exeter sent three ships, armed and manned at the city's expense, to fight against the Spanish Armada.

At the outbreak of the Civil War in 1642 the traditional loyalty to the Crown became deeply divided. First the Parliamentarians lost the city to the King's forces in 1643 (it became Royalist headquarters in the west) and then, in the winter of 1645, the Royalists themselves were forced to seek an honourable surrender. During the period of Royalist occupation, Charles I's Queen gave birth to Princess Henrietta in the city and, when the monarchy was restored in 1660, Charles II soon visited the city. He knighted the mayor and presented the city with a portrait of his Exeter-born sister. It can still be seen in the Guildhall.

James II was a less popular monarch than Charles and many Exeter men joined the Duke of Monmouth's rebellion in 1684. After Monmouth's failure to win the crown the infamous Judge Jeffreys held one of his "Bloody Assizes" in the city. Eighty men were hanged. In 1688 William of Orange spent twelve days in the city after landing at Brixham – he received an enthusiastic welcome from the citizens of Exeter, which encouraged him to continue his triumphant progress to London. In the early years of the 18th century Exeter's commercial prosperity was at its height. Ships sailed and unloaded on the canal, the wool trade flourished and trade with Holland, Portugal, Spain and Italy thrived. Decline in prosperity came at the end of the 18th century. Competition from Yorkshire towns hit the wool industry, the new larger ships could not use the canal and when the railway reached Exeter in 1844 it spelled the end of Exeter as a port of any real importance.

Exeter suffered considerable damage during the Second World War, because Hitler had ordered the destruction of the most beautiful and historic cities of England. The claim of the Third Reich that "Exeter was a jewel and we have destroyed it" was, however, somewhat of an exaggeration. One bomb fell on the Cathedral making the choir unusable, but the damage done has been completely restored and today the Cathedral Church of St Peter dominates the city, as it has done for 800 years.

The Cathedral as it appears today essentially dates from 1369, but there were earlier buildings on the site, including a monastery in 670, a minster in 932 and a church built by King Canute (see Southampton) in 1019. Nothing remains of these earlier places of worship. The Cathedral nave has the longest stretch of vaulting anywhere in the world (300 feet/ 91.2 m). The church was thoroughly restored by Gilbert Scott in the years 1870–77. Among the features of interest are the 15th-century clock, the John Loosemore Organ (1665) and its famous corbels (wood or stone decorated supporting projections). A rather splendid one is near the pulpit and depicts the tumbler who did acrobatic feats to show his love for Mary, the mother of Christ. (See Cathedral Library below.)

The city's most attractive area is the Cathedral Close which is flanked by the Georgian red brick terraces of Southernhay. Barnfield Crescent just to the northeast is also Georgian. Mol's Coffee House, mentioned earlier, is now an art shop and you can visit the room on the first floor where it is believed Drake, Hawkins and the others used to meet. The Cathedral Library, which is open to the public, contains priceless Anglo-Saxon manuscripts. The porticoed Guildhall in the high street has an excellent 15th-century roof and panelling. St Mary Arches, built of red Devon stone, is the most completely Norman church in Devon while St Mary Steps has an entertaining clock and the steep and cobbled stepcote was medieval Exeter's "high street." Adjacent to St Mary Steps is an Elizabethan house which was moved to this site when it was threatened with destruction by road development. Just a short walk down Fore Street is the Quay, a reminder of Exeter's past as a prosperous port. There is a splendid customs house dating from 1681 and the impressive 19th-century warehouses are being renovated as part of the Exeter Riverside project. The part-cobbled quayside was used as a location for the BBC production "Onedin Line" and indeed smallish ships still bring timber and oil up the five-mile (8 km) canal. The quay is the site of the Exeter Maritime Museum and is dotted with interesting pubs (see below).

WALK

Exeter Walk – As this is such a lovely city the walk I have described is quite long (3 miles/4.8 km). If you wish to break it in two, do so at the *.

Start at the multi-storey car park in Paul Street. Turn right into Paul Street and continue into Bartholemew Street East. You will see a section of Exeter's **Roman Wall** on your right and a restaurant that was once a malthouse. Follow the road around to the left and then turn right into Fore Street where you will find **Tuckers' Hall**. This is a reminder of Exeter's days as a wool centre. It is the hall of the Guild of Weavers, Fullers (one who cleans and scours cloth) and Shearsmen, founded in 1489 and still in operation today. At the foot of the hill, turn left into West Street. The sandstone church of **St Mary Steps** has quarter-jacks that strike the hours and opposite is **The House that Moved**, a timber-framed house that

MOL'S COFFEE HOUSE, CATHEDRAL CLOSE
EXETER

was moved on rollers to its present site in 1961 as its former location was threatened by road building. Beside the church is the flight of steps that gave the church its name. This was the centre of medieval Exeter and even today the area is redolent with atmosphere. Cross the busy Western Way and go down Cricklepit Street to the Quay, which lies beside the River Exe. Note the splendid 17th-century **Custom House**. You can take a ferry across to the **Exeter Maritime Museum**. Return via the footbridge and turn right and then left up Quay Hill. Turn right into lower Coombe Street and cross the small car park to the underpass. At the end of Coombe Street turn left into South Street. Continue across the road into North Street and then turn right into Paul Street. * Go to the end of Paul Street and turn left into Queen Street. The **Royal Albert Memorial Museum** is close by. Just past the museum turn right into **Northernhay Park**, said to be one of the oldest parks in England as it was laid out in 1612. There is a splendid **War Memorial**. By the memorial, turn right through an arch in the old city wall and walk into **Rougemont Gardens**, once the moat of Rougemont Castle. Take the left-hand footpath to the **Museum of Costume**. All that remains of **Exeter Castle** is a sandstone Norman gateway, while behind it, on the site of the Castle's keep, is the 18th-century **Assize Court**. Turn right into Castle Street, then into the High Street, where in a little alley adjacent to Boots, you will find the **Underground Passages**. Cross High Street into Princesshay, which is the oldest pedestrian shopping precinct in the country. Turn right into Post Office Street, where there is a fine long section of the old city wall. Turn left into Bedford Street and right into Southernhay West. The wide green is lined with fine Georgian houses. Turn right into the Cathedral Close and on into the Cathedral Yard and the Cathedral itself. The Elizabethan **Mol's Coffee House** is in one corner, close to the Royal Clarence Hotel and the **Ship Inn**. Cross Cathedral Yard into Broadgate and then turn right into High Street. The **Guildhall** is on your left. Note the splendid buildings at the corner of High Street and Queen Street. Turn left into Gandy Street, which is now a narrow pedestrian precinct, and then turn left again in Upper Paul Street. Cross Queen Street and return to the car park where the walk began.

MUSEUMS AND GALLERIES

St Nicholas Priory – Mint Lane off Fore Street, Tel 265858. The museum is the 15th-century guest hall of the former Priory built over a Norman undercroft. It is furnished with period fittings. Open Tues–Sat 10–5pm.

Royal Albert Museum – Queen Street, Tel 265858. This is one of the best Victorian buildings in the city (1864). Excellent collection of natural history, archaeology and ethnography. There is some attractive Exeter silver and also clocks, watches, lace, costumes and pottery, most with a local flavour. The Fine Art galleries specialize in works by Devon artists. Open Tues–Sat 10–5pm.

Rougemont House Museum – Rougemont Gardens, Castle Street. Tel 265858. This elegant house, built in 1769, makes a fine setting for a history of costume from the 1740s to the present day. Each room represents a different period, with models wearing the clothes of the time in appropriate backgrounds. Two rooms are devoted to lace and lacemaking with special attention to the lace produced at nearby Honiton. Open Mon–Sat and Sundays in July and Aug.

Guildhall – High Street, Tel 265858. The Guildhall is a 12th-century hall with a Tudor portico and is probably the oldest civil building still in use as a court and for city council meetings. Included among the items of historical significance are the sword presented to the city by Lord Nelson, the battle ensign of HMS *Exeter* sunk during the Second World War and the portrait of Princess Henrietta mentioned above. Open Mon–Sat 10–5:30 except when in use for civic functions.

Exeter Maritime Museum – The Quay, Tel 58075. The setting for a museum containing some 100 to 150 boats couldn't be better. The warehouses, cellars and canal basin provide a wonderfully atmospheric environment for the large and very beautiful exhibits. This is a "please touch" museum. You are invited to push and pull, clamber and climb and in general do all the things you will automatically want to do. Exhibits range from a birchbark Algonquin Indian canoe to an enormously heavy Danish steam tug – the *St Canute*. For me the highlight is the Hong Kong fishing junk – *Keying Two*. More than a boat really, it's a floating home. It's easy to imagine husband, wife, grandparents, children, grandchildren, aunts, uncles, dogs, cats, chickens and ducks all crammed inside. When you think of it that way it doesn't seem so big somehow.

Underground Passages – High Street (see Ephemera). Open Tues–Sat 2–5pm, Tel 265858.

THEATRE

Northcott Theatre – Tel 54853. The region's only full-time professional venue was built in 1967. It is situated on the university campus at the edge of the town but is fully independent. Over the years it has built up an enviable reputation in the theatre world for the excellence and originality of its productions. Productions by the resident company are supplemented by regular visits from touring ballet and opera companies. The theatre is a new building with excellent seating and sight lines. Among recent productions on the main stage by the resident company have been John Osborne's *The Entertainer*, Alan Ayckbourn's *A Small Family Business* and, as part of a summer season, Ben Travers' *Thark*, Agatha Christie's *Witness for the Prosecution* and Jerome K Jerome's *Three Men in a Boat*. Visitors to the main stage have been the Royal National Theatre, dance and opera companies and a variety of musical groups; at Christmas, there is generally a traditional pantomime. More experimental productions are to be found on the smaller stage of the **Northcott Studio**. There is a bar, and hot and cold food is available before and after each show and at lunchtime.

Exeter and Devon Arts Centre – Tel 219741, located at Gandy Street in the City Centre, stages a wide range of music, dance, film and theatre events, courses and workshops. The Arts Centre also houses an exhibition gallery and information centre.

Exeter Festival – Tel 211080, held in the late spring, has grown into a major and extremely popular event. The exciting two-week programme includes concerts by major orchestras, jazz, folk, theatre, exhibitions, sport, craft fairs, community plays and a beer festival with a torchlight procession and firework display providing a spectacular finale. Recent performers have included the Royal Philharmonic Orchestra, Jessye Norman, Hinge and Brackett, George Melby and the Academy of St Martin-in-the-Fields.

Barnfield Theatre – Tel 211080. A smaller auditorium in the city centre used for community, experimental, avant-garde and small touring productions.

MUSIC

Regular concerts of classical music can be heard at various venues within Exeter.

Exeter Symphony Orchestra – performs concerts throughout the year with top-quality soloists such as cellist Robert Cohen.

Visiting orchestras and soloists can also be heard in concerts at the **Cathedral**, Tel 55573, the **Great Hall of the University**, Tel 263263, **St George's Hall**, Tel 77888 and the **Northcott Centre**, Tel 54853. Besides the Exeter Festival (see above), an autumn series of music and arts events takes place at the end of September. During August the world famous Dartington International School of Music programme convenes at Dartington Hall, Totnes (26 miles/41.6 km to the south) Tel Totnes 865988.

CINEMA

Commercial cinema at the **Odeon** in Sidwell Street, Tel 54057. The Exeter and Devon Arts Centre shows major films on Wednesdays in conjunction with the Exeter Film Society. Tickets can be obtained at the door but if you are in Exeter for some time it is advantageous to join the Film Society. Tel 213916. There are also regular film showings at the **Northcott Theatre** (see above) which includes a very eclectic season of late-night films on Fridays.

BOOKSTORES

Chapter and Verse – 8 Princesshay, Tel 72676. An excellent chain (see Bristol). Good selection and helpful staff.

Fagins – 167 Sidwell Street, Tel 218248. Again a good selection and a good atmosphere.

Sherratt and Hughes – 48/49 High Street, Tel 218392. Probably has the largest stock in the city.

Dillon's – Roman Gate, 252 High Street, Tel 423044. Another excellent chain – good stock, helpful staff.

SPCK – 1–2 Catherine Street (Cathedral Close). Religious books of all persuasions and much more. Delightful premises.

Focus on Books – 7 South Street, Tel 217652. Mostly art books but some good remainders as well.

County Bookshops – 19 High Street, Tel 411707. The specialists in book bargains. A huge stock of remainders with some excellent buys.

ANTIQUARIAN AND SECONDHAND BOOKS

Dickens Centenary Bookshop – City Arcade, Fore Street, Tel 436021. A good general stock. Excellent browsing.

Exeter Rare Books – 12A Guildhall Shopping Centre, Tel 436021. A selection of beautiful and interesting books. Has an attractive café.

ART GALLERIES

One of the oldest established and best is **Fred Keetch (Exeter) Ltd**, which is conveniently located at 21 Cathedral Yard, Tel 74312. They specialize in oils and watercolours and generally have a good cross-section of British and European artists on show. **Kashan** at 2 Roman Passage in the High Street, Tel 213054, deals in watercolours and oils of the 18th, 19th and 20th centuries.

Spacex Gallery – 45 Preston Street, Tel 31786. A contemporary gallery with shows of painting, sculpture, prints and photography throughout the year.

Fore Street Gallery at 1436 Fore Street, Tel 215789 mostly focuses on engravings – local and national – and watercolours. They also have a framing service.

Note should also be made of **IC Cook**, Weircliffe House, St Andrew's Road, Tel 54573. They deal in the whole field of artistic endeavour - oils, watercolours, engravings and prints from 1500-1900. Call beforehand. Finally, of special interest to me, is **Vincent Gallery**, 15 Magdelen Road, Tel 430082. They specialize in West Country ceramics and represent local artists. Always something interesting on view.

ANTIQUE DEALERS

Peter Wadham Antiques – 5 Cathedral Close, Tel 439741. Period furniture, glass, pottery, metalwork, prints. Some excellent engravings of local views. Also at 10 Chudleigh Road, Alphington, Tel 221451 by appointment.

Priory Antiques – 19–20 Friernhay Street, Tel 53813. Oak and hardwood country furniture. Antique games, chess, tribal arts. A very good selection of early oak.

The Quay Gallery – 43 The Quay (next to the Old Customs House) Tel 213283. Marine antiques, art deco, Victoriana, prints.

The Antique Centre on the Quay, Tel 214180 with several dealers and a wide variety of antiques.

Nottingham and Walsh of Exeter – 1 Cathedral Close, Tel 51103. A fine selection of Exeter silver, flatware and raiseware.

C Samuels and Sons Ltd – 17–18 Waterbeer Street (Guildhall Shopping Centre) Tel 73219. Watercolours, prints and maps of Devon.

Billing Antiques – 154 Heavitree Road, Tel 73706. Clocks, paintings and furniture. General collection.

Ironbridge Antiques – 4 St Davids Hill, Tel 213673. Fine quality period pine and country furniture.

Brian Mortimer Antiques - 87 Queen Street, Tel 79994. Jewellery, silver and curios.

John Nathan Antiques – 153/154 Cowick Street, St Thomas, Tel 72228. Silver and jewellery including Georgian and Victorian.

Pirouette – 5 West Street, Tel 432643. Very different. Bridal headdresses, antique lace, ball gowns.

A T Whitton – 151/152 Fore Street, Tel 73377. Old established Exeter dealer in general antiques and stripped pine.

Micawber Antiques – New Buildings Lane, 25/26 Gandy Street, Tel 52200. Victoriana, art deco, plates, vases, jugs, Staffordshire and Devon pottery, clocks, prints, costume jewellery – ideal for browsing.

Youll's Antique Centre – Bakers Yard, Alphinbrook Road, Marsh Barton, Tel 438775. An extensive collection of antiques presented by nine dealers on one site. Worth a visit.

West Country Antiques and Collectors' Fairs are held bi-annually in St George's Hall Market in March.

Exmouth Collectors' Fair (11 miles/18 km south) is held the second Sunday of every month and every Sunday from June to October in the Pavilion 10:30–5pm.

For full details on fairs throughout the southwest call the **Dartmoor Antiques Centre** at Ashburton. Tel Ashburton 52182.

RESTAURANTS

Tudor House – Tudor Street, Tel 73764. In my opinion the best in Exeter. Streets ahead of the competition. Armorial crests and half-timbered on the outside. Beams, carved ceilings, reproduction Gobelin tapestries, floral upholstery and old furniture inside. The carrot and coriander soup was excellent and the rack of lamb was deliciously pink. To finish you off there's a thick alcoholic syllabub and a fruit Pavlova which is called "The Folly," on the menu. It certainly is if you are watching your waistline. Prices are very fair considering the quality of the cooking.

If you are in the area for a few days and fancy a day out pop down to Dartmouth (28 miles/45 km south). This ancient port not only boasts some beautiful quayside Elizabethan house fronts, but one of the most richly furnished old churches in Devon – St Saviour's. It is also the home of the Royal Naval College. As if this wasn't enough, the **Carved Angel**, 2 South Embankment, Tel Dartmouth 2465, is one of the best restaurants in England. Your meal will be a memorable experience. Some of the best cooking outside of France.

For the rest, I have eaten well at the **Gypsy Hill Hotel and Restaurant** at Gypsy Hill Lane, Pinhoe, Tel 65252 and at the **Imperial Hotel**, St David's Hill, Tel 211811. Many moons ago I had a wonderful jugged hare at the **Great Western Hotel** by the Railway Station, Tel 74039 but I confess I haven't eaten there lately. I also haven't had time to eat at the **Forte Hotel** in Southernhay which recently opened and is reckoned by my friends to be Exeter's premier hotel. Its Georgian Regency style is certainly impressive. Tel 412812. **Piaf's Brasserie**, Tel 7937 in Fore Street, Topsham is fun and Topsham itself is a delightful little place.

PUBS

White Hart Inn – South Street, Tel 79897. A 14th-century inn with a wonderful atmosphere. Big Windsor armchairs and built-in winged settles and masses of copper and brass. Sandwiches, good fish (especially the smoked mackerel and the plate of prawns). My favourite is the chicken and chestnut pie.
The Ship – Cathedral Lane, Tel 72040. Quickly served, good-value food until 9pm. Sir Francis Drake's favourite watering place (see above).
Turk's Head – City Centre. The long two-level lounge bar has bookshelves which is appropriate as Charles Dickens found the original for his "fat boy" in *The Pickwick Papers* here. Wide choice for bar food.
Double Docks – Canal Banks, Alphington, Tel 56947. This remote canal lockhouse, probably one of the oldest in the country, has a welcoming bar which resembles the interior of a retired seafarer's cottage. Good food. I had mushrooms on toast – very generous, but interesting fare such as stuffed peppers and leek and macaroni bake are on offer. Nice all the year round but especially in the summer.
Swan's Nest – Exminster (4 miles/7 km) Tel 83237. Very popular at lunchtime and in the evening. Very strong on food. Good home-made steak,kidney and mushroom pie. Chef's specials have included rabbit stew, braised oxtail and even venison. There is a wide selection of country wines – but be warned – the parsnip wine can be lethal if not sipped with caution.
On the B318 (Topsham Road) at the Countess Wear roundabout on the ring road is the **Countess Wear Lodge**, Tel 875441. This pub is named after Isabella, Countess of Devon, who built a weir (the spelling has changed over the years) on the River Exe in the 13th century. The village of Countess Wear is now a suburb of the city. I'm not sure why Isabella is honoured in this way as the building of her weir seemed to be directly responsible for the River Exe becoming impassable to shipping. The lodge named after her serves good value hot and cold food.

ARTISTIC ASSOCIATIONS

Sir Thomas Bodley and Richard Hooker were born and indeed, lived in Exeter in the second half of the 16th century. Bodley, diplomat and scholar, was the founder of the famous Bodleian library at Oxford to which his name is attached, while Hooker was a theologian and author of the famous *Laws of Ecclesiastical Politie* (policy). Thomas D'Urfey, a poet and dramatist of Huguenot descent, was also born here in 1653 and went to London to make his name. Sabine Baring-Gould, theologian and prolific writer, spent his early life here in the 1830s and George Gissing (b 1857) was a local novelist and the author of a number of Zolaesque portraits of poverty and misery. The best known are probably *Born in Exile* (1892) and *The Odd Women* (1893). His autobiographical novel, *The Private Papers of Henry Rycroft* (1903) is also well known. Gissing lived in Prospect Park and St Leonard's Terrace.

Exeter was the birthplace of the famous miniaturist, Nicholas Hilliard, who held the office of "Limner [ie painter] and Goldsmith" to Queen Elizabeth I. His father, Richard Hilliard, a goldsmith, had a shop appropriately enough in Goldsmith Street, but the family lived in the old market area of the city, most of which was destroyed in the Second World

War. Hilliard's famous *Man Leaning against a Tree with Rose Bushes* was chosen as the Stratford (Ontario) Festival Theatre poster a few years ago and his work can be seen in both the National Portrait Gallery and the Victoria and Albert Museum in London.

Thomas Hudson, the 18th-century portraitist to whom Sir Joshua Reynolds was apprenticed in 1740, and Francis Hayman, who was a founding member of the Royal Academy in 1768 and is best remembered for his decorative paintings of Vauxhall Gardens, were both born in Exeter. Around the same period, the watercolorist Francis Towne was earning his living as a drawing-master and by painting local landscapes and country-house views. Towne's most celebrated pupil, John White Abbott, whose work can be seen in the Royal Albert Memorial Museum, never relied totally upon the art world for a living. Although exhibiting frequently in London, Abbott never became a fully professional painter, but spent his whole life in Exeter where he practised as a surgeon.

EPHEMERA

Parliament Street, situated a few yards from the Guildhall, is the narrowest street in the world. These days Parliament Street runs from the High Street into the Guildhall Shopping Centre, although it was originally a medieval lane. Surprisingly, the name is relatively modern, dating from 1832 when the Reform Bill put Parliament very much in the news.

A fascinating survival from medieval times is the network of Underground Passages, probably first constructed about 1200 to supply water to the city. Closed for some years, the passages are once again open to visitors, with an entrance located off the High Street in the covered arcade next to Boots. There is also an audio visual presentation, museum and shop. A word of warning: fascinating as the passages are, they should not be visited by sufferers from claustrophobia, and dedicated followers of fashion may not find the tour hospitable. Regrettably, they are not suitable for disabled visitors. They may also provide too intense an experience for young children. Some years ago, I took eight children on a tour and when we emerged each child was sobbing and clinging like a limpet to some appendage of my person. However, the introduction of the latest safety equipment and lighting has remedied some of the frightening aspects of the experience.

Begun over 900 years ago in 1050 with a gift of 66 books from Leofric, the first Bishop of Exeter, the Cathedral library is far from the dull and boring place you might imagine. The greatest treasure is probably the *Exeter Book* (10th century) – the largest known collection of Anglo-Saxon poems. This is rivalled by the *Exeter Domesday Book,* the draft of the returns from the southwestern counties, made as part of the Domesday survey in 1086. It is particularly valuable as it catalogues many details, including statistics on animals, that were omitted from the *Great Domesday Book* itself. There are many medieval manuscripts including a beautiful 13th-century psalter and a fragment of Chaucer's *Canterbury Tales* in an interesting early printing of 1492. To be in the presence of such ancient faith, scholarship and artistic endeavour is both a humbling and a moving experience.

In 1941 an air raid reduced much of the old part of Exeter to rubble. Fortunately the cathedral survived, though it was badly damaged, and repairs were begun as early at 1943. While these were being carried out an extraordinary collection of wax models was discovered in a cavity of the stone screen surrounding the choir. They included representations of human and animal limbs, part of a horse's head and the complete figure of a woman. Almost certainly these were votive offerings that were once placed on the tomb of Bishop Edmund Lacey, who died in 1455. During his lifetime the Bishop was said to have shown much saintliness and, after he died, sick pilgrims used to kneel by his tomb to pray for recovery, either for themselves or for their sick animals. As a mark of faith they would leave behind them a wax image of the ailing limb or animal. At the Reformation in 1538, the zealous Dean of Exeter cleared the cathedral of all images and relics. These wax offerings probably survived because some faithful pilgrim deliberately hid them. They are now kept in the cathedral library.

The underground passages that brought fresh water to the medieval citizens of Exeter were partly fed from a spring at St Sidwell's. St Sidwell was martyred in the 6th century and a church was later built and dedicated to her. The story goes that her stepmother coveted some land the girl had inherited and hired two harvesters to murder her. As she knelt in prayer in a field they decapitated her with scythes and, where her head fell, a spring gushed forth.

About 12 miles (19.2 km) east of Exeter, just off the Honiton Road, is the pretty little village of Grittisham. Here, in 1750, was born Joanna Southcott, who for the first 40 years of her life lived in obscurity as a domestic servant and dairy maid. In the early 1790s, after experiencing certain visions, she began to prophesy and gathered around her a sect of followers called the Southcottians – who still exist today. In 1814 she announced she had been chosen to give birth to the second Messiah. No birth took place on October 19th, the date announced for the event, and ten days later the expectant mother died at the age of 64. She left a locked wooden box that was not to be opened until the time of a national crisis, and then only in the presence of all the bishops of England. Various attempts were made to persuade the episcopate to assemble for this purpose during the Crimean War and again in World War One. At last the box was opened in 1928, in the presence of one reluctant prelate, and found to contain some odds and ends including a horse pistol and a few unimportant papers. Among her 60 publications was *The Book of Wonders* written between 1813 and 1814, containing her prophecies.

TOURIST INFORMATION BUREAU: Civic Centre, Paris Street, Exeter, Devon, EX1 1J. Tel (0392) 265297

PENZANCE

County of Cornwall
287 miles (459 km) from London by M4, M5 to Exeter then the A38/A30 to Penzance
Train from London (Paddington) 5 hours 30 minutes

Penzance was the first Cornish town to become a resort. It has rather a grand promenade backed by Victorian and Regency terraces, looking to a fine bay and St Michael's Mount. The Mount, which looks like a fairy castle, is reached by boat but at low tide it is possible to walk across the causeway and up the steep cobbled pathway to the battlements. In 1044 a Benedictine monastery was established here, owned by the monks of Mont St Michel of Brittany to which St Michael's bears a striking resemblance. The island is a National Trust property and has a population of 48 people. Penzance's fortunes grew with the tin trade and probably smuggling. In 1595 four Spanish galleys that had escaped the debacle of the Armada attacked Penzance and devastated the nearby fishing villages of Mousehole and Newlyn. During the Civil War, Penzance was one of Cornwall's stannary or coinage towns where all smelted tin had to be brought to be tested for quality and taxed. It became prosperous, even allowing for the fact that in 1769 its mayor was a well-known smuggler.

Just 10 miles (16 km) from Penzance is Land's End, the most westerly point of the British Isles, while Penzance itself is the end of the railway line originally built by Kingdom Isadore Brunel (see Bristol). It is also the mainland port of the ferry *Scillonian Three,* the lifeline of the Isles of Scilly, over 30 miles (48 km) away to the west. Spring flowers and vegetables from the Scilly Isles reach the mainland weeks ahead of the normal season due to the equitable climate.

Picturesque Chapel Street has many antique shops (see below). Egyptian House, with its gleaming colours and coat of arms, is notable. Maria Branwell, mother of Charlotte and Emily Brontë, lived at No 25. In Market Jew Street stands the white imposing statue of the town's greatest son, scientist Sir Humphrey Davy, who holds the miner's safety lamp he invented. Outside Penlee House Museum (see below) is the ancient Market Cross, and not far away a cannon from the Spanish Armada.

WALK

Penzance Walk – Start from Alverton Road car park, close to the Tourist Information Centre. Walk out on to Alverton Road and cross to your right for the **Museum of the Royal Geological Society** housed in the Municipal Buildings. Walk ahead and turn right down Morrab Road. Penlee House is on your right with the **Museum and Art Gallery**, while further ahead on your left is **Morrab Gardens** with sub-tropical plants. Turn left onto Promenade Battery. Just past the seawater bathing pool is the **War Memorial**. Turn left again onto the Quay and Wharf Road for the **Trinity House National Lighthouse Centre**. Turn left on New Town Lane and walk into Market Jew Street. Turn left and walk ahead into the Market Place. Note **Lloyds Bank**, which was once the Market Hall, circa 1836, and the **statue of Sir Humphrey Davy**, inventor of the miner's safety lamp. Turn left into Chapel Street for the **Egyptian House**, built in a style that enjoyed a brief flourish of popularity after Napoleon's Egyptian campaign at the end of the 18th century. It is wonderfully flamboyant and is now owned by the National Trust, which has a shop on the premises. At No 19 is the **Nautical Museum** (see Museums below). Walk back up Chapel Street and turn left onto Alverton Road back to the car park.

MUSEUMS AND GALLERIES

The Penlee Museum and Art Gallery – Penlee Park, Tel 63625. Housed in Penlee House, the museum traces the history of man in the Cornish peninsula since Neolithic times. There are also exhibits illustrating the natural environment of the area and local industry – mining, fishing, and the domestic and social life of the past. The Art Gallery has a comprehensive exhibition of the famous Newlyn School of Painting.

Trinity House National Lighthouse Centre – The Old Buoy Store, Wharf Road (adjacent to the harbour), Tel 62207. The world's finest collection of lighthouse equipment and apparatus. The exhibitions illustrate how lighthouses were built, their history and how the keepers lived on their lonely outposts. One of the few national museums outside of London. Open daily 10–6pm.

Other museums in Penzance include the **Museum of the Royal Geological Society** in the municipal buildings opposite the Information Bureau and the **Nautical Museum** at 19 Chapel Street, Tel 68890, containing finds brought up by frogmen from the ship *Association,* sunk in 1707. On the outskirts of Penzance in Newlyn is the **Newlyn Art Gallery**, Tel 63715, splendidly situated on the shore of Mount's Bay. It is the base of Newlyn Orion, a major arts charity promoting contemporary art through an exciting programme showing the work of leading British artists. Special exhibitions of work by Cornish artists at Easter, July/Aug and Christmas.

Eight miles (12.8 km) north of Penzance is St Ives. **St Ives Society of Artists** was founded in 1927 by artists working in the *plein air* tradition associated with the Newlyn School, and is still committed to the support and exhibition of work with a bias towards principles of its founders. In the centre of St Ives, near the Parish Church, is **Barbara Hepworth's Museum**. Trewyn Studio was where Barbara Hepworth worked from 1949 until her death in 1975. Forty sculptures in wood, stone and brass can be seen indoors and in the adjoining sub-tropical garden. The stone carving workshop, virtually untouched since the artist's death, shows work in progress and retains a strong personal atmosphere.

THEATRE

Although Penzance is visited by just a few professional touring companies, mention must be made of the **Minack Theatre** at Porthcurno, just 7 miles (11 km) to the south of the town and 3 miles (5 km) from Land's End. A moonlit performance on the open-air stage of the Minack perched between cliff and hillside is truly memorable. This unique auditorium, carved from the rocks, has a matchless backcloth of sand and shore, glittering seas and the lights of passing fishing boats. Quite simply, there is no back wall to the stage except the Logan Rock to the left and the winking Lizard Lighthouse across the bay. The panorama is breathtaking by day or night but especially so as the moon rises on a clear night. Shakespeare, Mozart, Jane Austen, Charles Dickens, Robert Bolt, Gilbert and Sullivan, Anouilh, Euripides and Bernstein have all been performed here. There are some 20 different shows each summer, ranging from musicals to the classics, performed by companies from all parts of the country. On average only three performances a season are cancelled because of inclement weather. There is an Exhibition Centre telling the story of Rowena Cade who built the Minack, practically with her bare hands. The auditorium seats 750, and has sophisticated lighting and sound equipment; the season runs from the end of May to the middle of September. Tel St Buryan 810471.

MUSIC

As Penzance is small, with a population of some 15,000, musical events come into the town promoted by various sponsoring groups and are mainly single artists and small ensembles. Mention should be made of the St Ives Festival. The influence of painters like James Whistler and Walter Sickert and of their 20th-century successors like Ben Nicholson and Barbara Hepworth is still very much in evidence in the permanent colony of artists that has made St Ives internationally famous. The **St Ives September Festival** is not, however, limited to painting and sculpture. There are carnivals, puppets, poets, folk singers, mime artists, films, plays, concerts and exhibitions. A notable contribution is made by performers from the Prussia Cove International Musicians' Seminar from nearby Marazion and recent guests have included the Duchy String Quartet, the Brio Brass Ensemble and the Cornwall Youth Jazz Orchestra. St Ives is ten miles (16 km) north of Penzance.

CINEMA

If you want interesting cinema, Plymouth is the nearest place, but commercial cinema is at the **Savoy**, Causewayhead, Tel 63330 and the **Royal Cinema**, St Ives, Tel 796843.

BOOKSTORES

The best are **Book Centre** at 23 Market Jew Street, Tel 65607, **Katherine Wallace** at the **Penzance Bookshop**, 5 Chapel Street, Tel 65444, and **John Philpotts**, 2 Camelot court, Alverton Street, Tel 51237. There's also a **W H Smith** at 96 Market Jew Street, Tel 655797. There is a fascinating and comprehensive collection of books on the occult, mythology and comparative religion at the **Quay Bookshop**, 16 Quay Street (near the harbour), Tel 69446. Beside their focus on "New Age" material they also have a general stock.

ANTIQUARIAN AND SECONDHAND BOOKS

I couldn't find a specialist secondhand bookshop in Penzance. If you find one let me know. If you are browsing in Chapel Street (one of the centres for antiques), **Collector Gallery at No 61**, Tel 68138, and **The Old Posthouse** at No 9, Tel 60320, have book sections as well as a goodly collection of general antiques and bric-à-brac.

ANTIQUE DEALERS

In the Chapel Street area there are a number of retailers trading at **Penzance Antiques Arcade**, no phone, mostly china, glass and jewellery. **Peter Mansfield** – Tel 63267, is at No 61 with a general collection while **Viva Antiques** at No 52, no phone, has a similar stock. **Daphne's Antiques** at No 17, Tel 61719, specializes in 18th- and 19th-century furniture, glass, needlework, boxes and Georgian and Edwardian jewellery.

Little Jems at 1 Abbey Mall, Abbey Street (no phone) close by, also specializes in jewellery. **Barbara Howard**, nearby at 11 Abbey Mall (Tel 50888), has a general collection and interesting bric-à-brac. For furniture, the best bets are **New Street Antiques and Restoration** at 26 New Street (Tel 60173), **Mills' Antiques**, 1 Bread Street (Tel 60220) (they also have some nice pine), **MG Warnoke** at 17 Chapel Street (Tel 61719) and **Chapel Antiques** at 16 Chapel Street (Tel 631124). Ken Ashbrook at **The Red Brick Warehouse**, Leskinnick Place, Tel 65477, has a large stock of mainly 1800–1900 furniture and fittings but you need to call him beforehand as his times of opening vary. The other centre for antiques is the Bread Street area where you will find **Brown's Galleries**, Tel 788444, with a general collection, and **Attic Antiques**, which is associated with **The Old Posthouse** at No 6, Tel 61232. **Catherine and Mary Antiques** at 2 Old

Brewery Yard, Bread Street, no phone, has jewellery, textiles, linens and clothing as well as some pine, while **Brian Humphreys** at 1 St Clare Street has a quality general collection. Two of my favourite shops are **Kitts Corner** at 51 Chapel Street, Tel 63776, where Barbara Kirk deals in china, jewellery and accessories and husband David looks after ceramics and pottery, with some nice 20th-century ceramics as well as West Country Pottery, and **Derek W Davidson** at 1 Old Bakehouse Lane, Chapel Street, Tel 731171, who has uniforms, medals, militaria, nautical and even shipwreck items. Make a point of checking the local paper – *The Cornishman* or *The West Britain* for regularly held auctions of antiques, pictures and objets d'art, or check with the auctioneers **W H Lane and Son** at 61447, **David Lay** at 61414 and **Pooley and Rogers** at 68814 or 63816.

Finally, one of the most fascinating places I've ever been in: Mike Read is a buyer and vendor of antique scientific instruments and English barometers. At his premises are globes, barographs, sextants, theodolites, microscopes and drawing and medical instruments. Even if you have no idea of what various instruments are for, you cannot help but be impressed by their shining brass and wood and by the workmanship and precision which went into their construction. You will find Mike Read at **Ayia – Napa**, Wheal Whiddon, St Ives, Tel 798219.

ART GALLERIES

If you are interested in the work of the Newlyn and St Ives schools, my choice would be **Leon Suddaby Fine Arts** at 56 Chapel Street, Tel 50333, or **Tony Saunders Gallery** at 14 Chapel Street, Tel 66620. Both galleries also deal in 19th- and 20th-century oils, while Suddaby has etchings and watercolours and Saunders antiques. A bit less formidable is the **Gallery Lyonesse** in the Old Brewery Yard, Bread Street, Tel 69855, which also has old paintings, some Newlyn and St Ives examples, and antiquarian maps and prints. **Savels** at 23/24 Jennings Street, Tel 68636, has art, antiques and crafts. Finally, check out **Mill House Gallery**, Victoria Place, Tel 66668 and – a good name for an art gallery I think – **Wolf at the Door** on Bread Street, Tel 60573.

With its artistic background, St Ives is of course densely populated with art galleries. Rather than categorize them, as the town is so small, I have simply listed the best of them below in rough geographical groupings.

Burgess Gallery – 65 Fore Street, St Ives, Tel 795573.
Emanuel Judi Gallery – 30 Fore Street, St Ives, Tel 797303.
J P Fine Arts – 48 Fore, Street, St Ives, Tel 795577.
Tom Gower Studio – Wharf Road, St Ives, Tel 797939.
St Ives Fine Arts – The Wharf, St Ives, Tel 793456.
St Ives Gallery – The Wharf, St Ives, Tel 794665.
Crow Studios – The Warren, St Ives, Tel 798840.
Half Moon Gallery – 12 St Andrews Street, St Ives, Tel 793018.
Palette Studios – The Ropewalk, The Island, St Ives, Tel 794481.
Ponckle's Cat Gallery – Island Square Workshop, St Ives, Tel 794532.
The Salt House Gallery – Norway Square, St Ives, Tel 795003.
Wills Lane Gallery – Wills Lane, St Ives, Tel 795723.

RESTAURANTS

In my opinion the best food available is a short distance from Penzance. Twenty-four miles (38 km) to the southeast, a nice country run through Helston, is St Keverne. As well as the fine church, which was a centre of Celtic evangelism in pre-Saxon Cornwall, it also has **Laden Table**, Tel St Keverne 280090. Located in three converted cottages, it has a delightful ambiance. I still remember their prawns with aioli after three visits to France. Very hospitable. Opening times are a bit erratic so phone chef Tony Gulliford ahead of time. Open Tues–Sat June–Sept dinner only 7:30–9:30pm.

Much closer is **Enzo's**, just three miles (5 km) towards St Just, Tel Penzance 63777. The restaurant specializes in Italian cuisine and when it was sold to two Scots I wondered whether McEnzo's was a possibility. Today there is still an Italianate quality to the cooking, and the fish is wonderful. The bouillabaisse is excellent. There's also a good antipasto trolley as well as sinful desserts. Open all week, dinner only 7–9:30pm. Closed 2 weeks in Feb and 2 weeks in Nov.

In Penzance itself try **Ma Cuisine** at 5 Alverton Street, Tel 63814 for French cooking and fresh seafood and the **Admiral Benbow** and the **Turk's Head** both in Chapel Street. **Alverton's**, Tel 63926, down the road from Ma Cuisine does a good traditional Sunday lunch as well as nightly dinners. Finally, just outside of the town limits to the east past Marazion, is Perranuthnoe. There you will find **Bertie Wooster's Restaurant**, Tel 710242, which is really rather fun.

PUBS

Admiral Benbow – Chapel Street, Tel 63448. lots of atmosphere here – engine room telegraphs, ships in bottles, wreck charts, brass cannon, navigation lanterns and lots of rope. Various ploughman's, baked potatoes, curry and best of all, fresh fish, although the Guinness pie runs it close. Food at lunch and supper. Note the full-size smuggler figure on the roof.

Turk's Head – Chapel Street, Tel 63093. Oak beams and panelling and lots of old world atmosphere. Food is excellent. I found the crab soup wonderful, but there are also sardines, crevettes, mussels, crab, scallops, fisherman's pie and even lobster. All this plus the more traditional pub fare.

The Star – Market Jew Street, Tel 63241. Low beams, red plush wall seats, ship's pictures and nautical memorabilia with wood panelling and stripped stone. Good traditional home-cooked bar food.

Union Hotel – Chapel Street, Tel 62319. A pleasant Georgian building with Georgian façade and a niche in history. From a gallery in the dining room the news was first announced in England of Nelson's death at Trafalgar. Pleasant bar and good bar food and snacks.

ARTISTIC ASSOCIATIONS

Mrs Hester Thrale was the wife of a prosperous Southwark brewer. Dr Samuel Johnson developed an extraordinary passion for her and was a frequent visitor in her house for 16 years. "Frequent visitor" actually lacks a certain specificity. So enamoured was Dr J of Mrs Thrale that he essentially took up residence in her abode. When Mrs Thrale's husband died she upset the good doctor by marrying an itinerant Italian musician, Gabriel Piozzi. Considering that Dr Johnson softened many of his eccentricities in order to ingratiate himself with the good lady, the marriage was to him a bit of a blow – as I believe too, would have been Johnson's chagrin had he lived to read Mrs Piozzi's literary reminiscences. These consisted mostly of books written by her about Dr Johnson himself. *Anecdotes of Dr Johnson* was very popular, as was *Letters to and from Dr Johnson* and many others. Regardless of their popularity, the books obviously could not provide sufficient income for the Piozzi life style, for in 1820, Mrs Piozzi, having celebrated her 80th birthday in Bath well, but not too wisely, came to Penzance to recoup her depleted finances. She hoped to enjoy warm sea bathing and economical living. Alas, neither was available. Accommodation was expensive and hard to find and she was obliged to take a "little nutshell of a cottage." In a letter she said of Penzance, "No rooms, no theatre, no music, no pleasure but no expense." Because of the lack of amenities she did indeed achieve her object of settling her debts. In my darker moments I must admit that Penzance seems a little lacking in artistic amenities even today.

Stanhope Forbes, the founder of the Newlyn School of Painting, arrived in the village of Newlyn in 1884. He wrote, "Here every corner was a picture and, more important from the point of view of the figure painter, the people seemed to fall naturally into their places and to harmonize with their surroundings." Forbes spent most of his working life in Newlyn and gathered around him a group of like-minded artists such as Frank Bramley, Edwin Harris and Normen Garstin. The group was first attracted by Newlyn's similarity to Brittany, where several of them had studied. Art historians argue about whether the group was essentially the English branch of the Impressionist movement with direct artistic links to Monet and Renoir. Certainly the School established a reputation for *plein air* painting. This is a term used for paintings which convey an open-air feeling, particularly those actually painted out-of-doors. Although the term is used most frequently of the Impressionists, the Newlyn School was somewhat different. A painting by Forbes, such as *A Fish Sale on a Cornish Beach,* is indeed an "impression" of the scene and has a *plein air* quality about it, but technically it is very different from the work of say, Sisley or Monet. In order to judge for yourself, you can see Forbes's painting in the Plymouth Art Gallery.

Laura and Harold Knight (see Nottingham) came to Newlyn in 1907 as the second-generation Newlyn School artists. Harold's work changed a great deal through his Cornish experience. In Staithes, on the desolate North Sea Coast, he produced sombre scenes of the raw existence of the fisher folk. Here in Newlyn, with its more equitable climate and gentler, more colourful surroundings, his work took on a lighter quality. Laura began to see Newlyn developing as a holiday area and her work, especially *The Beach* (Newcastle-upon-Tyne Art Gallery) began to reflect the gaiety, joy and liveliness of a Britain at play, a characteristic she was to explore further, between the wars, with her paintings of itinerant actors, musicians and circus folk.

Some years later, in 1927, artists from Newlyn travelled to St Ives and established a colony in this most picturesque of small harbours. The work of this group of artists aimed to continue the *plein air* tradition but was also more diverse. It included a 16-year residence by Ben Nicholson, the abstract painter. The great abstract sculptress, Barbara Hepworth, also worked in the village (see Museums above). Bernard Leach, the most influential potter of his day, had a studio called the L Pottery at St Ives.

EPHEMERA

Cornish pasties have been the staple dish of the West Country for many generations. They were taken to work by the miners and later by farm workers and the fillings are many and varied. One thing they all have in common is that the meat, vegetables, fish, or fruit must be fresh. The pasty is not a way of using up leftovers. Traditionally, when pasties are made they are marked in one corner with the initials of the owner and then eaten in the hands from the corner opposite to the initials. In this way any leftovers can be identified and eaten later by their owners. It is said that the Devil is never found on the Cornish side of the River Tamar because "The Devil and all goes into a Cornish pasty." Even the Devil isn't about to take the risk.

Celtic whimsy – Cornwall is one of the most magical places in the British Isles and much of that raw and ancient magic has survived into the 20th century. Giants are still reputed to exist here. One-eyed Cormoran lives on St Michael's Mount, somewhat secretly, given the influx of summer visitors, and other large apparitions rejoice in the names of Den Dynas, Treerobm and Holiburn. There are mischievous *piskeys,* nasty *spriggans* and the *knockers* who still work tin mines long abandoned by men. There are mermaids at Lamorna Cove and Zenor, where the squire's son was bewitched by one. The sea-maiden's image is preserved on a bench-end in the church.

At Porthcurno, a phantom sailing ship materializes in sea fog and sails overland to vanish into thin air, while a guardian spirit – the Hooper – concealed in a bank of fog, watches over the fishermen of Sennen Cove. Witches in Cornwall, incidentally, fly on ragwort stems rather than the conventional broomstick.

The Cornish name for St Michael's Mount is *Carrick luz en cuz,* which means "the ancient rock in the wood." At low tide, there can still be seen the fossilized remains of the forest that once covered the coast around St Michael's Mount. Within the present castle is a rough-cut stone seat known as Michael's Chair. St Keyne, on a pilgrimage to the Mount, is believed to have endowed the seat with the same power that she gave to her holy well at St Keyne (two miles/3.2 km south of Liskeard). If the bride is the first to sit in Michael's Chair, she will henceforth dominate the marriage; if the groom is the first, he will.

The great King Arthur finished off Cornwall's giants (his castle is said to be at Tintagel, north of Bodmin), while Lyonesse, the legendary kingdom between Land's End and the Isles of Scilly, was sunk by a magician's spell on the day Arthur was slain by the traitor Mordred.

ST. MICHAEL'S MOUNT, PENZANCE

Whether you believe all this or not is up to you. As for myself, I'm taking no chances – it's all true.

About 20 miles (32 km) northeast of Penzance is the delightful coastal village of Perranporth. In the late 1930s Peter Bull, Robert Morley and Pamela Brown, among others, formed a summer theatre company in the village and performed in the town hall. One of the actors in the first season, John Penrose, who is now a theatrical agent, garnered a most delightful notice in a production directed by Peter Bull. According to the *West Cornwall Advertiser* (the local paper), "Mr John Penrose gave a sharp twist to both his parts." Mr Penrose gave up acting shortly afterward, perhaps because it was just too painful.

A more serious theatrical connection with this small coastal village is the Pirran Round, an Iron Age hill camp later used as a place for games. Performances of the Cornish trilogy of miracle plays have been given there. Dramatic in its own way is the Lost Church of St Piran, Perranporth. One of the oldest churches in Britain (built between the 7th and 10th centuries), it had by the 11th century been abandoned under drifting sand. It was cleared again in the 19th century, and in 1910 was encased for protection in a hideous concrete building which itself is often flooded. To visit St Piran's is a remarkable experience made disturbing by the fact that every so often the shifting sands reveal bones from the cemetery.

TOURIST INFORMATION BUREAU: Station Road, Penzance, Cornwall, TR18 2NF
Tel (0736) 62207

PLYMOUTH

County of Devon
218 miles (349 km) from London by M4, M5 and A38
3 hours 45 minutes by train from London (Paddington)

Because Plymouth was the base of Elizabethans like Sir Francis Drake, Sir Walter Raleigh, Sir John Hawkyns and Sir Humphrey Gilbert, it became the base of the English Navy during the 16th-century Spanish Wars. Later, in 1689, William of Orange decided to build the Royal Dockyard on the marshes that were to become Devonport, and so Plymouth gained the Navy officially.

PLYMOUTH

During the Second World War, German bombs smashed the centre of Plymouth even more comprehensively than the centre of Exeter. I visited Plymouth as a boy in 1946 and even today I can vividly recall the flattened city centre, the seeming total devastation. For a tremendous view of the modern rebuilt Plymouth, take the lift to the top of the tall Civic Centre. A map from the information bureau on the ground floor will show you the position of the Council Chambers, the Law Courts and the multi-domed Market. Opposite the Civic Centre is the Guildhall, which has interesting windows in its main hall and a rebuilt tower from the 1870s. The best modern windows in Devon, however, are those by John Piper on the rebuilt Parish Church of St Andrew's next door. Immediately southeast of St Andrew's is the 15th-century Prysten House which is the city's oldest building. In stark contrast to new Plymouth is the Barbican close by: this is the most attractive small urban area in Devon and indeed, is essentially the original town as Drake knew it. Its streets are narrow and sloping and its harbour packed with pleasure and fishing boats. There is a beautiful Elizabethan Merchant's House (furnished in period style) at 32 New Street, and in Southside Street the 16th-century refectory of a Dominican friary is incorporated into a distillery for Plymouth Gin (seems right, somehow). On the Quay, the Old Customs House dates from 1586, while the new is circa 1810. At the Mayflower Steps a plaque commemorates the sailing of the Pilgrim Fathers in 1620 as well as other famous sailings.

Finally, in the centre of the city is the Hoe, where tradition says Sir Francis Drake finished his game of bowls before dealing with the Armada in 1588. Standing on the Hoe, one is afforded one of Britain's great harbour views. There is also the Aquarium of the Marine Biological Association, which is outstanding. Dominating the Hoe is the Royal Citadel erected by Charles I after the Restoration in 1660. (Plymouth had, after all, resisted his father's forces for two years.) Its baroque main gateway, dated 1670, is exceptionally impressive. Smeatons Tower was originally the lighthouse on the Eddystone Rock (14 miles/22.4 km south) from 1759 to 1882. It was re-erected on the Hoe when its original site started to crumble. Finally, Drake's Island in Plymouth Sound was a fortress, then a prison, and is now an adventure centre for local schools.

Other interesting buildings are: the Royal William Victualling Yard (naval supply centre) built in 1826-1835 which is one mile west of the Hoe, Her Majesty's Dockyard in Devonport (three miles/5 km west) which contains much of naval, architectural and also macabre interest. Can at times be visited but only if you are British. The shell of Charles Church

(1664) in the middle of a roundabout in the city centre is kept as a memorial to those citizens of Plymouth killed or injured in the Second World War.

WALK

Plymouth Walk – Start from Notte Street car park. Cross Notte Street and turn right into St Andrew Passage for the **Merchant's House**. Take the passage to the left after the Merchant's House for **Prysten House**, which is in Finewall Street. Leaving Prysten House, turn left and left again into Royal Parade. Look for **St Andrew's Church** on the left and farther along, also on the left, the **Guildhall**. Turn left into Armada Way and go ahead to Hoe Park. Note the **World War Monument**, the **Armada Memorial** (see Ephemera) and, in a walled garden, the anchor of **HMS Ark Royal**, the Second World War aircraft carrier. From Hoe Park, cross the Promenade to **Smeaton's Tower** and go down the path to Hoe Road and the **Plymouth Dome**. Turn left on Hoe Road to the **Aquarium** and the **Royal Citadel**. On a bank on your left is an obelisk commemorating the Anglo-Boer War. From the citadel bear right into Lambhay Hill and follow it into the **Barbican**, turning left into New Street for the **Elizabethan House** and the **Armada Experience**. Turn right through Stokes Lane and left into Southside Street for the **Coates Gin Distillery**. At the end of Southside Street turn left into Notte Street and back to the car park.

MUSEUMS AND GALLERIES

City Museum and Art Gallery – Drake Circus, Tel 668000. Good displays reflecting the social history of the Southwest. The ethnological section has tribal artefacts from Oceania, Africa, America and Asia, although it specializes in prehistoric and later finds from Dartmoor and Plymouth. Fine art is represented, mainly by 18th- and 19th-century painters. Special attention is given to artists with Plymouth associations such as Sir Joshua Reynolds and Samuel Prout. The decorative art sections features a fine collection of Plymouth porcelain. The museum and gallery also offer art exhibitions, lectures and recitals. Open Mon–Fri 10–5:30 and Sat 10–5pm.

Elizabethan House – 33 New Street. 16th-century house of stone and timber frame furnished in period style (see above). Open Easter–Oct Mon–Fri 10–1 and 2:15–5:30 (closes 30 min earlier on Sat); Sun 3–5pm. Oct–Easter Mon–Sat 10–1 and 2:15–4:30pm.

Merchant's House Museum – 33 St Andrew's Street. A 16th-century house with 17th-century additions. It contains displays illustrating the social, economic and maritime history of Plymouth up to 1670. Open Mon–Fri 10–1 and 2–5:30pm; Sat 10–1 and 2–5pm; Sun 3–5pm (Easter–Sept only).

Plymouth Dome – Hoe Road, Tel 600608. A new building, of domes and turrets, shows the history of Plymouth over the centuries. There are the sights, sounds and smells of an Elizabethan street and tableaux of the Spanish Armada in 1588, the departure of the Mayflower in 1620 and Captain Cook's 18th-century voyages. Up-to-date innovations include a radar screen to track shipping in the Sound and a TV camera that can zoom in on ships in the harbour. Open all year daily 1–5pm.

Prysten House – Finewell Street, Tel 661414. Dating from 1498, this limestone-and-granite wine merchant's house contains the 28-foot (8.4 m) Plymouth Tapestry, which is based on a 16th-century document recording the appointment of Plymouth's first schoolmaster. An even more remarkable tapestry by local artist Tom Mor is in preparation, which will depict the colonization of America. Open April–Oct Mon–Sat 10–5pm.

Plymouth Aquarium - Hoe Road, Tel 222772. Some 250 fish of more than 50 different species are displayed in the laboratories of the Marine Biological Association of the UK. Each tank shows the fish in their natural environment with rocks adorned by exquisite sea anemones, starfish and sea urchins and crevices with crabs, lobsters and octopuses. Open all year Mon–Sat 10–5pm.

Saltran House – Plympton. A beautiful house designed by Robert Adam and dating from 1712. Some fine Reynolds portraits and superlative furniture, some of it by Adam himself. A wonderful orangery where the citrus trees are taken out of doors each summer. A notable kitchen and stables. **The Chapel Art Gallery** in the grounds of the house is a converted 19th-century chapel, housing summer art exhibitions. Open April–Oct Sun–Thurs and Bank Holiday weekends 12:30–6pm (garden daily 11–6pm); Nov–Mar garden only 11–6pm.

Dolls and Miniatures – 54 Southside Street, the Barbican, Tel 663676. Has an astounding collection of antique and reproduction dolls, doll's houses and doll's-house kits plus all accessories to make and finish doll's houses. There are Victorian and Edwardian miniature human figures, houses as well as furniture, fixtures and fittings. There are doll's dresses, wigs and shoes and a wide selection of Teddy bears.

Black Friars Distillery – Southside Street, the Barbican. Home of one of the finest dry gins in the world (Coates Plymouth Gin) and the guided tour of the distillery tells you everything you've always wanted to know about the traditional mother's ruin. Remains of the 14th-century Black Friars monastery can be seen. The building was also a debtor's prison in 1793, which is logical in a twisted sort of way. Unlike Harvey's Museum in Bristol, where you get a sherry, they don't give you a G and T at the end of this tour. Open Mon–Sat 10–4pm.

THEATRE

Theatre Royal – Tel 669595. Plymouth's acclaimed Theatre Royal is right in the heart of the city at the bottom of Royal Parade. The theatre regularly creates productions that go on national tours and to the West End of London. The main stage Theatre Royal has 1300 seats, while the Drum Theatre, presenting more experimental work, seats 200. There is a theatre shop with books, records, cards, etc, an art gallery on two floors, a craft display area and a number of catering areas ranging from a pizza bar and a light meal buttery to a sophisticated restaurant serving lunches, suppers and after show dinners. It's a new auditorium, very plush and modern with excellent sight lines. Visitors to the Theatre Royal's main stage have included Sadler's Wells Ballet Company, the Royal Ballet, Glyndebourne Touring Opera, Welsh National Opera and the English Shakespeare Company. Theatre Royal productions have included *My Fair Lady,* Alan Ayckbourn's *Bedroom Farce* and *Gold Diggers,* a swing era musical comedy. At the Drum Theatre, performances have included Arthur Miller's *The Price,* Strindberg's *Miss Julie* and Manuel Puig's *Kiss of the Spiderwoman* as well as visits by Kneehigh Theatre and Paine's Plough, two of the country's best touring groups.

Other theatres include the **Barbican Theatre**, Castle Street, Tel 267131, and the **Athenaeum Theatre**, both of which host touring and amateur productions.

MUSIC

A variety of musical events are staged in Plymouth under the auspices of the **Plymouth Musical Trust**. These range from orchestra concerts and chamber music to individual soloists and lecture/recitals. They are held at various venues such as the Barbican Theatre, the Athenaeum Theatre, the Theatre Royal, the Guildhall, Tel 227660, and St Andrew's Church. For full information on musical events contact the Theatre Royal box office or the Tourist Information Centre, Tel 264849.

CINEMA

Commercial cinema at the **Drake Odeon** (4 screens), Derry's Cross, Tel 227074 and the **Cannon** (3 screens), Derry's Cross, Tel 663300.

Of more interest is the **Plymouth Arts Centre**, 38 Looes Street, Tel 660060, which has ceased to be a theatrical venue. I remember playing in Ibsen's **Ghosts** there in the '60s but it now concentrates on film and the visual arts. Films run on most nights at 6 and 8pm. A recent sampling showed films from Australia, France, USA, Italy, Britain and Japan. Besides the extensive and interesting film programme there are workshops and exhibitions related to the visual arts and a very good vegetarian restaurant.

BOOKSTORES

Among the most comprehensive are the good chain bookshops. **Sherratt and Hughes** at 38 New George Street, Tel 673473, **Fagin's** at 141/3 Armada Way, Tel 661011, and **Chapter and Verse** at 38 Eastlake Walk (opposite Tesco's), Tel 220183. Book bargains and remainders can be found at **Bonus Books** at 138 Cornwall Street, Tel 660374 and **County Bookshops** at 18 Old Town Street, Tel 220282. If you are in the area of the Polytechnic, the **Polytechnic Bookshop**, 36–37 Mayflower Street, Tel 669199, has a good stock of general and academic books and is an agent for HMSO publications, while **Ron John's – The Bookseller,** just opposite the Poly at 42 Drake Circus, Tel 222012, is very helpful. If you are in the Pannier Market as I'm sure you will be, No 31 the **Book Stall**, Tel 221047, is worth a browse as is **In Other Words** at 72 Mutley Pain, Tel 663889. If you are interested in boating, **Boating Books – The Sea Chest** at Queen Anne's Battery Marina, Coxside, Tel 222012, specializes in nautical books and charts and also has a good secondhand section. Finally, **W H Smith** is at 73/75 George Street, Tel 669973.

ANTIQUARIAN AND SECONDHAND BOOKS

Surprisingly there is not such a large selection as one might hope for. For selection and ambience **John Glover Books** at 36 New Street on the Barbican, Tel 673204, is probably the best. **Alexandra Bookshop**, 1 Mutley Plain, Tel 664183, **Clement's** of 46 Southside Street, Tel 664957, **Fredk Harrison**, 43 Bridwell Road, Weston Mill (strong on antiquarian books) Tel 365595, and **Universal Book Stores**, 24 Frankfort Gate, Tel 223841, are all worth a browse and are the best of the rest.

ART GALLERIES

Most of Plymouth's art galleries and dealers seem to be gathered around the Barbican. My own especial favourite is the **Fox-Smith Galleries** at 53 Southside Street, Tel 267474. William Fox-Smith specializes in antique engravings and maps and a visit to the delightful little shop is a joy. He also has visiting cards which show a picture of the premises – a really nice touch.

Pilgrim Galleries – Island House, the Barbican, Tel 662226, specializes in oil paintings and watercolours of the 18th, 19th and 20th centuries, while the **Barbican Gallery** at 15 The Parade, Tel 661052, has a wide selection of paintings and prints as has The **New Street Gallery** at 37 New Street. The **Armada Gallery** at 19 The Parade, Tel 263031 specializes in posters, prints and framing while at the other end of the scale, although I'm not sure what scale, the **Odd'n Interesting New Age Centre** at 20/21 Southside Street, Tel 673003, is just what its name implies. Finally, another place well worth a visit is **Chris Robinson's Plymouth Prints** at 34 New Street (prints and engravings).

ANTIQUE DEALERS

Alvin Antiques – 148 Union Street, Tel 665628. A general selection of antique furniture. Some good porcelain.

Upstairs Downstairs Antiques and Curios – Devonshire Street, Greenbank, Tel 261015, has a general selection of china, paintings and furniture and also period costume, lace and linen.

Secondhand Rose – Out of town a bit at 22 Weston Park Road, Peverell, Tel 661453, but it has a good range of traditional furniture and antiques.

New Street Antique Centre – 27 New Street, Tel 661165, has a comprehensive range of antique furniture, glass, china and objets d'art, while similar quality and range is to be found at **Luella Antiques** at 40 North Hill, Tel 667536. As with the art galleries, there is a concentration of antique shops around the Barbican. Two of the best are **Colin Rhodes Antiques** at 53 Southside Street, Tel 862232, and **Galleon Antiques** at 5 Barbican Court, Tel 228993. Galleon also specializes in Doulton, Labbeth and Commemorative china. Finally, excellent browsing at **Antiques Galore**, Parade Antiques Centre, 17 The Parade, Tel 667499.

RESTAURANTS

There are two really excellent restaurants in Plymouth. Coming in at number one is **Chez Nous**, 7 Frankford Gate, Tel 266793. The cooking is French bistro, the menu on a blackboard in French. The set-price menu is excellent value and the dishes change with the seasons and with the fresh produce that is available. I had a wonderful John Dory with tomatoes and basil – simple but arrestingly fresh and imaginative. Desserts are classic French with excellent pastries. Good house French wine. Prices are not low but excellent value for the quality of the cooking. Open Tues–Sat 12:30–2 and 7–10:30pm.

Barrett's of Princess Street – This restaurant used to be Mister Barrett's until it moved to just behind the Mayflower Theatre. Ambience is art deco with piped jazz (good jazz though). Barrett's is open all day so you can get snacks and light meals all the time. There is often a sampling of local game – hare and wild boar – and the produce has a local flavour, fresh fish, organic ham, free range chicken and excellent local lamb (summer only). Ice cream is one of the best in England from Salcobbe Dairy – look for it in the stores. Comparatively inexpensive. Open Mon–Sat 10:30–10:30.

For the rest, good Indian food is available at the **Khyber Restaurant** at 44 Mayflower Street in the city centre, Tel 266036, and also at the **Ganges** at 146 Vauxhall Street, Tel 220907. The **Artillery Tower** at Firestone Bay, Devil's Point, Tel 667276, is a tiny converted 15th century gun tower. It specializes in fresh local fish but, be warned, it is popular and you should book in advance.

If you are in the mood for traditional British fish and chips, **Perillas** is both well established and popular with locals. They have two restaurants in the city centre, one at 33/35 Market Avenue, Tel 661307, and one at 34 Mayflower Street, Tel 667843. Finally, you'll find the traditional Cornish pasty all over the place. I know we're the wrong side of River Tamar but Plymouth seems to go for pasties in a big way. For a description see Penzance Ephemera above, and note that the best brands are **Ivor Dewdney** – they have an outlet at 99 Cornwall Street, Tel 6644725 and **Ginsters** – all over the place in pubs and shops.

PUBS

The Bank – Derry's Cross (behind the Theatre Royal). Renovated Lloyds Bank full of mahogany and brass with oak staircase to upper bar. Good cheap food.

The Distillery – in the Barbican on Southside Street, Tel 224305. Previous gin distillery slickly converted with wrought iron and palm trees in the main bar. Good basic pub food and steak.

Yard Arm – Saltram Place, back of Plymouth Hoe at 150 Citadel Road, Tel 262850. Naval theme pub with lots of atmosphere and decent food.

Sippers – West Hoe Road and Millbay Road, Tel 670668. Straightforward bar food – unpretentious – gets its name from the naval way of drinking rum.

ARTISTIC ASSOCIATIONS

Sir Joshua Reynolds, the famous 18th-century portrait painter, was born and educated in Plympton which is part of the city of Plymouth. The 17th-century school which he attended, and where his father was headmaster, is still there. Many of his portraits are in Saltram House (see Ephemera). Reynolds was a frequent visitor to Saltram and was often accompanied by his friends Dr Samuel Johnson, the lexicographer, critic and poet, and Fanny Burney, the novelist and diarist. Three other renowned artists also attended Plympton Grammar School – historical painter Benjamin Haydon, and James Northcote, whose picture, *The Princess in the Tower,* is well known, and Sir Charles Eastlake, who also painted historical subjects. In 1815, Eastlake seized the opportunity of painting *Napoleon on board the Bellerophon in Plymouth Sound.* This was based on a sketch made in a small boat moored near the *Bellerophon* during its short stop here *en route* to St Helena. Seeing Eastlake at work, Napoleon held a pose and had a uniform and decorations sent ashore for the young artist's use. The picture was a great success and provided funds for Eastlake to travel in Europe and begin the studies which made him not only a successful painter, but also a scholar and an administrator. Reynolds was the first president of the Royal Academy and Eastlake, also its president, was the first director of London's National Gallery.

Another friend of Sir Joshua Reynolds, William Cookworth, was a local chemist who discovered china clay deposits and established a porcelain industry in Plymouth. After five years the industry moved to Bristol.

Henry Austin Dodson, poet and essayist, was born in Plymouth. The city was also the native town of Thomas Hardy's first wife, Emma, and she had a great affection for it. Dodson was a special friend of Emma's and one of his most poignant poems, "The West-of-Wessex Girl" was written in Plymouth in March 1913, four months after Emma's death and laments the fact that Dodson and Emma were never in Plymouth together.

EPHEMERA

The Plymouth Theatre Company was committed to touring and for their production of *The Golden Pathway Annual,* six actors had learned 20 parts between them with the time taken to get into a hall and erect the scenery taking about ten hours. In Ashburton, a small market town some 20 miles (32 km) to the east of Plymouth, an expensive publicity campaign had blitzed the area with free tickets and a massive distribution of posters. When the curtain went up only one seat of the 200 available was occupied by a man sitting in the middle of the stalls. At the end of the play he applauded loudly and left. Not surprisingly, the actors declared Ashburton a cultural wilderness. According to the theatre's administrator, Ms Wendy Lost, the last time they went there, with *The Winslow Boy,* nobody turned up at all.

Sir Francis Drake, the Terror of the Spanish Main, was born at Crowndale, near Tavistock. His first command was a down-at-heel coastal vessel bequeathed him by the master to whom he was apprenticed. His early experiences in the West Indies gave Drake a hatred of Spain, but he gained revenge and wealth in 1572–73 by heading an expedition which snatched the King of Spain's treasure from the backs of mules plodding across the Isthmus of Panama. After sailing round the world, Drake "singed the King of Spain's beard" by destroying 33 ships in Cadiz harbour in 1587. When the Armada sailed against England a year later, Drake drummed them up the English Channel to disaster. This indomitable sea captain became fatally ill on a last expedition to the Caribbean in 1596, and just before the end, climbed into his armour "to meet death like a gentleman."

In 1581, Queen Elizabeth rode down to Deptford to dine aboard the *Golden Hind* and confer a knighthood on Drake, who had just returned from a round-the-world voyage. The banners Drake used to dress his "weather-beaten bark" can be seen in Buckland Abbey and are among the oldest in England. The next year, in 1582, Elizabeth gave Drake a New Year's gift of a silver gilt cup considered among the 100 best specimens of silver gilt in the country. It can be seen in Plymouth City Museum. Earlier that year the Spanish ambassador had complained to the Queen about Drake, calling him "the master thief of the unknown world." Elizabeth replied that "The gentleman careth not if I disown him," at the same time as she received a 400-percent profit on her outlay which had financed Drake's expedition.

Drake lived well on board the *Golden Hind.* He dined on solid silver tableware (stolen of course from Spain) and employed an orchestra of four to accompany him on his round-the-world voyages. The much publicized "I'll finish my game of bowls and then beat the Spaniards," has already been mentioned with respect to Sir Francis Drake, but contemporary suspicious opinion suggested that Drake had sold his soul to the Devil in exchange for the storm that drove the Spanish fleet north and westwards to their doom. Another popular story of the time has our hero sitting on the edge of the cliff on Plymouth Hoe whittling a stick. By some mysterious agency, each wood chip is, as it strikes the water, turned into a fully armed ship. Finally, Drake's drum accompanied the admiral on his circumnavigation of the globe in 1577–80. Legend tells us that Drake is not dead, but sleeping, and if his drum is beaten he will wake to his country's call. The drum was said to have been heard when the German fleet surrendered in 1918. It can be seen at Buckland Abbey on the outskirts of Plymouth. King Arthur too, is not dead but sleeping, and will come when his country needs him and I suspect that he and Drake would make a pretty formidable combination.

The Devonport Naval Column, erected to mark the renaming of Plymouth Dock in 1824, is one of the few commemorative columns in England shorter than it should be. The column was supposed to have a statue of George IV on top but the money ran out and the column has only a rather incongruous flagpole atop its 150-foot (45.6 m) height.

Plymouth's more famous column, the Armada Memorial on the Hoe, does have a figure on top but all they could think of was Britannia, and we all know that Britannias are two a penny.

In Southside Street, in the Barbican, is Jacka's Bakery, which claims to be the oldest commercial bakery in Britain. It is reputed to be where the ship's biscuits for the *Mayflower* were made but I think that claim should be taken with a pinch of flour.

TOURIST INFORMATION BUREAU: Civic Centre, Royal Parade, Plymouth, Devon, PL1 2EW. Tel (0752) 674303

SALISBURY

County of Wiltshire
London 83 (133 km) miles by road on M3 and A30
Hourly train service from London (Waterloo) approximately 80 minutes

Salisbury's history dates back to the 13th century, when it was decided to move the Bishop's See from Old Sarum to New Sarum in 1220. Old Sarum, the site of the Episcopal See after it was transferred from Sherborne at the end of the 11th century, consisted of a Norman cathedral and a castle. Gradually, the animosity between the castle soldiers and the clergy grew so acrimonious that the move was made to New Sarum which is still Salisbury's official name. Legend has it that the site of Salisbury Cathedral was chosen by the fall of an arrow from a bow drawn at venture. A bit like Robin Hood's gravesite. Incidentally, Old Sarum is only one and a half miles (2.4 km) from the centre of Salisbury and worth a visit. It's a good idea to visit Salisbury Museum (see below) first and get an idea, from an excellent model, of what the cathedral looked like in its heyday. Only the foundations of the old cathedral remain as stones from it were used in the construction of the new Cathedral and its Close.

Salisbury Cathedral was completed in 1258 after 38 years of uninterrupted work and this relatively short period of building is the reason for the cohesion of proportion and design in this, one of England's most impressive cathedrals. Mainly Early English in style, the magnificent 404-foot (121 m) spire, tallest in England, was added in the 14th century. The cathedral dominates the surrounding countryside and the first sight of it, as you approach the city from any direction, is breathtaking. One of the most renowned English landscape painters, John Constable, painted a famous picture of the Cathedral and Close in 1820 and the city has been a magnet for artists throughout the years (see Artistic Associations).

The city was built on the junction of the Avon and Nadder Rivers and, wonderfully, has still retained its character as a bustling market town. The streets are flanked by gabled houses and buildings of all periods are set in happy juxtaposition. Of course the architecture spans the centuries but it is all part of an original plan. Many English cities (Winchester is an example) grew up as a sort of medieval medley. Salisbury was planned on a grid or chequer, system which left space between the blocks.

Salisbury is a delightful city in which to wander. The Cathedral Close is one of the most beautiful in England and the buildings range in style from the Old Deanery, built in the 13th century, to Mompesson House, an elegant 18th-century merchant's house. Somewhat amazingly, houses from the various centuries harmonize gracefully, and a walk around the Close is highly recommended. Henry Fielding lived in the Close in the mid-18th century but I suspect the atmosphere was too tranquil for him to pen any of *Tom Jones* at this location.

The list of things to see in Salisbury is unending. St Martin's Church to the southeast of the city centre has sections dating back before the building of the Cathedral, while the beautiful parish church of Salisbury, St Thomas à Becket in St Thomas Square just off Bridge Street, has a remarkable medieval Doom painting over the chancel arch as well as early glass and embroidery, Tudor brasses, carving and heraldry and Georgian woodwork and wrought iron. In Thomas Hardy's novel Salisbury was renamed Melchester and St Thomas à Becket Church was the setting for *Jude the Obscure*. The Poultry Cross in Butcher Row just off the Market Square dates from the 15th century and the façade of the Joiners' Hall in St Ann Street is 16th century. The Banqueting Hall of John Halle, a 15th-century mayor of Salisbury is, unbelievably, the entrance to the Odeon Cinema in New Canal (just off the Market Square) and was restored by Pugin in 1834. The interior of the Odeon is magnificent mock Tudor – if that's not a contradiction in terms.

Finally, the Market Square itself is a delight. Try a visit to Salisbury on a Tuesday or Saturday (market days), even though at this time the parking is horrendous. When the square is bustling there are vendors in dozens of small tented stalls selling everything conceivable. Incidentally, the Tourist Information Centre is adjacent to the Market Square just behind the Guild Hall and is open 9–5pm daily.

WALK

Salisbury Walk – The walk begins at the Market Place car park where markets have been held since 1219 on every Tuesday, and on Saturday since 1361. Exit from the Market Square into Queen Street, passing in front of the **Guild Hall**. **Watson's China Shop** on your left dates from the early 14th century and was formed from two medieval houses. Turn right down **Fish Row** and **Butcher Row** which recall the days when the Market was segregated with respect to the commodities it sold. The **Poultry Cross** is 15th century, and as its name suggests, marks the spot where sales of poultry used to take place. There were also crosses for the sale of livestock, milk, cheese and wool, but all have disappeared. Turn right into Minster Street noting the **Haunch of Venison**, dating from the 15th century, on your left. Turn left into Blue Boar Row and then left again past **St Thomas Church** (see above). Continue up High Street towards the Cathedral Close. On your left is the **Bay Tree** occupying much of the former Old George Inn dating back to 1314. Ancient beams and plasterwork can be seen in the upstairs restaurant. Oliver Cromwell stayed here in 1645 and Samuel Pepys, who thought his bill exorbitant, in 1668.

Cross right into Crane Street. Houses in this street are among the oldest in Salisbury with **Church House** dating from the 15th century. Come back down Crane Street and on the corner with the High Street is **Beach's Bookshop** which is largely 14th century. On the opposite corner is **Mitre Corner** said to be the site of the first house built in Salisbury. Since 1451 the new bishop has been robed here before being led to the cathedral by the Dean and Chapter. Turn right into the Cathedral Close, which is guarded by a wall, gate and portcullis (relations between the Close and the rest of the city were not always harmonious). As you pass into the Cathedral precinct the **College of Matrons** is on your left – an almshouse founded

THE HIGH STREET GATE, SALISBURY

in 1682 by Bishop Ward who is said to have been moved to this generosity by an old flame whose clergyman husband had died. Turn right past **Mompesson House**, the **Wardrobe** (a military museum), the **North Canonry** and the **King's House** – so called because James I used to visit here. Turn left and enter the Cathedral. On your right as you enter are the **Cloisters** which are the largest in Britain. Off the Cloisters is the **Chapter House** with one of the four remaining copies of Magna Carta on view. The **Tower Vault** – just in front of the choir stalls – is 81 feet (24 m) high and the spire above five times as high, at 404 feet (121 m). Looking back down the nave, the simple **Shrine of St Osmund** is on your left. Much of the once elaborate ornamentation has gone, but the holes at the side of the tomb in which pilgrims placed the afflicted parts of their bodies for healing can still be seen. Further down the nave is the **Medieval Clock**, circa 1386, believed to be the oldest working clock in the world. Turn right as you come out of the cathedral and take the path across the north side. Cross St John's Street and you will see the **St Ann Street Gate**, which was built in the 14th century. Handel is reputed to have given his first concert in England here, in a room over the gate.

The **Joiners' Hall** in St Ann Street has a superb Jacobean façade. The sex of the carved corbels below the first-floor windows is difficult to determine; local legend claims that the carver wished to represent the councillors as a lot of "old women." Turn left at the Joiners' Hall and then left again into Trinity Street. At the corner of Trinity and Brown Streets is **Trinity Hospital**, circa 1379, built by Agnes of Bottenham, an ex-innkeeper and brothel owner, as an act of penance. The brothels were in fact in Culver Street, two blocks east. In 1452 their occupants were expelled from the city for refusing to wear the striped hoods of their profession. Turn left off Brown Street onto **New Canal**, so named for the wide channel of water that once ran through it. In fact nearly every street had such a channel, and Salisbury was known as the English Venice. The **Red Lion Hotel** on the left is a famous coaching inn and further down the road, the foyer of the **Odeon Cinema** was a 15th-century banqueting hall. Cross back into the Market Place, which once held the gallows, pillory, whipping-post and stocks, and you are back where the walk began.

MUSEUMS AND GALLERIES

Salisbury and South Wiltshire Museum – 65 The Close, Tel 332151. Situated in a building known as "The King's House," the museum has been the recipient of national awards for its galleries and has been noted Museum of the Year by National Heritage. Originally built for the Abbots of Sherborne in the 13th century, the building was completely reconstructed in the 15th century. The House was named after visits made to it by James I. Galleries reflect local interests such as Stonehenge, Old Sarum and the Salisbury giant. Also a porcelain and pottery collection with a good display of early Wedgewood. Open Oct–Mar Mon–Sat 10–4pm: April–Sept 10–5pm. Open Sun 2–5pm in July and Aug and during Salisbury Festival.

Mompesson House – The Close, Tel 335659. 18th-century merchant's house owned by the National Trust. Open April to Nov daily noon–6pm (not Thurs or Fri).

Museum of the Duke of Edinburgh's Royal Regiment (Berkshire and Wiltshire) – The Wardrobe, 58 The Close, Tel 336222. Regimental and military memorabilia.

Stonehenge – Ten miles (16 km) on A303. Two-hour tours available by bus. Tel 0722 336855. Possibly the most famous megalithic monument in the world. The circle of stones represents one of the most incredible achievements of early humankind. No one knows exactly what the use and purpose of Stonehenge was, but it is clear that it was some form of sacred temple or memorial for special purposes. Theories link it with fertility rites, astronomy and the solar calendar. In spite of its half-million annual visitors it is both a mystical and an awe-inspiring place, especially at dusk and dawn.

Wilton – Three miles (5 km) west of Salisbury on A30. King Egbert, ruler of the two ancient kingdoms of Wessex and Kent, had his Royal Palace here (circa 838). No trace remains and the foundations probably lie beneath the main street. King Alfred founded an important abbey here in the 9th century after defeating the Danes. When the abbey was dissolved in 1544 the lands were given to the First Earl of Pembroke by Henry VIII. The Earl built **Wilton House** on the abbey site which was destroyed by fire in 1647. The present house was designed by Inigo Jones and John Webb, and contains superb collection of pictures – Rubens, Van Dyck and Tintoretto are well represented. Especially interesting are the double and single cube rooms. The gardens are delightful (there is also a garden centre), with the famous Palladian Bridge (1737) of special note. Open April 10–Oct 14 (not Mon) also Bank Holidays (Mon included) 11am–6pm. Last admission 5:15pm. Tel 743115.

Also in the delightful village of Wilton is the **Royal Wilton Carpet Factory** which is also open to the public Mon–Sat 10–4pm. Tel 743204. For touring historic Wessex from Salisbury, pick up the **Wessex** booklet at the Tourist Information Centre. It's excellent.

The Hawk Conservancy – Weyhill, Hants. (15 miles (24 km) north on A338/A303). Tel 026477 772252. The largest and most comprehensive collection of birds of prey in southern England. Birds of prey from all over the world can be seen – hawks, falcons, eagles, owls, vultures and kites – and, weather permitting, flying demonstrations take place daily. Open Mar 1–last Sun in Oct 10:30–5pm.

Farmer Giles Farmstead – Tefont Magna (12 miles (19 km) on A30 Shaftesbury Road, then B3089). Tel 0722 716338. A working dairy farm where from 2:30 to 5pm you can watch 150 Friesians being milked. There are also Highland cattle, Shire horses, donkeys, Shetland ponies, calves, pigs, goats, rabbits and poultry. Open April 1–end of Oct daily 10:30–6pm.

THEATRE

Salisbury Playhouse – Box office 20333. One of the country's most successful repertory companies. In the main theatre one can see productions ranging in style from George Bernard Shaw's *Man and Superman* to Stephen Sondheim's musical *Sweeney Todd*. I saw a wonderful *Uncle Vanya* there which was challenging, thought-provoking and theatrically very exciting. The Salberg Theatre, the Playhouse's studio theatre, offers productions by visiting companies as well as in-house plays. A recent sampling included *Hamlet, The Life of Moll Flanders* by Claire Luckham who wrote *Trafford Tanzi* and a production showcasing the remarkable work of the Playhouse's Theatre-in-Education company. I saw Monstrous Regiment, one of the country's best touring companies mount a splendid production entitled *The Colony Comes a Cropper* there; a Marivaux one-act play followed by a one-act comment written by Robyn Archer. The production underlined the company's commitment to producing plays which present the richness of women's lives and experience.

There is also an art gallery which stages exhibitions during the year and the occasional jazz and folk concert. The theatre is centrally situated in the city at the Maltings site close to the Central Car Park. There is a restaurant serving simple but good fare.

Salisbury Art Centre – Box office 21744. A multi-art form venue located in a deconsecrated church building about three minutes walk from the Market Square. It offers programmes of theatre, dance, mime, comedy, jazz, pop and folk music. A programme sampling revealed two plays based respectively on Rasputin and Valentino, a folk group from the Andes, Humphrey Lyttleton's Jazz Band and a group called Blue Blud, described as Heavy Metal Mardi Gras – the mind boggles. The film series is a mix of classic and contemporary films from around the world (there's a late-night series too) and the Arts Centre boasts a small gallery with year-round exhibitions of painting and sculpture. At present it has serious financial problems and is threatened with closure.

MUSIC

Salisbury is too small to boast a resident symphony orchestra but the musical life of the city is rich, especially at the time of the **Salisbury Festival**, Tel 23883, which is held the first two weeks of September. The Salisbury Festival contains arts events of all kinds with international concerts being held in the splendid setting of the cathedral. During the rest of the year the Sarum Chamber Orchestra, the Salisbury Orchestral Society, the Farrant Singers and other groups give regular concerts at either the Cathedral or the auditorium of City Hall. Evensong is sung in the Cathedral each weekday at 5:30pm. An experience to be cherished.

CINEMA

Salisbury has only one cinema – the **Odeon**, New Canal, Tel 22080 – but it does have three screens and you are not likely to forget either its interior or exterior decor (see also Salisbury Arts Centre above).

BOOKSTORES

Everyman Bookshop – 5 Bridge Street, Tel 333531. A good feeling about Everyman. Good selection on four floors. Right in the middle of town, next to County Hotel.

Paperback Parade Ltd – 46 Fisherton Street, Tel 29368. Just what it says. Satisfactory if your tastes are pretty mainstream. Don't look for unusual items though.

Ottakar's – 9 New Canal, Tel 414060. Newish and rather elegant. Good selection of books. They also have CDs, records and tapes you can preview in armchair comfort. Superb surroundings and excellent service.

ANTIQUARIAN AND SECONDHAND BOOKS

Beach – 52 High Street, Tel 333801. One of my favourite secondhand book stores. Just the sort of place Helen Hanff would write to. Lots of little rooms with wonderful browsing (corner of High and Crane streets).

John and Judith Head – 88 Crane Street, Tel 27767. They specialize in books on hunting, shooting and fishing. Also some good, interesting and inexpensive prints.

ART GALLERIES

Wiltshire Gallery – 22 Fisherton Street, Tel 26346. Traditional English prints. They also do framing. There are some nice cricket prints I coveted last time I was there.

Courcoux and Courcoux – 90/92 Crane Street, Tel 333471. Quite a special place if you are interested in modern art. They specialize in all living artists and represent many top young sculptors and painters. They usually have work by Elizabeth Frink and Lynn Chadwick on hand, but be prepared for prices which are fair but not low. Last time I was there they had just sold a sculpture for £200,000. Still, one can always look. Four local exhibitions a year and you'll find the firm at the London and Bath Contemporary Art Fairs.

Ronald Carr – 6 St Francis Road, Tel 28892. Modern British etchings. Open by appointment only. One mile (1.6 km) north of town on A345.

ANTIQUE SHOPS

Ian J Brook Antiques and Picture Gallery – 26 North Street, Wilton, Tel 743392. Furniture, oil paintings, water colours, porcelain, pottery, silver, copper and brass.

Freddie Hastie – 46 St Ann Street, Tel 22957. Decorative items especially papier-mâché and toleware (19th century).

I G Hastie – 46 St Ann Street, Tel 22957. 18th- and 19th-century antique furniture and decorative works.

Joan Amos – 7A St John Street, Tel 330888. 19th-century porcelain and small furniture.

Derek Boston Antiques – 223 Wilton Road, Tel 22682. General furniture.

Robert Bradley – 71 Brown Street, Tel 333677. 17th- and 18th-century furniture and decorative items.

Berkshire Furnishings – 31 Winchester Street. Furniture, pictures and stipple engravings. 18th-19th century.

Castle Galleries – 81 Castle Street, Tel 333734. General antiques, coins and medals.

Edward Hurst Antiques – Stirling House, Paynes Hill, just off Ann Street. Country furniture 1650–1820.

T J Newsam – St Martin's House, 49 St Ann's Street, Tel 411059. Longcase and bracket clocks.

St John Street Gallery – 7 St John Street, Tel 412310. 18th- and 19th-century furniture, watercolours and objets d'art.

Salisbury Clock Shop – 107 Exeter Street. Antique clock specialists – also period furniture.

Memory Lane Antiques – 34 Chipper Lane, Tel 337587. Great fun.

Mr Micawber's Attic – 73 Fisherton Street, Tel 337822. Even greater fun.

Antique Market – 37 Catherine Street, Tel 26033. 30 dealers and a wide range of items.

Avonbridge Antiques Market – United Reform Church Hall, Fisherton Street, opposite hospital. 15 dealers, open Tues 9–4pm.

RESTAURANTS

Harper's – 7-9 Ox Row, The Market Square, Tel 333118. One of my favourite places for lunch, especially on a Tuesday or a Saturday when, if you are lucky enough to get a window table, you can look out on to the bustling market. Good home cooking. Lunch specials nearly always have fish – usually haddock or sole, as well as a daily roast and a steak and kidney pie. Try the excellent treacle tart for dessert. There's also a wonderful ale called the Bishop's Tipple – but only if you aren't driving. Open Mon–Sat 12–2 and 6:30–10pm.

Crustaceans – 2-4 Ivy Street, Tel 333948. An excellent, almost exclusively fish restaurant. Sole is very good and there are delicious prawns of all kinds. Their fish kebabs are also worth a try. Dinners only 7–10:30pm.

Yorkshire Fish Restaurant – Fisherton, Tel 25249. Traditional fish and chips. Open Mon–Sat 11am–11pm.

PUBS

Haunch of Venison – 1 Minster Street, opposite Market Cross adjacent to Market Square, Tel 22024. Building dates from circa 1430 when it was the church house for the church of St Thomas, just behind. Massive beams, oak benches, timbered walls, open fires and a unique pewter bar. The upper panelled room looks down on to the main bar. In 1903 workmen found a smoke-preserved, mummified hand holding some 18th-century playing cards here. It's behind glass on the wall. Good bar food ranging from sandwiches, soup, ploughman's and various pies to chicken curry and peppered beef. No food Sun evening.
King's Arms – St John Street, Tel 27629. Again lots of beams, settles and fireplaces. The panelled restaurant is very old. As the fireplace stone is the same age as the cathedral, the King's Arms, or part of it, may date from the 13th century. Bar food is good but not a varied as the Haunch of Venison. The pork chops cooked in cider are excellent.
Avon Brewery – Castle Street. The old theatre used to be next door and the pub still has a theatrical ambience. There is a garden at the back running down to the river. Good bar food. If you can sample their venison sausage, do! There is an excellent three-course supper menu. No food Sat evening or Sun.
The George – Used to be one of the country's finest inns but has now been rebuilt as a shopping arcade which is a shame as Shakespeare might have performed in its yard. Its façade is still worth a look and a visit to the upstairs coffee shop gives you an idea of what it was once like.
White Hart – St John Street, Tel 27476. The present building circa 1800 is on the site of an earlier inn. It has a very impressive façade with a carriage entrance added in 1820 which projects across the pavement. Above this there is a balcony with four pillars supporting a roof-level pediment. On the pediment is a white hart. Charles Dickens knew the inn, and refers to it in *Martin Chuzzlewit.*

ARTISTIC ASSOCIATIONS

John Fox, author of *Fox's Book of Martyrs* (1563) published his book the year he was made Canon of Salisbury Cathedral. Samuel Pepys, the great diarist, visited Salisbury in 1668 and stayed at the George Inn (see above), where he slept in a silken bed. There is a plaque in the arcade commemorating his visit. In his biography (1883), novelist Anthony Trollope recalls that he conceived the story of *The Warden* – from which came the "Barchester" novels – while wandering around Salisbury Cathedral. This is in spite of the fact that Barchester was based on Winchester. In Thomas Hardy's novels Salisbury is known as Melchester.

Probably the most famous painting of Salisbury Cathedral is John Constable's *Salisbury Cathedral from the Bishop's Grounds,* which can be seen in the Victoria and Albert Museum in London. Constable was friendly with Archdeacon John Fisher, a nephew of the Bishop of Salisbury, who lived at Ledenhall in the Cathedral Close. The artist was a frequent visitor to the house and Fisher bought several of Constable's works. The famous painting of the Cathedral was, however, executed on commission from the Bishop himself in 1823, to hang in his London home in Seymour Street. The Bishop, who appears in the picture strolling along a path with his wife, liked Constable's work, "all but the clouds" and said he would have preferred a clear blue sky.

This century Salisbury witnessed one of the most mysterious deaths among British artists. The victim was 29-year-old Christopher Wood. In 1930, after returning from France where he had produced his first truly mature and personal works, Wood went to see his family, who lived at Broad Chalke just outside the city. At Salisbury station he was met by his mother and sister who found him in a very agitated state. He claimed he was being followed by some strange Algerians and insisted on returning immediately to London. Whether intentionally or not, he subsequently fell under a moving train. On an envelope, found in his pocket, were scribbled two enigmatic sentences: "Are they positive?" and "Throwing away is not big enough proof." Wood was buried in the churchyard at Broad Chalke in a grave with a headstone carved by Eric Gill (see Chichester). This seems like a case for Ruth Rendell's Inspector Wexford, who has his patch at Romsey just a few miles to the southeast on the A30.

EPHEMERA

In the library of Salisbury Cathedral it is possible to see one of the four remaining copies of the Magna Carta, brought here for safety after it was signed by King John at Runnymede on June 15, 1215. The Magna Carta, the world's first Charter of Rights, is the Cathedral's most priceless treasure.

In Laurence Olivier's screen version of Shakespeare's *Richard III*, one of the most exciting moments is when Richard, hearing of the Duke of Buckingham's capture, hisses, in his most evil manner, "Off with his head." Interestingly this line does not appear in Shakespeare's play but was interpolated into the film version for dramatic effect. The Duke of Buckingham was duly executed on November 2, 1483, and the site of that execution is marked by a plaque, incongruously, on the wall of Dehenham's department store in the Market Square.

Reginald Salberg, who for many years was artistic director of the Salisbury Playhouse (the Salberg Studio – the Salisbury Playhouse's second stage – is named after him) tells this delightful story of a young and inexperienced actress who was on stage with a star player when for no reason at all the phone rang. The stage management had obviously made a mistake and the flustered actress was immensely reassured when the star picked up the receiver. His experience could cope with the situation. The star listened on the phone for a few seconds then, turning to the young actress, he handed it to her with a broad smile saying, "It's for you, darling."

The classical version of this story is that of an actor playing one of Shakespeare's kings. Kings in Shakespeare's plays are always receiving letters, and after having perused them, they share the contents with the audience. I always used to get the stage management team to write the actual words of text on my scroll so that when I was given it I could just read the letter as a letter. I justified this by convincing myself it was more realistic that way and put into the back of my mind the fact that I just didn't want to learn the words.

I therefore have tremendous sympathy with the actor who, due to a diabolical plot between the rest of the cast and the stage management, received an empty scroll at a matinee performance. His colleagues, barely disguising their smirks, wondered how he was going to give the audience the details of the Battle of Evesham as he had never memorized that section of the play. Equal to the occasion, the actor turned to the nearest unfortunate lord and handed him the empty scroll with the words, "My lord, my eyes grow dim, read this for me."

In Salisbury Museum there is a statue of a giant, which was carried around the city in the midsummer pageant of the Guild of Merchant Tailors. This Salisbury Guild is known to have existed as far back as 1496. Legend has it that the giant is St Christopher who, before his conversion, was the giant Reprobus who had a nasty habit of eating men. The story is told of St Christopher one day carrying a child over a river, and saying to him, "Child, you have put me in great peril, I might bear no greater burden." To which the child replied, "Marvel thou nothing, for thou hast borne all the world upon thee, and its sins likewise." The allegory behind the St Christopher legend is that the name means "Christ-bearer," and that the river is the river of death and the child, Christ. St Christopher is well known as the patron saint of travellers.

In museums at Avebury, Devizes and Salisbury can be seen the earthenware beakers or drinking cups which gave their name to the Beaker Folk. The Beaker Folk began to arrive in the Salisbury Plain area around 1800 BC, chiefly from Belgium and Holland. It was they who constructed the great ritual circle or temple at Avebury, an archaeological site that in my opinion is more impressive than Stonehenge. (To find Avebury, take the A338 north to Marlborough, go east along the A4 to Beckhampton Corner and take the Swindon Road two miles north.) The Beaker Folk were so called because the drinking cups were buried with their crouched bodies under round barrows, of which there are many on

Salisbury Plain. It has been suggested that the cups were to provide a means of drinking in the afterlife. Some members of the tribe, however, seem to have been less certain of the peaceful nature of any possible Valhalla and some skeletons have been found buried with archer's wrist guards and daggers.

TOURIST INFORMATION BUREAU: Fish Row, Salisbury, Wiltshire, SP1 1EJ.
Tel (0722) 334956

2
THE SOUTH

BRIGHTON
CANTERBURY
CHELTENHAM
CHICHESTER
FARNHAM

GUILDFORD
OXFORD
PORTSMOUTH
SOUTHAMPTON
WINCHESTER / WINDSOR

BRIGHTON

County of East Sussex
London 52 miles (83 km) by A23/M23. Train journey approximately 50 minutes from London (Victoria). Glyndebourne 8 miles (13 km) east of Brighton on A27 Lewes Road.

Although Brighton has some evidence of Roman settlement, and even of occupation by Neolithic tribes, there are few buildings earlier than the Regency, and it was at that period that the town achieved both fame and notoriety. Today Brighton is the largest town in Sussex and the largest seaside resort in the southeast. Its elegant Regency architecture clusters cheek by jowl with gift shops, modern places of entertainment and swimming pools, making it an amalgam of the refined and the raucous.

A fishing village, long buried under the sea, preceded modern Brighton. The Tudor town was built behind walls as a defence against French raiders, but this did not save it from being burnt down twice in the 16th century. The small fishing and farming village was "discovered" in 1754 when Dr Richard Russell proclaimed the therapeutic benefits of his amazing seawater cure (see Ephemera). Almost overnight the town became the fashionable haunt of London high society, and when Prince George (later to become Prince Regent and King George IV) decided to make himself a home here, Brighton's popularity soared higher than ever. In 1787 the Prince commissioned Henry Holland to build him a classically styled "pavilion" with the interior decorated in the Chinese style (*chinoiserie*) popular at that time. Between 1815 and 1822 this Royal Pavilion was rebuilt to the plans of John Nash in its present Indian Moghul style, with onion-shaped domes, spires and minarets, but still generally keeping the "Chinese" decor inside. After becoming king,

PAVILION, BRIGHTON

George still occupied the Royal Pavilion regularly until 1827. His brother William IV also spent much time there and later Queen Victoria stayed at the pavilion, but abandoned it in 1845. She claimed the building did not afford her enough privacy, that people would peer in at the windows and errand boys pester her when she took a walk. She sold the Pavilion to the town in 1850, first stripping it of everything that could be removed and leaving just an empty shell. In the following years many furnishings were returned from both Buckingham Palace and Windsor Castle and today the Pavilion appears much as it did when it was a royal residence (see Museums).

WALK

Brighton Walk – Park in the Kingswood Street car park which is between Brighton Polytechnic and the fruit and vegetable market. Walk right on Kingswood Street to Grand Parade, then left across the road to the **Royal Pavilion** (see above). Across the roadway from the Pavilion stands the **Dome**, originally built in 1806 as the Royal Stables. The Dome itself is 80 feet (24 m) high and 65 feet (19.5 m) in diameter and was modelled on the Halle au Blé in Paris. The building was remodelled in 1935 and is now a concert hall seating 2100. At the entrance to the Pavilion in Church Street are the **Museum** and **Art Gallery**, housed in rooms that were originally intended as an indoor tennis court for the Prince Regent. It is of course not just for the Royal Pavilion that we owe a debt of gratitude to Prince George. His friends shared his enthusiasm for the area and they built many of the beautiful Regency terraces for which Brighton is famous. If you walk down from the Pavilion to the Promenade you will see **Palace Pier** to your left and **West Pier** to your right. As I write, West Pier is closed and its future under review, but the Palace Pier still attracts enormous crowds with entertainment both live and mechanical in the summer season. Close to the Palace Pier is the **Aquarium** which has operated for more than 100 years and nearby is a **Waxworks**, devised by a great-grandson of Madame Tussaud and operated on similar lines to the London original. In the area between the Royal Pavilion to the north and the Palace and West Piers to the east and west are the **Lanes**. Based on the original street plan of medieval Brighton, the Lanes offer a fascinating glimpse of a vanished age. It's not difficult to imagine these narrow passageways and alleys as they might have been in the Middle Ages – the bustling thoroughfares of a thriving fishing community with the upper floors projecting out so far that they almost meet in the middle. Add to this the presence of Regency-inspired façades, elegant low windows and elaborate doorways and a sense of old Brighton is immediately engendered. Many of the small houses, some of which used to be fishermen's cottages, have been converted into antique and curio shops and the area has a special charm all its own. They are situated just south of the Royal Pavilion and are bounded by West Street, North Street, East Street and Kings Road.

From the Royal Pavilion walk up North Street and at the **Clock Tower** take the right hand fork into Dyke road. Here on a peaceful green you will find **St Nicholas' Church**, the Mother Church of Brighton. Although rebuilt in 1853 the church has parts dating from the 14th century. There is a Norman font and a fine 15th-century chancel screen (see Ephemera). Another church of interest in the town is St Peter's (in York Place on the A23 Crawley Road) which was built in 1823 in Gothic style by Charles Barry and replaced St Nicholas' as the parish church of Brighton in 1873. It has a mass of pinnacles and inside there is much 19th-century glass. **St Bartholemew's** (Anne Street) also Gothic in style, has the tallest nave in Europe, while the best Regency architecture can be seen in the **Grand Parade** (directly north of the

West Pier). From St Nicholas' Church retrace your steps to the Clock Tower, down North Street to the Royal Pavilion and back to the car park.

MUSEUMS AND GALLERIES

Art Gallery and Museum – Church Street, Tel 603005. The museum building was remodelled from stabling and coach houses which formed part of the Royal Stables built by the Prince of Wales in the early 1870s. There are sections devoted to art nouveau and art deco, Sussex archaeology and folk life, ceramics, ethnography and Brighton history. There are some Old Master paintings and watercolours and an unconventional costume gallery deliberately planned to provoke thought about the wearing of clothes. Open Tues–Sat 10–5:45pm; Sun 2–5pm.

Royal Pavilion – North Street, Tel 603005. The Royal Pavilion was designed by John Nash and built between 1815 and 1822 for George, Prince of Wales, later George IV. The picturesque exterior recalls Moghul India, whilst the so called "Chinese taste" prevails in the sumptuously furnished interiors. The remarkable Music Room was severely damaged by fire in 1975 and then, with restoration only just completed, suffered further misfortunes during the disastrous gales of October 1987. The displays include much of the original furniture lent by HM The Queen, and a magnificent collection of Regency silver and silver-gilt. The fully equipped Great Kitchens are a notable feature and have much the same appearance as when they were built. Open daily June–Sept 10–6pm; Oct–May 10–5pm.

Booth Museum of Natural History – 194 Dyke Road, Tel 552586. This museum was erected in 1874 by Edward Booth to house his collection of (stuffed) British birds. In addition to comprehensive displays of these birds mounted in settings that recreate their natural habitat, there are galleries of vertebrate evolution, butterflies of the world and Sussex geology, including bones of Iguanadon, the local dinosaur. There are also reference collections of insects, osteology, palaeontology, eggs and bird and mammal skin together with herbaria. Open Mon–Sat 10–5pm; Sun 2–5pm.

Barlow Collection – Library Building, University of Sussex. Falmer, Tel 6786678. On the A27, midway between Brighton and Lewes. The collection is considered to be the most important of its kind in Europe. It reflects 3000 years of Chinese civilization, with exhibits of bronzes, ceramics and figurines. The figurines in particular are of high quality. Open Tues, Thurs term time 11:30–2:30pm.

Preston Manor – The Thomas Stanford Collection – Preston Park, Tel 63005. Two miles (3.2 km) from the town centre on A23 London Road. Built circa 1739 and remodelled in 1905, the house incorporates 13th-century features in the basement. The home of the Stanford family for nearly 200 years, it was presented to Brighton Corporation by Sir Charles and Lady Thomas-Stanford in 1932 together with its collections of furniture, pictures, porcelain and silver. It is furnished and decorated to show the way of life of a rich family in the years before the First World War (the period of "Upstairs, Downstairs"). The rooms contain a wide-ranging collection of both English and Continental furniture, as well as notable 18th- and 19th-century silver and plated ware. The entrance hall displays walnut furniture from the 1680s to the 1730s. The paintings and watercolours are mainly by 19th-century English artists.

In 1939 the widow of the celebrated furniture historian, Percy Macquoid, presented her late husband's outstanding collection of English and Continental furniture and decorative art to the museum, which also has a good collection of 18th-century English drinking vessels. Open Wed–Sat 10–5pm; Tues,Sun 10–1 and 2–5pm.

Stanmer Village Rural Museum – Stanmer Park, Tel 509640. Three miles (4.8 km) north of Brighton on the A27 Lewes Road. The museum is in the yard of Stanmer House, built in 1722 for the Earls of Chichester. The house itself is not open to the public. There is a large collection of agricultural implements, blacksmith's and wheelwright's tools and photographs illustrating the history of Stanmer. A donkey wheel and a horse-gin have also been preserved. Open Easter–Oct Thurs, Sun, Bank Hols 2:30–5pm.

HMS Cavalier – Brighton Marina, Tel 699919. On the Marine Drive east of the Palace Pier. HMS *Cavalier*, launched in 1944, is the only surviving destroyer to have seen active service in the Second World War and the last representative of the long line of destroyers which originated with the HMS *Havock* in 1893. Visitors can tour the ship and inspect her accommodation and equipment. Open daily from 10:30am.

Brighton Aquarium and Dolphinarium – Marine Parade, Madeira Drive, Tel 604234. Brighton's elegant aquarium was opened in 1872. Nowadays it presents a wide range of aquatic creatures in conditions similar to their local habitat. These include local sea and fresh-water fish, tropical species, reptiles, molluscs and amphibia. The collections illustrate evolutionary development, types of locomotion, protective colouring and feeding habits. The Sea Pool area has dolphin shows at specific times of the day, and the aquarium has a breeding group of California sea lions, which are given opportunities to demonstrate their learning abilities and co-ordination both on land and in the water. Open daily 10–5pm.

British Engineerium – Off Nevil Road, Hove. North of the town off Shoreham Road. The Engineerium is in Brighton's 1866 water-pumping station with its 100-foot (30 m) chimney, classic panchromatic brickwork and 1876 Eastons and Anderson beam engine. The original coal store is now the museum's display area. It contains the Corliss engine, which won first prize when shown at the Paris International Exhibition of 1889, together with traction engines, steam fire engines, a hot engine bay and a display illustrating the history of the electric motor. Both the beam engine and the Corliss engine operate in steam on Sundays and Bank Holidays throughout the year. The Engineerium also has what is believed to be the finest collection of steam models in Europe, including the original model locomotive made by George Stephenson and the original design model of Timothy Hackworth's "Sans Pareil" which came second to the "Rocket" in the 1829 Trials. Open daily 10–5pm.

Hove Museum and Art Gallery – 19 New Church Road, north of the Leisure Centre, Tel 779410. The museum has outstanding collections of 18th- and early 19th-century British pottery and porcelain, 20th-century British drawings and paintings and historic dolls. Other sections contain toys, 18th-century paintings, furniture, glass, silver, watches, coins and medals. There are also military exhibits and displays illustrating the history of Hove and Sussex. Open Tues–Fri 10–5pm; Sun 10–4:30pm.

Old Ship Hotel – King's Road, on the sea front between the piers. Tel 29001. See Ephemera.

THEATRE

Theatre Royal – New Road, close to Royal Pavilion, Tel 28488. The Theatre Royal offers a first-class touring programme of plays, many of which are presented here before their West End openings. The theatre seats 1000 and has an intimate, Georgian-style interior, which is superbly maintained. The abundance of red plush and the feeling of history evoked by the building make it an experience to visit regardless of what play is being presented. The theatre's programme is similar to the Theatre Royal Bath with productions ranging from middle-of-the-road drama to ballet, comedy and a pantomime at Christmas.

Gardner Centre – University of Sussex, Falmer Brighton, Tel 685861. Situated on the university campus, four miles northeast of Brighton on the A27 to Lewes, the Centre offers an exciting programme of "alternative theatre" which has recently included works by Dario Fo, Harold Pinter, Sarah Daniels and Samuel Beckett. The varied and adventurous programme also includes music, jazz and dance.

Dome – 29 New Road, across from the Royal Pavilion, Tel 674357. The Dome is an entertainment complex comprising a large concert hall, a smaller theatre and the Corn Exchange which hosts trade shows and the like. Theatrical presentation occasionally takes place in the **Pavilion Theatre** while the Dome hosts large-scale events such as musicals, dance, ballet and concerts.

MUSIC

Gardner Arts Centre (see above) – Hosts individual artists, chamber groups, jazz, pop and ethnic music. Recent visitors have included the Chilingarian String Quartet, the Jaleo Flamenco Group, the East Sussex Wind Orchestra and Awatna, the music of the Aymara Indians. There is also an exciting dance programme (Shobana Jeyasing Dance Theatre and the Feather Store Laughs) and jazz and popular music such as the Hank Wexford Band.

The **Dome** hosts orchestral concerts by such ensembles as the Royal Flanders Philharmonic and the Brighton Philharmonic as well as dance companies such as Les Ballets Africains and the Red Army Ensemble. Popular music and musicals are also presented.

The **Brighton Centre**, King's Road on the sea front by the West Pier, Tel 202881, generally presents popular music concerts by such artists as James Last, Johnny Mathis and Paul Young.

CINEMA

Commercial cinema at the **Cannon**, East Street, Tel 27010 (4 screens) and the **Odeon** in the Kingswest Boulevard complex on King's Road, Tel 25890 (5 screens). There's also the **Duke of York's Cinema** in Preston Circus, Tel 602503, which is the nearest Brighton has to an art house.

The best time to visit Brighton is during the **Brighton Festival** which runs practically the whole of May. Thematic in nature, the Festival recently pursued an Eastern and Central European theme with orchestras from Moscow, Leipzig and Poland. There were also performances by Eastern European soloists, conductors and singers as well as Czech puppets and ballet. A comedy festival also runs throughout the month together with art and craft exhibitions, jazz, an international theatre season, master classes and events for children. Write Brighton Arts Information Centre, Box F, 111 Church Street, Brighton, BN1 1UD for more information or call 676926.

BOOKSTORES

The best are **Waterstone's** at 55/56 North Street, Tel 27867, **Fagin's** at 4 Air Street, Tel 772621, and **Hatchard's** at 17/18 North Street, Tel 720763. You expect these chain stores to be good but there are other gems in Brighton. I especially like **Ottakar's** at 34 Duke Street, Tel 728463, and **Read All About It**, Tel 205824, has a wide range of stock and is open seven days a week. Of the other independents, **Robinson's** of 11 Bond Street, Tel 29396, has an **HMSO** outlet, **City Books** at 23 Western Road, Hove is your best bet to the west, **Court House Bookshop** at 181 Edward Street is friendly, **The Booksmith** at 65 East Street, Tel 21680, is very efficient and the **English Language Bookshop** in George Street is what it says. Of the specialist shops, **Book Bargains of Oxford** at 1 Queens Road, Tel 207741, has remainders and sale books; religion is dealt with by **Scripture Union** at 8 Kings Road, Tel 29655, and **SPCK** in North Street, Tel 28764. Comics are at **Virgin Comics**, 157/161 Western Road, Hove, Tel 25300, and **Forbidden Planet** at 29 Sydney Street, Tel 687620 (well, sci-fi really). Railway books at **Dreambeam Media**, 29 Lodes Road, Tel 509552. Peace books at **Brighton Peace Centre** 28 Trafalgar Street, Tel 620125 and a good selection at **Collie Book** 34 Kensington Avenue, Tel 605422, rounds off a goodly choice.

ANTIQUARIAN AND SECONDHAND BOOKS

There's a cluster of good browsing situated in Trafalgar Street which is close to the Central Station. **Wax Factor**, Tel 673744 is at No 24, **C Walton Antiquarian Books**, Tel 600400, is at No 31 (a good selection here) and the **Trafalgar Bookshop**, Tel 684300, is at No 44 (a good secondhand stock). In about the same area is **Tenpenny Book Exchange**, Tel 691012, at 95 North Road which is off Queen's Road, south of the station, **David's Book Exchange**, Tel 690223, is at 3 Sydney Street which is off Trafalgar Street itself and **NF Brooks**, Tel 23105, at 12A Queen's Road which is just north of the Clock Tower. The two other shops I would recommend are in the Lanes. Both are excellent with some fine antiquarian volumes and selected secondhand stock: **Colin Page Antiquarian Books**, Tel 25954, is at 36 Duke Street and **Holleyman and Treacher Ltd**, Tel 28007, are at 21A Duke Street.

ART GALLERIES

There are many galleries presenting interesting work in Brighton. There is a lot of very good contemporary work on view and I'll start off at **Clairmonte Galleries**, 56 Gardner Road, Tel 622027. They have a nice collection of contemporary oils and watercolours. **Florentine Galleries** at 14 Brighton Square, Tel 23730, also deal with contemporary artists, but their collection deals with the way contemporary artists handle traditional subjects – an interesting philosophy and some fascinating and imaginative work. If your taste runs to contemporary jewellery then **Hugo Barclay** at 7 East Street in the Lanes, Tel 21694, has some stunning work. He also has contemporary ceramics and glass and usually has an exhibition of work by a contemporary print maker. This gallery is not to be missed. I'm also fond of **Window Gallery**, 3 Dukes Lane, Tel 726190 (the Lanes). They too deal in contemporary art but silk-screens, etchings, watercolours and limited edition prints. I'm fond of browsing here too. **Wandomir** at 78 Hollingbury Road, Tel 501629, deals in contemporary oil paintings and **M A Oxley**, 6 Sandgate Road, Tel 541739, has Victorian paintings and pictures. And to finish with something completely different, as John Cleese was wont to say, **C F Hussey** at 4 George Street, Tel 681852, deals in old Brighton photographs and very attractive they are too, vividly recalling the spirit of a bygone age.

ANTIQUE DEALERS

There are over 100 antique shops in Brighton. What I have attempted to do is to list them and where I consider it possible, give you an idea of their location. The Hove shops are not given any directions as they're easier to find, nor those Brighton stores where directions are complicated. The main areas for antiques are: 1. The Lanes, 2. Upper North Street which is northwest of the Clock Tower, 3. Gloucester Road which is east off Queen's Road and north of the Post Office and North Road which is east of Queen's Road just south of Gloucester Road, and 4. Hove.

1. *The Lanes*
Alan Adrian Ltd – l5C Prince Albert Street, Tel 25015.
Attic Antiques – 23 Ship Street, Tel 26378.
T Barnes – 24 Meeting House Lane, Tel 202929.
Bauermeister and Colwell Antiques – 2 Chapel Place, North Street, Portslade, Tel 411620.
Brighton Antiques Gallery – 41 Meeting House Lane, Tel 26693/21059.
Chalcrafts (Brighton) Ltd – 22 Meeting House Lane, Tel 28897.
David Hawkins and Sons – 15B Prince Albert Street, Tel 21357.
Elizabeth Corin – 29 Meeting House Lane, Tel 778354.
Hallmarks – 4 Unicorn Street, Tel 725477.
D Hawkins – 156 Prince Albert Street, Tel 21357.
Lancaster Antiques – 19 Middle Street, Tel 727791.
Le Jazz Hot – 14 Prince Albert Street, Tel 206091. Art deco and art nouveau.
Michael Norman Antiques – 15 Ship Street, Tel 29253.
H Miller – 22 Ship Street, Tel 26255.
P Moorhead – 22B Ship Street, Tel 26062 and 59A Ship Street, Tel 28209.
The Old Picture Shop - 2 Nile Street, Tel 725609.
Sue Pearson – 13A Prince Albert Street, Tel 29247. Antique dolls and teddy bears.
John Perver Antiques – 53 Ship Street, Tel 26985.
Resner's – 1 Meeting House Lane, Tel 29127.
J F J Sturmey – 59D Ship Street, Tel 202388.
Syd Jewellers – Prinny's, 3 Meeting House Lane, Tel 26729.
Tapsell Antiques – 59-59A Middle Street, Tel 28341.
Graham Webb – 59 Ship Street, Tel 21803.

2. *Upper North Street*
Ben Pontin – 53 Upper North Street, Tel 29409.
John Bird – 44 Upper North Street, Tel 739425.
Carmichael Peters – 33 Upper North Street, Tel 28072.
W Gilbert – 34 Upper North Street, Tel 21415.
Dudley Hume – 46 Upper North Street, Tel 23461.
E G Keys – 37 Upper North Street, Tel 21065.
Joachim Mendes – 66 Upper North Street, Tel 775978.
Peter Gee-Pemberton – 52 Upper North Street, Tel 720241.
Ben Pontin Antiques – 52 Upper North Street, Tel 20409.
Rutland Antiques – 48 Upper North Street, Tel 29991.
Raymond J Smith – 50 Upper North Street, Tel 204958.
Pamela Wright – 45 Upper North Street, Tel 738838.
Wyn Gillett – 34 Upper North Street, Tel 21415. Antique lace and linen.

3. *Gloucester Road*
Art Deco Etc – 73 Upper Gloucester Road, Tel 29268.
Cabinets – 37 Gloucester Road, Tel 692110.
Good Olde Days – 39 Gloucester Road, Tel 688076.
Simon Hatchwell Antiques – 94 Gloucester Road, Tel 691164.
House of Antiques – 16 Gloucester Road, Tel 695431.
Mall Gallery – Gloucester Road, Tel 609000.
Nadine's – 14 Gloucester Road, Tel 25304.
Percy Vear – 88 Gloucester Road, Tel 609863.
L Woolman Antiques – 29 Gloucester Road, Tel 609645.

4. *Hove*
Angel Antiques – 16 Church Road, Tel 737955.
Antiques Et Cetera – 190 Portland Road, Tel 773974.
Andrea Bondi – Flat 3, 27 Brunswick Square, Tel 204836.
Bradshaws – 53 Brunswick Street East, Tel 770002.

Browns – 76 Erroll Road, Tel 413163.
Memoirs – 67B Church Street, 775375.
Palmeira Antiques – 74 Western Road, Tel 822476.
Rin-Tin-Tin – 34 North Road, Tel 672424.
Classic Clock Co Ltd – 152B Church Road, Tel 735420.
Connoisseur Antiques Galleries – 113 Church Road, Tel 777398.
Shirley-Ann's – 69 Church Road, Tel 770045.
Sophie – 87 Portland Road, Tel 779323.
Kenneth Wigginton – 179 Church Road, Tel 783530.
Yellow Lantern Antiques – 34 Holland Road, Tel 771572.

Shops which do not fit easily into the above sections are listed below followed by their approximate geographic locations.
Amon Antiques – 6 Sydney Street. Gloucester Road, east of station. Tel 680043.
Antique Clothes and Lace – 35 Kensington Gardens. West of Queen's Road Post Office. Tel 695427.
Beckford-Weeks – Bella Vista, London Road. Take main road out to London north of town. Tel 508204.
Bel Air Antiques – 18 St George's Road, East of Royal Pavilion. Tel 687238.
Brian Page Antiques – 8 Foundry Street, off Queen's Road south of Central Station, Tel 609310. Japanese Art specialist.
Clive and Philip – 67 St James Street, north of aquarium, Tel 676833.
R Cushings – 5A Bedford Street, off Marine Parade, west of aquarium. Tel 688886.
David Wigdor Antiques – 30 Trafalgar Street, adjacent to Central Station. Tel 677272.
Deabe Gragan Antiques – 18 Marlborough Street, off Western Road west of Clock Tower, Tel 207207.
Direct Antiques – 4 Lewes Road, north of town by St Peter's Church, Tel 571629.
Down Lain – 28A North Road, east of Queen's Road just north of Post Office, Tel 697496.
El Gringo – 5-6 Regent Street, west of Clock Tower, Tel 676608.
Goodwoods – 11 Rock Street, east of aquarium. Tel 675903.
Hyndford Antiques – 143 Edward Street, east of Royal Pavilion. Tel 679936.
Michael Tidy – 87 St George's Road, east of Royal Pavilion. Tel 602389.
Oasis – 36 Kensington Gardens, west of Queen's Road Post Office, Tel 683885.
Odin Antiques – 43 Preston Street, north of West Pier, Tel 732738.
Pandora's Box Antiques – 112 St George's Road, east of Royal Pavilion, Tel 603305.
Peter Ivor Antiques – 84 Preston Street, north of West Pier, Tel 202520.
Pyramid – 9A Kensington Gardens, west of Queen's Road Post Office, Tel 607791.
Recollections – 1A Sydney Street, off Gloucester Road east off Station, Tel 681517.
Terry Skinner – 24 Chatham Place, west of Central Station, Tel 28591.
J Taylor – 82 Lewes Road, north of town by St Peter's Church, Tel 603950.
I Watson – 77-78 North Road, east of Queen's Road and north of Post Office, Tel 682566.
The Trading Place – 32 Prestonville Road, west of Central Station, Tel 822651.
David Watts – 5 Upper Gardner Street, just north of museum, Tel 600894.
    The area to the right of the Central Station, as you approach it up Queen's Road, is called North Lanes and roughly consists of North Road, Gloucester Road, Trafalgar Street and London Road to the east. Note that there is a Saturday morning flea market in this area in Upper Gardner Street and a Sunday morning "junk" market in the station car park.

RESTAURANTS

Langan's Bistro – 1 Paston Place, Tel 606933, is a cut above most bistros. The menu is small and it changes weekly with the ebb and flow of supplies. Generally equal space is given to meat and fish and the last time I ate there I had excellent duck. I have a feeling, in fact, that Langan's is strong on duck. I've always maintained that the true test of good restaurant is how they make a crème caramel or a crème brulée – here the crème brulée was topnotch and even the coffee was excellent. This is a place not to be missed. Open Tues–Sun 12:30–2:30 and 7:30–10:30pm. No Sat lunch or Sun dinner.
Food for Friends – 17A-18 Prince Albert Street (The Lanes) Tel 202310. This easygoing vegetarian café is worth considering even if you are not a vegetarian. Indeed, I got the impression that a lot of customers are not, but that they eat there because the food is good and excellent value for money. There are excel-

lent soups, of course, and substantial hot dishes like vegetable casseroles and stuffed pancakes. There are good dishes like vegetable casseroles and stuffed pancakes. There are good puddings, homemade cakes and the bread, naturally, is excellent. Try the fresh-squeezed juices. There is a small wine list. Open all week 9am–10pm.

If you are going to Glyndebourne, then it might be useful for you to stop in Lewes at an excellent restaurant called **Kenwards** in Pipe Passage, 151A High Street, Tel 472343. The cooking is extremely good with local ingredients to the fore – simply and classically cooked to bring out their full flavour and distinction. I had lunch there: a very satisfactory fill-your-own-plate cold buffet, although a shortened version of the evening menu was available. The wine list is quite remarkable. It must be the best for this type of restaurant in the whole British Isles. The puddings are wonderfully English. Open Mon–Sat 12–2:15 and 7:30–9:30pm. No Sat lunch or Mon dinners.

Back in Brighton, I hear good reports from friends about **Annie's**, 41 Middle Street, Tel 202051, a bustling cheerful British bistro right in the middle of the Lanes, a delightful trattoria called **Latin in the Lane** just south of Annie's at 10 King's Road, Tel 28672, where there is excellent freshly made pasta and **Melrose**, further along King's Road at No 132, Tel 26520, which is essentially a Cypriot café with interesting and unusual food.

PUBS

Bath Arms – Meeting House Lane, Tel 29437. A very pretty stone exterior in the Lanes fronts a charming bar with wooden furniture, fireplace, mirrors and bookshelves. Basic bar food. They brew their own pale ale aptly named Bathwater, which (in spite of its name) has a pleasant, malty taste.

Druid's Head – Situated at 9 Brighton Place, Tel 25490 in a little square originally known as "the knob," where the town well was situated. The Druid's Head probably began as an ordinary cottage in the 16th century. It has been much altered, but it is still one of the few houses in the Lanes to have retained its original flint front. Good bar food and excellent atmosphere.

Cricketer's Arms – 49 Church Road, Tel 417957. One of the most architecturally interesting pubs in the town. Its history can be traced back to the 17th century when it was known as the Last and Fishcart (a "last" was equivalent to 10,000 fish), although the present building dates from the 18th century. To the right of the main buildings the stableyard can still be seen, with its round-headed doors, and the premises above extend over the entire space. The yard was the last site of the Town Pound in 1882.

The **Belvedere** – A lively pub squashed into a long arch, below the road and right on the beach at 157 King's Road Arches (between the piers). Its sister pub next door is the **Fortune of War**, Tel 205065. It is lined with marine planking and it's quieter here than the Belvedere. Traditional bar food and a happy hour, beloved by North Americans, where you can purchase two drinks for the price of one, are two of the attractions.

Again, if you are Lewes-bound, then I recommend the **Dorset Arms** at 22 Malling Street, Tel 477110. It has excellent bar food, plus a restaurant, and it dates from the 17th century. It serves Harvey's Ales and as it's in sight of the brewery, one would expect the suds to be well kept.

ARTISTIC ASSOCIATIONS

Dr Johnson worked on his *Lives of the Poets* here while staying with the Thrale household at their seaside home in West Street (now the site of a dance hall). Mrs Thrale was an especial friend of the good doctor(see also Penzance). Fanny Burney also visited the Thrales and she and the family attended St Nicholas' Church, where there is a memorial tablet to Dr Johnson. In 1791 Charlotte Smith, whose nostalgic descriptions of the countryside were much admired, was visited here by William Wordsworth, who was on his way to France. Dickens stayed here many times (see Ephemera) and *Dombey and Son* was written here in 1847–48. Ivy Compton-Burnett, the novelist, lived here for many years in her parents' house in Hove. Richard Jeffries, the naturalist and novelist, author of *Bevis,* lived here in 1885, while another novelist, John Cowper Powys, taught at a girls' school in the west of the town in the 1920s. One of the most interesting of Brighton residents was A E Coppard, the short story writer and poet. He was born here in 1872 and lived in the town until after his marriage in 1906. He attended the Board School in Fairlight Place and was forced to leave at the age of nine. He started work as an office boy and then became a bookkeeper, all the while educating himself at the public library. The short stories "Nine Penny Flute" and "Pomona's Babe" are about Brighton. Sir Laurence Olivier lived for some years in one of Brighton's most beautiful Regency terraces. He travelled to the National Theatre by train each day.

As well as the numerous artistic and literary figures who have made Brighton their home, a large number of authors have made the town a setting for their literary works. Sir Arthur Conan Doyle's *Rodney Stone* (1896) and Thackeray's *Vanity Fair* (1847) have scenes set in Regency Brighton. Henry James's short story "Sir Edmund Orme" (1904), Arnold Bennett's *Clayhanger* (1910) and its sequel *Hilda Lessways* (1911), Somerset Maugham's *Of Human Bondage* (1915) and A S M Hutchinson's *If Winter Comes* (1920) also have scenes set in Brighton.

The Old Ship Hotel, King's Road, Tel 29001, is one of Brighton's strongest links with her past. There was an inn on this site in the 17th century. In 1755, when Brighton was becoming fashionable, it was rebuilt and became both an important social centre and the point from which London coaches left and arrived. By the end of the century there was a weekly ball and card assemblies twice a week, under the patronage, for a number of years, of Mrs Fitzherbert, the mistress of the Prince of Wales (later George IV). Charles Dickens stayed here when he was working on *Barnaby Rudge* and Thackeray wrote part of *Vanity Fair* in the hotel.

The great English landscape painter John Constable was a frequent visitor to Brighton in the 1820s during the periods his wife spent there for the sake of her health. The seashore provided him with plenty of material for his sketching and was the subject of one of his large-scale canvases *Marine Parade and Chain Pier, Brighton,* which can be seen in the Tate Gallery, London. On the whole, however, he thoroughly disapproved of the place. "Brighton is the receptacle of the fashion and off-scouring of London ... and the beach is only Piccadilly by the seaside... In short, there is nothing here for the painter but the breakers and the sky – which have been lovely indeed and always varying."

The stylish artificiality described by Constable had a formative influence on Brighton's greatest native artist, the art nouveau illustrator, Aubrey Beardsley. He was born in 1872 at 12 Buckingham Road (now No 31) and attended Brighton Grammar School. He indulged his early taste for High Church ceremonial at the church of the Annunciation of Our Lady in Washington Street. He left Brighton for London as a young man and in a working life of only eight years became one of the most important illustrators of his day with a penchant for fantastic and erotic subjects. His illustrations for Oscar Wilde's *Salome*, Pope's *Rape of the Lock* and Ben Jonson's *Volpone* are unique. He died of tuberculosis in 1898 at the age of 26.

In recent years Brighton has been the home of the Romanian artist Arnold DaGhani. He has decorated every available wall space and piece of furniture in his house (at 1 Palmeira Square) obsessively, and in a variety of media.

EPHEMERA

Near the entrance to the Palace Pier is the tiny terminus building, hardly larger than a hut, of Britain's first electric-powered railway. It was constructed in 1883 by the Brighton electrical pioneer, Magnus Volk, and runs along the seafront for about a mile. In 1896 Volk opened an extension along the coast as far as Rottingdean, and since the line was covered at high tide, he built a strange carriage on stilts known as the "Daddy Long Legs," which was discontinued after only four years following many breakdowns.

Brighton was "discovered" in the mid 1700s when Dr Richard Russel first proclaimed the benefits of his amazing "Seawater Cure." Indeed it is suggested that Prince George himself first came to Brighton to get the seawater treatment for his afflicted glands.

In his book *Dissertation on the Use of Seawater in Diseases of the Glands* published in 1750, Russel refers to a plethora of maladies and ailments which he claimed to have cured by the internal and external use of seawater. He describes the most revolting cases – tumours, eruptions, abscesses and the like – in great detail, and it makes for anything but pleasant reading. But in spite of this, or perhaps because of it, the book proved enormously successful and popular. Russel experimented with mixtures of crabs' eyes, burnt sponge, vipers' flesh, snails and wood lice as well, so the treatment was not an easy one. Usually patients had to swallow a medicine concocted by Russel and wash it down with a pint or so of seawater. That the treatment often worked was due in part, one suspects, to the fact that it acted as an extremely strong purgative and cleaned up symptoms associated with a troubled digestive system – a common complaint of the day, brought about by overindulgence and a hopelessly unbalanced diet. The dip in the sea, also part of the treatment, served to wash away grime and bacteria which often covered the body in an age when nobody washed very much. If you couple these with the fresh air, rest and relaxation that Russel prescribed, it is hardly surprising his patients felt better after their treatment. In the Prince of Wales' case, it was thought the iodine in the seawater was a valuable aid to the treatment of his thyroid gland disorder. A tablet on the Royal Hotel records that Russel once had a house on the site and quotes Sir Christopher Wren's epitaph, "If you seek his monument, look around." Perhaps, though, a personal epigram is more fitting. Dr Simon Manningham, a friend, said of him after his death in 1759;

> Admiring ages Russel's fame shall know
> Till Ocean's healing waters cease to flow

Stories and legends abound in Brighton. In the grounds of the Pavilion stands an ancient oak; like several similar trees scattered throughout the country, it is said to be the one in which Charles II hid after the Battle of Worcester. A Sussex location seems unlikely, but the story is vouched for by the descendants of the captain of the ship that took the King to France.

A monk haunts the Lanes. Tradition says he was walled up alive for running away with a local girl; his spirit has often been seen disappearing through a bricked-up doorway next to the Friends' Meeting House in Meeting House Lane.

Many legends surround the ancient stone plinth in St Nicholas' Churchyard in central Brighton. It is said that in the 14th century, Lord Pevensey and Earl de Warrenne met in single combat to resolve a long-standing feud. Pevensey drove his adversary into a corner and was about to deliver the death blow when Lady de Warrenne, watching the battle from afar, prayed to St Nicholas to save her husband, vowing that her first-born son would not marry until he had laid St Nicholas' belt on the tomb of the Blessed Virgin in Byzantium. At that moment, Pevensey lost his balance and, as he fell, de Warrenne ran him through.

Twenty years later, the Earl's eldest son, Lord Manfred, was betrothed to the beautiful Lady Edona, although he had not yet fulfilled his mother's vow. Halfway through a banquet held to celebrate the 21st anniversary of the Earl's victory, a chill wind suddenly blew through the great hall, lightning blazed across the tapestried walls and the terrified guests saw a vision of the Earl's battle. St Nicholas appeared not to be pleased. The very next day a ship was ordered to take Manfred to Byzantium; the wedding would have to wait.

Months passed, and finally Manfred's returning ship was sighted and Edona and her parents-in-law-to-be gathered to watch the ship sail into harbour. But disaster struck. The ship ran onto a hidden rock, keeled over on its side and sank so quickly that only one sailor escaped. The company watched in silent grief and then Edona gave one sigh and sank, dying of sorrow, to the ground. The Earl never smiled again and lived only long enough to build the Church of St Nicholas as a reminder to others never to neglect their vows. Lady Edona was buried where she fell; the ancient plinth in St Nicholas' Churchyard is said to mark her grave. As for Lord Manfred, his ghostly ship still sails towards the harbour at midnight every May 17, and each year it founders again on the same treacherous rock.

GLYNDEBOURNE

The Glyndebourne Opera Festival is very much an English institution. A place of pleasant lawns and wooded walks, nestling under the Sussex Downs, not far from Lewes; a fine country house which had the good fortune to fall into the hands of a wealthy music lover and his singer wife, and under their direction acquired its own opera house; a nursery for promising young opera singers from all parts of the world: the Festival is all these things. It is also the London Philharmonic Orchestra's home-away-from-home for the summer, and a kind of legend, its name synonymous with the highest standards of operatic performance. For half a century it has been associated with the genius of such men as Rudolf Bing, John Pritchard, Peter Hall and Bernard Haitink.

In June, you can see the audience eating a cream tea or a champagne supper on the lawn. It's easy to rub shoulders with the rich and famous, all dressed in "black ties" and elegant gowns. The quality of the opera is remarkable. Mozart with designs by David Hockney, bustling productions of Verdi, rarities like Janacek's *The Cunning Little Vixen* and new works like the recent Oliver Knussen/Maurice Sendak collaborations of *Where the Wild Things Are* and *Higglety, Pigglety, Pop!* There are no really big names like Domingo, Baltsa or Te Kanawa, but plenty of fresh, young, enthusiastic voices.

I guess Glyndebourne is not strictly a festival. It's a season of five productions (two new and three revivals each year) running all the way from late May to mid-August. It is, nonetheless, music-making under the most glitteringly festive of circumstances. It may be an élite event but it is by no means selfish – during the late 1940s its productions were regularly taken to the Edinburgh Festival at a time when Glyndebourne's operatic traditions were still at a formative stage. Forty-five years later, one of the highlights of the Promenade Concert season in London is a semi-staged performance of one of the operas currently in the Glyndebourne repertoire; most important of all, there is the touring company which each autumn does the rounds of a number of English and Welsh cities. One big problem for the casual visitor is the difficulty of getting tickets. Most are snapped up by the Glyndebourne Festival Society so it's necessary to get in an application for tickets months before the season opens. In this respect the Festival is perhaps an "exclusive" one. Nevertheless, the Festival is unique. Entire books have been devoted to Glyndebourne's history and achievements. Suffice it to say that it is one of a kind. Festival opera at its brightest and best.

TOURIST INFORMATION BUREAU: Marlborough House, 54 Old Steine, Brighton, East Sussex BN1 1EQ. Tel (0273) 777409

CANTERBURY

County of Kent
65 miles (104 km) from London by A20, M2O and M2
By rail 1 hour 30 minutes from London (Victoria)

Canterbury Cathedral is the Mother Church of the Anglican communion, so it is not surprising that the city itself is ancient and has more than 2000 years of history, with evidence of settlement going back to pre-Roman times. After Julius Caesar took the area by storm in 54 BC, a Roman regional centre, Durovernum, was established here. In 597 St Augustine arrived on his mission to spread Christianity in England and build his first cathedral. A few years later Canterbury became the metropolitan city of the English church in spite of suffering repeated Danish raids in the 10th and 11th centuries.

The city was damaged in the Civil War, mostly at the hands of the Parliamentary forces after they had gained control. The Industrial Revolution left little mark on Canterbury, but the city was severely damaged by bombing during the Second World War. Fortunately, the cathedral escaped unscathed except for some windows. It gives one pause to think that for nearly 14 centuries, through all its vicissitudes, Canterbury has remained the centre of Christianity in England, dominated by its great cathedral.

Of the medieval walls that once encircled the old city almost half are still standing in a continuous line from near Wincheape to Radigund's Street. Dating mainly from the 13th and 14th centuries, the walls are partly built on Roman foundations, remnants of which have been discovered during renovations. There are also a number of well-preserved bastions, the most impressive of which is the West Gate. Even though the walls in this area have disappeared, the West Gate is the only one of the seven original gates that remains as it was. It picturesquely but inconveniently straddles the entrance to St Peter's Street, the main thoroughfare, and it is an imposing structure of the late 14th century, with a fine view from its battlemented top. It once guarded the entrance to the city from the direction of London; later, it became a gaol. The structure itself now houses a museum.

Of the castle, only the keep remains. It was built during the 11th and 12th centuries, but it seems to have been pretty ineffective, as every time the castle was attacked the inhabitants quickly surrendered. The keep, though, is still a very solid structure, remaining intact over the centuries as the castle itself was demolished around it.

In addition to its cathedral, Canterbury has a number of very interesting churches. St Martin's, just off North Holmes Road at St Martin's Hill (about half a mile outside the city walls to the east) is said to be the oldest church in England still in use. It is believed there was a church dedicated to St Martin on this site in pre-Anglo-Saxon times. The chancel is in fact believed by some to pre-date St Augustine's arrival, and the nave is thought to have been completed shortly after. The tower was built in the Middle Ages, and to many this church rather than the cathedral is the cradle of Christianity in England.

St Dunstan's is another church which dates from the Middle Ages. Its porch is 14th century and there was considerable restoration in the 19th century. In 1174 Henry II entered St Dunstan's, removed his ordinary clothes and walked barefoot to the cathedral to do penance for his part in the murder of Thomas à Becket.

St Mildred's Church on Stour Street (by the castle) was reconstructed in the middle of the 13th century, but some of the old fabric remains. St Peter's, in St Peter's Street, and St Alphege's in Palace Street (very close to the cathedral) date from approximately the same time as St Mildred's and retain their medieval atmosphere. St Alphege's was declared redundant in 1982 and is now the Canterbury Urban Studies Centre. St George's Church, at the top of St George's Street close to the roundabout, was destroyed in Second-World-War bombing, but its tower remains and is incorporated in the new shopping precinct as a central landmark. Christopher Marlowe, the Elizabethan poet, was baptized in St George's. There seems to have been a plethora of churches in Canterbury. Holy Cross Church, close to West Gate, was also declared redundant and was given to the city council to serve as the Guildhall. The churchyard, with its yew trees and old gravestones, links the church with the Mayor's Parlour, a charming old house which is used for official receptions.

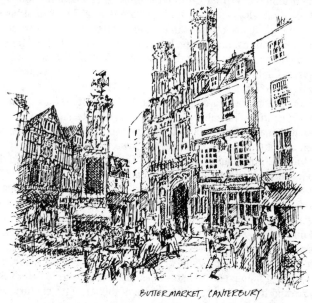

BUTTER MARKET, CANTERBURY

WALK

Canterbury Walk – Park in the car park at the junction of Stour Street and Castle Row and walk up Stour Street to St Peter's Street, then along St Peter's Street, much of which is now a pedestrian precinct, to **St Peter's Church**. Turning into St Peter's Lane one discovers the considerable remains of **Blackfriars**, a Dominican friary which dominated this part of Canterbury from 1237 until its dissolution at the Reformation. The **Guest House** of the Friary is well preserved, while on the other side of the river the **Refectory**, which was once connected to the other buildings by a bridge, is now used by the King's School as an arts centre. Close by is the **Marlowe Theatre** (formerly the Odeon Theatre) which is the main cultural centre for East Kent (see below). Back in St Peter's Street is the property known as the **Canterbury Weavers**. These are Tudor cottages, heavily restored, which house a restaurant and a gift shop, with a reconstructed ducking stool in front by the river. In earlier times so-called "nagging wives" were made to sit on the stool and plunged into the water of a nearby pond or river. Those suspected of witchcraft suffered a more severe form of this treatment, often with fatal results. The name Canterbury Weavers comes from the Huguenots, Protestant refugees from France, who were invited by Elizabeth I to settle in Canterbury to avoid religious persecution in their homeland. Elizabeth allowed the Huguenots to use the cathedral crypt for worship and services are still held there in French every Sunday. The Huguenots were mostly weavers and dyers, and some old looms can still be seen on the premises. There are also exhibitions of weaving open to the public.

On the opposite side of the road are the almshouses known as the **Eastbridge Hospital of St Thomas of Canterbury**. Founded in 1180 as a hostel for poor pilgrims visiting the tomb of St Thomas à Becket, this medieval complex has great atmosphere. For those unfamiliar with this period of English history, Thomas à Becket, Archbishop of Canterbury, was martyred in his cathedral by knights loyal to Henry II, who had interpreted a chance remark of the King's ("Who will rid me of this troublesome priest") as an invitation to murder. Canterbury soon became a place of pilgrimage for all of Christendom and the journeys of pilgrims to the city gave rise to Chaucer's *Canterbury Tales*; and T S Eliot's *Murder in the Cathedral* recounts the events leading up to this most heinous of crimes.

Leaving the peace and quiet of Eastbridge, pass the post office and turn right down Stour Street. Pass under an old gate and you will see a charming 13th-century house built over the river. This is all that survives of the church of the Grey Friars (see Ephemera). Across the river on the east side of Stour Street is the **Poor Priests' Hospital** which is now Canterbury Heritage Museum (see below). The hospital was founded in the 13th century as an almshouse for elderly celibate clergy. Further along Stour Street is another almshouse, **Maynard and Cotton's Hospital**, which was founded by a rich merchant in the 12th century and added to in the 17th and 20th centuries. At the end of Stour Street we pass **St Mildred's Church** and the remains of the **Norman Castle**. Walking up Rosemary Lane we come to **Dane John Gardens** in which there is a memorial to Christopher Marlowe, Canterbury's famous playwright. A ramp at the end of Worthgate Place will take you up onto the medieval walls of the city. Walk along the walls to the St George's Street roundabout, where you will see the tower of **St George's Church**, and by following the wall across busy St George's Street you will come in a short time to Burgate Street, which forms the south side of the cathedral precincts. Halfway down the street is the old tower of **St Mary Magdelene Church**, demolished in 1871. We pass Butchery Lane and in the Longmarket pedestrian precinct, which replaced the old covered market destroyed in the 1942 bombing, it is possible to see Roman remains with a tessellated pavement and mosaic panels (they are in the basement beneath the shops). The next street, **Mercery Lane**, is the most famous thoroughfare in Canterbury. Though much restored and modernized, it retains the feeling of a medieval street and the view of the cathedral as you look down High Street is most romantic. At the junction of Mercery Lane and High Street once stood the great pilgrim's hostelry called the **Chequers of Hope,** which occupied the whole west side of the lane. It had accommodation for 100 to sleep nightly, and although it was burnt down in 1860 some of its stone arches can still be seen on the ground floor of the shop opposite Lloyds Bank. In this part of High Street are **Queen Elizabeth's Great Chamber** (she is known to have stayed at St Augustine's Abbey, then a Royal Palace, on the occasion of her visit in 1573), and the **Royal Museum and Art Gallery**, which houses a museum for the Buffs Regiment. Opposite Mercery Lane is St Margaret's Street where can be found **St Margaret's Church** which is the home of the imaginative Pilgrim's Way exhibition. Back down Mercery Lane, we pass the market and turn into Sun Lane and then into Palace Street. At No 17 you will find **Conquest House**, which has a 12th-century crypt in the basement. Tradition has it that it was in this crypt that the four knights and their followers plotted the murder of Becket, before proceeding across the road to the Archbishop's Palace where the deed was done. **St Alphege's Church** is on Palace Street, as is, at the far end, **Sir John Boy's House**. Beside it you will see **King's School**, which claims to be the oldest public school in England. Continue past King's School, cross Broad Street and enter Northgate, where you will find, on the left, **St John the Baptist's Hospital**, the oldest almshouse still surviving in England and possibly in Europe. It was founded in 1084 by Archbishop Lanfranc, Abbot of Caen, who was a close friend of William the Conqueror. Come back into Broad Street, turn left and continue past King's School to Longport, which is also on your left. Here you will find **St Augustine's Abbey**, one of the most important ecclesiastical sites in England. An abbey was first built here in the time of St Augustine, but was subsequently torn down more than once. Much of the material was used to build St Augustine's College, originally a missionary college but now part of King's College, London. The excavations already completed give some idea of their construction over the centuries. The re-use of Roman bricks indicates that the Romans themselves may have had a building here at some time. The adjacent modern buildings of Christ Church College make an interesting contrast.

Coming back down Longport you come to Broad Street. Cross the road into Burgate and continue to the bottom where you will find **Christ Church Gate**, which is the principal entrance to the **Cathedral Precincts**. The tall, central **Bell Harry Tower**, the dominating external feature of the Cathedral, dates from 1498. This mighty tower (composed of some half a million Tudor bricks faced with stone), took ten years to build, being completed with the glorious interior vault in 1504. Not to be missed as you wander around the exterior of the cathedral is the **Norman Staircase**. This is situated in the buildings which are now in the hands of King's School. Originally these buildings were the granary, bakehouse, brewery and stables of the original monastery and the superb staircase led to the monastic almonry. Cross Green Court and return to the Cathedral itself.

Only one English monarch is buried in the Cathedral: Henry IV, who lies beside his queen, Joan of Navarre, in **Trinity Chapel**. However, the tomb of Edward III's son, the Black Prince (also called Edward), who died before his father, is here, and it is one of the most magnificent in England. Also in Trinity Chapel is the site of the **Shrine of St Thomas à Becket**. This was a scene of pilgrimage for more than 300 years until it was dismantled and plundered of its jewels by Henry VIII. Just behind the high altar is a roped-off space, worn and uneven from the multitude of pilgrims who knelt there. This is the actual spot where Becket was murdered. Besides Becket's shrine there are the tombs of more than half of the archbishops since St Augustine. Many are most impressive, while the tomb of Henry Chichele, showing him above in full regalia and below as a cadaver, emphasizes the transitory nature of human glory. A circular projection of Trinity College called the corona, contains **St Augustine's Chair**. Made of Purbeck marble, it dates from the 13th century and has been used for centuries for the enthronement of successive archbishops. The nave, completed early in the 13th century, is 187 feet (56 m) long, 71 feet (17 m) wide and 79 feet (24 m) high from pavement to vaulting. The font dates from the Restoration. **St Michael's Chapel**, beyond the nave in the southwest transept, is better known as the Warrior's Chapel, because of the number of memorials to famous soldiers. It is now the memorial chapel of the Buffs, the Royal East Kent Regiment, one of the oldest regiments in the British Army. Every morning at 11 o'clock a soldier sounds a bell that formerly belonged to HMS *Canterbury*, now hanging just outside the door of the chapel, and turns over a page of the Book of Memory, which records the names of men who died in battle. The Cathedral is rich in stained glass despite losses during the Civil War, the Commonwealth period and the Second World War. The glass ranges from medieval to modern with the Miracle Windows in Trinity Chapel of special interest. The splendid crypt has Norman pillars and a fine vaulted roof and is the largest of its kind in the country. The cloisters of the Benedictine monastery adjoining the Cathedral date from the early 15th century although traces of the 13th-century cloisters can still be seen. The colourful heraldic decorations of the vaulting are of interest as is the adjoining **Chapter House**, with 16th-century window tracery and the **Water Tower**, circa 1160, which housed a wash place for the monks. Water was conducted through leaden pipes to the tower and from here to all parts of the monastery, giving a water supply and system of sanitation far in advance of the times. The cathedral will always remain the city's crowning glory. Dominating the skyline, with its unique features, including magnificent architecture of diverse periods, fine stained glass, intricate carvings, ancient paintings and tombs, the 12th-century choir, 14th-century screening, slender Norman towers and the great 15th-century bell tower it is truly the jewel in the crown of English cathedrals.

MUSEUMS AND GALLERIES

Royal Museum and Art Gallery – High Street, Tel 452747. The museum occupies part of the interesting late Victorian building of Dr Beaney's Institute. There are displays of natural history, local archaeology and pottery and porcelain. The art collection includes paintings, engravings and topographical prints. The historical collections of the Buffs, the Royal East Kent Regiment, also form part of the museum. Look out for the Anglo-Saxon brooch with garnet inlay – it's beautiful. Open Mon–Sat 10:30–5pm.

Queen's Regiment Museum – Howe Barracks, Tel 457411. The museum's display of uniforms, weapons, medals, pictures, documents and equipment covers 400 years of military history. Open Mon–Fri 10–12:30 and 2–4pm.

Roman Mosaic – Butchery Lane, Tel 452747. Canterbury's Underground Museum preserves the foundations of a Roman town house with two mosaic floors and the remains of a heating system. There are displays illustrating everyday life during Roman times and Roman artefacts discovered during excavations in the city. Open Mon–Sat 2–4pm.

Canterbury Heritage – Poor Priests' Hospital, Stour Street, Tel 452747. The hospital was founded circa 1200 to house poor priests. The present building, dating from 1373, houses Canterbury Heritage which takes the form of a time-walk through the story of Canterbury with objects from the city's historical collections to support the displays and models. Open Mon–Sat 10:30–5pm (June–Oct Sun 1:30–5pm also).

Canterbury Tales – St Margaret's Street, Tel 454888. This exhibit is designed to allow you to step back in time to the 14th century and experience the sights, sounds and even smells of the period. Scenes of everyday medieval life are realistically portrayed by audio-visual techniques and five characters from Chaucer's great work are also created. Open 7 days a week – April–Sept 9:30–5:30; Oct–March Mon–Fri 10–4:30 Weekends 9:30–5:30.

West Gate – St Peter's Street, Tel 452747. The twin towers of this gate, built in 1380, were originally fitted with gates, portcullis and drawbridge. There is a display of arms and armour in the guard chamber. Open Apr–Sept 10–1 and 2–5pm; Oct–Mar 2–4. Closed Sundays.

THEATRE

Marlowe Theatre – The Friars, Tel 767246. The Marlowe Theatre, formerly the Odeon Cinema, has been imaginatively converted to a splendid new proscenium theatre seating over 1000. The theatre does not have a permanent company but acts as a major touring house. A very wide variety of musical activities can be found at the Marlowe, while theatrical offerings include West End plays such as *Sleuth,* Italian opera from Milan and a traditional Christmas pantomime.

Gulbenkian Theatre – University of Kent, Tel 769075. The Gulbenkian Theatre on the campus of Kent University is one of the major centres for drama and modern dance in the region. Visitors have included the Royal Shakespeare Company, Extemporary Dance Company, Shared Experience and the Mermaid's Molecule Theatre. There are also student productions of drama and opera, concerts, recitals and poetry readings. There is an open thrust stage that can be used at three different levels and art exhibitions are held in the theatre's specially designed foyer. The theatre seats 342.

MUSIC

Both the Marlowe Theatre and the Gulbenkian Theatre have a regular programme of musical events. The Marlowe generally has orchestras such as the National Symphony, the Kent Concert Orchestra and the Kent Youth Orchestra as well as jazz, folk, pop and ethnic music. The Gulbenkian also has jazz, chamber music and popular ensembles. Other venues in Canterbury which host musical activity include Christ Church College, North Holmes Road (a significant programme of events) and Canterbury Cathedral itself. For details of this additional musical activity call Forwood Bookings, 37 Palace Street, Tel 455600, who can provide tickets for all musical and theatrical activity in the city.

CINEMA

Commercial cinema can be found at **Cannon Cinemas**, St George's Place, Tel 462022 (2 screens). Of much greater interest to me is **Cinema 3** which is located on the campus of the University of Kent close to the Gulbenkian Theatre. Tel 769075. A sampling of a recent month's programme found films by directors such as Jim Jarmusch, Nicholas Roeg, Bertrand Blier, Jane Campion and Aki Kaurismaki.

For all artistic activity one would be advised to try to get to Canterbury during the **Canterbury Festival**, which is usually held for two weeks in the middle of October. There are often over 150 events during the fortnight and the festival is often thematic. A recent example had events in theatre, film, art and music focusing on the theme of relationships – past, present and future. There is also a Fringe Festival. Call 455600 for details.

BOOKSTORES

Waterstone's at 20 St Margaret's Street, Tel 456343, is very good. Excellent stock and knowledgeable staff. **Volume 1** at 24 St Margaret's Street, Tel 764800, is also excellent and as there is so little to choose between them I would visit both. **Dillon's** on the campus of the University of Kent is also excellent but out of town, although it is the only bookshop with a HMS0 outlet. Tel 462450. For religious books try **SPCK** at 7 St Peter's Street, Tel 462881, or **Christian Literature Crusade** at 18 Burgate, Tel 463535. Just up the road at 48 Burgate is the **Athena Booksellers** who are located at Mercery Lane, Tel 768631.

ANTIQUARIAN AND SECONDHAND BOOKS

You might as well start off on Northgate, which is essentially a continuation of Palace Street. Just past the crossroad and King's School you will find **David Miles** at No 37, Tel 464773, who has a good selection of antiquarian books and also pictures and ephemera. Go on down Northgate, past St John's Hospital on your left, and at 110 is **Bell Harry Books**, Tel 453481, with a general selection. Come back down to the crossroads and turn left onto Broad Street. Follow the city walls to the junction with Burgate. On your left is Longport where at No 7 you will find **Stephen Thomson** with a good general stock (closed on Thursdays). Just behind Stephen Thomson's is Ivy Lane, where at Latimer's Antiques Centre you will find **Bygone Books**, Tel 760378, with a secondhand and antiquarian selection. Come back to the Burgate crossroads, turn left and continue to follow the city wall until you get to the St George's Street round-about. Turn right onto St George's Street and follow it until it becomes High Street. At 44A is **Canterbury Bookshop**, Tel 459186, with a general selection of both antiquarian and secondhand books. Continue up High Street to the post office, turn left on Stour Street and halfway down you will see Beer Cart Lane (ask – it's not exactly obvious). **Chaucer Bookshop** at No 6 has books of antiquarian and local interest and it's well worth a browse. Tel 453912. My other four recommendations are a bit further out of town. Luckily three of them are comparatively close together. Come back on Stour Street and make your way back to the post office. Turn left onto St Peter's Street and just after it becomes St Dunstan's Street you will find North Lane on your right. At No 5 is **Books**, Tel 457913, which will be of interest especially to anyone with a penchant for social history or academe. The shop is only open Wed–Sun 11–5pm. Off to the right, behind the West Station (ask), is **J J Ridgen** at 17 Beverley Road, Tel 769911, who has a good selection of children's fiction, while coming back what is now St Dunstan's Way and turning right will lead you to the Whitstable Road where at No 79 you will find **Nick Spurrier**, Tel 462764, who specializes in history, politics and economics. Note that this is a private house and you have to call and make an appointment.

ART GALLERIES

Start in St Peter's Street where the **Nevill Gallery** at No 43, Tel 765291, specializes in watercolours, oils and prints with local and London artists especially well represented. Next door at No 42 is **St Peter's Street Gallery**, Tel 768033, which specializes in 19th-century oil paintings and prints with a little early 20th-century work. Moving up into High Street and turning left onto Palace Street brings you to **Cloisters** at No 26; they have a fine collection of old engravings. Their telephone number is 462729. **Drew Gallery** at 16 Best Lane, Tel 458759, on the other hand, specializes in contemporary painting and prints with local, national and international artists all represented. Finally, **Phillip Maslin Galleries**, at 60A Northgate, generally has a good collection of contemporary watercolours by both British and Continental artists.

ANTIQUE DEALERS

There are many antique stores in Canterbury, and given the city's long history this is hardly surprising. Most of them are closely grouped together, so it is as easy to wander through them as it is to read details of them. Start off at the St George's Street roundabout and follow the city wall north towards the Cathedral. Turn left at Burgate and at No 1OC you will find **Burgate Antiques**, Tel 456500, whose speciality is military memorabilia. Come back to the city walls and continue north. You are now on Broad Street, where at No 37A you will find **Henley's Antiques & Brass**, Tel 769055, and at No 92, **Antiques Odds and Ends**, Tel 767723. By now the wall will have stopped but carry on to the junction of Broad Street and Borough. Turn left onto Borough for a cornucopia of delights: within half a mile there are 14 antique shops! In Borough there are **Roger Clark**, Tel 455664, at No 1; **Michael Pearson**, Tel 459939, at No 2; **W J Christopher's**, Tel 451968, at No 9; **House Points**, Tel 451350, at No 13A; and right in the middle **Stablegate Antiques**, Tel 463009, which doesn't seem to have a number. What is even better for the avid collector is that the Borough becomes Palace Street, which is also rich with goodies. At No 12 Palace Street you will find **Leadenhall Gallery**, Tel 457339, while **Conquest House Antiques**, Tel 464587, is at No 17. Very close together are **Parker and Williams Antiques** at No 22 and **Canterbury Galleries** at No 23. Telephone 768341 and 462283 respectively. Carry on down Palace Street until it becomes Guildhall Street and very soon it will intersect with High Street. At No 44A High Street you can find **Rastro Antiques**, Tel 463537. Go back to Guildhall Street. Enter High Street again and turn right to the post office, were you left down Stour Street. **Nan Leith** is at No 68, Tel 454519 and the **Canterbury Antiques Centre**, Tel 452677, is in the Harvey Centre. Outside of the town centre, if you are driving to Whitstable via St Dunstan's Way you will find **Antique and Design**, Tel 762871, at Graham Bell House in Roper Close, which is on your right just past the House of Agnes Hotel. And, if you are on your way to Maidstone via Windcheape, you will find **Town and Country Furniture** at No 141, Tel 762340, just past the Norman castle. Two shops which I haven't had a chance to see but were recommended to me by friends at the University of Kent are **Acorn Antiques**, Tel 450121, at 19 Best Lane and **Coach House Antiques** at 2A Duck Lane, Tel 463117. Good hunting.

RESTAURANTS

When I am in Canterbury I generally eat at **Tuo e Mio**, 16 The Borough, Tel 61471. It's an authentic trattoria and its position near to the Cathedral makes it ideal for both concerts and theatre. There is always a range of daily specials which are usually interesting and the traditional cuisine of fresh pasta, veal, calf's liver and other standard Italian fare is of high quality. If you choose carefully prices can be reasonable. Open Tues–Sun 12 noon–2:30pm and 7–10:45pm (no Tues lunch). The restaurant is closed for two weeks at the end of August.

If you are on your way to Dover then there is a remarkable little bistro called **Old Coach House** at Barham (five miles/8 km out of Canterbury on the A2050). It's remarkable in that its position, in a lay-by behind a Happy Eater fast-food café, belies its excellent cuisine. The cooking convinces you that you are already on the other side of the Channel. You don't have to hang on and have that first meal in France – you can eat just as well here. French and English cuisines meet, with celery-and-lovage soup and moules farcies; the value and simplicity of the cooking are remarkable. Even if you are not going to Dover it's worth the journey.

Back in Canterbury, I've heard excellent reports about **River Kwai**, which is a Thai restaurant on Castle Street, Tel 462090, and **Greek Taverna** at 13 Church Street, Tel 464931, which has classic Greek cuisine. If you really have a yen for Chinese cooking, friends tell me that **Mandarin Dynasty**, 7 Upper Bridge Street, Tel 761214 is topnotch.

PUBS

Shakespeare Inn – Butchery Lane, Tel 463252. A 17th-century tavern in the Victorian coffee-house style. Excellent traditional bar food and snacks. A good traditional Sunday lunch. (Just off the High Street, close to the cathedral gates.)

Thomas Becket – 21 Best Lane, Tel 464384. A 15th-century town house, once used as a coffee house, now converted into a small pub with an intimate atmosphere and an open fire. Excellent homemade pub food. (From the High Street turn into Best Lane opposite the post office. House is 100 yards/90 m on right.)

House of Agnes Hotel – 71 St Dunstan's Street, Tel 464527. Built in the 16th century, this is one of the loveliest Tudor buildings in Canterbury. Ebony panelling in some rooms with good traditional bar food and restaurant. (Walk through West Gate at the end of St Peter's Street and the inn is on your left.)

The **Miller's Arms** – Mill Lane, Radigunds, Tel 456057. A country coaching inn right in the heart of the city. Good traditional bar food. (Turn right off High Street by the library and museum into King Street. Mill Lane is the second turn on the left.)

ARTISTIC ASSOCIATIONS

The murder of Thomas à Becket is the inspiration of many literary and dramatic works. Perhaps the most famous, T S Eliot's *Murder in the Cathedral,* received its first staging in the chapter house of Canterbury Cathedral in 1935. Becket's murder was also the subject of dramas by George Parley in 1840 and Tennyson in 1884. More recently Jean Anouilh, the French dramatist, had great success with his *Becket,* a play which essentially examines the relationship between the prelate and his king. This is perhaps the most widely known telling of the story as it was made into a film in 1964 starring Richard Burton and Peter O'Toole.

Christopher Marlowe, the Elizabethan dramatist, is perhaps Canterbury's most famous son. Born here in 1564, he was baptized in St George's Church. A Victorian tribute to him, representing the four main characters in his plays acted by Irving, Forbes Robertson, Alleyn and James Hackett, stands in Dane John Gardens by the old city wall. Richard Barham, the author of *Ingoldsby Legends* was born in Burgate in 1785. Some of the legends are set in the city. Charles Dickens set many scenes from *David Copperfield* in the city and the House of Agnes Hotel is said to have been Agnes Wickfield's home. The Sun Inn (built in 1503 but now a shop) has a plaque listing Dickens's associations with the inn. Joseph Conrad, the novelist and author of *Lord Jim* was buried in the cemetery here after a service in St Thomas's Church (Roman Catholic). King's School has provided a long list of famous ex-students. Besides Christopher Marlowe, novelists Hugh Walpole and Somerset Maugham both studied here, and both left bequests to the school. In 1961 Maugham returned to open the Maugham Library which houses his own books, and the manuscripts of *Liza of Lambeth* (1897) and *Catalina* (1948), his first and last novels.

In 1850, the animal painter Thomas Sidney Cooper left London and built himself a large house in Harbledown on the outskirts of Canterbury. The house was called Vernon Holme, and Cooper lived in it until his death in 1902 at the age of 98. The property contained a studio, stables and extensive fields for the herds of cattle and sheep that were his models; the house is now Junior Kent College. Cooper had been born in a house in Canterbury High Street and in 1882 he had a building erected on the site, designed for use as a school of art, and presented to the city. The building is now a community centre bearing his name. Some excellent examples of Cooper's work can be seen in the Royal Museum (above), especially a superb painting of a bull entitled *Separated but not Divorced.*

EPHEMERA

If you walk down St Peter's Street towards High Street and turn right after passing the post office, you will find yourself in Stour Street. Pass under an old gate and you will be in the Franciscan Gardens. Across the river you will see a charming 13th-century house, which once belonged to the Grey Friars. The first Franciscans to settle in England came here in the lifetime of their famous founder in 1224, and in the course of time, a church and community building grew up on this site. Today only this delightful little house survives with two rooms downstairs and the same above. The downstairs room at the rear of the house has a trap door which lifts up disclosing the sluggish stream flowing below and it is believed that in the early days of the community, before they became popular and prosperous, the friars used to let down rod and line in order to catch fish for food. The main room upstairs is now furnished as a chapel and services, open to all, are regularly held here.

Rupert Bear is a small bear, invariably clad in check trousers, red pullover and scarf, who has magical adventures in an English rural setting. He is the most enduring comic strip character in Britain, first created by Mary Tourtel for the *Daily Express* in 1920. Ms Tourtel was born at 51 Palace Street, Canterbury, on January 28, 1874 and she spent most of her life in the city. Books of Tourtel's drawings and stories about Rupert began to appear in the mid-1920s, but it was not until 1936 that the much-lauded and unbroken series of Rupert *Annuals* began. These were almost entirely the work of the outstanding artist Alfred Bestall, who had taken over responsibility for Rupert from the ailing Mary Tourtel in 1935. At the height of its popularity in the 1950s, the Rupert *Annual* sold one and a half million copies. Rupert's name and figure have long been exploited in merchandising and millions of Rupert dolls, mugs, towels and the like have been sold. Rupert has also appeared on TV and on the big screen. Rupert's standing has never been higher than it was in the late '80s. A celebratory book, *Rupert: A Bear's Life,* appeared in 1985 and a long-drawn-out correspondence appeared in the *Guardian* the same year. The letters concerned the important subject of what Rupert's father did for a living and it culminated in an authoritative communication from the ninety-three-year-old Alfred Bestall, the author who had done so much to make Rupert one of the best-loved children's heroes of the 20th century.

The passage between the old infirmary cloister and the Green Court in the cathedral is known as the Dark Entry. It is reputedly haunted by Nell Cook, a servant of a canon of the cathedral. Nell discovered that her employer was having an affair with his niece and in a fit of jealousy killed them both with a poisoned pie. The authorities buried her alive beneath the pavement of the Dark Entry and her ghost has haunted the passageway ever since. According to R H Barham, the visitations occur on Friday nights and anyone who sees the spirit will die. The story is widely believed, but it should be remembered that Barham wrote The *Ingoldsby Legends* in 1840 and could have made the whole thing up.

St Dunstan, who died in 988, was Archbishop of Canterbury in 961. He was a noted worker in gold and is now the patron saint of goldsmiths. He is usually represented in pontifical robes, carrying a pair of pincers in his right hand. The legend concerning the pincers is still remembered by local folk. It is said that once in Glastonbury, Dunstan's birthplace, he seized the devil by the nose with a pair of red-hot tongs and refused to release him till he promised never to tempt him again. For many years, due to this encounter, the devil was described as having a nose over a foot long!

St Dunstan was also noted for his skill in shoeing horses and legend has it that the devil asked him one day to shoe his single hoof. Dunstan, knowing who his customer was, tied him tightly to the wall and proceeded with the job but purposely caused his customer so much pain that he roared for mercy. Dunstan at last consented to release his captive on condition that he promised never to enter a place where he saw a horseshoe displayed. From this story arose the belief that it is lucky to pick up a horseshoe and, for good measure, to nail it to one's door. You just can't be too careful these days. After all, Lord Nelson had a horseshoe nailed to the mast of his flagship *Victory*. Mind you, now I come to think of it, I'm not too sure it did him a lot of good.

TOURIST INFORMATION BUREAU: 34 St Margaret's Street, Canterbury, Kent OT1 2TG. Tel (0228) 766567

CHELTENHAM

County of Gloucestershire
London 90 miles (144 km) by M40 and A40
Train 2 hours from London (Paddington)

Although Cheltenham was known to Alfred the Great, who wrote admiringly of it as a peaceful settlement on the banks of the River Chelt, little was heard of the town until after the Norman Conquest. It began to prosper under Henry III and in the 17th century local farmers grew tobacco and outraged the Americans by selling it to the London gentry as genuine Virginian. Yet despite a certain prosperity, there was little hint that the town – a single street of thatched houses and stepping stones over a malodorous stream – was soon to become the watering hole of royalty and the upper classes.

The change began in 1715 when a spring, bubbling up from ground now occupied by the famous Ladies' College, was discovered. Residents found that the outpourings of this salty spring appeared to ease a surprising number of ailments plaguing 18th-century society. One William Mason, a Quaker businessman, fenced off the healing waters and erected a makeshift thatched shelter to protect visitors from the elements. It was Cheltenham's first pump room. Mason, perhaps because of his religious beliefs, did not exploit the potential of the spring, but his son-in-law, a Captain Henry Skillicorne, did. He knew the hot springs of Clifton and realized the popularity of the water cure. He made the well covering more permanent and erected a ballroom and billiard room. More importantly, he created Well Walk, the first of the beautiful tree-lined walks, like the Promenade, for which Cheltenham is famous. Created to please the eye and encourage the gentle exercise associated with taking the waters, the walk led north and south from the well to the river and to the medieval Parish Church of St Mary.

Despite the Captain's efforts, by the middle of the 18th century Cheltenham was still little more than a one-street town. However, in a surprisingly short space of time, the "spa set" decided the place was fashionable. Distinguished people like Handel and Samuel Johnson patronized it and the final accolade came in 1788 when George III, an inveterate frequenter of spas, visited the town and gave it royal approval. In this period of imperial expansion, it was discovered that the mineral waters were extremely beneficial to the military officers and colonial administrators returning from the tropics with liver complaints, and it was from this period that Cheltenham's reputation for "curry and colonels" arose.

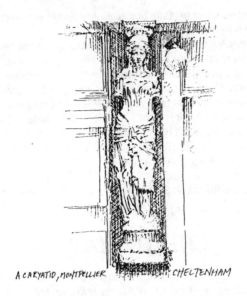

A CARYATID, MONTPELLIER   CHELTENHAM

The medical reputation of the spa grew so rapidly that a small number of brilliant architects were entrusted with plans to lay out an entirely new town. Here elegance and good
taste were to provide a setting in which people, steeped in classical culture and with
ample means for enjoying their period of retirement, could live in comfort. Between 1800
and 1840, Cheltenham was rebuilt in the Grecian idiom with occasional Gothic and Italianate
variations. The wide streets and tree-shaded open spaces which were so much a feature
of the town still remain. Landsdown Place, Montpellier Parade, the Rotunda (based on
the Pantheon in Rome) date from this period. Montpellier Walk, with its shops separated
by caryatids, must be one of the most unusual shopping precincts in the world. Many of
the houses and villas you will see still have their splendid Regency ironwork balconies and
verandas. All this careful planning culminated with the Promenade, which was completed
in 1825. The Municipal Offices date from this period too and I think they are best seen by
night when they are floodlit. The Promenade is dominated at one end by the Queen's
Hotel, circa 1838, with its classical columns, and one should not miss the Pittville Pump
Room, built in a parkland setting as an assembly hall suited to the growing social life of
the spa. Just out of the town on the Bath road are two of Cheltenham's famous schools;
the Cheltenham School for Boys, circa 1841, is built in the early Gothic revival style, while
the more famous Cheltenham Ladies' College dates from about the same time. Cheltenham,
in the mid-19th century, rivalled Bath architecturally, but the spa's popularity began to wane
as Victorian earnestness took over from Regency extravagance. The driving force behind
the new morality was the Reverend Francis Close, curate of Holy Trinity. Much offended
his fundamentalist eye. He railed unsuccessfully against the racecourse, failing to get it
closed down, but the notorious race week fair was finished. He also tried to get the Theatre
Royal closed (George III had freely patronized it and Sarah Siddons had acted there). In
fact, when the Theatre Royal burned down in 1839, some thought that Close had arranged
divine intervention. The good Reverend was also opposed to Sunday trains and was
responsible for delaying the building of a direct rail link with London. The *Times* referred
to Close as an "ignorant, meddling, claptrap preacher," while Alfred Tennyson, who wrote
his famous "In Memoriam" in the town, called Victorian Cheltenham "a parson-worship-
ping place of which Francis Close is Pope." The atmosphere of Victorian Cheltenham could
hardly have been more different from the Regency elegance.

Perhaps it was from the Victorian period that Cheltenham's reputation for stuffiness, snobbishness and dullness arose. Or perhaps it was the influence of its upper-crust public schools or its military retirees. Today, the visitor need not worry. The racecourse flourishes with the Cheltenham Gold Cup, the supreme event of the steeplechase season, as does the beautifully restored Everyman Theatre. The International Festival of Music carries on the Regency concert tradition: Johann Strauss and Paganini played for visitors such as the Duke of Wellington, who in 1828 called the town "the merriest sick resort on earth." The ambiance of Cheltenham as one of the finest spa towns in Europe is carefully controlled by planners and I suspect visitors will be able to enjoy Cheltenham's Regency elegance well into the 21st century.

WALK

Our **Cheltenham Walk** begins at the Regent Arcade multi-storey car park in Regent Street. Follow Regent Street into Rodney Road and turn right again into **Imperial Square** with a good view of the **Town Hall**. Walk down the right side of Imperial Square and right again into **Imperial Gardens**. Note the bust of Captain Skillicorne, who established Cheltenham as a spa. (It's in a walled garden behind the Town Hall.) Continue along Montpellier Avenue and cross to the right-hand side of Montpellier Walk. Note the **Rotunda** and then turn right into Montpellier Exchange with its tiny wrought-iron balconies and iron-hooded doorways and thence into Montpellier Street. There is a monument here in memory of General Gordon, hero of Khartoum. Cross St George's Road into Royal Well Place and then bear left along Royal Crescent with its white stucco buildings; continue along Crescent Place and cross Clarence Street into Well Walk where you will find St Mary's Church. Turn right, past the **Art Gallery and Museum** and turn right again into St George's Place. The red-brick building which resembles the Strozzi Palace in Florence is an electricity sub-station. Cross High Street into Henrietta Street and turn right beside the Cheltenham Brewery into St Margaret's Road. Turn left into Monson Avenue, then right along Clarence Square to Clarence Road with the **Holst Museum** at No 4. Leaving the museum, return and turn right along Evesham Road into the gardens. Go straight ahead through the gardens, noticing the houses on the right with stucco and decorated wrought-iron balconies – a significant Cheltenham architectural trait marking the Regency style. Go through the green gates ahead, cross the bridge beside the lake and go up the slope to the **Pittville Pump Room**. You can try spa water here (as well as in the Town Hall) and when you have drunk your fill of the salty waters, follow the left-hand path back to the lake. Go through the gate and turn right along Pittville Lawn to Pittville Gates. Continue along Winchcombe Street and and then turn right into High Street with the Regent Arcade opposite. Turn left along High Street and left again into the Promenade. Cross to the right-hand side of the pedestrian precinct and continue to the Tourist Information office. In front there are war memorials and at the end, the **Neptune Fountain** with the Edward Wilson Statue nearby. Cross the road by the Neptune Fountain, turn left into Imperial Square and return to the car park.

MUSEUMS AND GALLERIES

Cheltenham Art Gallery and Museum – Clarence Street, Tel 237431. Of especial interest is the collection relating to the Arts and Crafts Movement, including fine furniture and exquisite metalwork (including examples by William Letheren, who was declared England's greatest iron worker in 1866). The gallery contains paintings from the 16th century to the present day with a very important group of 17th-century Dutch masters. The Oriental Gallery contains ceramics, costumes and accessories from the Ming Dynasty to the reign of the last Emperor. A section is devoted to Cheltenham's history and to Edward Wilson, one of Cheltenham's famous sons. Wilson was a talented artist, an expert naturalist and, like his father, a physician. But the world remembers him best as the companion of Captain Robert Falcon Scott on his Antarctic explorations and his "brother in death" at the South Pole in 1912. His statue on the Promenade is by Scott's widow. Open all year Mon–Sat 10–5:20pm; Sun 2–5:20pm. Free.

Gustav Holst Museum – 4 Clarence Street, Tel 524846. Holst's birthplace is a Regency house, which now has displays on the composer's life and music, including his piano and other memorabilia. Each room in the house has been carefully restored to evoke a slightly different period of history from Regency to Edwardian times. Open all year Tues–Fri 12–5:20pm; Sat 11–5:20pm.

Pittville Pump Room – Pittville Park, Tel 512740. The museum, situated in a beautiful parkland setting, contains displays of Cheltenham history over the last thousand years; original costumes from 1760 to the present, shown against painted views of Cheltenham landscapes and buildings; and jewellery from Regency to art nouveau. Special exhibitions are mostly devoted to costume and textiles. Open all year Tues–Sat 10:30–5pm; Sun April 1–31 10:30–5pm.

THEATRE

The **Everyman Theatre**, Tel 572573, originally known as the Opera House, was designed by the leading theatre architect Frank Matcham, who in the 19th century designed more than 80 theatres throughout the country. Only a handful, such as the Bristol Hippodrome, Wyndham's and the Coliseum in London, and the Belfast Opera House, are still working theatres. The Opera House was opened in 1891 by Lillie Langtry and her company; the Cheltenham Corporation ran the theatre for a time but in 1960 it reverted to a repertory theatre and changed its name to the Everyman. A note in the programme at that time suggested that the old name conjured up the spirit of the 19th-century theatre and that if the theatre was to look forward, not back, it needed a new image. Today is the age of Everyman – hence the name. The theatre flourished in the 1960s and '70s but it became obvious that major redevelopments and renovations were needed, and it was closed from 1983 to 1986 while foyers were extended, production areas rebuilt and the auditorium restored to its original Victorian splendour. The main stage now seats 658 and the second performance space, the Richardson Studio (that fine English actor, the late Sir Ralph Richardson, was born here), holds a maximum of 60 and is used mostly for experimental productions and the presentation of new work.

The theatre's artistic policy is concentrated around ten in-house main-auditorium productions a year, with a traditional Christmas pantomime. The main programme is complemented by touring ballet and opera productions and touring West End shows, which occupy five or six weeks a year. There is a regular Sunday concert series. A touring company travels rural Gloucestershire and there is Theatre in Education work and a Youth Theatre group. In recent years I have seen an excellent adaptation of Hardy's *The Mayor of Casterbridge*, and a fascinating play about T S Eliot entitled *Tom and Viv*. Recent programmes have included productions as diverse as *Twelfth Night, Hay Fever, Guys and Dolls, The Country Wife* and an adaptation of Henry James's *The Turn of the Screw*, entitled *The Innocents*. The theatre is really lovely with a wonderful atmosphere. There are bars, a coffee shop and a good restaurant, all open 9:30am–11pm. Backstage tours can be arranged (contact the Stage Door) and a visit to the Everyman is always a pleasing experience.

Other theatres in Cheltenham are the **Playhouse** on Bath Road, which is the base for Cheltenham's thriving amateur companies, Tel 522852, and the **Shaftesbury Hall Theatre**, St George's Place, Tel 222795, which often has small visiting touring companies plus events as diverse as Olde Tyme Music Hall, rock music and contemporary dance and film. This theatre is especially busy during the International Festival of Music when it becomes a focus for fringe festival events.

MUSIC

Besides the **Cheltenham International Festival of Music** in July, there is a lively music scene in the town. Symphony concerts are held regularly in the Town Hall, Tel 523690, including ten concerts a year by the world-famous City of Birmingham Symphony Orchestra. There are three major choral societies in the town and four community orchestras. Individual recitals and chamber music concerts are given in a number of venues including the Pittville Pump Room, Tel 523690, and the Town Hall hosts regular lunchtime concerts.

The **Cheltenham International Festival of Music** was the first of the post-war festivals. In a sense it led the way for Edinburgh, Aldeburgh and Bath. From the outset the Festival has focused on contemporary British music and way back in 1945 it included works composed and conducted by Benjamin Britten, William Walton and Arthur Bliss. Since its modest beginning, the Festival has grown in both length and scope. It now occupies a full two-week period at the beginning of July each year, and its programme includes more music from the classical and romantic repertoire alongside the contemporary though its commitment to new works remains. It has become famous for the commissioning of works, many of which are now in the standard international repertoire. Orchestral concerts are held in the Town Hall, chamber music in the Pittville Pump Room, and dance, mime and opera can be seen at the Everyman Theatre. The Festival is complemented by a major fringe festival incorporating firework displays, street entertainment, jazz, folk, rock and theatrical events.

Founded two years after the Music Festival, the **Cheltenham Festival of Literature** was the first purely literary festival to be attempted in the late 1940s. The Festival includes talks and lectures, theatre performance, poetry readings, novelists in conversation, discussions, anthologies, exhibitions, music, literary criticism, and comedy; plus a large book fair and many events for children. Practically every significant literary figure has taken part over the years and many, such as Edna O'Brien, John Fowles, David Storey and Seamus Heaney were at the beginning of distinguished literary careers. The Festival takes place for two weeks in early autumn, generally early to mid-October, and full details can be obtained by writing to the Cheltenham Festival of Literature, Town Hall, Imperial Square, Cheltenham GL50 1QA or Tel 523690.

CINEMA

The **Odeon** in Winchcombe Street, Tel 658755, has five screens and this is augmented by occasional showings in other venues, especially at festival times.

BOOKSTORES

The best is **Waterstone's** on the Promenade, Tel 512722, with an excellent selection, very large stock and real style. **Sherratt and Hughes**, Tel 583930, with a comprehensive stock, right in the middle of town at 1, The Promenade is also excellent. **Hammick's Bookstore** at 38 Regent Arcade, Tel 571779, is also good, while, still in Regent Arcade at No 20 is **Reading Matters**, Tel 226561, an excellent children's bookstore while **The Works** at 206 High Street, Tel 224703, is an excellent shop for publishers' remainders and bargains. **W H Smith** has one of its better outlets in the High Street, Tel 584086.

ANTIQUARIAN AND SECONDHAND BOOKS

There are three good secondhand bookstores around the Promenade area; **Alan Hancox**, Tel 513204, is at 101 Montpellier Street, **Graham Bennett**, Tel 232429, is at 17A Montpellier Villas and **Simon Reynolds**, Tel 512088, is at 15 Montpellier Walk. All good and they all have shops which reflect the elegance of Cheltenham's past. If you are out visiting the Pittville Pump Room, then call into **Barrie's Fine Books**, Tel 515813, at 67 Malden Road. Two other shops have an excellent stock and are of interest; **Michael Rayner**, Tel 512806, is at 11 St Luke's Road and **Second Storey Books**, Tel 570754, is at 7 Selkirk Street. The only other shop to bother with is **Heynes' Bookshop**, Tel 515423, at 49 Clarence Street.

ART GALLERIES

The best area for galleries is the Montpellier section of town. **Whitcombe and Co**, Tel 524519, at 18 The Promenade, is a traditional gallery with excellent service. They are knowledgeable and friendly. The **Marier Jane Gallery**, Tel 221788, is also good and it's close by at 5 Rotunda Terrace. Just off Montpellier Terrace is Suffolk Parade, where you will find the **Parade Gallery**, Tel 241897, at 6 St James Terrace and **Turtle Fine Arts**, Tel 241646, at 29/30 Suffolk Parade. Both worth a visit. If you are in the Pittville area, then **Ogle Fine Arts**, Tel 231011, has an excellent contemporary exhibition, while **Clive Lawrence**, Tel 583562, at 12 St James Street has some very nice limited-edition lithographs and prints.

ANTIQUE DEALERS

There are a lot, so in order to be as helpful as possible I've grouped them, in so far as I can, geographically.

Group one can be found in the area bordered by Montpellier Gardens, Cheltenham College, Suffolk Road and Lypiatt Road and Tivoli Street.

The Elephant's Bag – 215 Bath Road, Tel 222165. General collection. Bric-à-brac.
Decorative Textiles – 7 Suffolk Parade, Tel 574546. They are specialists in antique cushions and textiles. Some lovely old needlework too.
Regency Antiques – 13 Suffolk Parade, Tel 221359. Fine general collection.
Carlton House Antiques – 21 Suffolk Parade, Tel 245667. A good general collection.
Triton Gallery – 27 Suffolk Parade, Tel 510477. Very good and comprehensive stock.
Tapestry Antiques – 33 Suffolk Parade, Tel 512191. A good general collection.
Patrick Oliver – 4 Tivoli Street, Tel 519538. Excellent general collection.
Manor House Antiques - 42 Suffolk Road, Tel 232780. Very good indeed.
Just a bit further away at 16A Landsdown Place Lane is **John McKenzie**, Tel 241499, in charming premises and with a collection that is well worth the five-minute walk.

Group two is out the London Road at Charlton Kings (five minutes by car). At 93 Horsefair Street is **Bottles and Bygones**, Tel 236393. As the name implies, they specialize in antique bottles and they have quite a collection. They also have general antiques, postcards, potlids and chimney pots, brass, copper, china, glass and advertising items. A fascinating browse. At 197 London Road is **Brocante**, Tel 243120. They specialize in fine table and bed linen and also in lace. You'll also find clothes (Edwardian-1960s), old needlework and tapestry. Next door at 199 London Road is **Charlton Kings Antiques and Crafts Centre**, Tel 510672. Comprehensive general antiques and bric-à-brac, while **M J Hanlon**, Tel 520302, is at Glenfall Farm, Ham Road. At 215 London Road is **Latchford Antiques**, Tel 226262, a good general collection.

Group three is situated in the town centre. They include **Country Life Antiques**, Tel 226919, very good indeed, at 8 Rotunda Terrace; **H W Kell** at 129/31 Promenade, Tel 522509, very well established, very elegant, impeccable service and a beautifully selected collection; and **Montpellier Clocks Ltd** at 13 Rotunda Terrace, who will show you all you want to see in the area of timepieces. **Sinclair Hardy and Co** at 5 Montpellier Walk, Tel 524738, also specializes in clocks and watches.

Group four is on the High Street leading out to the Tewkesbury Road. **Frontier Gallery**, Tel 513245, also has prints and can be found at 31 High Street, while further out at 420 High Street is **Heyden's Antiques**, dealing in militaria as well as having a general collection.

Finally, group five, on the way to Prestbury and Winchcombe. They are all on the Prestbury Road. There's **Bed of Roses Antiques** at No 12, Tel 231918, **The Old Butcher's Shop**, Tel 224353, at No 29, and **Struwelpeter**, Tel 230152 at No 35. **Grosvenor Antiques**, specializing in Victorian, Edwardian and 1930s furniture, has some lovely iron and brass beds at No 271.

There's a couple that don't quite fit in but are well worth a glance. They are both on Great Norwood Street – **Balley Architectural Antiques** (some very big pieces here) at No 11, Tel 584895; and **Cobwebs**, Tel 222450, at No 8.

RESTAURANTS

If you've been scouring the antique shops of Suffolk Road and even if you haven't, you will welcome the smart, attractive restaurant at Nos 24-26, **Le Champignon Sauvage**. The place is named after the dominant ingredient of the initial years of the restaurant. The menu is very complex – *chartreuse* of pigeons and pheasant with lentils is not easy to cook – and the price is not untoward for the effort and imagination that go into the creation of the cuisine. The soups are very good and the petits fours are the best I've tasted outside of a twin Michelin star in France. A good wine list. The set lunch and dinner are excellent value. Open Mon–Sat 12:30–1:30; 7:30–9:30pm. No Sat lunch. Tel 573449.

Finn's – 143 Bath Road, Tel 32109. High quality eating out at a reasonable price sums up this restaurant. The set price menus are very good value at lunch and dinner. The cooking is Anglo-French. Kingfish from the Seychelles served with a curry-and-coriander sauce and leek-and-potato soup are both, in their own ways, excellent. The strawberry shortcake nearly reaches the ceiling. Open all week 12:30–2; 7–10pm. No Sat lunch or Sun dinner.

Mayflower – 32 Clarence Street, Tel 522426. An excellent Cantonese restaurant, with the flavours well defined, as they should be. The hot-and-sour soup is not for the faint-hearted and the seafood is exceptional. Best of all is Szechuan crispy aromatic duck – a delight. Open all week 12–1:45; 5:45–10:45pm. No Sun lunch.

Elsewhere in Cheltenham try **New Land**, 119 Promenade, Tel 522426. It has authentic Vietnamese cooking as well as Chinese cuisine. Try set dinner A if you don't want to order from the à la carte menu. Open Tues–Sat 12–2; 6–11:30pm.

Good Italian food can be obtained at **Il Trovatore**, 20 Winchcombe Street, Tel 522525. Open Tues–Sat 12–2; 6:30–11pm.

And don't forget **Matcham's**, Tel 572532, at the Everyman Theatre. They have an imaginative set menu and you can return during the interval to have your dessert and coffee – what a civilized idea.

PUBS

Cotswold Inn – Portland Street, Tel 523998. A quite handsome Regency pub, comfortably furnished and with Victorian prints and flock-papered walls. Good home-cooked food including Sunday lunch.

Evergreen – (part of the Central Hotel) Portland Street, Tel 524789. Light and airy town centre bar with good food in bar and restaurant. Quiet courtyard garden for the summer.

Old Swan – 37 High Street. Excellent value meals at lunchtime. Friendly service. Tel 584929.

Cheltenham is not really the best place for pubs. The following wine bars and brasseries may be more in keeping with the atmosphere of the town.

Café Tabac – 42 Hight Street, Tel 224326. Good Sunday lunchtime jazz. Open 12-2pm all week (midnight on Sundays).

Everyman Theatre Café Bar – Regent Street, Tel 572532. 9am–11pm all week.

Latin Quarter – 45-47 Clarence Street, Tel 221507. Good Mexican food and a bar with world-wide selection of drinks. Open all week 12–2pm. (midnight on Sundays).

Montpellier – Bayshill Lodge, Montpellier Street, Tel 527774. Roast lunch on Sunday 12–2pm. Open Mon–Sat 11–11. An attractive brasserie in a cellar setting.

The Retreat – Suffolk Parade, Tel 235436. Open Mon–Sat 12–2:30pm; 5–11pm. Food only at lunchtimes.

Tailors – 4 Cambray Place, Tel 241186. Open Mon–Sat 11:30–3pm; 6–11pm.

It would be sad to come to Cheltenham and not visit some of the beautiful Cotswold pubs within easy distance of the town. At Withington (4 miles (6 km) south of A436) the **Mill Inn**, Tel 0242 89204, is situated in a pretty valley and has the river Coln running through its garden. At **Fossebridge**, the pub of the same name has an ancient Tudor bar and overlooks the lake. Tel 0285 720310 (on A429 Fosseway between Cirencester and Bourton). At Cowley (off A435, 3 miles (5 km) south), the **Green Dragon**, Tel 0242 87271, has walls festooned with pistols, hunting pinks and gleamy copper. At Ford (2 miles east of Winchcombe), the **Plough** is one of the oldest pubs in England. There was once a jail in the cellar and Shakespeare is supposed to have carved the plaque on the front of the house. They serve wonderful asparagus in season: A "must." Tel 0386 73215. At Alderton (2 miles (3.2 km) north of Winchcombe), the **Gardener's Arms** is a thatched Tudor house with a wonderful atmosphere, Tel 0242 62257. At Colesbourne (on A435, 4 miles (6.4 km) south) the **Colesbourne**, Tel 0242 87376, is very old with good food and finally, at Little Washbourne, **Hobnails** is known for its pub grub besides having a quarry-tiled traditional front bar. Tel 0242 62216.

ARTISTIC ASSOCIATIONS

Gustav Holst was born at 4 Clarence Road, the eldest son of a musician. His childhood was a difficult one. The boy's asthma and poor eyesight were ignored by his widowed father, who forced him to spend hours practising the violin. Gustav hated it. In a sense though, parental intransigence paid off and the young man was composing at the age of twelve. He made his name in 1918 with his brilliant orchestral suite, *The Planets*. No serious collection of recorded music is complete without it and Goodmusic (see above) will have half a dozen different recordings of it. To celebrate his genius, the people of Cheltenham paid for the Birmingham Orchestra to perform a special concert of his work, conducted by Holst himself. He called it "the most overwhelming event of my life." (See Holst museum above.)

No 11, Tivoli Road is a typical 19th-century villa with generous eaves, well-proportioned windows and a classical porch. In 1902 it was the birthplace of the great English actor, Sir Ralph Richardson. The studio theatre at the Everyman bears his name.

Adam Lindsay Gordan, known as the first Australian poet, spent his boyhood at 28 Priory Street. His poetry found its inspiration in the race meeting and one of his best-known poems, "How We Beat the Favourite," is based on the 1847 Cheltenham Steeplechase. Alfred Lord Tennyson lived for six years at 10 St James Square and his "In Memoriam" was written there. One of the greatest actors of his day was William Charles Macready. He spent his retirement at No 6 Wellington Square and it is said that he entertained Charles Dickens on several occasions. In April 1930, the young Cecil Day-Lewis took up a teaching appointment at Cheltenham College Junior School. After a brief stay at 96 Bath Road he bought the old, mellowed stone-and-brick Box Cottage in Bafford Lane, Charlton Kings where he lived for the next seven years. It was there, in order to pay for repairs to the Cotswold-tile roof, he wrote his first thriller, *A Question of Proof*, published in 1935 under the pseudonym of Nicholas Blake. He succeeded John Masefield as Poet Laureate in 1968.

James Elroy Flecker, poet and novelist, lived as a child at Dean Close School, where his father was the first headmaster. He spent his vacation from Oxford in Cheltenham and wrote about the town. His grave is in the town. Finally, John Nevil Maskelyne lived and worked as a watchmaker at No 12 Rotunda Terrace. Here his interest was directed towards the automata he subsequently used in his illusions at London's Egyptian and St George's Halls. In the late 19th and early 20th century, Maskelyne was the best-known and most respected magician and illusionist of his time.

EPHEMERA

Legend has it that Cheltenham's rise from obscurity (by means of the waters which established it as a fashionable spa) was due to a flock of discerning pigeons. Curious locals, viewing the spring which bubbled through a field on the site of what is now the internationally famous Ladies' College, noticed the birds gathering in large numbers to pick at the salt crystals drying in the sun. The pigeons appeared to thrive, the fascinated Cheltonians tried the spring for themselves and an era of elegance was born. Today the pigeon is incorporated in the city's crest standing on a roundel with bars of silver and blue symbolizing the waters. In the early days the waters were supposed to work wonders on gout, constipation and chronic rheumatism and for a long period they appeared to be recommended for practically everything. "A most commodious purge which works off without heat, thirst or dryness of the mouth, sickness, gripings, faintness or dejection of spirits" and which is of benefit in "rheumatic, scrophulous, erysipelous, scorbutic leprous cases" – sounds very nasty. People, especially locals, swore by the cure and when Dr Edward Jenner, the discoverer of the smallpox vaccine, who lived in the town from 1795 to 1815, began giving free vaccinations from his home in Alpha House, St George's Road (nicknamed "the Pest House") he found some people preferred Cheltenham's traditional remedy.

George III visited Cheltenham in 1788. At that time "Farmer George," later dubbed the "Mad Monarch," was truly a man of the people. Although already afflicted with porphyria, the physical disorder which eventually drove him insane, George was a popular ruler, who preferred the simple life of the rural landowner to the elaborate etiquette of court. Plagued by a series of bilious attacks, George's medical regimen gives some idea of the nature of "the cure" at this time. Rising at five, he walked to the well for a glass of water, then strolled for half an hour with his family, waving to the crowds and stopping to chat with passers-by. After another glass, George walked home to breakfast and spent the rest of the day on horseback. Some days he and his party went to church and several times he indulged one of his lifetime's passions by visiting Cheltenham's theatre – known thenceforward as the Theatre Royal. On being asked, before one of his walks, whether he would be taking his guards, George said he could have no better guards than his people. Perhaps one of the reasons for the popularity of the waters was that in the primitive days of medicine, the spa regime, with its tepid baths and early rising, was infinitely less uncomfortable than most other contemporary remedies.

In conclusion, I shall allow my obsession with the occult to take over again: the Everyman Theatre has an unseen ghost (unusual, this) supposedly of a labourer who fell off some scaffolding during redecorations in 1927. This spirit is supposed to occupy a seat in the back row of the stalls, but there is no evidence of this, despite the fact that a clergyman watching a performance of *Tom Jones* in 1965 collapsed and died in that seat. However, Ernest Dyson, who was handling night security for the re-opening of the theatre in 1959 will attest to the tangible actions of the unknown spirit. He was having a cup of tea with a couple of patrolling policemen, when the trio heard footsteps in the fly gallery above their heads. Splitting up, they scoured the area above the stage: to no avail. The unnerved policemen, deciding they had other pressing duties, left and Mr Dyson, hearing other unusual noises, locked himself in one of the dressing rooms for the night. When he emerged at first light he found, in the centre of the stage, two 18-foot (5.4 m) flats standing one on top of the other, without any means of support. As the average flat is no more than 18 inches (45.7 cm) thick, two would be impossible to balance and it would have taken a small army to construct a 36-foot-high (10.8 m) structure. As Mr Dyson approached, the flats crashed to the floor.

Cheltenham has a reputation for ghost stories, and not just theatrical ones. There's even a book, *Cheltenham: Town of Shadows*, on sale at the Tourist Office. The spooks range from a spectral old man searching for his dog off Bath Road to a ghostly carriage disappearing beneath the waters of Pittville Lake. The village of Prestbury, on the outskirts of town to the east, has 28 attested sightings of ghosts – something of a record, it seems to me. The Tourist Office has not been idle in this respect; it's possible to take a Ghost Walk around the town. So you can judge for yourself whether this seemingly elegant and tranquil town is all that it appears to be.

TOURIST INFORMATION BUREAU: 77 Promenade, Cheltenham, Glos GL50 1PP. Tel (0242) 522878

CHICHESTER

County of West Sussex
79 miles (126 km) from London by M3, M27 and A27
Train from London (Victoria) 1 hour 40 minutes

The Romans called Chichester "Noviomagus" and they established an important settlement here when they landed in Great Britain in AD43. There is much evidence of their presence, especially in the substantial remains of their defensive wall and one remaining bastion, but more especially at Fishbourne (one mile/1.6 km west of the city) where a Roman palace was built which is still the largest Roman building yet discovered in Britain and one of the largest anywhere. The Saxons also established themselves here. They called the town Cissa and added to it the word ceaster which meant Roman town. As both words were pronounced with a "ch," it is easy to see how the name of the town evolved. The city's history has been generally peaceful and prosperous. All traces of the city's castle, demolished in the 13th century, have disappeared, except for the mound on which it stood. The only serious disturbances were the two sieges of the Civil War, both comparatively short. There are some old buildings in the city, but it is chiefly notable for its Georgian architecture, especially in a delightful street called Little London (to your left as you walk away from the cross on East Street). The Pallants also has beautiful town houses (to your left as you walk away from the cross on South Street).

WALK

You will have gathered that it is easy to find your way around Chichester. The **Chichester Walk** starts from the **Market Cross**. (Park in the Friary Lane car park off East Street.) This is, in my view, the finest structure of its type in the country. Built at the end of the 15th century, it is often called Bishop Story's Cross after the Bishop of Chichester who gave it to the city. From the Cross, if you walk down West Street you will find the **Cathedral** with its unique detached **Bell Tower** to your left. Turn left at the end of West Street on to the Avenue de Chartres (named after Chichester's twin town) and you will find the remnants of the city's ancient town wall which can be traced around the whole city with parapet walks along the north and east walls. Return to the Market Cross and walk down South Street and turn right down Canon Lane. Pass through Canon Gate and on your right is **Vicar's Close**, a row of 15th century houses, renovated in the 18th century, once occupied by the vicar's chorale of the cathedral. Their refectory, the **Vicar's Hall**, can be seen at the far end of the pathway which leads to the cloisters. Further down Canon

THE MARKET CROSS, CHICHESTER

Lane is **St Richard's Walk**. The English saint, Richard de Wych, was Bishop of Chichester from 1245 to 1253 and this stone-flagged path may often have been used by the saint himself. Finally, at the end of the lane is the **Palace Gateway**. This ancient edifice dates from the 14th century and leads to the **Bishop's Palace** which itself is adjacent to the southwest corner of the Cathedral. Cross back into West Street and return to the Cross. Walk down East Street, turn right on to North Pallant and at the Junction with East Pallant you will find **Pallant House**, built in 1712 for Henry Peckham, a prosperous wine merchant. This is the spot where the four Pallants meet and Georgian houses abound. Further down East Street, to your left, is **Little London**; there is more Georgian architecture here and also the **Chichester District Museum** which was once a granary. Again return to the Cross and turn right up North Street, past **Market House** (circa 1807) and on your right close by is the **Saxon Church**. St Olave's Church was built around 1050 and is older than the cathedral. It was restored in 1850 but some Saxon work remains. It is now a book shop. Further down on the right is the **Council Chamber** with its mellow brickwork and stone Ionic columns. It was built in 1731. Finally, go past Lion Street and St Peter's Street and then turn right down Guildhall Street. In front of you, in Priory Park, is **Greyfriars**. This fine 13th-century building is all that remains of the great monastery of the Grey Friars. It formed the chancel of the monastic church and is now the Guildhall Museum. To the north is the site of the castle, demolished in the 13th century. Come back onto Priory Road and fork right into St Martin's Square. Follow the Square to St Martin's Street and at the junction with East Street, turn right and the Market Cross is just ahead.

MUSEUMS, GALLERIES AND PUBLIC BUILDINGS

Chichester District Museum – 29 Little London, Tel 784683. The museum is a converted 18th-century granary. Its displays provide an introduction to the geology, archaeology and history of the district. There are also strong collections relating to the Roman and Saxon Chichester, to the Church and to the Civil War. Look for the full-size figure of a Roman legionary in full armour, and the mobile city stocks and whipping post, used to pull offenders around the Market Cross to be pelted with rotten fruit and eggs by onlookers. Open Tues–Sat 10–5:30pm.

Guildhall Museum – Priory Park, Priory Road, Tel 784683. The Guildhall was built in the late 13th century as the church of the Franciscan Friary. Later, between 1541 and 1731, it was the city's Guildhall and then, until 1850, its Courthouse. It continued to be used for civic events until 1888. The museum now houses archaeological material from excavations in Chichester. Note the tombstones, inscriptions and an altar dating from the Roman period. The 18th-century bell from the Market Cross is also here. Open June–Sept Tues–Sat 1–5pm.

Mechanical Music and Doll Collection – Church Road, Portfield, Tel 785421. Housed in a former Victorian church one mile east of the city, just off the A27, the exhibits include mechanical musical instruments, musical boxes, phonographs, barrel organs, mechanical pianos and fair and dance organs which illustrate the craftsmanship and inventiveness of the Victorian period. The doll collection contains wax, bisque-headed, felt and velvet dolls dating from Victorian times to the 1920s. Open Easter–Sept daily 10–6pm.

Museum of the Royal Corps of Military Police – Rousillon Barracks, Tel 786311. The museum occupies the keep of the original barracks built by French prisoners of war in 1803. The display illustrates the history of the Corps from its Tudor origins to the present day. Exhibits compare life in the Corps in National Service days and in 1980, the methods by which modern soldier-detectives fight crime and the difficulties of protecting senior officials and diplomats in such difficult locations as Northern Ireland. Open May–Sept Tues–Sun 10–12:30 and 1:30–4pm; Oct–April Tues–Sat same hours.

Pallant House Gallery – 9 North Pallant, Tel 774557. Pallant House dates from 1713. It contains the collection of modern art formed by the late Dean of the Cathedral, Walter Hussey and given by him to the city. It includes works by Moore, Sutherland, Ceri Richards, John Piper and Geoffrey Clarke. Open Tues–Sat 10–5:30pm. Not bank holidays.

Royal Palace and Museum – Fishbourne, Tel 785859. The museum presents the remains of the north wing of a first century palace of Italianate design. There are also mosaics (the largest group in Britain) and underfloor heating. The museum shows the most important finds from the excavations including a reconstruction of a palace dining room, a Roman farm and a Roman garden. Open daily 10–4pm. (10–6pm in summer.)

Goodwood House – Chichester, Tel 774107. The house is three miles northeast of Chichester on the A27. A stable block was added in the 1750s. The remarkable octagon design, built around the Jacobean core, was never completed but the house remains a superb example of Restoration design. The house is the seat of the Dukes of Richmond and Gordan and the family still lives there. The contents of the house are impressive. Canaletto's first London porcelain, Gobelins tapestries and mementoes of many royal visits. The artists represented include Van Dyck, Lely, Kneller, Reynolds and Stubbs. The entrance portico by James Wyatt (circa 1780) is especially impressive. Open May 4th–Oct 6th Sun and Mon plus Tues–Thurs Aug 2nd–5th.

Chichester Cathedral – West Street, Tel 782595. After the Norman Conquest, William I ordered that all cathedrals should be removed from small villages to more important centres. The See of Chichester was thus established in 1075 and construction began in 1091. It was consecrated in 1184. A fire in 1187 did serious damage and the reconstruction was undertaken with the old heat-weakened stone which is causing structural problems even today. The spire collapsed in 1861 and was subsequently rebuilt in replica. On the right of the south choir aisle are two of the finest medieval carvings to be found in the country – Christ being greeted by Martha and Mary in Bethany and the miracle of Lazarus. In stark contrast, but yet strangely in harmony, are the John Piper reredos tapestries, Graham Sutherland's painting *Noli Me Tangere* and a superb Marc Chagall stained glass window.

THEATRE

Chichester Festival Theatre – Oaklands Park, Tel 781312. A remarkable thrust stage auditorium based on the Festival Theatre in Stratford, Ontario. Its first director was Lord Olivier and its Summer Festival season is now extended to five months with a wide range of productions including new plays, classics, comedies and musicals. Many productions transfer to London's West End or go on tour. Out of season, the fare is still sumptuous, with visits from great orchestras, opera, ballet, pantomime, pop stars, an autumn jazz week and a family show at Christmas. Recent visitors included the English Shakespeare Company, the Actors Touring Company, the London Mozart Players, Travelling Opera and the Royal Philharmonic Orchestra. Productions are also presented in the **Minerva Studio Theatre** which presents work of a more experimental nature.

MUSIC

Concerts are given in the Cathedral and the Festival Theatre but the most exciting time, musically, in Chichester is during the first half of July when the **Chichester Festivities** take place. Starting in 1975 as a three-day festival to celebrate the 900th anniversary of the Cathedral, the festival has been held every year since and is now one of the most important of its kind in the south of England. Concerts are given in the Cathedral and elsewhere in the city with international orchestras and artists, exhibitions, late-night shows and many outdoor and community events.

Among the artists who have appeared in the last few years are Janet Baker, the choir of King's College Cambridge, the London Symphony Orchestra, Paul Tortelier, James Galway, the Academy of St Martin-in-the-Fields and the Royal Philharmonic. Full details from Chichester Festivities, Canon Gate House, South Street, Tel 785718.

CINEMA

Chichester does not have a commercial cinema (it closed in 1980), but the **New Park Film Centre**, New Park Road, Tel 786650, shows a variety of foreign, contemporary and classic films which are open to the public during the centre's film season, which runs from September to July. Films are shown on Wed, Thurs and Fri. Phone Roger Gibson at 784881 for details.

BOOKSTORES

The best two shops are **Dillon's Bookshop** at 24A South Street, Tel 783136, and **Hammick's Bookshop** at the Token House, 65 East Street, Tel 780492. Both branches of respected chains, you should not need to look any further for your reading needs than these two stores. Christian books can be found at **SPCK**, St Olave's Church, North Street, Tel 782790 and **Chichester Bible Shop**, 33 West Street, Tel 780361, and good bargain books and publishers remainders are at **Omnibooks**, 1 St Peter's House, North Street, Tel 776452.

ANTIQUARIAN AND SECONDHAND BOOKS

I think the best is **St Peter's Bookshop** in St Peter's Arcade, West Street, Tel 778477. They have a good secondhand and antiquarian collection and are just opposite the Cathedral. The **Chichester Bookshop**, 39 Southgate, Tel 785473, and **Peter Hancock**, 40 West Street, Tel 786173, are both worth visiting (Peter Hancock especially).

ART GALLERIES

Canon Gallery – 4 Newtown, Tel 786063, has watercolours and prints of the 19th and 20th centuries.
Hornblower Gallery – Unit 25, Sadler's Walk, East Street, Tel 531316, has contemporary oils and watercolours mainly by local artists and also some interesting heritage drawings by the owner, in the style of David Gentleman.
Chichester Centre of Arts Ltd – St Andrew's Court, East Street, Tel 779103, has visiting shows covering painting, sculpture, collage and crafts. The Gallery is part of an arts centre whose activities include music, poetry reading and practical workshops.
Pallant House Gallery – 9 North Pallant, Tel 774557, is a new gallery housing temporary exhibitions of contemporary art.

ANTIQUE SHOPS

Almshouse Arcade is situated at the eastern end of the city at 19 The Hornet, close to the cattle market with a huge car park close by. There are seven dealers in residence, covering antique furniture, model railways, Dinky toys, ceramics, glass, militaria, postcards, prints, paintings, gentlemen's vintage clothes, general antiques and ephemera. Also at The Hornet is **Gallery Six Antiques** at **Nigel Purchase Gallery**. They have fine art, porcelain, furniture and work by local artists. Tel 782018. In the town centre in **West Street** you will find **Gems Antiques**, Tel 786173 at No 39. They have period furniture, Staffordshire and porcelain figures, books and pictures. At No 40/41 is **Peter Hancock Antiques** with silver, jewellery, porcelain, furniture, pictures, glass, clocks, books, ethnographica, art nouveau and art deco. Tel 786173. **St Pancras Antiques** at 150 St Pancras, Tel 787645, has militaria, arms and armour, medals, documents, uniforms and maps 1600–1914. Also stocked are china, pottery and ceramics 1800–1930, 18th- and 19th-century small furniture, and coins from ancient times to the present. One mile south on the B2145, just off the bypass, is **Antique Shop** at Frensham House, Hunston, Tel 782660. They have English furniture 1700–1830, bureaux, chests of drawers, tables and chairs, while **Heritage Antiques** at 57 Pound Farm Road (fork right at the top of The Hornet) has pine furniture and general antiques. Tel 783470.

RESTAURANTS

Through the Greenhouse – 24 St Pancras, Tel 531578. A theatrical bistro with imaginative food and a pleasing ambience. The grills are especially recommended and the place is lively, bustling and full of life.

Thompson's Restaurant – 30A Southgate, Tel 528832. Especially good for fresh seafood although there is a wide selection of landlubber fare as well. Open for late breakfasts through to lunch and dinner. Open daily 10–2pm and 7–10pm (6–11pm in theatre season). Closed Sunday evening.

St Martin's Tea Rooms – 3 St Martin's Street, Tel 786715. The Georgian façade hides a much earlier interior and an attractive brick paved garden. The food is mostly vegetarian, although the wild smoked salmon, an exception, was very good. There's a wonderful concoction called red dragon pie and a traditional Welsh rarebit which puts most dishes which go by this name to shame. Excellent pastries, especially the carrot cake topped with yogurt. Open Tues–Sat 9–6pm.

Shepherd's Tea Rooms – 35 Little London, Tel 774761. Chichester is big on tea rooms. Shepherd's makes a truly wonderful cup of tea. There's a wide range of snacks, good soup and enormous jacket potatoes. They also make a wonderful variety of rarebits and there's a sinful collection of pastries.

Clinch's Salad House – 14 Southgate, Tel 788822. As the name suggests, the salads are excellent, as are the daily vegetarian specials. I had a parsnip-and-tomato bake which was wonderful. Try the Belgian chocolate fudge cake or the delectable meringue iced walnut cake. Excellent value.

A good Indian restaurant to note is the **Indian Cottage** at The Old Toll House, 1 Westgate, Tel 780859. Their tandoori dishes are especially good and the cooking is well presented and pleasantly authentic. Open daily.

PUBS

Nags – 3 St Pancras, Tel 785823. A lively bar with pleasant garden and patio. They even have a stock of sporting reference books in the bar to settle sporting wagers. Traditional bar food.

Rainbow – St Paul's Street. Friendly welcoming pub with pleasant staff and good service. Good bar food and snacks. They even have an aviary in the garden where you can hear the birdies sing.

The **King's Head** – South Street, Tel 785753. Bustling city centre pub set in an old building circa 1740, with friendly staff and pleasing ambience. Full lunch and evening menu with traditional English cooking.

The **Dolphin and Anchor** – West Street, Tel 785121. Until the beginning of the present century there were two establishments side by side in Chichester, the Dolphin and the Anchor. Both dated from the 17th century when they were prosperous coffee houses and posting centres. They were amalgamated in 1910 and continued under their joint name. In the 18th and 19th centuries the Dolphin was the meeting place for the Whigs and the Anchor for the Tories.

Two good village pubs close by are at Oving (just east of the city) and Sidlesham (just south of the city on the B2145). At Oving the **Gribble** is an attractive village pub housed in a converted cottage. Very good bar food, fireplace and country garden. The unusual name derives from the old lady who used to own the premises. The **Crab and Lobster** at Sidlesham overlooks meadows and coastal flats and is blessedly off the tourist track. There is a nice homely atmosphere, a fire in winter and a pretty cottage garden in the summer. Good bar food – don't miss the Selsey crab.

ARTISTIC ASSOCIATIONS

The earliest of the many writers whose names are associated with Chichester is Reginald Peacock, Bishop of Chichester, who in 1450 wrote three works in English instead of the usual Latin. This was akin to heresy both with respect to the subject of the books and the lingua franca. Peacock was forced to resign the bishopric and was sent into retirement. John Selden, the jurist, was one of the major figures to dispute the legality of Charles I's actions and privileges which eventually led to the King's execution in 1649. Selden was educated in Chichester Choir School.

William Collins, the poet, was born in the city in 1721. His father was twice Mayor of the city and was a noted hatter. Collins studied at Oxford and was a friend of Dr Johnson and Gilbert White, the naturalist. Collins died in Chichester in 1756 and is buried in St Andrew's Church. William Blake, famous for his hymn "Jerusalem" and his collection of poems, *Songs of Innocence and Experience,* also has a Chichester connection: he was tried for sedition in the Guildhall in 1804 but was fortunately acquitted. Charlotte Smith, the poet and novelist, lived in Chichester after separating from her husband in 1787. Her sonnets had been printed at her own expense but they were so popular that five editions followed. Sir Walter Scott admired her novels and they proved so popular that she managed to keep her 12 children on the proceeds. Scott eventually wrote her biography. Finally, there is a plaque at No 11 Eastgate Street, commorating Keats's stay in 1819. It is thought that he visited the old Vicar's Close, with its crypt (it was then a wine store) and was inspired with the imagery for one of his most notable poems, "The Eve of St Agnes."

Eric Gill, the sculptor and artist, lived in Chichester from the age of 15 and married the daughter of the cathedral's head verger in 1904. Examples of his work can be seen in the cathedral and in the County Record Office in West Street.

EPHEMERA

William Huskisson, who was at the time Member of Parliament for Chichester, has the dubious distinction of being the first prominent person to be killed by a train, as he was knocked down and received fatal injuries at the opening of the Manchester and Liverpool Railway in 1830. He did a great deal for the city including promoting the building of the Wey and Arun Canal and its extension into Chichester. There is a memorial to him in the cathedral.

East on the A27, just past Fishbourne, is the village of Bosham where, in the waters of the creek in front of the church, is a place known as the Bell Hole. There, according to legend, lies the tenor bell of the church, which was stolen by Danish pirates in the 10th century. As they sailed away, the monks on shore rang the remaining bells to tell the villagers in the woods that it was safe for them to return. When the last peal rang out, the tenor bell in the boat joined in. It rocked and swayed until it capsized the boat, taking the pirates with it to the bottom of the creek. It is said that the tenor bell still joins in whenever the bells are rung in Bosham Church.

In the 18th century, needlemaking was a major trade in the city. It was largely conducted in the workers' own homes around St Pancras and the road joining St Pancras with The Hornet is still called Needlemakers. A diary of 1763, kept by a draper called Thomas Turner, notes that he paid 9 shillings 3 pence for 13,625 assorted needles to sell in his shop in East Hoathly (just northeast of Lewes). This industry came to a halt at the time of the Civil War, though there is evidence that it continued on a much smaller scale for another hundred years.

In 1874, says *The Anglo-Saxon Chronicle*, a marauding band of Vikings ravaged the Chichester countryside and the citizens put them to flight and killed many of them. Local tradition asserts that the battle was fought in Kingley Vale, four miles (6.4 km) northwest of the city and that the superb grove of ancient yew trees now filling the vale is descended from 60 yews planted on the graves of those that died in the fighting. At night it is said the trees change their shapes and move stealthily about the vale, in which lurk the ghosts of slaughtered Vikings and Saxon defenders.

In the Pallant House Gallery you will find the desk of the merchant Henry Peckham, just as he left it in the 18th century. Among the scattered papers is a doctor's bill listing his medical treatments – cuppings, purgings, leechings and dosings with Venice treacle. Perhaps Peckham's ill health was in some way connected to another letter on his desk, from one of his agents warning him of debts in his mercantile dealings in Lisbon.

TOURIST INFORMATION BUREAU: St Peter's Market, West Street, Chichester, Hants PO1 9AH. Tel (0243) 775888

FARNHAM

County of Surrey
By train, 50 minutes from London (Waterloo Station)
By road, 50 miles (80 km) from London on M3/A320/A31

Farnham is one of those towns which on first impression suggest one should continue to one's next destination. However, it has many delights if one simply perseveres and wanders. Farnham is especially noted for its Georgian houses and there are some excellent examples in West Street and Castle Street. Wilmer House, 38 West Street (see Museums), was built in 1718 and has a fine façade of cut and moulded brick. Inside there is much fine carving and panelling. The Castle, dating from the second half of the 12th century, has the distinction of having been occupied almost continuously until recent times. Until 1925 it was the seat of the Bishops of Winchester, then, until 1956, the Bishops of Guildford. The castle is now a centre which prepares people for official visits overseas. The keep is most impressive, and the great brick tower, erected in the 15th century, is especially noteworthy. Its top is decorated with one of the earliest and best examples of patterned brickwork in England. The Maltings began life as a tannery in the 18th century, although Tanyard House on nearby Red Lion Lane was built in 1500. Middle and Lower Church Lane (at the bottom of Downing Street) contains some very old cottages and nearby St Andrew's Parish Church is part Norman and part 15th century. William Cobbett's tomb is in the churchyard. Close to Wilmer House on West Street is Sandford House, one of the finest examples of Georgian design in the town, although Vernon House close by (now the public library) is also interesting. Although it has a Georgian facing, this in fact masks a 16th-century building, which has an enclosed courtyard. Charles I spent a night here on his way to trial and execution. Behind Vernon House is the West Surrey College of Art and Design, which has an excellent reputation in visual art circles. The Lion and Lamb Yard (off West Street) was originally an inn yard and the archway leading into it dates from 1537. The Spinning Wheel (junction of West and Castle Streets) is a double-gabled timber-framed building circa 1600. Many Farnham buildings must have looked like this before so many were refronted in the Georgian style. The Windsor Almshouses at the top of Castle Street were established in 1619 and are the only houses in the street which have not been given any form of Georgian facelift. Opposite the Town Hall (1930s) on The Borough is the Bush Hotel (bottom of Castle Street and turn left). The hotel's existence was recorded in 1603, and it was ancient even then. On the ceiling of the lounge is a very unusual sundial which used to be lit by the reflection from a pool outside. The back of the hotel (the South Street side) is most attractive. Also note the Redgrave Theatre and the William Cobbett Pub (see below).

WALK

The **Farnham Walk** begins at the car park off South Street, adjacent to the **Redgrave Theatre**. Turn left onto South Street from the car park, then right onto Union Road and left onto Longbridge. Ahead is the **William Cobbett** pub, birthplace of the politician and writer William Cobbett. Turn right onto Red Lion Lane for **The Maltings** and **Tanyard House** circa 1500. Retrace your steps to Longbridge. Cross the River Wey and at the Union Road junction turn left into Lower Church Lane and right into Middle Church Lane for **St Andrew's Parish Church**. These two lanes contains some very old timber-framed cottages, mostly refaced in the 18th century. At the junction of the two lanes, Vicarage Lane leads to a medieval timber frame house which was the Vicarage. Continue along Middle Church Lane into Downing Street. Turn left, and left again into West Street. On the opposite side of the road is the **Lion and Lamb Yard**, originally an inn yard. Continue out West Street to Wilmer House, No 38, and close by Sandford House. Retrace your steps down West Street and turn left into Castle Street. No 10 is a fine **Georgian House** circa 1720. Walk up Castle Steps ahead on your right to **Farnham Castle**. Return down Castle Street noting the

LION & LAMB COURTYARD, FARNHAM

Windsor Almshouses on your left, circa 1619, which are the only houses in Castle Street which have not been given any form of Georgian facelift. At the junction turn left into The Borough. Notice on your left the **Bush Hotel** (circa 1603), Farnham's oldest hotel. Just past the hotel turn right onto South Street and then left into the car park.

MUSEUMS AND GALLERIES

Farnham Museum – Wilmer House, 38 West Street, Tel 715094. The museum tells the story of Farnham's development from its geological beginnings to the 20th century. There are special exhibits on hop growing and drying, and on William Cobbett; there are also: a superb Georgian doll's house, an excellent collection of photographs of 19th-century farming and country life, and a beautiful garden. Open Tues–Sat 10–5pm.

Surrey College of Art and Design – Falkner Road (off The Hart) **James Hockey Gallery**. Contemporary art collection. Tel 722441.

New Ashgate Gallery – Waggon Yard, Tel 713208. A registered trust which aims to further the visual arts in the Waverley District. Open Tues–Sat 10–1:30 and 2:30–5pm.

Waverley Abbey – Ruins of the first Cistercian foundation in England in a riverside setting. Two miles southeast on B3001. Open during daylight hours.

Aldershot Military Museum – Queen's Avenue, Aldershot (two miles/3.2 km), Tel 314598. Housed in the only surviving example of Aldershot's original Victorian bungalow barrack blocks, the museum tells the story of the Home of the British Army from 1854 to the present. For those interested in the military there are at least eight other military museums in Aldershot ranging from the Royal Army Veterinary Corps Museum to The Gurkha Museum. Telephone the military museum for details (see also Ephemera). Open Mar–Oct 10–5; Nov–Feb 10–4:30pm.

THEATRE

The **Redgrave Theatre** is named after Sir Michael Redgrave. It is one of the new generation of provincial theatres and it opened in 1974. It is well designed with an open stage and a small but smart auditorium. Each production runs three or four weeks and plays range from the classics to new works with a traditional family entertainment at Christmas. I saw an excellent production of Sheridan's *The Rivals* there recently, co-produced with the Mercury Theatre in Colchester. In 1990 the theatre created *Freedom to Forget*, a play to mark the 50th anniversary of the Battle of Britain. There is a small studio theatre which offers occasional alternative productions but its use has recently been curtailed by funding cutbacks. There is a friendly coffee bar/restaurant in the late 18th-century house which is incorporated into the theatre. Good home cooked food is available all through the day up to the start of the performance.

MUSIC

In 1969, **The Maltings**, Red Lion Lane, stood derelict and only three weeks from demolition. Against all odds the building (circa 1729) was saved, thanks to the vision and determination of a group of local enthusiasts. Gradually the building was carefully and sympathetically refurbished into the unique arts and community centre it is today. The Maltings is home to some 30 clubs and organizations. The Great Hall is the venue for much musical activity, from jazz and popular music to the Guildford Philharmonic and Nigel Kennedy. There is also a craft centre with many studios and an art gallery. Tel 726234.

CINEMA

There is no commercial cinema in Farnham but there is in Guildford (10 miles/16 km), Camberley (8 miles/13 km) and Aldershot (2 miles/3 km). Fortnightly film showings by the **Farnham Film Society** take place in The Maltings, Wednesdays at 7:45pm. Tel 726234.

BOOKSTORES

The best is **Hammick's**, Tel 724666, in the Lion and Lamb Yard off West Street, with a comprehensive stock and pleasant surroundings. For publisher's remainders and bargain books, take a look at **Bookshelf Bargains** in The Borough, Tel 714811, and also in The Borough there is a branch of **W H Smith**, Tel 576217.

ANTIQUARIAN AND SECONDHAND BOOKS

The best is **Bygone Books** at 5A Castle Street, Tel 737865. They have antiquarian and other rare books as well as secondhand volumes and are especially strong on literature, travel, natural history and Victorian children's books.

ART GALLERIES

Perhaps it is the influence of the West Surrey College of Art and Design, formerly the Farnham College of Art, but the town, for its size, is unusually rich in visual arts. In Castle Street at No 17 you will find **Andrew Lloyd**, Tel 724333, who specializes in the finest contemporary prints. He is strong on British printmakers and can frame the work you purchase. **CCA Galleries** in The Lion and Lamb Yard, Tel 722231, was formed in 1972 as a subsidiary of the world famous auction house, Christie's, and became an independent public company in 1985. They have an excellent collection of limited-edition prints which, in my view, are the most satisfactory basis for a significant art collection.

The **Johnson Wax Kiln Gallery** at The Maltings, Tel 726234, exhibits a wide range of one-man and small group shows ranging from painting, sculpture and ceramics to textiles and furniture. The **Lion and Lamb Gallery**, Tel 714154, in The Lion and Lamb Yard (on the first floor above Biggs china and glass shop). They specialize in Victorian and contemporary watercolours and also have oils and prints. **New Ashgate Gallery**, Waggon Yard, Tel 713208. Changing exhibitions of paintings, prints, sculpture, photography, ceramics, glass, jewellery, textiles and wood.

ANTIQUE DEALERS

The **Farnham Antique Centre** at 27 South Street, Tel 724475, has 15 dealers under one roof so it's likely you'll find something of interest. Porcelain, china, brass and copper, jewellery, silver, dolls, toys and Teddy bears, and small furniture and collectables.

Likewise the **Treasury Antique Centre** in Downing Street, Tel 722199, has 14 dealers under one roof and is well worth a look. Also in Downing Street at No 60 is **R and M Putman**, Tel 715769, a nice little shop with an interesting collection. West Street is especially rich for collectors. At No 90, Tel 716272, is **P and B Jordan**. They have small antique furniture, pictures, maps and ornamental items. Just down the road at No 82 is **Bits and Pieces Antiques**, Tel 715043. They have antique furniture, pine, Victoriana, silver, jewellery, china, glass, art nouveau, collectables – also lace and costumes with costume hire available.

Village Pine is at 32 West Street, Tel 726660. As their name suggests they have lots of old stripped pine and a large stock of interesting and unusual furniture plus many small gift items. Next door to Sandford House is **Sandford Lodge**, which is the home of **Christopher's Antiques**. They specialize in 18th- and 19th-century French fruitwood provincial furniture and their collection is nice to look at even if you don't purchase. Tel 713794. **Annie's Antiques**, Tel 713447, can be found at 1 Ridgeway Parade. Here you'll find furniture, china, pictures, mirrors, jewellery, silver and collectables and a cellar of furniture in need of restoration, while at **Wrecclesham Antiques**, 47 Wrecclesham Road, Tel 716468, you'll find jewellery, clocks, china, brass, silver, shipping furniture and reproduction pine.

RESTAURANTS

If your tastes run to Austrian cuisine, then **Krugs** at 84 West Street, Tel 723277, can hardly be bettered. There are marinated herrings to start with, fondues, veal and steak. The wiener schnitzel, as you would hope, is excellent. Simple things like the red cabbage are prepared with imagination and flair. If you don't want to eat again for 24 hours, try the sauerkraut with bratwurst and dumplings – very good. Desserts, as you would expect, are exceptional. Open Tues–Sat for dinner only 7–10:30pm. Again on West Street at No 27 is **Bishop's Table**, Tel 715545, which is closed on Sunday and also has rooms. Their cuisine is classical French with a nod towards Nouvelle Anglais.

PUBS

The one pub you must visit is the **William Cobbett**, at Bridge Street, Tel 726281, the birthplace of the politician and writer (b 1762). It's a picturesque place with good cheap food and a young clientele. The **Wheatsheaf** on West Street, Tel 725132, is an unpretentious hostelry with interesting prints on the walls and excellent traditional bar food. Good Sunday roasts and a wonderful array of salads. On Castle Street is the **Nelson's Arms**, Tel 716078, which is a long, low beamed pub with polished tables and settles. It's next to the almshouses and last time I was there I had one of their triple-decker sandwiches for lunch and it lasted me all day.

ARTISTIC ASSOCIATIONS

Izaak Walton, the writer famous for *The Compleat Angler,* was Bishop Morley of Worcester's steward. When Morley was appointed Bishop of Winchester in 1662 and moved to Farnham Castle, Walton accompanied him and wrote two of his best-known works here – *The Life of Richard Hooker* in 1665 and *The Life of George Herbert* in 1670. Sir Walter Scott is thought to have taken the title of his series of novels from Waverley Abbey.

Jonathan Swift came to Farnham in 1690 to serve as secretary to Sir William Temple, the diplomat who lived at Moor Park House on the edge of the town. While there Swift met the young Esther Johnson, a daughter of a companion of Lady Temple. Esther was later to become the recipient of many of Swift's intimate letters, collected as *Journal to Stella.* Swift was disappointed at the extent of Temple's patronage and left Moor Park in 1694. He returned however and wrote *A Tale of Tub* and *The Battle of the Books* here in 1697. Both books he described as satires on corruption in religion and learning.

Augustus Toplady, author of the well-known hymn "Rock of Ages," was born at 10 West Street in 1740. In 1775 he was travelling in the Mendip Hills in Somerset when he was overtaken by a mighty storm. He sheltered in a cleft in the rock in the limestone gorge of Burrington Coombe, just north of Cheddar. The experience prompted him to write his famous hymn. The cleft where he took shelter can still be seen on the B3134 road at Burrington between Weston-Super-Mare and Shepton Mallett. A plaque of Burrington Stone can be seen at Toplady's birthplace.

Finally, J M Barrie wrote *Peter Pan* in the pine woods behind his country home in Blacklake Cottage (now Lobs Wood Manor) in Tilford Lane, one mile from the town centre. His Newfoundland dog, the original Nana, is buried there.

For details of William Cobbett see under Artistic Associations section of Guildford.

EPHEMERA

Eight miles (12.5 km) from Farnham on the A31 to Winchester is Alton. Just off the A31 at Alton is Chawton, a tiny village which contains the beautiful 300-year-old house that was the last home of the novelist Jane Austen. Jane lived here from 1809 until her early death in 1817 and in that short time she wrote *Mansfield Park, Emma* and *Persuasion* and revised *Sense and Sensibility, Pride and Prejudice* and *Northanger Abbey.* The atmosphere is cosy and friendly, and one is amazed at how small the table is where Jane did most of her writing. The writing was done in the parlour under semi-secret conditions. The wooden door to this room, known as the "creaking door," acted as a warning if anyone was coming, giving her time to hide her work under the blotter. The door is still there, but unfortunately has been rehung the wrong way round so it no longer creaks. Open April–Oct 11–4:30pm; Nov, Dec and March Wed–Sun 11–4:30pm; Jan and Feb Sat and Sun 11–4:30pm.

Also at Alton, take the B3006 to Selbourne. It was here at his country home, The Wakes, that the 18th-century clergyman-naturalist and author of *The Natural History and Antiquities of Selbourne,* the Reverend Gilbert White, lived for most of his life. White kept detailed notes on his garden for over 42 years – his successes and failures, books studied, methods used – making it one of the best-documented gardens of all time. Inside the house there are two museums. The ground floor is devoted to the life and works of Gilbert White, while the staircase and upper rooms are set aside for exhibits on two members of the Oates family. Frank Oates was a 19th-century naturalist and explorer in Africa and his nephew, Captain Lawrence Oates, accompanied Scott on his ill-fated Arctic expedition of 1910-1912. Captain Oates died on his 32nd birthday in March of 1912 from frostbite and gangrene. A display highlights the tragedy of his last words as he walked out of the tent into a blizzard, saying to his companions, "I am just going outside. I may be some time." Open Mar–Oct Tues–Sun 12–5pm.

Nine miles (14.4 km) south of Farnham on the A287 is Hindhead. Sir Arthur Conan Doyle built his house, Undershaw, here in 1896. The name of the house was believed to be a tribute to George Bernard Shaw. *The Hound of the Baskervilles* was written here in 1902 and although the setting for the book is nominally Dartmoor, it is easy to imagine that Hindhead, set high among commons of heather and pine trees, was the original inspiration for this classic novel.

If you are driving from Farnham towards the M3 motorway on the A287 in the direction of Basingstoke, or even if you are not, stop at the town of Odiham. You approach the town by way of a magnificent oak avenue. Buildings of all styles mingle happily in the wide high street of this market town; there is a 14th-century church with some fine brasses, an interesting but chilling Pest House and the remains of the only octagonal 13th-century castle in the country. Perhaps more mundanely, though I'm not at all sure of that, at 73 The High Street you will find Jewel in the Crown, Tel Odiham 703511. It is situated in a Georgian house with a narrow frontage, so you will have to look for it, but this restaurant serves some of the best Indian food in the country. Their special lamb is superb and the same goes for their muglai chicken. Biranyi and tandoori are also excellent and it's well worth taking a detour for. While editing this book I dropped in at Jewel in the Crown for lunch and found them closed for renovation and under new management. We can only hope that the tradition for superb food will continue, but while waiting, if you are looking for a pit stop in Odiham, just cross the road to the George, a charmingly appointed 16th-century building with good bar food and a restaurant.

Near Waverley Abbey is a deep cave, said in medieval times to have been the home of a white witch named Mother Ludlum. Local people would go to the cave at midnight and ask the good beldam for whatever they wanted, promising to return it within two days. The next day the article they asked for would be standing in front of the cave. Once someone failed to return a cauldron within the stipulated time and the witch never lent anything again. When the cauldron was finally returned it was ignored and tradition says it was taken to Waverley Abbey and afterwards to Frensham Church (three miles/4.8 km south on A287) where it can be seen today. The cave is so deep that it was said that geese that went in at Farnham reappeared featherless in Guildford two weeks later!

TOURIST INFORMATION BUREAU: Locality Office, South Street, Farnham, Surrey GU9 7RN. Tel (0483) 861111

GUILDFORD

County of Surrey
By road, 40 miles (64 km) by M3/A320
Train from London (Waterloo) 55 minutes with half-hourly service

Guildford is an old town, though its history is neither turbulent nor spectacular. There may have been pre-Saxon settlements here but it is first mentioned in the time of Alfred the Great. In medieval times the town became the favourite of a number of monarchs who had palaces and a castle here; the palaces have disappeared but parts of the castle remain. The medieval Pilgrim's Way that led from Winchester to Canterbury and the shrine of St Thomas à Becket crossed the River Wey just south of Guildford, and there is evidence that the medieval town was a prosperous centre of the wool industry. The town declined during Elizabethan times, but its strategic importance ensured its eventual prosperity. Today, it is a bustling town which has managed, unlike so many others, to retain its historic identity within its modern setting. One way it has achieved this is to make its most interesting street – the High Street – a pedestrian precinct, and indeed, the town is remarkably compact, with streets and lanes leading off the main thoroughfare. The High Street is cobbled, which gives it an added ambiance, as does the Guildhall with its famous projecting clock and the Angel Hotel, the only remaining coaching inn. In coaching days Guildford was the convenient stop between Portsmouth and London, but the advent of the railway in 1845 destroyed the coaching trade and consequently most of the inns. However, Guildford did become a cathedral town (not, contrary to popular opinion, a city) and a university was also established.

Most of the buildings in town are adjacent to the High Street and within easy walking distance. The Castle is at the bottom of the High Street reached by Quarry Street. Only the keep remains of a castle which, in its heyday, was considered one of the most luxurious in Europe. Guildford Museum is also in Quarry Street. Just behind the museum, in Castle Hill, is The Chestnuts, home of the six unmarried sisters of Charles Dodgson, better known to the world as Lewis Carroll, the author of *Alice in Wonderland*. Dodgson never actually lived in the house but he spent much time with his sisters, and died there in 1898. He is buried in the Old Mount Cemetery. The house is a private residence and not open to the public. In the centre of High Street is the Guildhall with its gilded clock and turreted roof, while further along the High Street, on the same side, is Abbot's Hospital, founded by George Abbot, a Guildford man and Archbishop of Canterbury under James I. Built in 1619, the present building still accommodates 23 old people of the town, who wear Tudor hats and gowns for services in the chapel. Just below the Guildhall is the Angel Inn, the last o,f the coaching inns, which still has the old courtyard (the arrival and departure point of the coaches), and on its front façade the proud words Posting House and Livery Stable can still be seen. Further up High Street, past Abbot's Hospital, is the Royal Grammar School, founded in 1507. The building was damaged by fire in 1962 but has been carefully restored. It is now used for art exhibitions and has a fine oak and elm staircase. St Mary's Church in Quarry Street near the castle, dating from the 11th century, is the oldest building in Guildford, and deserves a visit. Holy Trinity Church, opposite Abbot's Hospital, has the tomb of George Abbot even though only a chantry remains after the collapse of the tower in the mid-18th century. The Cathedral of the Holy Spirit, consecrated in 1961, is set on Stag Hill about a mile outside the town and was the first cathedral to be built on an entirely new site in the south of England since the Reformation. It is adjacent to the modern buildings of the University of Surrey.

HIGH STREET, GUILDFORD

WALK

The **Guildford Walk** begins at the Sydenham Road car park (Sydenham Road is a continuation of Castle Street). Turn right down Sydenham Road. Turn left into the **Castle Gardens** and go past the Victorian bandstand and the giant chessboard set out on the lawn. Continue under the arch to the castle mound and climb up to the **Castle**. Leave by the ruined building in the south corner of the gardens and turn into Castle Hill. Note **The Chestnuts** on the left, the home of Lewis Carroll's sisters. **Guildford Museum** is close by. Turn right into Quarry Street. Opposite **Castle House**, No 49, turn left down the steep steps of Rosemary Alley which brings you down to Millbrook, the River Wey and the **Yvonne Arnaud Theatre**. Before descending note, in Quarry Street, **St Mary's Church**, the oldest building in Guildford. Cross Millbrook to the **Town Mill** by the theatre, which houses a restaurant and is also the home of an excellent touring theatre company – Millstream Touring. Take the path to the left of the Yvonne Arnaud Theatre, cross over the River Wey and turn right along Millmead, past bronze figures from *Alice in Wonderland*. Turn left to **St Nicholas Church**, noting the decorative font and the large wall painting. The church dates from 1877. Now turn right into Bury Street, noting the **Almshouses** on your left, and right again into High Street. About halfway up on the right is the overhanging clock on the **Guildhall**, the **Angel Hotel** and, just ahead on the left, the red brick gatehouse of **Abbot's Hospital**, circa 1619. **Holy Trinity Church**, on the right, dates from 1763 and is classical in style. It has a so-called "Vinegar Bible" which is on display, open at the page which gives it its name: the misprint "Parable of the Vinegar" for "Parable of the Vineyard." Close by is the **Royal Grammar School**. Just below Holy Trinity Church turn into Milkhouse Gate, a medieval alleyway next to No 142 High Street, which will take you back to the car park.

MUSEUMS AND GALLERIES

Guildford Museum – Quarry Street, Tel 503497. Displayed in a Jacobean house with chalk fireplaces are exhibits covering archaeology, local history and needlework. The needlework is especially fine and there are good rooms devoted to Victorian childhood and a West Surrey cottage. Open Mon–Sat 11–5pm.

Guildford House Museum – 155 High Street, Tel 503406. Guildford House was built in 1660 and served as a shop from the mid-19th century to 1956. It has a permanent collection with a series of portraits by the Guildford artist John Russell RA. There is also craftwork, contemporary paintings and travelling exhibitions. Open Mon–Sat 10:30–4:30pm.

Guildford Cathedral – Stag Hill, Tel 64722. Open 8:30–5:30pm. See Introduction.

The Angel Inn – in the High Street, Tel 64555, was originally part of a monastic establishment and at one time frescoes could be seen in the cellar. The Inn gets its name from the Fish Cross erected in 1345 in front of the hotel. The cross was surmounted by a stone flying angel, hence the name. This cross was removed in 1595.

Loseley House – On the outskirts of town, dates from 1569. Sir Thomas Moore's kinsman, Sir William Moore, built this Elizabethan mansion by incorporating stone from Waverley Abbey near Farnham. Beautifully finished in period style.

Abbot's Hospital – High Street, Tel 62670, and **Royal Grammar School** – High Street, Tel 502424, can both be viewed by appointment. Finally, the **Watts Gallery** in Compton (three miles/4.8 km) is devoted chiefly to the work of the Victorian portraitist, allegorical painter and sculptor, George Frederick Watts. Watts was known as England's Michelangelo and the Gallery, which contains more of Watts's paintings than can be seen anywhere else, was built under the supervision of his wife and opened to the public three months before the artist's death in 1904 (See also Ephemera).

THEATRE

Yvonne Arnaud Theatre – Set in tranquil surroundings on the edge of the River Wey (turn left onto Millbrook at the bottom of High Street). It was named in memory of the delightful actress Yvonne Arnaud, who died in 1958. The Yvonne Arnaud is the epitome of middle-class theatre. As a producing theatre under the direction of Val May, it has earned a reputation for excellent murder, mystery and comedy productions, many of which are destined for London's West End. Recent productions included Edward Albee's *Who's Afraid of Virginia Woolf* and Willy Russell's *One for the Road* and there is always a lavish Christmas pantomime liberally dotted with popular TV and radio names. A recent panto had the TV astrologist Russell Grant, Olympic gold medallist Tessa Sanderson, and Dr Evadne Hinge in starring roles. (If your mind boggles, it was *Robinson Crusoe*.) Of more interest to me personally is the work carried out by the theatre's small-scale touring company, *Millstream*. They operate out of the theatre studio adjacent to the main auditorium and involve themselves in a variety of more offbeat and unusual productions than are normally on offer. I saw an excellent production of South African playwright Athol Fugard's *The Road to Mecca* there recently. Tel 69334.

The theatre has a coffee bar which is open from 10am till the end of the last interval in the evening and a very elegant restaurant called the Harlequin, which serves sophisticated food from 12:30–2 and from 6:15 for pre-, during and post-performance dinners. I recommend the table d'hôte dinner but the specialities, particularly the lamb, are tempting.

The Civic Hall – London Road (top of High Street), Tel 444555, is a large modern facility hosting a range of activities including symphony concerts, jazz and pop groups, lectures, fashion shows and antique fairs. The Guildford Philharmonic plays here and other recent artists have ranged from Norman Wisdom to Dave Berry and the Cruises.

MUSIC

The Guildford Philharmonic is the top professional orchestra of the Southeast and boasts the eminent maestro, Sir Charles Groves, as principal conductor. They play over a dozen concerts in Guildford during their season (Sept–May) with distinguished soloists such as Nigel Kennedy, John Lill and Kathryn Slott.

Musically, Guildford is most active during the **Guildford Festival** in early July. This cultural celebration includes music, theatre and all the arts. Tel 444007.

CINEMA

Commercial cinema at the **Odeon**, Epsom Road, Tel 504990 (4 screens). For alternative cinema contact the **Guildford Institute** of the University of Surrey on Ward Street, Tel 62142. They have occasional screenings and also a series of lunchtime concerts, lectures and the occasional literary lunch which generally takes place in October at the time of the Guildford Book Festival, Tel 444007. They will also know of any university screenings at Stag Hill.

BOOKSTORES

The most comprehensive is **Waterstone's**, 35-39 North Street, Tel 302949, with **Sherratt and Hughes**, 20 The Friary, running them a close second. I am especially fond of **Beaux Arts Books**, 20 London Road, Tel 35352, which has a cosy atmosphere and pleasant staff. The **Penguin Bookshop**, 41 North Street, Tel 32971, is excellent for paperbacks and **Reading Matters** in the High Street at No 39, Tel 60987, is pleasant to browse in. For religious books there are two excellent outlets – **Pilgrims' Bookshop** at 60 Quarry Street, Tel 32971 and **SPCK** adjacent to St Mary's Church in the same street, Tel 60316. I think **Bookends** at 1 Friary Street has a neat name and describes what you will find there, Tel 506484, while if you are at the cathedral, the **University of Surrey Bookshop** is close by, Tel 509169, and besides academic hooks, has a wide range of general reading. **W H Smith** is at 56 High Street, Tel 576217.

ANTIQUARIAN AND SECONDHAND BOOKS

There are two excellent locations. My favourite is **Charles W Traylin** whose premises look and feel just how an antiquarian bookshop should look and feel. He is in Castle House, 49/50 Quarry Street, just past St Mary's Church and just before the museum. His phone number is 572424 and he also stocks antiquarian prints and topographical views. **Thomas Thorp** at 170 High Street also has an excellent stock of secondhand and antiquarian hooks. He is especially strong on non-fiction and an excellent browse is to be had there. Reach him at 62770.

ART GALLERIES

Some fine work is on display in essentially three locations.

Michael Stewart Fine Art at 61 Quarry Street (opposite St Mary's Church) incorporates the Sir William Russell Flint Galleries and there is always a good selection of his work on show. The gallery also represents and shows the work of other artists. When I was last there, work by the equestrian artist Graham Isom and the West Country painter Ted Dyer were on view. Tel 504359.

Forest Gallery Fine Art – 180 High Street, Tel 66222, specializes in contemporary oils and watercolours. They also have limited edition prints, etchings, lithographs and silkscreens. Work by Celia Russell, Wendy Stevenson and John Yardley, as well as many others, can be seen or obtained.

Finally, **Palm House Gallery** at 85 North Street, Tel 506622, has etchings, watercolours, silk screen and limited edition prints from a wide range of contemporary artists.

ANTIQUE DEALERS

The best browsing for antiques near Guildford is five miles out of town to the northeast, on the A3 towards junction 10 of the M25. There you will find the village of Ripley with a positive plethora of antique stores. In the High Street, which is essentially the only street, you will find **Anthony Welling Antiques** who has a beautiful collection of 17th- and 18th-century oak and country furniture, Tel 225384, **Manor House Antiques**, Tel 225350, with a good general collection, **J Hartley** at No 186, Tel 224318, **Ripley Antiques** at No 67, Tel 224333, and **Sage Antiques**, Tel 224396, just down the road. All are interesting and as they are so close together they are worth a browse. If you are village-hopping, call into Compton (just on the outskirts of the town, off the A31 to Farnham – you can see the **Watts Gallery** at the same time). In Compton you'll find **Old Post Office Antiques** in a charming building, Tel 810303, and just down the road, **Compton Antiques**, Tel 810505. Both good general collections. South on the A281 towards Horsham, you'll find Shalford. You'll also find **M Granshaw Antiques** at the Old Malthouse, Tel 61462, close to the ancient Shalford Mill, which is well worth a look, and also **Angel Antiques** at 6 Station Road, Tel 62594. Finally, if you're not exhausted you can pop into Bramley, which is about a mile past Shalford on the A281. Herb you will find **Memories Antiques** in the High Street, Tel 892205. You can have lunch in the Jolly Farmer, a cheerful pub in the High Street and go on in the afternoon to **Loseley House**, a beautiful Elizabethan mansion and the **Winkworth Arboretum**, both close by.

For those of you not wishing to travel so far afield, there are two excellent shops very close to the castle. **Churchill Antiques Galleries** is close to St Mary's Church and the museum in Quarry Street, Tel 506662, while **Denning Antiques** is close, in nearby Chapel Street, Tel 39595. Both of these shops have elegant collections. Back on the High Street, off to the left just below the Guildhall is Market Street where you will find **Peter Goodall** at 12B – a nice little shop. Just above the Abbot's Hospital, Chertsey Road leads off to the left. **Back and Beyond**, Tel 300434, has interesting china, copper, toys and postcards, at No 64 while if you continue down Chertsey Road until it becomes Stoke Road you will find **David Nash** at No 81, Tel 38807. Finally, friends tell me there are bargains a-plenty at the **Antiques Centre**, Tel 67817, at 22 Haydon Place and that **J and S Antiques** at 38A Stringers Avenue is worth a visit.

RESTAURANTS

Whenever I am in Guildford I invariably eat at **Rumwong**, 16-18 London Road, Tel 36092. It is a Thai restaurant and that's a cuisine of which I'm especially fond. If you are uncertain what to order, go for the set menu. It's good value and it saves you the embarrassment of ordering the manager by mistake. If you want to be really adventurous then I recommend the poh-tack, a soup of mixed seafood served in a large pot for two or more persons. Duck with coconut milk and pineapple is also very good. Don't bother with the desserts. To drink, I recommend Singha beer imported from the East, excellent when you consider all the makings are imported. Open Tues–Sun 12–2:30 and 6–10:45.

I must admit to being very fond of the elegant restaurant at the **Yvonne Arnaud Theatre** (see above) – I often eat there.

Given that the **Angel** in the High Street, Tel 64555, is such an historic inn and has been so beautifully restored, it would be churlish not to eat there. It is run by the Trust House Forte chain which is as good a guarantee of quality as you are likely to get in the UK. The Angel serves lunch and dinner in its atmospheric dining room at the normal hours.

Friends of mine have been very enthusiastic about the **Mad Hatter**, 5-6 Sydenham Road, Tel 63011. The Michelin Guide also likes it and they're open for lunch and dinner Mon–Sat (not Sat lunch).

Finally, for when you're antique hunting, I'll mention two excellent restaurants you may run across – La Baita in the High Street at Bramley, Tel 893392, and **Withies Inn**, Withies Lane, Compton, Tel 21158.

PUBS

King's Head – Quarry Street, Tel 575004. Lots of beams and stripped brickwork in a pub which has been converted from former cottages. Lovely big inglenook. Good range of traditional bar food.

Royal Oak – Trinity Churchyard, Tel 66637. Very friendly pub with super big log fires in winter. Good simple bar food.

Harrow Inn – Compton. The village boasts an attractive pub with excellent food. Rustic atmosphere with the food itself certainly well above normal "pub grub" standards. Pasta with mussels and shrimp in a Provençale sauce and baked Brie with almonds are both excellent. Tel 810379.

ARTISTIC ASSOCIATIONS

Three miles (4.8 km) out of Guildford on the Hog's Back (A31) towards Farnham is the little village of Normandy. Here, from 1831 until his death, William Cobbett, journalist and political writer, farmed near the manor. He published *Rural Rides* in 1830, an account of journeys taken from 1812 to refute the landlords' policy towards agricultural labourers with a first-hand account of the distress and mismanagement. There is a story that Cobbett brought the bones of political radical, Tom Paine, to Normandy. Tom Paine wrote his famous treatise, *The Rights of Man,* in 1791/92 and it influenced Cobbett greatly. Cobbett died on his farm in Normandy in 1835. C L Dodgson (Lewis Carroll) has associations with Guildford (see above). Some of his letters and relics are in the museum, and P G Wodehouse, the humorous novelist, was born in a house just off the London Road.

The first large house to be built in what is today a very expensive residential area to the south of Guildford was Durbins, now called Quince House, 37 Chantry View Road. This was the home, from 1909 until his death in 1934, of the critic and painter Roger Fry. Durbins was designed by Fry himself and, like his painting, shows a strong French influence. With its split-level construction, mansard roof, shutters and formal gardens, it was architecturally adventurous for the time and soon became the butt of local disapproval. The staircase is decorated with painted figures by Fry and his friends Vanessa Bell and Duncan Grant. The three were of course central to the Bloomsbury Group, a gathering of English writers and artists who met regularly in the Bloomsbury area of London before, during, and after the First World War. Their unconventional lifestyle, socialist views and aesthetic sensibility combined to give Bloomsbury a connotation outside the circle of somewhat precious snobbery. Besides Fry, Bell and Grant, other prominent members of the group were Leonard and Virginia Woolf, Lytton Strachey, E M Forster and the economist John Maynard Keynes.

EPHEMERA

The Omen, a horror-thriller about the devil's son, was one of the biggest box-office hits of 1976. It starred Gregory Peck and Lee Remick and one of its most memorable scenes is when young Damien (the antiChrist) is being taken to the wedding of friends of his parents. As the car slowly ascends the long hill to the church, Damien, realizing he cannot enter a hallowed building, goes into a fit of rage which causes his parents to abandon their visit to the service. It's a memorable scene and the church is Guildford Cathedral.

In Queen Elizabeth Park, two miles (3.2 km) west off A322, there is the Women's Royal

Army Corps Museum. The displays of uniforms, photographs, documents and other items cover the period during which women have served in the British Army (1917 to the present). Open Mon–Fri 9–4pm. Tel 24431.

A few years ago the Yvonne Arnaud Theatre presented as its annual pantomime, *Sleeping Beauty*. The Wicked Fairy was in the process of concocting an evil spell over a bubbling cauldron. With a final triumphant "Abracadabra," she brought the spell to its conclusion but instead of the Good Fairy turning into something nasty, there was a faulty electronic flash under the cauldron, which blew the Wicked Fairy's knickers off. The property mistress for the company at that time – a Ms Dolly Dawkins – admitted she was not having a terribly good year, as in the preceding pantomime an exploding oven had malfunctioned and blown Mother Hubbard 20 feet across the stage.

An old charter says that "Whenever the King comes to Lothesley (Loseley) Manor near Guildford, the lord is to present His Majesty with 'Three Whores.'" No one knows when this custom fell into abeyance.

A 14th-century Earl of Surrey introduced bull-baiting to England from the Continent. The first "contest" took place in Guildford and thereafter each member of the Corporation, on appointment, was obliged to provide a breakfast for his colleagues and a bull for baiting. The custom lapsed when the awful "sport" died out in the 19th century.

Under the terms of a Guildford man's will, ratified in 1674, "two poor servant maids of good report" selected by the mayor and magistrates of Guildford, provided they "do not live in any inn or alehouse," may throw dice for the interest of £400. The contest takes place on or about January 27th each year at the Guildhall. The winner receives £12.

Shere is four miles (6.4 km) east of Guildford on the A25. A persistent legend of the area tells of a richly dressed stranger calling at the hut of a local woman (the area was once densely forested). While the woodman entertained his visitor, his beautiful teenage daughter went to a nearby lake – the Silent Pool – to bathe. No sooner had she slipped into the pool than her father's guest burst from the woods and stopped his horse over her clothes, laughing triumphantly. Frightened, she screamed and threw herself into the deepest part of the pool even though she could not swim. Her brother, hearing her cries, leapt to rescue her, but he was a poor swimmer and as she sank for the last time, he clasped her in his arms and they died together at the bottom of the pool. The stranger rode away. The distracted woodman finally found the bodies of his children and the matter might have ended there had he not noticed a feather caught in a tree and, realizing that it was from the stranger's hat, suspected his children had been the victims of foul play.

By asking questions, the woodman found that the stranger had been none other than Prince John, who was Regent of Britain while his brother, Richard the Lionheart, was at the Crusades in Palestine. The woodman told his story to one of John's enemies who arranged an audience for him at Guildford Castle. The woodman came to the audience in disguise, told his story and asked the Prince what should happen now. The Prince, forgetting the incident in which he himself had been involved, declared the murderer must be punished. The woodman then revealed his true identity, produced the hat feather, and denounced the Prince. Legend does not tell us the outcome of the audience except to say that the woodman had his revenge. The traditional story says that the tragic deaths of the children confirmed the barons in their hatred of John and paved the way for their triumph over him at Runnymede in 1215 with the signing of the Magna Carta.

A short distance from the Watts Gallery in Compton (see above) is the Watts Mortuary Chapel – not, as is often assumed, a memorial to George Frederick Watts, but simply a cemetery chapel – the work of Mrs Watts and a team of local assistants who built it between 1895 and 1906. With its strong Celtic flavour, the decoration of this unique building is an unforgettable example of British art nouveau; the exterior has ornamental terracotta work and the interior is encrusted with richly coloured gesso reliefs of angels and other symbolic forms. The altarpiece is a version of *The All-Pervading* by Watts himself.

TOURIST INFORMATION BUREAU: The Undercroft, 72 High Street, Guildford, Surrey GU1 3HE. Tel (0483) 302221

OXFORD

County of Oxfordshire
By train, 70 minutes from London (Paddington)
By road, 57 miles (91.2 km) from London by M40

In spite of its recent industrialization, Oxford's beauty and dignity have managed to survive. Matthew Arnold, one of England's greatest poets, described Oxford as "that sweet city with her dreaming spires" and in spite of cynicism which suggested that "dreaming spires" should be changed to "screaming tyres" (perhaps a tribute to the motor car industry, Oxford's main employer), a walk in the back streets or a stroll along the banks of Christ Church Meadows, where the River Isis becomes the River Thames, convinces one that there is still tranquillity, though it is harder to find since the age of the internal combustion engine. Seen from Boar's Hill three miles (4.8 km) away, the sight of Oxford is still an evocative and unforgettable sight.

Oxford's history begins in Saxon times when it was an ox-drover's fording place on the Thames. Sacked by the Danes in 1009, "Oxnaford" was rebuilt and began to expand. Its reputation as a seat of learning dates from 1167 when English scholars, banned from the University of Paris, began to congregate here.

Oxford University is the second oldest in Europe, acknowledging only the Sorbonne as its senior. Organized teaching was being conducted at Oxford in the 12th century, and with the appointment of a chancellor in 1214 the collegiate system started, initially through the various religious orders. It was this initial clericism that informed the evolution of the colleges, and set the pattern of the monastery-like layout of chapel, dining hall and inner quadrangle, with scholar's rooms set round them like cloisters, which is still apparent today. There was a great deal of conflict between "town and gown" in the Middle Ages as charters from successive monarchs conveyed privileges upon the university which caused hardship to the city merchants. During the Civil War Oxford was important as both the Royalist headquarters and the seat of Charles I's parliament.

There is so much to see in Oxford that any survey, short of a whole book, will of necessity be perfunctory. What I have done is to describe a walking tour which takes in most of the colleges and, let's face it, the colleges are what Oxford is all about, although there are other places which should not be missed. I have confined myself to the centre of the town and attempted to give as characteristic an impression as possible of the variety of sights, atmospheres and architectural styles within the heart of the historic city.

WALK

Oxford Walk – Start at **Carfax**, the central cross road in Oxford. **Carfax Tower** is all that survives of the 14th-century Church of St Martin. The clock has gilded quarter-boys that strike the quarter-hours and the view from the top of the tower provides an eagle's-eye view of the colleges. It's open from March to October, daily except Sundays, Tel 726871. Walk down St Aldgate's past the Town Hall on the left. Second on the right is Pembroke Square where you will find **Pembroke College**. Pembroke was originally Broadgates Hall, one of the medieval halls used to house the first students. It was named after the third Earl of Pembroke by James I in 1624. The refectory of the old Broadgate is now the college library and

THE RADCLIFFE CAMERA, OXFORD

the college itself occupies the site of six of the medieval halls. Part of the old city wall flanks the southern side of the college and the 18th-century chapel is very pleasing. Famous graduates include Dr Samuel Johnson, the critic, poet and lexicographer and John Pym, the eminent parliamentarian.

Opposite Pembroke across St Aldgate's is **Christ Church**. Founded by Cardinal Wolsey in 1525 and established by Henry VIII, Christ Church is one of the largest and most famous of the Oxford colleges. The 12th-century **Chapel** serves as Oxford's cathedral (England's smallest) and the **Medieval Hall** with its oak roof and armorial bearing is most impressive. **Tom Tower** was designed by Christopher Wren and is one of the dominant features on Oxford's skyline. The tower's bell, known as Great Tom, weighs over six tons and chimes 101 times every night to mark the old curfew. Charles Dodgson, better known as Lewis Carroll, the author of *Alice in Wonderland,* taught mathematics here between 1855 and 1881. Famous graduates include Sir Robert Peel, founder of the police force, W H Auden and John Wesley. Christ Church is proud in being able to name 13 of Britain's prime ministers among its past students.

Cross Tom Quad into Peckwater Quad, leave the college through Canterbury Gate and enter Oriel Square. On the left is **Oriel College**. Oriel was founded in 1326 by Adam de Brome, King Edward II's almoner. The hall has a hammer-beam roof and a carved Jacobean screen. Famous men who have studied here include Cecil Rhodes, the statesman, and Sir Walter Raleigh. Opposite Oriel, on the other side of Merton Street, is **Corpus Christi College** which was founded in 1517 by Richard Foxe. Foxe was, successively, bishop of Exeter, Bath and Wells, Durham and Winchester. The college has retained a priceless collection of gold and silver plate which would have been even larger if part of the collection had not been given to Charles I during the Civil War (see Worcester). In the chapel the altarpiece is the famous painting *The Adoration of the Shepherds,* which has been ascribed to Peter Paul Rubens. John Keble, the great English churchman and the poet Robert Bridges studied here.

The next college along Merton Street is **Merton College**, which is generally acknowledged to be the oldest college in Oxford; it was founded in 1264 by Walter de Merton, Lord High Chancellor to Henry III. The quadrangle is Oxford's oldest and houses the oldest library in the country, which still contains some of the original furnishings and chained books. The chapel is the first and largest of Oxford's chapels. Max Beerbohm, the writer and caricaturist and T S Eliot studied here as did Lord Randolph Churchill, the father of Winston. Continue along cobbled Merton Street and take the first left turn (Logic Lane) which will bring you to **University College**. Merton, University and Balliol all claim to be Oxford's oldest college. However, it is believed William of Durham bequeathed money for the founding of University College in 1249, but that the college site was not acquired until 1332. Tradition (which is both strong and important in Oxford) ascribes the college's foundation to King Alfred the Great. The front quadrangle houses the Shelley Memorial although the poet was actually sent down from the college in 1811 for writing an atheist pamphlet. Clement Attlee, Britain's first post-Second-World War prime minister, also studied here.

Coming out of Logic Lane, turn right and walk down the High Street past the Examination Schools where the students agonize each summer, go past the Botanical Gardens (see below) and cross over the High Street to **Magdalen College** (pronounced *mawdlin*) which was founded in 1458. The Bell Tower dates from the 15th century and forms a focal point of the May Morning celebrations (see Ephemera). The chapel, hall and cloisters are all 15th century and there is a superb library containing priceless and rare examples of early prints. There are fine gardens and a Deer Park which should be visited. Cardinal Wolsey studied here as did the poet John Betjeman and author Oscar Wilde. Incidentally Magdalen has some of Oxford's finest gargoyles and grotesques and its well worth cricking your neck to find them.

Further up the High Street is **Queen's College**, which was founded in 1341 as a theological seminary. The chapel, circa 1714, and the library, dating from 1692, are both impressive. King Henry V studied at Queen's as did astronomer Edmund Halley and essayist Joseph Addison. Looking up High Street from Queen's you will see one of Oxford's most famous views, but to appreciate the sweep of the High Street today you should do it at five in the morning when it is relatively free of traffic. If you now turn into the winding Queen's Lane you will find **St Edmund's Hall** on your right. This is the sole survivor of the medieval halls. It was only admitted to all of the same rights and privileges as the other colleges of the University as recently as 1957. The quadrangle, with its painted sundial, is one of Oxford's most charming corners and the beautiful 17th-century chapel has some fine oak and cedar screens. Continuing along Queen's Lane, turn into New College Lane where you will, not surprisingly, find **New College** which was founded in 1379. The chapel here contains Epstein's *Lazarus* and also some beautiful 14th-century glass. The Founder's Crozier and El Greco's painting of St James are two of the college's greatest treasures. The college garden, flanked, like Pembroke, by the 14th-century city wall, is most attractive.

Continue along New College Lane. Just before Hertford Bridge you will see a plaque on the wall to the right marking the site of Edmund Halley's observatory. Coming out of New College Lane you will find yourself in Catte Street. Directly ahead of you is the **Sheldonian Theatre** which was built in 1669 by the young Christopher Wren. This building, capped by a green domed cupola, is used for degree ceremonies and concerts. On one side of the theatre is the porticoed **Clarendon Building** designed by Wren's pupil, Nicholas Hawksmoor and today housing the University Administration Offices. To the left is the **Bodleian Library**. This library is one of the three in England entitled to a free copy of any book published in Britain. Its collection now occupies additional space in the **Radcliffe Camera**, the new Bodleian, and even extends underground beneath Radcliffe Square. The Bodleian possesses an estimated two million books including thousands of manuscripts and charters. Turning left down Catte Street you will find **Hertford College** which was given a college charter in 1740 because Magdalen Hall was burnt down and was only founded as Hertford College in 1874. The doors of the main entrance were made in the 17th century for the purpose of a gateway into Catte Street. The bridge over New College Lane which links the two blocks of the college is a model of the Bridge of Sighs in Venice. John Donne, the great metaphysical poet, studied here, as did the novelist Evelyn Waugh. Continuing down Catte Street you come to **All Souls College**, founded in 1437 by Henry Chichele, the Archbishop of Canterbury. All Souls is the most eminent of Oxford's graduate colleges; a Fellowship here is one of the highest academic distinctions. The College is famous for its Gothic architecture and its 15th-century chapel has one of the most impressive interiors in Oxford. The hall to the east contains many excellent portraits. T E Lawrence (Lawrence of Arabia) and Christopher Wren were both Fellows here. Cross over Catte Street to **St Mary's Church**. Superb "barley twist" columns form the entrance to this restored medieval building. Inside, high arcades above the nave and lofty chancel windows form a grand setting for the University Sunday sermon. There is a wonderful view from the tower. The church enjoyed a long association with the University and was used for degree ceremonies, disputations and trials (including the heresy trial of Latimer, Cranmer and Ridley) before the Sheldonian Theatre was built for this purpose. Opposite St Mary's is the **Radcliffe Camera**, which now forms part of the Bodleian Library. The great domed and drum-shaped Radcliffe Camera glorifies the centre of the square. It was the first round library in England, completed in 1749 with money left by royal physician Dr John Radcliffe. On the other side of the square is **Brasenose College**, founded in 1509. The college takes its name from the brazen nose door knocker which now hangs above the high table in the hall. The original knocker was stolen in the 14th century and fixed to a house in Stamford Street. It was only returned to Brasenose in the Victorian era when the college purchased the entire house (then a school) to regain its lost possession. The gate tower of Brasenose is still one of the finest in Oxford, although the addition of another storey in 1605 rather spoilt its proportions. The novelist John Buchan studied here, as did Robert Rurton, author of *The Anatomy of Melancholy*. Return up Catte Street, then turn left down Broad Street and cross over the road to **Blackwell's Bookshop**, one of the largest and most renowned bookshops in the world (see below). Continue along Broad Street to **Trinity College** which was founded on the site of Durham College, one of Oxford's richest colleges until it was suppressed by Henry VIII during the dissolution of the monasteries. The 17th-century chapel has some beautiful wood carving and on the ceiling is Berchet's painting *The Ascension*. The north side of the garden quadrangle was designed by Christopher Wren and the college's gardens have a famous lime walk. Cardinal Newman and William Pitt can be listed among Trinity's most famous "sons." Continue along Broad Street to **Balliol College** which was founded in 1263. The college housed many leaders of the Renaissance including William Gray, the Bishop of Ely, whose magnificent collection of manuscripts is still kept in the college. Although many eminent men studied here, Balliol remained one of Oxford's poorest colleges until the 19th century. In the gateway between the two quadrangles are hung the doors which were scorched by the flames of the pyre of the Protestant martyrs in the 16th century. An iron cross is set into the road where the martyrs were burnt at the stake. At the top of Broad Street is St Giles, where you will find the **Martyrs' Memorial**, a Victorian Gothic monument likened to the spire of a sunken cathedral. It commemorates Bishops Ridley and Latimer, burned at the stake during the reign of Queen Mary in 1555 for their Protestant faith and Archbishop Cranmer who suffered the same fate in 1556. Cranmer recanted his "crime against the true faith" but when asked to read the recantation he retracted and cheerfully went to the stake, where he thrust his right hand into the flame saying, "This hath offended! Oh, this unworthy hand." The deaths of Ridley and Latimer were, if anything, even more poignant. As the flames curled around the two men, Latimer turned to Ridley and said, "Master Ridley, we shall this day light such a candle in England as shall never be put out."

To return to Balliol ... its list of famous students is very impressive; Prime Ministers Lord Asquith, Edward Heath and Harold Macmillan, novelist Graham Greene and poets Hilaire Belloc and Matthew Arnold. From Balliol cross over Broad Street to Turl Street and **Exeter College** which was founded by Walter de Stapleton, Bishop of Exeter in 1314. The college hall has an impressive collar-beam roof but the chapel and Exeter's collection of manuscripts were destroyed by fire in 1709. The new chapel, in the French Gothic style, was built in 1856. William Morris, English craftsman and poet, and J R R Tolkien, the author of *The Lord of the Rings,* studied at Exeter as did actor Richard Burton. Further along Turl Street is **Jesus College**, founded by Queen Elizabeth I in 1571. Jesus has always had strong connections with Wales and even today nearly a quarter of the college's students come from Welsh schools. The chapel is a fine example of late Gothic architecture and the hall houses some excellent portraits including several Van Dycks. Beau Nash, who found fame in Bath, and Harold Wilson, the Labour Prime Minister, were both students here. On the left is **Lincoln College** founded by the Bishop of Lincoln as a theological college in 1427. The fine chapel is best described as Jacobean Gothic and there is some excellent 17th-century glass and a beautiful panelled ceiling. John Wesley was a Fellow of Lincoln. It is interesting to note that the first institution founded for women in Oxford was **Lady Margaret Hall** on Northam Road, in 1878. Like the members of the other five women's colleges, St Anne's, St Hugh's, Somerville and St Hilda's, its students were permitted to sit for examinations but not to receive degrees until 1920. Women account for about one-seventh of the undergraduate population at Oxford. Benazir Bhutto, Indira Gandhi and Margaret Thatcher all studied at Oxford.

It is virtually impossible to include all the buildings worth seeing in one tour. As well as the buildings already mentioned, the following are also of interest: *Worcester College* at the junction of Walton Street and Beaumont Street is noted for its beautiful garden and lake, and also for its row of original monastic buildings. **Keble College**, at the Junction of Keble Road and Parks Road, forms a striking contrast to all the other colleges in Oxford. It was designed by William Butterfield and founded in 1870 to commemorate John Keble, the English churchman. The huge chapel contains some remarkable mosaics and Holman Hunt's famous painting, *The Light of the World,* can be seen in the side chapel. Keble's new block has been widely praised and is a good example of Oxford's modern architecture. **St John's College,** at the bottom of St Giles, was founded in 1555 but the front quadrangle was part of an earlier college founded in 1437 for Cistercian Monks. The south wing is attributed to Inigo Jones and there are fine bronze statues of Charles I and Queen Henrietta Maria. Finally, if you wish to capture the true quality of summer Oxford, hire a punt and rowing boat, available at Folly Bridge and Magdalen Bridge.

MUSEUMS AND GALLERIES

Ashmolean Museum of Art and Archaeology – Beaumont Street, Tel 512651. The southern front of the Ashmolean is one of the finest neo-Grecian buildings in Britain. It is the private museum of the University of Oxford, but has been open to the public since 1683. Antiquities include objects from Greece, Rome, Crete and Cyprus as well as the Arundel classic marbles and the Alfred Jewel. Paintings are by Uccello and Tiepolo as well as Poussin, Pissarro and the French impressionists. Good 18th- and 19th-century English collection, and also the pre-Raphaelites. Drawings include works by Raphael, Michelangelo and Rembrandt and the Heberden Coin Collection is second only to that of the British Museum. Excellent department of Eastern art. Open Tues–Sat 10–4pm; Sun 2–4pm. Open Bank Holiday Mons 2–5pm.

The **Bate Collection of Historical Musical Instruments** – Faculty of Music, St Aldgates, Tel 247069. The most comprehensive collection in England of European woodwind, brass and percussion instruments and the finest Javanese gamelan in Britain. Fine collection of bows and bow making. Open Mon–Fri 2–5pm. Closed during some University vacations so check locally.

British Telecom Museum – 35 Speedwell Street, Tel 246601. A collection of exhibits illustrating the history and evolution of telephone and telegraph equipment. The 150 telephones displayed range from Alexander Graham Bell's 1875 "Gallows" telephone to modern instruments. Open by appointment only Mon–Fri 10–12 and 2–4pm.

Christ Church Picture Gallery – Christ Church, St Aldgates, Tel 242102. Collection of paintings and drawings, 14th-18th century. Very strong Italian influence but good examples of work from northern Europe including Van Dyck and Franz Hals. Open Easter–Sept Mon–Sat 10:30–1 and 2–5pm; Sun 2–5:30pm. Oct–Easter – closes one hour earlier in afternoon.

The **Frank Cooper Collection** – Frank Cooper Ltd, 84 High Street, Tel 245125. Along with many people, I think that Frank Cooper's Extra Thick Cut Marmalade is the best in the world. The Frank Cooper shop and memorabilia collection is now on the premises where the marmalade was once sold. The Angel Inn, claimed to be the first coffee house in England, had previously occupied the site. The museum tells the story of how Sarah Cooper's marmalade, sold over the counter in her husband's shop, achieved its worldwide popularity. There is even a tin of marmalade that was taken on Scott's Antarctic expedition in 1910.

Museum of the History of Science – The Old Ashmolean Building, Broad Street, Tel 243997. The museum building is one of the finest examples of 17th-century architecture in Oxford – originally the home of the Ashmolean Museum. There is an unrivalled collection of early astronomical, surveying, navigational and mathematical instruments and the largest collection of astrolabes in the world. Open Mon–Fri 10:30–1 and 2–4pm.

Museum of Modern Art – 30 Pembroke Street, Tel 722733. The museum was founded in 1966 in a converted brewery. Although the original intention was to build up a permanent collection of 20th century art, the focus quickly changed to exhibitions, usually including three or four artists, up to six times a year. All art is 20th century and is strongly international. Open Tues–Sat 10–5; Sun 2–5pm.

Museum of Oxford – St Aldgate's, Tel 815559. The museum is housed on two floors of Oxford's 1893 Town Hall. It tells the story of Oxford's growth from the earliest times to the present day. There are reconstructed furnished rooms including an Elizabethan Inn parlor and a 19th-century working-class kitchen as well as a corner of Capes' Cash Drapery. Jean de Wyck's painting, *The Siege of Oxford,* should be seen, as should the town seal – the oldest in the country. Open Tues–Sat 10–5pm.

Oxford Cathedral Treasury – Christ Church, Tel 724620. The 13th-century Cathedral Chapter House houses displays of college and cathedral plate and an interesting loan exhibition of church plate from parishes in the Diocese of Oxford. Open Easter–Sept daily 9–6pm. Oct–Easter daily 9–4:30pm.

The **Oxford City Council Plate Room** – at the Town Hall, St Aldgate's, Tel 249811. A collection of City plate and other civic possessions dating back to the 14th century. Can be visited by appointment.

Oxford University Museum – Parks Road, Tel 57529. The museum building is in the 19th-century Gothic revival style with carved decorations and ornamental ironwork. It houses the university's collection of zoology, entomology, geology and mineralogy. The collection is second only in importance to the Natural History Museum in London. Open Mon–Sat 12–5.

Pitt-Rivers Museum – South Parks Road, Tel 512541. The museum, which forms part of a university teaching department, possesses one of the six most important ethnographic collections in the world, a major collection of prehistoric archaeology and a fine British and European folk life section. The musical instrument collection is one of the three largest in existence. Open Mon–Sat 2–4pm.

Rotunda Museum of Antique Doll's Houses – Grove House, 44 Iffley Turn. The museum, dating from 1962, was built to harmonize with the adjoining 1780 house which was the home of the mother and sisters of Cardinal Newman. The museum is claimed to be the only one in the world showing solely doll's houses and their contemporary furniture. Open May–mid Sept Sun 2–5pm.

Regimental Museum of the Oxfordshire and Buckingham Light Infantry – Territorial Army Centre, Slade Park, Headington, Tel 778479. The museum contains exhibits of the militaria of the County Regiment, now incorporated in the Royal Green Jackets. Uniforms, medals, badges, pictures and silver. Open Mon–Fri 10–12 and 2:30–4pm.

Bodleian Library – Catte Street, Tel 277000. There is a permanent exhibition of the Treasures of the Bodleian in the Schola Naturalis Philosophiae in the Old Library Quadrangle. There are guided visits to the Divinity School, Duke Humphrey's Library and the Convocation House. Mon–Fri at 10:30, 11:30, 2 and 3pm. Sat 10:30 and 11:30.

Oxford Bus Museum Trust – 23 High Street, Tel 874080. The museum houses over 40 vehicles from the Oxford horse trams to the buses of the 1960s, some roadworthy, others in the course of restoration.

Oxford Story – 6 Broad Street, Tel 728822. The Oxford Story attempts to explain the University, past and present. The exhibition has been created in a disused warehouse. Part of the city wall, dating back to the 13th century and previously hidden from public view, stands in a small courtyard on the site. Exhibits are brought to life by audio-visual means, with subtle sound and lighting effects, and even authentic smells. The commentary, spoken by Alec Guinness, is intelligent and literate and I, who usually steer well clear of things like this, enjoyed the Oxford Story immensely. Open daily 9:30–5pm.

THEATRE

Apollo Theatre – George Street, Tel 244544, used to be called the New Theatre until it was completely refurbished and renovated a few years ago. It is Oxford's major touring house hosting such companies as the Royal Shakespeare Theatre Company, the Welsh National Opera Company, Glyndebourne Touring Opera and Ballet Rambert.

Pegasus Theatre – Magdalen Road off Iffley Road, Tel 722851. Oxford's "alternative" theatre and arts centre hosts a remarkable range of music, theatre, dance, jazz, poetry and art. A recent month's programme included two Afro-American poets, a jazz dance show of 1930s Harlem music and a performance by Temba Theatre.

Burton Taylor Theatre – Gloucester Street, Tel 793797. The Burton Taylor hosts the majority of university drama which covers a wide range of authors, styles and methods of presentation. In a single month presentations ranged from Euripides' *The Bacchae* to Pinter's *The Birthday Party* and plays by Jean-Paul Sartre and Peter Handke.

Two new ventures which, by the time you read this, will have come to fruition are the **Old Fire Station**, Gloucester Green, Tel 56400, which has jazz, an assortment of popular music and promises theatre when the premises are completely renovated and the **Oxford Playhouse**, Tel 247134, which was one of the most respected companies in the country and was known as the University Theatre. The link to the university has now been severed and the Playhouse is undergoing extensive renovations prior to opening as a new professional regional theatre. There are plans for a resident company, pre-West End tours, concerts, dance and opera, together with a range of bars, restaurants and bookshops open all day. The closure of the Playhouse left a gap not only in the life of Oxford but in the cultural life of the nation as a whole. The remedy is eagerly awaited. It is also hoped that the Playhouse will offer a home to the **Oxford Stage Company**, Tel 723238, one of England's premier touring companies which, until now, has not had a permanent base in Oxford. The company tours middle-scale touring venues for 32 weeks with four shows a year. Recent productions have included an adaptation of Sterne's *Tristram Shandy*, Moliere's *The Miser* and Percy Mtwa's *Woza Albert*. Recently the company has recreated the Elizabethan Rose Theatre in Oxford's Newman Room and presented a summer season of a Shakespeare play and a modern musical.

MUSIC

As you would expect, there is an extensive programme of music in Oxford. In fact, between September and April there is at least one major concert a week and often two or three. The excellent booklet, *Music at Oxford,* lists all concerts and it's obtainable at the Oxford Information Centre, St Aldgate's, Tel 726871. Generally, the large orchestras (the Royal Philharmonic and the Bournemouth Symphony, for example) play in the **Apollo Theatre**. Smaller orchestras, and many excellent ones such as the Orchestra of the Age of Enlightenment, the Bournemouth Sinfonietta, the English Concert and the Hanover Band visit Oxford, play in the **Sheldonian Theatre**. Chamber ensembles and individual concerts such as the Bartok Quartet, the Amaryllis Consort, the Clerkes of Oxenford, Peter Harford and Fou T'song, for example, also play in the Sheldonian. Other venues include **Christ Church Cathedral**, the **Town Hall** and Holywell. Oxford has both a community and a university orchestra which also play at the Sheldonian, the main venue for music in Oxford. Music at Oxford booking information – Tel 864056.

CINEMA

Commercial cinema can be found at the **Cannon Cinemas** in George Street, Tel 244607 (3 screens) and Magdalen Street, Tel 243067. More interesting are the **Phoenix 1 and 2** at Walton Street, Tel 54909. They have an excellent programme which recently included in one month films by Louis Malle, Woody Allen, Sergei Eisenstein, Alan Parker and John Waters. Recommended. Also of interest is the **Penultimate Picture Palace** on Jeune Street, Tel 723837, which is another art house and similarly recommended. The **Maison Française** on Northam Road shows films in French which are free. Check the *This Month in Oxford* or *What's on in Oxford* booklets for details.

BOOKSTORES

It is not surprising that Oxford is rich in bookshops; indeed, it would be most surprising if it were otherwise. The best in the city and one of the most famous booksellers in the country is **Blackwell's** at 48-51 Broad Street, Tel 792792. Just to enter Blackwell's is an experience in itself. They also have specialist shops dealing with art and posters (27 Broad Street), children's books (8 Broad Street), maps and travel (53 Broad Street), medical (John Radcliffe Hospital), modern art (30 Pembroke Street), music (38 Holywell Street) and paperbacks (23-25 Broad Street). There's a good **Dillon's** at William Baker House in Broad Street and the **Oxford University Press** has an excellent shop at 116 High Street, Tel 242913. For specialist tastes the **Catbap Bookshop** at 15 Cowley Road, Tel 793553, has everything you ever wanted to know about cars, trains, boats and planes. Religious books can be found at the **Christian Book Centre**, 57C St Clement's, Tel 247567, and **St Aldgate's Church** Bookshop at 94 St Aldgate's, Tel 722970, while the **Inner Bookshop**, 34 Cowley Road, has books dealing with alternatives for the mind, body, spirit and planet, Tel 245301. Comics, which are of growing interest in Britain, can be found at **Comic Showcase**, 19/20 St Clement's Street, Tel 723680 and at the **Fantastic Store Comic Shop** in the Westgate Centre, Tel 791302. **Her Majesty's Stationery Office** (HMSO) has a shop at 2 St Elsbes, Tel 250166.

ANTIQUARIAN AND SECONDHAND BOOKS

The High Street area is a good place to start. At No 41 is **Magna Gallery**, Tel 245805, with a good general collection while next door at No 43, **Niner and Hill Rare Books** are especially strong on art, travel, literature and history. Further down the road at 104 High Street you will find **Sanders of Oxford**, Tel 242590, which has a very special collection of rare books as well as some fine maps and prints. Running off the High Street, just below Carfax, is Turl Street where you can find Brasenose and Lincoln Colleges. At No 3 is **Classics Bookshop**, Tel 726466, and at No 15 is **Titles**, both of which are worth a visit. Carry on down Turl Street to Broad Street and at No 11 you will find **Thornton's**, Tel 242939; they have been university booksellers and bookbuyers since 1835. Besides a good general collection of new books, they have a good secondhand department and some excellent rare books and first editions on the third floor. Well worth a visit. If you are near the Covered Market near the centre of town you'll find the **Little Bookshop** at Lane 2, Tel 59176. They have a general collection of secondhand books. Also in the centre of town at 4 St Michael's Street (off Cornmarket Street) is **Arcadia Booksellers**, Tel 241757. Just a little way out of the centre by the station at 36 Park End Street you will find **Bookshop at the Plain** at No 11, Tel 790285 and **Artemis Books** at No 76, Tel 726909. Finally, if your travels take you to Headington (towards the M40) call in at **Bruce Ferrini**, 88 Old High Street, Tel 741924.

ART GALLERIES

In the centre of town is **Oxford Gallery** at 23 High Street, Tel 242731, which specializes in the decorative arts with ceramics, wood, textiles, jewellery and some fine limited-edition prints, and **Sanders of Oxford**, 104 High Street, Tel 242590, 18th-19th-century prints. At 50 High Street, Tel 242167, is the **Gallery of Chinese Art** which has some beautiful examples of workmanship. Also in the town centre at Gloucester

Green is the **Poster Shop**, Tel 793506, which has a colourful and varied collection. There are a couple of places out on the Walton Road which are worth a mention: one is **Art et Cetera** at 127 Walton Road, Tel 513936, and off the Walton Road, just past Worcester and Ruskin Colleges you will find the **Oxford Print Shop** at 46C Richmond Road, Tel 56099. It's well worth the effort to visit the **CCA Galleries** at 276 Banbury Road at Summertown. Banbury Road is an extension of St Giles Street (fork right after St John's College). CCA publishes contemporary etchings, lithographs and silkscreens. They also specialize in watercolours of Oxford. Well worth a visit.

ANTIQUE DEALERS

One might expect there to be more antique shops in Oxford than there are. The perceived paucity is explained by the surrounding area which is rich in villages and small towns offering antiques in an amazing variety of location and style. Close to Oxford I would recommend **Dorchester-on-Thames** (7 miles (11.2 km) to the south on the A423) or **Abingdon** (6 miles (9.6 km) south on the A34). Rich pickings can also be found in **Woodstock** (4 miles (6.4 km) north on the A34) which has the added advantage of being the home of Blenheim Palace, built for the first Duke of Marlborough between 1705 and 1722. The Palace was the birthplace of Sir Winston Churchill. Finally, **Witney** (6 miles (9.6 km) west on the A40) has many antiques and is also the home of the famous Witney blankets.

In Oxford itself, the major focus for antique activity is Park End Street which is essentially the A420 to Swindon. At No 27 is the **Oxford Antiques Centre**, Tel 251075, which has a large stock of general antiques. Just down the road at No 40 is the **Oxford Antique Trading Company**, Tel 793927. If you only have time to visit one location then you'd be wise to make it this one, as there are 60 businesses housed under one roof. They probably have the largest and most diverse stock of antiques in the south of England. Next door at No 39 is **Phillips**, one of the world's leading auction houses. They hold specialist and general auctions throughout the year and if you can coordinate an auction with your visit I would recommend it. Tel 723524. At No 52 is the **Pine Shop**, Tel 791327, with a good stock of original and reproduction pine furniture. Going back into the city, turn left on Worcester Street which becomes Walton Street. Off Walton Street, just before the Oxford University Press, you will find Nelson Street to your left. At the Old Pepot on Nelson Street are **Oxford Architectural Antiques**, Tel 53310, specializing in Victorian fixtures and fittings, garden ornaments, doors, leaded glass and ironwork. A fascinating place, whether you are buying or just looking.

If you come back onto Walton Street you will find **118 Walton Street**, situated, not surprisingly, at 118 Walton Street, Tel 54649; they have a general collection of antiques. Back in the town centre make your way to the High Street. At No 34 you will find **Reginald Davis**, Tel 248347, who has some really beautiful antique silver and jewellery, while next door at No 36 is **Laurie Leigh Antiques**, with a good general collection. Finally, on the east side of Oxford on the A420 which leads out to the main London Road you will find **Cherwell Antiques** at No 58 St Clement's, Tel 721924. It's just over the Magdalen Bridge.

RESTAURANTS

Unlike many provincial towns in the UK where one has to scrape around to find really excellent cuisine, you can eat very well in Oxford at a number of locations. I think the best, though not my favourite eatery, is **Gees** at 61 Banbury Road, Tel 53540. It has a beautiful locale, is always full and the service is cheery and intelligent. I enjoyed an excellent carrot soup, an even better chicken grilled with rosemary and lemon and a good crème brulée, which is always an indication of whether a restaurant is good or not. Open all week 12–2 and 6–11pm. No Sunday dinner.

My favourite eatery is **Munchy Munchy**, which is wonderfully frenetic, and in which the food is best described as "idiosyncratic Malaysian Peninsular." This is not the place for a romantic candlelit dinner as it's self-service and you're not expected to hang around – not that you would want to – but the food is top-notch. Wonderful spices such as cardamom, fenugreek, paprika and chopped pine kernels enliven all meals and you order from a blackboard setting out the daily specials. Take your own wine – the corkage fee is minimal. Munchy Munchy is at 6 Park End Street, Tel 245710, and is open Tues–Sat 12–2:10 and 5:30–9:40pm.

Just around the corner from Gees is **15 North Parade** situated at 15 North Parade, Tel 513773. The name of the restaurant may not seem inspired but it is incongruous when one realizes that North Parade is in fact south of South Parade. The food here is light and inventive with just a touch of nouvelle cuisine. There is always a vegetarian choice. Open 12–2 and 7–10pm all week except Sunday dinner.

If you want to rub shoulders with real Oxford undergrads you should visit **Cherwell Boathouse** at Bardwell Road, Tel 52746. There's a weekly menu at an affordable price and although the comfort level is not of the highest, the location by the river is worth putting up with anything. There's a good imaginative wine list and I'm delighted to say that smoking is discouraged. Open all week 12–2:15 and 6–8:30pm. No Sunday dinner Oct–March.

Al-Shami at 25 Walton Crescent, Tel 310066, is Lebanese and good Lebanese at that. If you haven't eaten Lebanese food before you might be put off by the lamb's brains cooked with sharp spices so go for the kebbeh, a stuffed groundmeat dish beloved of all Eastern Mediterranean countries. I tried the shawarma last time. It's lamb spiced with cumin and it was wonderful. Good medames and tabouleh too. Open all week noon–midnight.

Finally, for that special romantic dinner, try **Bath Place Hotel** at 4-5 Bath Place, Holywell Street, Tel 791812. Its setting is a small court and the restaurant (classic French) is essentially a collection of 17th-century cottages with rooms to stay in above the ground floor dining area. Excellent fish from Cornwall and the prices are not impossible. Open Tues–Sat 12–2:15 and 7–9:45.

PUBS

The Bear – Alfred Street, Tel 244680. In its coaching heyday the Bear used to stretch the whole way down Alfred Street. Parts of the pub date back 700 years and even the handpumps are 100 years old. In the panelled rooms you can see a collection of 7000 or so club ties and they're still adding to them. Good bar food including excellent steak and kidney pie and a plethora of students, mainly from Oriel and Christ Church. The menu welcomes guests in five languages.

Turf Tavern – Bath Place, Holywell Street, Tel 243235. Buried in its hidden courtyard, which it shares with the Bath Place Hotel (see restaurants above), the Turf, with its medieval building is still much as Thomas Hardy described it when Jude the Obscure discovered that Arabella, the barmaid, was the wife who left him years before. Dark beams, low ceilings and flagstoned floors. Good bar food, vegetarian too. Try the beef-and-beer pie.

King's Arms – Holywell Street, Tel 242369. Close by the Turf Tavern is what I think the most "studenty" of all Oxford pubs. Very full and lively in term time. A big warehouse of a room with a separate no-smoking room. Decent bar food and even a dictionary thoughtfully provided for crossword puzzle buffs.

Rose and Crown – North Parade, Tel 510551. Small, unspoilt traditional pub with authentic Oxford feel. Try the daily specials from the bar. Landlord is a real character.

The Crypt – Off Cornmarket Street in alley opposite Boots the Chemist, Tel 251000. More of a large underground restaurant with a wine bar than a pub, but good atmosphere, good service and good food, especially the pies.

ARTISTIC ASSOCIATIONS

Many of the hundreds of famous people connected with Oxford have been mentioned under the individual colleges but the Crown Inn in Cornmarket Street (now simply No 3) has a "painted room" on the second floor, so called because some 16th-century paintings were restored on the walls in 1927. It is said that Shakespeare slept here on his way each year to and from Stratford-upon-Avon.

One person who did not succumb to the charms of Oxford was William Cobbett who, in his *Rural Rides* (1830) said, "Upon beholding the masses of buildings at Oxford, devoted to what they call 'learning,' I could not help reflecting on the drones that they contain and the wasps they send forth."

W B Yeats lived with his wife and child on the corner of Broad Street, opposite Balliol College, in a tall narrow house (now gone). Many literary friends visited him there, but in April 1921 he moved to nearby Shillingford to save money by letting the house.

John Masefield, Poet Laureate 1930–1967, lived at Boar's Hill in the 1920s and his house is now called Masefield House. C S Lewis, author of *The Chronicles of Narnia* and *The Screwtape Letters,* used to drink in the back bar of the Eagle and Child in St Giles' with J R R Tolkien, author of *The Lord of the Rings.* Dylan Thomas and the poet Louis MacNeice used to favour the Port Mahon in St Clements'.

John Everett Millais, one of the founder members of the Pre-Raphaelite movement, had relatives in Oxford and was a regular visitor here as early as 1846, when he was 17. Around that date he became friendly with local art dealer, James Wyatt, who took an interest in his work and introduced him to patrons in the area such as Thomas Cobbe, superintendent of the Clarendon Press. Cobbe became a great patron of the Pre-Raphaelites and the Combe Bequest, 21 paintings and drawings by artists such as Millais himself, Rossetti, Collinson, Stephens and Holman Hunt, can be seen at the Ashmolean Museum. The first painting Thomas Cobbe purchased for his collection was Holman Hunt's *A Converted British Family Sheltering a Christian Priest from the Persecution of the Druids,* but the most celebrated was Hunt's *The Light of the World,* which is not in the Ashmolean but inside a chapel at Keble College. This and subsequent generosity towards the group earned him the nicknames "the Early Christian" and "the Patriarch."

The Pre-Raphaelite movement had a clear tie of sympathy with the Oxford Movement which was begun in 1833 by Anglican clergy at the University. The Movement sought to revitalize the Church of England by reviving certain Roman Catholic doctrines and rituals such as chanting prayers, wearing vestments and using elaborate rituals within the service. The revival of these ceremonial customs caused great controversy. J H Newman (later Cardinal Newman) published a series of pamphlets in the 1830s which suggested that Anglicanism was a kind of middle way between evangelism and Catholicism, but a storm of controversy brought the series to an end and Newman became a Roman Catholic. Both movements espoused a nostalgia for medieval Christianity and this interest can be seen in the work of the "second generation" Pre-Raphaelites, William Morris and Edward Burne-Jones. Morris (who was also interested in furniture design, stained glass, tapestries, carpets, wallpaper, textiles and book illustration) and Burne-Jones (who was interested in many of the same things) were both profoundly influenced by Dante Gabriel Rossetti. Rossetti, Morris and Burne-Jones decorated the Debating Hall of the Oxford Union (now the library) in 1857 but the murals were painted in an amateurish technique and in spite of attempts to restore them, are today virtually invisible.

John Ruskin, the critic and champion of Pre-Raphaelitism, was a Christchurch undergraduate in the late 1830s and in 1870 became the first Slade Professor of Fine Art in the University, a post he held for 15 years. In the 1850s, Ruskin had been actively involved with the building of the University Museum and soon after his appointment as Slade Professor of Fine Art he established his drawing school in the Ashmolean, endowing it with a large number of drawings, prints and photographs from his own collection. Perhaps Ruskin's most famous act as Professor was to set a group of undergraduates, including Oscar Wilde, to repair a stretch of road between Oxford and Ferry Hinksey so that they might feel "the pleasure of useful muscular work."

EPHEMERA

Many traditions exist in Oxford, as indeed they do across the whole of the British Isles. Many towns celebrate May Day but Oxford's festivities are among the most famous. At six in the morning on May first, Magdalen College choir sings a Latin hymn from the top of Magdalen Tower to the crowd gathered below. Morris dancers lead the crowd to Radcliffe Square where they give a display of dancing, which progresses from the Square to Broad Street and then to St Giles. A programme of music and dancing usually continues all day.

Eights Week, held at the end of May, forms the climax of the college's rowing season. The teams are divided into leagues which race along the Isis by Folly Bridge throughout the week, the object being to catch up with and bump the boat in front and so take their place in the next race. The leading boat in the first league becomes Head of the River. Established in medieval times, St Giles Fair is held on the first Monday and Tuesday after the first Sunday after the first full week in September. It is one of the largest travelling fairs in the country and is one of Oxford's most colourful events. The whole of St Giles is closed to traffic and for two days Oxford is a pretty wild place. Finally, the June Fair is held on a Saturday in early June in Oxpens. There is a large market and also exhibitions and displays of music and dancing.

The stage door of the Oxford Playhouse opens on an alleyway, on the opposite side of which there is a pub. I played a Christmas season there in *The Three Musketeers* some years ago and I can vouch for the suitability of the arrangement. In 1972, during a performance of *West Side Story,* as Maria and her friends were trying on dresses and singing *I Feel Pretty,* they were joined by a dancing First World War veteran who, staggering out of the pub, had been drawn to the theatre by the sound of music and the prospect of a good old "knees up." It proved impossible to get him off the stage and later in the show he enthusiastically joined in the "rumble" scene where he inflicted considerable damage on both Sharks and Jets.

Earlier, in 1951, Ronnie Barker (of "The Two Ronnies" fame) appeared at the Playhouse in Chekhov's *The Seagull.* The comments of the Oxford *Times'* theatre critic are probably not included in Mr Barker's theatrical scrapbook: "The most monumental bit of miscasting this week is Ronnie Barker as Yepidohov. Never has anyone been so much at sea since Colombus. He cried when he should have laughed, clowned when he should have been serious and generally had everything back to front including his guitar in the second act and his lady friend's favours in the third."

In 1966 Elizabeth Taylor played a walk-on part at the Playhouse – an event so unlikely it had the critics turning up in droves. The part was Helen of Troy in Christopher Marlowe's *Dr Faustus.* Helen appears as a brief vision to Faustus and has no lines. Faustus was being played by Richard Burton, Ms Taylor's husband at the time. The *Times* attempted to set the whole thing in perspective by commenting, "Those who visit the production to see Ms Taylor as a speechless apparition of Helen of Troy will not be out of the theatre before 10:45."

TOURIST INFORMATION BUREAU: St Aldgate's, Oxford, Oxfordshire OX1 1DY. Tel: (0865) 726871

PORTSMOUTH

County of Hampshire
70 miles (112 km) from London by M3 and M27
Train from London (Waterloo) 1 hour 30 minutes

Portsmouth has been important in the history of the British Navy since the earliest times. Richard I constructed the first dock here in 1194 and in 1495 the first dry dock in the world was built. There was further naval development in the 17th century and from then on Portsmouth went from strength to strength until today the dockyards comprise 300 acres (121 ha), very different from the eight acres (3.2 ha) they covered in the time of Henry VIII. Portsmouth has associations with many of the great men in naval history. The Navy's own museum is here, as are the historic ships HMS *Warrior,* HMS *Victory* (Nelson's flagship at Trafalgar) and the *Mary Rose,* the best preserved example of a Tudor flagship in the world. The Duke of Buckingham was Lord High Admiral to Charles I in the 1620s. He was an adventurer and the lover of the Queen of France, incidents which are recalled in *The Three Musketeers.* He was assassinated in Portsmouth in 1628 by a discontented subaltern, John

Felton, and the house in High Street where he died can still be seen. Admiral Byng, who was court-martialled for neglect of duty in 1756, was brought to Portsmouth for execution and shot on board the HMS *Manarque* in 1757.

Although not a naval figure, Charles Dickens was born here in 1812 and his modest house in Commercial Road, full of mementos of his life, is open to the public. Although not such a familiar name, the philanthropist Jonas Hanway, an unwearying friend to chimney sweeps and waifs, was born here in 1712. He was also the inventor of the umbrella.

WALK

The Hard, close to the harbour, is a good place to explore. There is the splendid Ship Anson Pub and HMS *Warrior*, while in the dockyard the 18th-century stores, the Semaphore Tower, the museum, HMS *Victory*, the Mary Rose Ship Hall, the Double Ropehouse and the Porter's House by the Victory Gate (the oldest building in the dockyard, circa 1708) and the Navigation School are all worth visiting. In the town itself you should see Broad Street, with the Square Tower that bears a gilded bust of Charles I and a sculpture in the shape of a chain link commemorating the sailing of the first fleet of convict ships to Australia in 1787; and the Sea Wall, with the Round Tower built to defend the harbour entrance in 1415.

The **Portsmouth Walk** is in two parts: the first explores the dockyard and historic ships; the second looks at the historic harbour and town. **Walk One** starts from the multi-storey car park off The Hard. Turn right into The Hard, opposite Portsmouth Harbour Station and the bus depot. Walk past **HMS Warrior** and enter **Portsmouth Historic Dockyard** through Victory Gate. Continue along Main Road to the **Royal Naval Museum**. After your visit cross the parade ground and bridge to **HMS Victory**. Close by is the **Mary Rose Exhibition**. Leave the dockyard by the Victory Gate and return along The Hard to the car park.

Walk Two begins at the car park in Grand Parade. Turn left into Broad Street. On your left is the **Square Tower** (see Introduction). Go through the arch by the tower and up to the top of the **Sea Wall**. Walk along the wall to the **Round Tower** looking out over Spithead. Come back down the Round Tower steps and back onto Broad Street. Turn left into West Street and continue ahead to the **Bath Square** and **The Point**. Return back along Broad Street and at the Square Tower turn left into High Street and the **Cathedral**. After the cathedral turn left into Lombard Street and right into St Thomas Street which has fine Georgian houses and cottages. At the top of St Thomas Street, turn right and right again into High Street. Note the **Portsmouth Grammar School** and **Buckingham House**. Turn left into Pembroke Road and right into Penny Street for the **Garrison Church** (see Ephemera). Climb the steps to the **Long Curtain**, a moated fortification built in Charles II's time. Walk along the Long Curtain and down the steps to the Grand Parade. On the left you can see the foundations of the main guardhouse of the **Portsmouth Garrison** built during the reign of George I, circa 1720, marked out in brick. Return to the car park.

H.M.S. WARRIOR 1860, PORTSMOUTH

MUSEUMS, GALLERIES AND PUBLIC BUILDINGS

City Museum and Art Gallery – Museum Road, Tel 827261. The museum is in a Victorian barrack block built in the style of a French chateau. Besides paintings and prints of Portsmouth, there are collections of English furniture, pottery, clocks, and glass, and displays of domestic equipment. Open daily 10:30–5:30pm.

Royal Naval Museum – HM Naval Base, Tel 733060. Some of the displays are housed in three Georgian storehouses, which form part of the original 18th-century Royal Dockyard. The displays illustrate the history of the Royal Navy from Tudor times to the Falklands campaign, with special emphasis on the social development of the Navy and on the Nelson and Victorian periods. There are personal items relating to Lord Nelson and his officers and men, ships' figureheads, ship models and fine paintings. Open daily 10:30–5pm.

HMS Victory – HM Naval Base, Tel 826682. Nelson's flagship was built in Chatham in 1759 and served at the Battle of Trafalgar. A plaque on the quarterdeck marks the place where Nelson fell (see Ephemera). The ship is still a commissioned flagship and the guides are serving officers of the Royal Navy and Marines. Open all year Mon–Sat all day and Sun afternoon.

HMS Warrior – HM Naval Base, Tel 291379. The world's first iron-clad warship, pioneer of a breed that made all other other fighting vessels obsolete, was launched in 1860 as a deterrent to the French. Napoleon III kept his navy in port because of HMS *Warrior* and she never fired a shot in anger. Six hundred men served on the ship, which has been superbly restored. Open daily all year.

Mary Rose Ship Hall and Exhibition – HM Naval Base, Tel 750521. The Ship Hall is housed in an old dry dock, itself a historic monument, while the Exhibition is in an early 19th-century timber building, which was originally a malthouse. In the Ship Hall is displayed what remains of the Tudor *Mary Rose* which sank in Portsmouth Harbour in 1545. The Exhibition Hall shows more than a thousand of the 14,000 objects recovered by divers from the wreck, which was raised in 1982. These include longbows, personal possessions and clothing of the crew, cooking and eating utensils and ship's fittings (see Ephemera). Open daily 10:30–5pm.

Fort Widley – Portsdown Hill Road, Tel 827261. Fort Widley was built on the orders of Lord Palmerston in 1861–65, designed to defend Portsmouth from the north. Now a museum, it contains a labyrinth of underground passages, magazines and gun emplacements. Open April–Sept Sat, Sun, Bank Hols 1:30–5:30pm.

Charles Dickens Birthplace Museum – 393 old Commercial Road, Tel 827261. The Dickens House was restored in 1970 and furnished to illustrate the kind of home John and Elizabeth Dickens would have created for themselves. Dickens memorabilia include a set of his waistcoat buttons, a signed cheque, a lock of hair and the couch on which he died in 1870.

Cathedral Church of St Thomas of Canterbury – High Street, Tel 823300. The east end of the church dates from the 12th century. The tower and the choir were rebuilt in the late 17th century and a new nave in the form of an arena was begun in 1935. The pulpit is also late 17th century and there is a superb golden baroque weather vane circa 1710. The vane is now kept indoors and legend says that no one who touches it will ever drown. This parish church was raised to cathedral status in 1927.

Garrison Church – Grand Parade, Tel 823973. The gaunt, roofless remains of the Domus Dei, or Royal Garrison Church, are the result of wartime bombing in the Second World War – the final blow to a church with a rich and varied history. It was founded in 1212 by the Bishop of Winchester as a hospice for travellers, pilgrims, the sick and elderly, and was dedicated to St John the Baptist and St Nicholas, the patron saint of sailors. The Domus Dei survived the dissolution of the monasteries in 1536 and became an armoury and residence of the military governors of Portsmouth. Later it became Royal Garrison Church, scene in 1622 of the marriage of Charles II and Catharine of Braganza (see Ephemera). Open daily April–Sept.

D Day Museum – Clarence Esplanade, Tel 827261. The only museum in Britain devoted to the Normandy landings. Its centrepiece is the magnificent Overlord Embroidery which tells the story of the invasion. Open every day 10:30–5:30pm.

The Royal Navy Submarine Museum – Gosport, Tel 529217. Guided tour of submarines new and old. Many fascinating artefacts. Open 10–4:30pm. (3:30pm in winter).

Royal Marines Museum – Eastney Barracks, Southsea, Tel 819385. Three hundred years of Royal Marine history. Open daily 10–5:30pm (4:30pm in winter).

THEATRE

King's Theatre – Southsea, Tel 828282. A restored 19th-century theatre offering a popular blend of mostly mainstream comedy and musicals. There are also variety shows, opera and a Christmas pantomime. **Portsmouth Arts Centre** – Reginald Road, Eastney, Tel 732236, is a good venue for small-scale and experimental touring companies.

In the city centre, the **New Theatre Royal** is undergoing extensive restoration. As I write the beautifully restored circle bar is serving coffee and lunch and by the time you read this, the theatre itself should be in full operation. Call 826722 for information and a progress report.

The **South Parade Pier**, Tel 732283, has the kind of entertainment you would expect a pier to have.

MUSIC

Occasional concerts by such ensembles as the Bournemouth Sinfonietta are presented in the **Portsmouth Guildhall**, Guildhall Square, Tel 824355. The **Portsmouth Arts Centre**, Reginald Road, Eastney, has a series of classical music recitals by soloists and small chamber ensembles. Tel 732236. For both music and theatre, the **Hornpipe Arts Centre**, 143 Kingston Road, Tel 817293, should be checked out, as should the **Centre Library Menuhin Room**, Tel 819311 and the **Mountbatten Centre**, Tel 665122.

CINEMA

Cannon – 335 Commercial Road, Tel 823538 (3 screens).
Cannon – Cosham High Street, Tel 376635 (3 screens).
Odeon – London Road, Tel 661539 (3 screens).
The **Ritz** – Walpole Road, Gosport, Tel 501231, often shows interesting films as distinct from box office blockbusters, as does the **Rendezvous Cinema** – The Hornpipe, 143 Kingston Road, Tel 833854.

BOOKSTORES

The best are **Chapter and Verse**, 6 Isambard Brunel Road, Tel 825552, and 7 Charterhouse, Lord Montgomery Way, Tel 832813, and **Volume One Bookshop** at 12 Arundel Street, Tel 862138 and 40/42 Palmerston Road, Southsea, Tel 824088. **Skinner and Craddock** are also worth a browse at 6 Grove Road South, Tel 817255, as is the **Oasis Bookshop** at 1 Upper Arundel Street, Tel 752114. **John Garland** at 115 High Street, Cosham, Tel 373749, has a large stock as befits a college bookseller and **Acorn Books** at 109 Palmerston Road has a good children's selection. Religious books can be found at the **Christian Book Centre**, 143 New Road, Tel 664647, comics at **Mondo Comics**, Unit F, Charlotte Street, Tel 851820, and **Nemesis Comics**, Royal Albert Walk, Albert Road, Tel 862854. Close by is **Arista** at the same location. New Age books can be found at **Gurukrupa Bookshop**, 44 London Road and bargain books and publishers' remainders at **Omnibooks**, 97A Commercial Road, Tel 293464.

ANTIQUARIAN AND SECONDHAND BOOKS

I really like **Miller's Rooks and Prints** at 55 Fawcett Road, Tel 755796. They have lots of old books, maps and prints and just down the road at No 69 is the **Star Bookshop**, Tel 737077. Just across the harbour in Gosport is the excellent **Richard Martin** at 23 Stoke Road, Tel 520642. He has a good collection of antiquarian and rare books plus a large number of secondhand volumes. Finally, the **Book Academy** at 13 Marmion Road, Tel 816632, and **E Gibbs** at 166 New Road, Tel 812265, are both worth a visit.

ART GALLERIES

Art Centre at 424 London Road, Tel 692614, has contemporary and traditional oils, watercolours and limited edition prints and **Scorpio**, 20 Ordnance Row, Tel 830236, has work from local artists but also military prints and hand-painted military figurines. Lastly, just across the harbour in Gosport, **Richard Martin** of 25 Stoke Road has 18th- and 19th-century and pre-1940 paintings, watercolours and etchings. Tel 520642.

Over the last couple of years a number of galleries in Portsmouth have closed and there is at the moment a dearth of fine art outlets in the city.

ANTIQUE DEALERS

Highland Road is as good a place as any to start. It's close by the bus depot and at No 130 you will find **Affordable Antiques**, Tel 293344. They have a large stock of Victorian, Edwardian and 1930s furniture and small items. At No 141 there is **Times Past**, Tel 822701. They have a stock of general antiques, especially furniture. At Nos 189-91 are **Pretty Chairs**, Tel 731411. They have a large stock of Victorian chairs, tables, wooden boxes, desks, bureaux, sofas, French-style furniture and cabriole-legged chairs. **Albert Road** is another good centre. It's adjacent to the King's Theatre and at No 105 you will find **Colin Macleod Antiques**, Tel 864211, with a stock of Oriental, Continental and English Victorian furniture, while at No 239, **Tony Amos Antiques**, Tel 736818, is to be found. Finally, **W R Priddy** at 144 Albert Road has bric-à-brac and small objects, Tel 738187. In Fawcett Road there is another branch of W R Priddy, Tel 738906, at No 65 dealing in general antiques and a bit further up on the same side of the road is **R C Dodson** at Nos 85/87, Tel 829481, also with general antiques. The **Gallery** has two shops at 11 and 19 Marion Road. At No 19 there are Victorian chairs and chesterfields and at No 11, Victorian and Edwardian furniture. Tel 822016. Just by the Clock Tower in Castle Road is **A Fleming** who has furniture, china, silver, porcelain, jewellery and general antiques, while **Leslie's** at 107 Fratton Road, close to Fratton railway station, has Victorian and antique rings and brooches circa 1850–1920. If philately is your interest **Portsmouth Stamp Shop** at 184 Chichester Road, Tel 663450, has stamps, coins, cigarette cards, postcards and banknotes while for the real specialist, **Wessex Medical Antiques** at 77 Carmarthen Avenue deals with 18th- and 19th-century medical items. They are open only by appointment. Call 376518.

RESTAURANTS

Barnardo – 109 High Street, Cosham, Tel 370226. Cosham is a suburb just north of the town centre. Barnardo is a small "front room" operation but the cooking belies the somewhat humble surroundings. The set lunch is remarkable value and even the evening meal is a bargain, given the quality of the cuisine. Friends have enthused about the salmon in dill sauce and the crab and tomato ravioli. Desserts are uniformly good. Open Tues to Sat 12–2pm and 7:30–10pm. No Sat lunch.

Pizza House – 14 Hillsea Market, London Road, Tel 695542. Well-prepared food with generous helpings. The minestrone soup is good and so are the pasta and the pizza (all made on the premises). There's also home-made ice cream which is wonderful. Open Mon–Sat 7–11:30pm. Open till midnight Fri and Sat.

Barnaby's Bistro – 56 Osborne Road, Tel 821089. Popular and crowded – with good reason. A very eclectic menu which spans the world with moules marinière, venison and garlic sausages, char-grilled lamb, steak teriyaki and a good cashew-nut and vegetable paella. Open all week 12–2:30 and 6–11pm. No Sun lunch.

Palash Tandoori – 124 Kingston Road, North End, Tel 664045. Good Indian cuisine with some excellent vegetarian dishes. Some very original curry flavourings which make the taste of Palash quite distinctive. Open daily 12–2:30 and 6–11:30pm. Midnight Fri and Sat.

PUBS

Oliver Twist – 373/375 Commercial Road, Tel 833708. Traditional friendly pub with good home-cooked food and real ales. As the name suggests, only 100 yards from the Dickens House and a three-minute walk from the dockyard and *Victory* and *Mary Rose*.

Thatched House – Lockways Road, Milton Locks, Tel 821527. Lively harbourside pub offering excellent views. Good snacks and bar food with fresh seafood a speciality. There's a nice garden for summer lounging.

Bat and Ball – Broadhalfpenny Down, Hambledown, Tel 070132 692. Four miles (6.4 km) north of the town on the B2150. One reason for visiting this pub is that it is the home of the world's greatest game – cricket. There are superb panoramic views over rolling farmland and the pub itself is charming and relaxing. Excellent restaurant and good bar food. (See Ephemera.)

Rosie's Vineyard – 87 Elm Grove, Tel 755944. A Continental-style wine bar with a pergola-covered garden for fine summer days. Good bar food including taramasalata, smoked haddock bake and ratatouille wholemeal pancake.

The Bridge – Canber Dock. on a busy quay in the old harbour, opposite the Isle of Wight ferry port, there is always something going on to fascinate you as you look through the window. Good traditional bar food with the "ploughman's" especially good.

Sally Port – High Street. Opposite the cathedral in a street full of interest, the pub has panelling, ship's lanterns and little "nautical" tables. Good cold buffet and interesting hot dishes.

Still and West – Bath Square. Marvellous waterside position with upstairs windows and terrace seeming almost within touching distance of the boats and ships leaving the harbour. Traditional bar food.

ARTISTIC ASSOCIATIONS

Portsmouth's most illustrious son is of course, Charles Dickens, who was born in the Commercial Road (see above). Dickens's father was a clerk in the Navy Pay Office. Born in 1812, Dickens came back to Portsmouth in 1838 to collect local colour for *Nicholas Nickleby*. (His family had by then moved to London.)

George Meredith, the novelist and poet, was born in Portsmouth in 1828 and baptized in St Thomas' Church (now the cathedral). Many of the characters in his best novel, *Evan Harrington*, are drawn from family and friends in the area, and Portsmouth is the "Lymport" of the book.

H G Wells, the novelist, served two years as an apprentice in Hyde's Drapery Establishment in the town. He hated it and the misery is reflected in the early part of his novel *Kipps*.

Sir Arthur Conan Doyle, creator of Sherlock Holmes, set up practice as a doctor in Portsea in 1882 and was married here in 1885. It was here that the character of Sherlock Holmes was conceived. Holmes was modelled on Dr Joseph Bell, under whom Conan Doyle studied medicine at Edinburgh University in 1876. Dr Watson, the narrator of the books and the foil of Holmes, was based on Doyle's friend, Dr James Watson, the president of the Portsmouth Literary and Scientific Society.

Portsmouth appears frequently in the seafaring novels of Captain Marryat, especially *Masterman Ready*. The character Fanny Price in Jane Austen's *Mansfield Park* lived in Portsmouth.

EPHEMERA

Catherine of Braganza was married to Charles II in the Garrison Church in 1622. Throughout his reign, Charles's numerous amours expanded the ranks of nobility with a dozen natural offspring. To them all he was solicitous and generous and no woman who had granted him her favours could justly accuse him of ingratitude or neglect. Catherine was Portuguese and as the marriage was arranged as a result of political expediency, Charles had not seen his bride before meeting her at Portsmouth. What happened at that meeting is luckily preserved in a letter Charles wrote to Lord Clarendon. "I arrived here yesterday about two in the afternoon, and as soon as I had shifted myself, I went to my wife's chamber, who I found in bed by reason of a little cough, and some inclination to a fever, which was caused by having certain things stopped at sea which ought to have carried away those humours. It was happy for the honour of the nation that I was not put to the consummation of the marriage last night, for I was so sleepy by having slept but two hours on my journey as I was afraid matters would have gone very sleepily. I can now only give you an account of what I have seen a-bed; which, in short is, her face is not so exact as to be called a beauty, though her eyes are excellent good, and not anything in her face that in the least degree can shock one. On the contrary, she has as much agreeableness in her looks altogether, as ever I saw; and if I have any skill in physiognomy, which I think I have, she must be as good a woman as ever was born. Her conversation, as much as I can perceive, is very good; for she has wit enough and a most agreeable voice. You would wonder much to see how well we are acquainted already. In a word, I think myself very happy; I am confident our two humours will agree very well together."

Admiral Horatio Nelson's finest hour was his victory in the Battle of Trafalgar in 1805. The British fleet approached the enemy in two divisions, one led by Nelson in his flagship *Victory* and the other led by the *Royal Sovereign*. While the *Sovereign* headed for the enemy's rear, *Victory* aimed for the centre, raking the ships on either side, and drawing heavy fire in return. Nelson stood on the quarterdeck in full dress uniform, a touch of vanity that invited musket fire from *Redoubtable* alongside. The admiral fell, mortally wounded, but survived long enough to learn that the battle had been won. In the *Victory* (which can be seen in the dockyard), there is still in Nelson's cabin, where he placed it, a portrait of Nelson's only child, Horatia, by his mistress Lady Emma Hamilton. Scandal was long averted by the parents' "adopting" her and after Nelson's death she was brought up by his sisters. She married the vicar of Tenterden in Kent. As he was dying, Nelson said to his surgeon, "I have to leave Lady Hamilton and my adopted daughter, Horatia, as a legacy to my country." After his death, Emma Hamilton tried for years to persuade the British government to comply with the admiral's dying request. To no avail. Emma died heartbroken and penniless in Calais in 1815.

In the 17th century, Spice Island, close to the present-day departure point of the Isle of Wight ferries, was an area of well-frequented inns and brothels crammed into the narrow streets of the small peninsula. In West Street is the weatherboarded Quebec House, built in 1754 as a sea-bathing establishment. The street leads to Bath Square and the Point where there are views of the harbour and dockyards from the cobbled promenade. The visitor can almost smell the hemp, tar and rum, hear the shouts of revelling seamen in the taverns, and feel the tramp of the press gang on the cobbles in the most evocative atmospheric part of this great naval city.

The Hambledown Cricket Club in Broadhalfpenny Down was where the game of cricket was first given its proper rules. The club was most important between 1772 and 1787 when, with its help, the MCC (cricket's ruling body) was formed. Opposite the Ball and Bat Inn is an imposing granite monument to commemorate a cricket match played here in the late 1800s.

TOURIST INFORMATION BUREAU: Clarence Esplanade, Southsea, Portsmouth P053PE. Tel (0705) 828441

SOUTHAMPTON

County of Hampshire
Three trains an hour from London (Waterloo), approximately 60 minutes
80 miles (128 km) by road on M3 and M27

From the sailing of the *Mayflower* to the sinking of the *Titanic,* and from the archers bound for Agincourt to the building of the Spitfire, the city of Southampton has played an important part in the unfolding history of the British Isles.

Southampton is one of the largest international ports in Britain. The safe haven of Southampton water has meant that for centuries the maritime tradition has been a major factor in the life of the city.

Southampton's wealth has always been built on trade and the accession of Henry II in 1154 stimulated Southampton's early development as a port by intertwining the fortunes of England and Anjou. The rich town merchants built stone houses which equalled any baronial hall in the country. Southampton Castle became important for shipping royal cargoes and it was in a large hall of the castle that Henry met his archbishop, Thomas à Becket, in 1162. Although successive kings made grants to Southampton to enclose their town the seaward side was left undefended. Perhaps the wealthy and luxurious life led by the merchants had dulled their sensibilities to the possible dangers posed by France. This fact was brought home to them however, on an October Sunday morning in 1338 when a French and Genoese force landed in Southampton and, in an orgy of destruction, brought an end to nearly 200 years of prosperity. The failure of the city fathers to defend their town resulted in martial law, an increase in the garrison of the castle and the building of a walled fortification around the town with seven main gateways and 29 towers. The town walls stretched for over a mile, standing up to 30 feet (9 m) high and six feet (1.8 m) thick. Southampton today probably has more substantial remains of medieval buildings than any other place in the country and certainly the jewel in the crown is the magnificent Bargate, which stands in the centre of the town. I think it is the finest and most complex gateway of its kind in Britain. Over the years it has been used for many purposes – tollgate, guildhall, courtroom and today, a museum. As Henry V was about to embark with an army for the Battle of Agincourt in 1415, a conspiracy of treason was unmasked and the Earl of Cambridge, Sir Thomas Grey and Lord Scroop were all beheaded in front of the Bargate. (See Shakespeare's *Henry V*, Act 2, Scene 2.)

Gradually, Southampton's shipping declined. By 1560 there was only one ship of more than 100 tons (90.7 m. tonnes) left in the port and the town had difficulty supplying even one vessel to the force that confronted the Spanish Armada in 1588. Elizabethan Southampton was often described as decayed, with sheep grazing in the castle, ship's hulks rotting in the quays and squatters sheltering from the elements in the once proud town wall towers.

Southampton's fortunes revived with the opportunities provided by the discovery of the New World. By then the town had established itself as a regional market centre. On July 29, 1620, a ship of 180 tons (163 m. tonnes), the *Mayflower,* arrived in Southampton from London. She was due to rendezvous with the *Speedwell,* arriving from Holland with a group of English Puritan refugees. On Saturday, August 15, the ships set sail for America, but the *Speedwell* was leaking and had to put in to Plymouth, and the Pilgrims crossed the Atlantic in the *Mayflower* alone, unknowingly creating great animosity between Southampton and Plymouth over which city was their actual port of departure.

When the Civil War broke out in 1642, Southampton, like many commercial towns, was basically Parliamentarian. Puritan preachers were installed in the town's churches. After the restoration of Charles II, one such preacher founded an independent church which grew into the **Above Bar Congregational Church**. One of the church's first deacons was the father of Isaac Watts, whose famous hymn, "O God, Our Help in Ages Past," now chimes from the Civic Centre clock tower. A plaque at the back entrance of Marks and Spencers in Vincent's Walk commemorates the church which was destroyed by enemy action in 1940.

In the 17th century recurrent epidemics of bubonic plague, losses of ships and their cargoes in the frequent wars and the disappearance of the woollen cloth weaving industry which had sustained Southampton in the past again led to economic and social depression. This was relieved in the 18th century with the development of a fashionable spa and a medicinal sea bathing resort which enjoyed royal patronage.

The first development of the modern port began in the early part of the 19th century, but not until Victorian times, with the introduction of steam navigation, did the real impetus for maritime growth come to Southampton. New docks were built, the rail link to London established and the great passenger shipping lines came into existence. P&O sailed to Alexandria and India and the Royal Mail Steam Packet Company provided service to the West Indies. If the sea lanes were the arteries of the British Empire, then the mailships from Southampton carried its life blood. Maritime expansion continued; in 1907 White Star Lines transferred its North Atlantic service from Liverpool to Southampton. In April 1912 the new and ill-fated *Titanic* set sail on its maiden voyage. During the first half of the 20th century all the world's greatest liners, the *Olympia,* the *Aquitania* and the *Canberra,* used Southampton's Ocean Dock and, of course, it is still being used today by Cunard's *Queen Elizabeth 2* and *Canberra*. During the First and Second World Wars Southampton was a vitally important port, servicing supplies, munitions and troops. A burgeoning aircraft industry produced, in the late '30s, the legendary Spitfire aircraft. After the Normandy landings in June 1944 more than two million men and millions of tons of equipment passed through Southampton. Severely damaged by bombing in the early part of the Second World War, the centre of Southampton was virtually rebuilt into the the unique blend of new and old that can be seen today.

Many important ancient buildings can be found in Southampton. Be sure to visit the Bargate, Westgate, God's House Gate, Arundel Tower, and Prince Edward Tower. King John's Palace and Canute Palace (preserved as a ruin) are not palaces but 12th-century merchants' houses. Behind the frontage of the Red Lion Inn in the High Street is the medieval house where the three traitors beheaded by Henry V were tried for conspiracy. Interesting late medieval buildings can be found in French Street and Bugle Street and the Tudor House in St Michael's Square (see Museums below) is another fine example. No 58 French Street has been restored by English Heritage and is believed to be the only example of its kind on its original site in Western Europe.

Southampton Castle fell into ruin during the reign of Elizabeth I, which is a pity, as Richard the Lionheart is said to have stayed there on his return from the Crusades – but the vaults survive. The Wool House, used as a store by the monks of Beaulieu Abbey and later as a prison in the Napoleonic Wars, is now a maritime museum and the Tudor Merchant's House, originally a fish market, was moved in 1634 to a spot by Westgate and has been superbly restored. It is used for concerts and other events. St Michael's Church is the oldest surviving building in Southampton and dates from the Norman Conquest, while the Holy Rood Church, near the High Street, was built in 1320 and is a shrine in memory of the men of the merchant navy. The Dolphin Hotel (rebuilt in 1775) in High Street reminds us of the prosperous period of the fashionable spa town. There are statues of Prime Minister Lord Palmerston and of the famous composer of hymns, Isaac Watts. The Mayflower Memorial commemorates the sailing of the Pilgrim Fathers (it's close to the Royal Pier) and in Watts Park, north of the main shopping centre, floodlights illuminate a memorial to those who died in the sinking of the *Titanic*. A walkway scheme to enable visitors to walk at high level along sections of the old wall should be completed by the time this book is in print.

THE BARGATE, SOUTHAMPTON

WALK

Your **Southampton Walk** is approximately two and a half miles (4 km) in length. Begin from the multi-storey car park in Western Esplanade. Come out into Western Esplanade, turn left and follow the foot-path below the medieval towers and walls to the **West Gate**, built in the 14th century. You can see grooves in the stonework where there was once a portcullis. Bear left onto the Town Quay, past the **Mayflower Memorial**, and note the gleaming white **Royal Pier**, built in 1833. The Pier has a moghul-type dome and a parapet studded with golden heraldic lions. Pass the **Maritime Museum** on the left, and at the junction of French Street bear left into Porter's Lane. Here one can see the remains of six medieval houses destroyed in the Second World War. Cross High Street into Winkle Street and **God's Tower House Museum**. Go through the arch at the end of Winkle Street and turn left into lower Canal Walk. On the right, in Orchard Place, is the Southampton Bowling Green, dating from 1299 and said to be the oldest in the world. Turn left into Briton Street and then right into High Street. The **Red Lion Inn** (see below), dating from the 15th century, is on your right. The elegant bow-windowed **Dolphin Hotel** dates from the 18th century. There are two imposing banks, in the classical style, and when you get to the Bernard Street Junction you will see **Holyrood Church** just ahead of you. As you turn left into St Michael's Street, you will see ahead of you **St Michael's Church**, which is the oldest building in Southampton, circa 1070. Behind St Michael's Street is the **Tudor House Museum**. Walk through St Michael's Square and turn left into Castle Way and then right into West Street and back into the High Street. Turn left and walk up to the medieval **Bargate**. Turn right into Hanover Buildings and left into Houndwell Park. Walk through Palmerston Park – Lord Palmerston, Prime Minister in the 1850s, was the member for Southampton – and East Park. In East Park turn left by the statue of Richard Andrews, a 19th-century coach builder who was five times Mayor of Southampton. Leave the park and walk into Above Bar Street with the **Titanic Memorial** on your right. Cross Above Bar Street and enter West Park by the Cenotaph, then take the left-hand turn into West Marlands Road and the Civic Centre. Turn left into Civic Centre Road and right again into Above Bar Street. Walk through the shopping precinct to Bargate and back to the car park.

Footnote: The *Southampton Official Handbook* is beautifully produced and exceptionally informative. If you are thinking of staying in the area at all, I heartily recommend it.

MUSEUMS AND GALLERIES

The **Bargate** – One of the oldest buildings still in use in Southampton (see above). The setting and space are mostly used for temporary exhibitions of local history rather than permanent ones. In 1977 the museum put on a joint commemoration, with Southampton's twin city of Le Havre, of the wartime raid on Bruneval. Other exhibitions have included the centenary of public transport in Southampton and Southampton's connections with the West Indies.

Tudor House Museum – St Michael's Square. A late medieval timber-framed house built for a wealthy merchant (see above). The banquetry hall is furnished in 16th-century style and the museum shows exhibitions of Victorian and Edwardian domestic and social life. There is a reconstruction of a Tudor garden in the grounds. Open Tues–Fri 10–5pm; Sat 10–4pm; Sun 2–5pm. Closed for lunch 1–2pm and all day on Mondays.

Medieval Merchant's House – 58 French Street. Built in 1290 as a merchant's house and a place of busi-ness. The house has a colourful history, having been used as a public house, a brothel and a theatrical store before being rescued and opened to the public. Open daily 10–4pm; April–Sept 10–6pm.

Museum of Archaeology – God's House Tower, Winkle Street. Housed in part of the town's 15th-century defences. Exhibitions tell the story of three towns – Roman Clausentum, Saxon Hamivic and Medieval Southampton. Displays focus on social and domestic life.

S S Shieldhall – Ocean Village, Tel 612628. Built in Glasgow in 1955, the Shieldhall is the last working steam-powered cargo vessel. Refitted and renovated to its original condition, the ship is in steam once a month.

Hall of Aviation – Albert Road South (near Ocean Village) Tel 635830. Presents the story of aviation in the Southampton area and incorporates the R J Mitchell Museum. Mitchell, who lived and worked in Southampton, was the designer of both the Spitfire and the S6 Seaplane, winner of the Schneider Trophy. The centrepiece of the museum is the spectacular Sandringham Flying Boat.

Maritime Museum – Wool House, Bugle Street. The museum is housed in a late 14th-century wool ware-house. The exhibits present the history of the port of Southampton, including a model of the docks at their peak in the 1930s. Opening times the same as Tudor House. Note that there are plans to open a new maritime museum in Ocean Village. At that time the wool warehouse will be given over to a museum devoted to Southampton at war, mainly based on the memories of local people.

City Art Gallery – Generally regarded as the finest in the south of England, it is visited by more than 10,000 people each year. The gallery owns many fine Italian, French, Dutch and Flemish paintings as well as Impressionist and post-Impressionist works. It is best known, however, for its collection of British paintings, unrivalled outside the Tate Gallery, London, in its representation of the 20th century in British art. Perhaps the most admired exhibits are Gainsborough's portrait of Lord Vernon, Philip Koninck's panoramic landscape and *The Church at Verheuil* by Claude Monet. Open year round 10–6pm. Closed Sundays.

Smaller galleries housing travelling exhibitions can be found at the University of Southampton – the **John Hansard Gallery** and the **Gantry** (see above).

THEATRE

Mayflower Theatre – Commercial Road, Tel 0703 229771. Seating more than 2250, the Mayflower, owned by the city council, opened in 1987 following a £3.9-million restoration programme. The theatre stages West End musicals, plays, opera, ballet, variety shows and rock concerts. Regular visitors to the theatre include the London Contemporary Dance Theatre, the Sadlers Wells Royal Ballet and the Welsh National Opera. Other companies have included the Royal Shakespeare Company, Glyndebourne Touring Opera and the Bolshoi Ballet.

Nuffield Theatre – The University, Tel 0703 671771. During the spring and autumn the Nuffield Theatre presents its own nationally acclaimed repertory productions, many of which have transferred to London's West End. Since its first season in 1975, the Nuffield has presented a healthy mix of classical plays, modern comedies and dramas, and has introduced the work of new playwrights. The Nuffield also presents work by university drama groups, local drama companies, visiting professional theatres and national touring companies.

Gantry Centre – Blechynden Terrace, Tel 0703 229319. Southampton's community arts centre. There is a 200-seat theatre and a cinema; many small-scale and alternative theatre events take place here. A recent programme sampling found performances by Trestle Theatre, the country's finest exponents of mask and mime theatre; the Medieval Players presenting *Courage*, a black farce drawn from the same source as Brecht's *Mother Courage*; and *The Last Dance*, a play by Teatre Blik, who are based in Koszalin, Poland. Varied programmes of theatre and film are also presented at the **Mountbatten Theatre**, East Park Terrace, Tel 0703 220640 for details.

MUSIC

The Guildhall – West Marlands Road, Tel 0703 632601. The Guildhall stages orchestral concerts throughout the year as well as organ recitals, pop and variety shows, brass band concerts and championship ballroom dancing. The area's local orchestras, the Bournemouth Symphony Orchestra and the Bournemouth Sinfonietta are the most regular visitors but other top symphony orchestras and soloists can also be heard throughout the year.

Turner Sims Concert Hall – Tel 0703 671771. Like the Nuffield Theatre, this concert hall is situated on the university campus. The hall has excellent acoustics and visitors have included pianists such as Peter Frankl and John Lill, Steven Isserlis, cellist, and Anthony Rolfe Johnson, tenor. Among visiting ensembles are numbered the Polish Philharmonic Chamber Orchestra, the Allegri String Quartet, the Franz Schubert Quartet of Vienna and the London Baroque.

Gantry Centre – (see above) has a Sunday lunchtime music series with bands ranging from blues and New Orleans jazz through mainstream to folk-rock and cajun music. The Gantry also hosts occasional evening music concerts.

In the summers **Ocean Village Marina** - Dock Gate 2, Tel 228353, stages special events and live entertainment on the waterfront.

The **Angel** – Palmerston Road, Tel 226708, has rock and pop music on Thursdays and Saturdays, **Chaplins** in York Building, Tel 225275, has jazz on Thursdays, **Goblets** – 180 Above Bar, has jazz on Wednesdays while the **Joiner's Arms** has blues on Sunday, folk on Fridays (Sept–June) and regular bands most other nights.

CINEMA

Commercial cinema:
Cannon Cinema – Above Bar Street, Tel 221026. Two screens.
Cannon Cinema – Ocean Village, Tel 634336. Five screens.
Odean Film Centre – Above Bar Street, Tel 333243/229188. Two screens, daily matinee.
Alternative Cinema:
The **Gantry** – (see above). Generally has showings Friday, Saturday and Sundays at 7pm.
Mountbatten Theatre – Generally weekly programming.
Southampton Film Theatre – Showings are in their comfortable auditorium at the Boldrewood Centre,
Basset Crescent East, Wednesdays at 8pm.

BOOKSTORES

The best is **Dillon's** at 7–9 Hanover Buildings, Tel 232188 (just down from the Bargate). Excellent selection, knowledgeable assistants and courteous service. **Sherratt and Hughes** at 94 Above Bar, Tel 639414, is also good, as is **Hammick's** at 100 Above Bar, Tel 634097. If you are at Southampton University there is a branch of **Bowes and Bowes**, Tel 558267, which is worth a look.

ANTIQUARIAN AND SECONDHAND BOOKS

H M Gilbert and Son, an old established business at 2 1/2 Portland Street, just off Above Bar by the Tourist Information Centre, is well worth a browse and **Oldfield Antiques, Maps, Books and Prints** also has an interesting collection of material. They're at Northam Road, Tel 638916.

ART GALLERIES

There's honestly not a lot to interest one in Southampton.
The First Gallery – 1 Burnham Chase, Bitterne, Tel 462723, is good for contemporary art with pictures, sculptures and pots. Very friendly gallery kept deliberately small in a private house. You might also try **Alfred James Morris Fine Art** at 280 Shirley Road, Tel 774772. It's in the same premises as Mr Alfred's Curiosity Shop (see below).

ANTIQUE DEALERS

Alfred's Curiosity Shop and Galleries – 280 Shirley Road, Tel 774772, is good for browsing.
Antiques at No 10 – 10A/B Northam Road, Six Dials, Tel 224707, has period furniture, gold and silver jewellery, glass and china and, more importantly, specializes in art nouveau and art deco.
Bassett Antiques – 15 Chetwynd Drive, Bassett, Tel 776287, besides having a general collection, also specializes in house clearances as does **Bazaar** at Highfields Lane, Tel 584347.
A really fascinating shop is **Cobwebs** at 78 Northam Road, Tel 227458. Perhaps, not so surprisingly, given Southampton's reputation as an ocean liner port, they specialize in ocean liner souvenirs, especially Cunard and White Star Lines, as well as general antiques and prints. As a matter of fact, Northam Road is an excellent browsing ground, for as well as the shops already mentioned, there are **Dials Antiques**, Tel 332293 at 80 Northam Road, **R J Elliot**, Tel 226642 at No 45, **Fair Deal Antiques**, Tel 632695 at No 50, **Miscellaneous**, Tel 228530 at No 29, **R K Leslie Antiques**, Tel 224784 at No 23 and **Relics**, Tel 221635 at No 54.

RESTAURANTS

Kuti's – 70 London Road, Tel 221585, is a handsome pink-and-mauve restaurant in the city centre. A sitar player performs twice weekly. The help-yourself buffet lunch is especially good value. The tandoori fish is excellent; and to drink, there is chaas, a diluted lassi best served Bombay-style spiced with ginger, cumin, coriander and mustard seeds. Open all week 12–2:15 and 6–11:30. Its sister restaurant, **Kohinoor**, is at 2 The Broadway, Portswood, and is also excellent.
Geddes – Town Quay, Tel 221159. A classical French restaurant set in a converted warehouse, with cellars, in the medieval town walls facing the old pier and landing stage for the Isle of Wight ferry. Beautiful decor and ambience. The set menu is good value and the dessert trolley spectacular.
La Margherita – 4-6 Commercial Road, Tel 333390. Italian food. Close to the Mayflower Theatre. Excellent fresh sardines and very good value Italian red wine. Recommended by *Les Routiers*. Very lively atmosphere and friendly service.

Los Marinos – A Spanish restaurant in Ocean Village, Tel 335045, it overlooks the marina and is very pleasant in the summer. For vegetarian food, **Town House** at 59 Oxford Street, Tel 220498, even offers gourmet vegetarian candlelit dinners while the **Flying Teapot** on Ounslow Road, Tel 335931, is also fun and good value.

PUBS

Red Lion – 53 High Street, Tel 333595. Set in a medieval hall with dark Tudor panelling and steeply pitched oak rafters. The walls are decorated with arms, armour and even a flag reputed to have been presented to the city by Queen Elizabeth I in 1585. Standard pub food with generous helpings.

Royal Pier – Town Quay (close to Geddes Restaurant). Lofty building with upper floor reached by spiral staircase. Standard pub food, reasonably priced. A nice sheltered terrace for the summer.

Cowherd – The Avenue. Set on the common, a vast tract of open land just to the north of the city centre which is the home of many rare plants and wildlife. Victorian decor with lots of alcoves and small rooms. Simple bar food, also a restaurant. Some tables set outside in summer. Very handy if you are visiting the Balloon Festival which is held in July.

Wellington Arms – Park Road, Fremantle (off Shirley Road), has lots of Wellington memorabilia, while the **Duke of Wellington** in Bugle Street has cellars said to be more than 800 years old.

ARTISTIC ASSOCIATIONS

Jane Austen lived at 3 Castle Square (gone) from 1807 to 1809. The house stood in modern Upper Bugle Street near the Juniper Berry Public House. Bugle Street is bounded on one side by the city walls, and Jane often used to walk there and admire the view.

Mention has been made of Isaac Watts, the author and composer of hymns, who was born in Southampton on July 17, 1674. As well as "O God, Our Help in Ages Past," Watts composed "Jesus Shall Reign Where'er the Sun" and "When I Survey the Wondrous Cross." His statue can be seen in Watts Park, north of the Civic Centre. The Church of the Ascension, Bilterne Park, has four memorial windows illustrating seven of his best-known hymns, and St Andrew's Church in Brunswick Place contains his sculpted head and shoulders rescued from the ruin of the Above Bar Congregational Church.

Charles Dibdin, the playwright and composer, was born in Southampton. He wrote nearly 70 dramatic pieces, novels and musical works and is particularly remembered for songs he composed during the Napoleonic Wars, which, it is claimed, boosted recruitment to the Royal Navy. His most famous song is "Tom Bowling."

The clergyman, wit and journalist Sydney Smith, the novelist William Makepeace Thackeray, and Sir John Everett Millais, the pre-Raphaelite painter, were all born in Southampton. Thackeray's memories of the town were not felicitous ones. He so hated the time he spent at Arthur's School that he used the unhappy experiences in his great historical novel, *Henry Esmond.* He also had a disastrous love affair with Jane Brookfield, the wife of a Southampton clergyman.

The leading 19th-century sculptor, Richard Cockle Lucas, spent the greater part of his life in Southampton. He is well known for his busts and medallions, many of which were exhibited at the Great Exhibition of 1851. Lucas was very eccentric and used to drive through Southampton's main streets standing in two-wheeled vehicle, like a Roman chariot, wearing a long flowing garment.

A quarter of a century after his death Lucas was at the centre of a controversy in the art world. It was then proved, more or less conclusively, that the bust of "Flora" in the Berlin Museum, which had been attributed to Leonardo da Vinci, and for which £9250 had been paid (a very considerable sum at the time), was actually Lucas's work.

EPHEMERA

Try to catch a performance by the Solent People's Theatre, one of the country's leading professional community drama companies. Solent's mandate is to take its theatre to the people. The company specializes in shows with strong visual and musical elements – especially open-air summer pageants and lively reconstructions of local history. They sometimes perform in historical locations such as the Tudor Merchants' Hall. They are supported by councils and agencies including Southampton City Council so, for their programme, phone the council at 223855 or the Tourist Information Centre at 221106.

Canute was King of England, Denmark and Norway in 1028. He gave England peace, restored the church to a high place and codified English law, besides establishing friendly relations with the Holy Roman Empire. Tiring of the extravagant praises of his greatness, power and invincibility, Canute ordered his chair to be set down on the seashore where he commanded the waves not to come in and wet him. The incoming tide soon demonstrated the limitations of human powers. The 12th-century chronicler who tells this story adds that from this time on, Canute never again wore his crown, but hung it upon a statue of the crucified Christ. Although there is no definite proof that this incident ever took place, Canute's demonstration of his powerlessness against natural forces could well have been emphasized by Southampton's "double" or prolonged high tide. On the front of the Canute Hotel there is a plaque which says, "Near this spot, AD 1028, Canute reproved his courtiers." It's a story one wants to believe.

In Peartree Churchyard, Peartree Green Church, there is a memorial to 17-year-old Richard Parker, who died a grisly death in 1884. Wrecked in the tropics, Richard and his three companions, starving and half-demented, drew lots to see who should be killed and eaten by the others. Richard, who was already dying, lost. Very soon afterwards the remaining three members of the stricken ship's crew were rescued.

It makes one wonder sometimes just which stage stories are true and which are part of thespian folklore. If one works in the theatre one is told, in deepest confidence, about something that happened in a particular playhouse last season and it turns out to be exactly the same incident that was supposed to have happened last season at a theatre 200 miles away. Not that all this matters, as many of the stories bear listening to regardless of where they took place. Who knows? ... this one *could* have happened in Southampton ... here it is:

The climax of the not terribly good comedy thriller has the leading actor reaching into the drawer of a desk and pulling out a revolver. Confronting the villain, he then issues the immortal words, "You cad, I intend to make sure you never blackmail another innocent woman!" and shoots the villain dead. One night the assistant stage manager had forgotten to place the gun, loaded of course with blanks, in the drawer, so when the actor reached for the weapon he found the drawer empty. Now at drama school they told us what to do in situations like that – stay calm, cool and collected, and ad lib. (This happened to me once on stage and I, like a mere novice, panicked.) So, I am glad to say, did the actor in our story, who for no apparent reason kicked out his foot at the villain and booted him in the behind. In a display of quite remarkable ingenuity and invention the villain fell to the ground clutching his bottom and uttering the words, "My god, the boot was poisoned."

The hero of ancient Southampton was Sir Bevis. He fought and slew the giant Ascapart who was terrorizing the surrounding countryside. The statue of Sir Bevis is on Southampton's Bargate, and just outside the town is Bevis Mound, a tumulus beneath which the skeleton of Ascapart is said to lie.

TOURIST INFORMATION BUREAU: Above Bar, Southampton, Hampshire, S09 4X5.
Tel (0703) 221106

WINCHESTER

County of Hampshire
60 miles (96 km) from London by M3
70 minutes from London (Waterloo) by rail

The story of Winchester runs like a golden thread through the history of England. Already an important town in Roman times, it became the capital under the Anglo-Saxons and in King Alfred's time (871–901), was a great centre of learning. William the Conqueror kept Winchester as his capital, though by this time London was almost of equal importance. As late as the 17th century Charles II planned a palace here.

Since it is so closely linked with history, buildings of interest are not hard to find. The city's focal point is the High Street, ornamented by a 15th-century cross and a statue to King Alfred. Nearby is the 19th-century Guildhall and not far away, a Plague monument. Many little alleyways are decorated by houses of all centuries; each is worth exploration.

Westgate, at one end of High Street, and Kingsgate, near the cathedral, are two of the original five city gates of William the Conqueror's castle from which the Empress Matilda escaped in a coffin in the 12th century. Not much remains, since it was demolished by Parliament during the Civil War in return for Winchester declaring for the King, but the Great Hall can still be seen. Another castle, Wolvesey, built in 1138, also had attention paid to it by Cromwell, but romantic ruins remain and in 1684 a new palace was built, which is still in use as the Bishop's Palace. Parts of the old wall remain. The Cathedral is of course magnificent and is surrounded by much of interest – the Old Deanery, Cheyney Court, the Pilgrim's School and of course, Winchester College.

WALK

Winchester is an easy town to walk. Start at the bottom of the High Street and park behind the **Guildhall**. Just east of **King Alfred's Statue** is Bridge Street. The present **City Bridge** dates from 1813 but an earlier bridge was built by St Swithin, Bishop of Winchester. The **City Mill** was built in 1744 on the site of a medieval mill. The River Ilchen made a natural defence here for the Roman city wall and Eastgate. King Alfred's statue, which shows the great man holding a sword aloft, is made of bronze raised on two blocks of Cornish granite, and was erected in 1901. It commemorates the death in 899 of the famous Saxon king, Alfred the Great. Winchester was Alfred's capital and it was he who defeated the marauding Danes, but he is most remembered for the prosperity, scholarly learning and justice that he brought to his kingdom of Wessex. Near the statue is the 19th-century **Guildhall**, which also houses the Tourist Information Bureau. Here too you will find a plague monument commemorating 1666 but erected in 1759.

Walk up Broadway to the ancient High Street. Down this street have walked Roman soldiers and citizens and in medieval times, pilgrims on their way to the shrine of St Swithin (see Ephemera). The clock was presented to the city in 1713 and from the turret above, the curfew bell is still rung at eight o'clock each evening, as it has been for 900 years.

The **City Cross** was built in the 15th century and restored in 1865. Adjacent to the cross is a fine 15th-century timber house. Close by is the **Prentice**, a row of shops sheltered by overhanging storeys. This was the site of William the Conqueror's Palace (see Ephemera). Just round the corner by the City Cross you will find the **Eclipse Inn**. This was once the rectory of the small but ancient church of St Lawrence, which is nearby. Formerly there was a rival inn called the Sun, hence the opposition named Eclipse. Just past the City Cross you will see on your right **Godbegot House**. This group of 15th-century tenements (much rebuilt) stands on the site of the ancient manor of Godbegot. It belonged to Queen Emma, mother of Edward the Confessor. In 1052, after the death of her husband King Canute, she gave it to the cathedral. At the top of the High Street is the **Westgate**. Fifteen hundred years ago a Roman city gate stood here. The present gate is about 600 years old. Look for the grooves dawn which the portcullis could be rushed in sudden emergency and also for the five openings from which missiles could be dropped on attackers. It is possible that the two grotesque heads with open mouths formerly

KING ALFRED, WINCHESTER

held drawbridge chains. The gatehouse contains a small museum and visitors can view Winchester from the roofwalk. To the left of the Westgate, set between the County Council Offices and the Crown Court stands the **Great Hall**. Built between 1222 and 1236 for Henry III, it is considered to be the finest medieval hall in England, after Westminster Hall in London. High on the west wall is a round table made of oak and measuring 18 feet (5.4 m) in diameter. The table is believed to have been painted for the visit to Winchester of Charles V and Henry VIII in 1522. The design is of a robed King Arthur with the names of his knights around the circumference.

Walter Raleigh was condemned to death here in 1603. (His sentence was commuted but carried out in 1618 after a voyage he made to South America was a failure.) The notorious Judge Jeffereys held court here in 1685. Jeffereys was sent by James II to try the followers of the Duke of Monmouth who had rebelled when Monmouth proclaimed himself king upon the death of Charles II. His tour of trials became known as the Bloody Assizes. Walk back down the High Street and at the City Cross turn right into the **Cathedral Close**.

A cathedral has stood here since Anglo-Saxon times, but in 1079, after the Conquest, the new building was started by Bishop Walkelyn, and consecrated in 1093. Work from this period can still be seen in the crypt, transepts and east part of the cloister. Between 1189 and 1204 Bishop de Lucy extended the choir and built the Lady Chapel. During the 14th century, William of Edington started to refashion the West Front and nave in Perpendicular style and this work was completed by his successor, William of Wykeham.

Thus the cathedral shows architectural styles from massive Norman to graceful Perpendicular. Winchester is the second longest cathedral in Europe and among its treasures are a magnificent 12th-century black marble font from Tournai, with vigorous carvings depicting legends from the life of St Nicholas – a boy saved from drowning and decapitated heads restored, and the great Winchester Bible also dating from the 12th century.

Many kings lie here, as do the famous, among them Jane Austen and Izaak Walton, but unfortunately St Swithin's tomb, though marked, has been destroyed. There is much else of beauty, including the paintings in the 13th-century Lady Chapel, the Chapel of the Guardian Angels and the beautiful chapels to William of Wykeham, Bishop Langton and others.

South of the cathedral is the **Deanery**. Originally the cloisters and buildings of the **Priory of St Swithin** lay here. The Prior's lodging with its first floor hall and the adjacent 13th-century porch now form the Deanery. **Dome Alley** has 17th-century houses and **Cheyney Court**, once the Bishop of Winchester's courthouse, is partly built into the medieval city wall. The ancient **Priory Gate** which adjoins Cheyney Court is another reminder of the great Priory of St Swithin which stood here before the Dissolution of 1539. There is a picturesque porter's lodge and alongside is the Priory Stable, perhaps the last addition to be made to the Priory before the Dissolution. Nearby is Pilgrim's School and at its side, the 14th-century hammer-beam roof (open to the public). At the corner of Kingsgate Street and St Swithin Street, just across from Cheyney Court, is **St Swithin-upon-Kingsgate**. This is one of the few remaining examples of a medieval church above a gateway; it is still in use as a place of worship. The Roman city wall had four gatehouses – Northgate, Southgate, Eastgate and Westgate. Kingsgate was added prior to 1148 for the convenience of the Bishop, the citizens and for the monks of the great priory of St Swithin.

Turn left along College Street and on your right you will see **Jane Austen's House**. The great English novelist died here in 1817, aged 42 years. In her last illness she had come here from Chawton to be close to her doctor. The house is not open to the public but there is a museum with Austen memorabilia in Chawton itself. Tel 042083262 (see under Farnham Ephemera). Behind the house and occupying most of the right hand side of the road as far as the river is Winchester College, founded in 1382 by Bishop William of Wykeham. Its purpose was to train scholars for the church; their studies would be completed at New College, Oxford (also founded by Wykeham). Many of the old buildings remain. The chapel has its original wooden vaulting, and above the main gateway in College Street there is an original statue of the Virgin.

Come back into College Street, turn right onto College Walk and you will find a footpath leading to the **Hospital of St Cross**. In 1136, Bishop Henry de Blois founded the hospital for the benefit of 13 poor men. Today they still wear black gowns decorated with a silver cross and a medieval cap, while those from the Almshouse of the Noble Poverty, founded in 1445 by Cardinal Beaufort, wear mulberry gowns and cardinals' hats with swinging tassels. The old buildings here are mellow and peaceful, and the vaulted Chapel of St Cross is quite outstanding. It has a 12th-century choir and transepts, a 14th-century tower, 15th-century glass and beautiful old wall paintings and woodwork. Anyone visiting this foundation and requesting it may still be given the Wayfarer's Dole – bread and beer served in a horn – which has been dispensed since the 12th century.

Walk back to the college and turn right on College Street. At the end turn left along a riverside footpath. On your left are the city walls, Bishop's Palace and the remains of Wolvesley Castle, which was built circa 1135 by Bishop Henri de Blois. It was largely destroyed in 1645 when Winchester was captured by the Parliamentary troops during the Civil War. Follow the footpath by the walls and it will lead you out into Broadway and King Alfred's statue, which was where you began your walk.

MUSEUMS AND GALLERIES

Winchester Cathedral – Tel 53137. Open daily 7:30am–6:30pm. At 556 feet (169 m), the second longest medieval building in the world. The **Crypt**, thought to be the oldest example of a Norman crypt in England, is open Easter–Sept (water level permitting). The **Treasury** houses the church plate and archaeological finds. Open May–Sept Mon–Sat 10:30–12:30 and 2:30–4:30, Sun 2:30–4:30. The **Library** – for opening times call the Cathedral office, Tel 853137.

Winchester College – College Street, Tel 864242. One of the oldest public schools in the country. Open April–Sept Mon–Sat 10–6pm. Guided tours at 11, 2 and 3:15pm. The **Treasury** was set up in 1982 to display the Duberlay collection of Chinese porcelain. Open Thurs, Sat, Sun: 2–4pm.

Great Hall and Round Table – High Street. Open March–Oct daily 10–5pm; Nov–Feb Mon–Fri 10–5pm and Sat, Sun 10–4pm. The 13th-century Great Hall is the only visible part remaining of a medieval castle built by Henry III. It houses the famous Round Table, circa 1280.

Winchester City Museum – The Square, Tel 868166. Open April–Sept Mon– Sat 10–5pm; Oct–March Tues–Sat 10–5pm and Sun 2–4pm. The museum's displays reflect the archaeology and history of Winchester, where excavations have produced a rich collection of Roman, Anglo-Saxon and medieval material. Among the exhibits are Anglo-Saxon jewellery and metalwork including a reliquary, a late Anglo-Saxon wall painting, Anglo-Saxon and Romanesque sculpture and Roman glass, metalwork and ceramics. The historical collections include reconstructions of a chemist's and a tobacconist's shop formerly in the High Street.

Westgate Museum – High Street, Tel 868166. Open same times as the City Museum. The museum is housed in the city's medieval Westgate, which dates mainly from the 14th century. There is a 16th-century painted ceiling that was originally in Winchester College, and the items on display include weapons and armour and a wonderful collection of ancient weights and measures once used in the city.

Winchester Heritage Centre – Brook Street, Tel 851664. Open March–Oct Tues–Sat 10:30–12:30 and 2–4pm, Sun 2–4pm. Contains varying displays and exhibitions on aspects of the city's history.

There are five military museums in Winchester – four of them on one site. The exception is the **Royal Hampshire Regiment Museum and Memorial Garden** in Southgate Street, Tel 863658. Open Mon–Fri 10–12:30 and 2–4pm. The museum is situated in Serle's House, circa 1732. The approach is through the

Memorial Garden, opened in 1952 to commemorate the members of the Regiment who have fallen in battle. The museum illustrates the history of the the Royal Hampshire Regiment and the Regiments which were combined to form it in 1881 (the 37th and the 67th). The displays include uniforms, medals, weapons, decorations, orders, colours, documents and photographs.

Essentially, the other four museums offer the same range of artefacts. They are all situated at **Peninsula Barracks**, Romsey Road (just behind the Great Hall).

Gurkha Museum – Open Tues–Sat 10–5 Sun 12–5, Tel 842832.

Royal Hussars Museum – Open Mon–Fri 10–4, Sat, Sun 12–4, Tel 863751.

Royal Green Jackets Museum – Open Mon–Sat 10–5 Sun 12–4, Tel 863846.

Light Infantry Museum – Open Mon–Sat 10–5 Sun 12–4, Tel 863846.

THEATRE

Theatre Royal – Jewry Street, Tel 843434. The original Theatre Royal was opened in 1914 and ran as a variety theatre until 1922 when it fell victim to the cinema craze. It saw service as a cinema for over 50 years and was rescued from demolition by the newly formed Winchester Theatre Fund. The theatre is unique in that it is believed to be the country's last surviving cine-variety theatre, in its original state, still in use. The theatre seats 419 and is a venue for touring drama, music, film and one night entertainment with the emphasis on a varied but light programme. Drama productions here recently ranged from *Nightingale*, a new musical, to Joe Orton's *Loot*. Popular films are presented at regular intervals.

Tower Arts Centre – Romsey Road, Tel 867986. A water tower was converted into an arts centre and small scale touring theatre and music of all kinds is presented here. There are also many workshop presentations, often given by the visiting companies themselves.

King Alfred's Arts Centre – Sparkford Road, Tel 868725. The **John Stripe Theatre**. A 300-seat auditorium and an intimate studio theatre play host to a varied touring programme of drama and music.

MUSIC

Winchester Cathedral – Tel 853137, is the venue of organ recitals, choirs and concerts throughout the year. The choir sings evensong during the week at 5:30pm (not Wednesdays or school holidays). Concerts are also held at the **Theatre Royal**, **Chapel of St Cross** and **New Hall Winchester College**. Details from Theatre Royal, Tel 843434.

CINEMA

Winchester Film Society shows films at the John Stripe Theatre, King Alfred's Art Centre, Sparkford Road, Tel 868725. All films are shown on Monday evenings at 8pm. There are usually four films per month and details can be obtained by phoning 864997. Winchester has no commercial cinema. The nearest cinemas are in Southampton.

BOOKSTORES

The two best bookshops in Winchester are **Hatchard's** at 97 High Street, Tel 840379 and **Sherratt and Hughes** at 1/2 King's Walk, Tel 866206. Both are well established chains with a good stock and knowledgeable staff. Local stores worth a visit are **H M Gilbert** at 19 The Square, Tel 852832, and **P and G Wells** at 11 College Street, Tel 852016. For a good selection of children's books you would be well advised to visit the **Children's Shop** at 6A Parchment Street, Tel 866297. Religious books can be found at **Worktown Christian Books** at 49 Upper Brook Street, Tel 863611 and **SPCK** at 24 The Square, Tel 866617. SPCK also have a good secondhand and antiquarian collection. Finally, for book bargains, there's **Omnibus** at 151 High Street, Tel 855882.

ANTIQUARIAN AND SECONDHAND BOOKS

Gilbert's Bookshop – at 19 The Square, Tel 852832, has an excellent selection of secondhand, rare and antiquarian books. **Wells Books and Prints** – Tel 864710, also has a good selection as well as nice local prints. They are at Kingsgate Arch, College Street and are closely related to the good store of P and G Wells which is mentioned above and is just down the road (P and G Wells are booksellers to Winchester College). **Upcroft Books** at 66 St Cross Road, Tel 852679, specializes in architecture and history books and **Jack Spencer** at 50A Stockbridge Road, Tel 866783 has a very large secondhand stock.

T L Craze – 27 Francis Gardens, Tel 864860, has a good general stock but specializes in military and Churchill volumes. **J G Barton** – 84 Old Kennels Lane, Tel 866543, has antiquarian and secondhand British topography, local history, general history, archaeology and related subjects. You need to make an appointment to see these dealers so call ahead.

Three dealers working out of antique stores are: **Children's Corner** – No 10, Antique and Craft Centre, King's Walk, Tel 862277, specializing in secondhand children's books, **Peter Daly** – Tel 866633, back of Ships and Sealing Wax, 20A Jewry Street, antiquarian and collector's books, especially natural history, and **R D and A J Shelly** – **Just Junk**, upstairs at the Antique and Craft Market, King's Walk, Tel 862277, general collection.

ART GALLERIES

Two recommended outlets: **Bell Fine Art** at 67B Parchment Street, Stonemason's Court, Tel 860439, deal in 18th- to 20th-century watercolours and have some excellent examples. They are friendly, helpful and knowledgeable. The same helpful service can be found at **Webb Fine Arts** at 8 Ramsay Road, Tel 842273, although their artistic focus is very different. Webb's deals in Victorian oil paintings and has excellent examples on hand.

ANTIQUE DEALERS

If you walk up High Street, just past the point where it ceases to be a pedestrian precinct you will find Jewry Street on your left. **J W Blanchard** is at No 12, Tel 854547. There is mostly furniture here, some of it very nice indeed. At 20A, **Thompson Antiques** incorporates **Ships and Sealing Wax**, Tel 866633. They have nice furniture and decorative items. **Keith Dyke Antiques**, Tel 851029, is at No 38, again some nice furniture. **Samuel Spencer's Antique and Decorative Arts Emporium and the Pine Cellars** is close by at No 39, Tel 867014. Here there are decorative items, interior design and of course, lots of pine and country furniture in the basement. On the other side of High Street, almost directly across from Jewry Street, is St Thomas Street, with **Burns and Graham** at No 4, Tel 853779, with furniture, fabrics and decorative items, and just down the street **Gallery Antiques** (mainly furniture), which has just moved from Jerry Street, Tel 842284. In the middle of High Street on the left and right of the pedestrian precinct are **The Square** (left as you look towards Westgate), **Kingswalk** (right) and **Parchment Street** (right). **G E Marsh** is at 32A The Square. He specializes in antique clocks, and very beautiful they are. Tel 844443.

The **Antiques and Crafts Centre** – Tel 862277, is in King's Walk with lots of variety and just up the hill, across the car park behind Marks and Spencer's, **Mary Roofe Antiques**, Tel 840613, is at Stonemason's Court, Parchment Street. There is some beautiful 18th- and 19th-century furniture here and also some lovely boxes and treen. Close by you will find some exquisite antique silver and **James W Potter & Sons**, Tel 840624. Andover Road leads out of the city (fork right past City Road, just past the Theatre Royal). At 2 Andover Road, **Todd and Austin**, Tel 869824, have furniture, porcelain and objets d'art, while nearby, at No. 13, **I S Trudgett**, Tel 854132, focuses on small collectables. If you fork left off City Road you will find Stockbridge Road, where **David Scott**, with a general collection, can be found at No 38, Tel 842880. If you fork left at the top of the High Street you will find yourself on Romsey Road where **W J Service** can be found at No 4, Tel 840714. **Phillips the Auctioneer** is at the Red House, 44 Hyde Street, Tel 862515 (off North Walls and parallel to Andover Road). They have regular, general and specialist antique sales. Finally, east of High Street at 2/3 Bridge Street is **Printed Page**, Tel 854072, with antique maps and prints.

RESTAURANTS

MiSo – 3 Jewry Street, Tel 861234. Open all week Noon–2:30 and 6–11pm. The restaurant offers some of the best Chinese food outside of London or Manchester. The Peking duck and sizzling beef are as good as you would imagine they should be, while there are interesting menu innovations such as venison with celery and deep-fried quail. I have always been very fond of Singapore noodles and here they are as good as anywhere I can remember.

Mr Pitkin's – 4 Jewry Street, Tel 869630. Open all week 11:30–2:30 and 6–11pm. Conveniently located close to MiSo's, the restaurant has bare wooden floors, poster-framed wine labels and an abundance of greenery. There's a very good brunch with kedgeree no less and, for both lunch and dinner, a good vegetarian selection.

Brann's – 9 Great Minster Street, Tel 864004. Open Mon–Sat 12–2:30 and 7–10:30pm. Opposite the museum and essentially part of the cathedral square is this pleasant eatery with a wine bar on the ground floor and a restaurant above: you can have an inexpensive meal in the wine bar, or a gourmet one in the restaurant, with the food coming from the same kitchen. The cuisine is "nouvelle anglaise" with excellent vegetarian selections, as befits a restaurant listed in *The Good Vegetarian Food Guide*. Only fresh local ingredients are used and dining here is a real pleasure.

Pizza Express at 1 Bridge Street, Tel 841845 and **Pizza Piazza** in Jewry Street, Tel 840037, are outlets of the two best pizza chains in the UK.

PUBS

Wykeham Arms – 75 Kingsgate Street, Tel 853834. A very well run and characterful pub hidden in the narrow cobbled streets near the cathedral. Stilton and quince pâté, and salmon fillet in filo pastry with ginger hollandaise are not your normal pub fare, although traditional dishes such as cottage pie and bangers and mash are given their rightful place. Highly recommended.

Royal Oak – Royal Oak Passage (off pedestrian part of High Street) Tel 861136. Cheerful town pub with well-kept real ale. Good traditional bar food including interesting range of open sandwiches. An excellent feature is the no-smoking cellar bar, with massive 12th-century beams and a Saxon wall that give it some claim to be the country's oldest drinking spot.

The Eclipse – 25 The Square, Tel 805676. Situated on a quiet corner just outside the Cathedral Close, this timbered building was built in the 14th century and was for some time the rectory of St Lawrence's Church. It became an inn sometime in the mid-18th century. One school of thought has the name coming from the Duke of Northumberland's celebrated racehorse, Eclipse, who was born during a total eclipse of the sun in 1763 and was never defeated. Just as authoritatively, other sources claim that there was a nearby rival inn called the Sun, hence the opposition name, the Eclipse. Either way there's a wide range of good value home-made food including good stuffed potatoes, game pie and fish (lunchtime snacks only). It was from an upper window of the pub that Lady Lisle was, in 1685, led to the scaffold on which she was beheaded after being wrongly condemned for complicity in the Duke of Monmouth's rebellion. Her ghost is said to haunt the top bedroom. Luckily perhaps, the inn does not rent rooms!

Rising Sun – 14 Bridge Street (continuation of the bottom of High Street past the statue and over the bridge) Tel 865691. Timber-framed Tudor pub with friendly split-level low-beamed bar; generous helpings of good home-cooked food. The cellar was once a prison and the pub has lots of atmosphere.

ARTISTIC ASSOCIATIONS

Izaak Walton, the biographer and great angler, lived in the city during his last years at 7 The Close. (His son-in-law was a Prebendary of the Cathedral.) He is buried in Prior Silkslede's Chapel in the cathedral's south transept. At the end of the 19th century the fishermen of England added the figure of Izaak Walton to the Great Screen at the east end and in 1914 the fisherman of England and America gave the memorial window in the chapel above his tomb.

Jane Austen died here in Winchester in 1817 at the house of her sister, Cassandra. She is buried in the north aisle of the nave where an inscribed brass tablet and a memorial window commemorate her passing. The text of her memorial, while lauding her personal virtues, makes no mention of her literary accomplishments. Three days before her death she wrote a light-hearted poem for St Swithin's Day (see Ephemera) which is published in a booklet available in the cathedral.

In 1819 Keats stayed with a friend in the city. He wrote "Ode to Autumn" here and also revised "The Eve of St Agnes." He described the walk he took daily across the front of the cathedral, left under a stone doorway, through two college-like squares, through one of the old city gates into College Street – Keatsian disciples can take the same walk today.

In 1808 thee was a scandal concerning the abuse of the mastership of the Hospital of St Cross (see above). It is believed that Trollope based his novel *The Warden* on these events.

The Cathedral Library has the oldest book room in Europe. Besides the exquisite copy of the Winchester Bible, circa 1150, one can also see a copy of Sir Walter Raleigh's speech from the scaffold in 1618 and a copy of the first edition of Gilbert White's *Natural History and Antiquities of Selbourne.*

The playwright Thomas Otway, the novelist Anthony Trollope and the poet Matthew Arnold were all pupils at Winchester College.

In Hardy's novel *Tess of the d'Urbervilles,* Tess is hanged in the city gaol. Winchester is the "Wintoncester" of the novel.

EPHEMERA

St Swithin was the Bishop of Winchester in the 9th century. One of the many miracles he is said to have performed concerns a market woman who dropped her basket of eggs near the church after bumping into a monk. Swithin happened to be passing by and was so moved by the poor woman's distress that he made the eggs whole again. On the altar screen of the cathedral the saint is shown with a pile of eggs at his feet and each of the four candlesticks in his shrine has a broken eggshell at its base. When Swithin died in 862 he was buried outside the church of that time in accordance with his wish to lie where the rain would fall on him. Nearly a century later, the monks decided to move his tomb to a worthier resting place inside the church. Legend has it that St Swithin's spirit, angered by the removal of his remains, made it rain so violently for 40 days that the monks gave up the plan. Ever since then, rain on St Swithin's day (July 15th) has been a sign of continuing bad weather.

Scholars have cast doubt on the authenticity of King Arthur's Round Table which hangs in the Great Hall – doubt with respect to it ever having been sat at by the great man himself. Similar aspersions have not stopped many other places in Britain from having a positive pre-occupation with Arthur and his Knights of the Round Table for legends about King Arthur abound in Great Britain. This is due to the fact that the King is essentially half legend with no real agreed record of his life. He is thought to have been born in Tintagel in Cornwall but his supposed castle there post-dates his life by more than 500 years. The best site we have for Arthur's fortress of Camelot is Cadbury Castle near Yeovil, but there are again, other claimants. According to Sir Thomas Malory in his *Morte d'Arthur,* the King was mortally wounded in the Battle of Camlam by his nephew, Modred. Arthur was then taken by knights to Glastonbury – the Vale of Avalon – where he was carried away over the waters by black hooded ladies in a barge. His death is not recorded by Malory but there are some wonderful words in the book which, roughly translated, say:

> Now more of the death of Arthur I could not find but that those ladies brought him to his grave. Yet some men say, in many parts of England, that King Arthur is not dead but was, by the will of our Lord Jesus, into another place and men say that he shall come again and he shall win the Holy Cross. I would not say that this shall be so but rather I would say here in this world he changed his life. And men say that there is written on his tomb these words – Here lies Arthur, the once and future King.

For centuries the story that Arthur's grave was in Glastonbury Abbey were dismissed as tales concocted by monks to attract more pilgrims to Glastonbury. In the 12th century the bones of a tall man were discovered together with the bones and hair of a woman who may have been Queen Guinevere. Also in the grave, according to the monks of the time, was a lead cross inscribed in Latin with the words, "Here in the Isle of Avalon the famous King Arthur lies buried."

Whatever the truth of the story, Glastonbury (25 miles/40 km south of Bristol) does have a sense of mystery about it. Joseph of Arimathea, who placed Christ in his own tomb, is said to have established a church here and hidden the Holy Grail, used in the Last Supper, in the spring which feeds the Chalice Well. Through the centuries the well was renowned for its healing qualities. Joseph, too, is said to have thrust his staff into the ground where it took root and grew into a Holy Thorn tree which blossoms only at Christmas. Cuttings from the tree still flourish in the area and the one in the churchyard of Glastonbury's parish church does bloom at Christmas. The original Holy Thorn bloomed on Weary-All Hill, near the Tor. It was cut down in Cromwell's time as the Lord Protector thought it to be an idolatrous image. Local legend has it that the Roundhead soldier who hacked down the tree also accidentally cut off his own leg. An even more persistent legend is that Christ himself visited Glastonbury as a boy, perhaps explaining why Joseph brought the Holy Grail here. Whatever the truth of the legends, Glastonbury still retains its aura of mystery from centuries of worship and is well worth a visit.

In the early part of the 20th century Winchester Cathedral was saved by the efforts of one man. The Norman foundations consisted of logs laid on bogland and by 1900 the cathedral was sinking. William Walker, an underwater diver, worked for five years under the foundations in black water (underwater lights were useless) removing the peat and decayed timber handful by handful so that the structure could be underpinned with concrete.

Finally, a totally irreverent but completely true story. During a college rag week in the sixties, students from King Alfred's College painted a series of footsteps leading from the plinth of King Alfred's statue across the road and back again. This would not have been so bad if the footsteps had not led into and then out of a strategically placed gents' toilet.

TOURIST INFORMATION BUREAU: Guildhall, The Broadway, Winchester, Hampshire, S023 9LJ. Tel (0962) 840500/848180

WINDSOR

County of Berkshire
By train, 50 minutes from London (Waterloo), half-hourly service
By road, 20 miles (32 km) by M4

Windsor owes its origins to the Saxon settlement of Windlesora, which stood on the present site of the village of Old Windsor and which was founded in the 7th century. Later in the Saxon period, a royal manor stood at Old Windsor where the Great Councils of England met in the 11th century.

After the Norman Conquest in 1066, William I thought that a steeply rising chalk hill some two miles north of the Saxon village would make an ideal outer defence to London and, around 1170, he crowned the hill with a mound and fortified it with a wooden keep. A century later Henry II replaced the wooden fort with stone defences which later formed the foundation of the Round Tower of Windsor Castle. The elegant landmark of the Round Tower as it is now seen however, is largely attributable to George IV who extended the tower between 1828 and 1832. Indeed the design and character of the Castle owes much to the influence of both George III and George IV. From its earliest beginnings, Windsor Castle has grown to cover some thirteen acres and to become the largest castle in England, if not in the world. Public access to the Castle precincts is normally gained through the Henry VIII Gateway in Castle Hill. This Tudor archway bears Henry's coat of arms and that of his first wife, Catherine of Aragon. Inside the archway is Lower Ward, flanked by the 19th-century guardroom, St George's Chapel and the Grace and Favour Houses of the Garter Knights. Each day in summer and on alternate days in winter, a guard-changing ceremony takes place at approximately 11am – indeed, the castle is still the setting for the reception of visiting heads of state from time to time and in most years there is a commemoration

WINDSOR CASTLE

of the founding by King Edward III of the Most Noble Order of the Garter, all of which involve colourful ceremonies and much pomp and majesty (see Ephemera).

Immediately opposite Henry VIII Gateway in Lower Ward is a gateway leading to Horseshoe Cloister and the famous west door of St George's Chapel. Beyond is Curfew Tower which is open to the public and contains splendid medieval vaulted dungeons with secret passages through its 13-foot-thick (3.9 m) walls. Towards the Round Tower, past St George's Chapel can be seen the entrance to Albert Memorial Chapel, converted by Queen Victoria as a memorial to her husband, who died in 1861. The chapel is open to the public and well worth a visit. To the left of the Round Tower, a gap in the stone wall leads to the North Terrace which commands a spectacular view towards Eton and across the Thames valley. Along this terrace are the entrances to the Royal apartments (which are open when the Royal Family is not in residence), Queen Mary's Doll's House and the Exhibition of Drawings. The state apartments comprise a magnificent suite of rooms housing priceless furniture, carpets, tapestries and works of art. There are painted ceilings, panelled walls, ornately carved wood and valuable ornaments. You can see the Waterloo Chamber with original portraits of monarchs, statesmen and warriors, the Throne Room where investitures still take place and St George's Hall where state banquets are often held. Queen Mary's Doll's House was designed by Sir Edwin Lutyens, whom many consider to be the greatest English architect since Christopher Wren, the designer of St Paul's Cathedral. The Doll's House is a residence in miniature, with every detail reproduced to a precise scale. It was given to Queen Mary as a symbol of national goodwill. The Exhibition of Drawings is a changing collection of drawings from the Queen's extensive collection and includes works by Leonardo da Vinci and Michelangelo.

Leaving the State Apartments, you will arrive in Engine Court. From here you can see the Quadrangle and the State Entrance to the Castle; here the guard changes take place when the Queen is in residence, and here, too, state visitors and those attending state banquets arrive via the Long Walk. St George's Chapel, one of the most beautiful ecclesiastical buildings in England, was started in 1475 by Edward IV and took 50 years to build. It is the chapel of the Most Noble Order of the Garter (see Ephemera) and the Garter Service is held here, most years, in June. The external appearance of the chapel bears a striking resemblance to that of Eton College Chapel (see below), founded by Edward IV's predecessor and rival, Henry VI, except that it is built to a much larger, grander and more splendid scale. Its perpendicular style of Gothic architecture is best appreciated inside the chapel where the fluted columns rise strikingly and fan out to support the vaulted ceilings. Over the West Door, the great West Window is magnificent with kings, saints, popes and ordinary citizens depicted in beautiful colours. Ten monarchs are buried here in the chapel, including Edward IV himself, Henry VIII with his favourite wife, Jane Seymour, Charles I, George V, Queen Mary and George VI. The most moving monument in the chapel is that of Princess Charlotte, only daughter of George IV, who died after the birth of her stillborn son. The stone figure shows her exhausted body beneath a winding sheet.

WALK

The Castle and St George's Chapel are not all there is to see in Windsor. Our **Windsor Walk** starts from the Henry VIII gateway on Castle Hill with parking at the bottom of Thames Street. The imposing statue of Queen Victoria, fashioned in bronze, designed by Sir Edgar Boehm and erected on a marble plinth to commemorate the Queen's Golden Jubilee in 1887 is close by. To the south of this statue stands the **Guildhall**. This beautifully proportioned building with its open arches and elegant columns was designed by Sir Thomas Fitch, surveyor to the Cinque Ports, but completed by Sir Christopher Wren, architect of St Paul's, in 1690. The Tuscan columns in the open ground floor stop short of the ceiling: Wren is said to have included them at the council's insistence, but left a two-inch gap to prove that they were unnecessary. The open ground floor was formerly used as a corn market.

The old town stands to the rear and sides of the Guildhall where an network of cobbled streets gives access to many buildings dating from the 17th century and before. Among the most interesting are the curiously crooked **Market Cross**, the **Old King's Head** which has a plaque recording the warrant for the execution of Charles I in 1648, **Burford House** where Nell Gwyn, orange seller and favourite mistress of Charles II lived and the **Engine House** where the town's fire engine was kept at the beginning of the 19th century. The **Three Tuns**, built in 1518, was the meeting place of the Merchants' Guild, while **Queen Charlotte Street** is recorded in the Guinness Book of Records as the shortest street in Britain. Behind the cobbled streets is St Alban's Street, named after the Duke of St Albans, son of Nell Gwyn. Here, in the Royal Mews, is an exhibition of the "Queen's Presents and Royal Carriages." Some of the presents are priceless while most of the carriages are still used on state occasions. For example, the Scottish State Coach was used at the wedding of the Prince and Princess of Wales and the ivory phaeton is now used by Her Majesty the Queen for her birthday parade of Horseguards each year. My own favourite is the miniature barouche given to the young Prince Edward by Queen Adelaide in 1847. A short distance from St Alban's Street, is Park Street, is the **Long Walk**. This three-mile (4.8 km) avenue, created by Charles II in 1685, runs straight as a die from the quadrangle of Windsor Castle through Windsor Great Park to a statue of King George III on horseback. Locally, the statue is known as the "Copper Horse" and on a clear day it can be seen silhouetted against the skyline from the Castle itself. The avenue is the route of important Royal visitors to the Castle, and the Royal Family travels this way each June to attend the nearby Royal Ascot race meeting.

Coming back along Park Street it becomes High Street and just before you get to the Guildhall you will find the **Parish Church** on your right. By contrast with the richness of St George's Chapel, the Parish Church of St John, founded in 1168 but rebuilt in the early 19th century, is plain and functional. Inside, the church is high-roofed and dark. The sculptured angels with musical instruments beneath the vaulting of the apse are delightful, while on the south side of the chancel is a royal pew carved by the great sculptor and wood carver, Grinling Gibbons, at the end of the 17th century. There are strong links between town church and royalty. The bells of St John's ring out on Royal occasions – at the Sovereign's expense! – and the church's proudest treasure, a painting by the 17th-century artist Franz de Cleyn, was given to the church by George III.

Continue back into the town down High Street, which becomes Thames Street. Just before you get to Victoria's statue there is a turning on the left which leads to the Windsor and Eton railway station, home of the **Royalty and Empire Exhibition** (see Museums). Also on Thames Street you can check your watch by a clock which is set into the pavement. Continue down Thames Street back to the car park at the bottom of the hill.

Three miles (4.8 km) southeast of Windsor is Runnymede, famous as the place where King John sealed the Magna Carta in 1215. The charter established the principle of constitutional monarchy and affirmed the individual's right of justice and liberty. The site of the sealing is marked on the wooded hillside by a memorial erected by the American Bar Association. Nearby is an acre of ground given to the USA by her Majesty the Queen in 1957: here stands a memorial to the memory of President John F Kennedy, while high on a nearby hill is the third Runnymede Memorial, this one erected as a tribute to the men and women of the Air Forces of the British Commonwealth and North West Europe who lost their lives in the Second World War. There are 20,455 names recorded on stone panels around a courtyard which offers breathtaking views across the Thames Valley.

A short stroll over the bridge across the Thames from central Windsor brings you to Eton, home of one of the most famous schools in the world. Founded in 1440 by Henry VI whose statue stands in the School Yard, the College can count among its former pupils no fewer than 20 prime ministers. During term time the boys can be seen moving about the school dressed in their traditional uniforms of wing collars, tail coats and pin-striped trousers. The main entrance to the school takes you into School Yard. On one side is Lower School, with classrooms dating from 1443 and still in use, and opposite, the magnificent College Chapel. If you walk straight ahead under Lupton's Tower, then through the cloisters, you will arrive at the venue of the Eton Wall Game, and looking beyond, see the famous playing fields of Eton.

Those not wishing to see Windsor through their own devices can join a walking tour which can be booked in advance from the Tourist Information Bureau in the Railway Station, Tel 852010, or tour the area in a horse-drawn carriage, Tel 865301. A trip by boat to Runnymede and other beautiful Thames villages, such as Bray, Wokham and Marlow, can be undertaken by ringing French's Boats at 851900 or Selter's Boats at 865832.

MUSEUMS AND GALLERIES

Windsor Castle – Areas open to the public include the State Apartments, St George's Chapel, Exhibition of Drawings, Queen Mary's Doll's House and Exhibition of the Queen's Presents and Royal Carriages (Royal Mews). Tel 831118.
State Apartments: Open Jan 3–Mar 9 and Oct 28–Dec 7 Mon–Sat 10:30–3pm. May 4–June 2 and June 29–Oct 26 Mon–Sat 10:30–5, Sun 1:30–5pm. The State Apartments are not open when HM the Queen is in official residence.
Queen Mary's Doll's House, Exhibition of Drawings and Royal Mews: Open Mon 3–March, Oct 27–Dec 21, Dec 27–31 Mon–Sat 10:30–3pm; Mar 31–April Mon–Sat 10:30–5pm; May 4–June 16 and June 18–Oct 25 Mon–Sat 10:30–5pm, Sun 1:30–5pm.
The Castle is always subject to closure, sometimes on short notice. Details of various areas of the Castle are contained within the main text above but I felt I would mention just two of my favourite exhibits. In the State Apartments it is possible to see the very bullet that killed Lord Nelson at the Battle of Trafalgar in 1805 and a chair made from the wood of an elm which stood in the British line at the Battle of Waterloo in 1815.
Royalty and Empire Exhibition – Windsor and Eton Central Station, Tel 857837. Windsor and Eton was a railway station of exceptional grandeur in order to meet the requirements of Queen Victoria, her court and her guests. The buildings, including the Royal Waiting Room, have been restored and refurbished and now house Madame Tussaud's Royalty and Empire Exhibition which recreates the celebrations of Queen Victoria's Diamond Jubilee in June 1897. A full size replica of the Royal Train stands at the platform and Queen Victoria awaits her guests in the Royal Waiting Room. On the covered parade ground in front of the station, 70 Coldstream Guards form an Honour Guard, standing waxily to attention as recorded orders are barked at them. In a 250-seat theatre, the audio-visual presentation *Sixty Glorious Years,* includes speaking representations of the Queen and some of her more illustrious subjects. Included in the Royalty and Empire Exhibition is the Royal Borough Collection formerly housed in the Guildhall. The exhibition, which illustrates the strong connections between Windsor and the Royal Family, is on permanent loan and concerns itself with living conditions in Windsor over the years, local shops, trade and social activities. It is interesting to note that during the early years of Victoria's reign Windsor was notorious for its poverty and slums.
Household Cavalry Museum – Combermere Barracks (on B3022 to Bracknell), Tel 868222.
Berkshire Yeomanry Museum – Territorial Army Centre, Bolton Road, Tel 860600. If the Royalty and Empire Exhibition has filled you with martial zeal, you can visit the museums devoted to the Household Cavalry

and the Berkshire Yeomanry. The Household Cavalry are the most glamorous of course, with displays illustrating the regiment's history back to 1660, together with prints, watercolours, firearms, swords, uniforms and equipment. Much the same at the Berkshire Yeomanry although they only go back to 1795.
Museum of Eton Life – Eton College, High Street, Eton, Tel 863593. The museum looks at the life of the school beginning with its foundation in 1440, and including displays celebrating some of its many famous ex-pupils. Open term time 2–4:30pm; holiday time (except Christmas) 10:30–4:30pm. Closed from Oct 1 to beginning of Easter holidays.

Apart from the Exhibition of Drawings in Windsor Castle, the most interesting public gallery in the area is **Stanley Spencer Art Gallery**, King's Hall, Cookham Village, Cookham, Tel 06285/245800. Sir Stanley Spencer was a fascinating painter who, besides producing many realistic landscapes, attempted to interpret the Bible in terms of everyday life using bold distortion. The gallery contains a permanent collection of the artist's work together with letters, documents and memorabilia. Each summer private and public collections are displayed.
Courage Shire Horse Centre – Cherry Garden Lane, Maidenhead Thicket, Maidenhead, Tel 062882 3917. Maidenhead is just six miles (9.6 km) west of Windsor on the A308. The wonderful shire horses on display here belong to Courage, the brewers, and they can be seen together with a collection of harness and rosettes and trophies won over the years. On two or three days each week it is possible to watch a farrier shoeing the horses.

THEATRE

Theatre Royal – Thames Street, Tel 53888. Legend has it that in the reign of Elizabeth I, strolling players used to set up their stage in the courtyard of an inn in Peascod Street, but the first recorded theatre performance was in 1706 when a Mrs Susan Carol, a widow, very successfully played the heroic role of "Alexander the Greek," in a travelling theatre set up by an actor/manager named Yates. It was a good engagement for Mrs Carol: while at Windsor she met her second husband, who was chief chef to Queen Anne. In the late 18th century, Windsor theatre performances took place in a small barn on the outskirts of the town, but in 1793 a new theatre was built in the High Street. George III, who loved the theatre, invariably attended when in residence at Windsor. Even though the theatre was very small it was only allowed to open for six weeks in the summer when Eton College was closed for holidays. The school authorities evidently feared that a constantly open theatre would threaten the school work of those hard-working scions of the aristocracy, who might never have won the Battle of Waterloo had their playing fields activity been interrupted by such a corruptive and seductive influence as the theatre. The theatre had its management problems, however, and in 1805 it was sold to a dissenting sect who evicted the actors and turned the building into a chapel. The citizens of Windsor were furious and in a short time £6000 was raised to build a new theatre on the site of the present building. Opened in 1815, it continued with fluctuating fortunes until its destruction by fire in 1908. It was rebuilt yet again and has remained a theatre, apart from a brief period in the '30s as a cinema, until the present day. From the '70s onward, constant improvements have turned it into the splendid Regency theatre it is today. It is both a producing theatre and a touring house and has a reputation for excellent light entertainment plays, many of which transfer to the West End. Successful productions which have transferred to London include *Sleuth, Rattle of a Simple Man, The Business of Murder* and *A Friend Indeed.* The theatre also plays host to performances by artists ranging from Paul Tortelier and Yehudi Menuhin and the London City Ballet to Humphrey Littleton and Bruce Forsyth. The traditional pantomime at Christmas has an excellent reputation. Licensed, and snack bars are open for all performances.

MUSIC

The most exciting time musically in Windsor is in the fall (late Sept and early Oct) when the Windsor Festival (Tel 432618) is held. This celebration of music, opera, dance (sometimes), lectures and the spoken word is unique for the remarkable venues in which the events are staged. To hear anything played in St George's Chapel is an experience not to be missed and the same can be said, to a slightly lesser degree, of the other venues which include the Waterloo Chamber, St George's Hall and the Chapter Library of Windsor Castle, the College Chapel and the School and Election Halls of Eton College and the Theatre Royal. Festival guests have included Alfred Brendel, the English Chamber Orchestra, the Philharmonia Orchestra, Janet Baker and the Amadeus Quartet. Recently the festival has expanded to include events in the surrounding towns of Cookham, Staines and Maidenhead. There is also a combined Fringe Festival and

Jazz celebration which is innovative and worthwhile.

Throughout the year the **Windsor Arts Centre**, St Leonard's Road, Tel 859336, sponsors a classical music series, which has included artists of the calibre of Philip Smith and the Sterling String Quartet. The Arts Centre also schedules other programmes throughout the year. Tel 859336.

CINEMA

There is no commercial cinema in Windsor. The nearest is three miles (4.8) away in Slough – the **Maybox Movie Centre**, 45 Queensmere Shopping Centre, Tel 0753 692244.

BOOKSTORES

The best is **Hammick's**, Tel 856456 at Unit 30, King Edward Court Shopping Centre (it's on Arthur Road and can be reached from Peascod Street or Station Approach). Good selection, wide choice and knowledgeable help. Personally though, I like **Eton Bridge Bookshop** at 77B High Street, Eton (just by the bridge). It's open seven days a week and it's smaller, friendlier and proudly independent. The **Resource Centre** on Dorset Road, Tel 830739, sells Christian books, cards and crafts and there's a branch of **W H Smith** at 6 Thames Street, Tel 869678. If you are in Eton College there is **Alden and Blackwell**, Tel 863849. If you buy books here you can casually say you picked it up while you were at Eton, which might do you some good in some company.

ANTIQUARIAN AND SECONDHAND BOOKS

Although Eton High Street is the antiques centre of Windsor, there is room for a couple of secondhand bookshops. **Eton Antique Bookshop** at No 88, Tel 855534, has not only a good secondhand collection but some excellent antiquarian books and prints. They also have a nice collection of framed antique maps. Just down the road at No 68 is the **Red Pale**, Tel 852610, which has a good general secondhand collection.

ART GALLERIES

Quite a few Windsor art galleries cluster between the antique shops on Eton High Street. At No 27 High Street is the **J Manley and Thames Gallery**, Tel 865647. They specialize in Victorian watercolours although they also have prints from the 17th century to the present day. A nice shop. Just down from them is **Greco Fine Art** at No 44, Tel 830746, who have modern and traditional paintings and prints while the **Eton Art Gallery** at No 58, Tel 860523, has an excellent collection of modern paintings. Close by too is **Maxwell's**, Tel 858680, at 3 Eton Court. They deal in both original prints and watercolours and they range from the traditional through to the modern. Back over the river in Windsor, **Jaspers Fine Art** at 67 Victoria Street, Tel 854925, has both traditional and modern paintings and prints while **Omell Galleries** at 134 Peascod Street specializes in contemporary art, Tel 852271. Finally, **Raynard Fine Arts** at 14 Park Street, Tel 831644, deals mainly in traditional prints.

ANTIQUE DEALERS

The last time I was in Eton I counted 13 antique dealers in Eton High Street alone. There are about the same number dotted about the town, and since I don't have the space to deal with all these in any specific detail, the following is a list of dealers clustered in Eton High Street, starting at one end and going to the other. It's so much nicer to browse and make up your own mind, rather than accept another's analysis. And everything is so conveniently adjacent.

4	High Street Eton	**A and C Antiques**	Tel 863016
17	High Street Eton	**Antiquus**	Tel 831039
40	High Street Eton	**Peter J Martin**	Tel 864901
41	High Street Eton	**Ulla Stafford**	Tel 859625
50	High Street Eton	**Eaton's of Eton**	Tel 860337
59	High Street Eton	**Times Past Antiques**	Tel 857018
60	High Street Eton	**Eton Cottage Antiques**	Tel 856329
65	High Street Eton	**Karen Morse Ltd**	Tel 857847
69	High Street Eton	**Art and Antiques**	Tel 855727
91	High Street Eton	**Roger Barnett**	Tel 867785
92	High Street Eton	**Mostly Furniture**	Tel 858470

| 101 | High Street Eton | **Studio** | Tel 863333 |
| 116 | High Street Eton | **Eton Galleries** | Tel 865247 |

Back in Windsor, the antique shops are again conveniently close. If I were you I would start in St Leonard's Road, which is a continuation of Peascod Street in the centre of town. At No 59 St Leonard's is **O'Connor Brothers**, Tel 866732. They have quality antique furniture, while next door at No 59A is **Pine Appeal**, Tel 862926, which also has a good antique selection. Finally at No 79 is **County Furniture**, Tel 830154.

Walk back down St Leonard's to Peascod Street, which will bring you into High Street. There at No 51 you will find **Lupin Antiques**, Tel 856244, one of my favourites. Carry on up the High Street past the Guildhall and it becomes Sheet Street. Sheet Street forks to the right to Francis Road and to the left to King's Road. At No 34 Francis Street you will find **Dee's Antiques**, Tel 865627. On King's Road you will see **C W Hoy**, Tel 865555, at No 17, and **Addison Bros**, Tel 863780, at No 25. Finally, back near the castle, check out the shops on Thames Street down by the Theatre Royal (a continuation of High Street). **Compton Gallery**, Tel 380100, is at No 42 Thames Street as is the **Berkshire Antique Co**, Tel 347232 and **Guy Bousfield**, Tel 864575, is at No 58. All worth a visit.

RESTAURANTS

The Windsor area is outstanding in that it has superb restaurants on its doorstep. I must confess that I'm inclined to save up and eat at one of these when I am in the area. The prices are high but not astronomical if you take into account the exceptional cooking. If you care about food, pamper yourself. First, let me deal with the town itself. If I'm going to the theatre or have an evening engagement I eat at one of three places:

Dome – 5 Thames Street (near the Theatre Royal), Tel 864405, is a lively café-bar-restaurant. A real French café atmosphere with good croissants and pain au chocolat. Try the Brie amandine with a salad – very good. Good sweets and fine coffee. Open 9am–11pm all week.

A similar kind of atmosphere but from the other side of the Alps can be found in **Angelo's Wine Bar**, 5 St Leonard Road (a continuation of Peascod Street). Angelo's is a simple Italian restaurant with honest cooking. The homemade minestrone is excellent as is the escalope Neopolitan – or try the spaghetti which is as good as you would expect. Open Mon–Sat 12–2:30 and 5:30–11pm.

But perhaps the best of the three is the **Eton Wine Bar**, 82-83 High Street Eton, Tel 854921. Generally there are half a dozen daily items on each course. I had baked, smoked salmon, which was excellent, and my companion raved about the scallop risotto. Very good and reasonable wine list.

And there are more treats ... Bray is five miles (8 km) west of Windsor on the A308 Maidenhead Road. Stonor is a couple of miles north of Henley-on-Thames via the A308 and A423, and Shinfield is just south of the M4 west at junction 11. At Bray you will find the **Waterside Inn** on Ferry Road, Tel 0628691. You know what to expect once you get over the surprise of the valet parking. The restaurant is right on the river, the ambience is unalloyed luxury, the food often brilliant. I confess to only eating there once, but it was an experience to cherish. The kitchen is masterminded by the brothers Roux, the most famous name in cuisine in England. You do not expect to come away from the Waterside with anything but a large hole in your savings but it is worth every penny. Open all week (except Sunday) 12–1:45 and 7–9:30pm.

If the Waterside is too rich for your blood then try the **Stonor Arms** at Stonor, Tel 049163 345. Here you can eat sophisticated bar food in the conservatory (fish soup, cold Cornish lobster or ratatouille) or you can dine regally on excellent beef and local game. Wonderful desserts. Excellent presentation, fresh ingredients and fine cooking.

Finally, Shinfield and **L'Ortolan** at the Old Vicarage Church Lane, Tel 0734 883783. For cooking I believe this to be one of the top half dozen restaurants in the country. Lobster, guinea fowl, pheasant and rabbit are all cooked with an imaginative sophistication. Haute cuisine at its best with a very French wine list and superb service. It is not inexpensive – but consider it an investment.

PUBS

Two first-class recommendations in the centre of town:

Horse and Groom – on Castle Hill opposite Henry VIII Gate, Tel 866264, is a small pub dating from 1520, with a nice uncrowded atmosphere, good inexpensive food and relaxed and friendly service.

Royal Oak – Tel 865179, is opposite the station near the Castle. It's very friendly and has a sister pub, the Greyhound, in Chalfont, St Peter, which is also good if you are ever that way. The bar food is excellent.

Cookham is just north of Maidenhead via the A308 and the B447. **Bel and the Dragon**, Tel 06285 21263, is one of the oldest pubs in England and you would expect the oak panelling and settles, pewter tankards and heavy Tudor beams that you find. The pub is opposite the Stanley Spencer Gallery and the bar food is good if not inexpensive. Just down the road at Cookham Rise is the **Swan Uppers**, Tel 06285 21324, an old pub with the black beams, flagstoned floor and log fires. The pub takes its name from the famous ceremony of "Swan Upping" which takes place in the third week of July with the Royal Swankeeper catching all the new cygnets and deciding ownership. Good bar food (no swan).

ARTISTIC ASSOCIATIONS

Geoffrey Chaucer, the poet and author of *The Canterbury Tales,* was Clerk of the Royal Works during the reign of Richard II. He is thought to have lived in the Winchester Tower of Windsor Castle around 1390.

The Scottish King James I, who was an accomplished poet, was captured as a youth by the English and spent the later years of his exile imprisoned in Windsor Castle by Henry V, a few years his senior. While at the castle he courted Jane Beaufort, daughter of the Earl of Somerset – I deduce that the terms of his imprisonment were not too harsh – and he married her in 1424 after his release. His poem, "The King's Quair," is truly beautiful and is about their courtship. Beautiful though it is, it was not published until 1783. In 1786 Fanny Burney, the novelist and diarist, obtained the post of Second Keeper of the Robes to George II's Queen, Charlotte, probably because she was a friend of the King. She writes of this time and of her failing health in her *Diary of Letters,* published after her death in 1846. As a portrayer of the domestic scene she was a forerunner of Jane Austen, whom she influenced, and her best novel, *Evelina,* is still a good read today.

A tradition peculiar to Eton College was that the most distinguished pupils should present portraits of themselves on leaving the school. This resulted in a most impressive series of paintings by the leading artists of the late 18th and early 19th centuries, including Sir Joshua Reynolds, George Romney, Thomas Gainsborough, Benjamin West and Sir William Beechey. The idea of the "leaving" portrait was first mooted by Dr Barnard who was headmaster in 1764 and the tradition remained current until 1868.

EPHEMERA

The Most Noble Order of the Garter, founded by King Edward III in 1348, is the highest British civil and military honour obtainable. The earliest records of the order were destroyed by fire, so it is not possible to reconstruct its original purposes. One theory is that Edward wished to revive the Round Table of Arthurian legend and that the garter symbolized the homage paid by knights to ladies. The most picturesque and abiding legend is that the order was formed to comemmorate an incident when Edward was dancing with Joan of Kent, Countess of Salisbury (later the wife of the Black Prince, one of the original Knights of the Order). One of her blue garters fell to the floor, and as bystanders snickered, Edward gallantly picked it up and put it on his own leg, admonishing his courtiers in French with the phrase, "Honi soit qui mal y pense," popularly translated as "Evil to him who evil thinks." He promptly made the order the most prestigious in the land and his original admonition has remained the order's motto. Historians cast doubt on this story (as historians are wont to do) but it remains very much the stuff of legend. The original medieval membership of the order was 12 companions (as if at a tournament) but that number has been increased to 25. As St George is patron saint of the order, there is a celebration in St George's Chapel on April 23, St George's Day, each year. Each knight has a stall assigned to him in the chapel and placed on it are his banner, helmet and a stall plate bearing his coat of arms. On the death of a knight, all insignia are returned and the banner and helmet taken down, but the stall plate remains, providing one of the most comprehensive examples known of the history of heraldic design. Although the greatest in the land have received the knighthood and the right to add "KG" (Knight of the Garter) after their names, 36 knights have been beheaded (Henry VIII being responsible for six). During the Second World War, Emperor Hirohito of Japan and King Victor Emmanuel III of Italy were removed from the order. In 1945 after an election defeat, Sir Winston Churchill refused the honour saying privately, "I can hardly accept the Order of the Garter from the king after the people have given me the Order of the Boot." Churchill relented however and was inducted into the order in 1953.

No one among her subjects enjoyed going to the theatre more than Queen Victoria. It was one of her greatest pleasures, and she was one of its greatest patrons. From the age of 12 to 42 she was not only an enthusiastic devotee of ballet, opera, circus and drama, sometimes going as often as three times a week, but was also an ardent supporter of the Windsor theatricals – plays performed by her family and staff. It is a mark of her abiding sorrow that after Prince Albert's death she denied herself one of her greatest enjoyments, and for the last 40 years of her life, over half of her reign, never entered a theatre again. Happily, however, the theatre was to come to her. In the 1880s the marriage of her youngest child, Princess Beatrice, to Prince Henry of Battenburg helped revive family theatricals, and celebrities such as Henry Irving and Ellen Terry acted in her presence at Windsor, Sandringham, Balmoral and Osborne. In this respect, at least, it is hoped that the Queen was, more often than not, amused.

In Oxford Road can be found Puffey's Old Bakery, Tel 865545. Dating from 1839, the shop has one of the oldest coal-fired bread ovens still in use in Britain. The building is reputed to be haunted, though I personally have never experienced any doughy apparitions while buying my stone ground loaf.

Chariott's Charity in William Street, off Windsor's main shopping area, Peascod Street, is a Gothic-style almshouse set up in 1863 with a bequest by Joseph Chariott, a successful property developer. The story goes that after his death his savings were loaded on a cart and weighed so much that the bottom of the cart fell out. While I'm on the subject of charity, some of you may not be aware of the phrase "grace and favour houses," used in the introduction to describe the house adjacent to St George's Chapel. A grace and favour residence is a house or apartment belonging to the Crown and bestowed on a notable person or faithful retainer as free accommodation. I often regret that I am neither notable or faithful servant enough to receive a perk of this kind.

Tradition has it that it was the Duke of Wellington who said, "The Battle of Waterloo was won on the playing fields of Eton." It is unlikely that he ever said any such thing. He had little time for the "public school spirit" and even less for Eton College itself – the school from which his parents removed him since his lack of academic ability did not justify the expenditure of money, considered better spent on his brothers, Gerald and Henry, who were brighter pupils. The Duke once made a point of refusing to give so much as a sixpence to a collection being made to raise funds to make improvements at the school. Like all good apocrypha, Wellington's quote did not make its appearance until the good Duke had gone to that great battlefield in the sky and was unable to refute the attribution.

The remark was first seen in 1855 in a book entitled "L'Avenir Politique de L'Angleterre" (Concerning the Political Future of England) by Count Charles de Montalembert, and takes the form of "It is here that the Battle of Waterloo was won" – written as if the words had been spoken by Wellington as he stood reminiscing on those hallowed acres. It is this that destroys any credibility in the assertion. When Wellington was at the school there were no playing fields – indeed, there were no organized games at all. Moreover, he only revisited the place once, in 1841, and never left the shelter of the buildings in the short duration of his stay. The whole thing originated in Montalembert's mind as the kind of thing that a Frenchman would imagine an Englishman saying about his alma mater.

It is hardly surprising that the ghosts within Windsor Castle, whose mighty bastions have protected monarchs from the time of the Norman Conquest, are wholly royal. The quick determined footsteps that hurry through the library are said to be those of Elizabeth I. By contrast, the steps in the cloisters are slow and halting - these are the echoes of Henry VIII, dragging his ulcerated leg through eternity. One visible manifestation is that of poor, demented George III, who in his periodic bouts of madness used to be shut into a room overlooking the parade ground. From there he would watch his soldiers drilling, and several modern subalterns have been startled to see his face at the same window, called there, apparently, by the sound of marching and drilling men.

For a pleasant evening out there are two theatres in easy distance of Windsor offering dinner and a show in a delightful setting. **The Mill at Sonning** is a beautifully converted 18th-century flour mill providing middle-of-the-road theatre in a wonderful riverside location. Sonning is one mile (1.6 km) north of the end of the M329 which is the road leading into Reading off junction 10 of the M4. After a cocktail by the river, have dinner in the elegant restaurant and then watch the show. Tel 0734 69800. A little further afield is the **Watermill Theatre, Mill House**, Bagnor, Newbury (go west on the M4 to exit 13 south). Again, this is a theatre by the river with drinks on the lawn, a play and dinner. Tel 0635 46044. In both these venues, the plays themselves may not be challenging but the setting and the food make for a memorable evening.

TOURIST INFORMATION BUREAU: Central Station, Thames Street, Windsor, Berkshire SL4 1PJ. Tel 0753 852010

3
LONDON

Because of its size, London demands a different treatment from that of any other city in this book. Whole volumes have been written on the subject of London's history alone, and to attempt to abridge that history into the few pages available seems pointless. (A number of informative, accessible volumes are noted in the bibliography.)

A complete walk around London would take about three weeks, assuming an eight-hour walking day, and I'm not sure that many visitors have that kind of time available to them, let alone that kind of stamina. Consequently I have divided London into nine areas. Within each area I have described the major points of interest and how to reach them. The recommended restaurants and pubs relate to the areas described. The areas themselves start with Westminster and more or less move eastwards as far as Greenwich. Depending on how much time you spend visiting museums and churches, etc, each area be can easily covered in a day, but if you wish you can take less time on the visits and complete each walk in half a day – about four hours. I should add that this timing does not include getting to the point of departure. I have assumed that you will not be driving in London – no one should unless it cannot be avoided – and consequently each walk begins from a convenient underground station or, in the case of Greenwich, a dock.

You will find that the theatre, music and cinema sections contain less description than those for other towns, but are as comprehensive as possible. There are hundreds of antique shops in London, so I have included details of just the antique markets which, if you have limited time, are the most sensible places to visit. Finally, artistic associations are included with the walks; so many artists have London connections that it would be impossible to do justice to them all.

WESTMINSTER WALK

Begin at **Westminster Underground Station**. Exit at the Bridge Street exit, emerge directly under **Big Ben**. **Westminster Bridge** spans the Thames. The view inspired Wordsworth to write his famous sonnet in 1802, but the bridge is a different one today, as is the view. The **Houses of Parliament** and **Westminster Hall** are on your left as you move into Parliament Square, correctly, the Palace of Westminster, with the legislative chambers of the **Commons** and the **Lords**. Note the statues of great men in the square, from Richard the Lionheart to Winston Churchill (why are there no women?). **St Margaret's Westminster** and **Westminster Abbey** should both be visited. The first, a medieval church renowned for its society weddings; the Abbey, scene of innumerable state occasions. Since King Harold, all British monarchs have been crowned here, and from the second half of the 13th century to the reign of George III it was used for royal burials too. Note **Poets' Corner**, the **Grave of the Unknown Soldier**, **Queen Elizabeth's Tomb** and outside, **Dean's Yard** and **Dean's Court**. Nearby, note **Old Palace Yard** where Guy Fawkes and Walter Raleigh were executed and in **Victoria Tower Gardens** see the statue of the suffragist Emmeline Pankhurst and Rodin's *Burghers of Calais*. Walk down **Millbank**. Ahead is the **Tate Gallery**, but turn up Dean Stanley Street to Smith Square. Note **St John's**, now a concert hall, and the handsome 18th-century building housing the headquarters of the Conservative Party and the Transport and General Workers' Union. Leave Smith Square. Walk, via Lord North Street, left into Cowley Street and right into Barton Street (Lawrence of Arabia lived at No 14) back to the Abbey. Walk down Victoria Street (Victoria Station is at the bottom). At first left, detour into Strutton Ground, where at the Grafton Pub, early Goon Shows were planned. Back on Victoria Street, cross to **Broadway** where in a park on the left, Colonel Blood, who attempted to steal the Crown Jewels in 1671, is buried. Further up Broadway is **New Scotland Yard** while the headquarters of **London Transit** nearby has Jacob Epstein and Henry Moore statues on the façade. Go up Dartmouth Street, left into Queen Anne's Gate and into **Birdcage Walk** (once James I's aviary). Turn left for the **Guards Museum and Chapel** and cross into **St James's Park**, a haven for wild fowl. To your left is **Buckingham Palace**. Cross the bridge and turn right into **Horse Guards Parade** for the **Cabinet War Rooms**. Climb the steps by the War Rooms, past the statue of Clive of India and go through King Charles Street – the **Foreign Office** is on your left and the **Cabinet Office** is on your right. Enter into **Parliament Street**; Whitehall is to your left with **Trafalgar Square** at the end. The **Cenotaph**, commemorating the dead of recent wars, is on your left as is **Downing Street**, the London home of the prime ministers of Great Britain. Turn right down Parliament Street and back to Westminster Underground Station.

ST JAMES WALK

Begin at **Green Park Underground Station**. Leave by Park exit. Ahead is the **Ritz** – why not try afternoon tea there? (But brace yourself for the bill!) Luckily, you turn right down Queen's Walk before you get to the hotel. Queen's Walk ends at the Mall. The great processional way starts with **Buckingham Palace** and the **Victoria Memorial** at one end and runs to **Admiralty Arch** and **Trafalgar Square** at the other. Turn left and then left again into Stable Yard. Go ahead and turn right along Cleveland Row for **St James's Palace**. Foreign ambassadors are still accredited to the Court of St James's but George III abandoned it as a residence in favour of Buckingham Palace. Here, Mary Tudor died, James I watched Ben Jonson's masques and Charles I spent his last night before execution. Close by is **Clarence House**, the home of the Queen Mother, and **Marlborough House**, built by Wren, with the lovely Queen's Chapel on its grounds. Cross Pall Mall into St James' Street (very elegant shops and restaurants) and turn right along King Street. Christie's, the international auction house, is on the right. Continue to St James's Square. During the siege of the Libyan Embassy in 1984, WPC Yvonne Fletcher was shot here and there is a small flower-decked memorial. Nancy Astor, the first woman MP, lived at No 4 and three prime ministers, William Pitt, Lord Derby and Gladstone, lived at No 10. Walk out of the square, cross Pall Mall and walk down Carlton Gardens. By Lord Carlton's statue turn left along Carlton House Terrace. Waterloo Place, at the end, is dominated by the Duke of York's statue on a tall column. Perched there to avoid his creditors, some say. Close by is the **Athenaeum Club**, packed with the privileged. Statues in Waterloo Place commemorate Edward VII and Captain Scott. Continue up Lower Regent Street and by the Plaza cinema turn into Jermyn Street. Very exclusive shops here. Ahead is **St James's Church**, a beautiful Wren creation. Many famous 18th-century figures are buried here, there are excellent Grimling Gibbons carvings, and lunchtime concerts. The churchyard, a garden of remembrance, is a popular place for lunch. Between the church and Fortnum and Mason's (they serve you in frock coats) turn right through Prince's Arcade, then turn left across Piccadilly and go right through Burlington Arcade, where you will see

Apsley House, the London home of the Duke of Wellington; Burlington House, now the Royal Academy Art Gallery; and the Albany bachelor chambers, built in 1802, into which no child, dog or journalist is allowed to enter. Burlington Arcade has elegant shops and rules against whistling, singing or hurrying, which are still enforced by top-hatted beadles. To the right at the end of the Arcade is the **Museum of Mankind**. Turn left along Burlington Gardens to **Old Bond Street** – beautiful people, beautiful shoes and expensive art galleries. Go left and then right through Stafford Street. You'll cross Albermarle Street, with more galleries, but go ahead to Dove Street. Turn right, then left down Hay Hill and right into Berkeley Square. **Annabel's Club**, very trendy, is at No 44; Clive of India committed suicide at No 45; and Prime Minister George Canning lived at No 50, which for years was haunted by a "thing" in the attic. Leave the Square by Fitzmaurice Place and go along Curzon Street with the fine **Curzon Cinema**. Opposite **Trumpers**, hairdresser to royalty, turn left into **Shepherd's Market**. This is London's nearest approximation to the Left Bank in Paris, with pretty restaurants and charming pubs. Note **Tiddy Dols**, a restaurant named after an 18th-century gingerbread seller of the area who also had a pitch at Tyburn where public executions were held – nice antiques here too. Go down White Horse Street to Piccadilly and turn left back to the station.

COVENT GARDEN WALK

Start at **Embankment Underground Station**. Walk along Villiers Street and turn right, down the steps, to **Watergate Walk** which was once at the edge of the Thames. At the end go up the steps, turn left into York Buildings and right into John Adam Street. Adam was one of the architects who built the Adelphi. Thomas Rowlands, the 18th-century cartoonist and satirist, lived nearby. The 1774 building of the **Royal Society of Arts** is on the left. Turn right into Adam Street. Sir Richard Arkwright, of cotton-spinning fame, lived at No 8. Go ahead to Adelphi Terrace and down the steps on the left to Savoy Place. The great **Savoy Hotel** is close by. Cross over into **Victoria Embankment Gardens** where there is a statue of Robert Raikes, founder of Sunday Schools in 1780. Cross onto Victoria Embankment and **Cleopatra's Needle**, circa 1500 BC, brought to England in 1878. **Waterloo Bridge** crosses the Thames to the **Royal Festival Hall**, the **National Theatre** and the **National Film Theatre**. Walk back to the Savoy and up into the Strand. Turn right on the Strand to Lancaster Place, the approach to Waterloo Bridge. By the river on your left is **Somerset House**, until 1973 the Register of all births, deaths and marriages, but now the **Courtauld Institute Galleries** with Impressionist, post-Impressionist and Old Masters paintings. Return along Lancaster Place, cross the Strand and go ahead to Wellington Street. At Russell Street turn left for the **Theatre Museum** and left into Covent Garden for the **Transport Museum**. Go through the Garden's Central Avenue and leave by King Street. The vegetable market has gone but the Inigo Jones colonnades remain, hosting one of London's most lively retail areas. Left on King Street is an alley leading to **St Paul's Church**, a superb Inigo Jones construction known as "the actors' church" with memorials to such names as Charles Chaplin, Noel Coward and Sybil Thorndike. Go through the church gardens and turn right into Bedford Street, then left into New Road and left again into Bedfordbury. Turn right through Goodwins Court with its 17th-century houses and left into St Martin's Lane, with the **Coliseum**, home of the English National Opera on your left, and the **Duke of York** and **Albery Theatres** on your right. Walk into Trafalgar Square. **St Martin's-in-the-Fields** is on your left and the **National Gallery** occupies the whole of the north side with its controversial contemporary addition. **Nelson's Column** stretches 185 feet (56.2 m) into the air, commemorating Britain's greatest sailor. Cross the square and walk through **Admiralty Arch**. At the end of the Mall is **Buckingham Palace**, London home of the Queen. At the **Guards Memorial** turn left across Horse Guards Parade, scene of the annual Trooping of the Colours ceremony, and walk through Horse Guards Arch into Whitehall. The entrance from Whitehall to Horse Guards Parade is guarded by mounted sentries, changed several times a day. Cross Whitehall to **Banqueting House**. Charles I was executed here on January 30, 1649. Continue down Horseguards Avenue, turn left on Embankment Gardens, pass the refurbished Charing Cross Station and return to Embankment Underground.

BLOOMSBURY WALK

Start at **Russell Square Underground Station**. Turn left along Bernard Street and cross to Russell Square, cross diagonally, turn left down Montague Street and right along Great Russell Street to the **British Museum**. The great museum is surrounded by little streets filled with antique bookshops and antique dealers. It is scheduled to move to new premises in the mid-1990s. Return along Great Russell Street through Bloomsbury Place, left up Southampton Row and right through Cosmo Place to Queen Square. Two pretty pubs, the **Swan** and the **Queen's Larder** are handy, and the Church of **St George the Martyr** is worth a visit. Cross the square into Great Ormond Street and the famous **Hospital for Sick Children** which still receives royalties from J M Barrie's *Peter Pan*. Turn left down Lamb's Conduit. The **Lamb** pub is worth a visit. Turn right along Guildford Street and right again to No 48, **Dickens House**, where the great man lived. Visit Dickens House and return down Doughty Street, cross Guilford Street in Mecklenborough Square with beautiful colonnaded houses and, on the left, follow the footpath between trees and Coram Fields to the **Thomas Coram Foundation**. Thomas Coram, with the help of such luminaries as Hogarth and Handel, established the hospital and orphanage in 1745. You can still see the uniforms the orphans wore and there is now a playground to which no adult is admitted without a child. Now turn right to the corner of Brunswick Square, known to Jane Austen and Virginia Woolf, go right again up Hunter Street, left through Handel Street and turn right. Turn left into Tavistock Place and right into Burton street, then left into Duke's Road and **Woburn Walk**. W B Yeats lived at No 5, and in Upper Woburn Place is **St Pancras Church**, looking like an Athenian temple and worth a visit. Return down Upper Woburn Place to the **Jewish Museum** on the right. Cross Tavistock Square with its cherry tree that commemorates Hiroshima. Note the statue of Gandhi at the copper beech nearby, planted by Pandit Nehru. At the far corner of the square turn right onto Gordon Square for the **Chinese Art Foundation**. Leave the foundation and glance around Gordon Square for the homes of the Bloomsbury Group. The abodes of Virginia and Leonard Woolf and Lytton Strachey are in the square and Clive and Vanessa Bell, E M Forster, David Garnett and John Maynard Keynes lived nearby. Cross into Woburn Square and continue into Thornhaugh Street. A plaque shows where T S Eliot worked as a publisher. Turn left by a green shelter where London cabbies gather for tea and chat (a rarity now) and go left to Russell Square Underground.

HAMPSTEAD WALK

Start at the **Hampstead Underground Station**. Exit from the station into the High Street and turn left up Flask Row; spa water was sold here and there's something stronger in the nearby **Flask Tavern**. **Burgh House** is a 1720s house which is the setting for a museum on Hampstead's history. Past Burgh House, Flask Walk becomes Well Walk. The **Well Tavern** was once a venue for clandestine marriages. Turn right down Christchurch Hill at Willow Road and turn right up Downshire Hill, past the **Freemasons Arms**. Turn left onto Keats Grove for **Keats House**. Visit the house, noting the plum tree in the garden under which Keats wrote "Ode to a Nightingale." Leave the house, continue down Keats Grove to South End Road, turn left up South End Road to East Heath Road. Turn left onto Heathside with splendid houses and bear right round Gainsborough Gardens. Turn right into Well Walk; the artist, John Constable, lived in a house on the left. Go behind the well with its inscription and walk up Well Passage, across Well Road and up Cannon Lane. The actor-manager Sir Gerald du Maurier lived at Cannon Lodge. Continue through Squire's Mount to East Heath Road and turn left. Turn right down a track to the **Vale of Health** where Shelley visited Leigh Hunt. Return and turn right to **Whitestone Pond**, constructed to refresh cart horses after the long uphill haul and where model boats are now sailed. Nearby is **Jack Straw's Castle Pub** and further on, towards Golders Green, the **Old Bull and Bush**. From Whitestone Pond, go down Lower Terrace and right towards Judge's Walk. In **Grove Lodge**, nearby, John Galsworthy wrote his Forsyte Saga. Turn right into Hampstead Grove. George du Maurier, author of *Trilby*, lived in the 18th-century house on the right (look for the plaque). **Fenton House** is a showcase for early keyboard instruments, furniture, porcelain and clocks, etc. Continue to Holly Bush Hill. Turn right and then left uphill to Mount Vernon. Robert Louis Stevenson lived here (blue plaque again). Turn left in Holly Walk and **St Mary's Church**. This Georgian church was founded in 1816 for refugees from the French Revolution. Walk ahead through **Church Row**. H G Wells, Gracie Fields and Oscar Wilde's friend, Lord Alfred Douglas have all lived here. At the top of Church Row, turn left onto Fitzjohn's Avenue and walk ahead to the tube station.

INNS OF COURT WALK

Start from **Holborn Underground Station**. Turn right along High Holborn, then right again into New Turnstile and left into Gate Street. Note the **Ship Inn** on the corner, once used for secret Roman Catholic services. Continue into **Lincoln's Inn Fields**, a spacious park; it has some grisly memories as Anthony Babbington was hanged, drawn and quartered here for plotting to overthrow Queen Elizabeth, and William Lord Russell was beheaded for plotting to assassinate Charles II. Walk down the west side of the square and ahead into Portsmouth Street. On the left is the **Old Curiosity Shop**, immortalized by Charles Dickens. Built in 1567, it claims to be London's oldest shop. Turn right into Portugal Street and left into

Clare Market. Continue into Clement's Inn Passage and down the steps. Follow Clement's Inn and cross the Strand to St Clement Danes. The Inns of Court are enclaves of 17th- and 18th-century houses set around courts and gardens and occupied by barristers and lawyers. In medieval times the "inns" were hostelries for barristers and students. Today the inns are governed by barristers, called "Benchers," who alone have the power to call students to the bar. **St Clement Danes Church** is the central church of the Royal Air Force and you'll probably remember the rhyme, "Oranges and lemons, say the bells of St Clement's." Wren designed the church in 1682 but it was destroyed in 1941 and rebuilt in 1958. Leave the church and cross to **Royal Courts of Justice**. In the middle of the road is **Temple Bar**. The Royal Courts of Justice are often open to the public and you can sit in the gallery and listen to a libel or slander case. Temple Bar, a griffin on a plinth, marks the western limit of the City of London. Retrace your steps and turn down Essex Street on your left. Note the **Edgar Wallace Pub**, named after the famous thriller writer. Continue ahead to the Victoria Embankment. Turn left and left again and go through the arch into Middle Temple Lane. Go through the second archway on the right into Elm Court, then up the steps to the left in Church Court for Temple Church. The **Temple**, in the 12th century, was the headquarters for the Knights Templar, founded to guard the Church of the Holy Sepulchre in Jerusalem. The great legal "societies" of the Middle and Inner Temple now occupy the complex of lanes and ancient buildings. **Temple Church** was built by the Knights Templar; it has a circular nave emulating the mother church in Jerusalem. Leave the church and go through another arch into King's Bench Walk, with beautiful Georgian houses and then right in Crown Office Row. Return through the archway to the embankment. Turn left and continue towards Blackfriars Bridge. Turn left into Temple Avenue, right into Tudor Street and left through Bridewell Place, the site of Henry VIII's **Bridewell Palace**. At New Bridge Street turn left and just before you get to Ludgate Circus turn left again, through Bride Court to **St Bride's Church**. St Bride is perhaps London's loveliest church and one of Wren's sublime creations. Built in 1703, it is called the "wedding cake church" because of its spire. It was badly damaged in 1940, but has been superbly restored. From the church go through St Bride's Avenue and turn left into **Fleet Street**, home of the newspaper industry (though some have moved out of central London). Cross Fleet Street and turn right into the narrow Wine Office Court. Note **Ye Olde Cheshire Cheese Pub**, frequented by Dr Samuel Johnson, whose house is just ahead in Gough Square. In the attic of the house, six clerks toiled to produce Johnson's famous *Dictionary of the English Language,* published in 1755 (it was Johnson who said "When a man is tired of London, he is tired of life"). Leave the house and go through Johnson's Court back to Fleet Street. Turn right and when you get to Chancery Lane turn right again. The **Public Records Office** is on your right with copies of the Doomsday Book and Shakespeare's will. Turn left into Carey Street and then right, through the arch to New Square. Keep right for **Old Hall**, built in 1492, and adjoining it **Lincoln's Inn Chapel**, a beautiful church built by Inigo Jones. Leave the square with the gardens on the left and turn right into Lincoln's Inn Fields. **Sir John Soane's Museum** is at the square's north end with a wonderful collection of artefacts and paintings from an inveterate collector. From Lincoln's Inn Fields turn right into Gate Street and Holborn Tube Station.

ST PAUL'S WALK

Start at **St Paul's Underground Station**. Walk into St Paul's Churchyard. Note the site of St Paul's Cross. Formerly the churchyard was a centre for booksellers and publishers. Visit **St Paul's Cathedral**. Old St Paul's, England's largest and finest Gothic building, was destroyed by fire in 1666 (the Great Fire of London). Wren's new cathedral was built between 1673 and 1708. Leave the churchyard beside the statue of John Wesley. Walk past the statue of Queen Anne and turn left down Dean's Court and right into Carter Lane. In **Wardrobe Place**, on your left, the monarch's clothes were once stored. Turn left down St Andrew's Hill. At the **Cockpit Pub** turn right into Ireland Yard. This is the site of the **Dominican Priory** which gave the Blackfriars area its name. Turn right, up Church Entry to Carter Lane, then right, and left up Creed Lane. Cross Ludgate Hill into **Ave Maria Lane**, then left into **Amen Corner** and round **Amen Court** (the names derive from the prayers of medieval clergy processing around the area). We suspect the wall at the rear of Amen Court might contain a section of the old **Newgate Prison**. Turn left into Warwick Lane, noting Cutler's Hall with fine terracotta reliefs. Turn right into Newgate Street and left onto King Edward Street for the **Postal Museum**. Note the statue of Rowland Hill who introduced the first modern stamp, the "penny black," in 1840. The museum has superb collections of stamps and postal artefacts. Cross the road into **Postman's Park** where there is an arcade of ceramic tablets recording acts of gallantry by ordinary people. Turn left to **St Botolph's Church**, which forms one side of Postman's Park. A wonderfully rich Georgian interior and glowing stained glass make it well worth a visit. Across from St Botolph's, a footbridge leads to the **Museum of London**. Turn right down Aldersgate Street, site of one of the old city gates, and left into Gresham Street, passing the rebuilt church of **St Anne and St Agnes**. Turn left into Noble Street, where the Roman Wall remains can be seen, right into Oat Lane and left through **St Alban's Court**. Cross Wood Street, past the 72-foot (21.8 m) tower of St Alban's Church and along Love Lane to the churchyard of **St Mary Aldermanbury** (the ruins of the bomb-shattered church itself were shipped to Fulton, Missouri, and rebuilt as a memorial to Winston Churchill). Walk down Aldermanbury and turn left into the courtyard of the **Guildhall**. The Guildhall itself has monuments to Pitt, Nelson and Wellington and the arms and banners of the city livery companies are displayed. The adjacent **Church of St Lawrence Jewry** was built in 1136 in the Jewish trading area of the City of London. It was destroyed in the Great Fire of 1660, rebuilt by Wren, destroyed in the Blitz and rebuilt in "the tradition of Wren" in 1967. It is the church of the City Corporation. Continue along Gresham Street, passing Prince's Street in Lothbury. Turn right into Bartholemew Lane for the **Bank of England Museum** with a doorkeeper resplendent in pink frock coat and displays of bank history, currency and a reconstruction of a late 18th-century banking hall. Turn left on Threadneedle Street to the **Bank of England** itself, the **Mansion House** (the official London residence of the Lord Mayor) and just round the corner in Walbrook, the **Church of St Stephen Walbrook**, a superb building rebuilt by Wren after the Great Fire. The dome was said to be a "test run" for St Paul's and the cream-coloured interior and the Henry Moore altar should on no account be missed. This is one of London's forgotten churches (by visitors anyway) and is a magnificent memorial to Sir Christopher Wren. Leave the church and walk to the junction with Threadneedle Street. Turn left on Bucklebury and left again down Queen Victoria Street. Note the remains of the **Roman Temple of Mithras**. Bear right up Watling Street (probably an offshoot of the old Roman road) and note **Ye Old Watley Pub**, said to have been used by Wren as an office. Turn right into Bow Lane, then along Cheapside, which is dominated by **St Mary-le-Bow**, another Wren church. Cheapside is the city's oldest market street and on the corner of Foster Lane is **St Vedast's**, another Wren masterpiece. Walk ahead to St Paul's Tube Station.

THE TOWER WALK

Start from **Tower Hill Underground Station**. Leave by the Fenchurch Street exit and turn right into Trinity Square. Take the first turning right, passing under Cooper's Row. By the fountain, in the square behind, is the most complete section of London's ancient defences yet uncovered. Begun by the Romans and completed in the Middle Ages, the mighty wall reached out from Tower Hill, encircled the city and returned to the river at Ludgate. Go through the gate in the wall, cross a paved area and turn left under the railway bridge. Go through America Square, over Crosswall, noting the **Angel Pub** and up Vine Street. Turn left along India Street and right up Jewry Street to Aldgate. **St Botolph's Aldgate** was built in 1744 but there has been a church on this site since Saxon times. Daniel Defoe, author of *Robinson Crusoe*, was married here, and many plague victims are buried in the churchyard. It's a lovely church and there is a refuge for the homeless in the crypt. Cross into Duke's Place, site of the city's ancient **Aldgate**, and turn left into Mitre Square. Here in 1888 Jack the Ripper slew his fourth victim. Go right up Mitre Street to Creechurch Lane and turn left. **St Katharine Cree Church** is not Indian, but the result of the medieval pronunciation of Christ as "Chreest," hence Cree. St Katharine's is an offshoot of Christchurch Priory, whose foundations lie under the surrounding streets. The superb organ has been played by Purcell, Handel and John Wesley. Turn right up Leadenhall Street, then left down Billiter Street. Fenchurch Avenue on the right, leads towards the remarkable steel and glass towers of the new **Lloyds** building. A public gallery looks down on "The Room" where insurance deals are made. The Lutine Bell, salvaged from a sunken French frigate, is rung once for bad tidings and twice for good news. Lloyds is so called because ship owners and merchants used to gather in Edward Lloyd's Coffee House in the 1680s to arrange marine insurance. Some of the atmosphere of those days can be recaptured by visiting the nearby **Jamaica Wine House** (see below) where insurance was arranged for West Indian shipping. From Lloyds, turn right up Leadenhall Place to Leadenhall Market where the fixings for trendy city lunches are purchased. (They have excellent oysters.) Go through the market into St Peter's Alley for **St Peter's Cornhill Church**. A church has stood here since the Roman occupation. Continue into Cornhill, turn left for **St Michael's Church** – the Stock Exchange's Church – then turn left again down St Michael's Alley to the Jamaica Wine House and the **George and Vulture Pub**, a favourite of Charles Dickens. Carry on through George Yard to the **Church of St Edmund the King**, another beautiful "forgotten" church and

TOWER BRIDGE, LONDON

turn left along Lombard Street with its many banking houses. At the end turn right down Gracechurch Street and cross over Fish Street Hill for the **Monument**, a 202-foot (61.4 m) column marking the outbreak, in nearby Pudding Lane, of the Great Fire of London in 1666. There are 311 steps to the top, but the view is worth it. Turn left and left again up Pudding Lane and then turn right along Eastcheap and Great Tower Street. Cross Tower Place by subway to **All Hallows-by-the-Tower Church**. This ancient church houses the **London Brass Rubbing Centre** and has connections with the **St Olave's Church** where the diarist, Samuel Pepys,was buried in 1703; a memorial garden to him is close by. Walk along Pepys Street and turn right through Savage Gardens to **Trinity Square**. Here are **Trinity House** (the English lifeboat head-quarters), the **Merchant Navy War Memorial** and a railed enclosure which marks the site of the scaffold where 125 prominent people were put to death between 1551 and 1747. Cross the road and visit the **Tower of London**, built in 1087 and a state prison since Norman times. See the **White Tower** and the **Crown Jewels**. Exit the Tower and walk down Tower Hill to the Thames. Turn left beside the Tower's river-side defences, including Traitor's Gate, as far as the tunnel and climb the steps to **Tower Bridge**. Look at the river from the bridge and walk along the riverside to St Katharine's Dock, a new development. Circle the Dock, cross the road and leave by St Katharine's Gardens. Use the underpass which will take you back to Tower Bridge Tube Station.

GREENWICH WALK

Travel by boat from **Westminster** or **Charing Cross Pier** – daily every half hour. Few London views are more impressive than the prospect of Greenwich from the Thames. Disembark at Greenwich Pier and visit the **Cutty Sark**, the clipper sailing ship that, in the 1880s, was the fastest to Australia (100 days!). On board everything is as it was during those epic voyages except for the splendid collection of ship's figure-heads in the hold. Close by is **Gypsy Moth IV**, the yacht that Sir Francis Chichester sailed single-handed around the world in 1966-67. Take Greenwich Church Street to **St Alfege Church**, built in 1714 by Nicholas Hawksmoor, Sir Christopher Wren's assistant, to replace the 12th-century church which stood on the site where the Danes murdered Alfege, Archbishop of Canterbury, in 1012. Turn left into Nelson Street, a street of fine Georgian buildings. Turn left down passageway for the market, right in Turpin Lane and left into King William Walk. Two pillars flank the entrance to the **Royal Naval College**. Wren created much of the present College as a hospital for naval pensioners, and the Painted Hall and the Chapel should both be seen. Continue down King William Walk, past the Cutty Sark, and turn right onto Riverside Walk. Note the **Trafalgar Tavern**, with its canopied bow windows and turn right into Park Row, then right again into Romney Road, for **Royal Naval College** and the **National Maritime Museum**. The museum's core is the lovely Queen's House, begun in 1616. The subject of the museum is the history of the Royal Navy and merchant shipping. There are superb 17th-century ship's models, marine paintings and actual ships. From the rear of the museum, turn right along a footpath, noting Isambard Brunel's steam ship, *Great Britain*, in a roofed building nearby. Turn left through a gateway into Greenwich Park, which was laid out in 1662 by the designer of Versailles. Follow the footpath to the **Old Royal Observatory**. The Meridian Line that divides the world into two hemispheres is marked in the courtyard. **Flamstead House**, built by Wren, is now a museum of astronomy. Greenwich Mean Time, by which the world sets its clocks, came into operation in the 1840s. The world's first visual time signal was the ball which still drops down a pole on a turret of the observatory at 1pm GMT each day. Note the bronze statue of General James Wolfe of Quebec fame. Continue along the wide avenue of chestnut trees, passing on the left the **Victorian Tea Room** and the ornate wrought iron **Bandstand**, both circa 1880. The **Ranger's House**, close by, is now an art gallery, which also has the Dolmetsch collection of early musical instruments. Turn right, past **Macartney House**, home of General Wolfe, and continue along the path, noting Henry Moore's *Standing Figure on a Knife Edge*. Keeping to the left, follow the path down the hill and turn left through the gate into Croom's Hill. Go ahead and turn right into Nevada Street and the **Greenwich Theatre**. Turn left into King William Walk. William IV's statue stands on a grassy plot. Follow the road to Cutty Sark Gardens and Greenwich pier for the boat trip back down the Thames to Charing Cross or Westminster.

MUSEUMS, GALLERIES AND PUBLIC BUILDINGS

The following museums, art galleries and public buildings are those *not* mentioned in the London Walks.
Bethnal Green Museum of Childhood – Cambridge Heath Road, Tel 081 980 2415 (Bethnal Green Tube)
Cricket Memorial Garden – Lords, St John's Wood Road, Tel 071 289 1611 (St John's Wood Tube)
Design Centre – 28 Haymarket, Tel 071 839 8000 (Piccadilly Circus Tube)
Florence Nightingale Museum – 2 Lambeth Palace Road, Tel 071 620 0374 (Waterloo Tube)
Freud Museum – 20 Maresfield Gardens, Tel 071 435 2002 (Finchley Road Tube)
Horniman Museum – Forest Hill, Tel 081 699 1872 (Forest Hill British Rail) Anthropological Museum.
Imperial War Museum – Lambeth Road, Tel 071 416 5000 (Lambeth North Tube)
London Museum of Jewish Life – East End Road, Tel 081 346 2288 (Finchley Central Tube)
London Toy and Model Museum – 23 Craven Hill, Tel 071 262 7905 (Paddington Tube)
Museum of the Moving Image – South Bank, Tel 071 401 2636 (Waterloo Tube)
National Army Museum – Royal Hospital Road, Tel 071 730 0717. (Sloane Square Tube)
Natural History Museum – Cromwell Road, Tel 071 589 6323 (South Kensington Tube)
Science Museum – Exhibition Road, Tel 071 938 8008 (South Kensington Tube)
Victoria and Albert Museum – Cromwell Road, Tel 071 589 6371 (South Kensington Tube)
Sherlock Holmes Museum – 221B Baker Street, Tel 071 935 8866 (Baker Street Tube)
Shakespeare Globe Museum – 1 Bear Gardens, Bankside, Tel 071 620 0202 (Mansion House Tube)
Design Museum – Bullers Wharf Shad Thames, Tel 071 403 6933 (Tower Hill Tube)
ICA Gallery – The Mall, Tel 071 930 3647 (Charing Cross Tube)
Hayward Gallery – South Bank Centre, Tel 071 928 3144 (Waterloo Tube)
National Portrait Gallery – St Martin's Place, Tel 071 306 0055 (Leicester Square Tube)
Tate Gallery – Millbank, Tel 071 821 1313 (Pimlico Tube)
Wallace Collection – Manchester Square, Tel 071 935 0687. (Bond Street Tube)
Whitechapel Art Gallery – Whitechapel High Street, Tel 071 377 0107 (Aldgate East Tube)
The George Inn – 77 High Street, Southwark, Tel 071 407 2056 (London Bridge Tube)
Hampton Court Palace – East Molsley, Surrey, Tel 081 977 8441 (Hampton Court, British Rail)
Prospect of Whitby Pub – Wapping Wall, Tel 071 481 1095. (Wapping Tube)
St George's Cathedral – Lambeth Road, Southwark (Elephant and Castle Tube)
Westminster Cathedral – Ashley Place (St James Park Tube)

THEATRE

West End Theatres:
Adelphi – The Strand, Tel 071 836 7611. Mainly musicals.
Albery – (formerly the New Theatre) St Martin's Lane, Tel 071 867 1115.
Aldwych – The Aldwych, Tel 071 836 6404. Formerly home of Royal Shakespeare Co.
Ambassadors – West Street, Cambridge Circus, Tel 071 836 6111. Home for many years of *The Mousetrap*.
Apollo Victoria – Wilton Road, Tel 071 437 2663. Formerly New Victoria Cinema, redesigned for epic musicals.
Barbican Centre – Silk Street, Tel 071 638 8891. Home of the Royal Shakespeare Company, consists of the **Barbican Theatre** and the **Pit**.

Cambridge – Earlham Street, Tel 071 379 5299.

Coliseum – St Martin's Lane, Tel 071 836 3161. Formerly the London Coliseum, now the home of English National Opera.

Comedy – Panton Street, Tel 071 930 2578.

Criterion – Piccadilly Circus, Tel 071 930 3216. London's only underground theatre.

Drury Lane – Catherine Street, Tel 071 838 8108. Home of *My Fair Lady, Forty-second Street* and *Miss Saigon.*

Duchess – Catherine Street, Tel 071 836 8243.

Duke of York's – St Martin's Lane, Tel 071 835 5122.

Fortune – Russell Street, Tel 071 836 2238. Small and intimate, remembered for *At the Drop of a Hat.*

Garrick – Charing Cross Road, Tel 071 379 6107.

Globe – Shaftesbury Avenue, Tel 071 437 3667.

Haymarket (Theatre Royal) – Haymarket, Tel 071 930 8800. Beautiful and prestigious.

Her Majesty's – Haymarket, Tel 071 839 2244. Home since 1986 of *The Phantom of the Opera.*

London Palladium – Argyll Street, Tel 071 437 7373. Home of variety.

Lyric – Shaftesbury Avenue, Tel 071 437 3686.

Mayfair – Stratton Street, Tel 071 629 3036.

National Theatre – South Bank, Tel 071 928 2252. Home of the Royal National Theatre Company. Three theatres on site, the **Olivier, Lyttelton** and **Cottesloe.**

New London – Parker Street, Tel 071 405 0072. Home of *Cats* for many years.

Old Vic – Waterloo Road, Tel 071 928 7616. Virtual national home of Shakespeare until opening of National Theatre. Refurbished in 1982 by Canadian Ed Mirvish.

Open Air – Regent's Park, Tel 071 486 2431.

Palace – Shaftesbury Avenue, Tel 071 434 0909. Home since 1986 of *Les Miserables.*

Phoenix – Charing Cross Road, Tel 071 867 1044.

Piccadilly – Denman Street, Tel 071 437 4506.

Playhouse – Northumberland Avenue, Tel 071 839 4401. Recently restored as a theatre after serving as a BBC Studio.

Prince Edward – Old Compton Street, Tel 071 734 8951.

Prince of Wales – Coventry Street, Tel 071 839 5972.

Queen's – Shaftesbury Avenue, Tel 071 734 1166.

Royal Court – Sloane Square, Tel 071 730 1745. The centre for innovative and controversial theatre, also **Theatre Upstairs** for new work, Tel 071 730 1745.

Royal Opera House Covent Garden – Bow Street, Tel 071 240 1911. The centre for Opera and Ballet.

Sadlers Wells – Roseberry Avenue, Tel 071 379 4444. Home of Sadlers Wells Ballet and Opera Companies.

St Martin's – West street, Tel 071 836 1443.

Savoy – Burnt down, in process of rebuilding. Original home of Gilbert and Sullivan operas.

Shaftesbury – Shaftesbury Avenue, Tel 071 379 5399.

Strand – Aldwych, Tel 071 240 0300.

Vaudeville – Strand, Tel 071 836 9987. *Salad Days* ran for 2329 performances in 1954.

Victoria Palace – Victoria Street, Tel 071 834 1317.

Westminster – Palace Street, Tel 071 834 0283.

Whitehall – Whitehall, Tel 071 867 1119.

Wyndham's – Charing Cross Road, Tel 071 836 3028.

Other Theatres:

Lyric Hammersmith – King Street, Tel 081 741 2311 and **Lyric Studio.** Excellent work.

Mermaid – Puddle Dock, upper Thames Street, Tel 071 236 5568. Only professional theatre in the City of London.

Almeida – Almeida Street (Angel Tube) Tel 071 359 4404. Excellent new work.

Bush Theatre – Shepherds Bush Road, Tel 081 743 3388. Excellent place to see new work.

Cockpit Theatre – Gateforth Street (Edgware Road Tube) Tel 071 402 5081.

Duke's Head – 42 The Vineyard, Richmond (Richmond Tube Station) Tel 081 948 8055. Excellent venue for new work.

Gate – above Prince Albert Pub, 11 Renbridge Road (Nottinghill Tube) Tel 071 229 0706.

Greenwich Theatre – Crooms Hill, Tel 081 858 7755. Excellent quality productions.

Hampstead Theatre – Avenue Road, Tel 071 722 9224. Excellent quality productions.
King's Head – 115 Upper Street (Angel Tube) Tel 071 226 1916. Excellent venue for new work. Also lunchtime show.
Man in the Moon – 392 Kings Road, Tel 071 351 2876. Good venue for new work.
Oval House – 54 Kennington Oval, Tel 071 582 7680.
Riverside Studios – Crisp Road (Hammersmith Tube) Tel 081 748 3354. Excellent for new work.
Theatre Museum – Russell Street, Tel 071 836 7891.
Theatre Royal Stratford East – (Stratford Tube) Tel 081 534 0310. Spiritual home of Joan Littlewood.
Tricycle Theatre – 269 Kilburn High Road, Tel 071 328 1000. (Kilburn Tube).
Young Vic - 66 The Cut, Tel 071 928 6363 (Waterloo Tube).
For the best listings of all the arts, consult *Time Out* (published weekly).

MUSIC

Major classical concerts are given in the following venues:
Royal Festival Hall – South Bank, Tel 071 928 8800. Orchestral.
Queen Elizabeth Hall – South Bank, Tel 071 928 8800. Orchestral.
Purcell Room – South Bank, Tel 071 928 8800. Chamber and solo.
Royal Albert Hall – Kensington Gore, Tel 071 589 8212. Orchestral.
Barbican Hall – Silk Street, Tel 071 638 8891. Orchestral.
Wigmore Hall – 36 Wigmore Street, Tel 071 935 2141. Chamber and solo.
St John's – Smith Square, Tel 071 222 1061. Orchestral.
St Martin's-in-the-Fields – Trafalgar Square. Orchestral and chamber.
British Music Information Centre – 10 Stratford Place (Bond Street Tube) Tel 071 499 8567.
St James – Piccadilly, Tel 071 734 4511. Chamber.
St Mary-le-Bow – Cheapside (Monument Tube). Chamber.
Lauderdale House – Waterlow Park, Highgate Hill (Highgate Tube) Tel 081 348 8716.
Amadeus Centre – 50 Sherland Road (Marda Vale Tube) Tel 071 286 1686. Chamber.
Kenwood House/Lakeside – Hampstead Lane, Tel 071 379 4444, (210, 271 bus) Orchestral.
St Giles Cripplegate – Fore Street, Barbican (Barbican Tube). Chamber.
Fairfield Halls – Park Lane, Croyden. Tel 081 688 9291. Orchestral and chamber.
Leighton House – 12 Holland Park Road, Tel 071 602 3316 (Kensington High Street Tube) Solo and chamber.
Rudolf Steiner House – 35 Park Road, Tel 071 723 4400 (Baker Street Tube). Solo and chamber.
Best for classical music is *Time Out,* published weekly.

CINEMA

Major cinemas are listed, with art houses recommended.
Barbican Centre – Silk Street, Tel 071 638 8891 (Barbican Tube).
Cannon – Baker Street, Marleybone Road, Tel 071 935 9772 (Baker Street Tube).
Cannon – Chelsea, 279 King's Road, Tel 071 352 5096 (Sloane Square Tube and bus).
Cannon – Fulham Road, Tel 071 370 2636. Fulham Road (South Kensington Tube and bus)
Cannon – Haymarket, Tel 071 839 1527 (Piccadilly Tube)
Cannon – Oxford Street (Tottenham Court Road Tube) Tel 071 636 0310.
Cannon – Panton street, Tel 071 930 0631 (Piccadilly Tube)
Cannon – Piccadilly, Tel 071 437 3561 (Piccadilly Tube)
Cannon – Shaftesbury Avenue, Tel 071 836 6279 (Leicester Square Tube)
Cannon – Tottenham court Road, Tel 071 636 6148 (Tottenham Court Road Tube)
Chelsea Cinema – Kings Road, Tel 071 351 3742 (Sloane Square Tube). Recommended.
Curzon Mayfair – Curzon Street, Tel 071 465 8865 (Green Park Tube). Recommended.
Curzon Phoenix – Charing Cross Road, Tel 071 240 9661 (Tottenham Court Road Tube). Recommended.
Curzon West End – Shaftesbury Avenue, Tel 071 439 4805 (Piccadilly Tube). Recommended.
Empire – Leicester square, Tel 071 479 9999 (Leicester Square Tube)
Gate Cinema – Notting Hill Gate, Tel 071 727 4043 (Notting Hill Gate Tube). Recommended.
ICA Cinema – Nash House, The Mall, Tel 071 930 3647 (Piccadilly Tube). Recommended.
Lumière – St Martin's Lane, Tel 071 836 0691 (Leicester Square Tube). Recommended.

Metro – Rupert Street, Tel 071 437 0757 (Leicester Square Tube). Recommended.
Minema – 45 Knightsbridge, Tel 071 235 4225 (Knightsbridge Tube). Recommended.
Notting Hill Coronet – Tel 071 727 6705 (Notting Hill Tube). Recommended.
Odeon – Haymarket, Tel 071 839 7697 (Piccadilly Tube)
Odeon – High Street, Kensington, Tel 071 602 5193 (High St Kensington Tube)
Odeon – Leicester Square, Tel 071 930 6111 (Leicester Square Tube). Also Odeon Mezzanine.
Odeon – Marble Arch, Tel 071 723 2011 (Marble Arch Tube)
Odeon – West End, Leicester Square, Tel 071 930 5252 (Leicester Square Tube)
Plaza – Lower Regent Street, Tel 071 497 9999 (Piccadilly Tube)
Prince Charles – Leicester Place, Tel 071 437 8181 (Leicester Square Tube)
Renoir – Brunswick Square, Tel 071 437 8402 (Russell Square Tube). Recommended.
Screen on Baker Street – 96 Baker Street, Tel 071 935 2772 (Baker Street Tube). Recommended.
Screen on the Green – Islington Green, Tel 071 226 3520 (Angel Tube). Recommended.
Screen on the Hill – 230 Haverstock Hill, Tel 071 435 3366 (Besize Park Tube). Recommended.
UCI Whiteleys – Bayswater, Tel 071 792 3303 (Queensway Tube)
Warner West End – Leicester Square, Tel 071 439 0791 (Leicester Square Tube)
Best check for films – *Time out,* published weekly.

BOOKSTORES

Only those in Central London are included. The best are:
Waterstone's at –
64/72 Leadenhall Market, Tel 071 628 5811.
128 Camden High Street, Tel 071 284 4948.
121/125 Charing Cross Road, Tel 071 434 4290.
9/13 Garrick Street, Tel 071 836 6757.
235 Kensington Church Street, Tel 071 229 9444.
193 Kensington High Street, Tel 071 937 8432.
99/101 Old Brompton Road, Tel 071 581 8522.
266 Earl's Court, Tel 071 370 1616.
The South Bank Centre, Tel 071 620 0403.

Dillon's at –
48 Kensington High Street, Tel 071 988 2228.
150 Kings Road Chelsea, Tel 071 351 3232.
28 Margaret Street, Tel 071 580 2812.
Long Acre, Tel 071 836 1359 (Art Books).

Hatchard's at –
187 Piccadilly, Tel 071 439 9921 (my favourite).
390 Strand, Tel 071 379 6264.
63 Kensington High Street, Tel 071 937 0858.

Claude Gill at –
19 Oxford Street, Tel 071 434 9759.
19 Coventry Street, Piccadilly Circus, Tel 071 734 5061.
10 James Street, Tel 071 628 8206.

Zwemmer's at –
26 Litchfield Street, Tel 071 379 7886 (Music).
80 Charing Cross Road, Tel 071 379 7886 (Art, Antiquarian, Secondhand).
72 Charing Cross Road, Tel 071 240 1559 (Oxford University Press).

Travel Bookshop – 13 Blenheim Crescent, Tel 071 229 5260 (Travel).
Sportspages – 94/96 Charing Cross Road, Tel 071 240 9404 (Sport).
Silver Moon – 68 Charing Cross Road, Tel 071 836 7906 (Women's books).
Sherratt and Hughes – 21 New Road, Tel 071 240 3656.
Publishers Book Clearance – 120 Baker Street, Tel 071 379 7650 (Penguins).
Motor Books – 33 St Martin's Lane, Tel 071 836 5376 (Cars, Railway, Aviation).

The Horseman's Bookshop – 1 Lower Grosvenor Place, Tel 071 834 5606 (Riding).
Forbidden Planet – 71 New Oxford Street, Tel 071 836 4179 (Science Fiction, Fantasy, Comics).
French's – 52 Fitzroy Street, Tel 071 387 9375 (Theatre, Drama). Recommended.
Foyle's – 119 Charing Cross Road, Tel 071 437 5660 (A great bookshop – an institution).

ANTIQUARIAN AND SECONDHAND BOOKS

Adrian John – 12 Cecil Court, Tel 071 836 2987 (by the Wyndhams and Albery Theatres).
Alan Brett – 24 Cecil Court, Tel 071 836 8222.
Ann Creed – 22 Cecil Court, Tel 071 836 7757.
Any Amount of Books – 56 Charing Cross Road, Tel 071 240 8140.
RA Gekoski – 33B Charing Cross Road, Tel 071 722 9037 (First editions).
Sotherans – 2 Sackville Street, Tel 071 439 6157 (Prints).
Marchpane – 16 Cecil Court, Tel 071 836 8661 (Children's and illustrated books).
Maggs – 50 Berkeley Square, Tel 071 493 7160 (Autographs, manuscripts, first editions).
John Thornton – 634 King's Road, Tel 071 736 6181.
Harrington Brothers – The Chelsea Antique Market, Tel 071 352 5689.
E Joseph – 1 Vere Street, Tel 071 493 8353 (Rare books, illustrators originals).
Dillons – 82 Gower Street, Tel 071 493 0876.
Check Books – 31 Museum Street, Tel 071 637 5862 (First editions and fine art).
Balantyne and Date – 38 Museum Street, Tel 071 242 4249.
Ash Rare Books – 25 Royal Exchange, Tel 071626 2665.
Foyle's – 119 Charing Cross Road, Tel 071 437 5669.
Recommended areas are Charing Cross Road (Cecil Court and area) and British Museum area.

ART GALLERIES

Arthur Ackerman – 33 New Bond Street, Tel 071 493 3288. English sporting paintings and prints 1700–1900.
Thomas Agnew – 43 Old Bond Street, Tel 071 629 6176. Paintings, watercolours, drawings, engravings and sculpture of all schools.
Albermarle Gallery – 18 Albermarle Street, Tel 071 355 1880. 20th-century paintings and sculpture. (Opposite Brown's Hotel)
Burlington Gallery – 10 Burlington Gardens, Tel 071 734 9228. Sporting and decorative prints 1600–1860.
Burlington Paintings – 12 Burlington Gardens, Tel 071 734 9984. Oils and watercolours 19th to early 20th century.
Lumly Cazelet – 24 Davies Street, Tel 071 491 4767. 19th and 20th century original prints.
Colnaghi – 14 Old Bond Street, Tel 071 491 7408. Paintings, drawings and sculpture 14th to 19th century.
Crawley and Asquith – 1 Davies Street, Tel 071439 2755. Paintings and watercolours 18th and 19th century.
Emanouel Antiques – 64 South Audley Street, Tel 071 629 3125. Islamic and fine works of art.
Fine Art Society – 148 New Bond Street, Tel 071 629 5116. British art and sculpture 19th and early 20th century.
Fritz-Denneville – 31 New Bond Street, Tel 071 629 2466. 19th-century and modern paintings especially German.
Frost and Reed – 16 Old Bond Street, Tel 071 629 2457. 19th- and 20th-century paintings.
Garton and Co – 39/42 New Bond Street, Tel 071 493 2820. 19th- and 20th-century original British prints.
Hahn and Son – 47 Albermarle Street, Tel 071 493 9196. English oil paintings.
MacConnal-Mason – 15 Burlington Arcade, Tel 071 499 6991. 19th- and 20th-century paintings.
Robin Kennedy – 29 New Bond Street, Tel 071 408 1238. Japanese prints and paintings.
Lefevre Gallery – 30 Bruton Street, Tel 071 493 2017. Impressionist paintings.
Maas Gallery – 15A Clifford Street, Tel 071 734 2302. Victorian paintings and prints.
Lane Fine Art – 1/9 Bruton Place, Tel 071 499 5020. Oils and portraits 1500–1850.
Mayfair Gallery – 49 South Audley Street, Tel 071 499 5315. Islamic and 18th to 19th century art.
Marlborough Fine Art – 6 Albermarle Street, Tel 071629 5161. 19th- and 20th-century masters.
Patterson's – 19 Albermarle Street, Tel 071 629 4119. 19th-century and contemporary work.
Piccadilly Gallery – 16 Cork Street, Tel 071 499 0431. Symbolist and art nouveau works.
Jonathan Potter – 21 Grosvenor Street, Tel 071 491 3520. Maps and prints (antique).
Rutland Gallery – 32A George Street, Tel 071 499 5636. British painting, especially primitives.

Sladmore Gallery – 32 Bruton Place, Tel 071 499 0365.

Scottish Gallery – 28 Cork Street, Tel 071 287 2121. Contemporary artists.

Taylor Gallery – 4 Royal Arcade, Old Bond Street, Tel 071 493 4111. Irish and British 20th-century paintings.

Welbeck Gallery – 18 Thayer Street, Tel 071 935 4825. Prints. Recommended.

The main areas to explore are Bond Street/Grosvenor Square (covered above), Kensington High Street and Kensington Church Street, Portobello Road and Westbourne Grove, St James's, Sloane Square, Pimlico, Kings Road (Chelsea) Fulham High Road and Bloomsbury.

ANTIQUE DEALERS

Listed are just the London Antique Markets as there are too many individual antique shops to make a considered selection. The areas to be explored are the same as for the Art Galleries and of course individual shops are generally adjacent to the markets themselves.

Bond Street Antiques Centre – 1244 New Bond Street, Tel 071 351 5353 (Bond Street Tube) 29 dealers selling a wide range of general antiques, especially jewellery.

Bond Street Silver Galleries – 111/112 New Bond Street, Tel 071 493 6180. Silver and plate.

Gray's Antique Market – 58 Davies Street, Tel 071 629 7034 and **Grays Mews** – 1/7 Davies Mews, Tel 071 629 7034. 200 dealers under two roofs (Bond Street Tube).

Kensington Church Street Antiques Centre – 58/60 Kensington Church Street. Over a dozen dealers, mostly jewellery, paintings, glass, ceramics, porcelain, silver and decorative objects. (Kensington High Street Tube).

Grays Portobello – 138 Portobello Road, Tel 071 221 3069 (Notting Hill Gate Tube) Nearly 30 dealers. Focuses on Oriental and Islamic art, pottery and jewellery.

Red Lion Market – 165/169 Portobello Road. Open Saturday 5:30am to 5pm. Over 200 dealers selling a wide range of general antiques and collectables.

Stouts Antique Arcade – 144 Portobello Road. Open Saturdays only. 10 dealers offering mostly jewellery, watches, clocks, porcelain, glass and silver.

Rogers Antiques Gallery – 65 Portobello Road, Tel 071 351 5353. Open Saturdays 7am–4pm. 60 dealers selling a wide range of general antiques.

Antiquarius – 135/141 Kings Road, Tel 071 351 5353. Next to Chelsea Town Hall. Over 40 dealers. Strong on paintings, jewellery, porcelain and glass.

Furniture Cave – 533 Kings Road, Tel 071 352 4229 (Gloucester Road Tube).

Bermondsey Antique Warehouse – 173 Bermondsey Street, Tel 071 407 2040 (Tower Hill Tube).

Cutler Street Antique Market – Goulston Street, Tel 071 351 5353 (Aldgate East Tube) Open Sundays only, 7am–1pm. Visit Petticoat Lane, a street market (Sunday only, Middlesex Street).

Camden Passage Antiques Centre – 357 Upper Street, Islington, Tel 071 359 2095 (Islington Tube). 300 dealers in shops, markets and arcades. Open Mon–Sat with Thursdays good for books.

Hampstead Antique Emporium – 12 Heath Street, Tel 071 794 3297 (Hampstead Tube). 25 dealers offering great variety. Open 10–6pm, Tues–Sun.

Alfies Antique Market – 13-25 Church Street, Tel 071 723 6066 (St John's Wood Tube) 200 stalls selling a wide range of general antiques. Open Mondays and Bank Holidays 6:30–5pm).

The London Silver Vaults – Chancery House, Chancery Lane (Chancery Lane Tube). Excellent location for silver and jewellery.

Camden Antiques Market – Camden High Street and Buck Street, Tel 071 351 5353 (Camden Town Tube). 100 dealers selling a wide range of general antiques. Open Thursday 7–4pm.

RESTAURANTS AND PUBS

With restaurants and pubs I have simply briefly recommended three of each kind to correspond with the walks described in the beginning of this section.

WESTMINSTER

Restaurants:

Carriages – 43 Buckingham Palace Road, Tel 071 834 0119. Stylish wine bar.

Wilkins – 61 Marsham Street, Tel 071 222 4038 (by Lambeth Bridge) Good vegetarian food.

Mijanou – 143 Eburg Street, Tel 071 730 4099 (near Sloane Square) Japanese.

Pubs:
Methuselah's – 29 Victoria Street, Tel 071 222 3550. Wine bar/bistro so close to Parliament it has a division bell.
Tapster – Buckingham Gate, Tel 071 222 0561. Traditional basement wine bar with good food.
Two Chairmen – Cockspur Street, Tel 071 930 1166. Just off Trafalgar Square.

ST JAMES
Restaurants:
Le Caprice – Arlington Street, Tel 071 629 2329. Stylish international cuisine.
Wiltons – 55 Jermyn Street, Tel 071 629 9955. Traditional game and fish cuisine at its best.
ICA Cafe – The Mall, Tel 071 930 8535. Good counter service eatery in an artsy setting.
Pubs:
Green's – 36 Duke Street, Tel 071 930 4566. A champagne and oyster bar – need I say more?
Golden Lion – 25 King Street (opposite Christies) Pleasant with a nice theatre bar.
Buckingham Arms – 62 Petty France. Good lunchtime food.

COVENT GARDEN
Restaurants:
Cranks – 11 The Market, Tel 071 379 6508. Long established vegetarian restaurant.
Neal's Yard Bakery – Neals Yard, Tel 071 836 5199. Good inexpensive vegetarian food.
Saheli Brasserie – 35 Great Queen Street, Tel 081 459 0340.
Pubs:
Maple Leaf – 41 Maiden Lane, Tel 071 240 2843. Canadian-style food moderately priced.
Lamb and Flag – 33 Rose Street. Another pub frequented by Dickens. Very good bar food.
Punch and Judy – 40 Covent Garden Market. Musicians, acrobats et al in courtyard. Very lively.

BLOOMSBURY
Restaurants:
Museum Street Cafe – 47 Museum Street, Tel 071 405 3211. Excellent bistro. Recommended.
Il Passetto – 230 Shaftesbury Avenue, Tel 071 836 9391. Imaginative Italian cooking.
Cafe Delancey – 3 Delaney Street, Tel 071 387 1985. Good bistro including breakfast any time.
Pubs:
Museum Tavern – Museum Street (opposite British Museum) Wonderful atmosphere, good bar food.
Princess Louise – 208 High Holborn. Old fashioned superb gents, good Lancashire hotpot upstairs.
Dolphin – Lamb Conduit Passage. Lots of atmosphere! Interesting bar food.

HAMPSTEAD
Restaurants:
Czech Club – 74 West End Lane, Tel 071 372 5251. Wonderfully authentic Czech food.
Mother Huff – 12 Heath Street, Tel 071 435 3714. Simple and delicious fare in rustic attic setting.
Keats – 3A Downshire Hill, Tel 071 435 3544. Elegant with wonderful food. Recommended.
Pubs:
Jack Straw's Castle – North End Way. Haunt of Dickens and many other writers.
Spaniards Inn – Spaniards Road. Wonderfully atmospheric. Patronized by Dick Turpin.
Holly Bush – Holly Mount. Real Edwardian feel. Good hot food all day.

INNS OF COURT
Restaurants:
Cafe Society – 32 Procter Street, Red Lion Square, Tel 071 242 6691. Good cafe/brasserie with a wonderful breakfast.
Oscar's Brasserie – 5 Temple Avenue, Temple Chambers, Tel 071 409 0750. Elegant French.
Savoy – The Strand, Tel 071 836 4343. Pamper yourself, it's an experience you won't forget.
Pubs:
Black Friar – 174 Queen Victoria Street, Tel 071 236 5650. Built on the site of the friary.
Old Bell Tavern – 95 Fleet Street, Tel 071 583 0700. Wren used this pub when building St Brides.
Ye Olde Cheshire Cheese Pub – 145 Fleet Street, Tel 071 353 6170. Dr Johnson's pub (see walk).

ST PAULS
Restaurants:
Balls Brothers – St Pauls Churchyard, Tel 071 248 8697. Wonderful sandwiches.
Place Below – St Mary-le-Bow Church, Cheapside. Stylish vegetarian restaurant in the crypt.
Le Poulbot – 45 Cheapside, Tel 071 236 4379. Very good brasserie with pricier restaurant downstairs.
Pubs:
Olde Watling – 29 Watling Street. Built by Wren in 1662. Lunchtime bar food.
Old Wine Shades – 6 Martin Lane. Wonderful old pub with excellent weekday lunchtime snacks.
Fox and Anchor – Charterhouse Street. Unknown pub with large helpings of good bar food.

THE TOWER
Restaurants:
Blueprint Cafe – Design Museum, Bullers Wharf, Tel 071 378 7031. Gutsy Mediterranean cooking. Recommended.
Blooms – 90 Whitechapel High Street, Tel 071 247 6001. Wonderful Jewish food.
City Brasserie – Plantation House, Mincing Lane, Tel 071 220 7094. Lunch only brasserie.
Pubs:
Dickens Inn – St Katharines Way. Fine dockland position with good bar food.
Chiswell Vaults – Chiswell Street. Subterranean pub with good food.
City Pride – Farringdon Lane. Attractive pub with inexpensive restaurant upstairs.

GREENWICH
Restaurants: (The first two entries are under the tunnel on the south bank of the Thames.)
Mandalay – 100 Greenwich South Street, Tel 081 691 0443. The only Burmese restaurant in London.
Escape Coffee House – 141/343 Greenwich South Street, Tel 081 692 5826. Good vegetarian restaurant.
Greenwich Theatre Restaurant – Crooms Hill. Good bistro style food from 6pm until after the show.
Pubs:
Mitre – 338 Tunnell Avenue. Victorian pub adjacent to St Alfege's Church.
Cutty Sark – Lassell Street (south bank) Wonderful atmosphere, excellent food.
Yacht – Crane Street. Maritime decor with decent bar food.

EPHEMERA

For a thousand years, London's fish market has stood near London Bridge on the site of the old river gate to the city. According to a medieval legend, Billingsgate takes its name from Bilin, a legendary king of the Britons, who "built a tower of prodigious height and a safe harbour for ships." The distinctive flat-topped leather hats worn by the fish porters are said to be modelled on those worn by the English archers at the Battle of Agincourt.

Dirty Dick's, a pub in Bishopgate, takes its name from a well-known city eccentric of the 18th century, Nathaniel Bentley. He was a Leadenhall Street merchant, who in his youth was noted as a scholar and a man of fashion and was nicknamed the "Beau of Leadenhall Street." But the shock of his fiancée's death on their wedding eve drove him to retreat into slovenly isolation. Dirty Dick, as he became known, never washed again, saying that if he did so he would only be dirty again the next day. On his death, the room in which the wedding feast had been laid was found as it had been left on the tragic day of his loved one's death 50 years before.

Close to Farringdon Tube is Cowcross Street, where the Castle Pub is the only one in Britain to have a pawnbroker's licence. The story goes that in the early 19th century, George IV, wearing a long cloak and large hat to conceal his identity, borrowed a pound from the landlord after gambling away all his ready cash at a cock fight in Clerkenwell. He left his watch as security and went back to the ringside. Next day a messenger redeemed the watch and the king awarded the publican a pawnbroker's licence for as long as the Castle should remain standing.

Ely Place (close to Holborn) is the location of St Ethelreda's Church, where on St Blaise's Day (Feb 3) people suffering from throat troubles kneel at the altar rail and the priest touches their throats with two candles tied together to form a cross. This service commemorates the 4th-century Christian martyr St Blaise, who on his way to execution touched the throat of a boy choking on a fish bone and saved his life.

Before the ardent Royalist Sir Nicholas Crisp died in 1666, he expressed a wish that his heart be buried at the foot of his master, Charles I. Instead his heart was entombed in an urn which stands underneath a bust of the king in St Paul's Church Hammersmith, and his body was buried in the churchyard outside. Crisp made provision in his will for his heart to be removed from the urn once a year and refreshed with a glass of wine. This ritual was dutifully carried out until the mid-18th century, when the urn was finally sealed forever.

On Highgate Hill a milestone topped by a bronze cat marks the spot where young Dick Whittington, summoned by London's bells, turned again to the city that was to make him mayor three times in the early 15th century. The legend of his cat may have arisen from a ship called a cat used in the coal trade, on which a part of Dick's fortunes was founded.

One of the many alleged burial places of Queen Boadicea is beneath Platform Ten of King's Cross Station. She is known to have fought her last battle against the occupying army on the site of the station, around 63 AD. She was defeated by Suetonius Paulinus and is reported to have taken poison.

Queen Elizabeth I was so pleased with the way that Middle Temple lawyers received her that she made them a Christmas pudding. Every year, part of the pudding was saved, to be mixed into next year's, so that the Queen's gift was constantly sampled afresh. The custom died out in 1966, but was revived in 1971 when the Queen Mother stirred a new pudding for the benchers.

The word *Cockney*, from Middle English, means a "cock's egg," or something to marvel at. Certainly cockney rhyming slang is a marvellous example of the ingenuity and independence of those who pride themselves on having been born within the sound of Bow Bells in East London. A conversation of rhyming slang is incomprehensible to strangers. It began in the 1850s with the use of place names to indicate objects. A tie was a "Peckham Rye," an arm a "Chalk Farm" and a horse a "Charing Cross." Further rhymes were introduced and to make it more difficult, the rhyme itself was often dropped: a suit became a whistle, from "whistle and flute," stairs were apples from "apples and pears" and half a dollar (the old half-crown piece) became an Oxford, from Oxford scholar.

Finally, a chance to throw some light on two nursery rhymes, often the most incomprehensible of British verse. "London Bridge is falling down" has a lot of truth in it. The Danes destroyed it in 850, it collapsed in heavy floods in 1091 and the replacement burned down in 1136. A stone bridge constructed 40 years later was paid for by a tax on wool, hence the line, "Build it up with packs of wool." The bridge collapsed again in 1281, but when restored with houses, shops and a chapel on it, stood until 1831. A later bridge lasted until 1971, when it was sold to become a tourist attraction at Lake Havasu City, Arizona, USA. Another nursery rhyme immortalizes the Eagle, a pub in Shepherdess Lane. "Pop Goes the Weasel" has a verse which goes,

> Up and down the city road
> In and out of the Eagle
> That's the way the money goes
> Pop goes the weasel.

The weasel was a tool used by saddlers to bore holes in leather. Apparently a saddler, who lived in nearby Nile Street, sometimes "popped" (pawned) his weasel to obtain drinking money; and the Eagle was his "local."

TOURIST INFORMATION BUREAU: 12 Regent Street, Piccadilly Circus, SW1Y 4PQ. Tel (071)730 3400.

4

THE EAST

CAMBRIDGE
COLCHESTER
IPSWICH AND ALDEBURGH
LINCOLN
NORWICH

CAMBRIDGE

County of Cambridgeshire
54 miles (86.4 km) from London by M11
By rail 1 hour 15 minutes from London (Liverpool or King's Cross)

Cambridge is one of the most important and beautiful towns not only in East Anglia, but in all of Britain and even Europe. The quality of the architecture, especially of the University buildings, and the very special atmosphere created by the combination of river and gardens make this a wonderful place to visit.

One of the phrases you are most likely to hear in a university town is "town and gown," which suggests the ancient division between those parts of the city devoted to the university (gown) and the rest of the inhabitants (town). The ivory tower versus the city of everyday life, if you like. In 1381, during Wat Tyler's revolt, there was considerable animosity between town and gown and I suspect this has recurred with monotonous regularity over the years whenever the students' boisterous behaviour has impinged on the residents of the town. In any university town one must accept the good with the bad. Outbreaks of immature behaviour have to be weighed against the considerable contribution, direct and indirect, that the university makes to the local economy. Certainly in Cambridge the university has profoundly influenced the character of the town: the theatre, cinema, concerts and restaurants are all made richer by the presence of a great seat of learning and the interests of the academic community.

In the century preceding the Roman Conquest there was a Celtic settlement just to the north of the present town and successive Roman developments probably included the building of a bridge at this point. The bridge was to be the only one to give its name to an English county. Its location was of great importance because it marked the place where the Via Devana (the Colchester-to-Chester road) converged with the system of rivers and canals. As the northernmost point before reaching the fens, the site was of great strategic and commercial importance.

With the departure of the Romans the town continued to spread to its present position on the East Anglian side of the river. The Normans, however, rebuilt the castle and moved over to the opposite bank of the river Cam. Nothing now remains of the castle but the mound. The 13th century saw the founding of the first Cambridge college, Peterhouse, which was established in 1284 by Hugh de Balasham, Bishop of Ely, and the consequent increase in the importance of the city as a seat of learning and a centre of communal life.

There is a great deal to see in Cambridge and I cannot hope to include everything in the two walks recommended below, but I will try to describe the most important university buildings. A word on the possible origins of the university itself might make a good starting place. In the 12th century, students were still attached to the schools of the monasteries and cathedrals and the gradual development of universities in Italy and France was followed by the migration of scholars from one centre to another. Thus in 1167 scholars moved from Paris to Oxford, and in 1209 a further group went from Oxford to Cambridge. Several religious orders settled in Cambridge in the 12th century and their houses attracted sufficient numbers of students for it to be recognized as a seat of learning by a writ for its governance made by Henry III in 1231.

In its early days the university used whatever accommodation was available in churches or private houses. The normal master's course was of seven years' duration and might sometimes be followed by a further ten years of study for a doctorate in theology. Students started earlier than they do now, at the age of 14, and most became schoolmasters. They lived in lodgings in the town and due to the unsatisfactory conditions under which they had to exist, hostels in the care of one of the masters came into being. Such were the origins of the college system that prevails today.

Many of the colleges are on the main street, Trumpington Street, which becomes King's Parade and then St John's Street, and runs parallel to the river. The "backs" are peaceful green lawns running down to the river, which with its small bridges and shady willows contributes significantly to the Cambridge idyll of punting and May Balls. The following are the most important of the colleges:

Christ's College – St Andrews Street. Founded in 1439 as "God's House" and re-established under its present name in 1505. There is an imposing gateway onto St Andrew's Street. Christ's has a fine collection of silver plate. Its most famous son was John Milton.

Clare College – Trinity Lane. Founded as University Hall in 1326. Re-founded under its present name in 1346. Its bridge dates from 1640. It has an excellent collection of candlesticks and silver.

Corpus Christi – Trumpington Street. Founded by the town's merchants in 1352. Old Court is essentially 14th century even though restored, while New Court is circa 1825. The college has the best selection of silver plate in Cambridge. Christopher Marlowe, who wrote *Doctor Faustus*, studied here in 1604.

Downing College – Regent Street. A late addition to the college scene, designed by William Wilkins in 1807. Classically Grecian in style, it has an imaginative addition, added in 1969.

Emmanuel College – St Andrew's Street. Founded in 1584. In 1666 Sir Christopher Wren designed the chapel in the new classical style. Fine collection of plate. John Harvard, founder of the American university which bears his name, studied here.

Gonville and Caius College – Trinity Street. Founded by Edmund Gonville in 1348, re-established by Dr Caius in 1557. The three gateways – the Gate of Humility, the Gate of Virtue and Wisdom and the Gate of Honour, symbolize a student's progress.

KING'S COLLEGE CHAPEL, CAMBRIDGE

Jesus College – Jesus Lane. Founded in 1496. With fewer students than some colleges, Jesus College is larger, and has a feeling of spaciousness. The chapel has some Norman portions but also decorations by Pugin, William Morris, Ford Madox Brown and Burne-Jones. Among its scholars were Coleridge, Lawrence Sterne, the author of *Tristram Shandy,* and Thomas Malthus, the great economist, who wrote *On Population.*

King's College – King's Parade. Founded by Henry VI in 1441 at the same time as he established the school at Eton, the Fellow's Building was designed in 1723 in a simple, classical style. The bridge dates from 1818. The chief glory of King's College and of Cambridge itself is the **Chapel**, considered by some the most outstanding building in Britain and the finest Gothic building in Europe. It was begun in 1446. Its unusual dimensions – 300 feet (91.4 m) long, 80 feet (24.3 m) high and 40 feet (12 m) wide – help to make the interior utterly breathtaking. Buttressed walls of white Tadcaster stone lead to the superb fan vaulting which arches over the 17th-century organ. Embossed with Tudor roses and portcullises, the vaulting stretches the entire length of the chapel. The massive carved oak screen, above which the organ towers, was the gift of Henry VIII, and the monograms "HR" and "HRAS" are carved on the screen's coving, the first stands for "Henricus Rex" and the second means "Henricus Rex Anne Sposa." Sposa is Latin for wife and the monogram is in honour of Henry's second wife, Anne Boleyn. The screen and the beautiful choir stalls date from 1536, so Anne Boleyn had then just a few months to live before her execution for treason on account of her alleged infidelity. The superb stained glass dates from 1515 and note should also be taken of Rubens's *Adoration of the Magi,* acquired in 1961.

Magdalene College – Magdalene Street. Founded in 1542 incorporating the original monk's hostel, which was established in 1428. The First Court and Chapel date from 1430 and, with its mellowed brickwork and tall chimneys, Magdalene has about it all the charm of a Tudor country mansion. In Second Court, the elegant 17th-century Pepys Building contains the library of the diarist Samuel Pepys, who was a student at Magdalene from 1650 until 1653.

Pembroke College – Pembroke Street. Founded in 1347 by Mary, Countess of Pembroke. A notable addition was made by Sir Christopher Wren who designed the chapel, a gift to the college from his uncle, the Bishop of Ely. Consecrated in 1664, the chapel is the earliest classical building in the city. Edmund Spenser, author of *The Faerie Queene;* Nicholas Ridley, who as Bishop of London was burned for heresy in front of Balliol College in Oxford in 1555; and the poet Thomas Gray, best remembered for his poem "Elegy in a Country Churchyard," were all Pembroke men.

Peterhouse College – Trumpington Street. This was the earliest of the colleges to be founded, established by the Bishop of Ely in 1281 and moved to its own hostels in 1284. The original hall is part of the south side of the Main Court but little remains, due to 19th-century restoration. The chapel dates from 1632.

Queen's College – Silver Street. You may have noticed that some of the colleges have been founded twice. Queen's was founded no less than three times, in 1446, 1448 and finally in 1485. Perhaps its most famous feature is the President's Lodge, circa 1540, a picturesque timbered building over the north cloisters. The famous Mathematical Bridge was constructed in 1749 without any nails. Erasmus, the famous humanist, resided here in 1510.

St Catherine's College – Trumpington Street. Founded in 1473, though none of its buildings from that time remain, most having been reconstructed at the end of the 17th century.

St John's College – The gilded arms of Lady Margaret Beaufort, mother of Henry VII and founder of St John's in 1511, adorn the turreted gateway of the college. First Court is a fine example of Tudor brickwork, with gables and stone mullioned windows. On the far side of the Cam is New Court, built in 1824 and linked to the older Courts by the Bridge of Sighs. Composed of white stone and unglazed Gothic windows, it has little in common with its Venetian namesake, though both are covered. The poets Robert Herrick and William Wordsworth studied here.

Sidney Sussex College – Sidney Street. Founded in 1596 by Lady Francis Sidney, Countess of Sussex, on the site of the Franciscan house. Much renovation took place in the early 19th century and the chapel was rebuilt in the classic style in 1912. Oliver Cromwell studied here in 1616.

Trinity College – Trinity Street. King's Hall, founded in 1336 by Edward III, was re-founded by Henry VIII as Trinity College in 1546. High on the turreted gateway of the largest college in Cambridge is a statue of Henry VIII with an orb in one hand and a chair leg in the other – an irreverent joke played by students of the last century. Beyond are the two acres of lawns and paths which make up the Great Court. On its north side, an 18th-century clock with great gilded hands and numbers strikes the hour twice. Undergraduates attempt to run the 380-yard (347 m) distance around the Great Clock while the clock twice strikes the hour of twelve – a feat enacted in the film *Chariots of Fire* and performed in 1988 by the athletes Sebastian Coe and Steve Cram. In Neville's Court beyond, the student Isaac Newton stamped his foot and timed the echo to calculate the speed of sound. The court's western end is dominated by the elegant Wren library designed by Sir Christopher in 1695. Wood carvings by the greatest of English carvers – Gringling Gibbons – adorn the building. A first edition of A A Milne's *Winnie the Pooh* is among the treasures on the library's shelves.

Trinity Hall – Trinity Lane. Adjacent to Trinity College and separated by Garret Hostel Lane, Trinity Hall was founded in 1350 by the Bishop of Norwich. The 16th-century library is the best remaining of its date. It is the only college known as a Hall, to distinguish it from Trinity College. It is famous for the number of chief justices it has produced and it has an outstanding collection of silver plates.

Eighteen-sixty-nine saw the funding of the first college for women, **Girton**, while in 1871, Miss Anne Clough founded **Newnham College. Selwyn Court** for men was founded in 1881, to be followed by **Ridley Hall, Westcott House** and **Westminster College**, all theological institutions. Though considerable building had taken place between the wars, it was 1954 before another college was founded. This was **New Hall**, a third women's college.

It is of striking design with a remarkable dome as its central feature and it is located past Castle Street on the Huntington Road. **Fitzwilliam Hall** was designed by Denys Lasdum, the designer of the National Theatre complex, in 1960. **Churchill College** is another splendid uncompromisingly modern building, while the **Old Schools**, though not specifically a college, were built in 1350 with many additions in succeeding years. **Senate House**, next to King's College in King's Parade, was built circa 1725 and handsomely adapts the tradition of Wren to the Palladian style. The **Old Library** was built in 1842 and the **New Library** in 1934. Of the many laboratories etc, perhaps the most famous is the **Cavendish Laboratory** where Ernest Rutherford, the atom physicist, was professor.

Although there are few public buildings of note in Cambridge, there are some interesting churches. In many ways the Round Church in Bridge Street is the most interesting. Built around 1130 with a circular nave to commemorate the Holy Sepulchre in Jerusalem, this is one of only four round churches in England. The nave is supported by eight massive pillars set around a sunken mosaic-tiled floor. The conical roof was built in the 19th century and replaced a 15th-century bell tower. The chancel and side chapels were also extensively restored in the 19th century although the 15th-century roof, with its angel supports in the north aisle, survives. Great St Mary's Church in King's Parade also merits a visit. This 14th-century university church with its 17th-century tower stands sentinel over the city. Its back is turned on the hurly-burly of the market place and its tall lancet windows look across the columned Senate House to the river and the Backs beyond. The Backs run behind the college and it's especially rewarding to lie there of a summer afternoon and watch the antics of someone new to punting. I have already mentioned the Mathematical Bridge which spans the river at Queen's College, but the oldest and prettiest bridge is Clare Bridge, built in 1639, which with its classical arches, stone balustrades and ornamental spheres links Clare College to the Backs. If you climb the tower of Great St Mary's there are splendid views.

Until the 18th century, students gathered in the church to receive their degrees. This ceremony is now held each June in the Senate, but the beautiful gilded clock of the west doorway of the church still sounds the time as it has done for centuries. University sermons are still given here. Finally, St Benet's Church in Benet Street: this is the oldest church in the country. The tower is Anglo-Saxon, circa 1000, and the interior arch is exceptionally well preserved.

WALK

Walk One – Begin at the car park in **Lion Yard**, which is off Corn Exchange Street. Turn right, and then left into the covered precinct of Lion Yard. Turn left into Petty Curry and right into Market Hill, past the cobbled **Market Square** with its colourful stalls. Turn right into Market Street and then left along narrow Market Passage. Turn left on Sidney Street, past **Sidney Sussex College** on your right and continue into Bridge Street. The **Round Church** is on your right and there is a delightful mixture of medieval, Georgian and Victorian shops and inns. Across the bridge, **Magdalene College** occupies almost the whole of one side of Magdalene Street, while on the other is a higgledy-piggledy row of 16th- and 17th-century houses in black and white. Retrace your steps across **Magdalene Bridge** and turn left down the steps to the riverside footpath. From **Jesus Lock**, a mooring place for pleasure craft, turn right to skirt Jesus Green. Turn right into tree-lined Victoria Avenue. To the right are the red brick buildings of **Jesus College**. At the crossroads go straight ahead into Short Street and Emmanuel Street. **Christ's College** is to your right. Turn left into St Andrew's Street and **Emmanuel College** is on your left. Turn right into Downing Street for the **Sedgwick Museum** and the **Museum of Archaeology and Anthropology**. Just beyond are the buildings of **Downing College**. Turn right into Corn Exchange Street and your car park starting point off Lion Yard.

Walk Two – Begin from the same place off Lion Yard. Emerge into Corn Exchange Street and turn right and then left into Wheeler Street. Turn right into Peas Hill and left along St Edward's Passage. Turn right to **Great St Mary's Church**. Beyond the church, turn left down Senate House Passage. The **Senate House**

is on your left and **Gonville and Gaius College** on your right. Turn left into Trinity Lane, past the ornate gatehouse of the **Old Schools** on the left and **Clare College** on the right to **King's College Chapel and College**. Leaving the chapel, follow Trinity Lane into Trinity Street. Turn left to **Trinity College**, and beyond it, to **St John's College**. Through St John's Gateway continue to Third Court, then turn left and cross the Old Bridge. Turn left and follow the footpath along the Backs. Cross a small bridge, passing **Wren Library**, then turn right along the Avenue. Turn left along a footpath beside the main road, past the 18th-century wrought-iron gates of **Clare College** and the gateway to **King's College**. The path soon veers left to the modern blocks of **Queen's College**. Continue to the bridge on Silver Street. Turn right onto Laundress Lane and then left along Mill Lane to Trumpington Street. Turn right past **Peterhouse College** to the **Fitzwilliam Museum**. Turn left into Fitzwilliam Street and left into Tennis Court Road, then left again into Pembroke Street and **Pembroke College**. An archway on the right leads to the **Museum of Zoology**. Turn right into Free School Lane to **Whipple Museum**. **Corpus Christi College** is adjacent to the museum and **St Catherine's College** is directly opposite, across Trumpington Street. From Whipple Museum turn right into Benet Street and **St Benet's Church** and into Wheeler Street and back to where you started. Most College grounds and chapels are open most days and entry is free. Libraries generally have more limited opening hours but all can be visited. Inquire at the porter's lodge of each college.

MUSEUMS AND GALLERIES

Fitzwilliam Museum – Trumpington Street, Tel 332900. The Fitzwilliam Museum is one of Britain's earliest public museums. The original building was designed by George Basevi and opened in 1848. The present collections contain Western European paintings, antiquities and the applied arts of Western Europe and Asia. The paintings range from the 14th century to modern; the antiquities are Egyptian, Western Asiatic, Greek and Roman; and the applied arts include sculpture, ceramics, textiles, fans, furniture, coins and medals. There are also illuminated musical and literary manuscripts and rare printed books. The whole collection now forms one of the most remarkable provincial museums in the country, and its permanent displays are supplemented by a lively series of temporary exhibitions throughout the year with special exhibitions and concerts for each Cambridge Festival. Open Tues–Sat 10–5pm; Antiquities, Applied Arts and Paintings 2–5pm, Sun 2:15–5pm.

Cambridge and County Folk Museum – 2/3 Castle Street, Tel 35515. Housed in a fascinating timber-framed building (formerly the White House Inn) dating from the 16th century, the museum's ten rooms of exhibits illustrate the work and everyday life of the people of Cambridge and its surrounding county over the last 300 years. On display are the tools and implements of the brickmaker, basket weaver, straw plaiter, bootmaker, chemist, barber, tobacconist, chimney sweep and thatcher. Other exhibits include a 19th-century kitchen, toys and games, city and university life, the Fens and local folklore. The collection of samplers on display here is one of the best in the country – remarkably dainty stitching, often worked by young children. Open Mon–Sat 10:30–5pm, Sun 2:30–4pm.

Polar Research Institute – Lensfield Road, Tel 336540. In June 1910, the Terra Nova set sail for the Antarctic – the start of Captain Scott's famous expedition to the South Pole. The five leading explorers eventually reached the Pole on 18th January 1912, only to discover they weren't the first – the Norwegian flag was there to greet them. All five, including Scott, died on the return journey. The full story of this and other more recent expeditions to the Arctic and Antarctic regions is told with diaries, letters, photographs, drawings, manuscripts and relics, including equipment and clothing. The museum also has major displays on the native people and the arts and crafts of the region from the early 19th century to the present day, plus an important section on scientific research being carried out today. The preparation for the Scott expedition was quite staggeringly detailed and efficient – take a look at the records of the plan of action. Open Mon–Sat 2–4pm.

Cambridge Museum of Technology – Riverside (off Newmarket Road), Tel 68650. Preserved Victorian pumping station with original steam, gas and electric powered pumps together with other examples of local industry, including a comprehensive collection of letterpress printing equipment. Open first Sunday of each month 2–5pm. Call for details of steam weekends.

University Museum of Archaeology and Anthropology – Downing Street, Tel 333576. The gallery of world prehistory and local archaeology provides a comprehensive survey from the origins of mankind to the rise of literate civilization. For the Cambridge region the story is continued through the Roman period into post-medieval times. There are extensive anthropological displays relating to all parts of the world. Open Mon–Fri 2–4pm, Sat 10–12:30pm.

University Museum of Zoology – Downing Street, Tel 336650. The museum consists of collections of zoological specimens used for teaching and research. There are displays of marine invertebrates, exotic birds and mammal skeletons included within a survey of the animal kingdom. Open Mon–Fri 2:15–4:45pm.

University Museum of Classical Archaeology – Sedgwick Avenue, Tel 335152. The museum houses and displays one of the largest and perhaps the finest collection of plaster casts of Greek and Roman sculptures in the world. Open Mon–Fri 9–5pm.

Whipple Museum of the History of Science – Free School Lane, Tel 334540. Housed in an historic 17th-century free school, the museum has an internationally known collection of early scientific instruments dating from the 14th century to the present day. The displays include items used in the study and practice of astronomy, electricity, gnomics, mathematics, medicine, microscopy, navigation, optics and general science. Open Mon–Fri 2–4pm.

Sedgwick Museum – Dept of Earth Sciences – Downing Street, Tel 333456. The museum houses a spectacular collection of fossil animals and plants of all geological ages and from all over the world. They include mounted skeletons of fossil mammals and birds, a mounted dinosaur skeleton, marine reptiles, flying reptiles, fishes, plants and a multitude of invertebrates. The museum also houses Britain's oldest intact geological collection, that of Dr John Woodward, still housed in early 18th-century walnut cabinets. It also displays material related to Professor Adam Sedgwick, the great pioneer of modern geology, after whom the museum is named. Open Mon–Fri 9–1pm and 2–5pm, Sat 10–1pm.

King's: The Building of a Chapel – King's College, King's Parade, Tel 350411. Visually and aurally, the chapel is easy to enjoy. But the process by which it came into existence was not easy at all. The wonderfully united impression it makes conceals a hundred years of starting and stopping, danger and survival for the people who built it. The exhibition reunites a great building with the people whose efforts made it; not just to the kings behind King's but to the craftsmen as well. The construction of the fan-vault, the woodwork of the screen and stalls and the glazing of the great windows are presented by excellent models. Open Mon–Sat 9:30–3:30, Sun (in vacations only) 1–3:30pm (winter) 10:30–4:30pm (summer).

Kettle's Yard – Castle Street, Tel 352124. Housed in converted 18th-century cottages, the gallery contains a permanent display of early 20th-century art collected by Jim Ede, whose home this was. There is an extensive collection of drawings and sculptures by Henry Gaudier-Brzeska as well as work by David Jones, Naum Gabo, Joan Miró, Constantin Brancusi, Albert Wallace and others. The house is maintained as Jim Ede lived in it, with ceramics, furniture and "found objects" he collected over many years. The adjoining exhibition gallery presents a changing programme of international contemporary art, including performance and video. Open: House – Tues–Sun 2–4pm, Gallery – Tues–Sat 12:30–5:30 (7pm on Thurs) Sun 2–5:30pm.

Dales Brewery – Cwydir Street, Tel 350725. This photographic gallery is attached to the **Cambridge Darkroom**, a centre for photography at the same address.

Check also the **Charrington Print Room**, the **Octagon Gallery**, the **Adeane Gallery** and the **Robertson Room**, all at the Fitzwilliam Museum, the **Rugg Centre**, Leys School, Trumpington Road, Clare College's **Latimer Room** and the **Gallery at the Central Library**, Lion Yard.

THEATRE

Arts Theatre – Peas Hill, off Market Square, Tel 352000. This traditional theatre with a welcoming staff provides an adventurous programme of professional touring theatre, dance and opera including a mix of comedies, thrillers and musicals plus interesting new work from the resident Cambridge Theatre Companies who spend at least eight weeks a year at the Arts and the rest of the time touring nationally and internationally. There is an annual pantomime and the excellent film programme is described below. Recent touring groups have included Cheek by Jowl, Theatre de Complicite, the Market Theatre Company of Johannesburg and the Oxford Stage Company. An innovation is the CTC co-producing a show with another regional theatre. Thus, recently, Jonson's *Volpone* was presented with the Theatre Royal, York and Joe Orton's *Loot* with the Wolsey Theatre, Ipswich. There are two excellent restaurants which are open all day.

Corn Exchange – Wheeler Street, Tel 357851. The Cambridge Corn Exchange is a large arts and entertainment centre. The programme includes rock and pop, ballet, orchestral music and children's shows. Recent visitors have ranged from the Cambridge Symphony Orchestra, the Moscow Festival Ballet and the London Mozart Players to Charlie Pride and Elkie Brooks. The Great British Orchestras series has included the City of Birmingham Symphony Orchestra and the Royal Philharmonic.

ADC Theatre – Park Road, Tel 352001. The ADC is England's oldest university playhouse and the main venue for university productions as well as small-scale touring companies. It is also the information centre for the Cambridge Fringe Festival in July.

Cambridge Drama Centre – Covent Garden, Mill Road, Tel 322748. Exciting new theatre from small-scale touring companies. Pretty avant-garde.

The Junction – Clifton Road, Tel 412600. Six or seven events a week ranging from funk rock, cabaret theatre and performance art. Very avant-garde theatre – very loud music. I especially like the "Gay Bykers on Acid."

MUSIC

University Concert Hall – West Road, Tel 335176, hosts a large number of concerts performed by the University Music Societies and other groups. Various musical events are often held in colleges and chapels. Contact Cambridge Tourist Office for details, Tel 332640.

Carpenter Hall – Victoria Street, Tel 232915, is the home of the Mackenzie Society, which has concerts on Tuesdays at 7:45 during term time plus other events.

Cambridge Symphony Orchestra – gives regular concerts throughout the year and has recently established a chamber ensemble called the **Eastern Sinfonia**, Tel 65374.

See also Cambridge Corn Exchange above.

Cambridge is most musically alive during the **Cambridge Festival**, Tel 463363, which takes place during the last two weeks of July. There is a Carnival Fair, jugglers, steel bands, folk and flamenco dancers, choirs, carnival costumes, jazz musicians, floats and evening fireworks – and that's just the opening day. Over the two-week period there are choirs, string ensembles, symphony orchestras, individual artists and chamber groups performing in locations all over the city. There is also an imaginative theatre programme, ballet, poetry readings, popular music, jazz and a large fringe festival. Tel 352001. The Festival really goes on all year with the MADD Youth Festival, a Folk Festival, children's events and promenade concerts but the last two weeks of July is really the time to be in town.

Later in August, Cambridge hosts the Cambridgeshire Summer Recitals. The organ is the festival's main theme and concerts are held in college chapels and city churches with some of the world's most famous organists taking part. Tel 240026.

CINEMA

The most exciting films in town can be seen at the **Cambridge Arts Cinema**, St Edward's Passage, Tel 352001. They offer as many as six shows a day of as many as three different films, with performances as often as 11am, 2pm, 4pm, 7pm, 9pm and 11:15pm. For variety and the number of performances I do not know how it could be bettered. The films range from "art" films by Rohmer, Godard and Almodovar to modern British cinema, Woody Allen and Costa-Gavras.

Commercial cinema: **Cannon** – St Andrew's Street, Tel 64537 (2 screens).

The information service of the Libraries and Information Service of the Cambridgeshire County Council presents an excellent little monthly booklet listing all music, opera, operetta, films, drama, dance, comedy and exhibitions in the area. Available from the Central Library, 7 Lion Yard, or the Tourist Information Office, Wheeler Street.

BOOKSTORES

There is a very good variety of booksellers in the Cambridge area – which is not really surprising when you think about it. The best are **Dillon's** at 22 Sidney Street, Tel 351688, **Heffer's** at 20 Trinity Street, Tel 358351 (they are agents for HMSO) and **Sherratt and Hughes**, 1 Trinity Street, Tel 355488. Heffer's, which takes first place, has large sections for children's books, paperbacks, general novels, maps and guides and new books on all subjects. We have heard of all of these before, but the local independents are just as good. **Galloway and Porter** at 30 Sidney Street, Tel 67876, are excellent as is **Browne's Bookstore** at 56 Mill Road, Tel 350968. For bargain books the best is **Harvey's Discount Books**, 14-16 Bradwell's Court, Tel 65129. For comics and science fiction there's **Comic Showcase** at 17 Norfolk Street, Tel 69206 and **Forbidden Planet**, 57-61 Burleigh Street, Tel 66926. Religious books can be found at **Scripture Union Bookshop**, 88A Regent Street, Tel 352727 and **A R Mowbray** at 14 King's Parade, Tel 358452 and there's real interest to be found at **Grapevine Radical and Community Bookshop**, 6 Dales Brewery, Gwydir

Street, Tel 61808. Finally, the **Green Street Bookshop** at 5 Green Street, Tel 68088, is good for philosophy, history and science and **Cambridge Music Shop** has books on music and sheet music.

ANTIQUARIAN AND SECONDHAND BOOKS

The **Bookroom** at 13A Eligius Street (off Bateman Street), Tel 69694, has a good selection of secondhand and antiquarian books as has **The Bookshop** at 24 Magdalene Street, Tel 62457. **G R David** in St Edward's Passage, Tel 354619, besides having a good secondhand and antiquarian selection, also has remainders. **Deighton Bell and Co** at 13 Trinity Street, Tel 353939, has a good antiquarian and secondhand collection as have **Galloway and Porter** at 3 Green Street, Tel 67876. They are the university booksellers and are mentioned above. **Brian Jordan Music Books**, 10 Green Street, Tel 322368, as the name suggests, has musical literature – all periods and a lot of secondhand music. **The Haunted Bookshop**, St Edward's Passage, Tel 312913, has some very beautiful antiquarian, illustrated and children's books while **Quinto** at 34 Trinity Street, Tel 358279 (just down the road from Deighton Bell), has antiquarian and secondhand books, prints and maps.

ART GALLERIES

Broughton House Gallery – 98 King Street, Tel 314960. Regular exhibitions of international contemporary art, usually once a month lasting three weeks between March and December. (Close to Sidney Sussex College)

Conservatory College – 6 Hills Avenue, Tel 211311. Paintings, sculptures and wall-hangings by over 50 of East Anglia's leading artists. Open Saturdays only 10–5pm and the first Sunday in each month at the same time.

Gallery on the Cam – Jesus Lock, Chesterton Road (on the river between Magdalene Bridge and Victoria Avenue), Tel 316901. This is unique – a floating gallery consisting of a 70-foot (21.2 m) barge moored to the banks of the River Cam and acting as an important gallery space for contemporary artists in Cambridge and East Anglia. Closed Mondays.

Ganz and Company – 51 Cambridge Place (close to Fenners Cricket Ground), Tel 316887. The policy of Ganz is to present a programme of exhibitions that feature the best of 20th century paintings and sculptures from both this country and abroad. They also have an extensive collection of master graphics by contemporary and modern artists.

Heffer's Art Gallery – 19 Sidney Street (close to Sidney Sussex College), Tel 358241. The gallery is a glass-roofed exhibition area situated on the fourth floor of Heffer's Stationers. Exhibitions include a broad spectrum of contemporary art from the traditional to new, more challenging work. There is a section on Cambridge and East Anglian artists. The Lower Gallery offers a wide range of posters, paintings and limited edition prints.

Jean Pain Gallery – 7 King's Parade (opposite King's College Chapel), Tel 313970. Some beautiful antique maps and prints together with modern art posters and Oxford and Cambridge University prints and posters.

The Oriel Gallery – 16 Fair Street (off Mards Causeway, close to Grafton Centre) Tel 321027. Oil and watercolour paintings, etchings and modern British art. The gallery deals mainly with the work of early 20th-century professional painters.

Primavera – 10 King's Parade (close to King's College Chapel) Tel 357708. Some fine examples of leading British contemporary ceramics, wood, glass, craftwork, metal, jewellery and paintings.

Sebastian Pearson – Free School Lane, Benet Street, Tel 323999. A delightful 16th-century building containing oil paintings, 19th-century watercolours, English porcelain and Oriental works of art. Finally, **Warwick and Son**, 102 Cherry Hinton Road (close to Zoology Museum) Tel 246896, has prints and originals, both traditional and contemporary.

Note that the **Cambridge Central Library Exhibition Room**, Lion Yard, Tel 65252, **Kettles Yard** (see Museums) and **Cambridge Darkroom Gallery**, Dales Brewery, Gwydir Street, Tel 350725, occasionally have work for sale depending on the nature of the touring exhibition they are hosting.

ANTIQUE DEALERS

There are a lot of antique dealers in Cambridge. I have attempted to group the ones listed below geographically. The description at the beginning of each section indicates its situation. I have also indicated the specialization of each dealer, although it should be borne in mind that most shops have a general collection as well as a specific focus and that some shops take a liberal view of the term "specialization."

1. Lensfield Road is a good area as is Regent Street, which is close by and a continuation of St Andrew's Street. Make for the Scott Polar Research Institute:

Jess Aplin – 8 Lensfield Road, Tel 315168. 17th- to 19th-century furniture.

Hyde Park Antiques – 12 Lensfield Road, Tel 312162. Furniture, pottery, porcelain, glass, clocks, pictures and jewellery.

Cottage Antiques – 16-18 Lensfield Road, Tel 316698. Glass, china, brass, copper, blue and white pottery (pre-1850), Staffordshire figures, prints, pictures and country furniture.

Pine Merchant – 60 Lensfield Road, Tel 314377. 19th-century pine furniture.

John Beazor and Sons Ltd – 78/80 Regent Street, Tel 355178. Fine antique furniture (English and Continental) and decorative items.

Collins and Clarke – 81 Regent Street, Tel 353801. All classes of fine antiques.

2. Trumpington Street, south of King's College Chapel, and Pembroke Street, to your left just before Pembroke College:

Dolphin Antiques – 33 Trumpington Street, Tel 354180. Furniture, brass, small items and glass.

Gabor Crossa Antiques – 34 Trumpington Street, Tel 356049. Early English ceramics, Delft ware and tiles, 18th-century glasses, Oriental porcelain, Japanese woodcuts and topographical prints.

Malcolm C Clarke – 3 Pembroke Street, Tel 357117. 18th-century furniture, brass, copper and china.

Pembroke Antiques – 7 Pembroke Street, Tel 63246. Jewellery, furniture, silver, glassware, china. Mostly pre-Victorian.

3. King's Street and Trinity Street, a continuation of Trumpington Street:

Antiques Etcetera – 18 King Street, Tel 62825. Victoriana, watches, clocks, silver, jewellery and Daisychain jewellery.

Book - Shelf – 62-64 King Street, Tel 352515. Silver, furniture and small items.

My Auntie Had One But She Threw It Away – 105 King Street, Tel 62388. Lamps, rugs and mirrors and a wonderful name!

Buckies – 31 Trinity Street, Tel 357910. Jewellery, silver, glass and general antiques.

4. Gwydir Street. Go out of town via Parker Street/Parkside and Mill Road to the Dales Brewery complex, which is on your left just before the railway line:

Collectors Market – Dales Brewery, Gwydir Street, no telephone. Antiques and bric-à-brac market.

Willroy of Dales – Dales Brewery, Cwydir Street, Tel 311687. Antiques, secondhand furniture and bric-à-brac.

Collectors Centre – Hope Street Yard, Hope Street, Tel 211632 (ask at Dales Brewery for directions). Antiques, toys, gramophones and secondhand furniture.

There are also a few dealers who don't fit neatly into the above categories. They are as follows:

Cambridge Doll's Hospital – 1 Jesus Terrace, Tel 350452. Antique dolls, toys and games and, of course, a doll's hospital. Close to Jesus College.

Chesterton Bygones – 190 Green End Road, Tel 424133. Furniture, porcelain and pictures. (First right past Magdalene, out via Chesterton Lane to Chesterton Road, and then ask for Green End Road past the football ground.)

Dado – 48A Eden Street, Tel 327725. Small antique furniture, jewellery, silver, decorative items. (Walk via Fitzroy Street from Grafton Centre car park off Newmarket Road.)

W R Parr – Unit 10, Ronald Rolph Court, Wadloes Road, Tel 212343. Cabinet maker and antique repairer. (Off Newmarket Road past the Rugby Ground.)

20th Century – 169 Histon Road, Tel 359482. Specialists in art deco, ceramics, furniture and lighting.

La Belle Epoque – 55A Hills Road. No telephone. Decorative items, jewellery, small furniture and lamps.

RESTAURANTS

One of the most beautiful places to eat in Cambridge is **Midsummer House**, Midsummer Common, Tel 69299. You reach the house by a towpath and the car park is distant. Once inside there is a choice to be made with respect to seating. The conservatory is bright and airy, looking out on to the gardens, while the downstairs dining room is cosy, and the upstairs private and very chic. Set lunches and dinner, depend for price on the number of courses taken and given the style and panache of the place, prices are reasonable. Friends have raved about the hot venison pie, the lamb persillade and the wild mushrooms. Open Mon–Sat 12–2pm and 6:30–9:30pm. No Sat or Mon lunch.

Twenty-Two – 22 Chesterton Road, Tel 357880. My favourite place to eat in Cambridge. Set in the rooms of a Victorian terraced house, the place is a little cramped but very friendly and the food is top-notch. I had a wonderful melon and ginger soup, an excellent saddle of hare at just the right gaminess and a superb chocolate mousse. I couldn't move afterwards. It's a wonderfully welcoming establishment and I wouldn't go anywhere else. Open Tues–Sat for dinner only 7:30–10pm.

Upstairs – 71 Castle Street (above Waffles Cafe), Tel 312569. Excellent Middle Eastern food and atmosphere. Dishes from Morocco (beef soup with lentils and chickpeas), Armenia (lamb with apricots) and Turkey (clove-flavoured beef and yoghurt) give the place a really authentic feeling. There are good crepes for dessert if the honey-dripping sweets are too much for you, authentic though they may be. Open all week for dinner only 6:30–11:30pm.

PUBS

Baron of Beef – 19 Bridge Street, Tel 63720. Unspoilt pub with one of the longest bars in the city. there's a panelled partition dividing the two drinking areas and a really mixed clientèle. Simple, good value food from a help yourself buffet.

Tram Depot – Dover Street, off East Road, Tel 324553. Part of the old tram depot with a built-in glazed mezzanine, a central skylight that runs the length of the building, bare brick walls, bare stone floors and old furniture. A really nice atmosphere. Excellent home-made bar food.

Boathouse – 14 Chesterton Road, Tel 460905. Little partitioned "snugs," net-curtained etched-glass windows, paisley wallpaper, bookshelves and prints. A really attractive setting looking across to Jesus Green with barges moored between the pub and a nearby lock. Good value bar food including baked potatoes, steak and kidney pie and an excellent aubergine-and-parmesan bake. Sunday lunches too.

Cambridge Blue – 85 Gwydir Street, Tel 61382. Two small rooms (one non-smoking) have a charming "kitcheny" feel about them. There are built in wall benches and lots of university sports pictures. Good bar food includes home-made pies with help yourself salads, spicy sausage and cauliflower au gratin. Sunday lunch.

Free Press – Prospect Row, Tel 68337. Lots of oars and rowing photographs, which is not surprising as the pub is the only one in the country registered as a boat club. Really excellent bar food – lots of interesting salads plus navarin of lamb, fresh salmon and smoked ham. Wonderful treacle tart. The rabbit in the garden is named Gismo.

Old Spring – Ferry Path (car park is on Chesterton Road) Tel 357228. Cushioned settles, pews and stools and cast-iron traditional tables give a pleasing ambience enhanced by the soft gas lighting and earth-coloured rough plaster walls. Good bar food including pita bread, Greek dips, chili con carne and swordfish. Sunday lunch. The method of lighting makes it a bit hot when it's crowded.

ARTISTIC ASSOCIATIONS

There are of course, a great many and I have linked this brief selection to the colleges attended by each.

John Milton had rooms at Christ's College from 1625 to 1632. He wrote both "Hymn on the Morning of Christ's Nativity" and his "Sonnet to Shakespeare" here. William Wordsworth was an undergraduate at St John's College in 1787. In 1788 he visited Milton's room and drank to his memory. Siegfried Sassoon was an undergraduate of Clare College and wrote his first poems there. He enlisted on the outbreak of war in 1914 and his bitter antiwar and antipolitical poems are a direct result of his experiences as an army officer in France and Palestine. Christopher Marlowe, author of *Doctor Faustus, Tamburlaine* and *The Jew of Malta,* had rooms in Corpus Christi College in 1578 and wrote *Tamburlaine* while at Cambridge. Marlowe was killed in a London tavern brawl in 1593, the same year that another fine Elizabethan dramatist, John Fletcher, author of *The Maid's Tragedy* attended Corpus Christi. Fletcher's plays, written in collaboration with Francis Beaumont, were, in their own day and throughout the Restoration period, more popular than Shakespeare.

Thomas Cramner, the English Protestant martyr burned at the stake for heresy in 1556, was made a Fellow of Jesus College in 1515. It is said that he used to meet with Hugh Latimer and William Tyndale at the Old White Hart Inn (demolished) to discuss the reforms they hoped to make in the church. Latimer, who studied at Clare, was burnt at the stake for heresy a year before Cramner while Tyndale, who first translated the Bible into English, was burned at the stake in Antwerp in 1536. Samuel Taylor Coleridge, author of "The Rime of the Ancient Mariner," "Christabel" and "Kubla Khan," studied at Jesus between 1791 and 1794. The famous writer of ghost stories, M R James, was an undergraduate at King's College and became Vice-Chancellor of the University in 1913. Rupert Brooke studied at King's too and founded the Marlowe Society, the undergraduate dramatic society. The Marlowe Society, which is still in existence, has had many of the country's finest actors among its cast lists. E M Forster, author of *A Room with a View* and *Howards End,* was made a Fellow of King's in 1927.

Charles Kingsley, author of the much loved children's book, *The Water Babies* and C S Lewis, author of *The Narnia Chronicles,* which are also wonderful for youngsters, both attended Magdalene College. Virginia Woolf's *A Room of One's Own,* written in 1929, is based on the papers she read to the Arts Societies at Newnham and Girton in 1928. Incidentally, the English writer Rosamond Lehmann and the social scientist Baroness Wooton both studied at Girton, the oldest women's college in Cambridge; the English novelist Margaret Drabble, and the Australian feminist and critic Germaine Greer both attended Newnham College, Girton's sister hall of learning.

Edmund Spenser, whose monumental opus, *The Faerie Queene,* is one of the greatest epics in the English language, entered Pembroke College in 1569, while Thomas Gray, author of "Elegy Written in a Country Churchyard" spent most of his life in Cambridge, became Professor of History and Modern Languages in 1768 and died here in 1771. Gray was previously at Peterhouse College, where a practical joke by other students caused him to move to Pembroke. Malcolm Lowry, who wrote *Under the Volcano,* was at St Catherine's College in the early 1930s and his first novel, *Ultramarine,* was accepted by his tutor in lieu of a thesis. Preceding William Wordsworth at St John's College were the Elizabethan dramatist Robert Greene in 1577, and the fine English poet Robert Herrick in 1613. Trinity College is the largest in Cambridge, which accounts for the many famous artistic figures associated with its hallowed halls. Francis Bacon, the English essayist and philosopher, was one of the college's earliest students in 1573, while George Herbert, the metaphysical poet, followed him in 1609. Even more famous was the poet, Andrew Marvell, who studied here from 1633 to 1638, while a few years later John Dryden was a student. Lord Byron, who came up to Trinity in 1805, had mixed feelings about his accommodation. He wrote, "I am now most pleasantly situated in super-excellent rooms, flanked on one side by my tutor, on the other by an Old Fellow, both of whom are rather checks on my vivacity." T B Macaulay, whose *History of England* and *Lays of Ancient Rome* are seminal works on their respective subjects, came to Trinity in 1818 and became a Fellow in 1824. Alfred, Lord Tennyson, was at Trinity for four years, beginning in 1827, but left without a degree because of his father's death. William Makepeace Thackeray, author of *Vanity Fair,* and Edward Fitzgerald, who wrote *The Rubaiyat of Omar Khayyam,* were contemporaries of Tennyson. More recently, in 1900, Lytton Strachey, the biographer and critic, formed a group including Clive Bell, Leonard Woolf and John Maynard Keynes, which was the precursor of the Bloomsbury Group. A E Housman, author of *A Shropshire Lad,* was appointed a Fellow of Trinity in 1911 and G M Trevelyan, who made history a pleasure for the general reader, was Master of Trinity from 1940 to 1951.

EPHEMERA

Granchester is a small village two miles south of Cambridge. It was immortalized by Rupert Brooke, although Chaucer, Spenser, Milton, Dryden and Byron all felt drawn to the village. Brooke's famous poem, "The Old Vicarage, Granchester," was written in 1910 while he was holidaying in Germany, and wonderfully expresses his nostalgia for the village and indeed the nostalgia of all expatriates for their homeland. Some of the most famous lines are –

> Oh! there the chestnuts, summer through
> Beside the river make for you
> A tunnel of green, gloom, and sleep
> Deeply above; and green and deep
> The stream mysteriously glides beneath
> Green as a dream and deep as death.

Best known, perhaps, are the lines -

> Stands the church clock at ten to three?
> And is there honey still for tea?

When Brooke returned to the Old Vicarage after his German holiday, he was surprised to be greeted by his landlady with the assurance that there was "honey still for tea." She had read the poem published in his college magazine. The village pub is called, yes, you guessed it – the Rupert Brooke.

In Magdalene College, appropriately enough in the 17th century Pepys Building, can be found the library of the diarist Samuel Pepys, who was a student of the college from 1650 to 1653. Some 3000 of his books are contained in bookcases Pepys designed himself. They include his famous diary, bound in six volumes and written in a shorthand devised by Pepys. Three years were spent deciphering the diary – only to discover that a complete key to the code was lying on the library shelves.

In Brookside can be found Hobson's Conduit, a reminder of the one time carrier and hansom cab entrepreneur who became mayor of the city. It was from his insistence that customers take the first cab offered that the expression "Hobson's choice" derives.

When I was a boy in school, classes were often taken to local village churches to take brass rubbings. During the Middle Ages, important people were often given a memorial in the form of a brass plate on their tomb which often had an engraving of their figure in costume. Because of this we now have original illustrations of what those people looked like in medieval costume – knights in armour, ladies in their best dresses, babies in swaddling clothes and priests in their vestments. Today it is no longer possible for this unrestricted brass rubbing to continue as the valuable brass pictures were becoming worn down. At Cambridge Brass Rubbing Centre in St Giles Church, Castle Street, there are over 100 exact facsimile brass plates from which you can make your own brass rubbings. A finished brass rubbing is a most attractive gift as well as a Cambridge souvenir and there is an enormous selection with the largest brass being more than two metres high.

Perhaps because of the town's gentler air, the phantoms of Cambridge colleges seem to have clung longer to their old lodgings than the ghosts of Oxford. Dr Butts, appointed Master of Corpus Christi in 1626, still haunts his old rooms in the college where he hanged himself on Easter Sunday, 1632. Apparently he had been depressed by the number of students who died of the plague that year and wrote to a friend that there was not an undergraduate to be seen in the college or the town. Another Corpus Christi ghost is that of a 17th-century student who fell in love with a Master's daughter. Interrupted at a secret meeting, he hid in a kitchen cupboard and was suffocated.

Dr Wood, who became Master of St John's before his death in 1839, has often been seen on the staircase of the college. He is said to appear not as the grand figure of his later years, but as the poverty-stricken student he once was. Unable to afford either fire or light, he used to wrap his feet in straw each evening and study by the feeble light of the rush candle which lit the staircase. Merton Hall, which belongs to St John's, is reputedly haunted by a large, furry, penguin-like creature. Whatever it is, it seems to have wandered from Abbey House in the Newmarket Road, where it has also been reported. The house is built on the site of an Augustinian priory and is said to be linked by a secret passage to Jesus College, once St Radegund's Nunnery.

TOURIST INFORMATION BUREAU: Wheeler Street, Cambridge, Cambs CB2 3QB. Tel (0223) 322640

COLCHESTER

County of Essex
52 miles (83.2 km) from London by A12
One hour by train from London (Liverpool Street Station)

Colchester calls itself "Britain's oldest recorded town" and the claim appears justified, as settlement in the immediate area goes back at least 3000 years. However, the real history of the town could be said to date from the first few decades of the Christian era when Camulodunum, Colchester's predecessor, developed greatly in size, strength and influence. A vast system of banks and ditches, known as dykes, was constructed to make this stronghold of the Celtic war god Camulos seem almost impregnable. Camulodunum reached a pinnacle of importance under the all-powerful king Cunobelin (Shakespeare's Cymbeline). Romans called him King of the Britons because he held sway over most of southeast Britain until his death in AD 40.

When the Roman Emperor Claudius invaded Britain in AD 43, Camulodunum was so important it was automatically chosen as the army's primary objective. Romans must have known the town well, as in the 1st century BC Roman merchants traded continental luxury goods such as fine pottery, glass and Italian wine for the corn, cattle, slaves, metal, hunting dogs and pearls (from the native oysters) that the town could export in return. The triumphant capture of Camulodunum was led by Claudius himself and it was here that he personally received the surrender of many of the British tribes, as well as establishing the first capital of Roman Britain in the town. The Roman fortress here was very large. Archaeological excavations have uncovered extensive remains of a full-sized legionary fortress lying beneath the town. There was also a magnificent temple dedicated to the deified Emperor Claudius. The temple was the centre of the Imperial cult in Britain and its remains were incorporated within the Norman foundations of Colchester Castle.

Camulodunum was now known as Colonia Victricensis. The garrison had been transferred in AD 49 and the new town was inhabited by native inhabitants and newly retired soldiers. In AD 60 Queen Boadicea of the neighbouring tribe of Iceni led a revolt against the Romans. The Romans had seized her territory and treated its inhabitants brutally. She wiped out the colony and also destroyed London and St Albans. According to Tacitus, as many as 70,000 Romans were put to death, but the revolt was short-lived as Boadicea herself was in turn defeated by Suetonius Paulinius, Governor of Britain, and rather than fall into Roman hands she took poison. When peace was restored the town was rebuilt and a triumphal arch was erected to mark the western entrance of the colony. This Balkerne Gate still survives and is Colchester's longest-surviving monument, along with

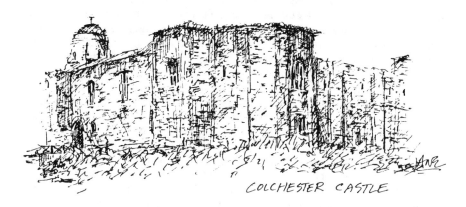

COLCHESTER CASTLE

a good stretch of Roman wall. Roman administration continued until the 5th century and then the Saxons occupied the town, setting up their timber huts amongst the now crumbling Roman ruins.

Colchester – a Saxon name meaning "the camp on the River Colne" – was a town of some importance in late Saxon times. It had a mint, was well fortified and contained buildings of quality – like the timber chapel in front of the castle, later rebuilt in stone, and Holy Trinity Church, whose original west wall and tower still survive. All Saints, St Martin's and St Peter's, all medieval churches, may have equally early origins. The great Keep of Colchester Castle and the old Moot Hall sprang up in response to the growing prominence of medieval Colchester. The Abbey of St John was founded in 1096 by the Benedictine Order (its perimeter walls still stand) and its last Abbot, John Beche, was hanged in 1539. Stone from the Abbey was used for the rebuilding of Bourne Mill in 1591 (see below). St Botolph's Priory was constructed in 1110 as the first house of Augustinian canons in Britain. Built of Roman stone, it is one of Colchester's most atmospheric places to visit and although it survived Henry VIII's dissolution of the monasteries in 1536, it was damaged in the Civil War. The remains of the Priory and indeed the Castle are both splendid and must be seen.

In the Middle Ages, Colchester grew in prosperity due to the cloth trade, and many fine timber buildings from those days can still be seen in the town. East Street has the Rose and Crown and, although dating from the late 15th century, the Red Lion in High Street still has beautiful workmanship. So does the George Hotel on the opposite side of the road, although the timber framework is partly hidden behind a Georgian façade. If you turn off High Street onto West Stockwell Street you will find the Dutch Quarter, which takes its name from the Flemish refugees who settled here in the late 16th century and revitalized the cloth trade with their new draperies known as "bays and says."

A century later Colchester was devastated during the Civil War by a siege lasting eleven weeks in which the Royalists, who had taken possession, were eventually ousted by their Parliamentary opponents. At the bottom of East Street you can see the Siege House, which is an Elizabethan building scarred by the attentions of Cromwell's army in 1648. Many houses were damaged or destroyed in the siege and the cost to the community was great. The cloth trade now suffered a gradual decline and by the early 19th century it was defunct, but not before many elegant Georgian houses had been built on the proceeds. Particularly outstanding is Hollytrees in the High St, Greyfriars, which occupies the site of the 13th-century Franciscan friary and Minories, in High St, which is now a fine art gallery.

In the 19th century Colchester again became a garrison town, this time as a result of the Napoleonic Wars. Since then the army has always played an important part in the life of the town and about 5000 troops are resident in Colchester, making it the third largest garrison town in Britain. The Colchester Tattoo is one of the most spectacular in the country. It takes place in the first week of August every second (even-numbered) year. Colchester continued to grow in the 19th century. The Water Tower, one of the town's most unusual buildings, was built at the end of the High Street in 1882. It was the second largest water tower in the country and although most Colchester residents regarded it as an eyesore they affectionately nicknamed it "Jumbo" after the famous Barnum and Bailey elephant who was at the height of his fame at this time (see Ephemera). The tower resisted England's worst earthquake, which had its epicentre here in 1884, and even the attempts of one owner to dynamite it for building materials. The view from the top of the water tower is stunning. Dominating the High Street, though, is the Town Hall, built in 1902. The carved ornamentation around the building and the stained glass windows commemorating the Dutch weavers make the building one of Colchester's most beautiful.

Nowadays Colchester is famous principally for its oysters, which have been highly esteemed since Roman times, and for engineering and the growing of roses.

WALK

For a **Colchester Walk**, start off at the bus station car park and walk towards the High Street. In front of you is **Colchester Castle** with the **Hollytrees Museum** on your right and the former **All Saints' Church**, now the **Natural History Museum**, on your left. Turn right into High Street and East Hill following the line of the Roman main street. **St James's Church** has a 14th century tower; beyond is the site of the Roman East Gate. Turn right down Priory Street, flanked by the stone and brick bands of the Roman walls. Opposite a pawnbroker's gilded sign are the skeletal remains of **St Botolph's Abbey**. Cross Queen Street to Vineyard Street. Note the remains of a Roman drain in the car park and in the middle distance a great gatehouse, all that remains of the medieval **St John's Abbey**. Climb Vineyard Steps and turn left along Eld Lane and right up Trinity Street. To the left is **Tymperley's Clock Museum**; opposite are the pyramid-capped turrets of **Holy Trinity Church**, now the **Social History Museum**. Turn left along Culver Street to Head Street and turn left. Through the arch is the former **King's Head Inn**. Turn right along Church Walk to **St Mary's Church**, its tower battered during the Civil War. Bear left through the churchyard and left down the steps, towards Balkerne Hill; turn right and follow the Roman wall to Balkerne Gate (the Mercury Theatre is on your right). Bear left at the **Water Tower** and pass through Balkerne Passage to North Hill and High Street to the **Town Hall**. Turn left down West Stockwell Street and visit the **Dutch Quarter**. Turn right at junction, right again up East Stockwell Street, then left along St Helen's Lane. Beyond St Helen's Chapel you will see the site of the **Roman Theatre** marked on the road. Cross Maidenburgh Street and go through the alley into upper **Castle Park**. Go round **Castle** and come back across High Street to the bus station.

MUSEUMS AND GALLERIES

Colchester Castle – The Castle, Tel 74218/2. Open April–Sept Mon–Sat 10–1 and 2–5pm: Oct–Mar Mon–Fri 10–1 and 2–5pm: Sat 10–1 and 2–4pm. Flower-clad outer defences, a red tile roof and bands of Roman brick make this, the largest keep in England, seem more like a Tuscan palace. But there is a grim episode attached to it: an obelisk in the bailey marks the spot where the Royalist commanders were executed after their surrender on August 28, 1648. It was on this site too, in the temple of Claudius, that Boadicea slaughtered Colchester's Romano-British population. The temple vaults are still intact and the **Colchester and Exeter Museum**, which is situated in the Castle, has a range of Roman treasures on display of exceptional quality and interest.

Hollytrees Museum – High Street, Tel 712481/2. Open same hours as the castle. The Hollytrees was built in 1718 and extended in 1785. There are displays illustrating the social history of Essex in the 18th and 19th century, as well as an endearing collection of Victorian doll's houses and tea sets, Georgian toy farms and early mechanical toys. There are also displays of tradesman's tools and firearms, paintings of old Colchester and a costume gallery.

Natural History Museum – All Saints' Church, Tel 712481/2. Open same hours as the Castle. Straight-tusked elephants, aurochs, mammoths and brown bears are the subject of vivid dioramas in the former church. Remains found in Essex of these animals are placed in front of the dioramas. There are also displays on exotic species to be found in Essex today, such as mink and muskrats.

Social History Museum – Holy Trinity Church, Trinity Street, Tel 712481/2. Open same hours as castle. The tower of Holy Trinity Church dates from 1000, the church itself from the 14th century. Water-mills, oyster fisheries and other local subjects form the main display.

The Minories – 74 High Street, Tel 577067. Open Tues–Sat 11–5; Sun 2–6pm. The gallery, accommodated in a distinguished Georgian house, has concentrated on building up a permanent collection of works by 20th century artists who have some connection with the region. The important research library includes the personal collections of Paul and John Nash. The Gallery also hosts many travelling/temporary exhibitions. There are also drawings by Constable.

Sir Alfred Munninqs Art Museum – Castle House, Pedham, Colchester, Tel 322127. Just north of the town on the A12 to Norwich. Open May–early Oct– Sun,Wed,Bank Hol Mon 2–5, also Thurs,Sat 2–5 in Aug. Castle House, part Tudor, part Georgian, was the home of Sir Alfred Munnings from 1919 until his death in 1959. It now contains a large selection of his paintings, sketches and other work in the setting of the house in which he had his studio. There are many studies of racehorses and of racing, equestrian portraits and hunting scenes. The exhibitions are changed from time to time and augmented by paintings by Munnings from other sources.

Tymperley's Clock Museum – Trinity Street, Tel 712943. Open April–Oct Tues–Sat 10–4pm. In this building dating back to 1500 there is a beautiful collection of locally made clocks, a unique collection in fact, and without parallel in Britain.

East Anglian Railway Museum – Chapel and Wakes Colne Station, Tel 242524. A comprehensive collection of 19th- and 20th-century railway buildings, locomotives, coaches, wagons, signal boxes etc. Steam locomotives can be seen in action on certain days. Open daily 9:30–5pm.

Bourne Mill – Bourne Road, Tel 572422. Open April–Oct 9–Sat, Sun and Bank Hol Mon 2–5:30pm. July–Aug also open Tues. This Dutch-gabled fishing lodge was built in 1591 from material taken from St John's Abbey. It was later converted into a mill. Much of the machinery, including the waterwheel, is intact and in working condition and the four-acre (1.6 ha) mill pond, too, still remains. The Gallery at the University of Essex hosts regular exhibitions. Phone the Arts Office – 873261 – for details.

THEATRE

Mercury Theatre – Balkerne Gate, Tel 573948. The Mercury is an attractive, open stage theatre, seating between 410 and 500 depending on the physical configuration of the production. Most of the drama here is home produced, although the main stage and also the Jenny Bone Studio space, which is tucked away under the main auditorium, do house the occasional tour. Generally there is a good four-weekly rep programme and an annual traditional pantomime. The smaller studio space which seats about 80 presents a more off-beat selection of plays. Recent productions have included a fine production of Timberlake Wertenbaker's *Our Country's Good* and a joint production with the Redgrave Theatre, Farnham, of Sheridan's *The Rivals*. There is a licensed restaurant serving lunch from 12–2pm and dinner from 6–11pm (not Mondays). There is also a snack bar open for morning coffee and from 6 pm and a licensed bar.

University of Essex Theatre hosts touring companies as well as "in house" productions by students. Phone 873261 for details.

MUSIC

Mercury Theatre offers touring opera and ballet and also Monday night concerts. (The theatre is dark on Mondays.)

Colchester Arts Centre – Church Street, Tel 577301. The Arts Centre runs an extensive and varied programme of classical music, poetry, theatre, folk, rock and blues on most nights of the week. Colchester does not have a designated concert hall but both touring and local artists perform in some of the town's churches, especially **St Botolph's**. Phone 712222 for details.

Along the estuary of River Colne is the **University of Essex,** one of the newest of the post-war universities. The University offers an admirable series of Tuesday concerts, a series of Wednesday lunchtime concerts and features performances by the University's resident string quartet. Tel 873261 for details.

CINEMA

Some film showings at the University of Essex (see above). Commercial cinema at Odeon, Crouch Street (3 screens), Tel 572294.

BOOKSTORES

The best is **Hatchards**, in neo-classical premises at 12/13 High Street, Tel 561307. If you are out at the University of Essex in Wivenhoe Park then **Sherratt and Hughes** is very good. They also have a branch at the Old Library, Culver Centre in the middle of town. Tel 864773 and 767623. You might want to take a look at the **Colchester Book Shop** at 47 Head St, Tel 572284, and the **Red Lion Bookshop**, 125 High Street, Tel 578584, while for art books and indeed supplies too, **Briggs** at 15 Crouch St, Tel 574530 is the place to go. Religious books can be obtained at the **Sign of the Fish Bookshop** at 40 Eld Lane, Tel 579665 and you'll find comic books at **Ace Comics**, 1 Headgate Buildings St John's St, Tel 561912.

ANTIQUARIAN AND SECONDHAND BOOKS

The best is the **Castle Bookshop**, 37 North Hill, Tel 577520 (closed Thursdays). Fitting snugly into a rambling 16th-century building with lots of nooks and crannies. A large and varied stock is held with emphasis given to archaeology and the topography of East Anglia. There are also some good maps and prints. At 926 East Hill, Tel 563138, you will find **Greyfriars Books** also well worth a visit. Also on the hill at No 48 is **Book Exchange**, Tel 867242 with a large stock and with a nice coffee lounge, while in the centre of town at 13 Trinity St is **Alphabets**, Tel 572751.

ART GALLERIES

Locksleys at 21 Eld Lane – prints of all kinds – some original. Tel 354071. The **Original Art Shop** at 34 Sir Isaacs Walk, Tel 571999 has a variety of posters, prints, oils and, especially, local watercolours. **Hayletts Gallery** at 34 North Hill, Tel 761837 has contemporary original art – watercolours, oils and prints. Open Tues–Sat 10–5pm. **Colchester Arts Forum** at 6 Trinity St, Tel 369188 has a studio which presents work by young Colchester and Essex artists who are just beginning to make a name for themselves.

ANTIQUE DEALERS

First let me deal with the antique centres, which generally means that a number of dealers have gathered together under the same roof to sell their wares and also reduce their overhead. One such centre is the **Trinity Antiques Centre** in the middle of town at 7 Trinity St, Tel 577775. Here there are eight dealers in jewellery, silver, glass, brass, copper, linen, small furniture and collectables. Another centre worth mentioning is the **Stock Exchange Antiques Centre** at 40 Osbourne Street, Tel 561997 which is a continuation of St John's St and is close to St Botolph's Priory and the station. Also in Osbourne St is **Cornucopia** at No 37, Tel 549781. Close by in Magdalen St at No 148 is **Victorian Interior Furnishings**, Tel 762351, while **E Smith** is at 123 Magdalen St, just down the road, Tel 45130. If you walk back down Osbourne St and St John's St you will come to Crouch St where **E M Cannon** is at No 85, Tel 575817. If you turn right after coming down St John's you will find yourself in Head St. North Hill is a continuation of Head St and at 14–15 you will find **S Bond and Son**, Tel 572925 who, besides furniture, generally have good oils and watercolours. Close by is **Partner and Puxon** at No 7 North Hill, Tel 573317 and not far away **Angel Antiques**, Tel 572403 at 38 North Station Road. Come back down North Hill and Head St and left into Sir Isaac's Walk which becomes Eld Lane where, at No 19, you will find **Eld Lane Antiques**, Tel 765929. At the end of Eld Lane, turn right into St Botolph's St and then immediately left into Priory St, where you will find **Fiffi Antiques**, Tel 384457. As the name may suggest, the store is an importer of fine French furniture and in fact specializes in carved French wood beds. Come back to Eld Lane and Scheregate is between the lane and St John's St to the south. At 3A Scheregate Steps is **Scheregate Antiques**, Tel 766474. Finally, **Ostrich Antiques**, Tel 869364 is at 10 East Street and **Ragna-Lee Antiques and Bygones** at 19 Church Walk, Tel 575582.

RESTAURANTS

Warehouse Brasserie – 12 Chapel St North, Tel 765656. This is my favourite place to eat in Colchester. The menu is eclectic to say the least, ranging from chicken satay through guinea fowl to moussaka. They have good old fashioned English desserts like rice or steamed pudding and the orange juice is fresh – a rarity for England. Open Mon–Sat 12–2pm and 7–10pm.

Red Lion Inn – High St, Tel 577986. The main reason for eating here is the sense of history which permeates the dining room. The New Inn dates from 1515 and survives today as the Red Lion. You eat in the great hall (circa 1465) which was incorporated into the New Inn and was originally built by Thomas

Howard, Earl of Surrey. The cooking is country-house English and every effort is made to use fresh local ingredients. There is an extensive international wine list.

Whig and Pen Restaurant – 2 North Hill, Tel 41111. The restaurant was formerly called William Scraggs, as a journeyman bricklayer of that name purchased the premises from the Borough of Colchester in 1882 and lived here until the ripe old age of 78. Mr Scraggs paid £135 for the house. The chef is strong on fish with seafood soup and of course local oysters to the fore. Also a bar with interesting food.

Karnak (Tilly's) – Crouch St, Tel 572780. One of Colchester's more unusual restaurants, the Karnak claims to be the only combined Egyptian and Lebanese restaurant in the country. The odd thing is that during the day the place is transformed into a typically English tea room, a transformation which includes changing all the decorations and artifacts. So remember, Eastern delights and promise only after 6 pm. It's called Tilly's during the day.

PUBS

Rose and Crown – East St, Tel 866677. A carefully modernized handsome Tudor inn, timbered and jettied with parts of a former jail preserved in its rambling beamed bar. Good value traditional bar food. Pleasant atmosphere.

Clarendon – Trinity St, Tel 860359. Wide choice of reasonably priced hot and cold food including good salads and vegetarian dishes. There's a no-smoking area, friendly service and very well kept beer.

Hospital Arms – Lexden Road, Tel 573572. A well-kept pub with very good-value food served in plentiful quantities. The pub is the home of Colchester Rugby Club so it's likely to be lively after a home win. In the summer it's popular with cricketers too.

Marquis of Granby – 25 Norton Hill, Tel 577630 (out past the Odeon cinema). The inn which contains interesting carved beams was not called by this name until the middle of the 18th century. It was named after the Marquis who was the eldest son of the 3rd Duke of Rutland, who commanded the British troops in Germany in the Seven Years War. He was popular with his men and after the war he set up a number of his disabled officers as innkeepers, a fact which explains why England has so many inns called the Marquis of Granby. Traditional bar food.

The Swan – Chappel (six miles (9.6 km) west on A604 to Halstead), Tel 222343. A friendly 500-year-old rambling pub with low dark beams, red velvet curtains and a lovely fireplace (log fires in winter). An abundance of good traditional bar food with home made pies especially good. There's a charming court-yard and a garden running down to the River Colne and below a splendid Victorian viaduct which carries the Colne Valley Steam Railway. (see above)

ARTISTIC ASSOCIATIONS

Jane and Anne Taylor lived at West Stockwell St, off the High St by the Town Hall. They wrote *Original Poems for the Infant Mind* in 1804, *Rhymes for the Nursery* in 1806 and *Hymns* in 1810. *Rhymes for the Nursery* included the famous "Twinkle, Twinkle Little Star." It must be noted that Lavenham in Suffolk claims that "Twinkle" was written there (see Ipswich Ephemera).

William Wilbye was born in Diss in 1574. For the last ten years of his life he lived in a house close to Holy Trinity Church and he is buried there in an unknown grave. Wilbye was one of the greatest of Elizabethan composers. His madrigals are marked by sensitive beauty and excellent workmanship and are still sung now, over 350 years after his death in 1638.

A few miles northeast of Colchester on the A137 is Cattawade. While farming here Thomas Tusser wrote *Hundreth Good Pointes of Husbandrie* in 1557. Although full of maxims to which many of our proverbs can be traced, it proved to be of little help to Tusser himself as he died in 1580, a prisoner for debt in London.

In the late summer of 1816, John Constable stayed at Wivenhoe Park (now occupied by the University of Essex). He painted a view of the house from across the lake. Although the area of the park is rather more thickly wooded now, the site of the picture can be located without difficulty. Unfortunately, Constable's original painting is in the National Gallery in Washington. Around the same time Constable painted a scene of another estate at nearby Alresford. The estate belonged to General Francis Slater-Rebow, who also owned

Wivenhoe Park, and Constable's painting featured "The Quarters," an exotic 18th-century fishing lodge. This and its surroundings also remain much as they were in Constable's time. Constable's father owned the mill in nearby Dedham (for directions see Sir Alfred Munning Art Museum, above). Although the old mill has been replaced by modern mill buildings, the original is preserved by Constable, as he made several paintings of it. Another of his favourite motifs was Dedham Church which appears in the mill paintings and in many more general Stour Valley landscapes. Constable was a devout Christian and regarded Dedham Church as a symbol of God's beneficent presence in the agricultural landscape.

EPHEMERA

One of the finest gravestones from Roman Britain, and possibly the earliest, can be seen in the Colchester and Essex Museum in Colchester Castle. It commemorates Marcus Favonius Facilis, a centurion of the 20th Legion. Made of Bath stone, the memorial is six feet high and was probably carved by a sculptor from the Mediterranean region; it dates from just before AD 60, from the military occupation preceding the colonial town of Colchester, for Facilis is not described as a veteran. Traces of plaster on the stone suggest it was once coloured, and the tombstone exerts a strange power and fascination over anyone who looks at it.

Local tradition tells us that St Helena was the mother of Emperor Constantine the Great. She became a Christian in the second part of the 2nd century but was not baptized until much later. When her son became Emperor he made her Empress Dowager and it was soon after this, in 326 according to Geoffrey of Monmouth, a 12th-century historian, that she visited Jerusalem and founded the basilicas on the Mount of Olives and at Bethlehem. Not only does tradition inform us that Helena came from Roman Colchester, but also that her father was "Old King Cole, the merry old soul" from the children's nursery rhyme. Local inhabitants believe that Old King Cole gave his name to the town. Whatever the truth of the matter, the figure of St Helena tops the tower of Colchester's Town Hall.

Colchester has long been famous for its oysters, and the season is opened by a traditional festival in early September. The Mayor, civic dignitaries and members of the Fishing Board go by boat to Pyfleet Creek, where the oyster fattening beds lie. Here the royal toast is drunk, gingerbread and gin are consumed and the Mayor makes the first ceremonial oyster dredge of the season. The gingerbread is traditional and may once have been an offering to the local sea god. Following this, on or about October 20th, the 400-year-old Oyster Feast takes place. This commemorates the granting by Richard I of the River Colne oyster fishing rights to the town. With the introduction of the Portuguese and Pacific oyster, the delicacy is now available throughout the year, though of course the real speciality of the area is the native oyster, in season when there is an R in the month.

Unfortunately the Colchester Oyster Feast, which is held in the Moot Hall of the Town Hall, can only be attended by invitation, but visitors wishing to sample oysters can go to Mussett's Oysters, Coast Road, West Merseon, Tel 384141, for an *al fresco* meal or telephone Colchester Oyster Fishery Ltd at 3841421, to arrange for a party, ideally numbering between 12 and 30, to visit the fishery by boat and enjoy a gourmet meal.

The affectionate naming of their massive water tower, Jumbo, by the citizens of Colchester is indicative of a nation-wide furore which shook England in 1882. Jumbo was the name of London Zoo's first African elephant who, with his mate Alice, was a popular feature of 19th-century life until purchased by Phineas T Barnum in 1882. Barnum was the manager of "The Greatest Show on Earth."

The removal of the elephant caused a great outcry with thousands of elephant fanciers, including Queen Victoria, united in their distress at losing him. Telegrams were sent to

Barnum by the editor of the *Morning Post*, inquiring on what terms he would return Jumbo. Barnum replied that with 50 million Americans awaiting his arrival, £100,000 could not stop the purchase. Protest songs were composed such as –

> Jumbo said to Alice "I love you"
> Alice said to Jumbo "I don't believe you do
> For if you really loved me as you say you do
> You wouldn't go to Yankee land and leave me at the zoo

Barnum remained adamant and the *Graphic,* an illustrated magazine featured eight drawings of Jumbo's final journey to the docks on April 1st, 1882. The elephant went on to become the star attraction of what later became known as Barnum and Bailey's Circus. When Jumbo died, he was stuffed and exhibited in the Barnum Museum of Natural History.

TOURIST INFORMATION BUREAU: 1 Queen Street, Colchester, Essex, CO1 2PJ. Tel (0206) 712920

IPSWICH AND ALDEBURGH

IPSWICH

County of Suffolk
77 miles (123.2 km) from London by road – A12
70 minutes by rail from London (Liverpool Street)
Aldeburgh is 16 miles (25.6 km) northeast of Ipswich by A12

Ipswich was founded at the head of the estuary of the River Orwell on a site which had been occupied since the Stone Age. During the period from 7th to the 9th century the town was the earliest and largest known Anglo-Saxon trading community in the country. The Vikings and Danes burned and pillaged the community many times, often during excursions to raid communities in the Midlands, but in 885 King Alfred's fleet defeated the Danes at the mouth of the Orwell. The situation was constantly changing however, for in 1016 the Danish leader, Chut, sailed up the river and seized Ipswich.

Ipswich was a thriving community at the Norman Conquest in 1066 but in 1086 the Domesday Book records it as a very poor community. Historians are uncertain what led to the decline. The town recovered, however, and King John granted the town its charter on May 25, 1200, in St Mary-le-Tower Churchyard. At this time Ipswich, surrounded by earthen walls with a palisade and stone gates, was granted "murage." That meant that for fixed periods the town could levy a toll on persons and animals passing through the gates. Street names perpetuate the memory of those times with Westgate, Northgate and Town Ramparts. Excavations are under way to uncover the original town wall and restore it.

Ipswich prospered through its trade with the Low Countries, France and Spain, particularly in the famous Suffolk cloth. The recession in the market for the commodity brought a temporary end to the town's prosperity towards the middle of the 17th century and the port declined. At the time of the Napoleonic Wars (end of the 18th century) things picked up as Ipswich found itself supplying great quantities of wheat, malt, timber, etc, to London. Industrial growth began in the 1780s and the Wet Dock, then the largest in the country, marked the expansion of the port in 1842. The railway, especially the link to Colchester in

THE CORNHILL, IPSWICH

1846, also helped prosperity and the town grew rapidly. By 1921 the population of Ipswich was seven times the 1801 population (80,000 in 1921) and today the population is more than double the 1921 figure.

Twelve medieval churches have survived, in various forms, in Ipswich. They were mainly built of flint and many were restored during Victorian times when there was a great revival in the church. Besides the churches mentioned specifically in the walking tour, efforts should be made to see the following churches as well (note that some are redundant and no longer in use). St Peter, in College Street close to the river, is early 14th century but has a 12th-century Tournai marble font. St Lawrence in Dial Lane between the Butter Market and Tavern Street is 15th century, while St Mary at the Quay in Key Street (just behind the Old Custom House) has the finest 15th-century roof in Ipswich. Finally, St Nicholas in Franciscan Way and St Stephen's in St Stephen's Lane are also worth a visit.

WALK

Ipswich Walk – To explore the town on foot, park in the Civic Centre car park and walk down Black Horse Lane. Turn left into Elm Street and walk ahead to **Cornhill**, the ancient Market Place which has been the town's main meeting place for more than a thousand years. Cornhill has been the venue for fairs, markets, religious and political meetings, bull and bear baitings and the burning at the stake of at least nine people in the 16th century, including Protestant martyrs whose memorial can be found in Christchurch Park. The **Town Hall**, with the **Corn Exchange**, now forms a multi-purpose entertainment arts and conference centre. Moving along Westgate Street you will see Museum Street on your left. The street took its name from the town's first museum. You can see the present museum on its new site if you look down High Street to your right. Museum Street has many buildings fronted with Suffolk white bricks. Behind the 15th-century church of **St Mary Elms** you will find the town's oldest inhabited cottage dating back to 1467. The flintwork on St Mary is both beautiful and striking, a reminder that flint is the local stone and was used extensively in town centre churches. The **Black Horse**, one of Ipswich's oldest pubs, is close by. Continue down Westgate Street and on your left is Lady Lane with a plaque commemorating the chapel of **Our Lady of Grace**, which contained a shrine that, to medieval East Anglian pilgrims, was second only to the Shrine of Our Lady at Walsingham in Norfolk. From here you will also get your first glimpse of the **Wolsey Theatre**. Come back to Westgate street and turn right onto Museum Street. Cross Elm Street and Princess Street and at the end of Friars Street turn right into St Nicholas Street. On your walk down you will see the **Unitarian Meeting House** on your left, one of the earliest Non-conformist chapels in the country, erected in 1699 at a cost of £257. St Nicholas Street has many fine half-timbered buildings and when you reach the junction with Silent Street you will see one of the world's most photographed groups of buildings. Look for the plaque marking the birthplace of Cardinal Wolsey in 1471. **Wolsey's Gate** in College Street (continue down the street and take the second left) is all that remains of what Wolsey intended to be the important **Cardinal College of St Mary**. Walk along College Street to the Custom House and you get a good view of the **Orwell Bridge**, under which all ships pass as they come into the port of Ipswich. You are now in Salthouse Street and at the junction with Fore Street is the **Jewish Cemetery** with Hebrew headstones from the 16th to 19th centuries. **Isaac Lord's House**, just to your right, is a typical 17th-century merchant's house still operating as business premises. Carry on past the house and turn left into Grimwade Street where the houses Nos 79–83 are often called the **Sea Captain's Houses** as they are linked by a single Bressumer beam. Turn left into Star Lane and you will find **St Clement's Church**, known as the "Sailors' Church." Thomas Eldred, who sailed round the world with Thomas Cavendish in 1586, is buried there, as is a Grace Pett who, it is reputed, died of spontaneous combustion in 1744! There is memorial to Sir Thomas Slade in front of the church's west end. He designed Nelson's flagship, HMS *Victory*. Nelson, incidentally, bought a house in the town in 1798 and was appointed High Steward of Ipswich in 1800. At the end of Star Lane turn right into Fore Street and then left into Orwell Place. On your left in School Street is all that remains of the Blackfriars Priory. In 1572 an almshouse, **Christ's Hospital** was established on the site and, just round the corner, two private almshouses built by 16th-century Ipswich merchants can be seen. These are **Tooley's** and **Smart's Almshouses**. Come back to Orwell Place and carry on left into Tacket Street. The **Congregational Church** on your right dates from 1720. One of their ministers, Reverend Will Gordon, went to America in 1764 and became George Washington's secretary. A little further down is the **Salvation Army Citadel** where in 1736 stood the New Playhouse. In 1741, a young man using the name Lydall made his first stage appearance in the theatre and went on to find fame and fortune under the name David Garrick. Tacket Street becomes Dog's Head Street, named after the public house called **Dog's Head in the Pot Inn**. The name presumably reminded erring husbands to hurry home before the dog got their dinner. Another pub close by in Upper Brook Street was called the **Cock and Pye**, as cockfighting was frequently held there on race days. Ipswich Racecourse existed from 1751 to 1911. Turn right at the end of Dog's Head Street and you enter St Stephen's, at the end of which is the **Butter Market**. This was the dairy market until 1810. The **Ancient House** on the right at the corner dates from the 15th century but the famous pargetting is a 17th-century addition. You will see Charles II's coat of arms on the house emphasizing the family's support for the Stuart cause. The Malyn family, forebears of Geoffrey Chaucer, owned this house and a number of inns in the vicinity. Turn right into Tavern Street. House No 44 has the Corporation Arms over it indicating the site of the town's water conduit where residents obtained their water. Some of the wood pipes which carried the water can be seen in the Ipswich Museum. The **Great White Horse Inn** is the only surviving inn which predates 1571. Its Dickensian connections are explained in Ephemera below, but it is interesting to note that Dickens gave his celebrated readings from his work in Ipswich in 1859 and 1861. Turn left up Northgate Street and near the top left is **Pykenham's Gateway**, recently restored and named after the former Archdeacon of Suffolk. The **North Gate** stood at the top of the street near the Halberd Inn until it was demolished in 1794. Cross St Margaret's Plain to **St Margaret's Church**, which is the finest-looking church in Ipswich, built in flint and stone and mostly 15th century (it was restored after enemy bombing in 1940); there is a wonderful double hammer-beam roof, and the clock dates from 1737. In the churchyard, 440 victims of the great plague of 1664–65 are buried. **Christchurch Park** is only a few minutes from the town centre. It contains **Christchurch Mansion**, built in 1548 (see Museums). Walk from St Margaret's Church down St Margaret's Plain, past Northgate Street and turn left into Tower Street which was originally the Hen Market. On your left is the civic church **St Mary-le-Tower**, which was rebuilt between 1850 and 1870. Turn right on Tavern Street and you will be back in Cornhill and (regardless of what time of day you started out) ready for a nice cup of tea.

MUSEUMS AND GALLERIES

Ipswich Museum – High Street, Tel 213761/2. The façade of the museum is distinguished by excellent late Victorian terracotta moulding. The displays feature ethnological material and worldwide natural history exhibits, especially tropical insects and shells and British birds. The archaeological galleries cover the archaeology of Suffolk from prehistoric times to the medieval period and include replicas of the Mildenhall and Sutton Hoo treasures. The Roman gallery includes reconstructions of a Roman bakery and a domestic interior. Open Mon–Sat 10–5pm.

Christchurch Mansion – Christchurch Park, Soane Street, Tel 313761/2. The house, which is now a museum, was built in 1548. The large collection of furniture and the decorative arts includes 18th-century chinoiserie and lacquerwork, 16th-century tapestries, lantern and longcase clocks, pottery, porcelain, glass – especially 18th-century wine glasses – and pewter. There are also interesting 17th- to 19th-century portraits. The servant's wing contains the kitchen with its copper pans, moulds and roasting spits and the servants' hall with the table laid for a meal. Washday at Christchurch Mansion at the turn of the century was quite an event. Tune in to the listening post in the laundry in the servants' wing to hear the Monday memories of Mrs Agnes Rogers, who worked here. The 18th-century state rooms on the first floor provide a striking contrast to conditions below stairs. Some rooms still contain original wallpaper of the 1730s. In the **Wolsey Gallery**, Suffolk artists are well represented with paintings by Gainsborough, Constable, John Moore and Alfred Munnings. There are also displays of 20th-century prints and sculptures, of costumes and of material illustrating the history of Ipswich and the surrounding area.

THEATRE

Wolsey Theatre – Civic Drive, Tel 253725. The Wolsey is one of the most popular and successful regional theatres in the country. The distinctive modern building with its modern open stage setting is home to two companies – one presenting monthly rep. Some recent productions have included Joe Orton's *Loot*, Neil Simon's *Barefoot in the Park*, Tom Stoppard's *The Real Thing* and Rodgers and Hammerstein's *Carousel*. The other, the Wolsey Theatre in Education company, tours schools with productions for all ages. There's a coffee bar open from 10–5pm, a restaurant open for lunch and pre-show dinners and a theatre bar open lunchtimes, evenings and after the show.

Odeon Theatre – St Helen's Street, Tel 53041 (shows) 215685 (films). The Odeon is one of the Rank Organization's Live Show theatres. It attracts international stars of light entertainment as well as opera, ballet, concerts and musicals.

MUSIC

Ipswich Corn Exchange – Cornhill, Tel 215544. A multi-purpose complex comprising ten halls. Musical events are usually held in the Grand Hall and range from Sir Charles Groves and the English Sinfonia through the Ipswich Orchestral Society to Val Doonican and Charley Pride. Musical events are also held at the Odeon Theatre and recently there was a very interesting series of programmes by the Concertante Ensemble at the Wolsey Theatre.

CINEMA

Commercial cinema at the **Odeon**, St Helen's Street, Tel 215685. More interesting for me is the **Ipswich Film Theatre**, which is part of the Corn Exchange complex in Cornhill, Tel 215544. The theatre is part of the network of Regional Film Theatres inspired by the British Film Institute's desire to bring good-quality films out of London's West End. There are two cinemas which provide a wide range of quality work. A sample showed, in one month, work by directors such as Alan Rudolph, Denys Arcand, Woody Allen, D W Griffith, Alan J Pakula, Rob Reiner, Bruce Beresford and Ingmar Bergman. There are generally performances at 6:15 and 8:30 most evenings.

BOOKSTORES

Ipswich is almost unique among large towns in that it doesn't have a major book chain branch within the city. That makes browsing more interesting in a way as, with locally based firms, one is uncertain what to expect. **Amberstone Bookshop** at 49 Upper Orwell Street, Tel 250675, has books on all subjects for children as well as adults plus classical music records, cassettes and CDs.

Ancient House Bookstore, Tel 257761, in the Butter Market, is housed in a superb building and also contains a branch of HMSO for government publications. These are the two best in town. Above the Ancient House Bookstore is a 15th-century chapel that was completely lost to view for many years. The chapel was partly boarded up, perhaps at the Reformation, and legend has it that the Sparrowe family, who lived in the building in the middle of the 17th century, hid Charles II here when he was being hunted by Cromwell after the Battle of Worcester in 1651. You may view the long-lost chapel and it is a unique and eerie experience to do so. There is a store dealing with publishers' remainders called **Booksale** at 46–48 Butter Market, Tel 226931. Religious books can be found at the **Church Centre**, 13–15 Tower Street, Tel 25650, while comics can be found at **Central City Comics**, 4 Eagle Street, Tel 233017. Finally, two shops in Grimwade Street (by Suffolk College); **Bookmart**, Tel 259430 at No 3, and **College Books**, Tel 217267 at No 32, are worth a look.

ANTIQUARIAN AND SECONDHAND BOOKS

There are one or two good antiquarian bookstores in the villages surrounding Ipswich. **R G Archer** is excellent if you happen to be in Lavenham (7 Water Street, Tel 0787 247229), while **Major Ian Grahame** of Daws Hall, Tel 0787 269213, is also excellent if you are passing through Lamarsh, which is a couple of miles west of Nayland (see Ephemera). In Ipswich itself I can really only wholeheartedly recommend Claude Cox at **College Gateway Bookshop**, 3 Silent Street, Tel 254776. Silent Street is just off the Old Cattle Market in the centre of town and Mr Cox has a respectable antiquarian and secondhand selection.

ART GALLERIES

Anglia Art – 13 Norwich Road, Tel 216655, has original oils and watercolours and also a wide selection of prints. I find the **John Russell Gallery** in Orwell Court, 13 Orwell Place, Tel 21205, the most interesting in Ipswich. They focus on contemporary art in East Anglia, both oils and watercolours and they also have limited-edition prints – a good selection. The **Fortescue Gallery**, 27 St Peter's Street, Tel 251342, could not be more different with a very winning collection of antiquarian prints and many fine examples of local topography.

ANTIQUE DEALERS

The best place to start looking for antiques in the centre of Ipswich is in St Peter's Street, which is a continuation of Queen Street and St Nicholas Street out of the Butter Market. At No 11 is **Charles Wall**, Tel 214366, with a good general selection. Close by at No 13 is **Cordell Antiques**, Tel 219508, and at 13C is **Country Bygones and Antiques**, Tel 253683. Just down the road at No 33A is **Tom Smith Antiques**, Tel 210172. If you turn left at the end of St Peter's Street you will be in Star Lane. At the end of Star Lane is Fore Street where at No 20A you will find **Ashley Antiques**, Tel 251696, with a good general collection. Turn left past the Odeon into St Margaret's Street. This in turn leads into St Margaret's Green where at No 16 is **Hubbard Antiques**, Tel 226033, with period furniture, fine art and accessories. Come back through St Margaret's Green and turn left into Woodbridge Road where at No 757, **A Abbot** is to be found with a good general selection. Tel 728900. Come back down Woodbridge Road and cross into Great Colman Street. Turn left onto Upper Brook Street and then right in the Butter Market. Halfway along on the left is St Stephen's Lane where at No 17 is **Atfield and Daughter**, Tel 251158. If you are on the way to Norwich on the A140, stop at 418 Norwich Place where **Thompson's Showroom**, Tel 747793, has all types of antique furniture, china, paintings and clocks. Just before you reach the Norwich Road, fork left into Bramford Road where, at No 388, you will find **Emma's Antiques**, Tel 241406, with a good general collection. Finally, by travelling west on the A1071 to Sudbury you will come to Hadleigh. Here at 97/99 High Street there is an excellent antiques collection at **Randolph**, Tel 82378, which specializes in Old English furniture, while at 102A High Street is **Playthings of the Past**, Tel 824435, which specializes in antique dolls, teddy bears, doll's houses and trains.

RESTAURANTS

My favourite noshery in Ipswich is the **Singing Chef**, 200 St Helen's Street, close to County Hall, Tel 255236. It's a delightfully eclectic bistro in terms of ambience and food, and yes, the chef – Kenneth Toye – really does sing on occasion and there are regular jazz evenings. A delightful touch is that the menu explores a different French province each month – a sort of gastronomic equivalent to presenting all of Shakespeare's plays. I sense the restaurant is strong on casseroles, as I had a wonderful *estouffade de boeuf artesienne* the last time I was here and there were a couple of "ragout" dishes on the menu. Great fun and value, especially the set dinner. Open Tues–Sat 7–11pm.

Mortimer's on the Quay – Wherry Quay, Tel 230225. Set in a converted warehouse, near the Old Custom House, this airy, glass-roofed restaurant serves fresh fish at fair prices and in lavish quantities. Their fish soups are excellent and their menu, which changes daily, offers a selection of plaice, sole, halibut, monkfish, turbot and salmon; there are also good oysters. Cooking ranges from simple to the classic. Excellent value. Open Mon–Sat 12–2pm and 7–9pm. No Sat lunch.

Orwell House Restaurants – 4 Orwell Place, Tel 230254. Two restaurants here contained within a Georgian townhouse, designed as open plan and split level. Downstairs the food is classic, simple, French bistro fare – watercress soup, lamb cutlets and orange bavarois, for example. Upstairs the menu is more elaborate and might include boned quail, lobster, oysters and smoked salmon. Service is attentive and value excellent. Open Mon–Sat 12–2 and 7–9:30pm. No Mon or Tues dinner.

If your taste is for the more exotic and far-flung, try **Kwok's Rendezvous**, 23 St Nicholas Street (follow Queen Street into St Nicholas Street off the Butter Market). Tel 256833. One of the best provincial Chinese restaurants in the country. Good crispy duck and excellent hot and sour soup have been reported to me. Open Mon–Sat 12–2 and 7–10:30pm. Try the set lunches and dinners for selection and value. For Indian food, the **Ipswich Tandoori**, 46A Norwich Road, Tel 257207, is a good bet. Follow Westgate Street into St Matthew's Street and then straight on into Norwich Road. Not surprisingly, there are excellent tandoori dishes and a good vegetarian selection. Open all week 12–2:30 and 6pm–midnight. I also hear good things about the **Baipo Thai Restaurant** at 63 Upper Orwell Street, Tel 218402. The entrance of Upper Orwell Street is opposite the Odeon Theatre in St Helen's Street. There's a wide selection of traditional Thai cuisine here. Finally, check out the after-show buffet at the **Cardinal's Table** which is the restaurant of the Wolsey Theatre.

PUBS

Right in the centre of town, opposite the Corn Exchange in King Street, is the **Swan**, Tel 252485. The pub dates back to 1707 and recent refurbishment has retained its authentic atmosphere. Good traditional bar food. From the Corn Exchange, walk down Elm Street to Black Horse Lane and you will come to the **Black Horse**, Tel 214741, which is one of the oldest pubs in the town. The Black Horse is the kind of pub one would normally expect to see in a small Suffolk village. It has a heavily beamed bar and the building is centuries old. There is good bar food – both sandwiches and hot meals. The dish of the day is a very good bet. If you walk down the Butter Market, away from the GPO, you come into Upper Brook Street where you will find the **Cock and Pye**, Tel 254213, so named because cock fighting was frequently held there on race days. This is one of the town's liveliest pubs and has traditional bar food. If you want to sup your suds in a nautical setting, then the **Malt Kiln** on Wherry Quay, Tel 259952, is a good spot. This quayside pub is close to the Old Custom House and has a bistro menu as well as traditional pub fare.

ARTISTIC ASSOCIATIONS

An interesting comment on Ipswich in the early 18th century is provided by Daniel Defoe, the author of *Robinson Crusoe*, who visited the town just after the turn of the century and wrote in his book, *A Tour Through the Whole Island of Great Britain*, that he abhorred the "noisome cookery of whaling." The oriental scholar, E B Colwell, joined his father's business in the town in 1842 and visited India in 1850. From India he sent a copy of the *Rubaiyat of Omar Khayyam* to Edward FitzGerald, whom he had met in Ipswich just prior to his departure. It was from Colwell's copy of the work that FitzGerald made his famous translation. There are some memorabilia of FitzGerald in Christchurch Mansion. In 1697 Jeremy Collier published a pamphlet entitled *A Short View of the Immorality of the English Stage*. This influential publication did much to stifle the overt sexuality of the Restoration theatre while simultaneously removing much of its wit and vitality. Sir Henry Rider Haggard, on the other hand, was best known for his romantic adventure stories such as *King Solomon's Mines*, *She* and *Allan Quartermain*, published in the late 1880s and no doubt drawing on experiences and ideas gathered during his five years in Africa. Both Collier, in the 1660s and Haggard, in the 1860s, were pupils at Ipswich School.

The great English portrait and landscape painter Thomas Gainsborough settled in Ipswich in 1752 and stayed seven years. According to tradition, his first residence was at 41 Lower Brook Street; by 1753 however, he was certainly living opposite the county gaol in Foundation Street. (Both houses have been demolished.) Early examples of Gainsborough's Ipswich portraiture show a stiffness in the poses and too detailed a handling of the paint, which by the end of his stay had given way to the more relaxed manner and fluency of technique for which he later became famous.

EPHEMERA

The Great White Horse Hotel stands in Tavern Street in the town centre, just down from the Town Hall and Corn Exchange. There is a reference to the hotel in a document of 1518, although it seems probable there was a resting house for travellers on the same site long before that date. The present three-storey building dates from the 18th century. The earliest part was in use before 1736 when George II stayed there, but most of the building belongs to the second half of the century. It was once a coaching inn, but the courtyard has since been roofed over. Famous guests include Louis XVIII and Lord Nelson, but Charles Dickens, who stayed here in 1830 when he was sent to report an election for the *Morning Star*, has probably provided the hostelry with its greatest claim to fame. In *The Pickwick Papers*, Mr Pickwick blunders into the wrong bedroom and encounters a "middle aged woman in yellow curl papers." It is easy to understand Mr Pickwick's mistake as he describes the inn as having "labyrinths of uncarpeted passages." He also describes the stone statue above the entrance as being "some rampacious animal with flowing mane and tail, distinctly resembling an insane carthorse." How accurate his description is in this case, only the visitor can judge.

Some of the loveliest villages in England lie clustered around Ipswich. Orford, 15 miles (24 km) east on B1084, was at one time an important seaport, but the sea has long since receded. Opposite the quay, where small boats still sail down the River Ore, is the Jolly Sailor Inn where secret cupboards attest to legends of former smuggling days. A superb view can be obtained by climbing to the top of the castle keep, which was built in 1165 by Henry II. It is said that in the dungeons of Orford Castle a merman was once incarcerated. The wild, hairy creature, half man, half fish, was trapped in the nets of local fishermen but after interrogation by the governor of the castle he managed to escape and return to sea. A portrait of the merman hangs on a sign over a shop in Market Square. Orford Church was the venue of some of Benjamin Britten's first compositions, among them *Noyes Fludde* in 1958 and *Curlew River* in 1964.

Dedham (15 miles/24 km south just off the A12) has been immortalized by the paintings of John Constable, who was born in 1776 at nearby East Bergholt. The Vale of Dedham is known as Constable country and the great artist wrote of it, "I love every stile and stump and lane ... these scenes made me a painter and I am grateful." The house where Constable was born no longer stands but many of the artist's favourite subjects remain. Especially noteworthy are Flatford Mill, Willy Lott's Cottage, and St Mary's Church. Another famous artist, Sir Alfred Munnings, lived at Castle House where a gallery of his work is displayed. The ancestors of General William Tecumseh Sherman, whose famous march through the southern states brought the American Civil War to a close, came from Sherman Hall, which is opposite the church. Three miles (4.8 km) away on the other side of the A12 is Stoke by Nayland whose church, St Mary's, was the focal point for Constable's famous *Rainbow* picture. In nearby Nayland the church contains Constable's *Christ Blessing Bread and Wine*.

Twelve miles (19.2 km) north of Nayland, through Sudbury, is Lavenham, once a prosperous wool town. It has one of the finest timber-framed guildhalls in the country, as well as a lovely church and many old weavers' cottages. Through an upper oriel window of a house that still stands in Shilling Street the stars were once watched by Jane Taylor in the late 18th century, prompting her to compose her famous poem, "Twinkle, Twinkle Little Star." On the way back to Ipswich on the A1141, just outside Hadleigh, is the old cloth-weaving village, Kersey. Kersey cloth was famous in its day and is mentioned in the plays of Shakespeare, notably *Love's Labour Lost,* Act 5, Scene 2. Just outside the south porch of the charming church a memorial stone in the graveyard is inscribed:

Reader pass on nor waste thy time
On bad biography or bitter rhyme
For what I am this humble dust enclose,
And what I was is no affair of yours.

ALDEBURGH

In the 16th century this little town was, like its northern neighbours Dunwich, Walberswick and Southwold, a prosperous port. Then came the sea and the storms which Benjamin Britten captured so unforgettably in his opera, *Peter Grimes*. The quaint little **Moot Hall**, now almost on the seawall, was at one time the centre of the town – which shows just how much has been eroded in the course of four centuries. The **Church of Peter and Paul** is mostly 16th century, but its tower almost 200 years older. There is a memorial to the great English poet, the Reverend George Crabbe, on the church wall. Crabbe was born in Aldeburgh in 1754 and returned there often over the years before settling in the West Country, where he died in 1832. One of his most famous works is *The Borough* which was Britten's inspiration for *Peter Grimes*. There are many quaint cottages, a fine Martello tower (built as a defence against Napoleonic invasion in 1810) and of course, the famous Aldeburgh lifeboat which is launched from a slipway near the Moot Hall.

Say "festival" to music lovers world-wide and many will reply "Aldeburgh"; say "Aldeburgh" and their unanimous response will be "Benjamin Britten." The village and its festival have become synonymous with the humanity and genius of this great figure of British music. Yet the **Aldeburgh Festival** has never been a one-man show. It was founded by Britten, his long-time companion Peter Pears and the librettist and critic Eric Crozier in 1948 as a home for new British music and opera. Practically every significant name in British music has appeared at Aldeburgh. The list includes Simon Rattle, John Shirley Quirk, Jeffrey Tate, Joan Cross, Clifford Curzon, Lennox Berkeley, William Alwyn, Nancy Evans and many, many others. At first concerts took place in the houses, halls and churches of the surrounding area but one of the festival's most important landmarks was reached in 1967 with the newly converted **Maltings Concert Hall** at Snape, five miles (8 km) west of Aldeburgh on A1094. These spacious Victorian storehouses, set amid bird-haunted marshes and flat grasslands made a splendid, warm-sounding auditorium capable of seating 800 people and adaptable for both concert and opera use. It says much for the festival's spirit and commitment that when the hall was destroyed by fire in 1969, a restored Maltings was ready for opening in 1970. Benjamin Britten died in 1976 and Peter Pears in 1986 and the Aldeburgh Festival is now run by the Aldeburgh Foundation who present a year-round programme of music at Snape Maltings Concert Hall and throughout the region. Adjacent to the Maltings is the Britten-Pears School for Advanced Musical Studies which runs courses from March to October in a wide range of discipline interests. The Britten-Pears Orchestra and Chamber Choir are also based here. The main Aldeburgh Festival takes place in June with the British Telecom Aldeburgh Proms in August. There is also a week of Easter concerts, as well as a year-round musical programme.

If you would like to eat in Aldeburgh, the best places are **Austins**, Tel 453932, and **Regatta**, Tel 452011, both on the High Street. Austins at No 243 is plush and elegant with a theatrical ambience. Good local fish is served as well as steak and lamb. They also have accommodation, and they are open Tues to Sun 12:30–2pm and 7:30–10:30pm. No Sunday dinner. Note that they close the first two weeks of February. Regatta at 171–173 is a cheerful wine-bar-cum-restaurant with a nautical ambience including a huge nautical mural. Good value food and a friendly atmosphere. The local fish is the best bet. I recommend Regatta strongly. They're open all week 12–2:30 and 7–10:15pm. Good cooking can also be found at the **Aldeburgh Festival Wine Bar**, 152 High Street, Tel 453734. It's very busy at Festival time and its hours are eccentric by some standards but it's worth a visit. During Festival times and bank holidays meals are served from 11am–7pm. Outside the Festival they operate Tues–Sun lunch.

If your mind is set on something a little less formal, the **Cross Keys** in Crabbe Street is your best bet. The pub is 16th century with beams, massive chimney and straightforward bar food with one or two hot dishes. The crab salad is very good, by the way. The **Brudnell Hotel**, which is a Trust House Forte Hotel on the Parade, has good bar food too, though the drinks in the large cocktail bar are a bit pricey. There are wonderful sea views.

The **Moot Hall** was built for the Borough of Aldeborough at some time between 1520 and 1540. Timber-framed with brick end walls, it has splendid Tudor chimneys on the southern end. The Hall occupies the upper storey of the building and is constructed over an arched ground floor which was designed to be used as a market. It now houses a museum focusing on local history, shipping and trade. The principal objects discovered during the excavation of the Snape Burial Ship are preserved here.

TOURIST INFORMATION CENTRES: Town Hall, Princess Street, Ipswich, Suffolk 1P1 1B2. Tel (0473) 250951

The Cinema, High Street, Aldeburgh, Suffolk 1515 5AV. Tel (0728) 453637

LINCOLN

County of Lincolnshire
131 miles (209 km) from London by M11/A1/A46
2 hours and 30 minutes by rail from London (King's Cross)

The ancient part of this historic city occupies a rugged hilltop, 200 feet (60.8 m) above the River Witham. The Celtic tribesmen who settled here called their settlement Lindon, "the hill fort by a pool," but with the coming of the Roman Ninth Legion in 47, the name was latinized to Lindum and later Lindum Colonia from which the name Lincoln was derived.

Roman Lincoln had fine colonnaded streets and elaborate baths; drinking water was supplied in earthenware pipes, under pressure, from a source one and a half miles (2.4 km) away from the hill. The dominant industry was agriculture and there is evidence of a major extension of the town walls to encompass a well-planned suburb. The present Stonebow stands on the site of the Roman south gate here, and beyond this, Newport Arch still bestrides the ancient Ermine Street, the only Roman gateway in Britain still used by traffic. The Romans also constructed an elaborate stone-built sewage system that was unique in Britain; they drained low-lying fenland and cut the Fossdyke Canal. When the Roman occupation ended in the 5th century, a period of cultured and organized life ended too. The Anglo-Saxon invaders were a pagan race and they robbed Lindum Colonia of much of its fine stonework and tile and allowed the Roman buildings to fall into disrepair. Lincoln, however, regained its position as a prominent trading centre with the arrival of the Vikings, circa 868. They made Lincoln one of their principal boroughs and established it as a thriving commercial centre with goods travelling to and from Scandinavia and Europe and the largest mint outside of London. Many Lincoln-produced coins have been found in Scandinavian countries.

In 1068, William the Conqueror ordered the building of Lincoln Castle: its defenses were constructed by throwing grass mounds over the Roman walls. Then the building of the cathedral began (in 1072). In 1206 appears the first mention of Lincoln's mayor, making the mayoralty older than that of the City of London. The woollen industry flourished during the Middle Ages with Lincolnshire sheep producing quality wool and the River Witham and the Fossdyke Canal providing excellent routes for export and trade. Also flourishing in the city at this time was a prosperous and influential Jewish community of traders, merchants and in particular, moneylenders.

Lincoln in the 13th century was a prosperous place, as the architecture such as the Jew House on Steep Hill, the black-and-white framed merchant's houses and fine parish churches, St Mary-le-Wigford especially, attest. Lincoln declined as one of the most important centres of culture and trade in Western Europe as, in the 14th century, the wool trade moved to Boston (35 miles/56 km south). By the 16th century Lincoln's population had shrunk to 2000 (from 6000 in 1086). The city was devastated by the plague and in the 17th century disasters arrived with the outbreak of the Civil War in 1642. Lincoln changed hands between Parliamentary and Royalist forces several times and a great deal of damage and disruption occurred. It was only with the passing of the Enclosure Act, and improvements of farming techniques, that Lincoln started its long climb back to prosperity through its agricultural industry. The market returned to prominence, the Fossdyke Canal was cleared and made navigable and road travel improved. By the census of 1831, Lincoln's population had risen to 11,217. The latent wealth of the Fens was being realized through improved drainage and the introduction of steam power. The production of agricultural machinery became important and with the arrival of the railways in 1846, a diversification into other forms of heavy engineering took place. Local foundries flourished and the city's products were exported all over the world. In the First World War a Lincoln firm designed, built and tested the first fighting tank, and in the post-war 1920s, a major housing programme cleared the city's poorer property.

In recent decades, although the horse fair, cattle market and racecourse were lost, the economy has diversified from its heavy engineering base to encompass high technology, retail and service industries with a dramatic growth in tourism. A modern commercial centre has grown up while the historic aspects of Lincoln have been preserved. Brayford Pool, which was the heart of the Roman harbour, is now a boating and relaxation centre, its 19th-century warehouses converted to shops, cafés and pubs. New cultural and commercial developments, such as the Lawn, have ensured the quality of life remains high and even now more discoveries from the past are ensuring that the interest for visitors in this ancient and fascinating city will extend well into the 21st century.

WALKS

There are two **Lincoln Walks**. Walk One is in the historic uphill Cathedral area. Walk Two travels down into the lower city towards the river and the main shopping area. Both walks start from the Tourist Information Centre, 9 Castle Hill. (Park in one of the Castle car parks off Westgate.)

Walk One – From the Information Centre, walk north along Bailgate, a pleasant shopping street, noticing the circular cobbled marks in the road indicating the sites of the columns that fronted the Roman forum building. At the junction of Westgate, notice the excavated **Roman Wall** and the site of **St Paul in the Bail** church, while across the road, the **County Assembly Rooms** are a fine example of Georgian architecture. At the northern end of Bailgate is the **Newport Arch**, the northern gateway to the city and the only Roman gateway in Britain still used by traffic. Turn right at Newport Arch and walk along East Bight, past sections of the Roman Wall. The **Eastgate Hotel** has the remains of the Roman East Gate in its forecourt. Cross towards **Cathedral Green** to see the statue of **Alfred Lord Tennyson**, born at Somersby near the city. The arch across the roadway is **Priory Gate**, one of the gates of the **Cathedral Close**. The wall was built in the 13th century. Walk round the southern edge of the **Cathedral** and cross the road to visit the **Bishop's Old Palace**, once the centre of the largest diocese in the country. Follow **Minster Yard**, noticing the many historic church properties like the **Chantry** and the **Deanery** and visit **Lincoln Cathedral**. Exit via **Exchequergate Arch**, another Close gateway, back towards the **Information Centre** which is housed in a 16th-century merchant's house. Cross the cobbles to Lincoln Castle, noting especially the prison chapel, the dungeons and the site of the city's gallows. Return to the car park.

HIGH BRIDGE, LINCOLN

Walk Two – From the Information Centre, descend the appropriately named **Steep Hill** (be warned, it is the steepest hill I have encountered in Britain). Many antique shops are here and some old pubs. The **Wig and Mitre** is 14th century and the stone between Nos 25 and 26 marks the site of the **Roman South Gate**. No 47 is the erroneously named **Aaron's House**, a splendid 12th-century Norman stone building. Bear left down the side of the **Harlequin**, a 16th-century former inn. **Harding House**, a 16th-century merchant's house is on your left. Keep descending The Strait and you will see on your right the **Jews House** and **Jews Court** (the Jewish Synagogue). These date from the 12th century and are probably the oldest domestic buildings in Britain. At the junction of the first road you cross (Corporation Street) turn left and the **Theatre Royal** is a few yards along on your left. Return and continue down The Strait. As it narrows to join High Street, note the 15th-century house and former inn named after Cardinal Wolsey, Bishop of Lincoln, in 1514. Just below, **Ruddock Shop (No 287)** was possibly the site of a Roman Temple and was later the location of the Danish Moot or meeting place. Ahead of you is **Stonebow**, a 16th-century arch on the site of Roman and medieval gates to the lower city. The building now houses the City Council Chambers, the Mayor's Parlour and the civic insignia, the finest collection outside of London. Pass under the arch and down to where the High Street crosses the river. Note the 16th-century black-and-white-framed building on **High Bridge** and descend the steps on the right hand side to the **Glory Hole** where there are good views of the vaulting of the bridge. The bridge is Norman and is the oldest bridge in the country still bearing buildings. Follow the riverside passage right to **Brayford Pool**. This is the former Roman harbour and once the heart of Lincoln's commercial trade in wool and grain. It is now a centre for pleasure boating. Return to High Bridge. To your left down High Street is **St Mary-le-Wigford Church** (near the level crossing). The church is essentially Saxon, though financed by Eirtig, a wealthy Dane. Further down High Street, **St Peter-at-Gowts** is of similar age, while **St Mary's Guildhall** was a religious and social guild for merchants and dates from the late 12th century. Return to High Bridge, go back up High Street and turn right on **Saltergate**. Turn left onto **Broadgate**. The **City and County Museum** is on your left, with the **Central Library** close by. Follow Broadgate to Lindum Road, with the **Usher Art Gallery** on your left. Just past the Art Gallery turn left up **Greestone Steps** to Minster Yard and the Cathedral. (The steps are an easier ascent than The Strait.) Turn left along the south of the Cathedral and through **Exchequer Gate** to the Information Office and Castle car park.

MUSEUMS, GALLERIES AND PUBLIC BUILDINGS

Lincoln Cathedral – Minster Yard, Tel 544544. Construction started in 1072 but the building was badly damaged by fire in the middle of the 12th century, restored, and then in 1185 ruined by an earthquake. Restoring the cathedral took a century. The Dean's Eye, the superb stained-glass window in the north transept is matched by the Bishop's Eye in the south transept. The tower contains Great Tom, the fourth heaviest bell in England. It took a team of eight horses to haul it into position. The 62 choir stalls, each with a carved misericord, are 14th century and some of the finest in the country. The shrine of St Hugh, the cathedral's founder, dates from 1280. Note the carving of musicians in the Angel Choir and the Lincoln Imp and the east windows (the largest and earliest eight-light window in Britain). The 1674 Wren Library contains an excellent copy of the Magna Carta and the Cathedral Treasury has superb gold and silver plate. The Chapter House dates from the first half of the 13th century and it was from here in 1301 that Edward I proclaimed his son the first Prince of Wales.

Old Bishop's Palace – Minster Yard, Tel 544544. The remains of the Palace of the Bishops of Lincoln are on the south side of the Cathedral. They include the 15th-century gate tower, built by Bishop Alnwick, a late 12th-century ceremonial hall and part of the residential wing. (The present Bishop's House is in Eastgate on the north side of the Cathedral.)

Lincoln Castle – Castle Square, Tel 511068. Established by William the Conqueror in 1068, the circuit of walls contained six acres (2.4 ha). At the northeast corner there is a low tower known as Cobb Hall and on two great mounds on the south side are the Observatory Tower (added in the 19th century by a prison governor with an interest in astronomy) and the uprights of the Norman Keep. Cobb Hall had a two-storey vaulted dungeon for prisoners, the iron rings which locked them to the walls can still be seen, and the roof of the tower remained a place of public execution until 1868. The remains of the first of the famous crosses erected to mark the halting places of Eleanor of Castile's funeral procession, from Harby in Nottingham to London, can be seen within the passage of the Castle Gateway. Do not miss the 19th-century prison chapel with its curious boxed-in pews arranged so the prisoners could see the preacher, but not each other.

The Lawn – Carline Road, Tel 560306. The Lawn Hospital, an 1820 lunatic asylum, became a pioneering centre for mental health care. It is now a complex which includes the Sir Joseph Banks Conservatory – a 5000-square-foot (464.4 m²)tropical glasshouse with plants and fish, the headquarters of the Lincoln Archaeology Unit and the Willis Centre, recalling the history of the Lawn Hospital. There is a concert hall, garden, shops and restaurants. Open all year.

Ellis Mill – Mills Road. Ellis Mill, a tower windmill built in 1798, was restored in 1977 and now transforms local grain to flour in the time-honoured tradition. Open Sat to Sun 10–6pm all year.

City and County Museum – Broadgate, Tel 530401. Housed in the oldest Franciscan friary in the country, which was built in 1230, the museum was the first public museum in Lincoln. The displays illustrate the history of human settlement in the area from prehistoric times to 1750. Open Mon–Sat 10–5:30pm, Sun 2–5:30pm.

Lincoln Transport Museum – Whisby Road. The collection consists of cars, public service vehicles and motorcycles from 1900 to 1950, most of which are locally registered and have local connections. Open May–Sept Sun 2–5pm.

National Cycle Museum – Brayford Wharf North, Tel 545091. The finest collection of cycles and cycling artifacts in the country. The exhibits range from early "boneshakers" of the 1820s through penny-farthings, the change from solid to pneumatic tires, diamon frames, up to the modern bikes and racing machines of today. Open daily 10–5pm.

Usher Art Gallery – Lindum Road, Tel 527980. Built in 1927 with the help of a gift from Lincoln jeweller and art enthusiast James Ward Usher, who made a large fortune from the sale of replicas of the Lincoln Imp. Usher himself donated his own collection of clocks, watches, miniatures, porcelain, silver and enamel to the gallery and there is an excellent coin collection. The paintings include works of the Italian, Dutch and Flemish schools and a good collection of 20th-century art. There is good representation of local artists including the largest Peter de Wint collection in the country. A section of the gallery is devoted to portraits and personal effects of Alfred Lord Tennyson.

THEATRE

Theatre Royal – Claskergate, Tel 525555. The theatre is one of the finest Victorian theatres in the country and has been expertly restored. It stages pre-West -End shows and national touring productions as well as concerts and amateur productions. There is a popular Christmas pantomime season.

Occasional theatre productions also take place at the **Lawn**, Carline Road, Tel 529828 for details. There are occasional performances of the Mystery Plays in a cathedral setting.

MUSIC

Concerts take place in **Lincoln Cathedral**, the **Lawn**, the **Usher Art Gallery** and other locations. Tel 529828 or 5255<5 for details.

The **Lincoln Festival** takes place during the first three weeks in May and includes performances by such groups as the Lincoln Symphony Orchestra (Lincoln's community ensemble) the East of England Orchestra, the Northern Philharmonic and the Capricci Chamber Ensemble. Also included is a folk festival, theatre events, puppets and literary events.

CINEMA

Ritz Theatre and Cinema– High Street, Tel 546313. The Ritz is a venue which successfully combines live stage performances by international artists with a regular programme of the latest film releases.

BOOKSTORES

The best is **J Ruddock Ltd** at 287 High Street, Tel 528 285, situated on a very ancient site. **Bookstore**, 9 The Stonebow Centre, Tel 532443, is also worth a look while the **Book Cellar**, 4 St Peter-at-Arches, Tel 531007, has some good book bargains. Books on philosophy and religion are best at **SPCK**, 36 Steep Hill, Tel 527486. **Hobby Books** at Unit 4, 3 Farmer Road, sells what its name suggests while **Advance Bookshop**, 17 Monks Road is often interesting.

ANTIQUARIAN AND SECONDHAND BOOKS

Steep Hill is the only location you need to explore. **Reader's Rest** at No 13 has a large collection of second-hand books while **Harlequin Galleries** at No 22, Tel 522589, is Lincolnshire's leading antiquarian bookseller with a good stock and delightful premises. Finally at No 46 is **Frippery Books**, Tel 537653, rounding off a charming selection of shops in close proximity to one another.

ART GALLERIES

Castle Gallery – 61 Steep Hill, Tel 535078, has some nice antique prints and also 19th- and early 20th-century oils and watercolours plus antiquarian maps and prints. **Frank Gadsby**, 260 High Street, Tel 527487, has contemporary oils, watercolours and limited edition prints. **Lincoln Fine Art**, 33 The Strait, Tel 533029, has a wide range of oils and watercolours while close by, **Harding House Gallery** has interesting contemporary work, Tel 788321 for details of this artist's cooperative. **Arc Gallery**, 38 Bailgate, Tel 542717, has very attractive ethnic pottery and jewellery while **Roy Collett** markets his own oils of English landscapes plus some nice traditional prints. He's at 34 Steep Hill, Tel 536250.

ANTIQUE DEALERS

Steep Hill and the Strait are rich ground for antiques. In Steep Hill at No 32, **David J Hansford**, Tel 530044, stocks 17th-to-19th-century English and Continental furniture and 18th-century clock, barometer and scientific instruments. Close by at No 44 is **RG Toogood**, Tel 528687, with small antiques, silver, collector's items, porcelain, glass, Victoriana and bric-à-brac. **Dorian Lambert Antiques**, Tel 545916, is at 64/65. He has beautiful 18th-to-20th-century furniture, clocks and porcelain. Close by in St Michael's Church Hall is **Collectors Cave**, Tel 539368, with furniture, paintings, silver, glass, china, jewellery, books and clothes. **A Doyle** is also nearby with a general collection, Tel 542226, while **Timepiece Clocks**, Tel 525831 with timepieces of all kinds, rounds out our Steep Hill selection. The Strait has the **Strait Antiques** at No 5, Tel 523130. They have 18th- and 19th-century porcelain, 19th-century blue-and-white transfer ware and general antiques and furniture. At No 27 is **Designs on Pine**, Tel 529252, with antique and reproduction pine, while at No 28, **Richard Pullen**, Tel 537170, has attractive jewellery, silver and plate. If you continue down the Strait you will come into High Street where at No 111 you will find **C and K Dring**, Tel 540733, who have Victorian and Edwardian inlaid furniture, porcelain and clocks, while at No 338, **Rowletts of Lincoln**, Tel 524139, has coins and jewellery. Just behind the Theatre Royal, off the right of The Strait as you descend, is St Martin's Lane with John R Bracey, Tel 530715, who has jewellery and silver. If you move into High Street, Silver Street is on your left just before Stonebow. At No 6 is **James Usher**, Tel 527547, who also stocks silver and jewellery. An ancestor of the present owner gave the Usher Art Gallery to the city. Finally, just to the north of the Cathedral is **Mansions Antiques**, Tel 514308 at 5A Eastgate. They have fine antique furniture and another outlet at 6 St Paul's.

RESTAURANTS

Harvey's Cathedral Restaurant – 1 Exchequergate, Castle Square, Tel 510333, is my favourite place to eat in Lincoln and one of my favourite places anywhere. It's delightfully situated in the shadow of the Cathedral and has a wonderful Victorian ambience. The set lunch is excellent value with such delights as crab bisque and coq au Riesling on offer. Wonderful old English cooking with pies like steak and kidney and sausage and bacon. Excellent desserts and wine list. Recommended. Open all week 12–2pm. and 7–9:30pm

Wig and Mitre – 29 Steep Hill, Tel 535190. Housed in an old building in one of the oldest parts of Lincoln, this restaurant serves a variety of food in conditions that can be formal or informal. Dishes such as gammon and eggs, braised tongue with red wine and oyster mushrooms, and chicken with Parma ham en croûte have all been praised, as have the salmon mousse and the quail salad. Open all week 8am–11pm.

Brown's Pie Shop – 33 Steep Hill, Tel 527330. Close to the Wig and Mitre, Brown's serves old-fashioned British food and serves it well. They are especially strong on pies and salads and have a whole range of sinfully fattening old-fashioned British puddings. Open all week 11am–11pm.

Jew's House Restaurant – 15 The Strait, Tel 524851. Apart from the classic cooking and the produce fresh from the market, it is an experience worth having just to sit in this 12th-century house and imagine what has gone on here for hundreds of years. Open Mon–Sat 12–2pm and 7–10pm.

PUBS

Lion and Snake – Bailgate, Tel 523770. Built in 1640, the pub is Lincoln's oldest. A friendly atmosphere tastefully refurbished and comfortable. Good bar food at lunch and in the evening until 8pm. A very good traditional Sunday lunch.

Green Dragon – Waterside North, Tel 524950. A 14th-century timber-framed former merchant's house set in a beautiful waterside location. Good food in the bar and in the friendly restaurant.

Jolly Brewer – 26 Broadgate, Tel 528583. A fascinating art deco pub given real atmosphere by its enthusiastic owners. Very friendly with good traditional bar food and real ale.

Adam and Eve – Lindum Road, Tel 537108. A contender for Lincoln's oldest pub set conveniently two minutes' walk from the Cathedral, castle and Usher Art Gallery. Pleasant garden in the summer with good home-cooked bar food served at lunch and in the evening.

ARTISTIC ASSOCIATIONS

The child martyr "Little St Hugh" (see Ephemera) was a favoured subject of poets. He is mentioned in "The Prioress's Tale" in Chaucer's *Canterbury Tales*, in Marlowe's *The Jew of Malta* and in *The Jew's Daughter*, a ballad in Thomas Percy's *Reliques*. Robert Grosseteste, the philosopher who was first Chancellor of Oxford and Bishop of Lincoln, is buried in the Cathedral. Alfred Lord Tennyson, a native of Lincoln, is commemorated by a statue on the green outside the cathedral. The Tennyson Research Centre in the Central Library houses a large collection of family books and papers. There is an Exhibition Room at the Usher Gallery which contains manuscripts, letters and memorabilia.

Peter de Wint, the landscape painter, became friendly with William Hinton of Lincoln while both were studying art in London. Upon visiting Lincoln, de Wint promptly fell in love with Hinton's sister and married her. The couple bought a house near the Cathedral on the corner of Drury Lane and Union Road (marked with a plaque) in 1814. For the next 30 years they divided their time between Lincoln and a house in London and Peter de Wint made many watercolours and paintings of local views.

An interesting but almost forgotten figure of late 19th-century British art is William Tom Warrener, who was born to a prominent Lincoln family in 1861 and studied at the local school of art. He lived in Paris for some years, and became a friend and follower of Henri de Toulouse-Lautrec. Lautrec made several portraits of him and featured him in a poster design as *L'Anglais au Moulin Rouge*. In 1906, Warrender returned to Lincoln to take over the family coal-merchant business and did little painting after that date. He lived at St Margaret's Lodge in Upper Lindum Street until his death in 1934.

EPHEMERA

Besides holding the finest of the four contemporary copies of the Magna Carta and the Charter recognizing the transfer of the see from Dorchester in Oxfordshire to Lincoln, the

Cathedral's Wren Library holds manuscripts not so closely related to the theological or constitutional. There are first editions of Milton's *Paradise Lost*, Cervantes's *Don Quixote* and part of Spencer's *Faerie Queene*.

The Jewish community in Lincoln in the Middle Ages was second in number only to the one in London. Jew's Court on Steep Hill is believed to have been a synagogue. The house next door, now a restaurant, is interesting in that it is built on two levels. The upper floor had windows, but on the street there were only loopholes. The house belonged to a rich Jewess, Belaset of Wallingford, who was hanged for fraud in 1290, the year the Jews were expelled from Britain. A little further up Steep Hill is Aaron the Jew's House, although Aaron's connection with it is unproven. Aaron was a moneylender (almost the only occupation permitted to Jews at that time). Without Aaron's loans, Lincoln Cathedral could not have been built, nor Kirkstead Abbey, Louth Park Abbey, Revesby Abbey and others. Without Aaron, Henry II could not have sent an expedition to conquer Ireland; his loans to Henry amounted to more that half the monarch's income, and although Henry II was the most powerful man in Europe, his debt to Aaron was far more than a mere monetary one.

The story of Little St Hugh, which Chaucer developed in "The Prioress's Tale," was actually a powerful piece of anti-Semitic propaganda. Hugh, an eight-year-old Lincoln boy, disappeared one August evening in 1255; a few days later, his mutilated body was found in a well. His death was at once declared to be a Jewish ritual murder. Time after time the accusation has been denounced – by at least two Popes and many scholars and men of goodwill – as a lie prompted by hatred, malice, envy and self-interest. A pogrom resulted, and a trail of faked evidence, false witness under torture, and farcical trials leading to judicial murders on a large scale. Hugh himself though, did exist. His shrine is in the Cathedral and the tomb was opened in 1791 by the Dean of the Cathedral and Sir Joseph Banks. The complete skeleton of a boy three feet three inches (98.8 cm) tall was discovered.

The one-foot-high Lincoln imp, carved high on a pillar in the Cathedral's Angel Choir, is a Lincoln tradition. The story goes that an imp flew into the Cathedral after causing havoc in the town. It became enamoured of the angel choir and flew high into the roof. Reaching the top of a pillar to rest, he was, in a moment, turned to stone. He is still there to this day. The Lincoln jeweller, James Ward Usher, who financed the Usher Gallery, made a fortune from the sale of replicas of the Lincoln Imp. A replica was supposed to bring good luck and perhaps there is some truth in the superstition. The Prince of Wales, afterwards King Edward VII, was given a Lincoln Imp tie pin on a visit to the city. Soon afterwards his horses won both the Grand National and the Derby.

In the choir stalls of Lincoln Cathedral is the splendid Precentor's Stall. A precentor was a member of the clergy who led congregational singing and was in general control of musical arrangements. Legend has it that the carvings on this particular Precentor's Stall refer to one particular precentor who had the reputation for being lazy, although he always turned up promptly on payday. The carvings, said to show the carver's dislike of this particular clergyman, show a number of monkeys working industriously. One monkey dodges his share of duty and steals a pat of butter. The miscreant is caught and hanged without further adieu and two monkeys take away the corpse. The carvings can be seen on the Precentor's Stall itself and on a nearby misericord. In case you are wondering, a misericord is a carved projection on the underside of a hinged seat, generally in the choir stalls, which, when turned up, gives support to one standing in the stall. Look for them in churches and cathedrals – they are generally quite unique and beautifully carved.

TOURIST INFORMATION BUREAU: 9 Castle Hill, Lincoln, Lincs, LN1 3AA. Tel (0522) 529828

NORWICH

County of Norfolk
By train, 100 minutes from London (Liverpool Street)
By road, 114 miles (182 km) from London via M11 and A11

From the air, Norwich looks very much like a medieval painting of a city with its castle, its cathedral, its narrow streets and the towers of 30 ancient churches (more than any other city in Europe). In medieval times, Norwich was second only to London in size and by the time of the Norman Conquest was a town of some importance. The building of the castle and the cathedral in the 12th century gave the city two focal points that remain to this day. During the years from 1300 to 1500 the Norfolk Broads (the miles of waterways that now constitute a haven for boating enthusiasts) were formed from the flooding of peat diggings. Industrial change dominated the 16th and 17th centuries, with French immigrants playing an important part in the regeneration of the Norfolk worsted industry. These centuries also saw the departure of many Norwich people seeking a new life in North America. During the 18th and 19th centuries Norwich was one of the most prosperous cities in the country, and many of the elements of its present-day economy trace their foundation to this time – including Gurney's Bank, the city's first shoe factory and the Norwich Union Insurance Company. Surprisingly, Norwich was bypassed by the main thrust of the Industrial Revolution, but during that period many prominent local firms were formed, the Port of Norwich was established and the railways reached the city which, at their peak, required three passenger stations to serve travellers. Norwich was lucky in escaping the worst effects of industrialization and there has been no large-scale development, pollution or blight. Likewise the city escaped the worst effects of war damage and there had to be little post-war construction.

Today Norwich boasts a thriving community where shoppers can wander through narrow, winding alleys, broad streets and modern malls. The firms Colman's of Norwich, famous for their mustard, and Rowntree Mackintosh, who are part of the Nestlé group and produce several well-known brands of chocolate and confectionery, employ nearly a quarter of the inhabitants of Norwich. Other industries include engineering, electronics, printing, publishing, pharmaceuticals, banking, insurance and financial services. The famous shoe industry is no longer as important as it once was but the city still has a reputation for high quality footwear. The famous Lotus sports cars are made here and just outside the boundaries of the city lies the firm of Bernard Matthews, beloved especially at Christmas, as the largest producer of turkeys in the country.

WALK

Our **Norwich Walk** is in two parts, both beginning at the Duke Street multi-storey car park. Turn left down Duke Street and left again into St Andrew's Street. Note the 14th-century **Suckling House** and its addition, which now houses a regional film theatre. Cross St Andrew's Plain and continue right along Princess Street. **Garsett House**, at the junction, dates from 1589 and is said to incorporate beams from an Armada galleon. **St Peter Hungate Church Museum and Brass Rubbing Centre** (one of the city's many redundant churches) is close by. Opposite is the **United Reform Church**, a great Victorian classical building of 1869. There are many half-timbered houses dating from Elizabethan and Stuart times in this street, including **Princes Inn**, which dates from the 15th century. Turn left along Tombland, Norwich's earliest market place. Tombland does not take its name from a graveyard but from the Danish word meaning open ground. Many street and place names bear witness to the Danish influence in the early history of Norwich. Of particular interest is No 14, the **Augustine Steward House** which dates from 1540. Opposite is the **Erpingham Gate** which leads to the cathedral precincts. Sir Thomas Erpingham's statue occupies a niche above the archway. This is only just, as he built the gate in 1420. Shakespeare,

PULL'S FERRY, NORWICH

in *Henry V*, refers to him as "stout Sir Thomas Erpingham" and establishes a warm relationship between Sir Thomas and the King in his play. As you pass through the gateway you will see the buildings of **Norwich School**, established in 1553; the school claims descent from a much earlier foundation and indeed the school chapel dates from 1316. Former pupils include the Elizabethan dramatist Robert Greene, and Lord Horatio Nelson, who was born at Burnham Thorpe in North Norfolk and whose statue stands nearby in the Upper Close. Visit the **Cathedral** and leave by the south door, outside which is **Edith Cavell's Grave** (see Ephemera); her memorial is in Palace Street, outside the Maid's Head. Walk down to Lower Close, which has Georgian houses on its south side and what was the monastic granary opposite. Follow the lane past the school playing fields to **Pull's Ferry**. Turn left along Riverside Walk to **Bishop Bridge** which dates from 1340, is the city's oldest and was reputed to be the fording point of a Roman marching route. Cross the road and continue along Riverside Walk, passing the 13th-century **Cow Tower**, the oldest brick building in Norwich which served in its time as a tollhouse and a prison. Nearby is the **Adam and Eve** pub, reputed to be the oldest inn in Norwich. Turn left past the Magistrate's Court into Bishopgate. Turn left along Bishopgate to the almshouse of Great Hospital (1249) and the nearby **St Helen's Church** (14th century). Continue along Bishopgate, Palace Plain and Palace Street and turn right into Wensum Street and left up Elm Hill. At the top turn right into St Andrew's Plain with **St Andrew's Hall**, originally the nave of the great convent church of the Black Friars, on the north side. Continue along St Andrew's Street to Duke Street and the car park. This walk will have taken you about two miles (3.2 km), so I think a break is called for.

Starting from the same point, again turn left down Duke Street but then right along Charing Cross to the **Strangers' Hall Museum**, a rambling, complex structure begun in 1320 but added to over the years, which now houses the museum of English domestic life. Come out onto Charing Cross and turn right along St Andrews Street and soon turn right down Exchange Street to the **Market Place** with its dozens of stalls selling everything from books, brassware and herbal remedies to vegetables. The Market Place has a dramatic setting. Ahead is the great **St Peter Mancroft Church**, to the right **City Hall** faces the flint-work, 15th-century **Guildhall** across St Giles Street while the Castle towers over the 18th-century houses of Gentleman's Walk to the left. Visit **St Peter Mancroft Church** and then walk down Gentleman's Walk and turn into the **Royal Arcade**. Built in 1899, the arcade is an art nouveau confection of glazed tiles and stained glass, beautifully restored. If you can bear to leave the arcade shops you will emerge into Castle Meadow. Turn left and then right up Castle Hill to the **Castle**. Return down Castle Hill, noting the **Bell**, a fine old coaching inn at the bottom; cross Castle Meadow and continue straight on into Red Lion Street. Turn left into Westgate and left again into All Saints Street, which has fine Georgian houses, and leads into Golden Ball Street. Ahead are the flint-and-metal offices of **Eastern Counties Newspapers** (circa 1900), who are national leaders in newspaper production technology; turn right here down Rouen Road and then left through St Julian's Alley to **St Julian's Church** (see Ephemera). Continue to King Street and turn left. At the corner of King Street and Old Barge Yard is **Dragon Hall**, a former medieval house and, until recently, the Old Barge Inn. It is now a museum and heritage centre. Further on, the **Manns and Norwich Brewery** offices occupy the site of a friary where brewing was carried out in medieval times.

Cross Prince of Wales Road to Upper King Street, noting the Anglia TV offices on the left, part of which was formerly the Agricultural Hall. At the top of Upper King Street, **St Ethelbert's Gate**, circa 1272, is the principal entrance to the Cathedral Close but turn left along Queen Street to **St Michael at Plea**, a redundant church which is now an antiques market. Note the attractive clock. Cross Redwell Street to **London Street**, a busy, pedestrian shopping precinct. A shopping centre since the 18th century, the street was once called Cockey Lane after the "Great Cockey" or stream which ran down part of its length. At the end of the precinct, bear right into Bridewell alley with the **Mustard Shop Museum**, a reconstructed 19th-century grocer's shop opened to commemorate the 150th anniversary of Colman's of Norwich. Close by is the **Bridewell Museum of Local Industry**, a superb flintwork building, originally a 14th-century merchant's house. The house became a Bridewell, that is, a prison for tramps and beggars, in 1583. After visiting the museum continue up the lane to St Andrew's Street and turn left and right to the car park.

MUSEUMS, GALLERIES AND PUBLIC BUILDINGS

Norwich Castle Museum – Castle Hill, Tel 611277. The Castle keep, constructed between 1100 and 1130, is the oldest part of the museum building. It contains displays of medieval armour, Egyptian mummies and an exhibition illustrating the links between Norwich and Europe which have existed since prehistoric times. Oddly, the Castle, one of the largest and strongest in England, played little part in the nation's history and for more than 500 years was in fact used as a prison. Not long after the last public execution in 1867 the building became a museum. There are exhibits relating to the ecology, natural history, archaeology, and social history of Norwich. There is a collection of paintings and watercolours, notably those of artists of the Norwich School, as well as Norwich silver and ceramics. The museum has the finest collection of Lowestoft porcelain in the world. Look especially for the Norwich "Snapdragons" – masks used in the Guild Day processions. Open Mon–Sat 10–5pm, Sun 2–5pm.

Bridewell Museum – Bridewell Alley. Essentially a museum of Norwich trades and industries. There are exhibits relating to clockmaking, engineering, brewing, printing and the once important textile and shoe manufacturing industries. There is a well-stocked pharmacist's shop and my own favourite exhibit is a case of stuffed Norwich canaries, a breed imported by Flemish weavers. The Norwich City Football Club is called the "Canaries" by its supporters. Open Mon–Sat 10–5pm.

Mustard Shop Museum – 3 Bridewell Alley, Tel 627889. The museum, at the back of the Mustard Shop, is entirely devoted to the history of mustard and illustrates the growing, processing and marketing of Colman's mustard from the beginning of the firm in 1841 to the present day. There is archival material, advertisements and a celebrated collection of mustard pots. Open Mon, Wed, Fri, Sat 9–5:30 Tues 9:30–5:30pm.

Strangers' Hall Museum – Charing Cross, Tel 611277. In this medieval merchant's house with a 14th-century vaulted undercroft, and a beautiful 16th-century Great Hall and Minstrel's Gallery, can be found a museum of urban life containing rooms furnished in the style of various periods from the 16th century onwards. There are 15th-century tapestries, an 18th-century Irish glass chandelier, Norwich shop signs, costumes and toys and the Lord Mayor's Coach. Open Mon–Sat 10–5pm.

St Peter Hungate Museum – Princess Street, Tel 611277. This 15th-century church is noted for its hammerbeam roof and Norwich painted glass. The museum's displays illustrate the theme of art and craftsmanship in the service of Christianity. Exhibits date from the 9th to 20th centuries and include illuminated books, monumental brasses and musical instruments. Many objects come from local redundant churches. Open Mon–Sat 10–5pm.

Royal Norfolk Regiment Museum – Shirehall, Castle Meadow, Tel 628455. The museum illustrates the history of the Regiment from 1685 to 1985. There are uniforms, paintings, Regimental silver and campaign medals including the six Victoria Crosses awarded to soldiers of the Regiment. Open Mon–Fri 9–12 and 2–4pm.

John Jarrold Print Museum – Jarrold Publishing Company, Whitefriars, Tel 660211. The museum of this old-fashioned printing company has displays of presses, types of print and hand and mechanical binding equipment dating from 1840. Open by appointment.

Norfolk and Norwich Heritage Centre – Dragon Hall, 123 King Street, Tel 663922. A newly opened museum housed in a former medieval house, latterly a pub! A beautiful first-floor hall with a fine timber-framed roof. An elaborate carved dragon on one of the roof spandrels gives the building its name. On the death of Robert Toppes, the wealthy merchant who built the house, it passed to William Boleyn, grandfather of Henry VIII's second wife, Anne. The museum examines the history and heritage of Norfolk and Norwich. Open Mon–Thurs 10–4pm and Sat in the summer 10–4pm.

City of Norwich Aviation Museum – Old Norwich Road, Horsham St Faith, Tel 625309. Situated on the northern edge of Norwich airport, the museum has displays relating to local aeronautical history and a collection of aircraft including a Vulcan bomber. Open Sun 10–3:30 and Tues and Thurs 7:30pm–dusk in summer.

Sainsbury Centre for Visual Arts – University of East Anglia, Tel 56060. The centre opened in 1978 and houses the Robert and Lisa Sainsbury Collection. The collection comprises objects and paintings from many cultures, with strong holdings of Oceanic, African, native North American and pre-Columbian art as well as works by 20th-century artists such as Moore, Epstein, Giacometti and John Davies. The building itself, designed by Foster Associates, is of considerable technical interest. Open Tues–Sun 12–5pm.

Norfolk Institute of Art and Design – St Georges Street, Tel 610561, also has occasional exhibitions and is open Mon–Sat 10–5pm when exhibiting.

Norwich Cathedral – Tombland, Tel 626290. The Cathedral was built between 1100 and 1174. In 1272 much of the Monastery and Cathedral was set on fire by local rioters and restoration work took until 1430 to complete. Further destruction took place after the Restoration and in Cromwellian times and the present appearance of what is architecturally one of Britain's finest cathedrals provides few clues to its turbulent and unfortunate history. Among the most remarkable features are the vaults in the presbytery and the south transept, the Chapel of St Luke, the stalls and canopies in the choir, the misericords and the roof bosses in the nave and cloisters.

Guildhall – Guildhall Hill, Tel 761082. The building, a fine example of Norfolk flintwork, dates from 1407. For over 500 years local government presided here in the form of 529 successive Mayors and Lord Mayors. Until 1985 the Magistrates' Court also sat here. The old Council Chamber has a Tudor carved ceiling and a window of 15th-century glass. The lower part of the building was once used as a prison and Thomas Bilney, the Protestant martyr, and Robert Kett, the rebel, were confined here prior to execution. The superb Corporation Regalia are housed here as is the Norwich Tourist Information office.

Assembly Rooms – Theatre Street. Built in 1754, the handsome Georgian frontage conceals some of the original timbers and masonry of the medieval College of St Mary-in-the-Fields, which stood on the site. The interior is well restored and preserves the flavour of the 18th century. Concerts are given in the **Music Room**, the **Noverre Cinema** occupies the west wing and there is also a restaurant and coffee lounge. I do not have sufficient space to mention in any great detail the beauty of Norwich's many churches. Below is a list of those I find the most interesting:

St Julian's – St Julian's Alley. Pilgrims come from all over the world to visit the cell of Dame Julian of Norwich, a 14th-century mystic (see Ephemera).

St Georges Colegate – Colegate. The church retains more Georgian woodwork than any other in the city. The building dates from the 15th century, and there are many interesting memorials. Close to St George's Colegate are two interesting Non-conformist chapels. The **Octagon Chapel** was built in 1754 on the site of a Presbyterian Meeting House of 1687. John Wesley called it "perhaps the most elegant chapel in all Europe." Those outside the Non-conformist circle however, nicknamed it the "Devil's Cucumber Frame." Today it is a Unitarian Chapel. Next door is the **Old Meeting House**, built in 1693 for an independent congregation, and still used for worship.

St Andrew's – Bridewell Alley. Completed in 1506, the church is the second largest in Norwich (after St Peter Mancroft). It was the centre of Whig Protestantism in the city and the sympathies of its parishoners are demonstrated by canvases over the south door condemning idolatry and popery.

St Clement's Church – Colegate. Said by many to be the oldest in the city, this simple little church has Victorian furnishings and monuments to the Iveses (woollen merchants) and the Harveys (merchants and bankers), two of the city's most influential families.

THEATRE

Theatrically, Norwich is on pause ...

Theatre Royal – Theatre Street, Tel 628205, is at the centre of a controversy involving a rebuilding appeal. The original appeal to raise £2.75 million failed and a management report now estimates that the appeal will cost £5.5 million. As I write, the theatre is closed, leaving Norwich as the only town of regional importance without a decent modernized touring theatre. Let us hope that by the time you read this new initiatives will see the Theatre Royal open again.

Another project which will probably have reached fruition by the time you read this is the **Playhouse Theatre**. The Playhouse aims to open in 1992 in an old warehouse with an architect-designed, 350 seat theatre. The plans for this professional regional theatre are exciting and details can be obtained from the Norwich Playhouse Office at 8A Castle Street, Tel 612580.

As I write, the only professional company is the delightful **Norwich Puppet Theatre**, one of only five in the country, which operates out of a redundant church, St James, Whitefriars, Tel 629921. They should not be missed and their 200-seat theatre also hosts visiting companies when the puppets are on tour.

Luckily, Norwich has one of the best amateur drama companies in the country. The **Maddermarket Theatre**, Maddermarket Alley, Tel 620917, is the home of the Norwich Players. In 1924, actor/manager Nugent Monck converted a former Roman Catholic chapel into a permanent home for his company. Monck's interest in performing Shakespeare's plays in their "original and pure form" was a major influence on the design of the building. The company stages 10 professionally directed productions a year covering the whole spectrum of classic and modern theatre. I saw their production of *Lark Rise,* an adaptation of Flora Thompson's book, and it was excellent.

Whiffler Open Air Theatre in the Castle Gardens, stages plays and concerts in the summer season. Tel 761082 for details. The **Kenney Theatre** at the University of East Anglia, Earlham Road, Tel 592510 also has student and some touring productions.

Norwich Arts Centre – Reeves Yard, St Benedict's Street, Tel 660352. A lively venue offering small-scale touring drama companies, music and jazz, together with art exhibitions (especially photography), workshops and classes. There is an outlet for buying crafts, a restaurant and bar. Well worth a visit.

Also check out **St Gregory's Arts Centre** at 15 Pottergate, Tel 628777.

MUSIC

Norwich has no concert hall and at present concerts are performed in **St Andrew's Hall**, an agreeably converted church on St Andrew's Plain, Tel 628477. Visitors have included the Royal Philharmonic Orchestra, but the hall's charm cannot mask the fact that it has poor acoustics and traffic noise. Occasional concerts are held in the Cathedral and at other churches and halls in Norwich. Tel 761082.

Norwich also has the second oldest festival in the country – the **Norwich and Norfolk Festival** began in 1770 as a triennial event until in 1988 it was changed to annual. The brave theme for the 1990 Festival was "A Celebration of the 20th Century." Elgar, Britten and Bliss all have written special works for the Norwich Festival and that tradition continues today. There are jazz, blues, classical orchestras, ensembles and soloists, theatre (the Berliner Ensemble did a cabaret evening in 1990), lectures and workshops. Over the years visitors have included the Philharmonia Orchestra, Alfred Brendel, John Lill, Cecile Ousset and the Allegri and Chilingerian String Quartets. A feature of the festival is the large Festival Choir which performs large-scale vocal works such as *Belshazzar's Feast* by William Walton and Frederick Delius's *Mass of Life.* The Festival usually runs for ten days early in October. Tel 614921 for details.

CINEMA

Commercial cinema at:
Odeon Cinema – Anglia Square, Tel 621903.
Cannon – Prince of Wales Road, Tel 623312, 4 screens.

Of more interest is the **Noverre Cinema**, Theatre Street, Tel 630128, and especially **Cinema City**, Tel 622047, which is in St Andrew's Street, housed in Suckling House, a 14th-century merchant's residence. Besides its unique location, Cinema City, as a regional film theatre, offers a varied programme of films covering the whole spectrum of world cinema.

BOOKSTORES

The two best are **Sherratt and Hughes** at 53 Stephen's Street, Tel 617028, and **Waterstone's** at 30 London Street, Tel 632426, and I don't know how many times you've heard that before. Of the local shops, **Blackhorse** at 8/10 Wensum Street, Tel 626871, is the best and they are also official agents for HMSO publications. Books on religion and philosophy are best found at **SPCK**, 19 Pottergate, Tel 627332, with **CLC Booksellers**, 68 Prince of Wales Road, Tel 623875, and **Living Bread**, Upper St Giles Street, Tel 764233, good alternatives. **Hungate** at 11 Princess Street, Tel 629651, and the department store, **Jarrolds**, in Exchange Street, Tel 660661, have a reasonably good selection of children's books as well, while **Bookmart** at 31 Market Place, Tel 667209, has good book bargains and publishers' remainders.

ANTIQUARIAN AND SECONDHAND BOOKS

For antiquarian books and some first editions, I like **Peter Crowe** at 75/77 Upper St Giles Street, Tel 624800, **T and J Hall**, 72 St Benedict's Street, Tel 624890 and **Tombland Bookshop**, 8 Tombland, Tel 7606110. Peter Crowe is best if you only have time for one. For prints as well as secondhand books, I recommend **Cathedral Gallery** which is also on Upper St Giles Street, Tel 612428. **J R and R K Ellis** at 53 St Giles Street, Tel 623679, have a good children's selection as well as a good paperback selection, while the rest – **Denise Crow** in the Norwich Market, **Scientific Anglian** at 30 St Benedict's Street, Tel 624079, and the **St Michael at Plea Exhibition Centre** on Bank Plain, Tel 619226, all have good selections which are worth a browse.

ART GALLERIES

Perhaps because of the influence of the Norwich School or the presence of the Norwich School of Art, the city has a better than average number and choice of galleries. They are listed below.

Rowans Gallery – 22 Wensum Street, Tel 764135. Paintings, watercolours and drawings. Specialists in East Anglian art. Permanent selection on view.

Contact Gallery – 56 St Benedict's Street, Tel 760219. Run by artists. Always a good selection of contemporary art by regional artists, with 13 exhibitions yearly. Covers all media.

Conroy-Foley Designer Craft – 6 Merchants Court, Tel 630338. Contemporary sculptures, wall hangings, tapestries, textiles, ceramics and glass.

Crome Gallery – 34 Elm Hill, Tel 622827. 18th- to 20th-century prints, paintings and sculptures.

Gallery 45 – 45 St Benedict's Street, Tel 763771. British and Continental oils and watercolours from 1850 plus prints and sculptures. Primitive and naive work plus Baxter and Le Blond. Always an interesting and unusual selection.

Bank House Gallery – 71 Newmarket Road, Tel 633380. English and Continental oils especially the Norfolk and Suffolk schools of the 19th century.

Glasshouse Gallery – Wensum Street, Tel 615200. Norfolk and Suffolk landscapes by local contemporary artists.

Little Gallery – 38 Elm Hill, Tel 625809. 19th- and 20th-century watercolours, drawings and etchings.

Mandell's Gallery – Elm Hill, Tel 626892. Oils and watercolours. Specializing in the Norwich and Suffolk schools.

A Room With a View – 20 St Benedict's Street, Tel 764471. Local contemporary watercolours and prints.

Stephen Reiss Fine Art – 14 Bridewell Alley, Tel 615357. 19th-century British paintings and drawings, selected 20th-century works, 17th-century Dutch paintings.

Tudor Galleries – 14 Bank Street, Tel 760041. Late 19th-century to contemporary paintings, drawings and prints.

Norwich Craft and Design Centre – St Mary's Plain, Duke Street, Tel 611276. Situated in the 12th-century round-towered church of St Mary Coslany, the only surviving church of this style in the city. There is a large crafts gallery as well as paintings and prints by local artists.

ANTIQUE DEALERS

First, the antique markets:

The **Cloisters Antique Fair** – St Andrew's and Blackfriars Hall, St Andrews Plain, Tel 425158, is open on Wednesdays 9:30–3:30 and attracts over 20 dealers. The **Norwich Antique and Collectors' Centre**, Quayside, Fye Bridge, Tel 612582, has 25 dealers and operates every day (not Sundays) 10–5pm. It's close to the cathedral. **St Michael at Plea Antiques Market** also operates six days a week and can be found on Bank Plain. There are 20 dealers, open 9:30–5pm.

A good place to start your antique trek is St Benedict's Street which is a continuation of Bank Plain and St Andrew's Streets. At No 2-24 is **Anthony Mann Antiques,** Tel 660046, close to St Andrew's Hall with Victorian and Edwardian lighting, brass and iron beds and old bathroom fittings, fireplaces and surrounds. At No 49 is **Queen of Hungary**, while at No 54 you will find **Robert Lowe Antiques**, with stock similar to Anthony Mann's. His telephone number is 624086. There are two dealers at No 86. **Englishman's Antiques**, Tel 633411, which has mainly Victorian and Edwardian furniture, and **Donna Hannent**, Tel 628100, with collectors' items, small silver and jewellery (mostly 1800–1940). Finally, for the numismatist, **Clive Dennett Coins** at No 66, Tel 624315, has a large stock from ancient Greek to the modern day plus some 19th- and 20th-century jewellery. Running parallel to St Benedict's Street to the south by the city hall is St Giles Street.

Here you will find **Malcolm Turner**, Tel 627007, at No 15. He has Staffordshire, Imari, English and Oriental ceramics and some nice 19th-century silver, while **Thomas Tillett** at No 17, Tel 625922 has 19th- and 20th-century diamond jewellery and 18th- to 19th-century silver, and very nice it is too. At No 40/44 is **Arthur Brett and Sons** with a fine collection of antique furniture (mahogany, walnut and oak), sculpture and metalwork. Finally, at 91 Upper St Giles Street you will find **Ninety One** with pine and oak furniture. Tel 625046.

Close to St Andrew's and Blackfriars Hall is Elmhill. **Elmhill Antiques**, Tel 664339, is at No 20. They have 18th- and 19th-century decorative items while **Nigel Handley** at No 32, Tel 628100 has 18th- and 19th-century furniture, china, pictures and decorative items. In a small courtyard at the bottom of Elm Hill on the right you will find **As Time Goes By Antique Clocks** at 5 Wrights Court, Tel 666508. They have a nice stock and close by, at the top of the street, is **Country and Eastern** at 8 Redwell Street, Tel 623107, with late 19th- and 20th-century Oriental rugs, kelims and textiles, primitive and country furniture and woolwork pictures – worth a visit. Also close to St Andrew's Hall is St George's Street. **Design House**, Tel 623181, at No 29, has furniture and decorative items with some lovely early 19th-century ornate gilt work. If you walk up St George's Street to Colegate and turn right you will come to Magdalen Street. At No 17 you will see **Michael Hallam Antiques**, Tel 621163, with furniture, porcelain, pictures and small items, all mainly 19th century. At No 24D is **Yesteryear**, Tel 622908, with a good general collection while further out at No 140 is **Another One**, Tel 615302, with general antiques and bric-à-brac. Magdalen Street leads into Tombland where at No 12/13 you will find **James and Anne Tillet** who have excellent English domestic silver and flatware from the 17th century, mustard pots, barometers, barographs, longcase clocks and jewellery from the 18th century. They are opposite Erpingham Gate, Tel 624914. Close by at 4A Exchange Street, Tel 618605, just off the Market Square, is **Robert Young Antiques** with beautiful 18th- to 20th-century jewellery and **This and That**, Tel 632201, at 56 Bethel Street with a general collection. Also near is the pedestrianized London Street with the old established **Henry Levine and Co** at No 55. They have excellent silver, jewellery and Sheffield Plate and are especially strong on Norwich silver – worth a visit. Tel 628709. Close by is the City Hall. To the right, 150 yards (137 m) down a paved street is Lower Goat Lane. Here at No 18C is **Maddermarket Antiques**, Tel 620610, with jewellery and silver, while at No 20 is **Oswald Sebley**, Tel 626504, also with 18th–20th-century silver and Victorian jewellery.

South of the castle is All Saints Green, where at No 10 you will find **Charles Cubitt**, Tel 622569 (opposite Bond's Store). He has jewellery, silver, china, glass and some antiquarian books. Not far away in Carrow Hill is **Carrow Hill Antique and Bygone Centre**, Tel 628628. They have a large stock of pine furniture, brass and iron bedsteads and bric-à-brac. Finally, the city centre and for movie buffs there's the **Movie Shop** at 11 St Gregory's Alley, Tel 615239, which has all kinds of movie bygones plus pre-1940 clothes and textiles and general antiques. Lastly, two specialist dealers – **D'Amico Antiques**, 20 Highland Road, Tel 52320, has clocks from the 17th to 20th centuries, and **Tooltique**, 54 Waterloo Road, Tel 414289, has old tools.

RESTAURANTS

Adlard's – 79 Upper St Giles, Tel 633522. Adlard's is a family restaurant run by a couple who really care about food and it is excellent. The premises were once a shop and offer levels and nooks for privacy with the dark green decor, inside and out, soothing to the nerves. The cooking is classical French with venison, duck, salmon and scallops all receiving rave reviews. The prices are good value given the excellence of the cooking and the quite superb flavouring. The set lunch and set dinner are priced according to whether you indulge in three or four courses. Highly recommended. Open Tues–Sat (no Sat lunch) 12:30–1:45 and 7:30–9pm.

Brasteds – 8–10 St Andrews Hill, Tel 625949. As at Adlard's, the flavouring and the sauces are excellent. The potted crab starter is well spoken of as is the fish soup. The chicken with Stilton and port sauce was delectable as was the lamb chops with tarragon and Vouvray sauce. There is an interesting wine list. Open Mon–Sat (no Sat lunch) 12–2 and 7–10pm.

Mange Tout – 22–24 White Lion Street, Tel 617879. An informal bistro offering generous portions of salads, hot French bread and good jacket potatoes. Daily specials are excellent. I had a super meal of fillets of plaice, stuffed and wrapped in vine leaves and friends raved about the sweetcorn and broadbean roulade. Very good value. Open Mon–Sat 11:30–10:30pm.

Andersens – 52 St Giles Street, Tel 617199. A nicely converted 18th-century town house and courtyard houses this Danish restaurant, which is appropriate when you consider the ancient ties between Norwich and Scandinavia. Breakfasts are served throughout the day and the Bornholm omelette (with kipper, radish and chives) is wonderful. There are excellent open face sandwiches, meatballs and a good smorgasbord. Good value. Open Mon–Wed 8am–7pm, Thurs–Sat 8am–9:30pm.

La Folie – 20 St John's, Maddermarket, Tel 622777. The restaurant is housed in a Georgian house, the cooking Anglo-French, with saddle of lamb, venison and lemon sole all well spoken of. A good friend also raved about the leek and mushroom tart. Open Mon–Sat (no Sat lunch) 12–2:30 and 7–10pm.

The Treehouse – 16 Dove Street, Tel 625560. Norwich's longest standing vegetarian restaurant, offering vegetarian and vegan food. Excellent value. Open Mon–Sat 11:30–3pm.

PUBS

Adam and Eve – Bishopgate (follow Palace Street from Tombland north of cathedral) Tel 667423. Though the gables are 14th century, the downstairs bar is over 700 years old, dating from when the pub was a refreshment house for the builders of the cathedral. Cosy bars with lots of atmosphere. The ghost of Lord Sheffield, who was killed during Kett's Rebellion in 1549, is said to wander around. Good bar food including vegetable bake, chicken curry, casserole of pork in cider and shepherd's pie. A nice terrace for the summer.

Bell Inn – Timber Hill. A former ancient coaching inn which was the headquarters of the anti-Methodist Hell Fire Club in the 18th century. The hotel itself dates from the 17th century and has cosy bars, good bar food and pleasant courtyard. Tel 614066.

Maid's Head Hotel – Tombland, Tel 76111. The Georgian and Edwardian "mock Tudor" façades conceal a much earlier building, for it was mentioned in the 15th century and was old then. Its foundations are probably Norman. The first regular stagecoach service to London set out from here in 1762. The bars are steeped in atmosphere and tradition and where the carvery lunch is served, coaches and horses once clattered through a courtyard. Interesting bar food, too.

Wig and Pen – 6 St Martin-at-Palace Plain, Tel 625891. Dating from the 17th century, the pub is next door to the house in which John Sell Cotman, a leading figure of the Norwich School of Painters, lived and taught for ten years. Cosy bars with traditional bar food.

Lamb Inn – Haymarket, Tel 625365. The building is Georgian and there is lots of atmosphere. A landlord in the 18th century was murdered by his brother-in-law and I couldn't ascertain whether a ghost is around, but I suspect it is. The pub stands on the site of a much earlier establishment. The area was the Jewish quarter in Norman and early medieval times and reverted to the city when the Jewish quarter, with its synagogue and schools, was destroyed by fire in 1286. Traditional bar food and pleasant atmosphere.

Louis Marchesi – 17 Tombland, Tel 613817. Named after the founder of the first Round Table, the service organization which now has branches world wide. A civilized pub with inexpensive bar food and a welcoming atmosphere.

ARTISTIC ASSOCIATIONS

John Skelton, the poet, was made Rector of Diss in Norfolk in 1498. While on a visit to Norwich, Skelton met Jane Scroop, whose husband had been executed for treason. Jane's pet sparrow, killed by a cat, inspired Skelton to write one of his best known works, "Phyllyp Sparowe." Robert Greene, the Elizabethan dramatist and poet, was born in the city in 1560 and went to Norwich Grammar School. Thomas Browne, the great philosopher and physician, lived in Norwich for more than 40 years. When Charles II visited the city in 1671, Browne was knighted by him in St Andrew's Hall. Browne, whose most famous work is *Religio Medici,* is buried in St Peter Mancroft Church and his statue is in a little paved garden nearby. George Borrow, the novelist and traveller, attended Norwich Grammar School in 1820. Mousehold Heath and the gypsies he met there feature in his partly autobiographical books, *Lavengro* and *The Romany Rye.* Mary Sewell, author of popular poems for children, lived in Norwich and her more famous daughter, Anna, wrote *Black Beauty* here in 1877. Daisy Ashford, author of the delightful *The Young Visiters* [*sic*], lived in Norwich for many years.

In Magdalen Street can be found the entrance to Gurney Court, a courtyard of fine medieval houses with Georgian façades now occupied by shops and doctors' and dentists' surgeries. Here lived the famous Quaker family of the Gurneys, the Norwich bankers who founded Gurney's Bank here in 1775. (It is now Barclay's.) Elizabeth Fry (nee Gurney), the great prison reformer, was born here in 1780 and she wrote many pamphlets and tracts setting out her liberal views. Luke Hansard was born in Norwich in 1752. He was a printers' apprentice who went to London to make his fortune and was later to begin publishing the reports of parliamentary proceedings which today bear his name.

In Pottergate is the site of the Infirmary for Sick Children established in 1853 by the famous Swedish soprano, Jenny Lind, who was the popular sensation of her day and, continuing the musical theme, at 91 Pottergate is the former home of Sarah Glover, a Norwich teacher, who in the early 19th century originated the Tonic Sol-Fa system.

The Norwich School was an English regional school of landscape painting founded by John Crome in 1803. Crome, known as "Old Crome," was an extravagant character. A notorious drinker, he was a great inhabitor of the Norwich pub scene and his association with licensed premises extended to painting the signs for the Three Cranes in the Cathedral Close and the Lame Dog on Queen's Road. All the greatest artists of the Norwich School were associated with the Norwich Society, founded by Crome, and dedicated to holding meetings where matters concerning art could be discussed. The Society also held an annual exhibition during the August Assizes. Crome called the first meeting of the Society in the Hole in the Wall pub and it is sad that none of the pubs, nor indeed the Crome inn signs, survive today. After Crome's death in 1821, his family – six of his children also became painters – suffered increasing financial hardship. That this was a source of pleasure to John Sell Cotman, the other most renowned member of the Norwich School, says much of Cotman's brooding, depressed and introverted personality. Although born in Norwich, Cotman wanted to make an impression in London art circles and moved there in 1798 at the age of 16. He was apt to despise the purely provincial aspirations of Crome and other members of the Norwich School but he exhibited at the Norwich Society Exhibition in 1807, albeit as a portraitist, which was not the school's strong point. In the 1820s he bought an enormous house at St-Martin's-at-Palace Gate (plaque) which he could ill afford. He became Vice-President of the Norwich Society in 1831 and President in 1833, but when he left for London in 1835 the Society came to an end. Cotman's later years were plagued with penury and madness. Most of his children became painters but they seem to have inherited their father's instability and the later history of the Cotman family is just as depressing as that of his rival, Crome. The paintings however, remain. Other important artists associated with the Norwich School include Cotman's brother-in-law John Thirtle, Robert Ladbroke, James Stark (a pupil of Crome's), George Vincent and Henry Bright.

EPHEMERA

In 1599 one of Shakespeare's colleagues, actor and dancer William Kemp(e), ended his "Nine Daies Wonder" – a Morris dance from London to Norwich – by leaping over the wall of St John Maddermarket Church in Maddermarket Alley. The name of both the church and the alley recall the market at which cloth workers bought red madder root for dyeing their fabrics. Kemp, a fellow shareholder with Shakespeare in the Globe Theatre, was Europe's most famous comic actor and Morris dancer. It is likely that several of Shakespeare's clown roles were specifically written for him but in 1599 the two men fell out. It may have been due to the fact that Kemp believed that no production of *Hamlet* was complete without his pulling onstage a dog on wheels! Whatever the cause of the quarrel,

Kemp decided to demonstrate that he, not the upstart bard, was still the people's favourite and in a sort of 16th-century publicity stunt, he set off to dance all the way from London to Norwich. In spite of primitive roads and winter weather, he achieved the feat in just nine days and wrote a book about the event which gave us the phrase "nine days wonder." A group of Norwich Morris dancers are named Kemp's Men in his honour and you can get details of their performances (I'm glad to say they work mostly in pubs), by ringing Peter Salt at 615066.

Four headless bridesmaids in a phantom coach driven by a headless horseman are said to haunt the old Norwich Road at Great Melton, just to the east of the city. The hapless young ladies are said to have been murdered by a highwayman several centuries ago while on their way home from a wedding. The coach was found immersed in a deep pond by the roadside and until frequent appearances of the spectres aroused local suspicion, it was assumed the deaths were the result of an accident. Coroners then were not as thorough as they are today. As usual with Norfolk's many headless ghosts, those who see the spectres are doomed to misfortune.

In the Church of St Julian, in St Julian's Alley off King Street, is the reconstructed cell of the anchoress and mystic, Dame Julian of Norwich. Very little is known about Lady Julian. She was born in 1342 and may have had some connection with the Benedictine nuns of nearby Carrow Abbey and may have received some education there. It seems unlikely she herself was a nun. She was the first woman to write a book in the English language – *Sixteen Revelations of Divine Love* – and on May 8, 1373, when she and those about her thought she was about to die, she received 16 visions (or "shewings"), centred on the Trinity and Passion of Christ and one final vision the following night. She wrote them down, it seems, after receiving them and these experiences are entitled *The Shorter Text*. She then dedicated herself to the solitary life, living in a small cell attached to the church and meditating on her visions. These later meditations were called *The Longer Text*. Opening out from Julian's cell was a window looking into the church. This enabled her to see mass celebrated and to receive communion. A second window opened on to the street and from that window, it seems, she counselled many people who came to her for help. One such was Margery Kempe of King's Lynn who travelled to Jerusalem in search of spiritual enlightenment and in her own *Book of Margery Kempe* (1501) records her meeting with Dame Julian. *Sixteen Revelations of Divine Love* was completed in 1393 and is regarded today as a spiritual classic throughout the Christian world. Julian was still living in 1413 and it may well be that she lived to the age of 80 or beyond. It is not known when this woman, who subjugated her own will and personality to God's work, and who wrote a book marked by the breadth of its compassion and the almost unrivalled beauty of its language, died. No trace of her burial place remains and no doubt she is content to have it so. Details of the Julian Cell are available at St Julian's Church and Shrine or by calling 622509.

Robert Kett, a Norfolk landowner, headed 16,000 insurgents in July 1549 in a protest against the land enclosure system. Kett twice captured Norwich and it was only when Queen Mary sent a large force of men under the command of the Earl of Warwick, that the rebellion was quelled. Kett was captured and hanged December 7, 1549.

Edith Cavell was born in 1865, the second daughter of the Rector of Swardeston, three miles south of the city. She became a nurse and was appointed matron of a hospital in Brussels where, at the outbreak of the First World War, she treated friend and foe alike. She was arrested by the Germans in 1915 and ruthlessly executed on October 12th for helping Belgian and Allied fugitives escape. She is often remembered for the words she uttered shortly before her execution: "Standing as I do in view of God and Eternity, I realize that patriotism is not enough. I must have no hatred or bitterness against anyone." Her death did much to rally English patriotic fervour and to bring the viciousness and brutality of the German forces into public knowledge. Her memorial stands in Palace Street outside the Maid's Head Hotel. She is buried in the Cathedral grounds.

TOURIST INFORMATION BUREAU: The Guildhall, Gaol Hill, Norwich, Norfolk, NR2 1NF. Tel (0603) 666071

5
WALES

CARDIFF
MILFORD HAVEN
PEMBROKE AND HAVERFORDWEST

CARDIFF

Capital of Wales
155 miles (248 km) from London by M4
By rail 2 hours from London (Paddington)

Cardiff was an important Roman settlement and on the Cardiff Castle site one can still see original Roman fortifications; part of the masonry wall, including the North Gate, ranks as one of the best preserved Roman structures in the country. The castle was built on the site of the Roman fort in about 1090. It is a huge fortress covering nearly nine acres (3.6 ha), yet today it is the Victorian restoration influences which predominate. Be sure not to miss the illuminated chamber which shows details of the Roman fortifications. The Norman Keep was built of stone on a steep mound and further protected by a moat. In my view, the keep is the best preserved in the whole of Britain. When the third Marquess of Bute, a coal and shipping magnate, decided to restore the castle in the second half of the 19th century, he chose as his architect William Burges. The castle's lavish interiors and the embellished clock tower that soars aloft are the result of a partnership between one of the world's richest men and an eccentric architectural genius, and are a perfect expression of Victorian energy and self-confidence. Lord Bute was only 18 when he commissioned Burges and the eccentric brilliance can best be seen in the gilded honeycomb ceiling, stained-glass windows and marble walls of the Arab room, the angelic mantelpiece of the dining room or the Chaucer room, so named from its stained glass windows depicting, in the style of Burne-Jones, the figures of the *Canterbury Tales*.

Cardiff was thought to be such a firm stronghold of the early Norman kings that William the Conqueror's eldest son, Robert Curt-Hose, Duke of Normandy, supplanted by his younger brother, Henry I of England, was imprisoned for life in the castle and remained there, blinded, for 28 years from 1106 to 1134. Saxton of Cardiff, a chronicler of the time, wryly writes, "You shall understand that royal parentage is never assured either of ends or safe security." The castle now belongs to the City of Cardiff and is open daily 10–6pm (4pm in winter).

During the Civil War Cardiff again showed its royal loyalty. Charles I was welcomed to the city in 1645 – a gesture to which the Parliamentary forces replied by taking the place exactly one month afterwards! During the 16th and 17th centuries the Bristol Channel, heavy with seaborne traffic, was designed by nature to favour the activities of pirates. Many of these came from Cardiff. There were many who were none too particular in what, or with whom, they dealt, and there is evidence that cannon were sent out from Cardiff to supply the Spanish Armada when it was preparing its attack on Britain in 1588.

In the 19th century Cardiff grew as its natural resources were exploited by the Industrial Revolution. Coal and iron from the Valleys were exported from Cardiff through the docks, which were begun in 1830 by the second Marquess of Bute (the father of the restorer of Cardiff Castle), who gambled his entire fortune on the project, and not without success. At the end of the 19th century, Cardiff was at the peak of its prosperity. There were, and indeed are, other productive industries in Cardiff and its environs. Coal, steel, copper, brewing, biscuits and chemicals have all flourished, but ships and shipping have remained an important factor of the life of the city from its early piratical days to the more refined present.

Today this maritime heritage can be seen in the Welsh Industrial and Maritime Museum (see below), but in the years around 1912 that maritime heritage manifested itself in a very different way. Bute Road, by the docks, where the museum mentioned above is situated, was the home of a community of seamen, who from time immemorial had wandered and mingled with other races, sailing on boats from *prau* to *felucca* to coastal tramp steamers. This colourful, restless and difficult-to-control group maintained its own customs against all comers, especially the police. Interracial rivalry seethed among its members. Often it was directed against the natives of Cardiff and the record of three-day riots, circa 1912, can be studied in contemporary newspaper reports, perhaps anticipating much of what goes on in American cities today.

WALK

For the **Cardiff Walk**, park in the Westgate Street car park by the rugby stadium, walk up Westgate Street to Castle Street and the main entrance of **Cardiff Castle**. Cross Castle Street and follow **Castle Arcade** round to the left. Castle Arcade is one of the six canopied Victorian and Edwardian arcades which are a feature of shopping in Cardiff.

The **Royal Arcade**, dating from 1856, is Cardiff's oldest, while the **Morgan Arcade** with its pretty first-floor Venetian windows was built in 1896. Both contain well-preserved Victorian shop fronts. Turn right into High Street and then left into Church Street, heading for the tower of **St John's Church**. The square tower of the church, with elaborate carvings at its summit, stands tall above the surrounding buildings. A religious site has existed here since Norman times, but the present church dates from the 1450s.

The **Herbert Chapel** contains 17th-century monuments to two brothers from a prominent local family; Sir William Herbert, Keeper of Cardiff Castle, and Sir John Herbert, Chief Secretary to Elizabeth I and James I. Walk along Trinity Street, past the **Central Market** to The Hayes, a wide pedestrianized area. Nearby in Charles Street is **St David's Cathedral**, the metropolitan church for the Roman Catholic Archdiocese of Cardiff and the centre for Cardiff's large Catholic population. Designed by Peter Paul Pugin, St David's was built as a parish church in 1884-87. It was raised to the status of a cathedral in 1916. During the Second World War it was badly damaged but has been restored. Its most notable architectural feature is its unusually wide nave which has, by accident, made the Cathedral particularly well suited to the form of Catholic worship prescribed by the Second Vatican Council. Opposite the cathe-

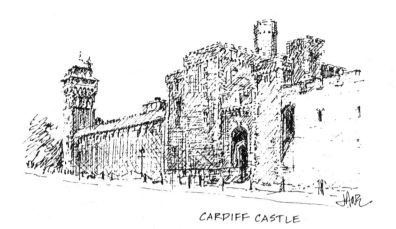

CARDIFF CASTLE

dral is the smaller, but very attractive **Ebenezer Welsh Independent Church**, while not far away in The Hayes is the beautifully maintained **Tabernacle Welsh Baptist Church**, built in the classic style of Welsh Nonconformity. Both the churches attract large congregations from Cardiff's Welsh-speaking community. After visiting the arcades in The Hayes, follow Mill Street to its junction with St Mary Street and Custom House Street, where a statue commemorates John, Second Marquess of Bute, the maker of modern Cardiff. Turn right along St Mary Street. Just after the **National Westminster Bank**, with its Italianate façade, turn left down Quay Street. Ahead is the stand of **Cardiff Arms Park** (see Ephemera). Continue along Womanby Street and out into Castle Street. Turn right and follow the castellated Castle walls (circa mid-19th century) through Duke Street and left into Kingsway and North Road. On your right is Cathays Park, which has become the focal point of the new Cardiff. Here you will find **City Hall**. Built in 1905, the building is finished in dazzling white Portland stone and parts of the interior are as splendid as the façade. Although the building houses the office of the Cardiff City Council, the public are admitted to the Marble Hall on the first floor. Mingling there with the monolithic columns of Sienna marble are the heroes of Wales – a collection of statues which includes St David (Wales's patron saint), Owain Glyndwr (Glendower), Wales's last national leader and Harri Tudur, the Welshman who became Henry VII, the first of the Tudor kings. Next to City Hall is the **National Museum of Wales** (see below), which has a fine entrance set between an imposing row of columns and a dome. The main hall is even finer than the façade. Cool, spacious and finished in marble, this galleried area spreads itself out beneath the dome, a distant 90 feet (27.3 m) above. Behind the museum are some of the finest neo-classical buildings in Europe. The **Law Courts**, the **University of Wales Registry** and the **Mid Glamorgan County Hall** are all imposing in their own way, as are the **University of Wales Institute of Science and Technology**, **Bute Building** and the elegantly simple **Temple of Peace and Health** across College Road. The Civic Centre is ranged around the delightful Alexandra Gardens, at the centre of which stands the **Welsh National War Memorial**, with bronze statues of a soldier, sailor and airman. Come back down North Road and Kingsway and turn left into Queen's Street which is Cardiff's pedestrianized main shopping street. At the bottom of the street is Windsor Place, facing the pretty St Andrew's Place, which encircles the church of **Eglwys Dewi Saint**. The wide Windsor Place is lined with handsome red brick Georgian houses, some of which still have their original wrought-iron balconies. Come back down Queen's Street, passing the entrance to **St David's Centre**, a covered shopping complex, and pass into Duke Street and the Castle where your tour began.

MUSEUMS AND GALLERIES

National Museum of Wales – Cathays Park, Tel 397951. The museum tells the story of Wales from the earliest times to the present day. The galleries illustrate Welsh geology, plants and animals as well as the story of humankind, their works and their art.

The art collection is of international standing and is particularly strong on works by French Impressionist and Post-impressionist painters, including Monet, Renoir, Cézanne and Pissarro.

The industrial section has original objects and machines relating to the older industries, together with dioramas and models. There is a mining gallery, and other displays tell the story of iron, steel and tinplate manufacture in Wales. The modern industries featured include electricity and oil refining. Open Tues–Sat 10–5pm, Sun 10:30–5pm.

The **Welsh Regiment Museum of the Royal Regiment of Wales** – Cardiff Castle, Tel 29367. The regimental museum is housed in the Black and Barbican Towers of the castle and in the Portcullis Chamber which links them. It illustrates the history of the Welsh Regiment from its formation in 1779 until 1969. Among the items of particular interest is the Colour of the Fourth Regiment of American Infantry, taken at Fort Detroit in 1812. There is also a fine collection of Welsh military insignia, dioramas, weapons and trophies. The museum building also includes a working portcullis. Open daily 10–6pm (10–4pm in winter).

Welsh Industrial and Maritime Museum – Bute Street, Tel 481919. This museum, in Cardiff's docklands, tells the story of motive power and the vital roles played by a variety of machines over two centuries of intense industrial progress in Wales. Exhibits have come from a wide range of industries including coal mining, iron and steel works and tinplate mills, etc. Two separate galleries portray the story of seaborne traffic around the coast of Wales and the evolution of Cardiff as a port and shipowning centre. Working exhibits tell the story of motive power and progress in South Wales. Many large outdoor exhibits are also on show including a pilot cutter, canal boat, cranes and an industrial locomotive and a working replica of Richard Trevithick's famous Penydarren Locomotive (see Ephemera). Open Tues–Sat 10–5pm.

Techniquest – Pier Head, 27 Bute Street, Tel 460211. Situated opposite the Welsh Industrial and Maritime Museum. Techniquest is the UK's largest "hands-on" science centre. All the exhibits on display are designed to be played with, touched and explored. There are over 70 specially designed exhibits including solar-powered pumps, thermal image cameras and mirrors that show you vanishing into infinity. There is even a mini studio where you can try your hand at reading the news. Open Tues–Fri 9:30–4:30pm, Sat and Sun 10:30–5pm.

Castle Coch – Tongwynlais, Tel 810101. This enchanting little castle – a combination of Victorian fantasy and timeless fairytale – peeps through the trees on the hills north of Cardiff. Its round towers and conical, needle-sharp turrets leap straight out of the pages of a story book. The Castle was the creation of the fabulously wealthy Lord Bute and his architect, William Burges. Work began in August 1875 on a site intended as a country retreat and companion piece to Cardiff Castle. The castle was completed in 1879 but Burges died suddenly in 1881 and the interior decoration and fittings were completed over the next ten years. An exhibition provides an illustrated history of Bute, Burges and the buildings they created. Open Oct–mid-March weekdays 9:30–4pm, Sun 2–4pm; mid March–Oct weekdays 9:30–6:30pm, Sun 9:30–6:30pm.

Llandaff Cathedral – Llandaff (two miles/3.2 km west of city centre). Away from the hustle and bustle of the centre, on the outskirts of the city, stands Llandaff Cathedral. Built on a site occupied by a religious community founded by St Teilo in the 6th century, Llandaff has demonstrated an amazing ability to survive. Oliver Cromwell's soldiers turned it into an alehouse in 1646, and it was severely damaged by bombing during the Second World War, but Llandaff Cathedral lived on and in the restorations following the war a remarkable new feature was added – Sir Jacob Epstein's magnificent *Christ in Majesty* – a superb and deeply impressive figure of the Christus cast in unpolished aluminum. The statue dominates the whole cathedral and should not be missed.

Welsh Folk Museum – St Fagan's, Tel 555105. The museum, which illustrates the traditional life and culture of Wales, is four miles (6.4 km) west of Cardiff near Junction 33 on the M4 motorway. The open-air section, covering a site of about 100 acres (40.4 ha), contains a number of buildings moved from other parts of Wales. These include farmhouses, cottages, a tannery, forge, tollhouse, cockpit, chapel and working woollen and flour mills. Among the craftspeople who give demonstrations on Saturday mornings throughout the summer months are a cooper and a woodturner. In St Fagan's, an Elizabethan mansion with formal gardens within the curtain wall of a Norman castle, are the Galleries of Material Culture, which have displays of costumes, transport, agricultural implements, furniture and domestic equipment. Music is very much a part of Welsh culture, so naturally there's an impressive display of musical instruments including the medieval Welsh *crwth* and *pibgorn*. Special events include an Old May Day Fair, which has traditional crafts, rural customs, folk dancing and music and sports and pastimes.

There is also a Day of the Valleys, a Midsummer Festival, a Harvest Festival and Christmas celebrations. Open April–Oct daily 10–5pm; Nov–Mar Mon–Sat 10–5pm.

THEATRE

New Theatre – Park Place, Tel 3948444. The New Theatre re-opened in April 1988 after massive refurbishment. Built in 1906, it is Cardiff's only surviving traditional theatre, with a stunning grand staircase and an auditorium that has been designed to match the original decor. The theatre's programme is based around regular seasons by the internationally acclaimed Welsh National Opera Company, for whom the New Theatre acts as home performing base. In addition to visits from companies such as Sadler's Wells Royal Ballet, London Contemporary Dance Theatre and Northern Ballet Theatre, the Royal National Theatre and the Peter Hall Company occur at regular intervals. In addition, a variety of plays on their way to London's West End are presented together with comedies, revues, musicals and a traditional family pantomime for Christmas.

Welsh National Opera Company (WNO) – John Street, Tel 464666. One of Britain's great operatic success stories. The Company tours extensively in Britain and has made guest appearances right across Europe. WNO was the first of Britain's regional opera companies ever to be invited to perform at the Royal Opera House, Covent Garden, and the company has also had considerable international exposure. I saw their recent production of Janacek's *From the House of the Dead*, and it remains one of my most stunning theatrical memories. WNO performs in Cardiff at the New Theatre.

Sherman Theatre – Senghennydd Road, Tel 230451. The Sherman Theatre is the home of Cardiff's Sherman Theatre Company, which presents regular productions of theatre ranging from Shakespeare and the classics to present-day plays. The company also tours both locally and nationally. The comfortable modern theatre is in fact two theatres in one. There's a beautiful fan-shaped main auditorium and an intimate studio theatre, the Arena. Generally, the main stage is reserved for the company's own productions, plus visits from such as Theatre Clwyd. The Arena usually hosts touring shows from some of the country's finest companies. I still vividly remember Shared Experience's production of Pinter's *The Birthday Party* and Monstrous Regiment's highly political interpretation of Marivaux's *The Colony* also played here.

Chapter Theatre – Market Road, Canton, Tel 396061. Part of the Chapter Arts Centre complex, the theatre hosts visits by small touring companies who generally present alternative theatre productions in a highly imaginative and innovative way. Recent visitors have included Red Shift Theatre with Frank Wedekind's *Lulu* and a double bill by the highly regarded Magdalen Project.

MUSIC

St David's Hall – The Hayes, Tel 371236/235900. St David's Hall opened in 1982 as the national concert and conference centre of Wales, providing a venue for all types of music from classical to pop and rock. There is a varied programme of classical concerts with the excellent BBC Welsh Symphony Orchestra as the resident orchestra. Many other major orchestras pay regular visits – the London Philharmonic, the City of Birmingham and the Halle, for example. There are also chamber music recitals and individual soloists. There is jazz (Oscar Peterson), pop music (Tom Jones – who else?), lunchtime concerts of piano and organ recitals and even dance, ballet and the occasional film. A splendid year-round musical programme.

Other musical events include the long running Tuesday Night Concert Series run by the Cardiff University Music Department in the **University Concert Hall** (near the city centre, Tel 371236) and student recitals given by the University Music Department and the Welsh College of Music and Drama on North Road.

CINEMA

Chapter Arts Centre – Market Road, Canton, Tel 396061, has three cinemas, a theatre and three galleries, as well as film and video workshops, bars and restaurants. Their nightly film programme includes an excellent blend of classic, foreign and modern films from around the world.

The same kind of excellent programming can be found at the **Sherman Theatre**, Senghennydd Road, Tel 230451. Because of their heavy schedule of theatrical events in both the main and arena theatres, film programming at the Sherman is less frequent than at Chapter, generally confining itself to midweek and late-night showings. Occasional film showings also at St David's Hall (see above). Commercial Cinema at:

Cannon Cinema – 65 Queen Street, Tel 377680. Three screens.
Odeon Cinema – 55 Queen Street, Tel 227058. Two screens.
Monico – Rhiwbina, Tel 693426.
Monroe – Albany Road, Tel 461690.

BOOKSTORES

Two joint firsts here – **Dillon's**, The Hayes, 1–2 St David's Link, Tel 222273 and **Lears**, 13–17 Royal Arcade, Tel 395036, are both excellent. **Lears** also has a specialist children's bookshop within the main store, an *HMSO* outlet at their **University Bookshop** on Senghennydd Road, Tel 228779, and a **Bargain Bookshop** at Hill Street in The Hayes, Tel 395036. There are also other shops worth a visit: **Claude Gill** at 115 Queen Street, Tel 394231, and **Chapter and Verse**, 23 Morgan Arcade, Tel 371563, have branches nationwide and are well respected. Of the Cardiff independents, try **Fry and Dart** at 20 Caroline Street, Tel 232881, and **Steps** at 80 Albany Road, Tel 484630. Religious books can be found at the **Christian Bookshop**, 7 Wyndham Arcade, Tel 220586, **Heath Christian Bookshop Trust**, 31 Whitchurch Road, Tel 621794, **Olive Branch** at 17 Heoi-v-Deri Rhiwbina, Tel 614659 and **SPCK** at 26 Morgan Arcade, Tel 27736. As well as **Lears Bargain Books**, there are two outlets of **Booksale**, dealing in remainders, publishers' overstock and promotional books. They are at 17 Church Street, Tel 228422, and 22 Queen Street, Tel 239530. Finally, fantasy, science fiction and comics at **Forbidden Planet**, 5 Duke Street, Tel 228885 and **Paperback Exchange** at 3 Dickens Arcade, Castle Street, Tel 223149.

ANTIQUARIAN AND SECONDHAND BOOKS

I think the best and most comprehensive shop is **Capital Bookshop** at 27 Morgan Arcade, Tel 388423. There are two shops in City Road that are worth a browse. **Roath Books** is at No 188, Tel 490523, and **Albany Books** is at No 206, Tel 498802. Cardiff, I should add, is not overflowing with good antiquarian bookshops, but surprisingly, there are two shops offering to find you out-of-print books, so if you've been searching fruitlessly, here's your chance. **Out of Print Service** is at 13 Pantbach Road, Birchgrove, Tel 627703, and more towards the centre of the city, you will find **Booksearch** at 29 Romilly Road, Tel 374249.

ART GALLERIES

Albany Gallery – 74B Albany Road, Tel 487158. Original oils and watercolours by leading Welsh artists from all parts of Wales. Monthly exhibitions. **Studio Gallery**, 18 Llandaff Road, Tel 383419, has oils, prints, etchings and print catalogues. The only other two galleries I can recommend are **Manor House Fine Arts** at 73 Pontcanna Street, Tel 227787, and **Millcraft Gallery**, Lon Fach Rhiwbina, Cardiff Tel 613373, but do remember that the Chapter Arts Centre has three galleries and that there is often an interesting exhibition at the Sherman Theatre.

ANTIQUE DEALERS

A good place to start is **Jacob's Antiques Centre**, Jacob's Market, West Canal Wharf, Tel 390039. They are open 9:30–5pm Wed–Sat and they are the largest antique centre in South Wales. There are five floors of antiques and even a café to relax in. Jacob's really has it all – antiques, period clothing, jewellery, old pine, china, glass and the bizarre. You will find **Tales and the Unexpected** here, Tel 340046, which is great fun and also **Back to the Wood**, Tel 390939, which has antique pine and architectural fittings. Another good centre is the Whitchurch Road, which not surprisingly leads to the suburb of Whitchurch. Here you will find **Hera Antiques** at No 140 Whitchurch Road, Tel 619472, **Past and Present Antiques** at 242 Whitchurch Road, Tel 621443 and **Alexander Antiques** at 312 Whitchurch Road, Tel 621824. In the suburb of Whitchurch itself you will find **Antiques Past and Present** at 242 Whitchurch Heath, Tel 621443, **Brookdale** at 297 College Road, Tel 623957 and **J McNiven** at 18 St Margaret's Road, Tel 627526. The inner suburb of Pontcanna is another good centre. **Atticus Antiques** are at 1 Pontcanna Street, Tel 225165, **Rhys Davies Antiques** is next door at the Red Barn, 2A Pontcanna Street, and **Manor House Fine Arts** (see Art Galleries) is at 73/75 Pontcanna Street. **Heritage**, Tel 390097, is at 85 Pontcanna Street and **Grandma's Goodies**, with antiques plus a wide selection of pre-1940 bric-à-brac, is in Pontcanna itself at 31 Mortimer Road, Tel 384142. The suburb of Canton has **Hour Glass** at 1 Kings Road, Tel 224697 and, in the same area are **W H Douglas** at 161 Cowbridge Road East, Tel 224861, and **King's Antiques** at 163 Cowbridge Road East, Tel 225014. **Crown Antiques**, at 32 Wyndham Crescent, Tel 342599, has a good selection as does **Tempus Antiques** at 11 King's Road, Tel 235832. In Crwys Road you will find **A Burge** at No 54, Tel 383268, and **Llanishen Antiques** at No 26, Tel 397244, while in Mackintosh Place you will find **E A Llewellyn** at No 27, Tel 496211, and **J Cronin** at No 12, Tel 498929. Finally, to round up, **P W Lichtenberg** is at 31 Brunswick Street and **Abbey Antiques** is at 22 Salisbury Road, Tel 224399 (close to the Sherman Theatre).

RESTAURANTS

There are a good number of worthwhile eating places in Cardiff, but my favourite is **Armless Dragon**, 97 Wyvern Road, Tel 382357. There is a short fixed menu, supplemented by a white board announcing the daily specials. The range of dishes is large and the chef seems to enjoy distant countries and their flavours. The cooking is essentially European, though. I had a wonderful lamb, duck and lentil hotpot the last time I was there, which was deliciously spiced with cumin, cardamom, coconut and tamarind. It can get very crowded and it's recommended that you book well in advance. Open Mon–Sat 12:30–2:15 and 7:30–10:30pm. No Sat lunch.

60 St Mary Street gives you two good restaurants at one location. On the ground floor is **La Brasserie**, Tel 372164, a lively place specializing in char-grilled meats, brochettes and fish. That's not all though, as there is also duck, suckling pig and venison. Cooking is French and the wine is good. Open Mon–Sat 12–2:30 and 7–midnight. Upstairs is **Le Monde**, Tel 387376, under the same management. The meats come on cast-iron plates and the fish is excellent with a really very fine fish soup. Open Mon–Sat 12–2:30 and 7–midnight.

As if these riches were not enough, there's even a good restaurant next door. **Champers** at 61 St Mary Street, Tel 373363, is a bodega-style Spanish wine bar with good food and realistic prices. Steaks, kebabs, ribs, pork chops with good fresh fish. Portions are huge and the service is very laid back. Open all week 12–2:30 and 7–midnight. No Sun lunch.

Le Cassoulet is an excellent French restaurant/bistro with fine food and good service. Yes, they do serve a very good cassoulet. Friends tell me that this is their favourite restaurant in Cardiff, indeed in South Wales and it's on my list for next visit. Le Cassoulet is at 5 Romilly Crescent, Canton, Tel 221905. They are open from noon–2 and 7–10pm. No Sat lunch.

If you are visiting Llandaff Cathedral, then **La Chaumière** at 44 Cardiff Road, Tel 555319, is close by. The restaurant is over a betting shop, but don't be fooled by the seemingly inauspicious setting. The food is French bistro style, with a nod to traditional English, and reports I have received are glowing. Open Tues–Sun 12:15–2pm and 7:15–10pm. No Sat lunch or Sun dinner.

Finally, at least with respect to European cooking, is **Salvatore** at 14 Romilly Crescent, Tel 372768 (close to Le Cassoulet). This Italian restaurant really makes you feel at home. The cooking is classical Italian, with a nod to South Wales. If you ask me what I mean by that I'll just refer you to one item on the menu which is laverbread with cockles and bacon (see Ephemera).

For Chinese food, the best bets are **Noble House**, 9–11 St David's House, Wood Street, Tel 388430, where a harpist performs every night except Saturday, amongst the plush decor and **Bo Zan**, 78 Albany Road, Roath, Tel 493617, where the food overshadows the decor with classical Szechuan cooking.

For Indian food, **Indian Ocean** at 290 North Road, Tel 621152, has excellent Tandoori, while **Tandoor Ghar** at 134 Whitchurch Road, Tel 615746, is wonderful if you are a vegetarian and very good even if you are not.

PUBS

Golden Cross – Custom House Street, Tel 394556. Victorian pub carefully and extensively restored by Brains, the Cardiff brewers. Fine ornate tilework, cast-iron tables, glittering glass and glossy woodwork. Good home-made sandwiches, rolls and hot meals.

Cottage – St Mary Street (near Howells Department Store), Tel 461744. Well-laid-out, friendly pub with excellent home-cooked food from ploughman's up, at lunchtime.

Glassworks – Wharton Street. One of my favourite watering places with a decor and ambience akin to a French brasserie. Excellent range of bar snacks and restaurant meals.

Arcade – Church Street. Well renovated city-centre pub with traditional atmosphere and good meals at the bar. Lots of rugby memorabilia.

Philharmonic – St Mary Street. Old-fashioned, dark and busy. Bread and huge chunks of cheese at lunchtime plus excellent sandwiches.

Queen's Vaults – Westgate Street. Well-run Victorian-style pub with friendly service and good value bar food. Close to law courts and Cardiff Arms Park.

ARTISTIC ASSOCIATIONS

Much of the artistic output of Cardiff is in the Welsh language. There are separate Welsh-language channels on both TV and radio and plays in Welsh are regularly performed. William John Gruffyd was one of the most prolific writers in Welsh and also a passionate champion of the language. His literary output was incredibly diverse, including poetry, stories, literary and philosophic essays, criticism, autobiography and scholarly works. His *History of Welsh Literature* and *History of Welsh Prose* have become standard works and his anthology of lyrical poetry, *Y Glodeugardd Gymraeg*, is one of the best anthologies in the Welsh language. For 30 years he was editor of the literary magazine, *Y Lenor* which was considered the most brilliant literary journal ever published in Wales.

The novelist Howard Spring was born in 1889. The author of *Fame is the Spur* entered the world at 32 Edward Street but the house has been demolished. After his father's death, Howard left school and worked in a butcher's shop. Later he became an office boy for the South Wales News and attended evening classes at University College, for which his editor paid. He became a reporter on the paper before moving north to Manchester.

In 1929, the novelist and playwright Jack Jones, best known for the novel, *Off to Philadelphia in the Morning* and the play, *Land of My Fathers*, came to Cardiff from Merthyr Tydfil and lived and wrote in the city until his death in 1970.

The Impressionist painter, Alfred Sisley (who was of English descent), came to Cardiff in 1897. He stayed first in Penarth (a seaside resort on the outskirts of the city) and then moved on to the Langland Hotel on the Gower peninsula. In a letter from Penarth to a French friend, Sisley wrote that "the countryside is pretty and the harbour, with its large ships which go in and out of Cardiff, is superb." Sisley's only complaint was that he found the weather too hot. The many landscapes he painted of the coast around Penarth and Langland constitute his swan song as a painter; he died in Paris early in 1899. An example of his Welsh work can be seen in the Gallery of the National Museum of Wales.

EPHEMERA

Rugby football has been elevated to the status of a quasi-religion in Wales, and its shrine is Cardiff Arms Park. This fabled ground is located in the heart of the city, which echoes to the sound of 58,000 Welsh voices singing "Land of My Fathers" on international match days. There are two rugby grounds here – both known as Cardiff Arms Park. The original Arms Park was officially renamed the Welsh National Ground when it was rebuilt in the 1960s. But the Arms Park it was and the Arms Park it shall forever remain to the followers of rugby. The Second Arms Park is a new ground, built next door for club rugby.

Two of the most brilliant of all 20th-century political orators were both Welsh. David Lloyd George, Prime Minister from 1916 to 1922, was noted for his speaking prowess, his radical views and his Welsh nationalism. Although he was nominally a pacifist, it was his influence while coalition Prime Minister and secretary for war that did much to ensure victory through his forceful foreign policy. Indeed, it was Hitler who later said of him that he was "the man who won the war." He lost the election of 1922, mainly because of his Irish policy, and he was created an earl in the year of his death, 1945. His statue can be seen in Gorsedd Gardens, adjacent to Cathays Park.

Aneurin Bevan was born in Tredegar in 1897. He was one of 13 children of a miner and was elected to Parliament in 1929. As minister of health in the 1945 Labour government, he introduced in 1948 the revolutionary National Health Service. He became minister of labour in 1951 but resigned over the proposed charges for the National Health Service; in 1956 he became shadow foreign secretary. He died in 1960. Bevan brought to the Commons a radical fervour, iconoclastic restlessness and an acute intellect. His statue is in Queen Street.

Nearly 200 years ago, the first known journey in the world by a steam locomotive took place between Merthyr Tydfil and Abercynon. To commemorate that historic event, a full-size working replica has been constructed at the Welsh Industrial and Maritime Museum and is "steamed" on a length of plate-rail track once a month and on other special occasions. It is on permanent display to the public in a specially constructed engine shed. The original locomotive was built at the Penydarren Works, Merlkyr, by the famous Welsh engineer, Richard Trevithick. Its subsequent fate is unknown and accurate details of its construction have not survived. The Penydarren Locomotive made its journey a quarter of a century before George Stephenson's "Rocket" made its debut on the Liverpool and Manchester Railway.

Laverbread is a misleading name, for it does not resemble bread at all. It is peculiarly Welsh, but the delicacy is called "stoke" in both Ireland and Scotland. Laver, of which laverbread is simply the puree, is a smooth, fine seaweed, sometimes called sea spinach, which clings to the rocks like silk. In earlier times it was cured in drying houses, but today more scientific methods are used. In the markets of South Wales it is generally sold already prepared – a brownish, spinach-like gelatinous puree. Contrary to what one would expect, it doesn't taste fishy at all; perhaps a vague caviar-like taste can be discerned. Laver sauce can be eaten with lamb, lobster or just by itself on toast. Laver and oatmeal made into little cakes and fried is delicious with ham or bacon. Laver makes wonderful soup if added to Welsh cawl (a traditional vegetable soup or broth), but it is an acquired taste, so if you're cooking with it, go easy. It has, needless to say, great health-giving properties and was regularly eaten in the fashionable 18th-century spa at Bath.

During the third week in June, 25 singers from the four corners of the globe travel to St David's Hall in Cardiff to compete in the Cardiff Singer of the World competition. The singers have to present a 20-minute programme consisting of an operatic aria and songs, accompanied by the BBC Welsh Symphony Orchestra. A winner is chosen each night of the week from among five contestants and on the Saturday night, the five finalists compete for a £5000 prize, a superb Stuart crystal bowl and also, a significant boost to a fledgling career for the winner. The BBC televises the proceedings each night, and devotes three hours to a telecast of the finals.

TOURIST INFORMATION BUREAU: 8-14 Bridge Street, Cardiff, South Glamorgan CF1 2EE. Tel (0222) 227281

MILFORD HAVEN, PEMBROKE AND HAVERFORDWEST

County of Dyfed
5 hours from London (Paddington) by train
252 miles (403.2 km) from London by M4, A48 and A40

The town of Milford Haven stands on one of the most magnificent natural harbours in Europe. When Daniel Defoe, the author of *Robinson Crusoe* and *Moll Flanders*, visited the town in the early part of the 18th century, he quoted an earlier antiquarian and traveller in saying that the harbour "contains 16 creeks, 5 great bays and 13 good roads for shipping and some say that a thousand sail of ships may ride in it and not the topmast of one

CHAPEL OF ST THOMAS À BECKET, MILFORD HAVEN

be seen from the other." The only sails nowadays are those of the recreational yachtsmen and the once famous naval and seaplane base is now more renowned for its oil refineries. But it was the harbour that made Pembrokeshire an object of desire for the Norman adventurers and the settlers sent by the first two Henrys of England concentrated their settlements around it in the middle of the 12th century. The great castle at Pembroke, circa 1090, stands guard over this huge natural harbour, with its mercantile container port on the south shore and Milford Haven facing it across the estuary. Henry VIII fortified the harbour with block-houses and the last military service the haven performed in British internal history was to shelter the Parliamentary fleet from storms just at the time when Royalist attacks might otherwise have taken Pembroke Castle in the 1640s.

In spite of the naval and military importance of the town, it was famous, in the great days of the British fishing industry, for its catches of skate, hake and conger. Indeed, it ranked fourth among Britain's fishing ports in respect to the amount of fish landed. There is also evidence that megrims (fanciful creatures) and witches formed part of the catch, though a description of these "odd fish" is not included in the report. Milford Haven is set against a smooth but steeply rising hill and its houses are ranked rather like barracks, in a square, low series of terraces that seem to date from the days of Nelson (last quarter of the 18th century).

Indeed, it was Charles Greville who began the development of Milford Haven on behalf of his uncle, Sir William Hamilton. Sir William was Britain's representative at the Court of Naples and, by a convenient arrangement with his nephew, he took Greville's mistress, the fascinating Emma Hart, as his second wife. Emma, by an equally convenient arrangement with Sir William, became Nelson's mistress after the Battle of the Nile. All four of them descended on Milford in 1802 in a memorable visit commemorated by the name of the Lord Nelson Hotel on the biggest inn in the town. Nelson seemed to like the town, and not just because Lady Hamilton was around. In 1803, he said that Milford Haven was the only seaport for commerce on the west coast of Britain and that it rivalled Trincomalee in Sri Lanka as the greatest harbour he had ever seen, and in 1808 he returned to the town to lay the foundation stone of the parish church; his visit is well remembered (he stayed at the Castle Hotel).

Henry Tudor was at Pembroke Castle in 1457. He was the grandson of Owen Tudor, who married Queen Catherine, the widow of Henry V. Henry traced his descent to the House of Lancaster, and after the Lancastrians were defeated by the Yorkist forces at the Battle of Tewkesbury, Henry was spirited away to Brittany where he remained safely in spite of numerous attempts on his life. In 1485, Henry landed unopposed at Milford Haven and waited to find out if Rhys ap Thomas, the Master of South Wales, would support him in his campaign to dethrone Richard III. But Thomas had sworn deep fealty to Richard and let it be known that the only way Henry would come to claim the throne of England through Wales would be over his dead body. Henry, on his arrival, had received a tremendous welcome from the people of Pembrokeshire, and now the Bishop of St David's himself informed Rhys ap Thomas that he was free of his oath to Richard, as Richard himself had committed perjury, was a usurper, and had murdered an infant king. Rhys, with all his followers, went to meet Henry and, it is said, thought it as well to make his own interpretation of the oath by lying before him and inviting Henry to step over his body. Henry's army now moved east, one part led by Rhys ap Thomas and the other by Henry Tudor himself. The armies met at Shrewsbury and from there the distance to Bosworth Field is short. In fact, tradition has it that it was Thomas who placed the defeated Richard III's muddy crown on Henry's head at the climax of the Battle of Bosworth Field. Shakespeare records Richard's dying words as being, "A horse! A horse! My kingdom for a horse!" – a cry never authenticated by historians but beloved of thespians. While on the subject of Shakespeare, it is interesting to note that in *Cymbeline* (Act 3, Scene 2) he refers to Milford Haven as "this same blessed Milford; and, by the way, tell me how Wales was made so happy as t'inherit such a haven."

Milford Haven essentially consists of three principal streets running parallel with one another and intersected by side streets. Hamilton Terrace, closest to the shore, was given the most stylish houses. Behind that, Charles Street was designed as the main shopping thoroughfare, while Robert Street, the third and highest terrace, was given the least pretentious housing. The main public buildings are at the east end of Hamilton Terrace: the Town Hall, Public Library and St Katherine's Church all date from 1801 to1808. The Friends' Meeting House (see Ephemera) and the Hakin Observatory are both worth a visit and the old row of cottages on Cellar Hill, above Castle Pill (river), is charming.

WALK

There are many beautiful walks around Milford Haven. To the west of the town, a footpath can take you around **Gellyswick Bay**, **Hubberston Fort**, the early 19th-century **Observatory** (now in ruins) through the cliffs of Hakin to the docks opposite **Hamilton Terrace**. On the east of the town, follow **The Rath** to the edge of **Castle Pill**, pass the site of **Castle Hall**, cross the Pill by **Black Bridge** and at the head of the Pill, cross to the Neyland Road on the town's eastern boundary. There is a pleasant booklet detailing walks in the area published to celebrate Milford Haven's Bicentenary in 1990 (available from the Tourist Office in the Torch Theatre foyer).

Our walk, however, focuses on the centre of town. Park adjacent to Chapel Street and walk up the street, past the **Methodist Chapel** via Wellington Road and right onto the **Rope Walk** to Victoria Bridge. There are fine views of the docks and town. Cross the bridge which links Milford and Hakin. Towering on the cliff ahead is the **Torch Theatre** and directly below a plaque commemorating the landing of George IV nearby in 1821. Close by is the entrance to the docks and the **Old Custom House** which now houses the **Town Museum**. In the docks are the remains of the old **Fish Market** and the last of the old **Smoke Houses** used to preserve fish. Between the wars the Milford Kipper was as famous as anything to come out of Scotland. Leave by Slup Hill and Pur Road, where in 1850 Colonel Greville built a 750-foot (228 m) wooden pier for a transatlantic passenger trade that never materialized. Go ahead into Hamilton Terrace from which vantage point it is possible to see the "grid iron" pattern of the town. The Terrace is designed as a promenade on the seaward side and the houses, simple and bold in design, were mostly built by Quakers. The same austerity of design can be found in the whaling ports of New England in America. On your left is the **Lord Nelson Hotel**, opened as the New Inn in 1800 and visited by Lord Nelson, Sir William

Hamilton and his wife, Emma, in 1802 (hence the name). The mail coach ran to London from here and the journey took 48 hours. Turn up Priory Street by Barclays Bank, cross Charles and Robert Streets and on your left is the **Friends Meeting House**, built by early Quakers in 1811. Note the gravestones in the churchyard marked only with initials. Return to Hamilton Terrace and note the fine **War Memorial** and stones, set in the wall, marking the length of Brunel's famous ship, the *Great Eastern* (see Bristol) which lay in the docks here in 1861. At the junction with Slip Hill is the **Belgian Monument**, erected by the people of Ostend in grateful thanks for the hospitality extended to them during the Great War when Belgian fishermen worked out of Milford. At the end of Hamilton Terrace is **St Katherine's Church**, circa 1808, which has Nelson memorabilia. Turn right onto Murray Crescent which leads to **The Rath**, a wonderful promenade which used to house the gun battery defending the town. The Royalists defended the town from Parliamentary attack here in 1644 and the tiny **Chapel of St Thomas à Becket** is a delight. From the sheltered shores of the two **Pills** on either side of the modern town, people have lived and gone to sea since distant times. Turn right on the Beach Hill and take the footpath on your left which skirts Castle Pill to Black Bridge. Turn left onto Coombes Road and then left again onto Great North Road. Turning right on Robert or Charles Streets will bring you to Dartmouth Street. Turn left on Dartmouth Street and then right onto Hamilton Terrace and back.

Almost a suburb of Milford Haven is Neyland which, like Milford itself, seemed to have a promising future that never materialized. When the railway was extended to Haverfordwest in 1856, the great engineer, Brunel, planned to make Neyland an Atlantic terminus. The streets still bear names like Brunel Avenue and Great Eastern Terrace, reminding one of a dream that did not come to fruition. The huge Great Western Hotel on the waterfront is another reminder that the Atlantic trade did not develop. The Irish ferry used to leave from here but in 1906 it was transferred to Fishguard, and even the ferry that used to cross the Haven to Pembroke Dock has been made redundant by the new bridge, which now spans the Haven. Just on the other side of this new bridge is Pembroke, with the oldest castle in West Wales (see below) while seven miles (11 km) to the north on the A4076 is Haverfordwest, the county town of Pembrokeshire before it was merged into the new outsized county of Dyfed. The parish church is one of the finest in Wales and there are some fine early 19th-century houses. The castle looks impressive but is really only a shell, having received attention from Oliver Cromwell. In the grounds of Picton Castle at Rhos on the eastern approach to the town is the Graham Sutherland Art Gallery which is one of great interest.

MUSEUMS AND GALLERIES

Milford Haven Maritime and Heritage Museum – The museum is in the process of moving to a new location on the docks as I write. The museum is essentially maritime in nature and looks at the history of Milford Haven mainly from this viewpoint. Tel 0646 693128.

National Museum of Gypsy Caravans, Romany Crafts and Lore – Commons Road, Pembroke, Tel 0646 681308. Open Easter–Sept Sun–Fri 10–5pm. The museum aims to provide a representation of traditional gypsy life with the aid of an outstanding collection of caravans, together with carts, tools and many other types of artefacts relevant to the gypsy way of life. Visitors can also see displays of Romany crafts. The museum is also actively concerned with the building, decoration and restoration of gypsy wagons and carts as a means of keeping the tradition alive.

Pembroke Castle – Tel 0646 684585. Open daily 9:30–5:30pm; Oct–Easter closed Sun. Constructed in stages between 1093 and circa 1250, this was one of the largest and strongest fortresses ever built in Britain. The keep, 80 feet (24.3 m) high and with walls 20 feet (6 m) thick at the base, is remarkable. There is an inner and outer bailey, the outer wall being protected by five projecting angle towers, a gatehouse and a barbican. The inner bailey stands at the tip of a promontory jutting into the Pembroke River, while on the town side the walls of Pembroke itself form a 13th-century extension of the castle defences. In 1457 Henry Tudor, who defeated Richard III at the Battle of Bosworth to become King Henry VII, was born in the tower named after him.

Castle Hill Museum – 7 Westgate Hill, Pembroke, Tel 0646 681200. Open Easter–Oct 10:30–5:30pm. Closed Thurs and Sat. This unique collection of over 2000 artefacts of a bygone time in a beautiful domestic setting, just across the road from Pembroke Castle, gives fascinating glimpses of life in our forefathers' homes over the past 300 years.

Castle Museum and Art Gallery – The Castle, Haverfordwest, Tel 0437 3708. Open June–Sept Mon–Sat 10–5:30pm: Oct–May Tues–Sat 11–4pm plus Bank Holidays. Construction of the Castle began in 1128 but most of the building dates from the 13th century. The museum occupies the former County Gaol, built in 1820 in the Outer Ward of the Castle. The displays relate to the town and former County of Haverfordwest and to the collections of militaria formed by the Pembroke Yeomanry Trust and by the museum itself. The latter are arranged to illustrate two themes – the Norman Conquest of Wales and the associated building of castles, and the origin and development of uniform from armour and heraldry. There are also exhibits of coins and medals and recently discovered archaeological material. Selections from the fine and applied art sections are shown in temporary exhibitions arranged to illustrate themes. The Art Gallery maintains an up-to-date Register of Pembrokeshire Artists, available to researchers and those interested in buying works.

Graham Sutherland Gallery – Picton Castle, The Rhos, Haverfordwest. Tel 0437 86296. Open April–Sept Tues–Sun 10:30–12:30 and 1:30–5pm. The gallery possesses the largest public collection of works by Graham Sutherland, many of them given by the artist as a thanks for inspiration gained from many visits to Pembrokeshire. There are indeed many pictures of the surrounding countryside painted in Sutherland's unique style (see Coventry Cathedral).

Penrhos Cottage – Maenclochog, Haverfordwest, Tel 0437 82328. Open at Easter, then May–Sept Tues–Sat 10–12:30 and 2:30–6pm. Sun 2:30–6pm. Penrhos Common is now almost completely enclosed, but it was formerly a bleak and exposed area on a high north/south ridge to the east of the B4313. According to local tradition, the cottage was built overnight on common land. The intending occupier would gather together all his friends and relations and proceed to the site. The house had to be built in one night between sunset and sunrise and smoke had to be rising from the chimney. The builder could then lay claim to all the land within a stone's throw of the door. Such homes produced many famous Welshmen and women.

Scolton Manor Museum – Spittal, Haverfordwest, Tel 0437 82838. Open June–Sept Tues–Sun 10:30–6pm. Scolton Manor was built in 1840. Its grounds are managed as a country park and the attractive stables and carriage house are also open to the public. The developing displays illustrate the history and natural environment of Pembrokeshire with a well equipped local history research centre. Among the major exhibits is the 0-6-0 St Fox Walker Locomotive, "Margaret," supplied in 1878 to the Maenclochog and Rosebush Railway.

THEATRE

The Torch Theatre – St Peter's Road, Tel 0646 695267, was built in the mid-'70s as part of a network of regional arts centres. It is a very friendly, community-oriented theatre with a good mixture of plays and musicals from the resident company and a varied programme of dance, music and drama from visiting companies. There are regular showings of popular films. The summer and Christmas shows are designed especially for children and are excellent. I saw a wonderful show for Christmas called *Merlin's Return* which used many of the legends of West Wales and merged them with a captivating mystery story. Some fine adult work has recently included Athol Fugard's *Master Harold and the Boys* and a celebratory 100th production of Dylan Thomas's *Under Milk Wood*. There is also a gallery which has changing exhibitions and a bar. When I was there recently the theatre was trying to work out a catering arrangement which would incorporate an outdoor summer café. The Torch Theatre is the only professional theatre west of Swansea. Swansea has the **Grand Theatre**, Singleton Street, Tel 0492 475715, if you're going that way.

MUSIC

Fishguard is 22 miles (35.2 km) north of Milford Haven and hosts a Music Festival in late July with mainly Welsh performers and orchestras. Tel 0348 873612.

Jazz, classical music, opera and dance are offered at regular intervals by the **Torch Theatre**.

BOOKSTORES

Locally, the **Book Shop**, 34/36 Market Street, Haverfordwest, Tel 0437 765001 and **Bookmark**, 1 Quay Street Haverfordwest, Tel 0437 762633, are best. The **Pembroke Bookshop**, 73 Main Street Pembroke, Tel 0646 684585, is also good.

ANTIQUARIAN AND SECONDHAND BOOKS

Carmarthen (30 miles/48 km east on A477/A40) is your best bet with **Carmarthen Books**, 1 St Mary Street, Tel 0267 235676, or travel an extra 20 miles (32 km) to Swansea where **Rowlands Bookshop**, 16 St Helen's Road, Tel 0792 654427, and **Dylan's Bookstore** at the wonderfully named Salubrious Passage, Tel 0792

655255, are both excellent. Incidentally, if you turn off the A477 at St Clears where it becomes the A40 and go due south for four miles (6.4 km), you will come to Laugharne. Much of the atmosphere of the town is evident in Dylan Thomas's *Under Milk Wood*. Thomas wrote the radio play in The Boathouse, which is now a museum dedicated to his memory. Dylan Thomas's Boathouse looks out over the estuary to the sea beyond and if you are interested in things maritime, then **Seafare Books and Crafts**, 18 Riverside Market, Haverfordwest, Tel 0437 768359, will please you no end.

ART GALLERIES
Locally, and rather surprisingly, there is little in the way of visual art. **Hayloft Fine Arts** in Pembroke at 2 Northgate Street, Tel 0646 686700, is worth a browse as is the **Old Smithy Studio**, just north of Haverfordwest on the B4329 at Bethlehem, Cardigan Road, Haverfordwest, Tel 0437 82398. I'm never certain where to draw the line between art and craft, risking being called elitist by some and overly populist by others. In fact I don't really care that much what people think so I'll recommend a visit to **Shirley Norman**, 2 Holbrook Close, Broad Haven, Haverfordwest, who does the most beautiful calligraphy with decorations in watercolours and gold leaf. There's also a good selection of watercolours and prints of local (especially coastal) scenery.

ANTIQUE DEALERS
Milford Haven – A good general collection at **JRD Jenkins**, 8 Mansfield Street, Tel 0646 692152, and out of town towards Neyland, a fascinating collection of militaria, police and fire brigade collectibles at **Camelot Antiques**, Gwynmay, Hill Mountain, Tel 0646 601170.

Pembroke – The best centre for antiques in Pembroke is **Pembroke Antiques Centre**, Tel 0646 687017. There are 30 outlets on three floors and one can find furniture, pine, brass, copper and paintings. Apart from the market, **J P and J Howells** at 10 Northgate Street in the middle of town has a good general collection, Tel 0646 684416, as has **Camelot Antiques**, 83 Main Street, Tel 0646 687317.

Haverfordwest – Before I come to the town itself, I must strongly recommend that you take the seven miles (11.2 km) journey east on the A40 to Narberth, where you will find, at 32 High Street, **Chereton Antiques**, with one of the best collections in Wales. Twelve showrooms in a home setting with some superb period furniture. In Haverfordwest itself, **Kent House Antiques**, Kent House, 13 Market Street, Tel 0437 768175, is very good as is **Gerald Oliver** at 14 Albany Terrace, Tel 0437 763794. Also in town are **John and Sylvia Davies** at 28 Dark Street, Tel 0437 768550, and **Dyfed Antiques**, the Wesleyan Chapel, Perroths Road, Tel 0437 760496. Finally, at Unit 2, the Riverside Market, Swan Square you will find **Heirloom Antiques**, Tel 0437 763285.

RESTAURANTS
I make no excuse for recommending mainly country restaurants in this part of Wales. The coastal scenery is stunning and if you can enjoy the sun dipping into the ocean as you enjoy your pre-dinner G and T, so much the better. An excellent place to do this is the **Druidstone Hotel**, Broad Haven (4 miles/6,4 km west of Milford Haven) on the coast, Tel 0437 781221. It's a wonderful place for a summer evening and they even have tables outside. What we are looking at is essentially a well-run family hotel with excellent cooking. They have their own herb garden and local produce – lamb and fish – is beautifully cooked. They also have bar meals, which are very popular. Open all week 12:30–2:30 and 7:30–10pm.

Portfield Gate is on the westerly outskirts of Haverfordwest. Here you will find **Sutton Lodge**, Tel 0437 68548, which is a delightful early 19th-century country house. They offer a four-course set menu which doesn't leave a choice but don't worry as the cooking is excellent and you can voice your likes and dislikes when you book (which you must). The cooking is essentially French and the wine list is good and inexpensive. Open dinner only Mon–Sat 6:30–9pm.

Also close to Haverfordwest you can find **Jemima's** at Nash Grove, Freystop, Tel 0437 891109 (south of the town on the Burton Road). Locally this converted house is known to be situated on Puddleduck Hill, hence the name, but the decorative influence is more Laura Ashley than Beatrix Potter. The bread is home-baked, the vegetables and herbs mostly come from the garden behind the house and the fish is from Milford Haven and you can't get much fresher than that. The menu is short which always commends the chef to me and suggests that freshness is important. The cooking is Franco-British. I thought their chicken with tarragon was wonderful and beautifully set off by the melon and elderflower sorbet I had to start with. There are some really interesting items on the menu. Pork with borage dumplings and geranium ice cream, for example. Excellent value and heartily recommended. Open Tues–Sat, dinner only 7–9pm.

Finally, if you are looking for antiques in Narberth, I recommend **Gregory's** in the Market Square, Tel 0834 3814. The restaurant is located in a converted brewery, the cooking is good and the value, excellent.

PUBS

Milford Haven:

Lord Nelson Hotel – Hamilton Terrace, Tel 0646 695341. The hotel is named to commemorate Nelson's visit in 1802. There is a dining room and a lounge serving bar meals. There are attractive lawns and a beer garden in the summer.

Sir Benfro Inn – Herbrandston, Tel 0646 694242. Old-style Pembrokeshire farmhouse converted into comfortable and relaxing country inn. Traditional bar food.

Haverfordwest:

Bristol Trader – Old Quay, Quay Street. The massive walls are a clue to the age of the pub; it's been open for 600 years. Bar food is very good, partly I suspect because they grow some of the ingredients themselves. Steak-and-kidney pie is recommended, as is the gammon. Tel 0437 762122.

Little Haven:

St Bride's – (adjacent to Broad Haven on the coast, 4 miles/6.2 km west). There's a cottagey atmosphere in this black-beamed pub which has an unusually interesting collection of horse brass on the wall. If there's local fish or seafood on the menu, go for it – the crab is especially good. There's even a well at the back which may be Roman or at least medieval. Tel 0437 781226.

Swan – This pretty pub, perched on the side of a hill just above the beach, has a lovely view. There's an open fire in winter and you can sit outside in summer. Good bar food with the fresh fish or shellfish the best bet. Tel 0437 781256.

Pembroke:

Old King's Arms – Main Street. This old pub in the centre of town has good traditional bar food at modest prices and real ale. Tel 0646 683611.

The Ferry- (at foot of bridge over estuary). A nice riverside setting with a good range of bar food. They have especially imaginative fresh fish dishes. There's friendly, helpful service, a good restaurant and excellent Sunday lunch. Tel 0646 682947.

ARTISTIC ASSOCIATIONS

George Owen was born in Pembrokeshire in 1552. He was neither a powerful politician nor a particularly wealthy member of the gentry, but his fame rests on the fact that he was an inveterate scribbler. He wrote furiously on all sorts of topics and much of his manuscript material has survived to this day. He wrote in Welsh and his *Description of Pembrokeshire* is the fullest and most clearly documented picture we have of Elizabethan Wales. He was a man fascinated by the environment, the customs, the economic life and the life-style of his own times. His work is an undiscovered gem of, essentially, oral history and deserves wider recognition.

The great English artist, Graham Sutherland, has a gallery dedicated to him at Picton Castle (see above). Sutherland made his reputation as a painter of romantic, mainly abstract landscapes with superb, if arbitrary, colouring. His tapestry *Christ in Majesty* hangs behind the altar in Coventry Cathedral, while his portraits of Somerset Maugham (1949) and Winston Churchill (1955) are notable, albeit controversial. Churchill so hated his that it was destroyed. Sutherland and his wife gave a collection of his paintings "for the benefit of Pembrokeshire and the nation" and the gallery opened in 1976, four years before Sutherland's death. On March 17, 1976, Sutherland said "From the moment I set foot in Wales I was obsessed. I have worked there particularly in Pembrokeshire, every year since 1934 – with one long and regrettable gap, brought about by the fact that I thought I had exhausted what the countryside had to offer both as 'vocabulary' and inspiration.

I was sadly mistaken and in the last ten years I have made up for it, continuing my visits in order to make my studies and to soak myself in the curiously charged atmosphere – at once both calm and exciting, to meet the people – so kind and optimistic and to benefit on good days from the extraordinary clear and transparent light. About four years ago, the thought came into my mind that, having gained so much from this country, I should like to 'give something back.'"

Waldo Williams, the Welsh language poet, was born at the School House of the Boys' School in 1904. When he was seven he moved, with his family, to the village of Mynachlogddu, south of Cardigan. Welsh friends tell me that Williams's work (he died in 1971) is very beautiful and that his collections, *Leaves of a Tree* and *Children's Poem* are memorable. Unfortunately, I have been unable to track down an English translation.

EPHEMERA

You might not expect to find a great cathedral tucked away in a hidden valley at the end of a rocky, cliff-girt peninsula, filled with the sound of the sea. Yet it is at St David's – the Land's End of Wales – that the patron saint of Wales chose to establish his monastery, "far from the haunts of men." St David's Cathedral is a very special place with its leaning arches, sloping floor, oak roof and carvings on the seat ends. Edmund Tudor, the father of Henry VII, is buried here and it is thought that the bones of St David himself rest in Holy Trinity Chapel. There is a trout stream (surely the only Cathedral trout stream in the kingdom) which you cross and come to the ruins of the Bishop's Palace – one of the finest medieval ruins in Wales. The inhabitants of St David's village claim that the cathedral gives them "city" status. If it does, it must be the smallest city in Christendom. St David's should not be missed (16 miles/25.6 km northwest of Haverfordwest on the A487).

A fascinating and comparatively unknown segment of history concerns the development of Milford Haven as a town by Sir William Hamilton and Charles Greville, his nephew and agent. Greville realized that he would need more than stones and bricks in founding a new town. Hamilton, in 1790, had been authorized by Parliament "to make and provide Quays, Docks, Piers and other erections and to establish a Market with proper roads and avenues there . . . " and Greville realized that in order for his new town to flourish he would need commercial development. For that, he turned his attention towards a group of American Quaker whalers from Nantucket Island, whom he hoped to persuade to carry on their trade in the southern seas from his new town. The Quakers had established themselves in Nantucket, having first fled religious intolerance in 17th-century England, only to find it again in Puritan Massachusetts. Life was difficult in 18th-century Nantucket until by chance the settlers discovered that sperm oil from the whales inhabiting the neighbouring waters was in demand as a source of light. The streets of London were illuminated by lamps burning sperm oil (spermaceti). Whaling prospered in Nantucket until 1775 when the War of Independence broke out. The Quakers refused to take part and consequently they were harassed and looted by the American and British navies alike. When the war came to an end in 1783, the Quakers of Nantucket were in a pitiful state of poverty and no doubt welcomed Greville's offer to colonize his new town. The first settlers arrived in 1792 and it was the Quaker colony that was mainly responsible for building the town under Greville's instructions. When the demand for sperm oil as a source of light declined, the Quakers integrated themselves into the community of Milford Haven by finding occupations as farmers, fishermen and merchants. Dr Stephen Griffith's fascinating book, *A History of the Quakers of Pembrokeshire*, is available from local bookstores in Milford Haven or from the Quaker Meeting House in the town.

A final footnote: the first Quaker settler to arrive in Milford Haven was Daniel Starbuck and his family in 1792 and the Starbucks remained a prominent family in the area through the early 19th century. (I would love to know where they went as there is no mention of them in the 1991 telephone directory.) You will remember that the chief mate in Herman Melville's magnificent whale-hunting novel, *Moby Dick* was named Starbuck and that he hailed from Nantucket and was from a long line of Quakers. Melville wrote the book in 1851 when he was living near Pillsfield, Massachusetts, and considering that he is now regarded as one of America's greatest novelists, it's hard to understand why the book was so unappreciated. Melville was so disillusioned that he only wrote poetry until his death in 1891 and *Moby Dick* was not recognized as the great book it is until some 30 years after his death. Stephen Griffiths, in his book mentioned above, cites the diary of a John Grubb of Clonmel, Ireland, who wrote in 1793 on a visit to Milford Haven, "I slept one night in an American bed with old Sam Starbuck, a sensible man who had several years followed a seafaring life in the whale fishery." Perhaps this experience, which so closely mirrors that of Melville's narrator, Ishmael with the harpooner, Queequeg, is just coincidence – or maybe it's not.

TOURIST INFORMATION BUREAU: Old Bridge, Haverfordwest, Dyfed SA61 2EZ. Tel (0437) 763110

6

WEST MIDLANDS

BIRMINGHAM
COVENTRY
STRATFORD-UPON-AVON
WARWICK
WORCESTER

BIRMINGHAM

County of Warwickshire
105 miles (168 km) from London by M1 and M6
2 hours from London by train (Euston)

With a population of well over 1 million, Birmingham is Britain's second-largest city. Although mentioned in the Domesday Book in 1086, the city developed slowly until the middle of the 16th century, by which time it had established its reputation as a small industrial town. Then as now, the Bull Ring was the centre of many of its activities. By 1642, the city's metal industry had already advanced to such a state that it could temper 16,000 sword blades for Cromwell's forces during the Civil War. Birmingham's Roundhead allegiance led to a clash of arms in the Bull Ring area in 1643. Charles I's general, Prince Rupert, had been ordered to clear a communications route for the Royalists between Oxford and York after the citizens of Birmingham had seized the King's plate and coin while the King was travelling with his forces to relieve the besieged Banbury Castle. In the ensuing battle some 900 houses were destroyed and the town was fined £30,000, about 1 million in terms of today's value. It was the Industrial Revolution, however, that produced Birmingham's most rapid expansion, and in 1889 Queen Victoria declared it a city. Eleven years later it had its own university, and in 1909 it gave England its first official Town Planning Act.

Then as now, there was a tremendous concentration of industry in the city, with factories, workshops and the head offices of international companies. Today metal remains a high priority, but jewellery, toys, chemicals, brass, plastics and rubber products are also

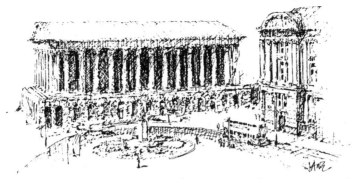

TOWN HALL, BIRMINGHAM

manufactured. The chocolate-and-cocoa capital of England is Bourneville, a few minutes from the city centre, while the suburbs of Longbridge and Solihull are host to a large automotive manufacturing industry. Although some of the largest factories in Europe are based in the city, production companies of all types and sizes abound. The new city centre – the Bull Ring – is dominated by wide roads and banked by large buildings of concrete and glass with the new shopping centre terraced underneath by the flyovers. This traffic-free area is linked by subways to the older shopping street where many of the large department stores are located. There is also a vibrant market, part of it open and part covered.

Among the city's remarkable buildings are the Town Hall and the Council House. Birmingham's growth through the Industrial Revolution to become the workshop of the world reached its zenith in the early part of the 19th century. By the middle of that century "Made in Birmingham" was a guarantor of respect from the Arctic to the Sahara, and to celebrate, the city built a Victorian feast: the Council House, in whose pediment Britannia bestows laurels upon Birmingham manufacturers. Even more remarkable is the Town Hall, built in 1830 by Joseph Hansom (of cab fame). The building is a pure classical "temple," more a concert hall than a seat of civic government and modelled, it is said, on the Temple of Castor and Pollux in Rome. Some of the world's leading orchestras played at the Town Hall before the recent completion of the Birmingham Symphony Hall, a superb building that provides a home for the internationally renowned City of Birmingham Symphony Orchestra and also presents famous orchestral ensembles from all over the world. The Assay Office, a pleasant red-brick building on the corner of Charlotte Street, bears the royal coat of arms, the outward sign that this is one of Her Majesty's Assay Offices, in which objects made of precious metals, especially in the jewellery quarter round about, are hallmarked to indicate their provenance. Birmingham's own hallmark is a rather handsome anchor. In the jewellery district it is still possible to buy direct from the craftsmen. Birmingham also boasts what is probably the largest indoor retail market in the country. Surrounding the ancient parish church of St Martin's and overlooked by the Rotunda Office Building of the Bull Ring, there are separate markets specializing in fish, meat and dairy produce, fresh fruit, vegetables and plants, clothing, soft furnishings, china, gifts, bric-à-brac and second-hand goods. There is an antiques market on Mondays.

Finally, the canals. Birmingham, it is proudly said, has more miles of canals than Venice. Rather than let them die, the city has restored miles of towpath to form an urban trail through scenes of unalloyed Industrial Revolution. One can walk along part of the Birmingham and Fazeley Canal, built in 1789 by John Smeaton. On its way through back-yard Birmingham it shows ancient warehouses, still and shuttered, tunnels echoing with dripping water, ponderous timber lock gates and the mighty brick arch built in 1852 to carry the platforms of the old Snow Hill Railway Station.

WALK

I have devised the **Birmingham Walk** in two sections. The first section stops at the Great Western Arcade, which is close to the car park. You can stop here for tea, coffee, or what have you, and then return to the car or carry on to the second section, which takes in the canals. Both sections are about one and a half miles (2.4 km) in length.

Start at the car park at Snow Hill Queensway opposite the police station. Go through Colmore Circus and turn right down Colmore Row to **St Philip's Cathedral**. The **Grand Hotel**, circa 1872, is rather splendid. Continue down Colmore Row to Victoria Square, the **Town Hall**, **Council House** and the "**Big Brum**" clock tower. Behind the Council House, in Chamberlain Square, is the **Museum and Art Gallery**. Here also is a fountain to the city's great benefactor, Joseph Chamberlain, and statues to other Birmingham worthies. Cross Chamberlain Square, past the monumental **Central Library**, to the green space surrounding the **Hall of Memory**. Across Broad Street, a bronze conversation piece depicts the industrial pioneers James Watts, Matthew Bouton and William Murdoch poring over a plan. Just ahead on your right is the **Birmingham Repertory Theatre**, the **International Convention Centre** and **Symphony Hall**. Retrace your steps to Victoria Square and bear right down New Street. Ahead is the drum-like **Rotunda** office building which overlooks **St Martin's Church** and the markets. Turn left up Cannon Street, then right up Temple Row to the **Great Western Arcade**. This is a totally Victorian arcade of brown wooden shop-fronts. There are wrought-iron ornamental lamps, splendid arches, all kinds of shops and a lovely gold clock. To return to your car, go through the arcade to Colmore Row, turn right and then left down Snow Hill. The adventurous and fit may continue on through the **Great Western Arcade**, turn left onto Colmore Row, then right down Livery Street. When you get to Edmund Street, turn left past the classically styled **Eye Hospital** and the old terra-cotta **Telephone Exchange** to Newhall Street. Turn right up Newhall Street and take the subway under Great Charles Queensway and soon you'll find yourself at the back of the Art Gallery. Bear right down Summer Row, cross the road at the first traffic lights and continue down the left side of Summer Row to Saturday Bridge. Go down the steps to the canal towpath and turn left under the bridge. You will see, built end to end, the 13 locks of **Farmer's Steps**, which once raised canal barges 40 feet. Note the ridges in the brick path to help the barge horses. At Newhall Street Bridge, go up the steps to the **Museum of Science and Industry**. Cross Newhall Street to the Assay office and turn right along Charlotte Street to St Paul's Square and **St Paul's Church**. Go back to the Science Museum, descend to the towpath again and turn left. You will pass lofty warehouses and then the brick arch which carried the platforms of the old Snow Hill Railway Station. Go up the steps at Snow Hill and take the underpass to **St Chad's Cathedral**. Take the underpass again to St Chad's Circus and back up Snow Hill to the car park.

MUSEUMS, GALLERIES AND PUBLIC BUILDINGS

Birmingham City Museum and Art Gallery – Chamberlain Square, Tel 215 2834. The recently restored Victorian museum makes a fine setting for the splendid collection of glass, ceramics and costumes. There are also natural history, archaeology, ethnography and local history exhibits. The Art Gallery includes an impressive Pre-Raphaelite section, a large number of Old Masters and excellent examples from Italian, French and Dutch Schools. There is a splendid tearoom. Open Mon-Sat 9:30–5pm, Sun 2–5pm.

Birmingham Museum of Science and Industry – Newhall Street, Tel 236 1022. Exhibits cover all aspects of science, engineering and industry, including transport (road, rail, air) machine tools, firearms, etc. The James Watts Building houses the world's oldest working steam engine. There are good Engineering and Locomotive Halls. Engines are on steam the first and third Wednesday of each month. Open Mon–Sat 9:30–5pm, Sun 2–5pm.

Birmingham Railway Museum – 670 Warwick Road, Tyseley, Tel 707 4696. The museum occupies part of the Great Western Railway Depot, built in 1908. The collection includes six express locomotives in various stages of restoration, together with rolling stock including a Post Office van, a GWR Royal Saloon and a Pullman bar car. Open 10–5pm, summer only.

National Motorcycle Museum – Coventry Road, Bickenhill, Tel 704 2784. Strategically placed at the junction of the M42 and A45, the museum has a collection of 600 British motorcycles (foreign makes are excluded) dating from 1898 to the present day. All exhibits have been restored to their original condition and specifications. Open daily 10–6pm.

The Patrick Collection – 180 Lifford Lane, Kings Norton, Tel 459 4471. A unique collection of vehicles from 1904 to the present day, displayed in period settings in a Victorian paper mill. Open Easter to end of Oct 11–5:30pm (7pm in summer).

Cadbury World – Bourneville, Tel 433 4334. The ultimate experience for chocolate lovers. Discover how they get the filling into the Caramilk bar and how Chocolate Creme Easter Eggs are made. Factory visit and tasting. Open every day Mon–Sat 10–5:30pm, Sun 12–6pm.

Sarehole Mill – Cole Bank Road, Hall Green, Tel 777 6612. The mill is one of the last survivors of more than 50 Birmingham watermills. Last used commercially in 1919, the mill now contains displays relating to agriculture. The mill has associations with J R R Tolkien, whose family lived nearby, and who recalled the area when creating the Shire in *The Hobbit* and *The Lord of the Rings*.

Central Library – Paradise Circus, Tel 235 4511. A vast reference library housing over a million volumes. Includes the Shakespeare Memorial Library with 40,000 books and a wealth of pictures and prints relating to the Bard.

Aston Hall – Aston Park, Trinity Road, Aston Tel 327 0062. The house was built between 1618 and 1635 and contains Jacobean decorative plaster and woodwork together with some superb sculpted fireplaces. Nearly 30 rooms have been redecorated and rearranged in order to give a clearer impression of what it was like to live in an 18th-century house. Many fine paintings, furniture, textiles, ceramics and silver. One room of Aston Hall is definitely not open to the public; it measures just four feet by four feet (1.2 m by 1.2 m) and is said to house a 300-year-old ghost. It was here, according to legend, that a former owner, Sir Thomas Holte, imprisoned his daughter for not marrying the man of his choice. She eventually went mad and died and her ghost has frequented this part of the house ever since (see Ephemera). Open Easter–Oct daily 2–5pm.

Blakesley Hall – Blakesley Road, Yardley, Tel 783 2193. A timber-framed yeoman's house, circa 1575, furnished to show what a 16th-century home was like. A fine first-floor long gallery and 16th-century wall paintings in one of the bedrooms. There are displays on domestic interiors and the techniques of timber-framed building. Open Easter–Oct daily 2–5pm.

Weoley Castle – Alwold Road, Tel 427 4270. The castle was a semi-fortified medieval manor house. Excavations have uncovered many domestic objects from the Middle Ages, and these are displayed in a museum set in the castle ruins.

Cathedral Church of St Philip – St Philip's Square, Tel 236 4333. St Philip's was built between 1711 and 1725 as a parish church and became a cathedral in 1905. The church was designed as a preaching hall with galleries. The style is essentially classical, with a Baroque tower, free-standing Corinthian columns and some excellent Burne-Jones windows.

Metropolitan Cathedral Church of St Chad – Queensway, Tel 236 2257. Designed in 1839 by A W Pugin, the Cathedral Church of the Roman Catholic Diocese of Birmingham has been perceptively described as 14th-century Baltic German Gothic in style! Some excellent 19th-century stained glass, a Flemish pulpit and the relics of St Chad. Additions were made in 1933 and 1964.

St Paul's Church – St Paul's Square, Tel 236 5782. The church is pure 18th century, from its magnificent altarpiece to its galleries and its sombre painted-glass windows. The box pews, still bearing the numbers, are a rare survival, and their freeholds were sold to pay for the church. Many were bought by rich jewellers, giving the church its nickname of the Jewellers' Church.

St Martin's Church – Edgbaston Street. The most ancient part of this ancient church dates from the 13th century, although only the interior of the lower part of the tower is intact.

Barker Institute of Fine Arts – Edgbaston Park Road, Tel 472 0962. The Institute has a small but important collection of paintings from Western Europe up to the early 20th century. There are also drawings, sculpture and decorative arts. Open Mon–Fri 10–5pm, Sat 10–1pm.

THEATRE

Alexandra Theatre – Suffolk Street, Queensway, Tel 633 3325. National touring productions such as *South Pacific* and *Evita,* dramas, thrillers and pre- and post-West End productions.

Birmingham Hippodrome – Hurst Street, Tel 622 7486. Opera, ballet, contemporary dance, musicals and one-night concerts by international stars. The Midlands base for the Welsh National Opera Company and the home of the Birmingham Royal Ballet, formerly the Sadlers Wells Royal Ballet.

Birmingham Repertory Theatre – Broad Street, Tel 236 4455. An important theatre, which stages a mixture of classical and contemporary works, new plays and some musicals. Productions can be seen in the 900-seat main house and also in the 140-seat Studio Theatre, whose programmes include more experimental productions and work by other local professional companies.

Midlands Arts Centre – Canon Hill Park, Tel 440 3838. Major centre for alternative theatre, dance, music and film. Recent programming included visits by Women's Theatre Company, Temba Theatre Company, Images Dance Company and the Albion Wind Ensemble. There is a major art exhibition space, courses and workshops. The Centre is the home of the annual **Birmingham Readers and Writers Festival**, which is held in early May, the **Birmingham Film and TV Festival**, which is held in Sept/Oct and the world-famous **Cannon Hill Puppet Theatre**.

MUSIC

Birmingham is home to one of the world's great orchestras, the City of Birmingham Symphony Orchestra. There is no doubt that the orchestra has been led to world-wide acclaim by its dynamic young conductor, Simon Rattle. The orchestra plays in the superb new 2,200-seat **Birmingham Symphony Hall**, which is part of the **International Convention Centre** in Bridge Street, Tel 782 8282. Concerts are also held at the **Birmingham Town Hall** in Victoria Square, Tel 236 2392. Visiting orchestras such as the London Sinfonietta and the Icon Symphony Orchestra also play at Symphony Hall and the City of Birmingham Choir gives a minimum of four concerts a year. There is a season of GBSO Proms in early summer, and the Birmingham Contemporary Music Group and Birmingham Jazz give concert series in the Adrian Boult Hall of the Town Hall. The Birmingham Festival Choral Society gives a series of concerts, mainly in **Birmingham Cathedral**, throughout the year, Tel 777 6840 for details. More extensively, the **Birmingham Conservatoire** offers a comprehensive programme of more than 200 musical events each year. There are chamber music concerts, celebrity recitals and concerts by individual students and by the Conservatoire's many ensembles. There are many lunchtime concerts in the Adrian Boult Hall as well as evening performances. For details phone the Birmingham Conservatoire in Paradise Place at 331 5908/9. The **Birmingham International Jazz Festival** is held at the beginning of July.

CINEMA

Commercial cinemas: **Cannon** – Quinton, Tel 442 2562 (4 screens). **Cannon** – John Bright Street, Tel 643 0292 (2 screens). **Capitol** – Alum Rock, Tel 327 0528 (3 screens). **Odeon** – New Street, Tel 643 6101/2/3 (6 screens). **Tivoli** – Station Street, Tel 643 1556 (2 screens).

For me, the two most interesting cinemas in Birmingham are the **Midlands Arts Centre Cinema** in Canon Hill Park, which has three screens, Tel 440 3838, and the **Triangle Cinema**, Aston Triangle, Tel 359 3979. Both cinemas offer a compelling mix of contemporary foreign and classic films, and both are heavily engaged in the Birmingham International Film and TV Festival, which takes place in September and October of each year. In 16 days more than a hundred films are shown, ranging from new commercial work to groupings of films from specific areas (recent festivals have looked at Canada, Barcelona and Catalonia) and a selection of film from international film festivals. There are also tributes, retrospectives, lectures, discussions and workshops.

BOOKSTORES

The best are **Waterstone's** at 24-26 High Street, Tel 633 4353 and **Dillon's** at 116 New Street, Tel 631 4333, and **City Plaza**, Cannon Street, Tel 633 3830. Other local stores worth a look are **Athena Books**, 98 Corporation Street, Tel 2361578, **Athena Bookshop**, Unit 11, The Pavilion, High Street, Tel 643 6640, **The Book Cellar**, The Bridge Link, Birmingham Shopping Centre, Tel 643 1098, **Burchell and Martin**, 34 Granville Street, Tel 643 1888 and **Hornby's Bookshop**, Fast Mall, Birmingham Shopping Centre, Tel 643 1266. Religious books can be found at the **Book Room**, 7 Carrs Lane, Tel 643 9235 (they also have a good juvenile selection) while books on transport of all kinds are at **Ian Allen**, 47 Stephenson Street, Tel 643 2496. Comics can be found at **Nostalgia and Comics**, 14-16 Smallbrock, Queensway, Tel 643 0143, and children's books at **Positive Image Children's Books**, Unit 1, Zair Works, Bishop Street, Tel 622 5921. When I was last there I bought some excellent bargain books at **The Works**, 137 New Street, Tel 643 3092, but the bargain bookstores do move around a bit.

ANTIQUARIAN AND SECONDHAND BOOKS

Birmingham Bookshop – 565-567 Bristol Road, Selly Oak, Tel 472 8556. Out-of-print books of all periods. Close by is **Stephen Wycherley**, 508 Bristol Road, with a large selection of antiquarian and secondhand books. **Blitzgeist**, 189 High Street, Harborne, Tel 426 4122, has antiquarian and secondhand books of all kinds as has **Maxwell's Bookshop**, 22 Shaftmoor Lane, Acocks Green, Tel 706 8379, with a good antiquarian and secondhand selection while **Reader's World**, 11 St Martin's Parade, Bull Ring Centre, is certainly worth a visit.

ART GALLERIES

The **Halcyon Gallery** – 59 The Pallasades, Tel 643 4474, has modern British oils, watercolours and limited-edition prints, especially Sir William Russell Flint, David Shepherd and Stephen Lowry. The **Moseley Gallery**, 6 Ernest Street, off Holloway Head in the city centre, specializes in 18th-, 19th- and 20th-century watercolours and drawings, Tel 666 6630, while the **Carleton Gallery**, 91 Vivian Road, Harborne, Tel 427 2487, has excellent antiquarian prints and maps. **Ikon Gallery** at 58/72 John Bright Street, Tel 643 0708, is an excellent contemporary gallery, the best in Birmingham I think, and has 20 shows a year. The **Ling Gallery**, Highcroft Hospital, Highcroft Road, Tel 378 2211, is fascinating in that it attempts to celebrate the creative work in this hospital and to explore the bridge between art therapy and fine art generally (ask for Mandy Roberts). **Midlands Contemporary Art** at 59 George Street, Tel 233 9818, is another good contemporary gallery while **Madden Gallery**, 77 Digbeth, Tel 631 2098, **Warwick Fine Arts**, 313 Shaftmoor Lane Hall Green, Tel 777 3178, and **Woodland Fine Arts**, 1348 Stratford Road, Tel 777 2927, are often worth a browse.

ANTIQUES

Shops in Birmingham have been divided into stores that are in the centre of the city (within the inner ring road) and those in the suburbs, listed under individual geographic locations.

City Centre Antique Shops:

First, the **City of Birmingham Antique Market**, St Martin's Market, Edgbaston Street, Tel 624 3214, is open Mondays 7am–2pm and has a large general and art deco stock with many dealers in attendance. Adjacent to the Bull Ring and general market.

Dalton Street Antiques – 66 Dalton Street, Tel 236 2479. General antiques, stripped pine, fireplaces, beds and architectural items.

The Collectors' Shop – 63 Station Road, close to New Street Station. Tel 631 2072. Coins, militaria, jewellery, silver.

Garratt Antiques – 35 Stephenson Street, Tel 643 9507. Jewellery.

Rex Johnson and Sons – 28 Lower Temple Street, Tel 643 9674 and 23 Union Street, Tel 643 7503. Silver, jewellery, porcelain, glass and coins.

Nathan and Co – 31 Corporation Street, Tel 643 5225. Silver and jewellery.

The Old Clock Shop – 32 Stephenson Street, Tel 632 4864. Clocks, especially longcase, mantel and wall; scientific instruments, microscopes and sextants – all 18th- and 19th-century – vintage wrist-watches.

Piccadilly Jewellers – Piccadilly Arcade, New Street, Tel 643 4791. Jewellery and silver.

Smithsonia – Piccadilly Arcade, New Street, Tel 643 4805. Jewellery, small collectables and furniture.

Jomarc – Newtown Shopping Centre, Newtown Row, Tel 743 292. Close to Aston University. Pianos.

Edgbaston:

Ashleigh House Antiques – 5 Westbourned Road, Tel 454 6283. Close to Five Ways. Furniture, oils, water-colours, clocks and objets d'art.

Edgbaston Gallery – 42 Islington Row, Five Ways, Tel 454 4244. Oil paintings, watercolours, small furni-ture, clocks and collector's items. All 19th century.

Erdington:

Fine Pine – 75 Mason Road, Tel 373 6321. Pine and satin walnut furniture, iron, tiled fireplaces and general antiques.

Kestrel House Antiques – 72 Gravelly Hill, Tel 373 3876. Oil paintings of all schools, furniture.

Chesterfield Antiques – 181 Gravelly Lane, Tel 373 3876. General antiques.

March Medals – 113 Gravelly Lane, Tel 384 4901. Orders, decorations, campaign medals, militaria, mili-tary books.

Hall Green:

The Original Choice – 1340 Stratford Road, Tel 777 3821. Fireplaces, fenders, tiles, stained glass, mirrors and interior fittings.

Woodland Fine Art – 1348 Stratford Road, Tel 777 2027. Oil paintings, watercolours and decorative prints, decorative lamps and mirrors, collectables, trunks, brass and porcelain, 19th to 20th century.

Harborne:
Austy House Antiques – Princess Corner, Harborne Park Road, Tel 427 5325. French furniture, oil paintings, porcelain, chandeliers, general antiques.
Harborne Place Antiques – 22-24 Northfield Road, Tel 427 5788. Victorian and other period furniture and general antiques.
John Hubbard Antiques – 224-226 Court Oak Road, Tel 426 1694. 17th–19th-century furniture and paintings.
Stuart House Fine Art – 123 Queen's Park Road, Tel 426 3300. 17th- to early 20th-century furniture and paintings.

Hockley:
Maurice Fellows – 21 Vyse Street, Tel 554 0211. Jewellery and objets d'art.

King's Heath:
Always Antiques – 285 Vicarage Road, Tel 448 8701. Victorian and Edwardian furniture, dolls, linen, lace and curios.
Harbrow Antiques – 294 Vicarage Road, Tel 444 1619. Furniture, gold, silver, porcelain and paintings.

Moseley:
Chandry House Antiques – 116A Alcester Road, Tel 449 3462. Period and Edwardian furniture.
Peter Clark Antiques – 36 St Mary's Row, Tel 449 8245. Mid-17th-century to early 20th-century furniture; 19th- and 20th-century silver.
Christopher Gordon Antiques – 133 School Road, Tel 444 4644. Early shop and pub fittings and fixtures, advertising signs and mirrors; architectural and decorative items; pine, stained glass and fireplaces.
James Architectural Antiques – 15 Alcester Road, Tel 444 4628. Stained-glass panels, fireplaces and surrounds, general architectural items.
Moseley Antiques – Unit 5, Woodbridge Road, Tel 449 6186. Furniture and clocks.

Oldbury:
S R Furnishing and Antiques – 18 Stanley Road, Tel 422 9788. General antiques and furniture.

Rubery:
R Collyer – 185 New Road, Tel 453 2332. Clocks, including longcase, watches, barometers and jewellery.

Selly Oak:
Collecting World/ Rings and Things – 743 Bristol Road, Tel 471 1645. Militaria, collectables and jewellery.
Treasure Chest – 636 Bristol Road, Tel 458 3705. General furniture and antiques.

Sheldon:
Bob Harris and Sons – 2071 Coventry Road, Tel 743 2259. Furniture and general antiques, mostly 18th and 19th century.

Warley:
Victoria's Curios – 287 Bearwood Road, Tel 429 8661. Furniture, silver, bric-à-brac, textiles, jewellery and Victorian tiles, cast-iron fireplaces.

RESTAURANTS

As there are now signposts helping you find your way, it seems that Birmingham has an official Chinese quarter. Mind you, it was always a good place to eat Chinese food and long before it became trendy to struggle with chopsticks, I was enjoying the cuisine at the **Chung Ying**, 16-18 Wrottesley Street, Tel 622 5669. The Arcadia Shopping Complex now dwarfs the restaurant but it continues to serve authentic Cantonese food with a minimum of fuss. There's a huge menu to choose from and if you've never tried dim-sum, this is a wonderful place to start. In Thorp Street, at No 17, Tel 666 6622, is **Chung Ying Garden** which is a sister establishment and equally good. Together these two restaurants offer the best Chinese cooking in Birmingham. If your taste runs to Indian cuisine, then the **Maharaja** at 23-25 Hurst Street, Tel 622 2641, will do very nicely. It's very close to the Birmingham Hippodrome and the food is consistently well above average. The cuisine is essentially Punjabi, and I think the curries and vegetables are better than the tandoori offerings. The sauces are fiery and authentic and a sign of the establishment's quality is that lots of Indians eat here. Open Mon–Sat 12–2:30pm and 6–11:30pm. **Days of the Raj** at 51 Dale End,

Tel 236 0445, is also excellent. It's close to the law courts and it has a very good buffet lunch. Tandoori cooking is probably the best bet here. I had a memorable tandoori special last time I was here (five items from the tandoor with nan bread). Open all week 12–2:30 and 7–11:30pm. No Sat or Sun lunch. Finally in the Indian section, we turn to what is probably the most authentic restaurant of all. **Adil** is in the Sparkbrook-Sparkhill area of Birmingham, which has the largest concentration of Indian cafés and sweet centres in the city. Adil, which is at 140-150 Stoney Lane, Tel 449 0335, specializes in the Balti cooking of Kashmir. Dishes are cooked and served in cast iron pots which are rather like flattened woks. The kitchen makes little compromise to Western taste and as the proper accompaniment to a balti is bread, not rice, the chapatis and nan are wonderful (they are also *huge*). Adil is excellent and very busy, but there is another branch at 130 Stoney Lane.

The standard-bearer of Anglo-French cooking in Birmingham is unquestionably **Sloan's** at 27-29 Chad Square, Hawthorne Road, Tel 455 6697. The fish here is excellent – brill with champagne sauce (the best I've tasted since Le Darnetal in Montreuil-sur-Mer, Pas de Calais) trout, monkfish, sole and salmon. There is a set menu at lunchtime which is good value. Open Mon–Sat 12–2 and 7–10pm. No Sat lunch.

For vegetarians I recommend **Nutters**, 422 Bearwood Road, Bearwood, Tel 420 2428. They are very friendly and their food is delightfully spicy. The prices are reasonable too. Last time I was in the town centre I had a quick lunch at **Thai Paradise**, 31 Paradise Circus, Tel 643 5523. It's right opposite the Town Hall and I thought the cooking was authentic and excellent value for money if you are hooked on Thai cuisine (even if you are not). Friends tell me good things about **La Galleria** which is also in Paradise Circus, Tel 236 1006. It's an Italian snack bar serving delicious light meals and good ice cream. Finally, **Franzl's** at 151 Milcote Road, Bearwood, Tel 429 7920: Franzl's is authentically Austrian, both in cuisine and decor, even though the "Tourist Board" music gets a little wearing. The food is excellent though. Zigeuner goulash is suitably gypsyish in taste with unstinted paprika - now I come to think of it, more Hungarian than Austrian, but let's not quibble. The schnitzel is very good and remember, this is not as easy a dish to prepare as you might think, while the iced coffee is the best I've tasted outside of Vienna. Open Tues–Sat for dinner only, 7–10:30pm.

PUBS

Barton Arms – Park Lane, Tel 359 0853, on A34 North, close to Aston High Street. A magnificent Edwardian pub with an opulent atmosphere and superb, elaborate, painted tilework. There are booths with cut glass "snob screens" which you swivel open to ask for a drink, lots of mahogany, mirrors, plush seating and heavy brass lamps. Traditional bar food.

Longboat – Cambrian Wharf, Kingston Row (off Broad Street). Tel 236 2421. City centre pub which overlooks the canal. There's a summer terrace and balcony over the water and straightforward bar food.

White Swan – Edmund Street, Tel 236 5782 (close to Town Hall). Furnished in Edwardian style with gas lamps, stained glass and small booths for sitting. Traditional bar food.

Cathedral – Church Street (near Eye Hospital). Right in the city centre. Very friendly with surprisingly reasonable bar food which makes it very busy at lunchtime.

Church – Church Lane, Perry Bar, Tel 356 4389. Refurbished and decorated with interesting bric-à-brac. Small panelled room with open fire. Nice gardens and a truly magnificent chip butty (French-fry sandwich).

Peacock – Lea End Lane and Icknield Street. The pub is actually over the Hereford and Worcestershire border even though it's just a few minutes from the city centre. (It's worth getting the car out for.) It's small and comparatively isolated with friendly staff, low ceilings and pub games. Traditional bar food and picnic tables in the summer.

ARTISTIC ASSOCIATIONS

Dr Johnson, the lexicographer, critic and poet, lived in Birmingham for a while around 1734 and contributed essays to the Birmingham *Journal*. Indeed, he met Miss Porter, the future Mrs Johnson, in the city and they were married in 1735. Washington Irving, the American man of letters, wrote *Rip Van Winkle* in Birmingham while he was visiting his brother-in-law in 1818. In fact, Aston Hall (see above) is thought to be the original of Irving's "Bracebridge Hall," published in 1822. J R R Tolkien, the scholar and novelist, lived in the suburb of Hall Green when he was a child, and he reflects that those years were "the longest-seeming and most formative part of my life." Tolkien lived very close to Sarehole

Mill and it seems that when reflecting on his childhood, he saw the Mill as the heart of an unspoiled English countryside, almost certainly the inspiration for Hobbiton in *The Hobbit.* Francis Brett Young, the novelist, graduated in medicine from Birmingham University and the city is the "North Bromwich" of his novels. Louis MacNeice was lecturer in Classics at Birmingham University from 1930 till 1935, and published a volume of poems here.

Edward Burne-Jones and William Morris were two of the leading members of the Pre-Raphaelite movement, having met at Exeter College, Oxford. They were both influenced by Dante Gabriel Rossetti and information on them and the movement they so avidly supported can be found under Oxford (Artistic Associations). One of the obsessions of the Pre-Raphaelites was with anything medieval. They avidly read Chaucer and Sir Thomas Malory, studied illuminated manuscripts and made pilgrimages to medieval sites. Many art historians think that Burne-Jones, who was born in Birmingham, developed his distinctive views only after meeting other like-minded students at Oxford. He was born in 1833, the son of a carver and gilder, and attended King Edward's School, then in New Street near the Burne-Jones family home at 11 Bennett's Hill. (The house has gone, and the site is now a building society.) Burne-Jones's wife described the environment in which he grew up as "destitute of any visible thing that could appeal to the imagination." Yet there is evidence that while still at school, Burne-Jones was already developing an interest in medieval religion and used to playfully sign his letters, "Edward, Cardinal de Byrmyngham."

Joseph Smith came to Birmingham with his parents in 1862 when he was one year old, and lived for most of the remainder of his life at 13 Charlotte Road in Edgbaston. Deeply impressed by a visit he made to Italy in 1883, he abandoned his original intention of becoming an architect and turned to art. He spent the next eight years mastering the technique of tempera painting, "this most beautiful and permanent method, in which most of the Italian pictures were wrought up to the middle of the sixteenth century." Tempera is a painting technique in which powder colour is mixed with a binder, normally the yolk of an egg or both white and yolk together, thinned with water and applied to a white plaster ground. It is opaque, permanent and fast drying, though the colours dry lighter than they appear when wet. As a teacher at the Birmingham School of Art, Smith influenced many young artists and led a "tempera revival," which flourished around the turn of the century. During the First World War he was commissioned to paint frescoes of Birmingham scenes in the City Art Gallery; in addition to these works, the gallery also contains a room devoted to Smith and other tempera revivalists.

EPHEMERA

The London-to-Birmingham Railway, the first long-distance railway out of London, opened in 1837. The Company marked the importance of the occasion by erecting a great Doric arch at Euston, the London terminus. Designed by Philip Hardwick, it was destroyed in 1962 when Euston was rebuilt. But Hardwick's monumental Ionic portico at Curzon Street, Birmingham, the other terminus, survives, together with the three-storey wing added in 1840 as a hotel. Curzon Street was superseded by New Street in 1854 and thereafter the station was only used for freight. The station building is now used as offices.

Bourneville was built from 1894 onwards by George Cadbury, around the chocolate and cocoa factory to which he and Richard Cadbury had moved their business from the city centre in 1879. Cadbury employed the architect, W Alexander Harvey, to create a garden suburb of carefully designed houses set in large gardens, with a generous provision of schools, shops and places of worship and even a pair of old timber-framed buildings from the Warwickshire countryside. It was always intended that Bourneville should not be restricted to employees at the chocolate factory. George Cadbury was a Quaker who hoped that the example which he set at Bourneville would be followed elsewhere, and in many respects his achievements have been so influential that the streets of Bourneville seem quite commonplace. When they are compared with the neighbouring areas of late Victorian and Edwardian Birmingham it becomes clear how much of a novelty they were at the time they were built.

Birmingham is a theatre town. The Birmingham Repertory Theatre has a long reputation for excellence going back to 1913 when it opened. Laurence Olivier, Ralph Richardson and Paul Scofield all got their start at the Birmingham Rep and Lord Miles of Blackfriars (Bernard Miles, the actor, director and manager) recalls a time in the 1930s when Charles Victor was stage manager of the Rep. It was opening night and Victor, worn out after a wearying weekend of dress rehearsals, was standing in the prompt corner half asleep, with the prompt book open at the wrong page when, suddenly, the play stopped. Someone had dried. Roused from his reverie, Victor saw five actors gazing into the wings at him beseechingly – two of them even holding out their hands to collect a well-thrown prompt. He glanced at the prompt book, realized it was open on the wrong page, and said clearly and incisively to the floundering performers, "Go back to act one, scene one."

The Alexandra Theatre, Birmingham, opened as the Lyceum in 1901 to such dismal audiences that within a year it had been sold for a little less than £4000 – less than half of what it had cost to build. The first owner, a flamboyant character named Lester Collingwood, had two main interests – his theatre and women. He was killed in a traffic accident in 1910 while driving to Sheffield for an assignation with an actress. This afforded him the dubious honour of being one of the first road accident victims in Britain. In 1911 he was succeeded by Leon Salberg, whose accomplishments at the theatre were enormous. He died in his office in 1938 and his ghost inhabits the theatre. Many sightings have occurred, including the sighting of a shadowy figure, the sound of the clinking of keys on a chain and an invisible hand which touched a security guard's shoulder. Everyone assumed the ghost was Loon Salberg's, as he was still tied to the theatre, in a manner of speaking, but in 1987 a cleaning woman saw a figure of a woman dressed completely in grey. From her description, many think it was the ghost of a former wardrobe mistress, but I like to think it was a mistress of a different sort – that of Lester Collingwood, who seems to have been unfairly left out of the ghost stakes.

Birmingham Readers and Writers Festival, which is a celebration of words written, spoken and sung, takes place throughout the city during the first two weeks in May. Recent participants have included actors Antony Sher and Sheila Steafel, director and filmmaker Mike Leigh, and writers Jeanette Winterson, Andrew Davies, Fay Weldon and Derek Walcott. There is a book fair, writer's workshops and events for children.

At Aston Hall (see above) there hangs a portrait of the first owner of the house, Sir Thomas Holte. Before building Aston, he had lived at Duddleston Hall, where he was said to have murdered his cook by running him through with a spit. When Duddleston Hall was razed in 1850, many expected to find the cook's skeleton under the cellar floor where Sir Thomas was supposed to have buried him. But the story was never proved. In 1606, Sir Thomas took a neighbour to court for saying he had split his cook's head with a cleaver. Although Sir Thomas won his case, the rumour persisted and by the 19th century it was said that, because of the supposed murder, he was forced to wear the "bloody hand" in his coat of arms. Actually the bloody hand is the Red Hand of Ulster, the badge of baronetcy, but it has given rise to murder tales all over England. At Aston Church the hand (minus a finger) depicted in the Holte arms in one of the windows was explained by saying Sir Thomas's descendants were allowed to remove one finger or thumb for each generation until the hand was gone.

TOURIST INFORMATION BUREAU: 2 City Arcade, Birmingham, West Midlands, B24TX. Tel (021) 643 2514

COVENTRY

County of Warwickshire
95 miles (152 km) by road from London via M1/M45
One hour 30 minutes by train from London (Euston)

Coventry's history probably began in the 7th century, with the erection of an Anglo-Saxon convent. However, it was the Benedictine abbey, founded in the 11th century by Leofric, Earl of Mercia, that gave the town its first impetus to growth. Leofric was the husband of Godiva, Coventry's most famous inhabitant (see Ephemera). You can see a statue of the good lady in Broadgate.

During the Middle Ages, wool, needles and leather all contributed to the city's prosperity, but with the industrial revolution great changes took place. The Daimler company produced the first English motorcar here in 1898 and the rapid increase of the car industry in turn gave rise to aircraft production. In November 1940 much of the city was wiped out by a devastating air raid, leaving only the medieval tower and spire of the Cathedral Church of St Michael standing. St Michael's had only become a cathedral in 1918 having previously been part of the diocese of Lichfield. In 1951 an open architectural competition for a new cathedral was won by Basil Spence who was knighted in 1960. The new cathedral is one of the most striking examples of modern architecture in the world and the impression it leaves with you is long lasting. Built of rosy, delicately coloured sandstone, it looks like a long cliff of Gothic buttresses. The canopied link between the entrance to the new church and the charred, preserved remains of the old is a gesture of pure genius. The engraved entrance doors by John Hutton are superb, and as one enters one's eye is held by a suggestion of great length. In fact the nave is only 270 feet (82 m), which is not considered long by cathedral standards. The glass is beautiful, suffusing the interior with deep greens, golden yellows, vivid reds and blues and sombre purple. The windows, most of which stretch from floor to ceiling, are by Laurence Lee, Geoffrey Clarke and Keith Naw, with the great baptistry window by John Piper. These windows did much to give back to England her medieval fame for the making of stained glass and the last time I was in the cathedral there was an exhibition by makers of stained glass from all over the country. The massive block of the altar stone is surmounted by Geoffrey Clarke's metal abstraction of Christ crucified. The final focal point is the tapestry designed by Graham Sutherland, and woven in France. The work is 75 feet (22.8 m) high and represents, in almost Byzantine terms, Christianity's "Redeeming Savior of the World." The green background sets off the muted whites, reds and purples woven into Christ's robes and the four medallions of the Evangelists. Beneath the feet of Christ stands man, diminutive, yet stark and dynamic against the background.

The Lady Chapels have, by design, a sense of immediacy and involvement in modern life. The Chapel of Christ the Servant gives the names and positions of all the industrial plants in Coventry while the theme of the Chapel of Unity is understanding among all races and religions. Outside against the walls immediately to the right of the steps leading to the entrance is the bronze sculpture of St Michael and the Devil by Sir Jacob Epstein. There is an audio-visual presentation in the visitor centre, a restaurant and a gift shop.

Few buildings remain from the medieval city. Holy Trinity Church is immediately behind the new cathedral. The proximity of two such important churches as the old, destroyed St Michael's and Holy Trinity itself is the reflection of a medieval feud when the townspeople were roughly divided between the prior and the earl and were continually at loggerheads. Holy Trinity has a timbered ceiling, a 15th-century brass eagle lectern and a splendid pulpit of the same period. The Collegiate Church of St John the Baptist was built by the

COVENTRY CATHEDRAL

wife of Edward II. Nearby stand two black-and-white-gabled houses. Bond's Hospital (facing the north side of St John's) is the most important. Founded in 1506 by the Coventry draper, Thomas Bond, for the care of 12 elderly poor men, it has some excellent period furniture. The other house is Bablake School for Boys. Coventry has two well preserved medieval gates which survived both Charles II's attempt to have them destroyed after the Civil War in 1660 and the Blitz in 1940. St Mary's Guildhall in Bayley Lane was built in 1340 as the hall of the Merchants' Guild. It has some fine early stained glass and a superb 15th-century tapestry depicting the Assumption of the Blessed Virgin with a kneeling figure of Henry VII and his queen. There is also a minstrel gallery. Legend has it that Mary Queen of Scots was once imprisoned here. Of interest nearby is Spon Street, where medieval shops, taverns and dwellings have been relocated and reconstructed beam by beam. Whitefriars, a renovated 14th-century Carmelite friary is situated on the London Road, just before the London Road/Ring Road roundabout (Open Thurs–Sun all year). Ford's Hospital in Greyfriars Lane is a Tudor almshouse founded in 1509. Considered to be one of the finest examples of domestic architecture, the building is viewable from the outside only. The architecture of the traffic-free central shopping area is undistinguished, but the scale is human, and the place is easier to use than some more pretentious centres.

WALK

Coventry Walk – Start from Whitefriars car park, off the Ringway. Turn left into Whitefriars Lane and go through Whitefriars Gate which now houses a **Toy Museum**. Turn right into Much Park Street, then left into Earl Street. Continue ahead into High Street noting the 1920s **Council House** in Tudor style on the right. Go ahead into Broadgate at **Lady Godiva's Statue**, follow Broadgate round to the right, then turn left into Trinity Street and at the traffic lights cross Hale Street for the **Museum of British Road Transport**. Turn left into Chauntry Place, pass on the right the **Lady Herbert Gardens**. Pass through the medieval **Town Gate** and return back through the gardens themselves. Cross Hales Street into Fairfax Street and at the traffic lights turn right into Priory Street for **Coventry Cathedral**. Go through the cathedral precincts to St Michael's Avenue. Just ahead is the **Coventry Cross**, a replica of the original cross of 1541. Turn left and immediately left again into Bayley Lane for **St Mary's Guildhall**, circa 1342. Go ahead to the right along Bayley Lane and turn left into Jordan Well for the **Herbert Art Gallery and Museum**. Turn right in Whitefriars Street and then right into Whitefriars Lane for the car park.

MUSEUMS AND GALLERIES

Herbert Art Gallery and Museum – Jordan Well, Tel 25555. The gallery concentrates on the work of British artists. They include watercolours, paintings, sculpture, 20th-century figure drawings and an interesting section on paintings using the theme of Lady Godiva. Graham Sutherland's studies for his Coventry Cathedral tapestry are on display and the gallery has the Poke Collection of English furniture, silver and paintings. There are good displays on the story of Coventry, animal migration and an excellent vivarium. Open Mon–Sat 10–5:30 and Sun 2–5pm.

Coventry Toy Museum – Whitefriars Gate, Much Park Street, Tel 27560. Whitefriars Gate, which houses the museum, was built in 1352 as the main gateway of the friary. It contains a collection of dolls, toys and games (1750–1960). There is also a display of amusement machines (which I really enjoyed, having a weakness for fairs and midways). Open April–Oct Mon–Sat 10–6, Sun 2–6pm; Nov–Mar by appointment.

Museum of British Transport – St Agnes Lane, Hales Street, Tel 832425. The museum pays tribute to more than 50 motor vehicle and cycle manufacturers who have made their home in Coventry, including legendary names such as Daimler, Jaguar, Hillman, Rover, Singer, Standard and Triumph. There are more than 150 motorcars, 90 motorcycles and 200 cycles including Queen Mary's 1935 Daimler and Viscount Montgomery's Victory car. You can even hear and see what it's like to travel at 633 mph (1012.8 kmph) in Richard Noble's land speed record breaking jet-car (simulated, of course). Open April–Oct 10–5; Nov–Mar Fri, Sat, Sun 10–5pm.

Midland Air Museum – Coventry Airport, Tel 832425. The museum incorporates Sir Frank Whittle's Jet Heritage Centre. Whittle was the inventor of the jet engine. On display are Vulcan bombers, Canberras, Meteors, Starfighters, Lightnings, and the huge Armstrong-Whitworth Argosy freighter of 1959. Also displays of local aviation history. Open April–Oct Mon–Sat 10–4, Sun 11–6; Nov–Mar Sat and Sun 11–5pm.

Lunt Roman Fort – Coventry Road, Baignton, Tel 303567. This 1st-century Roman cavalry fort has been reconstructed *in situ*. There are timber ramparts, a two-storey gateway and a *Gyrus* – a training ring for cavalry. Open May 24–Sept 28 12–6pm.

THEATRE

Belgrade Theatre – Corporation Street, Tel 20205. The West Midlands is extremely well served by high-quality theatre and the Belgrade, in both its 899-seat main theatre and its 60-seat studio, is no exception. This lively repertory theatre offers an adventurous and varied programme. Recent production have included Alan Ayckbourn's *A Chorus of Disapproval,* a special stage adaptation of Hardy's *Tess of the D'Urbervilles* and a new play from Mike Harding called *Last Tango in Whitby.* There is a traditional family pantomime as well as some visiting companies and some "starry" one-night stands. The studio is the home of the Belgrade Youth Theatre and there is also a famed Theatre in Education Team which works in local schools. The theatre is named after the Yugoslav capital, which presented the timber used in its interior. Built in 1958, the Belgrade was Britain's first civic theatre. There is a good restaurant and coffee bar.

Arts Centre University of Warwick – Oddly, the Arts Centre of Warwick University is only three miles (4.8 km) from Coventry and eight miles (12.8 km) from Warwick. It is in fact one of the largest and most impressive arts complexes outside of London. Generally, between October and December, some 90 different events are scheduled in the centre's theatre, gallery, hall or studio. Recent theatrical productions have included Athol Fugard's *The Road to Mecca,* Harold Pinter's *The Birthday Party,* the London Contemporary Dance Theatre, the Red Army Ensemble and the English Shakespeare Company in *The Merchant of Venice* and *Volpone.* The hall (for concerts, etc.) seats 1517, the theatre 573, the studio 200 and the film theatre 250. The centre is just west of the crossroads between the A45 and the A46. Tel 524524.

MUSIC

Coventry does not have a professional symphony orchestra (perhaps because of its proximity to Birmingham and its superb City of Birmingham Symphony). Concerts are given in the cathedral but the real centre for music is the **Great Hall of the University of Warwick Arts Centre**. Recent visitors have included the CBSO under Simon Rattle, Peter Donohoe, who inaugurated the centre's new Steinway concert grand, the Coull String Quarter, the Sofia Philharmonic, the English Chamber Orchestra and the Royal Flanders Orchestra. There is also dance, ballet and jazz. **Coventry Festival,** a celebration of music, theatre and film, takes place during the last two weeks in June.

CINEMA

Commercial cinema is at the **Odeon**, Jordan Well, Tel 222042 and **Theatre One**, Tel 224301 on Ford Street. More interesting fare can be seen at the **University of Warwick Arts Centre**, Tel 524524 (see above) which has a wide ranging and extensive film programme in their film theatre.

BOOKSTORES

The best is **Dillon's** at 38 Hertford Street, Tel 227151. They also have a store at 26 Earl Street, tel 229092. An excellent selection and efficient service. Christian and religious books can be found at the **Christian Bookshop**, 21 City Arcade, Tel 222064, while there are two branches of **W H Smith**, the main one at 62 Hertford Street, Tel 221927. the **University Bookshop**, Tel 523388, close to the Warwick Arts Centre is excellent.

ANTIQUARIAN AND SECONDHAND BOOKS

Coventry is not noted for antiguarian hooks. Warwick is a better bet. **Gosford Books**, 116 Gosford Street, Tel 220873, is worth a look, as is **Armstrong's Books and Collectables**, 163A Sovereign Road, Tel 714344. One industry which is rapidly growing is the trading of sporting memorabilia. If you want to acquaint yourself with the current prices and selection then **Sports Programmes** at 3 Chapel Street can answer your questions. Tel 228672.

ANTIQUE DEALERS

In the centre of town, at 160 Spon Street, is **Kingsway Antiques**, Tel 221450 – a general collection – while at 107 Spon is the **Antique Shop**, Tel 525915, which has bric-à-brac and a very varied selection. **Memories Antiques**, Tel 687994, has clocks and paintings as well as a large general collection. They are also dealers of Royal Doulton figurines and character jugs and are at 400A Stoney Stanton Road. **John Abberley** at 5 Beanfield Avenue, Green Lane, Tel 419438, specializes in pine furniture as well as general antiques, while **Antiquarian** at 60 Mayfield Road has an interesting general collection, Tel 691239.

There are two places worth visiting on the Daventry Road, **Antiques and Collectables** at No 44, Tel 504350 and **Queenstand Antiques** at No 50, Tel 503166 – both general collections. Likewise Hearsall Lane gives you **Hearsall Lane Antiques** at No 4, Tel 673241, and **Carlson Antiques** at No 36, Tel 675456. They have an enormous collection of bric-à-brac and collectables. In Gosford Street you will find **Cobwebs** at No 58, Tel 222032, and **Spires Antiques** at No 138, Tel 258744. Again, general collection and bric-a-brac. Finally, **Candlelight Antiques**, 4 Cramper's Fields, Tel 591112, and **JG Supplies** at 44 Britannia Street, Tel 258930, round off a list that is somewhat lacking in elegance and quality but full of interesting junk.

RESTAURANTS

Trinity House Hotel – Herbs Restaurant, 28 Lower Holyhead Road, Tel 555654. It's good to see someone taking vegetarian cooking seriously. Here we have a highly original menu, based on top quality natural ingredients and even if you are not vegetarian you'll appreciate the change. West Country Hot-Pot, stuffed pine-nut loaf and curried vegetable pâté are all delicious and they even have a couple of meat dishes for those who lack flexibility. Open for dinner only 6:30–9:30pm Mon–Sat.

Oak – Coventry Road, Baginton, Tel 301817. If you are visiting the Lunt Roman Fort or the Midlands Air Museum at Coventry Airport (or even if you are not) you will find good home cooking at this cheerful restaurant.

PUBS

Old Windmill – Spon Street, Tel 252183. Ouaint and popular timber framed 16th-century pub – all nooks and crannies. Generous helpings of simple lunchtime fare. Unlike so many buildings in this street, which have been moved here, this pub began life here.

Town Wall – Bond Street (behind the Belgrade Theatre), Tel 220963. Unspoilt, compact Victorian pub still much as it must have been in the 1840s with open fire in the lounge and a flower filled back yard. Good and very inexpensive bar food at lunch and early evening.

Greyhound – Coventry Road (close to M6 junction 3) Tel 220963. Situated at the junction of Coventry and Oxford canals. Good food at good prices. In the summer, waterside tables in a lovely garden.

ARTISTIC ASSOCIATIONS

The Coventry Miracle Plays of the 15th and 16th century are thought to be named after the town where they were performed. Alfred Lord Tennyson visited Coventry in 1840 and soon afterwards wrote a poem about Lady Godiva. Walter Savage Landor also used the good lady in one of his *Imaginary Conversations*. Mary Ann Evans (George Eliot), who wrote *Middlemarch* and *The Mill on the Floss,* lived for eight years at Bird Grove, Foleshill Road. The American poet and essayist, Ralph Waldo Emerson, visited her here. At Bird Grove Mary Ann completed her translation of Strauss's *Life of Jesus.* The great actress, Dame Ellen Terry, was born in Coventry. Her son Edward Gordon Craig was the greatest stage designer of his time. From 1878 to 1902 Dame Ellen established herself as the leading Shakespearean actress in London, in partnership with Sir Henry Irving. J M Barrie and George Bernard Shaw both wrote roles especially for her. The influential British poet, Philip Larkin, was born in Coventry in 1922.

A most notable artist associated with Coventry is David Gee. He was born here in 1793, attended a local charity school and, before taking up art as a full-time profession, worked for a while in his father's watchmaking business. Like many provincial painters he had to be versatile, tackling inn signs, banners and heraldic coach painting as well as landscapes, portraits and pictures of local events – such as the annual Lady Godiva procession. For most of his life Gee lived in a house on the north side of Spon Street, near the junction with Barras Lane (the house has gone). His work, including the *Lady Godiva Procession,* can be seen in the Herbert Art Gallery and Museum in Jordan Wall.

EPHEMERA

St John's Church in Spon Street is a 14th-century red sandstone building and is where the famous expression "sent to Coventry" originated. During the Civil War St John's Church was used as prison for Royalist troups defeated by Cromwell. These prisoners were then shunned by Coventry citizens, and so the saying arose.

Coventry's two cathedrals stand side by side. The burnt-out remains of the old 14th-century cathedral, victim of wartime destruction, is adjoined by the bold, modern architecture of the new cathedral, and together they symbolize sacrifice and resurrection. The altar of the old cathedral is made of broken stones gathered in the wake of the night of horror and devastation. It is surmounted by a cross of charred roof beams and a cross of medieval nails behind which are inscribed the words from Calvary, "Father forgive." The Cross of Nails has become the symbol of the ministry of reconciliation and renewal carried out by members of its community worldwide, and replicas have been carried to all corners of the globe.

The most famous story connected with Coventry is that of Lady Godiva's naked ride through the city in protest at the merciless tax her husband, Leofric, had imposed on the inhabitants of the city. We know that Lady Godiva existed. She was actually called Godgifu and was indeed married to Earl Leofric of Mercia, one of the four all-powerful lords who ruled England under the Danish King, Canute. She was also a rich landowner in her own right and, according to reports, was wise, virtuous and charitable – unlike her husband.

According to the legend, which may not be far from the truth, when Godgifu begged her husband to rescind the tax, the exasperated earl replied that first she would have to ride naked through Coventry on market day. That, he was certain, was something that this modest woman would never do. The legend was first written down, in Latin, by monks in St Albans Abbey in Hertfordshire, some 900 years ago. Historically, it is possible that the good lady may have performed some sort of public penance for the misdeeds of her husband. Perhaps she appeared in the street stripped of her usual badges of rank and that in the minds of the people of Coventry this voluntary act of self-humiliation became mixed up with a Christian version of Eve – naked and beautiful and bravely preserving her modesty by means of her long hair. It should be remembered that the Coventry cycle of Miracle Plays was performed in the streets and the story of Eve was consequently a familiar one to the townspeople.

Whatever the actual facts of the story, it seems that Leofric did undergo some sort of religious conversion during his life, but whether this was as a direct result of his wife's actions is not known. The hated tax was removed and we know that the couple founded a Benedictine monastery in which they were both buried. Sadly, not even the ruins of their joint creation remain.

The story of peeping Tom, the only citizen who looked at Lady Godiva, and who was struck blind for his temerity, did not come until 600 years after the event took place. The idea may have sprung from an attempt to explain the unseeing eyes and agonized expression of the strange wooden statue of a man, the true meaning of which is unknown, but which can still be seen in the Leofric Hotel.

In Holy Trinity Church a sinister but beautiful misericord shows a mysterious face looking out through leaves. Such images are descended from the practice of tree worship. Identified with the Green Man of folk custom, the leaf mask is thought to represent the youth who was clothed and masked in leaves to personify the tree spirit and led out to bless the fields. Despite its probable origin, it appears in numerous churches on capitals, misericords (Exeter Cathedral) and roof bosses. Normally the face is wreathed with oak leaves and many old oak trees in England are linked by legends to tree cults.

Although the church replaced the old field rites with the Christian Rogation-tide ceremonies, in some places the Green Man lingered on into this century, walking or riding through the streets in procession, his head and shoulders hidden in a leaf-covered wicker cage – a link back to a spirit whose malevolent dispostion struck fear into the hearts of the primitive ancestors.

TOURIST INFORMATION BUREAU: Bayley Lane, Coventry, West Midlands CV1 5RN. Tel (0203) 832303

STRATFORD-UPON-AVON

County of Warwickshire
2 hours 40 minutes from London (Euston, changing at Birmingham)
90 miles (144 km) from London by M1, A425 and A46

The charm of Stratford-upon-Avon lies in the streets that were here long before William Shakespeare was born on the 25th of April, 1564. By then the town was already a thriving market centre and many of the fine half-timbered merchants' houses which survive today had already been built. It is, however, due to Shakespeare that Stratford is the most heavily tourist-visited place in England. Many who have never seen Chester or Plymouth, Milford Haven or Norwich, have made their one excursion out of London to see Stratford.

Stratford-upon-Avon originated as a river crossing. Stratford, or Stretford in Old English, means "the ford at which the street crosses the river." Situated at the intersection of seven main roads, Stratford was, from earliest times, a place of some importance. There was a Bronze Age settlement here, a Romano-British village and an Anglo-Saxon monastery. By 1196 the town had the right to hold a weekly market and in 1214 King John granted the right to hold a three-day fair. The only fair to survive is the annual Mop Fair, held in the streets of the town on the 12th of October. Today it is essentially a fun fair, but traditionally it was a labour market: farm hands and domestic servants came to offer their services for hire.

In addition to the markets and fairs, the rise of the Guild of the Holy Cross greatly assisted the town's development. The Guild was founded in the 13th century and until its suppression in 1547 it virtually governed the town. The Guild Chapel was built in 1269 but almost entirely reconstructed in the 15th century. The half-timbered Guildhall was erected beside the chapel in 1417–18, and at the same time a number of almshouses were built for the Guild's aged and sick members. A few years later a school was founded nearby. When the Guild ceased operation the school was transferred to the upper floor of the Guildhall and classes held in a large room, now known as Big School which today is still used by the King Edward IV Grammar School. It is thought that Shakespeare attended school here in this upper room and that in the hall below he watched his first play, performed by one of the travelling companies under the protection of great noblemen such as the Earl of Derby or the Earl of Leicester.

John Shakespeare was a farmer in the small village of Snitterfield located a few miles north of Stratford. By 1551 he had moved to Stratford and established himself as a glover and a dealer in wool. In 1557 he married Mary Arden, daughter of a wealthy yeoman farmer who lived at Wilmcote (three miles/4.8 km northwest of the town). At the time of Shakespeare's birth, John and Mary were living on Henley Street in a property consisting of the family home and their shop and warehouse. In 1582, at the age of 18, William Shakespeare married Anne Hathaway, the daughter of Richard Hathaway, a yeoman farmer of Shottery, a small hamlet to the west of Stratford. The farmhouse was originally called Hewlands Farm, but is now known as Anne Hathaway's Cottage. On May 26, 1583, Anne and William's first child, Susanna, was baptized. Two years later they had twins, Hamnet and Judith. Shortly afterwards Shakespeare left Stratford for London. His reason for leaving is not known, but legend has it that he had been caught poaching deer at nearby Charlecote Park, a couple of miles to the east of the town – the deer are still there, or at least their descendants are (see Ephemera). From 1592, at the age of 28, Shakespeare can be traced in London, first as an actor and then as a reviser of plays. He became a writer and part-owner of the Globe Theatre, built on the south bank of the Thames at Southwark in 1599. The publication of *Venus and Adonis* in 1593 was followed by a prodigious stream of poems and plays and within a few years he had become a wealthy and successful man. Shakespeare did not, however, forget Stratford: in 1597, a year after the death of his son Hamnet, he purchased New Place, one of the largest houses in the town. Once owned by Sir Hugh Clopton, who gave the town the four-arched bridge that crosses the Avon, New Place stood beside the medieval Guild Chapel and the grammar school. Originally the house had extensive grounds but today only the foundations remain. The house was pulled down in the mid-18th century by the Reverend Francis Gastrell who became irritated by tourists seeking the house. The loss was not as great as might be thought, as Shakespeare's original house had nearly completely disappeared in rebuilding. Shakespeare's daughter Susanna became the wife of one of the town's leading physicians, Dr John Hall, in 1607 and lived in Hall's Croft. It is not known whether Shakespeare was ever treated by Dr Hall, but after his retirement in 1610 Shakespeare would have been a frequent visitor to the house.

William Shakespeare died on the 23rd of April, 1616, his 52nd birthday. Two days later he was buried in the chancel of Holy Trinity Church on the banks of the Avon. Buried nearby are his wife, his daughter Susanna, her husband, and Thomas Nash, the husband of Shakespeare's granddaughter who lived in Nash's House next door to New Place.

Each year on St George's Day, England's Day and the day of Shakespeare's birth and death, his grave is overwhelmed by a mountain of floral tributes from over a hundred countries. Sir Walter Scott came with his sister to view the poet's grave in April 1828 and wrote in his journal, "We visited the tomb of the mighty wizzard. It is in the bad taste of

King James I's reign, but what a magic does the locality possess." Ben Jonson, the "mighty wizzard's" friend and contemporary, said of him:

Thou art a monument without a tomb,
And art alive still, while thy book doth live,
And we have wits to read, and praise to give.

And we still do read and we most certainly continue to praise. Although there is no record of when the first tourists began to visit the town, it is known that the great 18th-century actor, David Garrick, organized a Stratford Jubilee in 1769 "in honor of the memory of Shakespeare." The Jubilee was a distinctly odd affair. Garrick had a mighty ego, and according to contemporary reports not a word of Shakespeare was uttered during the three days of festivities, but there was a lot to be heard from Garrick. Interestingly, it was not until 1879 that a theatre in memory of Shakespeare was built in the town of the world's greatest playwright. This Victorian Gothic building was destroyed by fire in 1926, and six years later its simple red brick successor was opened.

Comparatively little is known of Shakespeare's life and career but in Stratford he is celebrated everywhere in monuments, street and pub signs, cafés – even dry cleaners! His birthplace and the homes of his relatives bathe in his reflected glory, but perhaps his presence is strongest in the lovely landscape, truly the country of a midsummer night's dream.

WALK

Stratford Walk – Begin at the car park in Bridgeway, just off the A34. From Bridgeway, the life-size figure of William Shakespeare at the entrance to the Bancroft gardens soon comes into view. It is an impressive introduction to Stratford, with "sweet Will" sitting on a plinth of Portland stone and behind him the lawns sweeping down to the Avon and the Royal Shakespeare Theatre. At the base of the plinth are four compelling figures, sculpted in bronze representing Hamlet, Lady Macbeth, Prince Hal and Falstaff, symbolizing philosophy, tragedy, history and comedy. In the gardens a bridge crosses a lock on the Stratford-upon-Avon Canal to a footpath leading along the riverside to the **Royal Shakespeare Theatre**. Climb the steps to the riverside terrace and continue through the theatre gardens. By the gate leading into Southern Lane note the "Nine Men's Morris" (See Ephemera). From Southern Lane a gate leads into Avonbank Garden for the **Brass Rubbing Centre**. The footpath continues to **Old Town** and **Trinity Church** where Shakespeare was baptized and where he is buried. Return along Old Town for **Hall's Croft** – the home of Shakespeare's daughter, then turn right into Church Street and ahead into Chapel Street for **New Place**, the remains of the house in which Shakespeare probably died and **Nash's House**, next door, home of Shakespeare's granddaughter, Elizabeth. Continue along Chapel Street, passing the **Shakespeare Hotel** with its resplendent black-and-white timbering, and then turn right into Sheep Street. Turn left on Waterside and then left again into Bridge Street. Walk ahead to Wood Street, towards the **American Fountain**, given to the town by George W Childs, a Philadelphia journalist, in 1887 (Queen Victoria's Jubilee Year) and unveiled by Henry Irving, who read a specially composed poem by Oliver Wendell Holmes. Turn sharp right – a U-turn, along Mier Street to Henley Street to the crossroads and sharp right again into Guild Street, noting on the right the gardens of the Birthplace. At the end of Guild Street bear right towards the bridge and so back to the car park.

MUSEUMS, GALLERIES AND PUBLIC BUILDINGS

Hall's Croft – Old Town, Tel 292 107. This 16th-century half-timbered house was the home of Dr John Hall who married Susanna, the poet's daughter. The rooms are furnished in the style of a middle-class Elizabethan home, with a garden which attempts to portray something of the formality of Shakespeare's day and at the same time create the atmosphere of a more homely garden, with familiar trees, flowers and shrubs. One of the rooms is furnished as an Elizabethan dispensary. Open Mar–Oct Mon–Sat 9:30–5pm; Sun 10:30–5pm and Nov–Feb Mon–Sat 10–4pm; Sun 1:30–4pm.

New Place and Nash's House – Chapel Street, Tel 292325. Shakespeare spent his retirement here, and died here in 1616. The house was demolished in 1759 and its foundations are preserved in a garden setting approached through the house of Thomas Nash, which is next door. Nash was the husband of

SHAKESPEARE'S BIRTHPLACE
STRATFORD-UPON-AVON

Shakespeare's granddaughter, Elizabeth Hall. Nash's House is now Stratford's local museum and has displays illustrating the archaeology and history of the area. Part of the site of New Place contains a replica of an Elizabethan knot garden, based on designs shown in contemporary gardening books. The square-shaped garden is divided by stone "knots" or beds. The Great Garden which leads from it was originally the orchard and kitchen garden belonging to New Place. Open as Hall's Croft.

Shakespeare's Birthplace – Henley Street. The shrine for Stratford visitors. Above the living room is the tiny bedroom where it is believed Shakespeare was born. It is simply furnished with a plain oak bed, a carved chest and a 17th-century cradle. The lattice window has its original glass with the signatures of Sir Walter Scott, Henry Irving, Thomas Carlyle and Ellen Terry among others scratched on it. It is still unnerving to think that the infant Shakespeare, "mewling and puking," grew to become the "whining schoolboy with his satchel and shining morning face creeping like snail unwillingly to school" in this very place. And that then, as a lover he "sighed like a furnace" and made a "woeful ballad" to Anne Hathaway's eyebrow. The house is entered through the modern Shakespeare Study Centre and has changed little since the days when the bard's father, John, plied his trade as a glovemaker here. There is also a museum with records illustrating the history of the house as well as furniture, pictures and books, including a First Folio of Shakespeare's plays published in 1623. At the rear of the house is the Shakespearean Garden. A stately cedar of Lebanon holds pride of place, surrounded by trees, plants, herbs and flowers mentioned in Shakespeare's works. Open Mar–Oct weekdays 9–5:30; Sun 9:30–4pm and Nov–Feb weekdays 9:30–4; Sun 10:30–4pm.

Anne Hathaway's Cottage – Cottage Lane, Shottery, Tel 292100. The cottage is situated about a mile from the centre of the town, left of the Alcester Road (A422) or right of Evesham Road (A439). This thatched, half-timbered cottage was the home of Shakespeare's wife, Anne Hathaway, before her marriage. It was originally a farmhouse and the earliest part dates from the 15th century. Most of the present furnishings belonged to the Hathaways, whose descendants lived here until 1892, but other 16th- and 17th-century furniture has been added. Open same times as Shakespeare's Birthplace.

Mary Arden's House – Station Road, Wilmcote, Tel 293455. Mary Arden's House is a mile off the main Stratford to Birmingham Road (A3400), three and a half miles (5.6 km) from the town centre. The house was the home of Shakespeare's mother before her marriage. Continued occupation by farmers until 1930 ensured its presentation in, substantially, its original condition. The rooms contain 16th- and 17th-century farm furniture and domestic utensils of the period. There is also a Shakespeare Countryside exhibition which illustrates the traditional rural life and farming methods of the district with an emphasis on country crafts, which are demonstrated from time to time. Open same times as Hall's Croft.

The five properties described above are all under the control of the Shakespeare Birthplace Trust. For further information Tel 204016.

Brass Rubbing Centre – Avonbank Gardens, Tel 2927671. The circular building in which the centre is housed was once the conservatory of a house, now demolished, that was the home of Charles Edward Flower, the local brewer who built the first Memorial Theatre. Open April–Oct daily 10–5pm and Mar Sat and Sun only.

Arms and Armour Museum – Sheep Street, Tel 293 453. The museum houses a collection of mostly European weapons, armour and accoutrements. The earliest gun dates from circa 1380 and the development of firearms is shown from this time to the present century. The image of medieval warfare is provided by suits of armour, helmets, maces, bows and crossbows. There is a remarkable collection of weapons belonging to the Sultan of Tipu. Open daily 9:30–5:30pm.

Stratford-upon-Avon Motor Museum – 1 Shakespeare Street, Tel 69413. The museum, housed in a converted Methodist chapel and Victorian school hall, specializes in cars of the 1920s and 1930s. Examples of the more distinguished makes and models are displayed in settings which recapture the atmosphere of a golden age of style and engineering in the automobile world.

Teddy Bear Museum – 19 Greenhill Street, Tel 293160. In an original Elizabethan setting, hundreds of teddy bears from around the world, including some of the oldest, most valuable and most unusual on earth, jostle for attention. Open daily 9:30–6pm.

The World of Shakespeare – Waterside, Tel 269190. Travel back in time to the authentic atmosphere of Elizabethan England – 25 life-size tableaux combined with light and sound techniques bring the period vividly to life. Performances on the half hour every day of the week. Open daily 10–5pm.

Harvard House – High Street. The house was built in 1596 by Thomas Rogers, an alderman of the town. His daughter married Robert Harvard of Southwark and it was their son, John Harvard, who founded the American university of that name.

Holy Trinity Church – Old Town, Tel 66313. An avenue of limes leads to the door of the church - 12 on the left representing the tribes of Israel and 11 on the right for the faithful apostles, with a 12th tree set back representing Mathias, who took the place of Judas. It was here in 1564 that John and Mary Shakespeare brought their son to be baptized and it was here in 1616 that he was laid to rest. His simple gravestone, set in front of the altar, bears the inscription:

> Good friend, for Jesus' sake forbear
> To digg the dust enclosed here
> Bleste be ye man yt spares thes stones
> And curst be he yt moves my bones

The words are said to be Shakespeare's own. On the chancel wall is a statue of the poet erected by his family in 1623 and therefore, probably a good likeness. He wears a dark red doublet and black sleeveless tabard and holds a quill in his right hand. The quill is, and always was, real. The Latin inscription below the bust reads "In justice a Nestor, in wit a Socrates, in art a Virgil." His wife Anne and his daughter Susanna are also buried in the church. Holy Trinity also possesses a stained glass window which links Old Testament characters to the Seven Ages of Man described in *As You Like It*.

THEATRE

Stratford is the headquarters of the Royal Shakespeare Company. The RSC operates two theatres, the **Royal Shakespeare Theatre** and the **Swan Theatre**, Tel 295623. There is also a third theatre, the **Other Place**, in Southern Lane which was opened in 1974 to make possible the production of contemporary plays in a workshop setting. Due perhaps to the company's financial difficulties of late, the theatre has not been in operation since the opening of the Swan in 1986. Ask at Box Office. Each season there are five new productions of Shakespeare's plays at the **Royal Shakespeare Theatre**. Visiting companies present drama and musical events at both theatres in February and March between the Shakespeare seasons. The **Swan Theatre** is set within the shell of the Memorial Theatre which was destroyed in 1926. It has a Globe-like auditorium and thrust stage and resembles the theatre of Shakespeare's day. Besides the plays of Shakespeare, the Swan presents work by contemporaries of Shakespeare such as Marlowe and Jonson and also the work of modern playwrights. Backstage tours give fascinating insight into the way the theatre works and include an Aladdin's cave of costumes, props and stagecraft. Tel 296655.

The **RSC Collection** has props, costumes, pictures and historical exhibits. Open weekdays 9:15–8pm; Sun noon–5pm. From Nov–Mar daily 11–4pm.

MUSIC

Stratford is a small town and what musical events there are take place in the Shakespeare Memorial Theatre or the Civic Hall, Rother Street, Tel 414513. Visitors have included pianist Peter Donohue and the Birmingham Symphony Orchestra. The excellent facilities of the Warwick Arts Centre (see Warwick) and Symphony Hall, Birmingham (see Birmingham) are only a few miles away.

CINEMA

There is no commercial cinema in Stratford. Leamington (eight miles/12.8 km) has the **Regal**, Portland Place, Tel 0926 426106 and the **Robins**, Newbold Terrace, Tel 0926 334418.

BOOKSTORES

The best is inevitably **Waterstone's** at 18 High Street, Tel 414418. There are book bargains at **Booksale**, 13 Waterside, Tel 298489 and books on religion and philosophy at **Jubilate Christian Bookshop**, 55 Ely Street, Tel 298351. There's also a branch of **W H Smith** at 4-5 High Street, Tel 292134. That's about it – Stratford really is a small town.

ANTIQUARIAN AND SECONDHAND BOOKS

Robert Vaughan – 20 Chapel Street, Tel 205312 has a good stock of antiquarian and out-of-print books as well as maps and prints and is the best in town. Also worth a visit is **Chaucer Head Bookshop** at 21 Chapel Street, Tel 415691 and **Anticus - BDC Books**, 59 Ely Street, Tel 266950, both with general second-hand collections.

ART GALLERIES

The following antique dealers have some pictures and prints and you'll find them fully listed in the antiques section below – **Bow Cottage Antiques**, **Burman Antiques** and **Ferneyhough**. Apart from that, the only ones I can recommend are the **Loguens Gallery**, the Minories, Rother Street, Tel 297706, which has a good stock of late 18th- to early 20th-century watercolours and oils, **Peter Dingley Gallery**, 8 Chapel Street, Tel 205001, with work from Britain's leading contemporary artists and craftspeople and **Pickwick Gallery**, 32 Henley Street, Tel 294861, which specializes in antique maps and prints, but also has limited edition prints, oils and watercolours.

ANTIQUE DEALERS

First the antique markets: **Stratford Antiques Centre**, Ely Street, Tel 204180, is one of the biggest antique markets in the country with 50 dealers (opposite the Shakespeare Hotel). The **Antique Market**, 4 Sheep Street, has 14 dealers and includes jewellery, silver, furniture, books, toy soldiers and lace. Of special interest for me in the antique market is **Bow Street Antiques**, Tel 297249, with 18th-to-19th-century porcelain, 18th-to-20th-century glass and English silver and oils, watercolours, engravings, maps and general antiques and **Rosemary Antiques and Paper Moon Books** with pottery, porcelain, small furniture (late 19th century to 1940) and Victorian poetry and illustrated children's books, Tel 297249. Stay on Sheep Street and at No 40 you will find **Abode** situated in the Shrieve's House, Tel 268755. They have furniture, pine and interior design items while close by, at No 41 is **Jean A Bateman**, Tel 298494 – very nice with Victorian and Georgian jewellery, objets d'art and vertu, including scent bottles. Finally on Sheep Street at Polt's Arbour is **Arbour Antiques**, one of the few I've found who deal in arms and armour. If this is your interest you should also call **James Wigington** at 293881. He is at 276 Alcester Road, and besides arms and armour he deals in cannons, early fishing tackle and general antiques. He is open by appointment. With your back to the river, walk up Sheep Street to the crossroads. Turn left and you will find yourself on Chapel Street. At No 5A is **Burman Antiques**, Tel 293917. They have furniture, pictures, prints, maps, silver, porcelain, brass, copper and clocks, while at No 11 is **Ferneyhough**, Tel 293928, with mahogany furniture, pictures and works of art from the 18th to early 19th centuries. Walk back down Chapel Street through the crossroads into High Street and then across Bridge Street into Union Street where at 6C can be found **La-di-da**, period interior decorators offering some architectural items. Retrace your steps and at Bridge Street turn right. This becomes Wood Street where at 44A you will find **Howard Jewellers**, Tel 205404 with a good stock of 19th-century jewellery, silver and objets d'art. Coming into the Market Place, turn left onto Rother Street where at Shop 2 in the Civic Hall Shopping complex you will find **Jazz**, Tel 298362, which has art deco ceramics, lighting, jewellery and furniture. Finally, return to the Market Place and turn left onto Greenhill Street where at No 7 is **Arden Antiques**, Tel 267067, with copper, brass, metalware, Victoriana, curios and small furniture. You'll find them next to Safeway.

RESTAURANTS

I've been very fond of **Sir Toby's** for a long time, perhaps because he was one of my best roles, but more probably because the food at this tiny restaurant at 8 Church Street, Tel 268822, is so good. It's conveniently placed for the theatre and you can save a lot of hassle by coming straight out of the matinee and waiting there till the evening show. The restaurant is strong on smoked meat and fish as they do it themselves and the smoked salmon is excellent. There is an Oriental touch to some of the cooking and ginger is liberally used. Bravely, they don't serve chips, as they don't consider them real food. Open Mon–Sat for dinner only 5:30–9:30pm.

I once played a theatre season where the nearest food was prepared by catering students. Rehearsing all afternoon after duck à l'orange and crème brûlée is a problem, but I have no doubt at all that the best food value in Stratford is at the **South Warwickshire College Training Restaurant**, The Willows North, Alcester Road, Tel 266245. Under the watchful eyes of tutors, this restaurant, though not romantically named, is enthusiastically run. The set lunch and dinner are both remarkable value and you get whatever meal the students are working on that day, which adds to the fun. Open Mon–Fri for lunch 12:15–1:30 and Mon, Tues, Thurs for dinner 7:30–9:30.

For a brief excursion away from the crowds, travel four miles (6.4 km) west on the A422 Alcester Road to Billesley. Here you will find **Bellesley Manor** which is a charming 16th-century mansion, Tel 400888. The cooking is excellent but don't expect bargains! One of the best tests of a good restaurant is that they do the simple things well. Here, for example, an avocado with smoked salmon mousse was delicious. The poached salmon even came with a champagne sauce which was also excellent. I prefer lunch here to dinner. Open all week 12:30–2pm and 7:30–9:30.

Slug and Lettuce – 38 Guild Street, Tel 299700. I know this should really be under the Pubs section, but the feel of the place is more like that of a bistro than a watering hole. Really interesting food with the dishes listed on the blackboard. There is a real international flavour to the cooking with, on the one hand, squid stuffed with rice, prawns and spinach; and on the other, black pudding with mustard sauce. An actor friend raved about the chicken breast with avocado and garlic. He eats there all the time and he looks very good on it. Open all week noon–2:15 and 5:30–9:15pm. Thurs–Sat open noon–9:15pm.

PUBS

Garrick – High Street, close to Town Hall, Tel 292186. The name originates from 1769 when the actor David Garrick visited Stratford and inaugurated the Stratford Festival. There are heavy wood beams, stone walls and sawdust on the floor. There's even a talking mynah bird. Good steak-and-kidney pie and game pie. Next door to Harvard House.

White Swan – Rother Street (leads into the A34), Tel 297022. During renovations, a 1560 wall painting of Tobias and the Angel was discovered behind the Jacobean panelling; the painting can still be seen. There are ancient oak settles, heavy beams and a handsomely carved fireplace. Good bar food with quiche, a daily hot dish and traditional puddings.

Black Swan – Riverside, Tel 297312. Known familiarly as the "Dirty Duck," the pub is in a lovely position with an attractive terrace overlooking the Riverside public gardens and handy for the Memorial Theatre. Lots of actors hang out here. Traditional bar food.

Shakespeare Hotel – Chapel Street, Tel 294771. The smart Trust House Forte Hotel occupies a lavishly modernized Tudor merchant house. The Froth and Elbow bar has settles and armchairs and is very comfortable. Bar food is good and there are some tables in the back courtyard for sunny days.

Queen's Head – Ely Street, Tel 204914. One of the few town centre pubs which is still a real local. Fewer tourists here and there's a real fire when the weather's cold. Traditional bar food and a really friendly atmosphere.

ARTISTIC ASSOCIATIONS

William Shakespeare's connection with Stratford has been fully documented elsewhere, but he was not the only artistic figure to have a relationship with the town. Washington Irving, the American essayist and historian, stayed in the town in 1818 and wrote about it in *The Sketchbook of Geoffrey Crayon*. His compatriot, Nathaniel Parker Willis, poet and playwright, stayed in Irving's room about ten years later. He reported how surprised the landlady was to discover she had been "immortalized" in Irving's book. Some of the artefacts Irving mentions in his story – his chair and the sexton's clock – can still be seen on the first floor landing of the Red Horse in Bridge Street where he stayed. Mrs Elizabeth Gaskell, the novelist and author of *The Life of Charlotte Bronte,* attended Avonbank School (demolished in 1866) which was near Holy Trinity Church. While at school she wrote an account of a visit to Clopton House, one mile north of the town, which was part of a school excursion. The writer William Howitt included the piece in his *Visits to Remarkable Places* and it thus became her first published work. The great historian G W Trevelyan, author of *English Social History,* was born at Welcombe House (now a hotel) in 1876 and May Mackay, who wrote romantic fiction under the name "Marie Corelli," settled at Mason Croft in Church Street which is now the Shakespeare Institute run by the University of Birmingham. A full account of her Stratford activities can be found below.

EPHEMERA

Marie Corelli (Mary Mackay) was born in 1855, the natural daughter of Dr Charles Mackay who encouraged her as a musician, a career she abandoned for fiction in 1886 with the publication of *A Romance of Two Worlds* after which, as they say, she never looked back. Her novels, sensation-seeking, ever so faintly naughty and full of half-baked metaphysics, attracted a strong following. The elderly Gladstone and Tennyson were among her fans, and Queen Victoria solemnly announced to an appalled Empress Frederick that she supposed Marie Corelli would be remembered when novelists like Dickens and George Eliot were forgotten. She is indeed still widely read in the Far East. Settling at Mason Croft in 1899, she became self-appointed doyenne of Shakespeareland, philanthropic but managing and litigious. Her enthusiasm for rescuing old buildings from development was not always welcomed, but Samuel Clemens (Mark Twain) appreciated her renovation of Harvard House which she persuaded an American, Edward Morris, to buy in 1908. He gave it to Harvard University in 1909. She was not only a romantic novelist but affected a romance-filled style herself. She drove Shetland ponies four in hand, until she replaced them with a Daimler, and her voluminous decolletage was one of the sights of the Festival. Her greatest extravagance was perhaps her full-sized gondola (imported from Venice), *The Dream,* in which she was transported up and down the Avon. Frequent complaints about her gondolier's lack of competence and a drunken argument in which he pulled out a knife seem to have brought this form of transportation to a close. Marie Corelli died at Mason Croft in 1924 and is buried in Stratford Cemetery.

Set in the grass by the gate leading from the Memorial Theatre into Southern Lane are the stones of an ancient game called nine-men's-morris, mentioned in *A Midsummer Night's Dream,* Act Two, Scene Two. ("The nine men's morris is filled up with mud.") The game itself consisted of an imperfect chess board cut out on the turf with the players involved in a cross between chess and draughts.

There's a persistent but unsubstantiated tradition that the young William Shakespeare was caught red-handed poaching deer from Charlecote Park, the home of Sir Thomas Lucy. From his writings it is clear that Shakespeare's knowledge of deer was considerable. He seemed to know more about driving deer into nets or shooting them with a crossbow than chasing them with dogs for sport. In *Henry VI, Part III,* he writes:

> Under this thick-grown brake we'll shroud ourselves
> For through this laund anon the deer will come;
> And in this covert will we make our stand,
> Culling the principal of all the deer.

From *Love's Labour's Lost* it appears that if he did poach deer he preferred to kill them outright with a crossbow rather than let them suffer:

Thus will I save my credit in the shoot:
Not wounding, pity would not let me do it.

And in *As You Like It* he describes the plight of an injured animal:

Under an oak whose antique roots peep out
Upon the brook that brawls along this wood
To the which place a poor sequest'red stag
That from the hunter's aim had ta'en a hurt
Did come to languish.

Shakespeare was aware that for the poacher the hunter was also the hunted, and the successful kill was accompanied by the thrill of outwitting the gamekeeper. In *Titus Andronicus* he writes:

What, hast not thou full often struck a doe
And borne her cleanly by the keeper's nose

Although Shakespeare reveals a thorough knowledge of poaching in his plays, there is no real evidence that he put that knowledge into practice, but taking into account the positions Shakespeare's father held in the town (he was mayor in 1568), perhaps the crime was hushed up. There is a reference in *The Merry Wives of Windsor* to "a dozen white luces." Luces were fish, pike in fact, and is it just coincidence that they appear in the Lucy family's coat of arms? The legend goes on to suggest that young Will was hauled before Sir Thomas Lucy who was not only lord of the manor but a magistrate as well. It is said that this was the reason for Shakespeare's sudden departure from Stratford and it is certainly more romantic than the idea that he left because of his father's imminent material and psychological collapse. The legend goes further: it is said that as an act of revenge, Shakespeare caricatured Sir Thomas Lucy as Justice Shallow in *Henry IV Part II* and made him the laughing-stock of London's playhouses. It is also reported that the Lucy family were so annoyed that in their library copy of *The Merry Wives of Windsor*, they tore out the offending pages relating to their family coat of arms. To go even further, some rather scathing lines about Sir Thomas, which would further support the poaching theory, are attributed to Shakespeare:

A Parliament Member, a Justice of Peace,
At home a poor scarecrow, at London an ass;
If lowsie is Lucy, as some folks miscalle it,
Then Lucy is lowsie, whatever befall it.

I make no judgement as to the veracity of the story, you :m:st decide for yourself.

Shakespeare is also said to have composed a satirical epitaph on a neighbour, John Combe, who died in 1614 and is buried in Holy Trinity Church. Despite the charitable bequests recorded on his tomb, he was locally unpopular as a money-lender. We think Shakespeare was resident in Stratford in 1614 so he would have known of Combe's death and perhaps penned the following verse:

Ten in the hundred lies here engraved
'Tis a hundred to ten his soul is not saved;
If any man asks who lies in this tomb
Oh! Oh! quoth the Devil, 'tis my John-a-Cobbe.

TOURIST INFORMATION BUREAU: Bridgefoot, Stratford-upon-Avon, Warwickshire, CV37 6GW. Tel (0789) 293127

WARWICK

County of Warwickshire
From London, 99 miles (158 km) by M1/M45
Train to Leamington Spa, 2 hours from London (Paddington); then bus to Warwick

Warwick is one of the least spoiled county towns in England. It stands on a dominant position overlooking the River Avon, and this was the reason for its early importance. One of King Alfred the Great's daughters built a fortress here to ward off attacks from the Danes, and by the time of the Norman Conquest, Warwick was a regal borough of some importance. Like Northampton, Warwick suffered a terrible fire in the 17th century (1694) which burned more than 250 dwellings; most of the town had to be rebuilt. Castle Street contains some of the most delightful pre-1694 houses. Note especially the building housing the Doll Museum (Thomas Oken's House). Most famous of all the remaining medieval houses is Lord Leycester's Hospital by the Westgate in the High Street. Founded in 1571 as a retirement home for his aged retainers by Robert Dudley, Earl of Leicester (a favourite of Queen Elizabeth), the hospital is set among a group of timber-framed buildings dating from 1383. The fine galleried Guildhall was originally used as private chambers for business meetings by the guilds of the Holy Trinity and Our Lady; the chapel is still used by the retired soldiers who live in the building – 12 "bretheren" and a "master" who still wear traditional Elizabethan dress on occasion. The kitchen and great hall of the building are also still in use as, respectively, a restaurant and a place for wedding receptions, dinners etc. Other houses of the period worth seeing are Tinker's Hatch, at No 105 High Street, and Tudor House, in West Street.

When Warwick was rebuilt after the fire, the buildings reflected the power of the wealthy burgesses. The Court House in Jury Street was built between 1725 and 1728. It has a Doric-colonnaded façade of rusticated stone and a statue of Justice. It houses the Museum of the Warwickshire Yeomanry. The one-storied pedimented Shire Hall in Northgate Street was built in 1753. It has a fine coffered and stucco ceiling. The Old Market Hall in the Market Place dates from the 17th century and survived the great fire. It has housed the town's museum since 1835. Note that the arches on the ground floor were once open. Landor House in Small Street was the birthplace of the poet and essayist Walter Savage Landor. The building is now part of a girls' school. Other examples of this remarkable period of reconstruction are Eastgate House in Jury Street and the Pageant House, which is late Georgian. See also St John's House (Museums below). The lovely Church of St Mary stands on one of the highest points in Warwick, and with its 174-foot (53 m) tower, it is a dominant architectural feature of the town. It was built on the site of an early Norman church, and although the nave and aisles were destroyed in the fire, the crypt, chancel and south transept still give some idea of the splendour of the original building. The crypt suggests it supported an enormous building, and the chancel's soaring roof is a perfect example of the vision of Perpendicular architecture. The tomb of Richard Beauchamp (the Earl of Warwick, who figures in the story of the burning of Joan of Arc) is one of the most beautiful in Europe. There are also impressive tombs to the memory of Ambrose, the first Earl of Dudley (he was given the vacant title by Queen Elizabeth I) and of his brother, Robert – in fact, this Beauchamp chapel is incomparable. The restored Chapter House contains a monument to Sir Fulke Greville, the Elizabethan poet, who was counsellor to both Queen Elizabeth and James I and who was born in Warwick.

In stark contrast to St Mary's is the old Friends' Meeting House in the High Street. Built by the Quakers in 1695, it still has its original simple furnishings and is still used for worship. Warwick Castle must compare favourably with any of the great fortress houses

THE CASTLE AND RIVER AVON, WARWICK

of Europe. In my view it is the finest medieval castle in England and the main reason for visiting Warwick. Although much of the present building dates back to before the 13th century, the outlines of the original keep, circa 1068, can still be seen. The outstanding features are Caesar's Tower, the Gatehouse, Guy's Tower, which is 128 feet (39 m) high, and the South Range which housed the living quarters and is dramatically set above the winding river. The Great Hall must be seen, so too the State Dining Room. The library was carefully restored after a fire in 1871. There is a fine collection of classical paintings and the magnificent gardens were laid out by Capability Brown in 1753.

WALK

Warwick Walk – Start from Castle Lane car park off Castle Hill. Turn right into Castle Hill. On the right by the crossroads is **Mill Street** with fine Tudor houses. Cross Castle Hill and go left down St Nicholas Church Street for **St John's House**. Cross the road and turn sharp left down Smith Street to the 15th-century **East Gate**. Continue ahead to Jury Street with its fine houses and note the **Court House**, then turn right into Church Street. **St Mary's Church** is ahead on your right. At the church turn right in Northgate Street to **Shire Hall**. Turn left in Barrack Street and left again into Market Place for the **County Museum**. Just off the Market Place is Swan Street with superb buildings, mainly Tudor. Leave the Market Place by Market Street and bear left in Bowling Green Street. At West Gate turn left into High Street for **Lord Leycester Hospital**. Continue along High Street and turn right into Back Lane, then left into Castle Lane for the **Warwick Doll Museum** in Oken's House. Cross the road to the **Castle** and when you have visited it return to Castle Lane and the car park.

MUSEUMS AND GALLERIES

Lord Leycester Hospital – High Street, Tel 491422. See Introduction to Warwick above. Open Easter–Sept Mon–Sat 10–5:30pm; Oct–Easter Mon–Sat 10–4pm.
St John's House Museum – Smith Street, Tel 4916543. The building dates from 1546. Of especial interest are the reconstructions of a Victorian classroom, parlour and kitchen. There are some good costumes. On the upper floor is the museum of the Royal Warwickshire Regiment. There is a comprehensive display of uniforms and medals, etc, from the 18th century onwards. There is also a collection of memorabilia of Field Marshal Viscount Montgomery. Open Tues–Sat 10–12:30pm. (May–Sept Sun 2:30–5pm as well.)
Warwick Castle – Castle Lane, Tel 495421. See Introduction to Warwick above. The castle is now owned by Madame Tussaud's which accounts for the re-creation, with costumed lifelike figures, of "A Royal Weekend Party" in the former private apartments. The State Room and Great Hall contain memorabilia of Elizabeth I, Queen Anne, Bonnie Prince Charlie, Oliver Cromwell and Marie Antoinette. Open daily Mar–Oct 10–5:30pm; Nov–Feb 10–4:30pm.

Warwick Doll Museum – Oken's House, Castle Street, Tel 495546. The House was the home of a Tudor mercer (one who has a shop for silks, woollens, linens and cottons) Thomas Oken, circa 1573. Bequeathed to the town by a 16th-century benefactor, the house now contains a comprehensive collection of mainly 18th- and 19th-century dolls, doll's houses, prams, toys, children's books, puzzles and miniatures. Open Mar–Nov daily 10:30–5pm; Dec–Feb Sat and Sun 10:30–5pm.

Warwickshire Museum – Market Hall, Market Place, Tel 493431. The museum's collection reflects the natural history of Warwickshire. It is especially strong on geology. Note the giant plesiosaurus fossil and the celebrated Sheldon tapestry map made circa 1650. Open Mon–Sat 10–5:30pm. (May–Sept also Sun 2:30–5pm.)

Warwickshire Yeomanry Museum – The Court House, Jury Street, Tel 492212. The museum presents the history of Yeomanry from 1794 to 1968. There are swords, uniforms, firearms, paintings and a wide range of campaign relics. Open Good Fri–Oct Fri–Sun 10–1 and 2–4pm.

THEATRE

As Coventry is only nine miles (14.4 km) away, refer to the **Belgrade Theatre** and the **Warwick University Arts Centre** under Coventry.

MUSIC

As well as the fine music programme outlined under the **Warwick University Arts Centre** (see Coventry, Music), the **Warwick Arts Society** sponsors a series of string quartet concerts. Details Tel 410747.

The **Warwick Festival** (early July) is usually thematic in nature. Previous festivals have focused on Handel, Bach, Weber, Liszt and Prokofiev. Visitors have included the London Mozart Players and Jane Glover, the Academy of St Martin-in-the-Fields, the Endellion String Quartet, Judi Dench and Raphael Wallfisch. There is a Fireworks Concert and a Shakespeare production in Warwick Castle and many other musical, dramatic and visual arts events. Tel 410747 for details.

CINEMA

The nearest cinema to Warwick is the **Regal Cinema**, Portland Place, Leamington Spa, Tel Leamington 426106. Of greater interest is the extensive film programme offered by the **University of Warwick Arts Centre**, Tel Coventry 524524. In the past they have had series on popular Indian cinema, the Spanish director Pedro Almodovar, modern horror films and the Italian master, Pier Paolo Pasolini. They operate seven days a week and often have two showings an evening.

BOOKSTORES

The best is **John Gould**, 9 High Street, Tel 492904. A real small-town bookshop with a good stock and excellent service. **John Menzies**, Tel 492318, has a branch at 37 Market Street, mainly for your newspaper and stationery needs.

ANTIQUARIAN AND SECONDHAND BOOKS

The best, and it really is excellent, is **Duncan M Allsop** at 26 Smith Street, Tel 493266. It's one of the largest bookshops of its kind in the Midlands and has seven rooms of rare and secondhand books.

ART GALLERIES

I think the most comprehensive and best is **Eastgate Fine Arts** at 6 Smith Street, Tel 499777. They reflect a lot of my interests: they specialize in maps dating from the 17th century, and they have original engravings, including a good selection of Warwick prints. They also have 19th- and 20th-century paintings and an extensive range of posters; they even mount occasional exhibitions. What more could you ask?

If you are interested in contemporary art, then the **Warwick Gallery** at 14 Smith Street is a good place to try. Tel 495880. The other art gallery is more traditional but certainly worth a visit; **Mason Walt's Fine Arts** is at 60 Smith Street, Tel 403160.

ANTIQUE DEALERS

Warwick antique dealers are mainly located in the High Street, Smith Street and West Street. The High Street is especially rich in offerings. A large selection of good quality pieces can be found at **Dorridge Antiques**, the **Antique Centre**, High Street, Tel 499857. They are close to **Warwick Antiques**, where the browser will find a large and interesting selection including clocks, chandeliers and garden furniture at 16/18 High Street, Tel 492482. Also close by is **Helen Brady** at 20/22 High Street, Tel 491382, whom you should also not miss. Finally in High Street, there's **Russell Lane Antiques** at 2/4, Tel 494494, which specializes in antique and modern jewellery and silver but also has porcelain, pictures and furniture.

Next, West Street and West Rock: **Apollo Antiques** at 20 West Rock, Tel 494746, and **Chris Rhodes** close by at 19 West Rock, Tel 492079, are both worth a visit. Chris Rhodes also has some books and will send your purchases anywhere in the world. On West Street you will find **Patrick and Gillian Morley**, 62 West Street, Tel 494464. They have an elegant showroom and a very large stock of 17th-, 18th- and early 19th-century furniture, works of art and decorative items. They should not be missed. Also on West Street, at No 28, is **Westgate Antiques**, Tel 494106. They have some period furniture but they really specialize in antique silver and if your interest lies here you should not miss them. The Smith Street area gives you **Smith Street Antique Centre** at No 7, Tel 497864. They specialize in glassware, jewellery, silver plate, porcelain and militaria and their stock is eminently packable. At No 68 is **Antiques and Collectables**, Tel 401828, a good general collection with some bric-à-brac.

Of course there are some dealers who don't fit neatly into this three-street pattern. The best of these is **James Reeve**, Tel 498113, at 9 Church Street – very elegant and some lovely pieces. **Martin Payne Antiques** at 30 Book Street, Tel 494948, is also worth a detour and **Warwick Desks** at 33 Saltisford, Tel 494666, specializes in what the name suggests, and have some lovely pieces on view.

RESTAURANTS

I think the best restaurant in town is **Fanshaw's**, 22 Market Place, Tel 410590. I ate at a restaurant in Kenilworth where the owner of Fanshaw's was chef before moving to Warwick and he knows all there is to know about cooking. The restaurant is a nicely converted shop with flowers, chintz and a cottage atmosphere. The atmosphere is friendly and there are British favourites on the menu such as steak and kidney pie, as well as more adventurous dishes such as tandoori-style chicken in puff pastry and beef filet with green peppercorn sauce. There are good vegetarian choices and a wonderful homemade apricot ice cream for dessert. Open Tues–Sat 11:30–2 and 6–10pm.

Very close to Fanshaw's but totally different in cuisine is the **Jolshah Tandoori** at 20 Market Place, Tel 491797. They serve good Indian food and I advise you to try the chef's daily special. You may need to book ahead on weekends. Open evenings only, all week 6–12:30pm.

The **Aylesford** – 1 High Street, Tel 492799, is an elegant, intimate cellar restaurant offering both a table d'hôte and à la carte menu. Cuisine is classical French and there is an excellent wine list. Open 12–2:30 and 7–10:30pm. It's best to book.

PUBS

Zetland Arms – Church Street, Tel 491974. Originally a bakery, the Zetland Arms is a historic pub with beamed ceilings built after the great fire. Very good traditional pub food at lunchtime and early evening. They also have rooms which are very inexpensive.

Saxon Mill – Guys Cliffe (just north of town on A429) The centrepiece here is the great wheel turning slowly behind glass and the mill race rushing under a glass floor panel – though it hasn't worked as a watermill since 1938. Nice, rambling, cottagey rooms with beams and flagstones. Lots of brass, books and open fire-places. Standard range of bar food. Picnic tables on a terrace and fine views of the Avon weir.

The Barn – St Nicholas Church Street. Very good bar food in converted barn with beams, exposed brick-work and flagstones. They have sewing machine trestle tables with candles and fresh flowers, old farm tools and stripped wood chairs. Tables in the courtyard and a nice restaurant. Even the pub part has a restauranty feel. I really like it.

ARTISTIC ASSOCIATIONS

Walter Savage Landor, poet and essayist, was born in Warwick in 1775 and lived at Landor House in Smith Street. Landor wrote his best work, *Imaginary Conversations*, in Italy, where he lived for a good part of his life. Fulke Greville was born in 1554 at Beauchamp Court near Warwick, and was made first Baron Brooke by James I in 1620. He wrote over a hundred sonnets and two tragic plays; his *Life of Sir Philip Sidney* is still read. Richard Corbett, the English poet (Bishop and Dean of Christ Church, Oxford, and Bishop of Norwich) met Fulke

Greville at Beauchamp (the house has gone) and it is likely Sir Philip Sidney, the poet, was also a visitor. Greville, incidentally, was assassinated by a servant who thought himself excluded from Greville's will, proving that life in 17th century Warwick was not *all* beer and skittles. He is buried in St Mary's (see introduction to Warwick above). John Masefield, poet laureate from 1830 until his death in 1967, was a boarder at Warwick School for Boys from 1888 to 1890. He first began writing poetry at this time.

EPHEMERA

Warwick is the home of Guy of Warwick, a legendary knight of great size, who became a hermit. There is a wonderful verse romance of the early 14th century which tells of his exploits against the giant Colbrand, the monstrous dun cow and the winged dragon – it's stirring stuff. He is commemorated at Guys Cliffe (one mile/1.6 km north) by a 15th-century chantry erected by Richard de Beauchamp, Earl of Warwick, who claimed to be a descendant, and by a statue erected in 1964.

Just ten miles east of Warwick on the A425 to Daventry is Napton. Here you will find a fascinating museum called the Nickelodeon, Tel 092681 2183. Long before the invention of radio and television, many mechanical devices existed for producing live music without the need for musicians. These instruments thrilled audiences in the home, on the streets and in cafés and theatres. There are barrel organs, one-man bands, mechanical violins, player pianos and (the flagship of the collection) a Compton cinema organ that once graced the orchestra pit of the Hammersmith Regal and is now installed in a replica of the picture house of the 1930s. You can watch newsreels and silent films accompanied by the organ, and recapture the sadly lost heyday of the neighbourhood cinema. Open to individuals on Bank Holidays and the last Saturday of each month, but you can also join group tours. Telephone for details.

For a touch of historic realism, you can enjoy a medieval banquet at Warwick Castle. Focused around the theme of the Battle of Agincourt, which was fought on the eve of St Crispin's day on October 24, 1415, the evening offers food and jesters much like those Richard Beauchamp, Earl of Warwick, enjoyed all those years ago (although your meal will be much cleaner; medieval cooks were not fastidious). The menu is usually a barley broth flavoured with sherry, braised mutton ribs, roast fowl, lemon syllabub and fresh fruit. You can wash this down with red or white wine, and you get a beaker of English mead as a starter. You *must* book in advance. Telephone Warwick Castle at 495421 for details.

After the Battle of Edgehill in 1642, a Cromwellian dragoon corporal named Jeremiah Stone came to the Anchor Inn (gone) with a bag of money he had pillaged from the dead. Being wounded himself, he entrusted the bag to the landlord, but when he recovered, his host denied all knowledge of it and threw him out of the house. The soldier drew his sword and tried to break down the door, whereupon the landlord had him arrested for attempted burglary. While he lay in prison, the soldier was visited by the Devil, who offered to act as his attorney when the soldier came to court. The offer was gratefully accepted and, next day, in pleading Stone's cause, the Devil suggested to the court that the inn might be searched to settle whether the money was there or not. The landlord denied stealing the money and wished that the Devil might take him if he told a lie. The Devil promptly obliged, "seized upon his body and carried him over the Marketplace, nothing left behind but a terrible stinke." This story is vouched for in a broadsheet published in 1642, which states, "This is the truth, John Finch (a shoemaker) in St Martin's being an eye witness doth testify the same."

The Shire Hall offers as comprehensive a reminder of medieval justice as any that can be found in the country. Beneath it is a dungeon, shaped rather like an underground beehive. In a circle on the floor are eight posts, each with a ring through which a chain was passed. The chain was then threaded through the manacled legs of the unfortunate prisoners. The chain continued up the stairs, through an inner door and was then padlocked to the wall outside. You can still see the grooves the chain made as it rubbed against the steps. In the centre of the posts was a drain, which not only served as a primitive form of sanitation, but had the additional use of draining away the water when the dungeon flooded, which it did quite often. The prisoners themselves were often packed in so tightly that there was only room for them to lie on their sides. It's impossible to see the dungeon without giving an involuntary shudder at the plight of the poor wretches condemned to exist in this inhuman way.

In the Saltisford area of the town you will find a white, elegant, beautifully restored building, now used for offices, which has an impressive central block and two diagonal towers. Unbelievably, in the early 19th century these towers were gasholders for the town's gas supply, and are in fact England's oldest surviving gasholders.

TOURIST INFORMATION BUREAU: The Court House, Warwick, Warwicks CV34 4EW. Tel (0926) 492212

WORCESTER

County of Hereford and Worcester
110 miles (176 km) from London by M40 to Oxford/A40 to the M5/M5 to Worcester
By rail, 2 hours from London (Paddington)

Worcester was well established as a settlement as early as the 9th century, although there had been first an Iron Age settlement, then a Roman encampment on the site in earlier times. By 1070 a castle and a cathedral were in existence, although both were destroyed by a fire in 1113. Medieval Worcester does not seem to have had the best of luck, as it was sacked and burned again in 1139 and, just after Richard I granted Worcester's first Royal Charter in 1189, there was yet another disastrous fire. Henry III granted the city his Royal Charter in 1227 and this permitted the establishment of both a guild of merchants and a guild-hall. During the Middle Ages, Worcester was a great religious centre with the cathedral shrines of St Oswald and St Wulfstan, the cathedral monastery, at least three friaries, and four hospitals. Part of Greyfriars still exists. In the Middle Ages iron-smelting was the city's main industry but when this ceased the cloth trade took over, with gloving in particular gaining great importance. Queen Elizabeth visited the city in 1575, during a slump in the fortunes of the cloth trade, and she endowed the Free School as a Grammar School. Much later, in 1889, Queen Victoria granted the school its "Royal" appellation and the Royal Grammar School still exists today in a building dating from the end of the 19th century.

Worcester reached the height of its fame during the Civil War of 1642–1651. Early in the nine-year conflict, Charles I won an important battle at Worcester, which enabled a gift of plate from Oxford University to reach the Royal Mint at Aberystwyth. The battle was not a large one but it was significant in that, had the Parliamentarians captured the plate, the Royalist cause might well have petered out for lack of money. The victory was a mixed blessing in that it allowed the bloody conflict of the Civil War to continue for another nine years. Worcester was in fact a Royalist city from 1642 until 1646 when the defeated Charles I placed himself in the hands of the Scots. Even though Parliament ordered all Royalist strongholds to surrender, Worcester held out till the last and only surrendered after a siege of two months. Between 1646 and 1651 there was an uneasy peace in England. Charles I was beheaded in 1649, and in 1651 Charles II marched into England at the head of an

WORCESTER CATHEDRAL AND CRICKET GROUND

Anglo-Scottish army, having declared himself King of Scotland in 1649 at Edinburgh. The mayor of Worcester proclaimed Charles King in August of 1651 and Charles set up his Court in the city. The Bishop's Palace and the Deanery were requisitioned by troops and the Royalist batteries were set up in the grounds of the Commandery, from which vantage point the King's Commander, the Duke of Hamilton, directed operations. The decisive battle of the Civil War was fought in the vicinity of Worcester in 1651. Against Cromwell's army of 30,000 men, Charles could muster only 16,000, but in spite of this the fortune of war fluctuated between the two sides until on September 3rd, Charles, realizing that further resistance would be hopeless, rode away from the city for the last time. The Civil War was over and Charles and his mainly Scottish army were fugitives. During the battle at Worcester, 3000 of the Royalist army died and 10,000 were captured.

Although the various battles of the Civil War had left Worcester battered, its position as a commercial centre for a large area aided its recovery and by the end of the 17th century and the beginning of the 18th great rebuilding had been done and prosperity had returned. Many fine buildings date from this period. Of special interest is the Guildhall: Worcester's allegiance to the Royalist cause is marked by the statues of Charles I and Charles II that stand in niches flanking the entrance. In not so kind a manner, a stone head, said to be that of Cromwell, appears nailed by the ears above the doorway. The Great Assembly Room inside is decorated in Queen Anne style and in summer tea can be taken in the room to the tinkling of a piano in the best Palm Court tradition. Open all year Mon–Fri, some Sats. Tel 723471.

Other notable buildings dating from this period are St Nicholas's Church, St Swithin's, All Saints, and St Martin's Cornmarket. The spire of St Andrew's Church, nicknamed "The Glover's Needle," was erected in 1751. Many new Non-conformist chapels were built and John Wesley personally opened the new Methodist Chapel in New Street in 1772. Other buildings to visit include Greyfriars (all that remains of a Greyfriars friary) Tel 23571; the Commandery, used by Charles II and his generals in 1651 but originally a 15th-century hospital, Tel 355071, and of course, Worcester Cathedral, begun in 1084. The cathedral suffered under Victorian restorers but it is a magnificent building and its position, high above the town, dominates the surrounding countryside. It is interesting to note that the grounds of the Worcestershire Cricket Club, which are situated across the river from the cathedral, are considered the most beautiful in the country and touring cricket sides from the Commonwealth always open their tours on the ground against the county side.

Today, Worcester is well known artistically for its Three Choirs Festival (see below) and its association with its most famous son, the English composer, Sir Edward Elgar. The Royal Worcester Spode porcelain factory (see below) is still in operation in the city and Worcester sauce really has been made in the city by Lea & Perrins since 1837. The historic craft of glove-making still continues and this most loyal of cities seems set for an exciting passage into the 21st century.

Other buildings of especial interest are Countess of Huntingdon Hall at Deansway, Edgar Tower in Edgar Street, the Shirehall in Foregate Street, St Helen's Church in Fish Street, Laslett's Almshouses in Friar Street, King Charles' House and John Nash House in New Street, Berdeley's Hospital in The Foregate and Queen Elizabeth House in the Trinity.

WALK

Worcester Walk – Begin at the Cornmarket car park, off City Walls Road on the A38. Cross the Cornmarket into New Street. On the left is **King Charles House**, where Charles II briefly took refuge after the Battle of Worcester in 1641. Note should also be taken of the old **Pheasant Inn** and **Nash's House**, built by a 16th-century cloth merchant. Continue into Friar Street. On the corner with Pump Street you will see the **Eagle Vaults Public House** which is adorned with splendid Victorian tiling. As you walk down Friar Street, **Greyfriars** is to your left and a little further on, the **Tudor House Museum** on your right. Friar Street becomes College Street, so bear left, past City Walls Road into Sidbury. At the end, just across the river, is the **Commandery**. Retrace your steps and turn left off Sidbury into Edgar Street. Ahead of you is **Edgar Tower**, the 14th-century gateway to **Worcester Cathedral**. Turn left off Edgar Street into Severn Street, where you will find the **Dyson-Perrins Museum** with its superb collection of Royal Worcester china. Continue to the bottom of the street and then turn right along the riverside walkway. A gateway and steps lead into the Cathedral. After visiting the Cathedral, continue along the riverside path through South Quay and South Parade to Worcester Bridge. Cross the bridge into Bridge Street and soon turn right again into Quay Street, bear left into Copenhagen Street which is dominated by the spire of St Andrew's Church, known as "The Glover's Needle." Cross Deansway and turn left into the bustling pedestrian precinct of High Street. Note the **Guildhall** and next door, the Tourist Information Office. High Street becomes The Cross. Just before you turn right into St Nicholas Street, note the imposing bank building in cream-coloured stone. As you walk down St Nicholas Street you will see the Georgian **St Nicholas's Church**. Turn right into Trinity Street. On the corner is **Queen Elizabeth House**. Turn left into Mealcheapen Street and back to the car park.

MUSEUMS, GALLERIES AND PUBLIC BUILDINGS

Worcester City Museum and Art Gallery – Foregate Street, Tel 2<371. The Natural History Gallery uses the Severn Valley as its central theme, while there is a good display of the Stone Age history of Worcester. There is a wonderfully complete and authentic recreation of the interior, furnishings and stock of a late-19th-century chemist's shop. The Art Gallery has changing monthly exhibitions and visiting regional and national exhibitions. The Museum also houses the collections of the Worcester Regiment and Worcestershire Yeomanry Cavalry. Open 9:30–6pm (5pm Sat). Closed Thurs and Sun.

Tudor House Museum – Friar Street, Tel 20904. A 16th-century timber-framed building (some original "wattle and daub" constructions can be seen) serving as a setting for displays showing aspects of domestic and social life in Worcester from Elizabethan times. A very interesting children's room. Open 10:30–5pm. Closed Thurs and Sun.

The **Commandery, or Hospital of St Wulfstan** – Sidbury, Tel 355071. Originally a medieval hospital for the care of the sick and poor, circa 1085, although the surviving buildings date from 1460–70. The building served as the Royalist headquarters during the Civil War and played a vital role in the Battle of Worcester in 1651. A wide-screen multi-projector show lets you relive the battle in glorious colour. Open 10:30–5pm Mon–Sat; 2–5pm Sun.

Greyfriars – Friar Street. Once the great house of the Franciscan Friary, the building dates from 1480. A fine example of a town house of its period with early fireplaces, panelling and other features. Open 2–6pm Wed and Thurs, April–Oct.

Dyson Perrins Museum – Severn Street, Tel 23221. Housed in a former Victorian school, the museum offers the world's largest collection of Royal Worcester porcelain. Take note of the giant vase made for the Chicago Exhibition of 1893 (called the World's Columbian Exposition in honour of the 400th anniversary of Columbus's voyage). Tours of the modern factory give visitors an opportunity to see how Royal Worcester is made today. Open Mon–Fri 9:30–5pm; Sat 10–1 and 2–5pm.

The **King's School** – College Green, Tel 28854. There was probably a monastic school at Worcester in the 7th century. The present school was founded in 1541 by Henry VIII after the suppression of the Priory. The refectory of the Priory has been used almost continually by the school since its foundation. Dating from 1141–42, it was partly reconstructed during the 14th century. Note also *Edgar Tower,* which contains the school library. College Hall is open by arrangement with the steward during summer holidays. College Green is open all the time.

Elgar Birthplace Museum – Lower Broadheath, Tel 0905 66224. The countryside around Worcester was the inspiration for much of Elgar's music and the modest county cottage in which he was born, and which he never tired of visiting, has at his own wish been established as his memorial and houses a unique collection of manuscripts, scores, concert programmes and memorabilia. The cottage garden is a delight and the atmosphere of the house retains something of the spirit of this most gentle of men. Open 10:30–6 (May–Sept) 1:30–4:30 (Oct–April). Closed Weds and mid Jan to Mid Feb.

THEATRE

Worcester has a long theatre tradition. Although theatrical performances were banned in the city for part of the 17th century, a play, *Oedipus, King of Thebes,* was performed in the yard of the now vanished King's Head, in the High Street, which served as Worcester's theatre until the opening of the **Theatre Royal** in Angel Street in 1780. Sarah Siddons, then Sarah Kemble, actually played there at the age of 12 in 1767. The Theatre Royal closed in 1945 to be replaced with the **Swan Theatre**. Situated on the edge of the racecourse, the theatre has a main auditorium of 353 seats plus a studio theatre for smaller productions. Two companies use the theatre; the professional Worcester Repertory Company presents fortnightly rep for 34 weeks of the year whilst the Swan Theatre Company, an amateur group, also provides regular productions. Visiting companies providing ballet, opera and concerts fill out the year's programme, and there is also a Youth Theatre. The theatre has a restaurant, which serves good and interesting food and is open all day. Recent productions have included Farquhar's *The Recruiting Officer,* an adaptation of Henry Fielding's *Tom Jones,* and a most exciting production of *Our Country's Good* by Timberlake Wertenberger, which is set in 1789 Australia and concerns the efforts of a young lieutenant to produce *The Recruiting Officer* (the first play ever staged in Australia) with a cast of convicts. Conditions are hardly ideal, as one of his cast may be hanged at any moment! Box Office Tel 27322.

Worcester Arts Workshop – A community arts centre, 21 Stansome Street, Tel 21095. A variety of artistic activity takes place at the centre including children's activities and a regional centre for dance. Tel 21095.

MUSIC

The most significant musical event of the year takes place during the **Three Choirs Festival** in late August. The festival rotates between Worcester, Gloucester and Hereford. It is Europe's oldest music festival, dating back to at least 1722; it was attended by George III and his family in 1788. Over the years it has commissioned a number of great works and played host to virtually all of England's greatest musicians. In Worcester in 1990, festival visitors included the BBC Philharmonic, the Royal Liverpool Philharmonic, Simon Preston, the Alberni String Quartet and the Hanover Band. There is also a Three Choirs Festival Fringe, Tel 21095, which stages alternative events.

During the year many musical events take place in the **Countess of Huntingdon's Hall**. Built in 1804, the hall captures the atmosphere and architecture of early-19th-century urban evangelicalism. Sir John Betjeman, the poet, wrote in 1964, "The hall is a unique Georgian gem both inside and outside." Concerts of all kinds are held here, ranging from individual artists, chamber music, orchestral concerts, folk and jazz. Tel 611427.

Over 50 years after his death, Sir Edward Elgar is universally recognized as a composer of the first rank. He was born in Lower Broadheath, three miles (4.8 km) west of Worcester, and spent a good deal of his life in the city. The **Elgar Trail** allows visitors to follow the great man's footsteps around the area. Tel 723471.

CINEMA

The **Odeon** in Foregate Street has three screens. Tel 247733.

BOOKSTORES

The most comprehensive is **Sherratt and Hughes** at 95 High Street, Tel 72397, although I have a special fondness for **Worcester Other Book Shop** at Unit 11, The Hopmarket, Tel 29660. The **Midlands Educational Co** at 51 High Street, Tel 21358, sells more than educational books while **SCCK** at 105 High Street has a wider stock than its raison d'être as a Christian book shop might suggest. Finally **W H Smith** can be found in the High Street, Tel 723624.

ANTIQUARIAN AND SECONDHAND BOOKS

Two of the best are **Andrew Boyle** at 21 Friar Street, Tel 611700, and **David Lloyd** at 26 George's Square, Tel 20920. Both have a wide stock with some rare and antiquarian volumes. Around the Tything area of the city you will find a small shop with my favourite name. **Abookortwo** at 6 The Tything, Tel 20816, while **Holbourne Books** is at 47A Upper Tything, Tel 27824.

ART GALLERIES

There is not a wide choice with respect to the visual arts in Worcester itself. Practically the only place worth a glance is the **Framed Picture Gallery** at 46 Friar Street, Tel 28836, which has some interesting prints. Apart from that, the A449 is your best bet! Eight miles (12.8 km) north of the city at Ombersley is the **Ombersley Galleries**, Tel 620655, while two miles (3.2 km) south of the city on the same road is **Ham Martin**, Sandpits Farm, 25 Colletts Green Road, Tel 830029.

I have a sense that one would be better employed paying a visit to **Lowesmoor Wharf**, Tel 611889, in the city, which is a canalside development comprising 20 craft workshops depicting a variety of "craft" used in a traditional manner. On Sundays many antique market stalls spring up and the setting and atmosphere are most pleasant.

ANTIQUE DEALERS

There are three main areas in the city of interest to collectors. At **Lowesmoor Wharf** is the **Vesta Tilley Antiques, Arts and Craft Centre** (see Art Galleries). The centre is housed in a large, imposing building some 150 years old, originally the site of an old Victorian inn. It was rebuilt in 1864 as the Worcester New Concert Hall and Vesta Tilley, a famous music hall artist and male impersonator, performed there. She was born in Worcester, and later spent her retirement in the city. As music hall declined, the building was taken over by the Salvation Army – rather an apt and fitting change I think – and remained a place of worship until 1984.

The second interesting area of the city is The Tythings. **Antiques of Worcester**, Tel 611323, is at No 48 and has a wide and comprehensive collection of general antiques with some very nice pieces. **Clive's Curios** are at the same address and telephone number. At 46 Upper Tything you'll find **Heirlooms**, Tel 23332, and at 50 Upper Tything is **Antiques and Curios**, Tel 25412, both general collection and bric-à-brac. Lastly for Upper Tything, there is **Derek Lines** at 50A who has a discriminating and well chosen selection. Sorry, I almost forgot **Meriden House Antiques** at No 41, Tel 29014. They are certainly worth a browse.

Finally, Sidbury Street will give you **Bygones of Worcester** at No 55, Tel 23132 (they also have a branch called **Bygones by the Cathedral**, Tel 25388, in the Cathedral Square). Both shops have a good and comprehensive general collection. At No 61 is the **Antique Map and Print Gallery**, Tel 612926, where you can be certain to find both local and national view prints and engravings. I like their shop a lot.

Apart from these main areas there are two shops in the Barbourne suburb. **Antique Warehouse**, Tel 274493, on Alma Street and **Gemma Antiques** at 316 Barbourne Road. Both general collections. If you want clutter and fun, try **Antiques in St John's** at 17 Bromyard Road, Tel 427796 and **B Browning and Sons** at 35A Wyldes Lane, Tel 355646. In the centre of town you would expect things to be more elegant and you'll certainly find elegance at **Christy's of Worcester Antiques**, Tel 29544, at 14 Bridge Street. Also elegant in their own way are the two shops on Friar Street, **Cottage Antiques** at No 17 and **Friars Gate** at No 19.

RESTAURANTS

I've always enjoyed **Brown's** at 24 Quay Street, Tel 26263. Maybe it's because the ambience of this converted cornmill is so pleasing, or perhaps it has something to do with the view of the county cricket ground where one can imagine the brilliance of Ian Botham and Graham Hick in full flower. (Ask anyone in Worcester about them.) Less fancifully, it's probably because of the food, which is simple, healthy and imaginative. I can recommend both the langoustine and bacon kebabs with a light curry mayonnaise and their excellent spring lamb. If their caramel and meringue parfait is on, order it. It's deliciously sinful and so packed with calories it will take you the first taste to convince yourself it's really good for you and that the scales in the hotel bathroom were out of whack. Service is efficient and relaxed but the prices do tend to reflect the excellent quality of the cooking, which is as it should be. Open all week 12:30–1:45pm and 7:30–9:30pm. No Sat lunch or Sun dinner.

Friends tell me that the cooking at **Ye Olde Talbot Hotel**, Friar Street, Tel 23573, is quite acceptable, especially at Sunday lunch. The Talbot is one of a number of carefully restored coaching inns operated by Whitbread's, the brewers, so you can be sure the bitter is in topnotch condition.

At 111-113 Sidbury Street is **McTaffish**, Tel 350816, a fun fish restaurant with a neat decor. Excellent fish and chips. New, and as far as I'm concerned, unproven, is **Fownes Resort Hotel**, City Walls Road, Tel 61351. Interestingly, the site of the hotel was formerly the centre of a thriving glove manufacturing business and the architecturally imposing Victorian building has been transformed with luxury and elegance in mind. Formal dining is in the very elegant King's Restaurant, and there's also Tilley's Brasserie, which celebrates Worcester's very own Vesta Tilley (see above). Reports to me about Fownes would be useful.

If you want to get close to the stage you could do a lot worse than to eat at **Café Encore** which is upstairs at the Swan itself. Café Encore is not your bangers-and-mash restaurant. Last time I was there I had a delicious pheasant and orange casserole for a ridiculously low price. What's more, the restaurant overlooks Worcester Racecourse, so you can even watch the ponies go through their paces while you eat. Swan Theatre, Tel 611223.

Santini's – Severn Terrace, Tel 612300. Santini's is a traditional Italian restaurant. One thing, apart from the food, that makes Santini's a delight is that it is situated by the entrance to the theatre car park and serves pre- and after-theatre meals.

Heroes – 26-32 Friars Street, Tel 25451, is a bistro set in a delightful 16th-century Tudor building. The restaurant serves a wide range of Continental and English dishes. If you are going to the Swan Theatre and if you present two tickets for an evening performance and order two courses (one being a main course), Heroes will present you with a free bottle of house wine.

Just a note to say that there are a number of pubs below which offer excellent cuisine.

PUBS

Farrier's Arms - Fish Street, off High Street just north of Cathedral, Tel 27569. Excellent food (it received an award from Alisdair Aird, the guru of Britain's best pubs). Black beamed bars with not only traditional soups, pies and ploughman's, but more exotic offerings such as hummus with hot pita bread and brown rice nut risotto. I did sample their treacle tart (flavoured with lemon and ginger) before the theatre one day and pronounced it excellent. (I slept through half the first act.) Open for food 12–2pm and 3–9pm.

Ombersley is about eight miles (12.8 km) north of Worcester on the A449. The Sandys family have been in Ombersley since 1560 and the village breathes much family history. The quality of the village may be judged by the fact that it has 20 listed buildings of special historic or architectural interest. (Do seek out the Georgian rectory and the charity school built in 1729.) Besides its historical and architectural interest, Ombersley is renowned for one other thing. It has, within a stone's throw of each other, two excellent and highly recommended hostelries.

King's Arms – Tel 620142. Charles II is reputed to have made this comfortable and popular Tudor pub his first stop when he was on the run after the Battle of Worcester – hence his coat of arms all over the place. Black beams, timber and lots of bric-à-brac in a delightfully rambling setting. Excellent food (it has an Aird award) Greek shepherd's pie, lamb kebab, pheasant casserole and if that's not enough, a wonderful Sunday lunch. Open for food 12–3pm and 7–11pm all year.

Crown and Sandys Arms – Tel 620252. Similar to the King's Arms in decor with a partly flagstoned floor. Very strong on soups and wonderful veggies. Other delights include dressed crab, pancakes filled with

Stilton, walnuts and broccoli and stir-fried beef. Seasonal log fires and the locals play dominoes and crib-bage and I'm sure will let you in if you buy them a pint.

Back in town, the **Little Worcester Sauce Factory**, Tel 350159, on the London Road about half a mile from the centre is great fun. The food has a Japanese influence – sushi and sea spinach soup – and the decor, majoring on sauce bottles, is flamboyant to say the least. And who could resist the delicately named **Slug and Lettuce** at 12 Cornmarket, Tel 28362, which has good value traditional food and very well kept draught beer.

ARTISTIC ASSOCIATIONS

Near the cathedral is the city's oldest church, St Helen's, which is now the Diocesan Registrar's Office. The office holds the bond of 1582 pledging two Stratford-upon-Avon men to ensure the marriage of one William Shagspere (Shakespeare) and Ann Hathway (Hathaway). The document is on show and photocopies can be purchased. Samuel Butler, the satirist, who wrote *Hudibras* and Samuel Foote, the wit, playwright and actor, were both pupils at King's School (see above) circa 1620 and 1730 respectively.

Izaak Walton, the writer famous for *The Compleat Angler,* lived at Hartlebury Castle (10 miles/16 km north of the city) where he was Bishop Morley's (of Worcester) steward. Walton wrote the inscription on the tablet in the cathedral's Lady Chapel commemorating the death of Morley's wife. After a list of the good lady's virtues comes the anguished aside, "Alas, that she is dead." Also in the cathedral are tablets commemorating three local novelists: Mrs Henry Wood, although born in the city (she was Ellen Price, the daughter of a glover) rarely returned after leaving at the age of 20. Many of her novels though, use the city, which she disguises as "Helstoneleigh," as their background. One of her best known books, *Mrs Halliburton's Troubles,* is about glove-makers. Mary Martha Sherwood spent most of her life in the neighbourhood with the exception of the years with her husband's regiment in India. The last volume of her popular moral saga, *The Fairchild Family,* was written while she was living in Britannia Square. Finally, many of the novels of Francis Brett Young are set in Worcester. His ashes were interred in the cathedral.

EPHEMERA

Tradition has it that it was during Queen Elizabeth's visit to Worcester in 1575 that the city acquired a second coat of arms, that of the three black pears. It is said that during the Queen's "walkabout" she saw a pear tree, laden with enormous fruit, which had been planted in the Foregate in her honour. She was so pleased with the appropriateness of such an ornament in the city in the centre of a fruit growing area that she bade the city add the emblem of pears to its arms. Whether or not this story is true, the city, in 1634, had both coats of arms registered, and so it has been ever since – the three black pears existing besides the older coat of arms – "A quarterly sable and gules over all a castle triple lowered argent." That's heraldic language but you can see both coats of arms in many places in the city. Incidentally, members of the County Cricket Club wear the three-pears coat of arms on their sweaters.

Worcester sauce really is made in Worcester. The famous thin brown liquid has been produced in Worcester since 1837, when chemists John Wheeley Lea and William Perrin prepared a recipe believed to have been brought back from India by Lord Sandys, former governor of Bengal.

Berrows Newspapers Ltd are located in Hylton Road. Their newspaper, the *Worcester Journal,* was established in 1690 and is now the oldest newspaper in the world. An evening tour, lasting about an hour and a half, is available, giving the opportunity to see the printing of a newspaper from start to finish. The tour operates on Wednesday and advance notice is preferred. Tel 748200.

Two miles south of Evesham (10 miles/16 km) is Ashton-under-Hill. Nestling under

Bredon Hill, the village has, after some years of speculation, been acknowledged as the model upon which "Ambridge" of the long-running radio series "The Archers" is based.

In Ombersley, which I have already mentioned, there is at the central crossroads, on a little green, a large rectangular trough of solid stone known as the "Plague Stone." It formerly stood at the edge of Ombersley, and in the 14th century, at a time when the plague of the Black Death swept the area, the "Plague Stone" acted as a place of exchange. Traders, reluctant to enter the village for fear of disease, would deposit their wares in the stone after collecting coins placed there by the villagers.

In medieval times, two old women lived in Castle Street, which was then called Salt Lane. They were white witches and made their living by freeing the carts which regularly became stuck in the mud outside the hovel in which they lived. For a sum of money, one of them would come and stroke the cartwheels and bless the horse, after which the cart would roll away easily, however heavy its load and however deeply its wheels were stuck. One day a waggoner came by carrying a load that was so light he knew there was little risk of his cart becoming stuck. He was wrong. Just outside the witches' cottage the wheels sank in the mud and no attempt of pulling could shift them. As usual one of the women came to the door and started bargaining over the price to be paid for freeing the cart. As they argued, the waggoner noticed the witch had placed a long piece of straw over the horses' shoulders. It occurred to him that this might be the source of the witches' power so he cut the straw in half with his knife. The witch immediately let out a bloodcurdling scream, his wagon became free and as he raced away down Salt Lane he saw, lying in the mud, the body of the witch, which he had severed in two.

Stories abound of the second witch. She is supposed to have turned a captain and his troop of soldiers into stone when they came to Worcester to collect taxes. It was said the petrified figures used to stand alongside the Tything, now the A38 which runs through the city. A local merchant once tried to break the spell and free the petrified figures, but when one of them turned into an enormous horse and reared up at him, he fled the town in terror.

TOURIST INFORMATION BUREAU: The Guildhall, High Street, Hereford and Worcester, WR1 2EY. Tel (0995) 726311

7

EAST MIDLANDS

LEICESTER
NORTHAMPTON
NOTTINGHAM

LEICESTER

County of Leicestershire
97 miles (155 km) from London by the M1
87 minutes from London (St Pancras) by hourly inter-city express trains

Leicester owes much of its history to its geographical situation. It is, in fact, in the centre of England. The Romans came to Leicester as they built the Fosse Way from Exeter to The Wash. Ratae Coritanorum, as the Romans called Leicester, can still be seen in the shape of the Jewry Wall in St Nicholas Circle. This well-preserved length of Roman wall had no defensive purpose; it formed one side of the wall of the exercise hall of the public baths. Although there is little evidence of them, the Roman baths at Leicester were the largest in England, and formed part of an extensive forum and shopping area. The Jewry Wall Museum is on the site.

The hub of the city is the Clock Tower, a Gothic structure erected in 1868 to commemorate four benefactors of Leicester since the Norman Conquest. The most famous was Simon de Montfort, Earl of Leicester, who, as one of the most powerful barons in England, forced Henry III to establish the first English Parliament in 1275. The others, William Wigglestown, Sir Thomas White and Gabriel Newton, all founded schools or charitable institutions in the city.

The original Leicester Castle dates from 1088, but the red brick frontage, added circa 1690, has diminished the grandeur of the original concept. The Great Hall in Castle Yard, which was once part of John of Gaunt's country residence, is now the Assize Court. The hall itself dates from 1140 to1160 and the roof of braced beams which span the whole

THE CLOCK TOWER; LEICESTER

ceiling is particularly imposing. A few yards away is the new work, or "Newarke,"as it is known today, a walled enclosure of about four acres (1.6 ha) in which stood the noble Collegiate Church of St Mary, founded by Henry, Earl of Leicester and Lancaster in the 14th century. The finest monument of the Newarke is the high stone gateway on the east side, with three arches, a vaulted canopy and ornamented square-topped windows.

The beautiful church of St Mary de Castro in Castle Street is well worth a visit. From completely Anglo-Saxon beginnings, the church was rebuilt by succeeding Earls of Leicester. The pinnacled tower and the belfry were begun in the 13th century and the slender spire was added a hundred years or so later. Of especial interest are the five sedilia or priests' seats and the superb 700-year-old font. St Nicholas Church, St Nicholas Circle (end of High Street) goes back through Saxon times to the Roman period. It is the oldest church in Leicester. When the diocese of Leicester was re-established in 1926, the natural choice for the cathedral was the civic church of St Martin in St Martin's East (by the Guildhall). Although much restored, the graceful old arches and rich decorations of the interior remain and the bishop's throne is magnificent. The Guildhall itself, in Guildhall Lane, was built in the 14th century as the Hall of the Corpus Christi Guild. It later became the Town Hall and was extensively altered so that today the building is essentially Tudor. The superb Great Hall is open to visitors and should be seen. The Abbey in St Margaret's Way was founded in 1143 and was of great importance in medieval times. It was here in 1530 that Cardinal Wolsey died; his tomb can still be seen. At the dissolution of the monasteries it was demolished, but the Earls of Huntington built a mansion on the site, which in turn was destroyed during the Civil War. The ruins of both the Abbey and the mansion can be seen in Abbey Park. Also in St Margaret's Way is St Margaret's Church. Originally part of the stipend of the Bishop of Lincoln, the church dates from the 13th and 15th centuries.

Two hundred years ago the only industry in Leicester was the making of hosiery, then, during the Industrial Revolution, the bulk manufacture of boots and shoes became impor-tant. Today the majority of Leicester's people are employed in engineering.

WALK

Leicester Walk – Set off from the multi-storey car park in St Nicholas Circle. Take the footbridge to **Jewry Wall**. Return and walk down St Nicholas Circle to St Augustine Road. Note beyond the bridge, to your left, the **Great Hole of Leicester**, a brick structure whose upper half once stood above the city's vegetable market. **Bow Bridge**, close by, has the arms of Richard III on the side. Cross the road and turn right through **Castle Gardens**, walk along parallel to the Grand Union Canal and by the castle mound is a magnificent bronze statue of Richard III. Turn left out of the gardens and follow The Newarke to **Newarke Houses Museum**. Retrace your steps and turn right into Castle View and go through **Castle House** gateway. Close by is **St Mary de Castro Church**. Turn left into Castle Street and right into St Nicholas Circle. Cross Southgates and you are in Peacock Lane; turn left into Applegate for **Wygston's House**. Turn right into Guildhall Lane for **Guildhall**, then right into cobbled St Martin's West and St Martin's for the **Cathedral**. Turn left along St Martin's, then right into Hotel Street. St Martin's Square Shopping Centre is close by as is the Tourist Information Bureau. Turn left into Market Place and continue through the market to the **Corn Exchange**, then left along Cheapside to the **Clock Tower**. Just along the Haymarket is the **Haymarket Theatre**. Turn left into High Street and immediately left again into Silver Street. Note the **Silver Arcade** and then turn right into Carts Lane and back into High Street. Turn left and then right into Highcross Street and the 16th-century, old **Free Grammar School**. On the left, on a factory wall, a plaque marks the site of Blue Boar Lane where, in the Blue Boar Inn, Richard III spent the night before riding out to the Battle of Bosworth Field and his death. Come back to the High Street, turn right, cross Vaughan Way and return to the bridge to the car park.

MUSEUMS AND GALLERIES

Jewry Wall Museum of Archaeology – St Nicholas Circle, Tel 541333. A brick-and-flint Roman Wall towers over the foundations of a large bathhouse. The wall has nothing to do with Jews, the name is a corruption of Jurat – a medieval councillor. There are some fine mosaics in the museum (look for the peacock especially). Open Mon–Sat 10–5:30, Sun 2–5:30pm.

Guildhall – Guildhall Lane, Tel 541333. Built in the 14th century, it was once the meeting place for the mayor and aldermen. It also served as a police station and the gibbet irons should be noted (see Ephemera). Open Mon–Sat 10–5:30, Sun 2–5:30pm.

Leicester Museum and Art Gallery – New Walk, Tel 554100. Has sections devoted to British and foreign natural history, minerals and paleontology (including an articulated dinosaur display.) An internationally celebrated collection of German Expressionist paintings can be seen and a collection of English and European paintings from the 16th century to the present day. There are also some excellent ceramics and a good display of English silver. Open Mon–Sat 10–5:30pm, Sun 2–5:30pm.

Leicestershire Museum of Technology – Abbey Pumping Station, Corporation Road, Tel 661330. The museum is housed in the late Victorian pumping station for the sewerage system of Leicester. It contains the original four-beam engines together with other steam engines and Steam Days are held five times a year. There is also a collection of horse-drawn and mechanical transport and a display illustrating the history of machine knitting.

Newarke Houses Museum – The Newarke, Tel 541333. Housed in a 16th-century chantry house and a 17th-century dwelling-house, there is a good social history collection of Leicestershire from 1500 to the present day, as well as hosiery, knitwear, toys, clocks and musical instruments. Open Mon–Sat 10–5pm, Sun 2–5:30pm.

Wygston's House Museum of Costume – St Nicholas Circle, Tel 541333. A late medieval building, housing displays of 18th–20th-century costumes. Open Mon–Sat 10–5pm, Sun 2–5:30pm.

Museum of the Royal Leicestershire Regiment – The Magazine, Oxford Street, Tel 541333. The Magazine was a 15th-century gatehouse to the Newarke which, at that time, was a walled area outside the town of Leicester. The displays include uniforms, weapons and medals, etc, relating to the Royal Leicester Regiment. Open Mon–Sat 10–5pm, Sun 2–5:30pm.

Belgrave Hall – Church Road off Thurcaston Road, Belgrave, Tel 541333. One and a half miles (2.4 km) on the A6 Leicester to Loughborough Road. Built 1709–1713 in fine grounds. Wonderful furniture in the drawing room with a "lion mark" suite of chairs (circa 1720) outstanding. Open Mon–Sat 10–5pm, Sun 2–5:30pm.

THEATRE

Haymarket Theatre – Belgrave Gate, Tel 539797. Opened in 1973 in conjunction with the modern shopping complex of the same name. The theatre seats 701 and it is a thrust stage design with the orchestra pit set into the thrust (an unusual feature). The Haymarket is a high-quality producing theatre with many of its productions transferring to London's West End. As well, the theatre welcomes touring companies such as the Rambert Dance Company. Recent productions have included *Little Shop of Horrors*, Shakespeare's *The Taming of the Shrew* and *Seven Brides for Seven Brothers*.

The Haymarket Studio is part of the same complex but seats only 130, giving an extremely intimate setting for productions such as *The Mystery of Irma Vep*, a stage adaptation of Oscar Wilde's *The Picture of Dorian Gray* and Edmund White's *Trios*. There's a coffee bar and a bistro-style restaurant.

Phoenix Arts Centre – Newmarket Street, Tel 554854. An independent trust created in 1979 to run the Phoenix Theatre and its associated buildings. The best films in Leicester can be seen here (see below). There is also dance – a celebration of South Asian Dance was recently held here; theatre, alternative theatre, storytelling and comedy; and music, which is mostly ethnic, folk and jazz.

Little Theatre in Dover Street, Tel 551302, is professionally managed and seats 347. It stages ten plays each season plus a music hall and a Christmas pantomime. Most plays are staged by amateur groups within the city.

De Montford Hall – off Regent Street, Tel 544444, is the largest-capacity venue in Leicester (2500 seats) and stages a variety of events from symphony concerts, brass bands, pop concerts and wrestling, etc.

MUSIC

The **Leicester Proms**, with a variety of visiting symphony orchestras, are held each June in the De Montford Hall. As well there are regular concerts throughout the year. Call box office for details.

The Leicester Bach Choir performs a series of concerts, mainly in **Leicester Cathedral**, between October and June, Tel 707396 for details. The Department of Music of **Leicester University** has occasional concerts on its campus in the middle of the city. Details, Tel 522522.

CINEMA

Commercial cinema at the **Odeon**, Queen Street, Tel 622892 (4 screens) **Cannon**, Belgrave Gate, Tel 624346 (3 screens) **Cannon**, Abbey Street, Tel 620005 (2 screens). Excellent cinema at **Phoenix Arts Centre**, Tel 554854. Recent thematic series have included the films of Pier Paolo Pasolini and a wonderful and eclectic selection of quality films from around the world.

BOOKSTORES

The best are **Dillon's** at 26 Market Street, Tel 212197, **Fagin's Bookstore** close by at No 27 Market Street, Tel 541468 and **Sherratt and Hughes** at 11 Horsefair Street, Tel 518997. The best for children's books is **Rhyme and Reason** at 22 Malcolm Arcade, Silver Street, Tel 624591. **Midland Educational** at 17 Market Street, Tel 555544, also has a good children's selection as well as adult books. For books on education, law, science, etc, **Leicester University Bookshop** on University Road, Tel 523456, and **Leicester Polytechnic Bookshop** on Mill Lane, Tel 548718, are both good. Discount books and publisher's remainders can be found at **Harvey's** at 12 Market Place, Tel 627729, while **Murray's** in the centre at 23 Loseby Lane is worth a browse, Tel 620360. Christian and religious books are best at **Christian Literature**, 43 Belvoir Street, Tel 558481 and **SPCK**, 68 High Street, Tel 626161. If you are interested in quality fiction, "green" books and women's studies, then **Blackthorn Books**, 70 High Street, Tel 621896, is your best bet. They also have a good collection of jazz records. If you've lost your way here in the centre of England then the **Map Shop**, 15 Malcolm Arcade, Tel 628077, will be able to help. Finally, if it's all too much and you want to get away in your imagination to fantastic places, then the Silver Street area, close to the Tourist Information Bureau, can help. Here you will find **The Final Frontier**, Tel 510775, at 43/44 Silver Arcade and **Another World** at 23 Silver Street, Tel 515266.

ANTIQUARIAN AND SECONDHAND BOOKS

There is a good selection in the city centre – Silver Arcade in Silver Street offers **Forest Books**, Tel 627171, at 41/42 (they also have sheet music). The **Black Cat Bookshop** at 37/38, Tel 512756 (they also have records) and **Century 2000 Books** at No 22, Tel 517034 (they specialize, not surprisingly, in science fiction and comic books). For antiquarian, as well as secondhand, I especially like **Maynard and Bradley** at 1 Royal Arcade (Silver Street end) Tel 532712. Their shop has the right kind of atmosphere and they also have prints. I also like **Edgar Backus** at 44–46 Cank Street, Tel 518137. Backus also has prints and engravings and does framing and binding (rare these days). Close to the junction of Charles and Belvoir Streets is **Harvey's Bookshop** at 90 Charles Street, Tel 533095. A comprehensive secondhand collection of some nice antiquarian books – well worth a browse. Finally, out of the centre of town – but not too far – are **Clarendon Books** at 144 Clarendon Road, Tel 701856 (closed Mon), and **Tin Drum Books** at 68 Narborough Road, Tel 548236.

ART GALLERIES

There's not a huge selection. **West End Gallery** at 31A Braunstone Gate, Tel 546546, has watercolours and prints, while the **Lighthouse Gallery**, Tel 510594, is slap bang in the middle of town and has a nice atmosphere. Apart from those your best bets are **Antique Pictures**, 202 East Park Road, Tel 734105, which sometimes has interesting stock and **Antique Galleries**, 3 Loseby Lane, Tel 628380, whose stock is also constantly changing.

ANTIQUE DEALERS

I'll deal with two of the best established first (convenience, not in order of rank!) **Withers of Leicester** at 142A London Road, Tel 544836, and **E Smith (Leicester) Ltd** at the Antiques Complex, 9 St Nicholas Place Tel 533343, both have large selections ranging from clocks to oil paintings and from music boxes to bureaux. I enjoyed, too, visiting **Architectural Heritage of Leicester** at 107 Highcross Street, Tel 515460. There are two antique centres which are worth a visit – **Churchgate Collectors Centre** is at 66 Church Gate, Tel 514839, and **Oxford Street Antique Centre** is at 16–26 Oxford Street, Tel 553006 (a big stock here). Another large stock can be found in the 4000-square-foot (372 m²) showroom of **Robert Neville Antiques** at Unit 4, Old Dairy, Western Boulevard, Tel 514201(day)/477159 (evenings). If you would like to see some beautiful antique fireplaces, call in at **Britain's Heritage**, Shaftesbury Hall, 3 Holy Bones, Tel 519592 (what a wonderful address), and if you're interested in pottery, porcelain and especially jewellery, then right in the middle of town at 36 Silver Arcade is **Julie's Antiques**, Tel 515291. Just room to mention three more with good general collections – **Curiotique** at 214 Narborough Road, Tel 825169, **Moores and Sons** at 89 Wellington Street, Tel 551402, and **Montague's Antiques** at 60 Montague Road, Tel 706485.

RESTAURANTS

Water Margin – 76–78 High Street, Tel 516422. Ask for the dim-sum and noodle menu. This is one of the few places that do dim-sum and one-plate dishes and they are excellent. It doesn't matter if you don't understand from looking at it what it is, go ahead and order it anyway. Cheerful and fun. Open noon–11:30pm. **Rise of the Raj** – 6 Evington Road, Tel 553885. Out of town a bit towards the suburb of Evington, this North Indian restaurant is strong on tandoori dishes. More unusual are the dishes cooked in a skillet, of which Karachi chicken is the best. Leicester has a large ethnic population and there are many restaurants which reflect that cosmopolitanism. Open all week 12–2pm and 6–11:45pm.

If you want Indian food in the town centre, try the **Curry Fever** at 139 Belgrave Road, Tel 511699. You may even want to sample Caribbean food at the **Rum Runner Creole Restaurant** (try a blackened Cajun dish) at Braunstone Gate, Tel 470318. For vegetarian tastes there is **Blossoms** at 17B Cank Street in the city centre, Tel 539535, and **The Hayrick** at 4 Churchgate, Tel 538585. If however, your taste runs to traditional English cooking, then I can recommend the **Old Bakery** on the Main Street at Countersthorpe which is just south of Blaby off the A426 (five miles/8 km), Tel 778777. There's homemade game pie and traditional puddings with real custard. Open Tues–Sun 12:15–1 :45 and 7–9pm. No Sat lunch or Sun dinner.

PUBS

Although it's out of the centre at 131 Beaumanor Road, the **Tom Hoskins**, Tel 681160, is worth a visit because it adjoins the Hoskins brewery. Not only is the beer top class but you can arrange to be shown round the late-Victorian brewhouse (Tel 661122). A traditional but limited menu of bar food can be sampled, but only at lunchtimes. In Charles Street in the centre of the city is the **Rainbow and Dove**. There's a brightly decorated open-plan bar with a wide range of bar food at lunchtimes only, Tel 555916. I think best of all, though, is the **Globe** in the centre of town on Silver Street. It has period features including gas lighting and original woodwork and it's very comfortable. Again reasonable food but at lunchtimes only – don't people go out for pub grub in Leicester in the evenings? The **Black Swan**,

Belgrave Gate, Tel 513240, is an old, daunting building surrounded by ultra-new offices yet steeped in history. It now has a complete Paris street scene in the bar and is used by actors appearing at the nearby theatre. Traditional bar food.

ARTISTIC ASSOCIATIONS

Six miles (9.6 km) north of Leicester on the B5328 is Rothley. The old manorhouse, home of the Babingtons from 1565–1845 (now the Rothley Court Hotel) was the birthplace in 1800 of Thomas Babington Macaulay, the historian and essayist, author of *History of England* and *Lays of Ancient Rome*.

Despite being such a young theatre (it opened in 1973) the Leicester Haymarket has a reputation for paranormal occurrences. In 1975, Brecht's *Caucasian Chalk Circle* was running in repertoire with *Joseph and the Amazing Technicolor Dreamcoat*. Perhaps because of the large number of children in the production, the Haymarket's resident ghost made its appearance. He is a small boy in an Edwardian sailor suit and he has often appeared to both actors and technicians. There is some speculation that in the 19th century there was a well at the back of the theatre that supplied a row of houses, long since destroyed. Local legend has it that a child drowned in this well but that it was the boy in the sailor suit is mere speculation.

Five miles (8 km) east of Leicester on the B674 is the small village of Twyford. At Burrough Court, an erstwhile hunting lodge close to the village, the then Prince of Wales met Mrs Wallis Simpson for the first time in 1930.

Of unusual interest is the lead casting practiced by Norman and Underwood of Freeschool Lane. The company was established 160 years ago and lead is cast just as it was in Roman times. The end product is used on buildings throughout the world, including Buckingham Palace. The works can be viewed by appointment, Tel 515000.

EPHEMERA

In 1485, on August 22, the Wars of the Roses between the Houses of York and Lancaster culminated in the Battle of Bosworth Field. Richard III, the last English king to die fighting in battle, lost his crown to the young Henry Tudor, who became Henry VII. The field of Bosworth can be visited (at Market Bosworth Battlefield Centre, Tel 0455 290429). There are battle trails marked out to show the position and movements of the opposing armies and the spot where Richard was cut down. Whether he uttered the immortal words, "A horse! A horse! My kingdom for a horse!" (*Richard III*, Act 5, Scene 4) I am sure is doubted by historians, but as Shakespeare said he did, it must be true! An exhibition hall brings the 15th century to life with dioramas, life-size tableaux and a display of arms and armour. Richard spent the night before the Battle of Bosworth in the Blue Boar Inn in Blue Boar Lane (a plaque marks the spot in Highcross Street opposite the old Free Grammar School). In the morning of August 20th, Richard rode out through Castle Street to battle with Henry Tudor. On August 22nd, the victorious Henry VII arrived, followed by the naked corpse of Richard thrown over a horse. Richard's coat of arms on Bow Bridge (in St Augustine's Road) recalls that the king passed this way twice (as a monarch and as a corpse.) Richard's body was placed on display in Newarke for two days and finally buried in Grey Friars Church, which was later demolished during the Dissolution of the Monasteries. The king's last resting-place is unknown, although at the destruction of Grey Friars in 1538, a mob was reported to have removed his bones and flung them from Bow Bridge into the River Soar. In the floor of the choir of Leicester Cathedral is a memorial tablet to Richard – one of the few memorials in England dedicated to this perhaps unjustly vilified king. There is, however, a magnificent statue of him in Castle Gardens.

Each October, Leicester hosts a Think Green Festival. Held in Granby Halls, Welford Road (Tel 552644), and other venues, the festival focuses on environmental issues with a film festival, live theatre and music performance, exhibitions, workshops, a schools festival and a large exhibition with over 70 stalls.

The East Midlands Gas Museum on Aylstone Road, Tel 549414, is fascinating. Housed in a fine example of a Victorian gasworks gate-house, the displays cover the history of gas distribution in the East Midlands and collections relating to domestic lighting, cooking and heating, For example, did you know that there were gas hairdryers, gas magic lanterns and even a gas-driven radio? Open Tues–Fri 12:30–4:30pm.

Gibbet irons were particularly gruesome devices whereby the body of a murderer or the like could be hung up for public view. There is a set preserved in the Leicester Guildhall. They were essentially an iron frame, in the shape of a man, into which the recently hanged corpse fitted. The last man to occupy Leicester's set of gibbet irons was one James Cook, who murdered a commercial traveller for his money, then cut up the body and attempted to burn it in his bookbinder's shop. Rashly, he went out while the remains were still smouldering and the chimney caught fire. He returned to find a crowd had gathered, attracted not only by the smoke, but by a strong smell of burning flesh. Cook claimed, optimistically I think, that he was merely cooking meat for his dog, but a doctor was called and identified the flesh as human. The murderer somehow made a run for it, got as far as Cheshire and was actually boarding a ship when he was caught. He was hanged before a crowd of 30,000 people in 1832 and left to dangle in the gibbet irons until, no doubt, his flesh was in even worse shape than that of his victim.

TOURIST INFORMATION BUREAU: 2–6 St Martin's Walk, St Martin's Square, Leicester, LE1 5DG . Tel (0533) 511300

NORTHAMPTON

County of Northamptonshire
65 miles (106 km) from London on MI
One hour from London by train (Euston)

Northampton is an ancient Anglo-Saxon town which, by the 8th century, had become an important centre for the ancient Kingdom of Mercia; it even had its own mint. Under the Normans the town grew in status, as it was halfway between the important northern and southern capitals of York and Winchester. For a while it was even the centre of government. Northampton's Norman Castle (now the site of the railway station) was a favourite of the royal family. In 1291, Edward I caused a decorated cross to be set up outside the town at Hardingstone to mark one of the resting-places of his wife's body on the journey from Harby in Nottinghamshire, where she died, to burial in Westminster Abbey; he built a cross at every place where the funeral cortege had stopped for the night. The Hardingstone Cross (recently restored) is one of only three that remain. In 1460, Henry VI was captured in Northampton by the Yorkists in one of the most important battles of the Wars of the Roses. During the Civil War the trade for which Northampton is now so famous – the manufacture of boots and shoes – became important, since Northampton shod most of Cromwell's army. After the Civil War in 1660, Charles II ordered the castle to be destroyed as Northampton had aligned itself firmly on the Parliamentarian side. In 1675 a disastrous fire burned down much of the town's medieval heritage. All Saints Church, in a square in the middle of town, was destroyed along with many other buildings. Charles II gave 1000 tons of timber for the rebuilding and his gift was later commemorated by a statue of him on the church's wide portico. Perhaps he felt sorry for ordering the destruction of the castle. To this day the statue is decorated with oak-leaf garlands on every 29th of May (his birthday), though what Charles would make of a representation of himself in full-bottomed wig and Roman tunic is hard to assess.

I am very fond of All Saints. By 1680 the church had been rebuilt; the portico was added in 1701 and the cupola in 1704. The west doors of the nave are richly carved and the nave is wonderfully handsome. There is a medieval crypt below the chancel but it contains the church's heating equipment and little can be seen of it. By the church, in George Row, is the Sessions House, a small attractive building with cherubs perched on its balustrade and a hipped roof. Opposite is the Guildhall, an ornate building in an architectural style best described as Venetian Gothic. It is surprising just how many churches of note there are in Northampton. At the bottom of Bridge Street is St John's, which was a hostel for travellers in the 12th century and an almshouse at the time of the Reformation. It is now a Roman Catholic Church with some good medieval windows. Hazelrigg Mansions in Marefair (a continuation of Gold Street which is at the top of Bridge Street) was built just prior to the 1675 fire, and survived it. Its original owner was a Cromwellian, Sir Arthur Hazelrigg, who died in the Tower of London. A little further along Marefair is St Peter's. It is Norman in style with massive buttresses on the exterior and a 17th-century squat tower. Interestingly, there is no chancel arch inside. Instead there is a range of fine Norman carvings and also a 14th-century font. St Peter's was also one of the buildings surviving the great fire. In Sheep Street is the interesting and unusual Church of the Holy Sepulchre, one of the four surviving round churches in England. It was built at the time of the crusades, and modelled on the Holy Sepulchre in Jerusalem. St Giles' Church, in St Giles' Street, is a 12th-century church rebuilt in 1616 after the original tower collapsed, virtually destroying it. There is a magnificent east window which is a fine example of Victorian glass painting. Robert Browne, founder of the Congregational Church, is buried in the churchyard. St Matthew's Church, on the Keltery Road, is an impressive landmark, having a 183-foot (55.6 m) spire. Consecrated in 1893, the church possesses two famous works of modern art. One is of Sir Henry Moore's controversial stone *Madonna and Child* and the other, Graham Sutherland's abstract painting of the Crucifixion. The church also has a long-standing musical tradition and it hosts an extensive programme of concerts. The church has also commissioned work by composers such as Benjamin Britten, Richard Rodney Bennett and, most recently, Malcolm Arnold. Finally on the clerical front is College Street Baptist Church in College Street opposite Swan Yard. The church was built in 1863 and its classical façade might be said to represent the ultimate in Victorian non-conformist "chapel" buildings.

The Market Square is believed to be the largest in England. It dates from 1235 when Henry III forbade the selling of goods in All Saints Churchyard and ordered the market moved to its present site. Markets are held every Tuesday, Wednesday, Friday and Saturday. Tuesday is books, records and antiques and the other three days offer mainly fruit, vegetables, flowers, clothes and dress-making materials. Bargains abound. There are many interesting buildings around the square. Welsh House, built in 1595, survived the fire and today is a china shop (a very good one). It is decorated with obelisks and heraldic shields on the front. It belongs to the days when the Welsh brought their cattle to the market. Animals were in fact penned and sold in the square and in the surrounding streets, hence *Sheep Street* and *Marefair*. Next door to Welsh House is the 18th-century Beethoven House, so called because it was thought to have been a music school. The great fire of 1675 started in the Market Square when piled up wood ignited. Welsh House was the only building in the square to survive and people fled through its gardens to escape the conflagration. Various shopping arcades lead off the square making it the shopping hub of the town. The Guildhall was built in 1864 by the 28-year-old Edwin Godwin. It has arched windows,

ROYAL THEATRE AND OPERA HOUSE
NORTHAMPTON

turrets, gables and a "chateau style" tower. Its architectural form is best described as highly exuberant Victorian. The Great Hall is cathedral-like and has a timbered roof, circular stained-glass windows and an enormous proscenium arch framing the stage.

Northampton grew from a population of 5000 people in the 18th century to 15,000 during the Napoleonic Wars, when craftsmen poured in to make army boots. By 1901, the population was 87,000. Over the last half century, light engineering and distribution have taken over from the traditional shoe-making as the major industry. In the 1960s the government decided the town should expand, mainly to house people from London. Today nearly 200,000 people live in the area.

WALK

The **Northampton Walk** starts from the Swan Street car park. Exit the car park and turn left onto St John's Street leading to Bridge Street and the **Museum of Leathercraft**. The statues on the building's façade are of Blue Coat boys, as the building was once a school. Turn right into Bridge Street with its old coaching inn, the **Angel**, and right again for **All Saints' Church**. Cross Mercers' Row and follow Drum Lane into the **Market Square**. Note **Welsh House**, circa 1595, and **Peacock Place**, a shopping arcade with Victorian-style ornate ironwork balconies. Recross Mercers' Row into Wood Hill and then turn left into **St Giles Square**. The ornate **Guildhall** is on your left. Turn right into Guildhall Road, and the Derngate Centre and the exquisite **Royal Theatre** of 1844. Opposite is the **Central Museum and Art Gallery**, in my view one of the most attractive small museums in the country. Visit the museum and then continue down Guildhall Street and turn left into Swan Street for the car park.

MUSEUMS AND GALLERIES

Central Museum and Art Gallery – Guildhall Road (opposite Royal Theatre) Tel 34881. The museum is particularly distinguished, possessing the largest historical collection of boots, shoes and shoe-making machinery in the world. There are Cromwellian boots, Elizabethan sandals, Queen Victoria's wedding shoes, the ballet shoes worn by Moira Shearer in the film *The Red Shoes*, and an outsize boot worn by an elephant in a 1959 reconstruction of Hannibal's crossing of the Alps. The art gallery contains 15th- to 19th-century European paintings and a considerable collection of works by 18th- to 20th-century British artists including John Crome, George Morland, Walter Sickert, John Nash and Burne-Jones. Open Mon–Sat 10–6pm.

Museum of Leathercraft – 60 Bridge Street, Tel 34881. The former Blue Coat School which houses the museum was built in 1812. There are displays of leather goods from early historical times to the present day. Special sections are devoted to gloves, costume, saddlery and leather wall paintings. Of special interest are a coracle, a 3500-year-old Egyptian loincloth, a collection of leather bottles and a leather casket given by the Holy Roman Emperor, Charles I, to Isabella of Portugal as a betrothal gift. Open Mon–Sat 10–1 and 2–5:15pm.

Abington Museum – Abington Park, Tel 31454. Abington Manor House, which houses the museum, dates from the 15th century. Modifications were carried out in the 16th, 17th and 18th centuries and also when the house and park became the property of Northampton Corporation in the 1890s. Exhibitions are mainly socio-historic. There is a good lace collection and the museum also houses the collection of memorabilia of the Northampton Regiment. The house was closed for extensive renovation in 1990 and a re-opening date had not been set. Open Mon–Sat 10–12:30 and 2–6pm, Sun 2:30–5pm Apr–Sept.

Althorp – Five miles (8 km) north-west of Northampton on the A428. Althorp is the family home of the Spencers and has attracted increasing numbers of visitors since the marriage of Lady Diana Spencer to Prince Charles. The house, built in 1508, has an important collection of pictures by Anthony Van Dyck, Paul Rubens, Sir Thomas Gainsborough and others, plus excellent porcelain and rare furniture. The celebrated Spencer library of 40,000 early printed books, including 58 Caxtons, was sold complete in 1892 and is now the John Rylands Library at the University of Manchester. Open daily 1:30–5:30pm.

Castle Ashby House – Castle Ashby, Tel (060129)234, was built between 1570 and 1630, and the grounds were landscaped by the great Capability Brown. The 1860 terracotta terraces are especially fine. Late 17th- and 18th-century furniture and Old Masters as well as some 19th-century sculpture. Open by appointment.

THEATRE

The **Royal Theatre** – Guildhall Road, Tel 32533. The home since 1927 of the Northampton Repertory Players. The programme is essentially composed of West End successes, classical texts and, recently, mainly in the Studio, more thought-provoking and original work. There is also a traditional pantomime at Christmas. The theatre itself, which was opened in 1884 as the "Opera House," is wonderful. Its modest exterior belies its beautifully preserved and decorated auditorium, resplendent with red plush seats, ornate boxes and an elaborate ceiling. The highlight of the auditorium, in a way, is the lavishly decorated safety curtain, which looks like a theatrical version of a trade union banner. It certainly gives one something to talk about in the interval. I saw a good adaptation of Richard Llewellyn's famous novel, *How Green Was My Valley* at the theatre. It starred the ex-boy-soprano, Aled Jones, who was really very good. Recent programmes have included plays by Tom Kempinski, Jeffrey Archer and Noel Coward and a notable adaptation of Dickens's *Hard Times* in the studio.

Derngate Centre – In Guildhall Street (adjacent to the Royal Theatre) Tel 24811, the centre is Northampton's large entertainment space. It was opened in 1983, and its ingenious design allows the stage and setting to be adjusted to produce four distinct layouts, which can host a vast range of different events from boxing to ballet and symphony concerts to conferences. The centre hosts visiting theatre productions, opera and ballet, and music of all kinds.

Northampton Arts Centre – Adjacent to the Northampton College of Further Education in Booth Lane South, Tel 407544, hosts mainly alternative theatre, but also comedy, dance and music. Recent productions have included a one-man-show on Brendan Behan, an Irish Cultural Festival, a Gamelan Ensemble and theatre by Ionesco, Kevin Fagan and the African People's Theatre.

MUSIC

The **Derngate** (see above) hosts visits by many of the country's leading orchestras. The Bournemouth Symphony Orchestra, the English Sinfonia, the Royal Philharmonic, the Liverpool Philharmonic and the BBC Philharmonic have all played at the centre in recent years. There are also visits by foreign orchestras such as the Amsterdam Baroque Orchestra and the Sofia Philharmonic. Northampton also has a Bach choir which performs at the Derngate, and two community orchestras, the Northampton Symphony and the Midland Philharmonic.

BOOKSTORES

On Tuesdays, excellent browsing is to be had in the Market Square. All week at Unit 7, Peacock Place 31 (one of the new shopping malls) is **Hammicks**, Tel 231972, with a good general selection and pleasant service. Best for children's books is **Bookscene the Bookstore**, Tel 758118. They are at St James Mill Road. There are two good bookshops dealing with Christian and religious literature. Manna House (rather nice, I think) is on St Giles Street, Tel 22666, and **Chapters** which also has cards and music is at 2 College Street Mews. I guess **Occultique** at 73 Kettering Road, Tel 27727, has some items of a religious nature. They (obviously) deal in matters of the occult and are a fascinating browse. **W H Smith**, Tel 21822, has a branch at 14 Newland Walk in the Grosvenor Centre off the Market Square. I didn't buy any books the last time I was there but I did pick up some bargain-priced cassette tapes. Finally, if you are walking in the Wellingborough Road, call in at **Bibliopol**, Tel 32932, at No 327 and **Books Unlimited**, Tel 26167, at No 84.

ANTIQUARIAN AND SECONDHAND BOOKS

First, the Market on Tuesday; then, if you're not in town on that day **Wooton-Billingham** is your best bet. They're at 79 St Giles Street, Tel 34531, and they also have maps and prints. I enjoyed them. I also enjoyed **Abington Bookshop**, Tel 32932, at 327 Wellingborough Road. They're in the same premises as Bibliopol so you can kill two birds with one stone. They also have old maps and prints.

ART GALLERIES

I think I like **Ariadne and Naxos**, 73 Kingsthorpe Road, Kingsthorpe Hollow, Tel 710740, because they have such a nice woodcut advertising their shop. They're a couple of miles out on the A43 towards Kettering and the last time I was there they had some fine paintings of all periods on view. The best gallery in town is **Evergreen Gallery** in St Giles Square, Tel 20236. They have some fine English watercolours and oils by traditional and contemporary artists. They also have signed limited editions by L S Lowery and Russell Flint, among others. Some nice antique maps and engravings are also on view. Close by at 39 St Giles Street is **Four Seasons Gallery**, Tel 32287, with a selection of traditional and contemporary pictures. **Savage Fine Art** in Alfred Street, Tel 29327, is an old established business with a wide collection of pictures. Finally in town, **World of Pictures**, Tel 230365, at 3 College Street Mews and **Abington Galleries** at 140 Abington Avenue, Tel 27550, are both worth a look.

ANTIQUE DEALERS

One of the best centres for antiques in Northampton is the Kettering Road. There's **Caves** at 111 Kettering Road, Tel 38278. They have a very large stock and their basement is chock full of bargains. At 164 Kettering Road is **Buley Antiques**, Tel 31588. They sell practically everything pre-1930 and their stock ranges from clothing, linen and lace to clocks and old dolls to antique jewellery. While I'm thinking about jewellery, back in the town centre at 1 Gold Street (how appropriate) you will find **Michael Jones** who specializes in antique and secondhand jewellery. He can be reached at 32548. If it's a brass or iron bed you are after, then **Laila Gray** at 25 Welford Road may well have what you want. Welford Road is in Kingsthorpe which is just on the edge of Northampton on the A43 to Kettering. Laila Gray also specializes in pine and her telephone number is 715277. A bit further out from Northampton on the Market Harborough Road (A508) is Boughton. Here you will find **Peter Cooksley**, Tel 842705, at the quaintly named Poacher's Gap. He not only has furniture, but also pianos which are notoriously difficult to take on board as hand luggage. Off the Daventry Road, two miles (3.2 km) from the city centre, is Harpole. Here you will find **Pamela Havard**, 23 The High Street, Tel 830007, well worth a visit and at Guillsborough, which is off the A50 Leicester Road, you can make the acquaintance of **Roberta Condor Antiques**, Tel 740809, again worth the drive. Finally, back in town, check out **Abbey Antiques**, Tel 764321, at 116 Towcester Road (a large general collection) and **Gillian Cave** at Regent House, Royal Terrace, Tel 37992.

RESTAURANTS

I must admit to eating outside of Northampton when I am in town for shopping. If I'm going to the theatre I invariably eat at one of the two good Caribbean restaurants. **The Go Go Nut**, Tel 33010, is at 15 Wellington Place, Barrack Road, while **Bupsie's Restaurant** at 186 Wellingborough Road, where the food is really authentic, is cosy and fun. Bupsie's is only open in the evenings and is a bit rushed for a pre-theatre supper. They are open till 11pm though, Tel 230578. Handy for the theatre and serving good Indian food is **Royal Bengal**, 39/41 Bridge Street, Tel 38617. They're open for lunch and dinner (6pm–midnight).

If you're not going to the theatre in the evening, then let me recommend two excellent country restaurants. Horton is on the B526 to Newport Pagnell, about four miles (6.4 km) from the city centre. Roade is about the same distance from town on the A508 Buckingham Road.

At Horton is the **French Partridge**, Tel 870033. Set in a converted farmhouse, the food is a judicious blend of French and English cooking. They are only open for dinner (7:30–9pm) and they only offer a four-course table d'hôte menu, but the cooking is excellent and the wine list exemplary. What is even more wonderful is that the tip is included in the price. But be sure to book, the restaurant is well established and very popular.

At Roade you'll find **Roadhouse Restaurant**, a dull name for one of the best country establishments in England. I've only eaten here once but it was memorable. There are little touches that make you know how much the place cares. My gravalax was homemade and my favourite dish of breast of roast guinea fowl came with a casserole of the dark meat. The desserts are wickedly wonderful and the prices are fair. Eating here will be an experience you will long remember with relish. Open Tues–Sat 12:30–1:45 and 7–12pm. No Sat lunch.

PUBS

You must visit the **Fish** in Fish Street, Tel 234040. On the outside you are confronted with what can only be called architectural whimsy, but in the interior there is good value bar food and a cosy restaurant.

A mile past Roade (see above) you will find Stoke Bruerne and the **Boat Inn**, Tel 0604 862428. It's right on the Grand Union Canal which makes it delightful in the summer and it's cosy in the winter with low ceilinged bar, tiled floor and the walls painted with vignettes of barge life. Small range of homemade food. The **Waterway Museum** here is worth a visit. Open Easter–Oct 10–6pm. Call to check opening times Oct–Easter. Tel 0604 862229.

Back in town, try the **Abingdon Park** on Wellingborough Road. It's a large pub in elegant buildings near the Northants Cricket Ground and the Abingdon Park brewery. You can arrange to tour the brewery here and there's a spacious Victorian lounge with good hot and cold lunchtime bar food (the pies have been praised) and a restaurant.

ARTISTIC ASSOCIATIONS

Anne Bradstreet, one of the first poets to write in English in North America, was born here. She emigrated to Boston in 1630. In 1841, the poet John Clare, who had previously been cared for in a private institution, was brought to the county asylum in Northampton. At first he was able to walk the mile to the town where he used to enjoy sitting under the portico of All Saints Church. His wonderful poems, especially those collected in *Poems of John Clare's Madness*, reveal the sadness he felt on being abandoned by his family, and on being far from the familiar sights and sounds of home. When he died he was buried in Helpston, just north of Peterborough, where he was born. In 1927, Jerome K Jerome died suddenly in Northampton while on a motoring holiday. He is best known for his novel, *Three Men in a Boat* and his play, *The Passing of the Third Floor Back*.

EPHEMERA

Castle Mound, close to the railway station (nicknamed the Castle by locals) is all that remains of the once famous Norman Castle. St Thomas à Becket was tried here in 1164. At the corner of Derngate and Cheyne Walk is Beckett's Well where Becket is supposed to have gained respite as he fled from King Henry II's agents after his trial.

In the late 17th century there were six inns fronting the Market Square. They became trading centres, with the innkeepers often acting as bankers. Trade by sample grew at the expense of the market, the avoidance of tolls being an added incentive. Inns became associated with particular products. The Hind and the Wool Pack were known as places to buy turnip seed, the Chequer sold clover and grass seed and the Star Inn was the centre of the leather market.

In 1828, Northampton Market Square was the venue for an attempted balloon ascent. The balloon rose from the ground but failed to gain height and landed on the roof of a house in the square's southwest corner. The woman aeronaut escaped from the balloon through an attic window. In 1845, another unusual visitor was Mr Gyngell, the tightrope walker and fireworks expert. He ascended a tightrope whilst holding two lit fireworks.

Halfway across the rope he threw one of them into the watching crown, hitting Mrs F Smith in the face and causing her demise. There is no record of Mr Gyngell's fate.

The patron saints of Northampton's shoemakers are Crispin and Crispinian, two cobbler brothers who lived in Soissons, France, during the third century. Both were Christian converts and noted for their compassion to the poor. They were beheaded in 303 during the Roman emperor Diocletian's persecution of Christians. Their feast day is October 25th. A modern engraved glass panel depicting them is in Northampton Art Gallery.

The Norman Church of St Peter, in St Peter's Way, stands on the site of an earlier Saxon Church. In the 11th century the parish priest determined that his devout Norwegian servant should make a pilgrimage to Rome. Before his ship sailed, however, the servant was commanded by a dream to return home. Sensing some divine purpose, the priest asked his servant to keep vigil in the church. There the man had another dream in which he was told to search a certain part of the church. Doing so, he discovered an ancient tomb. Convinced of some great revelation, the priest sent for a crippled servant girl named Alfgiva, in the hope that she might be cured. At sunset the three of them knelt at the altar and waited. As midnight struck, the church was suddenly filled with light and a snow-white dove appeared and sprinkled the watchers with holy water from the font. Alfgiva was immediately cured. The priest then opened the tomb and discovered from a document within that it contained the bones of St Ragener, a nephew of the martyr-king, St Edmund. A stone coffin lid in the present church is believed to be that of St Ragener's reliquary.

TOURIST INFORMATION BUREAU: 21 St Giles Square, Northampton, Northants, NN1 1JA. Tel (0604) 22677

NOTTINGHAM

County of Nottinghamshire
122 miles (195.2 km) from London by MI
By train 2 hours from London (St Pancras)

The first signs of settlement in Nottingham date from pre-Roman times, and although there was no large Roman settlement, evidence suggests that Roman occupation of the nearby Fosse Way spilled over into the town. The town's name dates from a later Anglo-Saxon settlement when a chieftain with the unfortunate name of "Snot" gathered his people on the hill where the Lace Market now stands. The name *Snot-ting-ham* means, in literal translation, "the town of Snot's people" and there must have been a collective sigh of relief when the town's name was abridged to its present form. Snot's people were an independent lot and they resisted William the Conqueror's army in 1066 so successfully that he was forced to establish his castle on Castle Hill, leaving the Anglo-Saxon settlement intact. After a couple of years peace was restored and the two settlements became one, but the idea of twin cities continued for hundreds of years with the city being granted two sheriffs. Today Nottingham has just one sheriff, reminding people of the legendary Sheriff of Nottingham and his heroic adversary, Robin Hood.

The town flourished in the 13th century with cloth making as its major industry. Later, in the 1300s, the tanning and leather industries increased as the woollen industry declined. At this time the famous Nottingham alabaster carvings were being made and exported right across Europe. Nottingham Castle was one of the castles left in charge of John, brother of King Richard, when Richard himself went off to the crusades. This was the period when the legend of Robin Hood and his Merry Men gained its place in the local folklore. Throughout the turmoil of the Wars of the Roses, the castle was a Yorkist stronghold, but with the coming of the Tudors it fell into disrepair. The castle was sold in 1603, but still retained loyal links. It was from here that Charles I came to raise his standard on August 22nd, 1642, and thus start the Civil War. His Royalist forces soon moved their headquarters to Newark and the Parliamentarians took over the castle. In one battle, the Royalists had fired into the castle from the tower of St Nicholas's church. After the skirmish, Parliamentary soldiers demolished the tower, and in 1651, when the war was over, Parliamentary forces demolished the castle too, to prevent its use in any future rebellion. When Charles II was restored to the throne in 1660 the economy of Nottingham improved. It also became fashionable for local gentry to build town mansions and imitate the social activities of London society. The first Duke of Newcastle built his ducal mansion on the site of the castle in 1674. During this period the appearance of the town was radically altered by the growth of building in brick. By 1700, brick was the most commonly used building material and the old wooden houses were gradually replaced.

William Lee had invented the stocking frame for making hosiery in 1589, and by the middle of the 17th century Nottingham was the national production centre for silk hosiery, with many small houses and even sheds filled with busy knitters using Lee's frame.

Industrialization had begun. In 1764 James Hargreaves had invented the "spinning-jenny," the first machine that could produce cotton thread capable of being used as warp and in 1809 John Heathcote invented the "bobbin-net" machine which allowed lace-making to be industrialized. Nottingham's lace industry was on the rise. In 1811 the Luddite Revolution began: gangs of cottage industry workers destroyed the machinery they feared would put them out of work. The rioters were called "Luddites" after Ned Lud, the lunatic who had won notoriety by breaking machines some 30 years earlier, and the English language thus acquired a term that is still current. (A Luddite is anyone who aggressively opposes technological progress.) Further riots took place in 1831 when the news came that the Reform Bill, a measure aimed at increasing the parliamentary franchise, had been defeated. The town centre was ransacked and the Duke of Newcastle's mansion burnt.

Conditions in what was the town's medieval centre were appalling. Workers in the factories lived in back-to-back houses facing narrow courtyards with access through a tunnel to the streets. In 1845 the town expansion outside its medieval confines was finally approved, and decent-quality housing, open spaces, sewers and a pure water supply followed. Civic pride was restored in the rebuilding of the Duke of Newcastle's mansion as the Castle Museum in 1878. In 1887, a man named Frank Bowden began making bicycles in Raleigh Street and called his company the Raleigh Bicycle Company. It was to become the greatest producer of bicycles in the world. About the same time another man named Jesse Boot opened a herbalist's shop in Goose Gate that was to develop into one of the world's largest pharmaceutical manufacturers. Nottingham was raised to the status of city in 1897 and the new industries of pharmaceuticals and bicycles, plus engineering and tobacco, gave the new city a strong industrial base that enabled it to flourish even when the huge lace industry declined.

Nottingham was also the site of the Goose Fair, a huge agricultural market and social gathering that was last held in its original form in 1927. It has now been replaced by a new fair, the largest in Europe, held for three days in October. The Lace Market district declined too, and in the 1960s it was declared a conservation area. Restoration of the fine buildings in the city centre has gone on apace and with the Victorian Theatre Royal, the Nottingham Playhouse and the newer Royal Concert Hall, Nottingham has performance facilities equal to any in the country.

ROBIN HOOD, NOTTINGHAM

WALK

Nottingham Walk – Begin from the multi-storey car park in Pilcher Gate. On leaving the car park turn right and cross Weekday Cross into Byard Lane. Turn right again into Bridlesmith Gate, which was the centre of the medieval town. There are a number of attractive buildings, especially those of King John's Arcade. Turn left into St Peter's for **St Peter's Church**. Here there is some 13th-century work preserved and two interesting fonts. Bear right into Wheeler Gate. "The Nottingham Story" (a film history) is at the Tourist Information Centre at No 16. Continue along Wheeler Gate and turn right into **Old Market Square**. The square is dominated by the tower of the **Council House** which was completed in 1928, and is modelled on St Paul's in London. The building has a Robin Hood fresco in the cupola above the arcade and the Robin Hood theme is carried through to the great bell which is named Little John after Robin's outlaw companion. Return to Wheeler Gate and walk down Friar Lane and turn left into Spaniel Row. As you turn right into Hounds Gate, the **Salutation Inn**, with its old rock cellars, is on your left (see Pubs). At the junction of Hounds Gate and Maid Marian Way, the **Tales of Robin Hood** is on your right. Continue across Maid Marian Way to Castle Road and ahead to Castle Museum. Leave by the Gatehouse Entrance and follow Castle Road to the Brewhouse Yard Museum, passing the statue of Robin Hood on your right with reliefs from the legend on the castle walls and small groups of his Merry Men nearby. The **Olde Trip to Jerusalem** pub is close by. The **Lace Centre** is housed in a 15th-century house that has been moved and opposite is the **Costume Museum**. Continue up Castle Gate, cross Maid Marian Way and note the **Royal Children** pub on your left (see Pubs). Walk ahead into Low Pavement with its charming Georgian, Victorian and Edwardian buildings. The post office was once the Ladies' Assembly Rooms, the scene of balls and receptions, and its columned façade betrays its Georgian origins. The **Broad Marsh Shopping Centre** is on your right but go ahead through Middle Pavement and cross Middle Hill into High Pavement and the **Lace Hall**. Retrace your steps to Middle Hill, turn right into Weekday Cross and right again into Pilcher Gate to the car park.

MUSEUMS, GALLERIES AND PUBLIC BUILDINGS

Nottingham Castle Museum – Castle Road, Tel 483504. Built on the site of a high rock, the castle once rivalled the great castles of Windsor and the Tower of London with all the Kings from William the Conqueror to Henry VII staying there at one time or another. Totally destroyed after the Civil War, it was replaced by the present magnificent Ducal Mansion in 1674; then, in 1875, it was converted into the first municipal museum and art gallery outside London for fine and applied arts. Collections of ceramics, silver, glass and military displays (the Regimental Museum of the Sherwood Foresters). Fine medieval alabaster carvings and a collection of watercolours, oils, prints and sculpture. Open April–Sept 10–5pm daily; Oct–Mar 10–4:45pm daily.
Museum of Costume and Textiles – Castle Gate, Tel 483504. Situated in a row of elegant 18th–century

houses, the costume displays from 1790 to mid–20th century are presented in a series of period furnished rooms. There are displays of hand- and machine-made lace as well as tapestries, embroidery and needle-work. Open daily 10–5pm.

Nottingham Caves – Nottingham Castle, Tel 483504. Guided tours of some of the 400 caves known to exist beneath the city depart from the Castle. For a history of the famous Mortimer's Cave, see Ephemera. Open daily 2, 3 and 4pm in summer; 2 and 3pm in winter. For other cave tours call 470661.

Brewhouse Yard Museum – Castle Boulevard, Tel 483504. Nestled in the rock below the Castle and housed in a group of restored 17th-century cottages, the museum presents a realistic glimpse of everyday domestic and commercial life in Nottingham over the last 300 years. There are recreated shops, a "between-the-wars" shopping street and displays covering education and recreating living conditions. Open daily 10–12 and 1–5pm.

Tales of Robin Hood – Maid Marian Way, Tel 483284. You are carried in a small "car" through exhibits which examine the sights, sounds and stories of the legend of Robin Hood. Open daily April–Sept 10–4:30; Oct–Mar 10–4pm.

Lace Hall – High Pavement, Tel 484221. The story of Nottingham lace is told in the splendid setting of a former Unitarian Chapel with a fine Burne-Jones stained glass window. Visitors can watch lace being made, and buy it too. Open daily 10–5:30pm (5pm in winter).

Lace Centre – Severns Building, Castle Road, Tel 413539. Situated in a medieval building opposite Robin Hood's statue near the castle. The centre offers an introduction to the history of lace. Hand lace-making demonstrations on Thursday afternoons in the summer and opportunities to buy lace. Open daily 10–5pm (4pm in Jan and Feb).

Wollaton Hall – Wollaton Park, Tel 281333. Built in 1538, the Hall is one of the most spectacular and ornate Tudor buildings in England. It now houses the city's Natural History Museum with displays covering many aspects of the natural world. The surrounding park has herds of red and fallow deer. Open daily April–Sept 10–7pm (closes at dusk in winter); Sun 2–5pm (4:30pm closure in winter). In the stable block and estate buildings of the Hall is the **Nottingham Industrial Museum**, Tel 284602, which reflects the city's many industries from curtains to computers. Working steam engines are regularly in steam; also on display are a horse gin and mining and agricultural machinery. Transport exhibits include horse-drawn carriages, motorcycles, cars and bicycles. Open the same days and hours as Wollaton Hall.

Canal Museum – Canal Street, Tel 598835. Set in a restored warehouse on the banks of the Nottingham and Beeston Canal, the museum presents a broad insight into the history of local canals, the River Trent, bridges, floods, natural history and archeology. There is an audio-visual programme and seasonal canal trips. Open Easter–Oct Wed–Sat 10–noon and 1–5:45pm; Oct–Easter Wed and Thurs same hours, Sun 1–5pm all year.

Green Mill Science Centre – Windmill Lane, Tel 503635. Set in the 19th-century working windmill once owned and operated by the mathematical scientist George Green, the centre explores the life of Green and aspects of windmills and milling generally. Open daily Wed–Sun 10–5pm.

THEATRE

Theatre Royal – Theatre Square, Tel 482626. Part of the Royal Centre which includes the Nottingham Playhouse and the Royal Concert Hall, the Theatre Royal (opened 1865) is a beautifully restored Victorian playhouse. In 1908 the 64-year-old Sarah Bernhardt captured the heart of the young D H Lawrence here, while he sat enamoured in the audience. Today the theatre is a top-rate touring house attracting such visitors as the Royal Shakespeare Company, the D'Oyly Carte Company, the London City Ballet and Opera North.

Nottingham Playhouse – Wellington Circus, Tel 419419. Nottingham's repertory company is among the best half dozen in the country and has been since it opened with Alan Sillitoe's *Saturday Night and Sunday Morning* in 1963. Offers a varied programme of classical, modern, foreign and avant-garde theatre.

Lace Market Theatre – Halifax Place, Tel 507201. A community theatre offering good-quality, interesting drama.

MUSIC

Royal Concert Hall – Theatre Square, Tel 482626, opened in 1982 as Nottingham's premier venue for classical music. Visitors have included the Leningrad Symphony Orchestra, the Halle and Nigel Kennedy.

Albert Hall – Wellington Circus, Tel 482626, was opened in 1876 and has recently been refurbished. It is the home venue for the East of England Orchestra and also plays host to visiting ensembles and soloists. There is a wonderful organ.

University of Nottingham – University Park, Tel 506101, offer classical concerts in their Music Studio. Telephone the university for details.

Nottingham Festival – Tel 470661, is held in May and June and offers music, dance, theatre, film, art, media events, lectures and workshops as well as many community events. There is a whole "Parks and Pavements" section in the festival with outdoor performances by bands, dancers and musicians.

Contemporary Archives – Tel 470661, challenges audiences to test their own perceptions of what is new and avant-garde in music, art, film, theatre and the media. It is presented in mid-June.

CINEMA

Commercial cinema at:

Odeon – Angel Row, Tel 473273 (6 screens).
Cannon – Chapel Bar, Tel 475260 (3 screens).
Savoy – Derby Road, Tel 472580 (3 screens).
Showcase – Clifton Boulevard, Tel 866766 (12 screens).

Of more interest is the **Broadway**, Broad Street, Tel 412536, which shows an interesting mix of classic, foreign and contemporary films of real quality, which you are not likely to see at the commercial cinema. A recent programme showed work from Canada, France, Japan, Germany, Argentina and the USA.

BOOKSTORES

The best are **Dillon's**, 25 Wheelergate, Tel 473532 (opposite the Tourist Information Office), **Waterstone's**, 1/5 Bridlesmith Gate, Tel 484499, and **Sherratt and Hughes**, 7 Cheapside, Tel 470694. Of the local bookstores, you might like to try **Bookscene**, 70 Alfreton Road, Tel 422575, **Parker's** in Russell Street, Tel 424140, **The Potter's House**, 16 St James Street, Tel 411048, **The Private Shop**, 18 Carrington Street, Tel 599853 and **Dealerfield**, King Street, Tel 473951. There's a good **Penguin Bookshop** for paperbacks at 54 Bridlesmith Gate, Tel 599295, while books on philosophy and religion are best found at **Scripture Union**, 26/30 Heathcoat Road, Tel 501919, and **Christian Book Centre**, 63/65 Chilwell Road, Tel 256961. If you are out at the university, Clulows is a fine bookshop. At University Park, Tel 587063. There are lots of dealers in science fiction, fantasy and comics in Nottingham. The best are **Forbidden Planets**, 129 Middle Walk, Broad Marsh Centre, Tel 584706, **Strange Tales**, 3 Hurts Yard, Tel 411325, and **Virgin Comics**, 6 Wheeler Gate, Tel 476246. Finally, you'll find "new age" literature at **Yamaa Book Shop**, 14 Radford Road, Tel 780058, and all kinds of books on sport at **Sport in Print**, 3 Radcliffe Road, Tel 455407.

ANTIQUARIAN AND SECONDHAND BOOKS

The best is **Heather Cowley**, 235 Mansfield Road, Tel 473836, with a large stock of antiquarian and second-hand books, maps, engravings and antique prints. Close by are **Jermy and Westerman**, 203 Mansfield Road, Tel 474522 and **Geoff Blore's Bookshop**, 484 Mansfield Road, Tel 691441, both with good second-hand collections.

Maynard and Bradley are also excellent. They're at 30 Friar Lane. Finally, **T Vennett Smith**, 11 Nottingham Road, Gotham, Tel 830541, has postcards, cigarette cards and is also an autograph auctioneer.

ART GALLERIES

Anthony Mitchell Fine Paintings – Sunnymede House, 11 Albermarle Road, Woodthorpe, Tel 623865. Oils and watercolours (by appointment). **Focus Gallery** – 108 Derby Road, Tel 417913. Some nice contemporary etchings and contemporary pottery and ceramics.

Oldknows Studio Group – Oldknows Factory, St Ann's Hill Road, Tel 419217, has contemporary oils, watercolour prints, sculptures and textiles, many direct from the artists' own studios. The **Original Art Shop**, 249 Victoria Centre, Tel 419127, has contemporary oils and watercolours and limited edition prints. Finally, **Zuma Gallery**, King's Place, 16 Stoney Street, Tel 503667, has contemporary oils, watercolours and limited edition prints.

ANTIQUE DEALERS

The antique markets first – the **Top Hat Antiques Centre** is at 66 – 72 Derby Road, Tel 419143. It is right in the middle of Nottingham's antique district and has 25 dealers under one roof with 15 rooms of

Georgian, Victorian and Edwardian furniture, period brass and copper, art nouveau, art deco, paintings, prints, linen, lace and Victorian clothing. Stay on Derby Road for **Pegasus Antiques** at No 62, Tel 474220, with 17th- to late 19th-century furniture, and 19th-century brass, copper, silver and jewellery. At No 74 is **Trident Arms**, Tel 474137, with arms and armour of all ages and nations. Close by are No 76 and No 78. **David and Carole Potter** are at No 76, Tel 417911, with clocks, silver and plate, furniture, glass, paintings and porcelain, while at No 78 you will find **D Wise**, Tel 472132, with 18th- and 19th-century furniture and decorative Victorian and Edwardian carved oak furnishings, silver, plate and general antiques. **Melville Kemp** – at No 79/81, Tel 417055, has Victorian jewellery, Georgian and Victorian silver, Sheffield plate and beautiful porcelain. At No 82 is **Woodwards City Jewellers** with a good collection of antique and modern jewellery, while **The Golden Cage** at No 99, Tel 411600, has beaded dresses, Victorian clothes, tweeds and dinner jackets. **Lustre Metal Antiques** at Canning Circus, Derby Road, Tel 704385 (by the police station), has copper, brass, silver and plated and cast iron-items, especially fireplaces and beds. Also at Canning Circus is **Sheila Harris Antiques**, Tel 412094, with 19th-century furniture, porcelain and metalware. **Michael Pollock Antiques** at No 110, Tel 474266, has china, silver, gold, furniture, instruments, tinplate, toys and dolls. Finally, to round off Derby Road there's **Val Smith** at No 170, Tel 781194, with coins, postcards and general antiques. In the city centre at 145 Lower Parliament Street is **Antiques and General Trading Company**, Tel 585791, with furniture from the 17th century and decorative objects and **Hockley Coins** at 16 Hockley Street, Tel 507097, with coins, bank notes, militaria, toys and postcards.

Close to the Midland Station is Carrington Road with **Station Pine Antiques**, Tel 582710, at No 103. They have stripped pine and satin walnut furniture. Just round the corner from Carrington Road is Queen's Road with **Trade Winds Antiques**, Tel 862850, at No 2 (opposite the station). They have clocks and general antiques. Just to the east of the city on the A612 is the suburb of Carlton where at 308 Carlton Hill is **Granny's Attic**, Tel 265204, with dolls, miniatures, general antiques and furniture, while at No 306, next door, is **S Pembleton**, Tel 265204, with a collection of general antiques. Finally, if you are interested in beautiful 18th-century porcelain, you should visit **Breck Antiques**, 726 Mansfield Road (A60), Tel 605263.

RESTAURANTS

Les Artistes Gourmands – 61 Wollaton Road, Beeston, Tel 228288. Unquestionably the best place to eat in Nottingham, with a beautifully cooked cuisine of classic and modern French dishes. It's handy for the university but only those of professorial rank could afford to eat here. You don't get this kind of quality at bargain basement prices. The last time I ate there I had smoked salmon, duck with blackcurrant sauce and a superb tarte tatin. Friends have raved about the goose and the wild boar. The **Café des Artistes** is run in tandem with the restaurant but the atmosphere is more informal, the emphasis is on bistro dishes and it is less expensive. In Les Artistes Gourmands the set lunch and dinner are good value and the wine list exemplary. Open Mon–Sat 12–2 and 7–10pm. No Sat or Mon lunch.

Loch Fyne Oyster Bar – 17 King Street, Tel 508481. I wish every major city had an enterprising fish restaurant like this. The parent company is at Cairndow, Strathclyde, Scotland and the fresh seafood is airlifted down each night. Excellent value oysters – not to be missed – and the langoustines, clams, crab and moules marinières are all excellent. You can get a full meal or an open sandwich. Recommended. Open Mon–Sat 9–8:30pm.

Ocean City – 100/104 Derby Road, Tel 475095. Friends of mine from the university go there twice a week for the excellent lunchtime dim sum. The large menu of mostly Cantonese dishes is strong on "sizzling" dishes. Especially good is the monkfish with chili and there are wonderful and exotic specialities such as braised whelks with ginger, crabmeat braised in milk and stewed belly pork with yams (it tastes better than it sounds). There's a good vegetarian selection. Open daily Mon–Sat noon to 2:30 and 6–11:30pm., Sun noon–10:30pm.

Saagar – 473 Mansfield Road, Tel 622014. Good northern Indian cooking with excellent tandoori and tikka dishes with all the trimmings. They bake their own nan bread and a friend from the Playhouse said the korma chicken was the best he'd ever tasted. Open daily noon–2:30 and 5:30–midnight.

Jack Sprats – 23/25 Heathcote Street, Tel 410710. Close to the Lace Market – there are good fish and vegetarian dishes. Good reports on the trout with peanut sauce and the aubergine parmesan. They also have organic wines which should be tasted. Open Mon–Sat dinner only 7–10pm (10:30 on weekends).

PUBS

Olde Trip to Jerusalem – Brewhouse Yard, Tel 473171. The present building is mainly 17th century although there has been an inn here since 1189. It was originally a brewhouse for Nottingham Castle and was a favourite resting place for crusaders en route to the Holy Land, hence the name. The unique upstairs bar is cut into the sandstone rock on which the castle is built and the ceiling is lost upwards in the gloom. Probably the most unique pub in the country. Good bar food with pies, baked potatoes, ploughman's and a daily special. Changed hands in 1990 after being with the same family for over a hundred years.

Royal Children – 52 Castle Gate, Tel 580207. So called because the children of Princess Anne, daughter of James I, are supposed to have played with the children of the Duke of Newcastle, builder of the "new" castle, in the grounds of the pub. The pub dates from 1696, it's full of atmosphere and has good bar food at lunchtime.

Salutation Inn – Hound's Gate, Tel 504627. In spite of a modern façade, this is a genuine ancient beamed and flagstoned pub, with reasonably priced traditional bar food. The old rock cellars can be visited at quiet times by arrangement.

Grand Central – Great Northern Close (off London Road), Tel 410064. An imaginative conversion of a former railway building. Good atmosphere in two roomy railway-arch areas. There's a rather nice mock-up of an Orient Express dining car and better-than-average bar food. There's also rather an elegant dining area and, all in all, this is a nice place to be.

New Market – 40 Broad Street. The austere, neo-classical façade could be that of a bank but inside the prices for the drinks are pleasurably inexpensive and won't break your bank. The bar food is traditional, but it's well cooked, simple and as inexpensive as the drinks. Friendly atmosphere and very comfortable.

ARTISTIC ASSOCIATIONS

The diarist and traveller, Celia Fiennes, knew the city well and thought the beer of Nottingham among the best in the country. She probably quaffed a tankard at the Olde Trip to Jerusalem. Her book, *The Journeys of Celia Fiennes*, makes fascinating reading for anyone travelling in Britain. Lord Byron lived in a house in Pelham Street with his mother in 1798 (the house is now gone). They worshipped at the Unitarian Chapel in High Pavement where Coleridge had preached (now the Lace Hall). Byron had succeeded to the title of 6th Baron Rochdale on the death of his great-uncle. The family seat was Newstead Abbey (four miles/6.4 km north on B683) but at this time Byron could not afford to live there. He did, however, make Newstead his home later and in fact he made the Abbey and its ghostly legends famous. His apartments, the elegant salon and the great hall are open to the public. Tel 0623 793557.

William Howitt, the author of *Visits to Remarkable Places* and *The Forest Minstrel* (written with his wife), lived in Nottingham with Mary, his wife, for 13 years. The couple ran a chemist's shop in Parliament Street. Howitt wrote a long poem on Byron's death and attended his funeral but disapproved of the disorderly scenes which accompanied the procession and the interment. (Byron had been suspected of a more than brotherly love for his half-sister Augusta Leigh and had been ostracized by conventional society). Wordsworth stayed with the Howitts in 1831 and later that year they witnessed the Reform Bill riots and the burning of the castle. In 1835 Howitt was made an alderman.

John Drinkwater, the poet and dramatist best known for his historical plays *Abraham Lincoln* and *Robert E Lee*, was on the staff of the Northern Assurance Company in Victoria Street but resigned as soon as his success enabled him to. D H Lawrence, author of *Sons and Lovers* and *Lady Chatterley's Lover*, was born in Eastwood, three miles (4.8 km) to the northwest of the city. He attended Nottingham High School and University College (now Nottingham University).

Dame Laura Knight, the portrait painter and creator of many celebrated circus and ballet canvases, was born in Nottingham in 1877. The household in which she was brought up was an unusual one and the source of much local gossip. Her mother was estranged from a husband who had married her in the mistaken belief that her family, the Bateses, were rich. They did in fact own a lace-machine factory in Nottingham, but Laura's grandfather, an inventor, had neglected to take out patents for his machines, and other people had been quick to plagiarize his ideas and undersell him. Laura's mother took over the running of her father's increasingly insecure firm, but she was also an art teacher who not only encouraged Laura's artistic aspirations but was determined that her daughter should receive a proper art education, something she had been denied by lack of money. In 1890, young Laura was sent to Nottingham School of Art. On almost her first day she met her future husband, Harold Knight, who was then the school's most talented student. Harold and Laura entered a rather diffident courtship which lasted, apparently on a purely platonic basis, for over 13 years. Harold, whose father was a successful Nottingham architect, was temperamentally very different from Laura; he was a shy, reserved man who found Laura's ebullience and ceaseless chatter (generally about herself) rather overwhelming. Moreover, his mother had instilled in him a strongly puritanical nature and a fear of sex. Harold was in many ways the more serious and dedicated artist but Laura, who fell completely under his spell, even to the extent of imitating his works, had a more extrovert manner of painting, which was to win her greater public renown. After leaving school, Laura moved with her sister Nellie to a most unusual residence, in a cave underneath Nottingham Castle. Laura had already begun to receive commissions for portraits and she thought that having such a distinctive and convenient address at the edge of the city's most exclusive park would enable her to attract more clients. The actual living conditions of the cave dwelling – cold, damp and infested with rats – turned out, however, to be less than desirable.

Gradually, both Harold and Laura gained official recognition. Harold received an eight-month travelling scholarship to Paris while Laura was awarded a gold medal by the Prince of Wales. In 1895 both were invited to the holiday resort of Staithes on the Yorkshire coast by an aunt of Laura's. Both Laura and Harold liked Staithes so much that they lived there almost constantly for the next 14 years. In 1903, Laura submitted a work to the Royal Academy in London; it was accepted and later bought by the painter Edward Stott for the then princely sum of £20. The purchase of this work finally enabled Laura and Harold to marry; they returned to Staithes for a further seven years, then moved to Newlyn in Cornwall and finally settled in London. Laura was made a Dame of the British Empire in 1929.

EPHEMERA

It is usually assumed that Robin Hood and his merry band became outlaws in Sherwood Forest in protest against the treatment of the common people by the Sheriff of Nottingham, an agent for King John, who had been entrusted with the care of the kingdom while Richard I (Lionheart) was fighting in the crusades. There are nearly 40 different Robin Hood ballads, most of which tell the familiar tale of robbing the rich to feed the poor and of conflict with the Sheriff of Nottingham and his retinue. Most of these, however, were written after 1600 when singing Robin Hood ballads became popular. Only five tales are known to have existed before 1500 and these are the main evidence for our outlaw hero. Long before the tales were written down they enjoyed huge popularity, being spread by word of mouth. The poem *Piers Plowman*, written about 1377, says that the "rhymes of Robin Hood" were well known and the earliest reference of all is in a Berkshire court document circa 1261. That someone like Robin Hood lived is pretty certain. Who he was is another matter. There are also inconsistencies in the tales themselves. In modern versions Robin's loyalty is always pledged to King Richard, but in three of the early tales the King is referred to as Edward. The famous story of the disguised king's visit to the Greenwood is imaginary and a familiar medieval theme, but the story of the King travelling north to inspect the loss of his deer was based on an actual journey made by Edward II in 1323. Whatever the truth of the story, the legend of romance, adventure and loyalty has proved enduringly attractive and is likely to continue to do so well into the 21st century.

No one knows where the famous Nottingham Goose Fair got its name. Legend has it that it comes from the hundreds of geese which were at one time driven from Lincolnshire and Norfolk to be sold at Nottingham, and it is a fact that the fair was held at the time of year when geese were at their prime, and roast goose was for centuries a traditional Michaelmas treat. In its earlier day the Goose Fair's main purpose was trade and it enjoyed a reputation for its cheese. There was always an element of merry-making, and from earliest times there were shows to amuse the visitors. Up to 1927 the fair was held in the market square and up to 1876 it lasted eight days. It is now held on the first Thursday, Friday and Saturday in October on the Forest Recreation Ground a mile or so to the north of the market square, and is among the biggest amusement fairs of its kind in Europe.

No discussion of medieval Nottingham is complete without mention of the caves cut into the sandstone on which the city was built. In 868 Alfred the Great's biographer wrote that the ancient Britons had called Nottingham "Tiqquocobauc" or dwelling of caves. Sandstone is very easily cut and it is likely that caves were dug into the sides of the steep slopes leading down to the Trent Valley from early times. However, It was probably only in the 13th century that people began to cut caves under their houses, mainly for storage. By 1250 caves were used for roasting malt for brewing, and by 1500 we even know of one cave used as a tannery. Caves continued to be used during the 17th and 18th centuries and many were filled with rubble by the Victorians. In the Second World War they were used as air raid shelters and some are still used today, mostly as garages. The most famous cave is "Mortimer's Hole" which leads from the top of the Castle Rock to the Brewhouse Yard Museum at the base of the cliff. Roger Mortimer, nobleman and adventurer, was the lover of Isabella, Edward II's Queen. Mortimer brutally murdered the King at Berkeley Castle in 1327. Isabella's son, Edward III, was 15 when he came to the throne and the country was ruled by Isabella and Mortimer during his minority, but in 1330 Edward and his companions crept through the cave up to the castle, seized Mortimer and put him to death. Isabella was banished by her son to Castle Rising in Norfolk.

William Lee was born in 1564, the same year as Shakespeare. He gained an MA from Cambridge but even though legend suggests he was a clergyman, there is no record of his having taken holy orders. Lee invented the stocking frame, which enabled knitting to be done by machine and not only by hand. Legend has it that he was a romantic figure. There are suggestions that he invented the frame to ease his wife's burden as a hand-knitter, another story says its invention was to enable his sweetheart to spend more time with him, and yet another that it was to spite a woman who took more interest in her knitting than she did in him. Whatever the reason for his invention of the stocking frame in 1589, it did indeed improve the lives of the hand knitters greatly. For reasons about which there are many theories, Lee failed to persuade Queen Elizabeth I to grant him a patent and he emigrated to France, taking his frame with him. Lee had great hopes that the French King, Henry IV, might be interested in his invention but this hope was dashed in 1610 when Henry was assassinated. Lee died a few years later, a bitter man, without ever having derived any personal benefit from his invention. In 1989 Nottingham celebrated the quarter-centenary of the invention of the knitting frame, giving long overdue credit to a man who was responsible for starting the knitting industry that employs 90,000 people in Britain, and is the base of many industrial economies around the world.

One of Nottingham's most famous sons (he went to school and university in the town) was the novelist, poet and playwright, D H Lawrence. One of Lawrence's best-known novels is of course *Lady Chatterley's Lover*. A prosecution was brought against Penguin Books for daring to publish the work which was deemed to be obscene. The trial of *Lady Chatterley's Lover*, a book which chiefly concerns the dalliance of a lady of quality with her crippled husband's gamekeeper, elicited this tongue-in-cheek review from the book critic of *Field and Stream*, a magazine devoted to hunting, shooting and fishing and the management of stately homes and their vast estates:

"D H Lawrence's account of an English gamekeeper's daily life is full of considerable interest to outdoor-minded readers as it contains many passages on pheasant raising, the apprehending of poachers, ways to control vermin and other chores and duties of the professional gamekeepers. Unfortunately, one is obliged to wade through many pages of extraneous material in order to discover and savour these side lights on the management of a midland shooting estate."

Elsewhere in this book (see Edinburgh Ephemera), I note the reaction of some eminent artists to the role of the critic. It seems appropriate, while our thoughts are focused on D H Lawrence, to make note of the great man's feelings about critics in general. He wrote: "Curse the blasted, jelly boned swine, the slimy, the belly-wriggling invertebrates, the miserable sodding rotters, the flaming sods, the snivelling, dribbling, dithering, palsied, pulseless lot that make up England today. They've got white of egg in their veins, and their spunk is that watery it's a marvel they can breed. They can nothing but frogspawn – the gibberers. God, how I hate them."

My goodness, I do wish David Herbert was not so reticent. Why didn't he come out and say what he really felt?

TOURIST INFORMATION BUREAU: 16 Wheeler Gate, Nottingham, Nottinghamshire NG1 2NB. Tel (0602) 470661

8

THE NORTH

CHESTER AND MOLD	MANCHESTER
HARROGATE	NEWCASTLE-UPON-TYNE
LANCASTER	SCARBOROUGH
LEEDS	YORK
LIVERPOOL	

CHESTER AND MOLD

CHESTER

County of Cheshire
188 miles (300 km) from London by M1, M6, M56
Train from London (Euston) approximately 3 hours

A combination of Roman and medieval relics and many fine timber-framed buildings makes Chester, the Roman fortress of Deva, one of England's most interesting old cities. Chester contains the architecturally important work of Thomas Harrison, who rebuilt the castle and constructed a single-span bridge here in the 19th century, as well as some excellent examples of Victorian black-and-white buildings.

Roman occupation in the later part of the 1st century made Chester an important military stronghold; with its fortress sited on a sandstone ridge in a loop of the River Dee, and its deep harbour, it was a perfect location for a military base. It commanded one of the crossing points of the river and was a base for the Roman fleet. Deva was a typical Roman fortress, rectangular in shape with the Praetorium or commandant's quarters in the centre; the Town Hall covers part of this site today. The fortress was smaller than the present-day walled area of the city, stretching west only as far as the inner ring road and south just to Pepper Street. Deva was principally associated with the 20th Valeria Victrix legion which served here for 200 years and was one of the three Roman legions in Britain. The Romans' original intention in building a fortress at Chester was to control the native populations, especially the Ordovices in North Wales and the Brigantes of northern Britain, but as time went by a large civilian settlement and following grew up around the fortress, and there must have been considerable inter-marriage between the Roman and British populations.

The Roman forces left Britain in the early 5th century and settlements such as Deva were largely abandoned, but gradually the Anglo-Saxon invaders recolonized the Roman towns. It is thought that Chester was never totally deserted even during the Dark Ages and we believe that it was refortified by Aethelflaeda, Lady of the Mercians, daughter of Alfred the Great, at the beginning of the 10th century. Anglo-Saxon Chester was a rich and prosperous community and a thriving port. In 973 King Edgar came to Chester after his coronation and was rowed in state on the river by kings from Wales, Ireland and the Isle of Man who had come to swear allegiance to him.

After the death of the last Anglo-Saxon King, Edward the Confessor, the English throne was won by William of Normandy, who defeated Harold at the Battle of Hastings in 1066 (see Ephemera). William's conquest of the whole country was gradual and bitterly resented. Chester is reputed to have been the last of the important towns to fall to the Norman invaders: it was not until 1070, four years after the invasion, that the town was subdued. In 1071 the earldom of Chester was created. William the Conqueror bestowed the title on his nephew, Hugh of Avranches, who was nicknamed "the Wolf" for his rapacity. Yet it was this same Wolf who refounded the ancient church of St Werburgh as a great Benedictine abbey. After the Dissolution of the Monasteries in 1540 the Abbey Church became the Cathedral. Chester Castle, begun by William, became the centre for the earldom of Chester and Norman earls were among the most powerful men in the kingdom, but when the seventh earl died in 1237 without issue the earldom reverted to the throne. Since 1301 the heir to the throne has held the title Prince of Wales and Earl of Chester. Until Edward I's conquest of North Wales in 1284, Chester Castle was the starting point for many expeditions against the Welsh. Unrest continued through the Middle Ages and as late as 1516 Chester people were forbidden by the Civic Assembly to attend Welsh weddings. During the Middle Ages, Chester became the most important port in the northwest and trade flourished with Spain, Germany and Ireland. In 1506 Henry VII granted Chester its Great Charter, which confirmed the framework of the city's government. Alongside city government, the city trade guilds began to emerge. Twenty-three of these guilds, or companies, survive to the present day. They were originally formed to protect different trades or crafts, by regulating wages and prices, and looking after their poor members. The guilds contributed to the artistic life of the city by producing the famous Mystery Plays. The plays, which recreated the story of the life of Christ, were performed over three days at a number of locations in Chester. Each guild was responsible for a play or part of a play including construction of the lavish props as well as the performance (see Ephemera).

The quarrel between Charles I and his Parliament, which became open warfare in 1642, had a profound effect on Chester. There was a Puritan faction in the city assembly but the Royalists retained control and Chester declared for the King. Charles I came to Chester twice during the war, in 1642 and 1645 when the city was under siege. The King is said to have watched the Battle of Rowton Moor, in which his forces were defeated, from the tower on the city walls which now bears his name. After the battle, the King retreated into Wales, but Chester continued to hold out against its besiegers until surrendering to the Parliamentary forces in February 1646. Not surprisingly, the siege placed intolerable burdens on the city treasury and Chester was also expected to subscribe to Royalist causes in general. The city had possessed a fine collection of silver but most of it was melted down to make coins during the war.

Chester's prosperity had begun to decline before the start of the Civil War. The channel of the River Dee had been gradually silting up for centuries. During the 18th century the New Cut, a new channel in the river, and the Chester Canal were excavated. Both proved unsuccessful in reviving Chester's flagging status as a trading port. New industries such as the leadworks and the Flookersbrook foundry were established and both contributed to Britain's success in the Napoleonic Wars. New streets and buildings were built as the Industrial Revolution gathered steam and the grid-like street pattern, dating back to Roman and medieval times, changed; medieval buildings such as St Bridget's Church and White Friars were lost. The arrival of the railway in 1840 created both prosperity and poverty. The poverty was most apparent in the slums and courts along Foregate Street and behind the Town Hall, and outbreaks of typhus and other diseases were common. The prosperity showed itself in the rebuilding of many city centre landmarks, with the result that Chester's black-and-white appearance, best seen on both corners of Bridge Street at the Cross, is not as old as it appears at first glance and was in fact created by Victorian architects. Chester is one of the very few cities in the world which have managed to retain their sense of historical identity through the protection of past treasures, yet have still developed into modern, dynamic commercial and retail centres.

WALK

Chester Walk – Parking in Chester is not easy. By far the easiest course is to park in one of the many car parks just outside the walls and make your way to the Market Square. Every main route into the city has a car park just before the walls. Driving in the city centre is both difficult and restricted. The centre of Chester is the **Market Square** in which stands the **Town Hall**. This giant Victorian Gothic building, circa 1867, is composed of bands of red and grey sandstone and is surmounted by a tower 160 feet (48.6 m) high. In the **Waiting Hall**, beneath friezes of the city's history, hangs the Chester tapestry, woven in 1975 from brightly coloured Wilton carpet wool and depicting the River Dee meandering past the city's landmarks. In the resplendent **Assembly Rooms** hang portraits of the Grosvenor family – local aristocrats who owned much of Mayfair and Belgravia in London. The Tourist Information Centre adjoins the Town Hall as does the **Forum**, a modern complex of shops leading to the **Gateway Theatre**. Remains of the **Roman Principia** are displayed in the wall of the Forum in Hamilton Place. Opposite the Town Hall, Barclays Bank occupies the premises that used to house the King's School, which moved there in 1876. The school is the oldest in Chester; it was founded in 1541 and originally occupied the Cathedral rectory (the school moved to new premises in 1960). Adjacent to the old King's School is **Abbey Gateway** which leads to Abbey Square, a pleasant cobbled area within the Cathedral precincts with some fine 18th-century houses. Abbey Square leads into Abbey Street from which you can pass through **Kaleyards Gate** or climb to the **City Walls**. Tradition says that Edward I allowed the monks of the Abbey to make this breach in the walls about 1275. Control of the gate passed from the monks to the Dean of the Cathedral and it is still locked at 9pm. To the north is **King Charles Tower** (see above). From Kaleyards Gate you can walk south along the wall and see the **Cathedral Gardens** and in a short distance you come to Eastgate and the **Eastgate Clock**. The simple 18th-century archway forms an airy walkway which emerges from between upper storeys of the houses opposite. A gate has stood here since the first century. The Romans called their fortress Deva, after the goddess of the River Dee and from the gate, against a distant background of the Welsh hills, one can now see the magpie façades of Eastgate Street's black-and-white timbered buildings, together with turrets and spires, classical columns, Dutch gables and buildings of other shapes and styles. The Eastgate Clock was erected in 1899 to commemorate Queen Victoria's Diamond Jubilee. The **Grosvenor Hotel** (1866), **Browns of Chester** (1828), the **Midland Bank** (1833) and the 17th-century **Boot Inn** are all of interest, while to the south is the ruined **Wolf Tower** dating from the 14th century. Close by is the Newgate, a modern structure with a wide stone archway flanked by towers, which is built alongside the Wolf Gate. Just outside the Wolf Gate are foundations of the Roman fortress, the reconstruction of a Roman central-heating system and, a little further away, the **Roman Amphitheatre**. Built around AD 86, it could hold 7000 spectators, making it the largest amphitheatre discovered in Britain when it was excavated in 1929. Today half the amphitheatre lies beneath the grounds of a convent, but walking into the arena from one of the surviving entrances, one can still picture the tiered onlookers, the gladiatorial contests and the wild animal fights that once took place here. Its day-to-day use was to train Roman legionaries in weapons use, and an interesting coincidence is that the same spot was used as a bear pit in the 18th century. Close by are the ruins of **St John's Church**, probably an Anglo-Saxon foundation. From 1075 to 1102 it served as the cathedral for Chester. Later it became a parish church, and part fell into disuse (the West Tower collapsed in 1881 and was never rebuilt) but the remaining structure, especially the nave, is a superb example of Norman architecture and services and concerts take place here throughout the year. Adjoining St John's is **Grosvenor Park**. The Shipgate and an arch from the medieval St Mary's Nunnery have been re-erected here. Return to Newgate and walk south along the wall. Leaving the wall by the **Wishing Steps** (1785) you will come to the **Groves**, a pleasant promenade along the river. To the north is the **Anchorites' Cell** (see Ephemera). Westwards from the Groves is the **Old Dee Bridge** where a crossing of the river has existed since Roman times, and close by is **The Weir**, dating from the 11th century. From the bridge, where the 18th-century **Bridgegate** stands, walk west along Castle Drive, passing County Hall to Grosvenor Bridge where Grosvenor Road leads to the imposing entrance of **Chester Castle**. Buildings of Greek Revival splendour now stand around the former outer bailey of Chester's medieval castle which was mostly demolished last century. The 12th-century **Agricola Tower** still stands intact, dwarfed by the Crown Court and Council building. The gaol at Chester Castle was visited by the prison reformer, John Howard, at the end of the 18th century. He compared it to the Black Hole of Calcutta. The gaol was closed in 1877. Opposite the entrance to Chester Castle is the **Chester Constabulary Building**, on the site of the 12th-century St Mary's Priory. Cross Grosvenor Street roundabout to **Grosvenor Museum** (see below). Walk along Castle Street and turn into St Mary's Hill, which links Castle Street with Lower Bridge Street, to St Peter's Church and the cross at the heart of the city. You will pass the **Bear and Billet**, a black-and-white-tiered building of 1664, and **Ye Olde King's Head**, which was originally a family home.

Walk along Bridge Street to Pepper Street and you will find St Michael's Church, now **Chester Heritage Centre** (see below). Close by is the **Toy Museum** in Bridge Street Row. Bridge Street intersects with Watergate Street to the left and Eastgate Street to the right. In these streets you will find the **Rows** which are unique to Chester. They consist of covered galleries above the shops at street level and are reached by steps from the street. The upper level shops have galleries in front where you can watch the busy street below. At the top of Bridge Street is the **Cross**. The High Cross, where merchants made bargains, stood on this site from 1407 until the English Civil War. After a sojourn in the Roman Gardens adjoining the Newgate it was re-erected in the centre of the city in 1975. For many centuries the Cross was the centre of city government. The mayor and aldermen used to meet in the **Pentice**, a timber-framed structure built against St Peter's Church. The Pentice was demolished in 1803. St Peter's Church was probably an Anglo-Saxon foundation and it was restored in 1886–87 although its interior dates from the 15th century. Other buildings at the Cross are mostly Victorian but if you walk down Watergate Street you will see **God's Providence House** (1652). The inscription, "God's Providence is Mine Inheritance," celebrates the legend that the houses's inhabitants were spared by the plague. Next door is a wine merchant's premises which has the largest medieval crypt in Chester. Walk on to **Leche House** which is late 13th century and has associations with Catherine of Aragon, first wife of Henry VIII. Further along is **Bishop Lloyd's House** (16th century) while across the street is the Georgian elegance of **Booth Mansion**, once a fashionable Assembly Room but now the home of Sotheby's, the London auction house. Trinity Church is medieval, but was rebuilt in the 1860s. In 1963 it became the Guildhall of the Freemen and Guilds of the City of Chester. The **Custom House** of the Port of Chester is built into an angle of the church. In the Middle Ages the River Dee was close to the **Watergate** at the bottom of the street. Ships unloaded their cargoes there and they were brought into Chester through the gate. The present Watergate dates from 1788. Turn right before the Watergate into City Walls Road. Walk past the Queen's School and the Royal Infirmary, and rejoin the City Walls. You will see the **Water Tower**, built of the same warm-coloured sandstone as the rest of the city wall. The Tower once protected the entrance to Chester's medieval port but the river long ago wandered off to the west leaving the Water Tower dry and a little forlorn. From this section of the wall you get a good view of the canal and railway and also of **Bluecoat School**, built in 1717. Stay on the wall until Northgate, a severe classical arch (1808–10). Northgate Street was the Roman Via Decumana. The **Pied Bull** on the right is one of Chester's oldest inns (see below). South of the Pied Bull is the Town Hall, and opposite it, St Werburgh's Street leads to the **Cathedral**. Modest nobility rather than grandeur is the impression given by the elegant tower of Chester Cathedral and by the decorated stone work of the building's reddish walls, parapets and turrets. The Cathedral was originally a Benedictine abbey, founded in 1092, and some of the abbey's Norman architecture survives inside. Rebuilding began in the 13th century in the Early English style of pointed arches and light vertical lines, rising to the magnificent

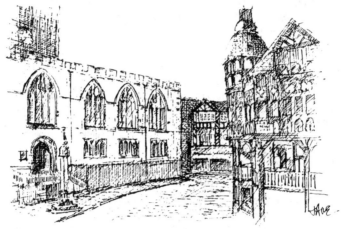

THE CROSS, CHESTER

roof of the nave. This was built by the architect Sir Charles Gilbert Scott, who restored the cathedral during the last century. In the choir, the 14th-century wood carvings of dragons, kings, angels, fabulous monsters and human caricatures look out from the stalls. Above rise ranks of thickly pinnacled canopies, designed to keep the draught off the monks' shaven heads. The cloisters are surrounded by the monastic buildings of the old abbey. The refectory, a many-windowed hall with a 20th-century hammerbeam roof, serves modern-day pilgrims' lunches to cathedral visitors. Set into one of the walls is the reader's pulpit, from which monks used to read to their brethren during mealtimes. Leave the Cathedral and walk back to the Market Square and Town Hall where the walk started. The Cathedral, the Rows, the mix of Roman and medieval antiquities and the most complete circuit of walkable walls in England make Chester a must on any tourist itinerary.

MUSEUMS

Cheshire Military Museum – The Castle, Tel 327617. The museum displays the colours and standards, uniforms, badges, equipment, weapons, medals, silver, pictures and various other militaria of four famous regiments whose historic home is Chester and the County of Cheshire. They are the Fifth Royal Inniskilling Dragoon Guards, the Third Carabiniers, the Cheshire Yeomanry and the Cheshire Regiment. The display covers the 300 years of the regiments' history with exhibits ranging from the remains of a standard carried at the Battle of the Boyne to present-day weapons and uniforms. Almost all of the parts of the world where the British Army has been engaged in one way or another are represented, including the Antarctic, where Captain Laurence Oates, the polar explorer, lost his life. His unique Polar Medal is displayed in the museum. (Oates was an Inniskilling Dragoon Guard.) Open daily 9–5pm. Closed Christmas week.

Grosvenor Museum – 27 Grosvenor Street, Tel 321616. Founded in 1886, the museum contains displays of international importance illustrating the organization of the Roman Army and a large collection of Roman tombstones and inscriptions. Other collections cover the natural history, local history and archaeology of Chester and Cheshire. The museum is noted for its local paintings and watercolours and for its silver, much of which was made and assayed in the city. The Mayor's Parlour from the King's Arms Kitchen is a reconstruction of the 19th-century room where the Honourable Incorporation, a debating and wagering club, staged a satire on the city council, electing its own mayor, sheriff and other officials. The Castle Street Georgian House, the former town house of the Swettenham and Comerback families dating from circa 1680, is part of the museum. It contains 17th- and 18th-century panelled rooms, a fine late 17th-century staircase, Stuart, mid-Georgian and 18th-century period rooms, with many examples of local furniture and reconstructions of a Victorian kitchen and laundry together with a gallery of 19th- and 20th-century costumes. Open Mon–Sat 10:30–5pm; Sun 2–5:30pm.

Chester Visitor Centre – Vicar's Lane, Tel 318916. Housed in the former Grosvenor St John's School (circa 1813). The building was rebuilt in the 1880s and now houses a tourist information office, a video show, and a life-size reconstruction of the Rows of Chester in Victorian days together with a restaurant. Open daily 9–7pm.

Chester Heritage Centre – Bridge Street Row, Tel 317948. The centre is housed in St Michael's Church, which has a nice 15th-century aisle and decorated chancel roof. St Michael's was declared redundant in 1972 and the centre opened three years later. There is a small theatre giving a vivid description of Chester's history and buildings. In addition, permanent and temporary exhibitions describe the city's conservation programme. Open April–Sept weekdays 10–5pm; Sun 2–5pm (closed Wed). Oct–March daily (except Wed) 1–4:30pm

Toy Museum – 42 Bridge Street Row, Tel 316251. The museum has an outstanding collection of more than 5000 toys reflecting child's play through the ages – everything from Victorian and china dolls, doll's houses and Teddy bears to 1920 pedal cars and German, French and English tin plate toys. The museum also contains the largest exhibition of Matchbox and Lesney toys on public display in the world. Open daily 11–5pm.

St Mary's Centre – St Mary's Hill, Tel 603321. Housed in another redundant church and used for occasional exhibitions. Open weekdays 2–4:30pm.

King Charles Tower – City Walls, Tel 321616. Named because, in 1645, Charles I watched from its roof as his army was defeated by Parliamentarians at the battle of Rowton Moor. In earlier times it was called the Phoenix Tower. The phoenix is the emblem of the Painters', Glaziers', Embroiderers' and Stationers' Company, a medieval guild which used this tower as a meeting place. A phoenix and the date 1613 are carved above the door of the tower chamber. The room and the chamber above house a small exhibition describing the siege of Chester during the Civil War. Above the upper door appear the royal arms of Charles I. (Accessible by a stairway leading from the City Walls.) Open April–Oct Mon–Fri 1–5pm; Sat 10–5pm; Sun 2–5:30pm. Nov–March Sat 1–4:30pm; Sun 2–4:30pm.

THEATRE

Gateway Theatre – Hamilton Place, Tel 340392/3. The Gateway Theatre brings drama to a city long associated with the beginnings of English theatre (see Ephemera). The theatre offers plays from classics such as Shakespeare and Shaw to modern comedies by the best contemporary authors, hard-hitting dramas about important social issues, specially devised community shows which tour the area, and full-scale musical productions. In addition to the season of repertory productions in the main house, the theatre presents a programme of late-night shows, open rehearsals and after-show discussions. The Gateway is also the focal point for many other activities; the prestigious **Chester Summer Music Festival**, Chester Symphony Orchestra, concerts and Cheshire Dance Workshop events for **Danceabout North West**.

A recent production of *A Midsummer Night's Dream* garnered high critical praise while the pairing in repertory of **Cabaret** and C P Taylor's **Good** – two very different plays about Germany in the '30s – was an excellent piece of programming. There is a traditional pantomime at Christmas. The Gateway offers a 440-seat auditorium with every seat offering an excellent and unimpeded view of the stage. The Foyer Coffee Shop is open from 10am–6:45pm (5pm on days of no performance) for tea, coffee, sandwiches and hot snacks and there is a lively upstairs bar.

MUSIC

Musically, Chester is most alive during the week-long **Chester Summer Music Festival** at the end of July. Concerts and recitals take place in the Gateway Theatre, St Mary's Centre, the Cathedral and St John's Church. Main attractions are the choral and orchestral concerts in the Cathedral with the Halle, Royal Liverpool Philharmonic, BBC Philharmonic, Royal Philharmonic and the Academy of St Martin-in-the-Fields all being recent visitors. Chester now has its own 130-strong Festival Chorus which performs works as widely different in mood and idiom as Fauré's *Pavane*, Mendelssohn's *Elijah*, Walton's *Belshazzar's Feast* and Handel's *Solomon*. There are always individual soloists (a wide range: Pascal Roge and Nicholas

Kyneston, for example) and both chamber and specialist groups such as the Barbican Percussion Ensemble and Las Saguenoutiers de Toulouse in a programme of Renaissance music. There are also jazz, folk, pop and a thriving Fringe Festival. During the year concerts of classical music are given by visiting orchestras, chamber groups and soloists at the above locations. For Festival and year-round events, phone 313126.

FILM

The **Chester Film Festival** takes place in August and September each year with a wide range of films from classics to modern and foreign masterpieces.
Commercial cinema at –
Odeon – Northgate Street, Tel 324930 (3 screens).
Cannon – Foregate Street, Tel 322931 (2 screens).

BOOKSTORES

There's not a lot to choose between the top three. **Waterstone's**, 43-45 Brighton Street Row, Tel 328040, we have heard of lots of times before. Big, efficient with a large stock and a staff that never seems quite enough. **Hatchard's** is another excellent chain with service that's a touch more personal than at Waterstone's. They're at 12 Watergate Street, Tel 348402. The local firm is excellent, with probably the best service of the lot. They are **Scrivener and Burgis** at 49 Bridge Street Row, Tel 349976. They certainly have the finest premises. There is a galleried room with an exposed timber ceiling, a 17th-century series of six stations of the Cross and, most unusually of all, the rear wall of the building now stands unaltered in the centre of the shop which was extended during the reign of Queen Victoria. The premises were of course a rectory, built under the Protectorate of Oliver Cromwell – an apt architectural setting for this traditional and richly stocked bookshop. Besides these three there is also **Bookland** at 121 Bridge Street, Tel 347323, which is the local agent for HMSO and a **W H Smith** branch at 11 Foregate Street, Tel 321106. Religious books can be found at **SPCK**, 7 St Werburgh Street, Tel 323753 (close to the Cathedral) while **Logos Books and Craft** is at 49 Frodsham Street close to the AA Office.

ANTIQUARIAN AND SECONDHAND BOOKS

One of my favourite locations is **Iain Campbell** at 5 Delamere Street, Upper Northgate Street, Tel 390727. (Walk through Northgate and Delamere Street is off Northgate Street on your right.) A good selection of antiquarian and secondhand books as well as old prints and ephemera. If you walk back down Northgate Street to the City Wall you will find **Avalon** at 1 City Walls, Northgate Street, Tel 318406. Besides books they also have postcards, stamps and assorted ephemera. Further down Northgate Street on your right is Chester Market Hall where at stalls B15/16 you will find **Earl's Eye Books**, Tel 319688. Turn left into Eastgate Street and on your left is the **SPCK Bookshop** which has an antiquarian and secondhand department. They are at 7 St Werburgh Street, Tel 323753. Walk down Eastgate Street to the Eastgate Clock and you will find **Made of Honour Antiques** at 11 City Walls, next to the clock at wall level. They have antiquarian and secondhand books as well as antiques. Finally, walk back down Eastgate Street into Watergate Street and turn left into Nicholas Street where at No 4 you will find another favourite shop of mine, **Stothert Antiquarian Books**, Tel 340756, with a fine collection of books both antiquarian and secondhand.

ART GALLERIES

First of all let me deal with two excellent galleries selling antique prints and maps. The **Antiquarian Map and Old Print Gallery** is at 54 Lower Bridge Street, Tel 344006 (under Gamul House), and **Richard Nicholson of Chester** is at 25 Watergate Street, Tel 326818. Both are excellent and should not be missed. I really must also mention **Paul C Delrue** at No 1 City Walls, Northgate Street. He is a hand bookbinder who also repairs and restores and his work is excellent. What's more he offers summer and evening classes in bookbinding. For contemporary art the **Ayling Porteous Gallery** at 33 City Road, Tel 314556, offers contemporary work by leading artists. (City Road is essentially a continuation of Foregate Street.) **Algora Contemporary Art**, Canal Warehouse, Whipcord Lane, Tel 382579, is also worth a visit. It is just north of the city walls past the Royal Infirmary. The **Art Shop** in the middle of town at 38 Watergate Row, Tel 320504, also has contemporary art and a lot more. **Baron Fine Art** at 68 Watergate Street has some fine Victorian and 20th-century paintings, Tel 342520, while **City Wall Galleries** have two shops on Northgate Street adjacent to Northgate. They deal in contemporary watercolours and oils and have some excellent limited edition prints plus Russell Flint prints. They can be reached at 349212. Finally, **St Peter's Fine Art Gallery** can be found in St Peter's Churchyard, Northgate Street, Tel 345500.

ANTIQUE DEALERS

Considerately, many of Chester's fine antique stores are conveniently clustered together. By far the greatest conurbation of shops is gathered in Watergate Row and Watergate Street.

Watergate Row first: At No 29 is **Christopher Pugh Antiques**, Tel 314137. Besides general antiques he also has ceramics, paintings and decorative items. He also keeps a shop at No 68 Watergate Street. Just down the road at No 49 is **Chester Antiques**, Tel 311768, while **Olwyn Boustead** is at No 61, Tel 342300. **Adams Antiques of Chester** is at No 65, Tel 319421. They specialize in 18th- and 19th-century decorative and traditional furniture, clocks, objets d'art, watercolours and oil paintings, and have some lovely pieces. Finally, **Filkin's Antiques**, Tel 318782, at No 22, Tel 315201, is worth a visit as is **Richard Nicholson**, Tel 326818, at No 25. Just down the street is **Watergate Antiques**, Tel 344516 at No 56. Still in the centre of the city, **Kayes of Chester** at 9 St Michael's Row, Tel 327149, has very attractive antique jewellery of all kinds as well as silver, silverplated ware, candlesticks, claret jugs and tea and coffee services. They also have some old wristwatches. Close by is **Bernard Walsh** at 11 St Michael's Row, Tel 326032, with a good collection of general antiques.

Next Lower Bridge Street, which is off Watergate Street in the centre of the city. They don't come much closer than here: **Dollectable Antique Dolls**, Tel 344888, are at No 53. Inside this Tudor building (circa 1621) is one of the foremost antique doll shops in the country. Even if you don't intend to buy you should visit. The range is remarkable: everything from early dolls, character dolls, baby dolls through to the 1930s plus French and German dolls. Remarkable! Close by at No 54 is **J A Hulme**, Tel 344006, with a good general collection, and not far away is **Soldier of Fortune** at No 56, Tel 328205, with some nice militaria.

Christleton Road is essentially the A41 Whitchurch Road which leads to the village of Christleton, two miles (3.2 km) from the city centre. At No 6 is **Second Time Around**, Tel 316394. They have a good general collection. At No 23 is **Farmhouse Antiques**, Tel 322478, while at No 25 is **Barn Antiques**, Tel 344928. Finally, **Chester Furniture Cave** at No 97A probably has the largest selection of quality furniture in the area. There are always over 500 items permanently on display.

City Road is essentially an extension of Foregate Street beyond the roundabout. At No 32 is **Barnhill Trading Company**, Tel 340666, and **Melody's Antique Galleries**, Tel 328968, both with good general collections. I have already mentioned **Made of Honour**, Tel 314208, which is at 11 City Walls. **Pearl Antiques**, 20 Handbridge, Tel 677088, is close to Chester Castle. Finally, **Moulin Rouge**, Tel 310197, is at 46 Gullden Sutton Lane and **Richmond Galleries** is at Watergate Buildings, Crane Wharf, Tel 317602.

RESTAURANTS

I don't think there's much doubt that the best restaurant in Chester is **Arkle** at the Chester Grosvenor in Eastgate Street, Tel 324024. Meals are by no means inexpensive. The best value is the set lunch which can include crab, salmon and mussel fritters and pigeon salad for starters, a roast, sweetbreads or turbot to follow and an excellent dessert to top things off. Dinner is of course more expensive, but memorable. Open Mon–Sat 12–2:30 and 7–10:30pm. No Mon lunch.

Abbey Green Restaurant – 2 Abbey Green, Northgate Street, Tel 313251, is set in a cobbled alley with civilized surroundings of soft Victorian furnishings and classical music. The focus is gourmet vegetarian cuisine, and very good it is too. Some of the meals produce totally new taste sensations and one begins to think that if all vegetarian cooking were like this it would be a cuisine one would be happy to embrace. Excellent. Open Mon–Sat 12–2:30 and 6:30–10:15pm.

Blue Bell Restaurant – 65 Northgate Street, Tel 317758. This is the oldest surviving domestic structure in Chester dating back to at least the 15th century. It is the city's sole remaining example of medieval domestic architecture, and its open fires, sloping floors, oak beams and a resident ghost make the quality of the food, in a sense, immaterial. But fear not, the cuisine has traditional English food at very good value. Open Mon–Sat 10am–11pm.

I really enjoyed **Francs** in Cuppin Street, Tel 317952 (just off Grosvenor Street). It's a traditional French restaurant serving home-made boudins (very good sausages), crepes, French casseroles and good fish. I thought the cooking was good and the whole experience great fun. Open weekdays noon to 11pm; Sun noon–3pm and 6:30–10pm. Finally, if you would like to spread your wings and eat in the beauty of the Cheshire countryside then **Crabwall Manor** at Mollington, Tel 851666, is your best bet. Mollington is a few miles northwest of Chester on the A450 to Parkgate in Parkgate Road. The red brick Tudor/Elizabethan house is beautifully maintained and friends tell me that Crabwall Manor offers the best value Sunday lunch in the area. The set dinner is excellent value for what it offers. Recommended. Open all week 12–2pm and 7–9pm.

PUBS

Boot Inn – Eastgate Row North, unlisted number. One of the oldest inns in Chester, dating from the 17th century. Oak flooring and flagstones, heavy beams, stained-glass windows and ancient wattle-and-daub walls exposed behind glass panels. Traditional bar snacks (not evenings).

Falcon – Lower Bridge Street, unlisted number. A splendidly ornamental timbered building dating from the 17th century, though the cellars go back some 700 years. Very carefully restored inside – staff even wear uniforms. Traditional hot meals and snacks (not evenings).

Bear and Bullet – Lower Bridge Street, Tel 321272. Small black-and-white-timbered pub by the river. A really charming atmosphere with traditional bar snacks.

City Arms – Foregate Street, unlisted number. Bright, clean interior set out in three themes – bookshop, toys and apothecary, and haberdashers behind the bar. Good range of hot and cold bar food.

King's Head – Lower Bridge, Tel 534013. Black-and-white-timbered premises dating back to 17th century. It even has original woodwork. Open all day. Traditional bar snacks. The accommodation even boasts four-poster beds. I wonder why three pubs in Chester feel the need to request British Telecom to withhold their telephone numbers? Too many relatives calling up to check on erring relatives perhaps....

ARTISTIC ASSOCIATIONS

Daniel Defoe, author of *Robinson Crusoe,* visited Chester in 1725 and was much taken with the walls. "The walls, as I have said, are in very good repair and it is a very pleasant walk round the city, upon the walls and within the battlements." Jonathan Swift of *Gulliver's Travels* fame used to travel to and from Ireland by way of Chester and in his *Journal to Stella* (1710) he often mentions the city. His friend, the poet Thomas Parnell, died here in 1718 after falling ill on his way to Ireland. James Boswell, biographer of Dr Johnson, expressed his delight to his mentor in a letter written during a stay in 1779. Boswell liked the city, but he was even more taken with the feminine society he came into contact with. "I am in a state of much enjoyment," he writes. "Chester pleases my fancy more than any town I ever saw." Thomas De Quincey, the famous essayist, ran away from Manchester Grammar School in July 1802. He made his way on foot to his mother's house in Chester, which was called the Priory, and was attached to the walls of the ancient Anglo-Saxon church of St John. After staying a while, he left to wander through Wales on an allowance of a guinea a week which his uncle had given him. In March 1803 he came back "to rest briefly after the storms" before going on to Worcester College, Oxford. His mother's house is now occupied by the Chester Police Headquarters. Thomas Hughes, author of *Tom Brown's Schooldays* came to live in Chester when he was appointed a county court judge in 1882. He and his wife, Fanny, moved into Uffington House (in Dee Hills Park), which they had built for them. The wrought-iron gates of the house embody the initials of Hughes and his wife – T H and F H. Henry James, the American novelist, author of *Washington Square* and *The Portrait of a Lady,* visited Chester in the 1870s and in his 1903 novel, *The Ambassadors,* he describes "the wicked old Rows of Chester rank with feudalism." Although the description in the novel does not seem to be one the local tourist office might publicize, James did not seem to hold that view personally. In an 1872 letter he writes, "The wall enfolds the place in a continuous ring which, passing through innumerable picturesque vicissitudes, often threatens to snap, but never fairly breaks the link; so that starting at any point, an hour's easy stroll will bring you back to your station. I have quite lost my heart to this charming creation..." It was almost as if James had read the booklet, "Chester Walls Walk," published by the Cheshire County Council. However, it was not published until 1989 and is well worth the small amount it will cost you to purchase it. Chester was the birthplace of the popular Victorian illustrator and painter, Randolph Caldecott. Best known for his children's picture books, Caldecott was among the first to make use of colour wood engravings. He was the son of a merchant hatter and attended the Henry VIII School. In 1861 the Liverpool animal painter, William Huggins, arrived in the town. His work can be seen at the Walker Art Gallery in Liverpool. He is buried close by in the little village of Chistelton, where he lived for the latter part of his life. He was, by all reports, a kindly and gentle man. His gravestone describes him as "a just and compassionate man, who would neither tread on a worm nor cringe to an emperor."

EPHEMERA

Most people are aware that the Saxon King Harold was defeated at the Battle of Hastings by William of Normandy (the Conqueror) and that Harold was slain by an arrow through his eye. According to a local legend he did not die in 1066 but came to Chester where he lived as a hermit in the Anchorite's Cell, a simple sandstone building to the north of the Groves. The legend does not tell us just whose body Harold's wife, Edith Swan-neck, identified after the battle, nor who is buried in Harold's grave at Waltham Abbey! But it is still a nice story.

The Chester Mystery Plays (religious plays performed by the craft guilds of the area) were of some importance in the life of the city and large sums of money were spent in staging them each year. They were also known as the Whitsun plays as they took place during three days of Whitsun week, nine on Monday, nine on Tuesday and six or seven on Wednesday. It is likely that the plays originated from a desire to make the Latin teaching of the church more intelligible to the people, and all were based on the Bible. Each city company undertook responsibility for staging a play, and the allocation was not wholly without appropriateness: for example, the story of the Flood was performed by the Water-drawers of Dee, the Last Supper by the Bakers, and so on. Each play was mounted on a large two-tiered wagon, the lower part being used as a dressing room (and as Hell, if required) the upper part as the main stage, and there is speculation among scholars that heavenly beings would appear on a ladder above the backdrop on the main stage. The first performance of the first play of the day was given at the abbey gateway, and from there the wagons would be drawn through the town, stopping at regular stations for further performances, so that the spectators, by remaining in one spot, would see a succession of plays performed before them. There are, of course, several cycles of mystery plays, but that of Chester is believed to be the oldest, dating from about 1375 and preceding other cycles at York, Coventry and other towns by several years. They continued to be performed regularly for 200 years until 1575 when they were suppressed by authorities as being "popish plaies." By this time too, the plays had developed a degree of secularity which was worrying clerics. A glance at the *Second Shepherd's Play* of the Wakefield Cycle will give you an idea of their concerns. Some of the plays have been revived in recent years, sponsored by the Chester City Council, and revised versions presented in the cathedral precincts and at the Cross.

During Chester's early history the ecclesiastical authorities wielded great power but there was a good relationship between the Church and the city. At the beginning of the 17th century a strain was placed on this seeming rapport. In 1607, a canon of the Cathedral challenged the ancient right of the mayor to enter the Cathedral preceded by the great civic sword carried point uppermost. Shortly afterwards, the sword-bearer died and when his corpse was carried to the Cathedral for burial, attended by the mayor and his council, the prebendary caused the west doors of the Cathedral to be shut against them. Nothing daunted, the mayor and his party gained entrance by another door and marched to their usual place in the choir with the sword borne before them and the body was eventually brought in. These incidents gave rise to considerable resentment in the town and legal action was taken to decide the issue. The two judges who heard the case upheld the city's claim, and the right of the mayor and his sword-bearer to carry the civic sword, point up, in the cathedral is still observed.

The Roodee is a feature unique to Chester. It takes its name from the rood, or cross, whose base can still be seen there and the word "eye" which means land partly surrounded by water. It was once the harbour of the Romans and after the legions left and the land silted up, the citizens used the area to graze their cattle, as a place of recreation and as a training ground for soldiers. In the 16th century, the football match between the Shoemakers' and Drapers' Companies began at the Cross on the Roodee. Football violence caused the City Assembly to ban the match in 1540. It was replaced first by foot races and later by horses. Chester Racecourse on the Roodee is therefore one of the oldest in the country. The main meeting is held every May – its richest prize, the Chester Cup, originated in the Chester Tradesmen's Plate, which was first run in 1824. The first grandstand on the Roodee was built in 1817 to provide accommodation for the gentry attending the races. What is nice is that parts of the Roman quay wall are still visible.

A local Chester saying is "When the daughter is stolen shut the Pepper-gate." This local version of horses and stable doors stems from a medieval mayor's bid to force his daughter to wed an English noble called Luke de Taney, instead of the Welsh knight she loved. During a ball game with de Taney and others in an orchard inside the city walls, the girl escaped. She flung the ball over the wall and persuaded the young Englishman to search for it. While he searched she slipped out of the tiny Pepper-gate and ran to her lover. Later, her angry and frustrated father, wise after the event, ordered the gate to be kept locked for evermore. Hence the expression.

MOLD

County of Delyn, North Wales
214 miles (342 km) from London by M1, M6, M56 and A550
3 hours by rail from London (Euston) to Chester, then bus

Mold used to be the county town of Flintshire before local government organization made Flint a part of the new county of Delyn. We suspect there was a settlement at Mold in Roman times, as a major Roman road passed within a mile of the town. An obelisk one mile to the west of the town shows where, in about AD 430, a victory was won by the British of the neighbourhood against some enemy advancing from the north. It is known as the Alleluia Victory since it is recorded (by the Venerable Bede, no less) that St Garmon, sent to propagate the Catholic faith in Britain, routed the opposing forces by hiding his troops until, with great cries of "Alleluia" echoing around the surrounding hills, they startled the enemy into flight. Scholars are doubtful about this incident, but it is a good story and certainly a battle was fought along that Roman road between supporters of one Christian belief and those of another. Just southwest of Mold is Llanarmon-yn-lal. The church there is double-naved and contains a figure of the Virgin thought to have been brought from the Monastery of Valle Crucis nr Llangollen at the time of the Dissolution. The church contains the tomb of Gruffydd ap Llywelyn (who lived about 1350). A little beyond the church at Llanferes is We Three Loggerheads Inn, with a signboard allegedly painted by the Welsh artist, Richard Wilson (see Artistic Associations). He died here in 1782 and is buried in the churchyard at Mold. (There is a fine window dedicated to him.)

Wilson began his career as a portrait painter and anticipated Gainsborough and Constable in forsaking strait-laced classicism for a lyrical freedom of style. He became one of the most famous painters of his day and his *View of Rome from the Villa Madama* is very well known.

The high street in Mold is picturesque and the parish church, dating from the 15th century, has an interesting roof, fine glass and interesting animal frescoes. The Mostyn Arms Inn bears a notice of the National Eisteddfod of 1873 of which Daniel Owen, the novelist and social critic, was chairman. Owen is often called the Thomas Hardy of Wales and his novels, written in Welsh, reflect the changes of his time and are full of shrewdly contemporary character sketches. Like Hardy, Owen was deeply concerned with the simplicity of life his generation seemed to be leaving behind. Owen received little education and at the age of 12 was apprenticed to a tailor. His novels, like those of Dickens, first appeared serially in periodicals.

Although not wishing to offend Welsh sensibilities, I must confess the real reason for including Mold in the towns listed in this book is that it gives the reader the chance to visit the wonderful arts complex at **Theatre Clwyd**. Built on a hill overlooking Mold and the Clwydian hills beyond, the theatre probably houses more aspects of art and entertainment than any other arts complex in the country. This dynamic centre houses a main theatre seating 535, a studio theatre, the **Emlyn Williams Theatre**, which is totally flexible and seats 250, a general-purpose room for music, lectures, conferences, etc, seating 350, a 129-seat film theatre, a professional and a community art gallery, an excellent restaurant, a variety of bars and a good bookshop. The complex is the home of the Theatre Clwyd Company which is a professional repertory company producing about eight plays each year and touring for some 15 weeks to other theatres in the UK. The productions range from the classics – Shakespeare, Sophocles, Molière and Ibsen – to modern playwrights such as Brian Friel, Joe Orton, Alan Ayckbourn, Tom Stoppard and Harold Pinter. There is also either a pantomime or a family show at Christmas and musicals such as *Cabaret, Little Shop of Horrors* and *Hair*. Productions are of an excellent quality and the company is highly regarded throughout the UK. Theatre Clwyd's film theatre shows more than 100 films a year ranging from the latest releases to works by David Lynch and Derek Jarman. Touring companies include opera (Music Theatre Wales), ballet (Ballet Rambert) and music (BBC Welsh Symphony Orchestra). There are also jazz, comedy, lectures, poetry, folk concerts and dramatic presentations in Welsh. Not content with this multiplicity of activity, the complex is also the home of the regional television company, HTV, which produces principally Welsh-language programmes and news coverage in its own TV studio and also in the theatres of the arts centre. It is quite remarkable that on an opening night of a Theatre Clwyd Company production, there might be a professional company playing in Welsh in the other auditorium, a jazz or folk concert in the Clwyd Room, a lecture taking place in the small lecture theatre, a film playing in the Film Theatre and perhaps two art exhibitions on view in the Oriel Gallery and elsewhere in the building. It is not unusual for well over 1000 public performances to take place in a year at the complex, making it one of the most dynamic arts centres in the whole of Britain.

I would recommend three places to eat. One is **Theatre Clwyd** which has excellent catering service and offers full-course meals and also snacks and sandwiches. Further afield, **We Three Loggerheads** (see above) is a beautifully refurbished pub situated four miles (6.4 km) away on the Ruthin Road (A494). Lots of beams, farm machinery and tiled floors give a country pub feeling and the food is excellent, ranging from sandwiches to curry and tandoori kebabs. What's more, it's served until 10pm. Finally, in Mold itself, the **Sybarite** (a person devoted to luxury and pleasure) is at 33 New Street, Tel 3814, and has a very good set dinner menu which is excellent value.

ARTISTIC ASSOCIATIONS

Beset by old age, poverty, alcoholism and ill health, Richard Wilson, "the father of British landscape painting," returned to Llanferres (4 miles/6.4 km south of Mold on A494) in his native Wales to spend his last days at Colomendy Hall, home of his cousin, Catherine Jones. According to local tradition, the Loggerheads Inn, near the entrance to the grounds of Colomendy, was much frequented by the artist, and an inn sign preserved in a glass case attached to the front wall is said to have painted by him, in part payment of his debts to the landlord. The work shows the heads of two men in profile facing away from each other with the inscription "We three Loggerheads" (the third being the spectator himself).

EPHEMERA

The animosity between the men of Chester and those living in the Welsh Borders is significant. Not only were Chester people not allowed to attend Welsh weddings but Welshmen were banned from the streets of Chester after sunset and allowed to carry no weapon apart from "a knife for their meat" during the day. Henry IV thought this necessary to keep the cross-border feuds to a minimum but the strife continued. In the early 15th century a Welshman called Reinallt, involved in a quarrel at Chester Fair, seized the mayor, carried him off to his castle at Mold and hanged him from the battlements. Reinallt and his followers then left the castle and hid in the woods to await their angry pursuers. Two hundred men of Chester quickly broke into the undefended castle, only to be trapped as Reinallt's band slammed the gates on them and set fire to the place. Those who managed to escape the blaze were butchered as they staggered out of the castle.

TOURIST INFORMATION BUREAU: Town Hall, Earl Street, Mold, Clwyd CH71AB. Tel (0352) 59331

HARROGATE

County of North Yorkshire
203 miles (325 km) from London by M1 and A61
2 hours 30 minutes by rail from London (King's Cross)

Harrogate's mineral springs were discovered by William Slingsby in 1571. He was a travelled man and he noticed that the water from Tewit (a local name for lapwing) Well tasted like water he had tasted in Continental spas. Tradition has it that Slingsby only stopped and tasted the water because his horse stumbled on the marshy ground. Slingsby arranged for the area to be paved and walled, and in about 1596 it was formally called a "spa," after the town of Spa in Belgium.

Interestingly, the nearby town of Knaresborough served as a spa long before Harrogate was developed. The Tewit Well is on the South Stray. Other wells were developed which became more popular because they were in High Harrogate where lodging houses, hotels and a theatre were built for spa visitors. These wells were impregnated with iron and were more pleasant-tasting than the sulphur waters of low Harrogate. Taste notwithstanding, in 1842 the Royal Pump Room was built over the Old Sulphur well. The water available at the Royal Pump Room is now the only spring still available to the public. If you try the sulphur water you will appreciate why it was once called "the Stinking Spaw" – it has a disgusting taste. From the early 17th century on, people flocked to the Old Sulphur well. The well in the basement is still the original and was once at street level. Its potent waters were used for both internal and external cures. As late as 1926 no less than 1500 glasses of sulphur water were served here in a single morning. The Royal Pump Room itself replaced the simple circular stone canopy that had been erected over the four tapped well heads erected in 1804. It is now a museum. The canopy can now be seen over the site of the original Tewit Well, which is opposite the Royal Crescent off the Leeds Road at the west end of the Stray. Before the Royal Pump Room and the Royal Baths and Royal Hall and other amenities were opened, people used to bathe in their lodging-houses or hotels. They would lie in a tub, the water warmed as hot as was bearable, for anywhere from 10 to 30 minutes. This was followed by sweating in a blanket bed. Whether taken externally or internally, the waters seemed helpful in relieving rheumatism, gout, digestive ailments, constipation, lumbago and skin diseases, or just to restore jangled nerves. Exercise was considered an important part of the cure and in 1770 the Stray was declared "open and unenclosed" by George III – as it is to this day. The demand for the cure declined as new drugs were developed but you can still take a Turkish bath in the sumptuous Royal Baths and brave the taste of the spa water at the Royal Pump Room (now a museum). Unlike some spa towns, Harrogate has adapted well to the decline in the spa's popularity. Attractive in itself and handy for some of the best scenery in Yorkshire and the North, Harrogate is a popular convention centre where modern facilities such as the Harrogate Convention Centre sit easily with the dignified late 19th-century houses and hotels built of dark stone. It is easy to imagine crinolined ladies and frock-coated gentlemen strolling the gardens and elegant streets as they did in the town's Victorian and Edwardian heyday. Unlike many other towns, Harrogate has entered the last part of the 20th century with all its former charms still evident.

WALK

Our **Harrogate Walk** begins at the Tower Street multistorey car park off West Park Road (becomes Leeds Road) in the Stray. Come out into West Park and turn left. At the roundabout, walk diagonally left across the **Stray**, with Leeds Road on your right, to **Tewit Well**, the first well discovered. During the 18th and especially the 19th century, Harrogate's fame as a spa rivalled such towns as Bath, Buxton, Tunbridge Wells and Cheltenham. Retrace your steps to West Park and go ahead, noting the fine Georgian and Victorian houses on your right and more of the **Stray** on your left. Of the houses, **Cathcart House** once played host to Russian royalty while the **Congregational Church** (1862) is especially fine. As you pass into Parliament Street the tall obelisk is the **War Memorial**. The Post Office is nearby as is the Gothic **Westminster Arcade**. Turn left into Crescent Road. On the left are the **Royal Baths** (the Tourist Information Centre is inside) and the **Royal Hall**. You will see the name Kursaal (German for casino) in stone, which was the original name of the hall when it opened in 1903. It was changed during the First World War. Ahead are the **Valley Gardens**. Harrogate's somewhat dour and serious buildings are considerably lightened by the magnificent displays of flowers, well-kept lawns and shady trees of its many parks. If you continue through the Valley Gardens to the Pine Woods and Birk Crag you will come to the splendid **Harlow Car Gardens** – but it is two miles (3.2 km) there and back. At the far end of the Valley Gardens is the **Sun Pavilion**, a large glass-domed building, and in the bottom of the valley is an octagonal building, with wrought-iron terraces and a dome and cupola, built in 1895 to serve waters from the Magnesia Well. Today it sells tea and ice cream! In the centre of the Gardens (venue of the celebrated Spring Flower Show) is an area, marked by a plaque, known as **Bogs Field** where there are 36 different mineral wells.

Come back to the entrance to the gardens and cross the road to the **Royal Pump Room Museum**. Just to the left, on Swan Road, is the **Mercer Gallery**, housed in a building that began life in 1806 as the Promenade Room, was reincarnated as a theatre for a time and then, at its most mundane, served as the rates and housing benefits office, known as the Old Town Hall. Pass to the left of the Royal Pump Room and walk into **Royal Parade**, passing the old grocery firm of Farrah's, makers of famous Harrogate toffee since 1840, to the **Crown Hotel** where Byron stayed in 1807. Cross the roundabout into Montpellier Parade with its gardens on the right. This is another area redolent with Victorian and Edwardian ambience. The area at the top of Montpellier is known to the locals as "the pierhead." You are now back at

CROWN PLACE AND ROYAL PUMP ROOM MUSEUM
HARROGATE

the War Memorial. Back down Parliament Street on the right is Oxford Street, which has a notable **Wesley Chapel** and the **Harrogate Theatre**, originally the Opera House. Return to the junction of Montpellier Hill and Parliament Street and continue ahead to West Park. Pass the junction with Victoria Avenue and turn left into Tower Street and the car park.

MUSEUMS, GALLERIES AND PUBLIC BUILDINGS

Royal Baths and Royal Hall – Crescent Road, Tel 565757. You can still get a Turkish bath here although the sulphur baths and poultices of local fango (hot mud) have disappeared. The Royal Hall serves as a concert hall.

Royal Pump Room Museum – Royal Parade, Tel 503340. The museum is Harrogate's historic Pump Room, built in 1842. The original wellhead is in the basement and water from it is available. The museum is pleasantly laid out with a diverse selection of exhibits. These include Harrogate's last Bath Chair, a collection of 19th-century bicycles, a superb Victorian doll's house and a doll collection and the contents of a saddler's shop that once stood in Royal Parade. Open Mon–Sat 10:30–5pm, Sun 2–5pm.

Mercer Gallery – Swan Road, Tel 503340. Opened in the spring of 1991, the gallery is housed in the Spa Promenade Room, built in 1806. The collection is representative of English art with works by Thomas Rowlandson, George Romney, Burne-Jones, John Piper, Walter Sickert, Sidney Nolan, John Singer-Sargent and Ivon Hitchens. There is a collection of naive paintings and the Kent Collection of antiquities. Open Mon–Fri 10–5pm, Sat 10–4pm.

THEATRE

Harrogate Theatre – Oxford Street, Tel 502116. Built as the splendid Grand Opera House in 1900, the theatre opened with an entertainment, the proceeds of which were given to the Boer War Fund. For the first 45 years of its existence the theatre played to many members of the armed forces as Harrogate was an important convalescent centre for troops in both world wars. Harrogate in fact has had four theatres since its establishment as a spa. The first Georgian Theatre was in Mansfield House (1788) in Church Square and is now a private house – Edmund Kean played there. The Promenade Room in Swan Road (now the Mercer Art Gallery) flourished in the third quarter of the 19th century and the Empire Theatre in the town centre is now a restaurant. The present Harrogate Theatre provides a professional repertory season from September to May and fills the vacant months with amateur productions, children's shows, professional touring companies and jazz.

MUSIC

International concerts are presented at the Royal Baths throughout the year, Tel 564433, but the best time, musically, to visit Harrogate is during the **Harrogate International Festival**, Tel 565757, which is held during the last week of July and the first week of August. Recent visitors have included the Northern Sinfonia, the English Sinfonia under Sir Charles Groves, the Endellion String Quartet and the London Concert Orchestra. Britten's *The Turn of the Screw* has been produced by the Festival and there are film, jazz, cabaret and dance.

The **Harrogate Spring Festival**, Tel 565757, runs in May and a recent theme was the work of the cellist Julian Lloyd Webber. The Festival acts as a curtain-raiser to the larger International Festival. Five miles (8 km) to the south of Harrogate on the A61 to Leeds is **Harewood House**, an opulent 18th-century mansion, home of the Earl and Countess of Harewood. Magnificent Robert Adam decorations and a notable collection of paintings (El Greco, Tintoretto, Titian, Turner, Sargent and Munnings) are well worth a visit, while in the summer, open-air concerts are also held. Tel 0625 573477.

CINEMA

Commercial cinema at **Odeon Cinema**, East Parade, Tel 521590 (2 screens).

BOOKSHOPS

The best are **Austick's**, 16 Oxford Street, Tel 502314 (they also have very good shops in Leeds), **Dillon's**, 40 James Street, Tel 509435 and **Hammick's**, 15 James Street, Tel 531953. Bargain books are best at **Book Sales**, 11 Cambridge Street, Tel 527921 and **S G Hitchen** at 16 Oxford Street, Tel 502314 and **Premium Books**, 11 Magnus Court, Cold Bath Road, Tel 500757, are also worth a look.

ANTIQUARIAN AND SECONDHAND BOOKS

Harrogate Bookshop – 29 Cheltenham Crescent, Tel 500479, has a large general stock and specializes in music, literature, history and local history.

J E Courtney – Fine Books – 5 Mount Parade, Tel 500341, also has all subjects but especially literature, topography, transport, maritime, history and sport.

Rippon Bookshop – 6 Station Bridge (1st floor) Tel 501835, has all subjects but especially Yorkshire local history and topography, while **Bookstop Bookshop**, 11 Mayfield Grove, Tel 505817, has all subjects and a good paperback selection; it specializes in military, Yorkshire and the occult.

ART GALLERIES

Chantry House Gallery – Ripley, Tel 770141, has contemporary oils, watercolours and pastels as well as limited edition prints. **Amaron Arts**, 6 Strawberry Dale Avenue, Tel 507949, on the other hand, has just watercolours by the local artist who is also the proprietor. **Creskeld Gallery**, 2A High Street, Patelely Bridge, Tel 711353, focuses on Yorkshire artists with oils, pastels and watercolours. **Godfrey and Twatt**, 7 Westminster Arcade, Parliament Street, Tel 525300, have very attractive contemporary ceramics, original paintings, jewellery and glass, while **Gordon Reece Ceramics**, 8 Kirkgate, Tel 868084, has ceramics from around the world, as far afield as Afghanistan and India, as well as antique ceramics. **Sutcliffe Galleries**, 5 Royal Parade, specializes in paintings of the Victorian era and earlier, Tel 562976, while **Walker Galleries**, 6 Montpellier Gardens, Tel 5679333, has 19th-century oils and watercolours, Oriental ceramics and some period English furniture. **McTague of Harrogate**, 17/19 Cheltenham Mount, Tel 567086, has a fine collection of antique prints and paintings. **Harrogate Fine Arts**, 77 Station Parade, Tel 530355, deals exclusively in 20th-century oils while **Old Masters Gallery**, 4 Crescent Road, Tel 521142, has contemporary oils and watercolours and limited edition prints.

ANTIQUE DEALERS

There are a lot of antique dealers in Harrogate. A greater concentration in fact than practically anywhere in the north. I have divided the dealers into seven areas, geographically, so they can be found easily. I start with the Antique Markets:

West Park Antiques – 20 West Park, Tel 561758. Six dealers selling English furniture, paintings, Oriental antiques, pottery, jewellery, maps, silver, copper, brass, porcelain, art nouveau and Art Deco and clocks.

Montpellier Mews Antiques Market – Montpellier Street, Tel 530484. Twenty dealers selling general antiques, paintings, porcelain, Oriental carpets and jewellery. There is also a restaurant.

Grove Collectors Centre – Grove Road, Tel 561680. Eight dealers selling general antiques, stamps, militaria, silver, collectables and furniture.

Now for the areas:
West Park:
Rodney Kent – 20 West Park, Tel 560352. 18th-, 19th- and 20th-century paintings, drawings and watercolours, Oriental antiques and English furniture.

Town Centre (east of West Park, west of Station parade, north of Victoria Avenue):
Christopher Warner – 15 Princess Street, Tel 503617. Silver and jewellery.
Ogden of Harrogate – 38 James Street, Tel 504123. Antique jewellery, silver, clocks, 19th-century pictures.
John H Preston – 39 James Street, Tel 503187. Old cameras, scientific and meteorological instruments, ship's clocks, compasses, sextants and octants. Well worth a look even if you are not buying.

Low Harrogate (Montpellier, south of Crescent Road, west of West Park):
London House Oriental Rugs and Carpets – 9 Montpellier Parade, Tel 567167. Persian, Turkish, Caucasian carpets and rugs, Kelims and tribal trappings.
Armstrong – 10/11 Montpellier Parade, Tel 506843. 18th-century furniture, glasses and works of art.
Bill Bentley – 16 Montpellier Parade, Tel 564084. Period oak and country furniture, brass, copper, treen (wooden objects) and textiles.
Shaw Brothers – 21 Montpellier Parade, Tel 567466. Porcelain, silver, antique jewellery and objets d'art.
Derbyshire Antiques – 27 Montpellier Parade, Tel 503115. Early oak and walnut furniture. Georgian to 1820 and decorative items.
Weatherell's Antiques – 29 Montpellier Parade, Tel 525004. Period furniture.
Charles Lumb – 2 Montpellier Gardens, Tel 503776. Old English furniture and metalware.
Thorntons of Harrogate – 1 Montpellier Gardens, Tel 504118. 17th-, 18th- and 19th-century furniture, clocks, porcelain, bronzes, arms and armour, paintings, scientific instruments and ivories.
Garth Antiques – 2 Montpellier Parade, Tel 530573. 19th-century furniture and general antiques.
Windmill Antiques – 4 Montpellier Mews. 18th- and 19th-century furniture, metalware, collector's items, children's chairs, rocking horses, boxes, inkstands and fenders.
Ginnel-Harrogate Antiques Centre – The Ginnel off Parliament Street, Tel 567182. Wide range of antiques on two floors. Coffee Shop.
Elaine Phillips – 1 and 2 Royal Parade, Tel 569745. At No 1, mahogany and decorations; at No 2, period oak furniture, metalware and associated items.
David Love Antiques – 10 Royal Parade, Tel 565797. 18th-century English furniture, 18th- and 19th-century English and Continental furniture, Oriental ceramics.
W F Greenwood – 2-3 Crown Place, Tel 504467. Period furniture, silver, jewellery, pottery and porcelain.
Omar Ltd – 8 Crescent Road, Tel 503675. Oriental carpets and rugs.
B R Morrison – 11 York Road, Tel 503123. English longcase and bracket clocks. By appointment.

Cold Bath Area (south of West Park):
Haworth Antiques – 26 Cold Bath Road, Tel 521401. Furniture, clocks.
Paraphernalia – 38A Cold Bath Road, Tel 567968. Bric-à-brac, postcards, cutlery, plates, small furniture and collectors' items.

King's Road, Cheltenham Parade and Cheltenham Mount Area (south of King's Road, east of West Park):
Bloomers – 14 Cheltenham Crescent, Tel 569389. Antique lace, period fashions, fans, bed and table linens, samplers and quilts.
Antiques and Collectables – 39 Cheltenham Crescent, Tel 521897. Jewellery, watches, silver and collector's items.
Antique and Furniture Centre – 44 King's Road, Tel 509708. 19th-century mahogany, oak and pine furniture, collectables, decorative items and old tools.
Ann-Tiquities – 12 Cheltenham Parade, Tel 503567. Antique linen, silver, brass, copper and small collectables.
Ages Ago Antiques – 2 Granville Road, Tel 507077. Collectables, bric-à-brac, willowcraft, collector's bears, dolls, doll's houses and country crafts.
Paul M Peters Antiques – 15 Bower Road, Tel 560118. 17th- to 19th-century Chinese and Japanese ceramics and works of art, European ceramics, metalware and collectable objects.

High Harrogate:
Dragon Antiques – 10 Dragon Road, Tel 562037. Art glass, topographical postcards, pottery, up to the 1950s.
Smith's Ltd – Dragon Road, Tel 503217. Large stock of old English and continental furniture.
D Mason – 7/8 Westmoreland Street, Tel 567305. Victorian, Edwardian and secondhand furniture, jewellery and antique clocks.
Antique Pine – Library House, Regent Parade, Tel 560452. Period pine, decorative items, old kitchen treasures, collector's antiques.
Cottage Antiques – 3 Devonshire Place, Skipton Road, Tel 568195. Period oak, country furniture, rural bygones, 19th-century blue-and-white pottery, collector's items.

Knaresborough Road and Starbeck (east on Knaresborough Road A59):
Singing Bird Antiques – 19 Knaresborough Road, Tel 888292. 18th- to 20th-century pottery and porcelain, pewter, silver and small antiques.
John Daffern – 38 Forest Lane Head, Starbeck, Tel 889832. Period furniture, clocks, pottery, porcelain.

RESTAURANTS

Drum and Monkey – 5 Montpellier Gardens, Tel 502650. Excellent for fish. I had a fresh steaming bowl of moules marinière which was as good as any I've tasted outside of France. The monkfish kebabs have been well spoken of and everything is fresh. The set lunch and dinner are good value, given the quality of the food. It's good to see a wine list in a fish restaurant that is 90 percent white. Friendly and efficient service. Open Mon–Sat 12–2:30 and 7–10:15pm.
Millers – 1 Montpellier Mews, Tel 530708. Small restaurant with excellent cooking. The fish soup is excellent, as is the guinea fowl. I've noticed in a number of restaurants that pig's trotters are making a gastronomic comeback and here they're stuffed with crab and ginger! The crème caramel is excellent – always the mark of a good restaurant. The fixed price menu offers the best value but the wine list is pricey. Open Mon–Sat 12–2 and 7–10pm. No Mon dinner.
Betty's – 1 Parliament Street, Tel 502746. You can't come to Harrogate and not have a real afternoon tea any more than you can in Bath or Cheltenham, and Betty's is one of the best. Don't expect a bargain, but the quality makes up for what at first seems expensive. Their cream teas are delicious and served by a friendly and jolly staff. Good sandwiches and interesting things on toast. They bake their own bread, scones, cakes, etc, so everything is fresh. Good evening meals too. Open all week 9am–9pm.
William and Victoria – 6 Cold Bath Road, Tel 506883. A stylish basement bistro/wine bar close to the Pump Room. The cuisine is Anglo-French, with good reports about the salmon with cucumber sauce. Aubergine and tomato bake will delight you even if you are not a vegetarian and the desserts range from the sophisticated to the simple. Open Mon–Sat 12–2 and 6–10pm. No Sat lunch.

PUBS

Montpellier Arms – Montpellier Terrace. A real "local" with friendly efficient service. They have a wonderful Yorkshire pudding with liver and onion gravy for lunch which will set you up for the day.
Gardener's Arms – Bilton Lane, Tel 565860. Small house converted into a pub with a wonderfully peaceful setting. Totally unspoilt, with a tiny bar, three small panelled rooms, lovely garden. Friendly atmosphere.
Tap and Spile – 31 Tower Street, Tel 526785. Another small unspoilt local with wooden floors and friendly atmosphere. Very good homemade pies and sandwiches.
Squinty Cat – Whinney Lane (off the B6162 west of Harrogate towards Beckwithshaw) Tel 565650. Hard to find, but worth it. 18th-century pub with stone walls fashioned from an old railway bridge, lots of grain sacks, barrels, bottles and pine. Wonderful atmosphere. Excellent sophisticated bar food. Close to Harlow Gardens.
The Crown – Crown Place, Tel 567755. Elegant 18th-century hotel with ties to Lord Byron, Sir Walter Scott and J B Priestley. Very elegant bar with good quality bar food. The Brontë Bar is most pleasant. It's a Trust House Forte Hotel which is as good a guarantee of quality as you're likely to find in Britain.

ARTISTIC ASSOCIATIONS

The characters of Tobias Smollett's *Humphrey Clinker* visited Harrogate at the height of its fame as a spa. The novelist Elizabeth Hamilton, best known for *The Cottagers of*

Glenburnie, came to live in the town in 1816, persuaded that a warmer climate than Edinburgh would benefit her health. She died here the same year and is buried in Christ Church High Harrogate. A marble tablet in the church, placed by her sister, identifies her as "one who was the ornament, the instructress and the example of her sex." The Crown Hotel in Crown Place has connections with Lord Byron, Sir Walter Scott and J B Priestley. In 1926 Agatha Christie, the great crime writer, was found at the Old Swan Hotel after her mysterious disappearance. She had gone away without telling anyone of her whereabouts and (possibly because of her vocation) foul play was suspected. She had in fact taken refuge at the hotel for peace and quiet. Michael Apted's 1979 film *Agatha,* with Dustin Hoffman and Vanessa Redgrave, documented the story and was made on location in the town.

EPHEMERA

John Metcalf ("Blind Jack") was born in Knaresborough in 1717 and though sightless from the age of six, won lasting fame as a roadmaker. He has been called the most remarkable Yorkshireman of all, which places him on a very high pedestal. Even as a boy Jack showed that his blindness was no handicap. He rode, climbed trees and swam. Later he guided travellers across the wilds of Knaresborough Forest, became a popular fiddler in local inns, especially the Granby Hotel in Granby Road and eloped with his bride, Dolly Benson (daughter of the landlord of the Royal Oak in Dacre Banks), the day before she was to have married another man. But his most solid achievement was his skill in laying roads over boggy ground, something never successfully managed before, by means of laying a foundation of bundles of heather or ling. I wonder what he would think of the motorways traversing his native county today.

Ursula Southeil, the grotesque woman who was destined to be England's most famous prophetess, was born in 1488 in a small cave in Knaresborough, three miles (4.8 km) east of Harrogate on the A59. Her mother, Agatha, died giving her birth and her death was apparently attended by strange and terrible noises. Ursula was placed in the care of one of the townswomen who, returning from market one day, found Ursula and her cradle suspended inside the chimney, nine feet above the ground. Mysterious events continued to plague the cottage as the child grew up. Furniture moved of its own accord and food vanished from the plates of startled guests. In 1512 Ursula married Toby Shipton – hence Mother Shipton – and her renown as a fortuneteller and prophetess began in earnest. Neighbours were forever prying into her private life, and she is said to have taken revenge on them by causing them to burst into paroxysms of laughter as they sat at table and then making them flee the house pursued by a hideous goblin. When brought before the local magistrate, Mother Shipton is reported to have told him that far worse things would happen if she wasn't left alone. She then shouted out the magic words, "Updraxi, call Stygician Helluci," and was carried off by a winged dragon. This was a contemporary report of her trial, you understand. She predicted trains, the telegraph, automobiles, ocean liners, the Great Exhibition of 1851, the Crimean War and the Klondike Gold Rush, among other events. Most of the prophecies ascribed to her are now known to have been written by a man named Hindley in 1871, but despite this she continues to be Yorkshire's most famous witch; Mother Shipton's Cave in Knaresborough is her memorial. Close by the Cave is the Dropping Well, whose waters, trickling over a limestone rock, are so charged with calcium that they encrust with lime or "petrify" objects hung beneath them. Bowler hats, toys and gloves are all allowed to petrify and when an auction of petrified objects was held for a Yorkshire charity, a Teddy bear who had been in the well for four years was found to have gained 24 pounds in weight. He sold for £15.

The inventor of one of the most useful motoring innovations was a passionate Yorkshireman who often visited Harrogate. Percy Shaw was born in Halifax (15 miles/

24 km southwest of Leeds) and one foggy night was driving from Bradford to Halifax along a road with a sheer drop on one side. Usually he had no difficulty seeing his way, even in fog, because the steel tramlines shone in his headlights and he could follow them down the road. But on this night the lines had been taken up for repair. He drove with great caution, knowing that a mistake could put him over the edge. He was actually heading straight for the fence guarding the drop when his headlights picked up two points of light; they were the eyes of a black cat sitting on a fence-post.

Percy Shaw made his first cat's eyes in 1934 and it is estimated that these little reflectors, sunk in the road, have saved thousands of lives. Shaw's invention can be found in virtually every country in the world and it has been estimated that his wealth approached £11 million. In spite of his millions he steadfastly believed that he could find everything he wanted in his native Yorkshire, and probably the longest journey he ever made was to London to receive his OBE. Likewise his lifestyle changed very little after he became wealthy. He continued to live in the same house as his father had done, refused to have curtains in his windows as they obscured the view and would not allow carpets on his floors because they attracted tobacco ash. He did buy a custom-built Rolls Royce, however, with a fitted cocktail cabinet, reading lamps at the back and front, and three television sets, all kept permanently tuned to the three different channels then available.

As his business expanded, the workshop where he made his first cat's eyes using handmade tools was torn down and replaced by a substantial factory. Next to his workshop was a sycamore tree he used to climb as a boy and he refused to let it be felled. The factory was consequently built around it and the sycamore still proudly flourishes, its upper branches poking out of the factory roof in the heart of a 20-acre industrial site – an unusual monument to a remarkable man.

TOURIST INFORMATION BUREAU: Royal Bath Assembly Rooms, Crescent Road, Harrogate , North Yorks, HG1 2RR. Tel (0423) 525669

LANCASTER

County of Lancashire
236 miles (378 km) from London by M1 and M6
By rail, 3 hours 10 minutes from London (Euston)

The history of Lancaster goes back more than seven and a half centuries. There were early occupations of Castle Hill – prehistoric flint implements have been found in the vicinity – and the Romans chose the site for its strategic position overlooking the place where their main route to the northwest crossed the River Lune. The river could be forded here at low tide, yet approached by transport ships at high tide. We do not know what name the Romans called their settlement but there is evidence that, roughly where Church Street stands today, there was a town of temples, shops, inns and private houses, where the families of the soldiers lived. Like garrison towns throughout history, it also attracted many merchants and shopkeepers who served the needs of the soldiers and their families. A Saxon church, a Benedictine monastery, and later a mighty Norman castle followed on the same site. William I bestowed Halton Manor, which included Lancaster, on Roger de Poitou and the latter began the building of the castle in the 11th century. The great keep was built in 1170 and the massive Lungers Tower also dates from this period. The castle was strengthened around 1400 and its most distinctive feature – the twin-towered

THE OLD PALM HOUSE
AT THE ASHTON MEMORIAL
LANCASTER

gatehouse known as John of Gaunt's Gateway – was built a few years later. In the 1790s the neo-Gothic Shire Hall, the Crown Court and the high enclosing walls which isolate the prison were erected. Throughout most of its history, Lancaster Castle has been a prison and that tradition continues up to today. It is said that more people have been sentenced to death here than in any other English town, including (in 1865) the last man to be publicly hanged. The "Witches of Pendle" were sentenced here in 1612 in the former Crown Court which is now the Barristers' Robing Room and George Fox, the founder of the Society of Friends, or Quakers, was twice imprisoned here in the 1650s. Hadrian's Tower, which was drastically restored in the 18th and 19th centuries, is now a museum and contains a Roman altar found during rebuilding. John of Gaunt is much associated with the castle (see Ephemera). The memory of the hundreds doomed to the torture chamber and gallows gives the castle a somewhat malignant air: the ankle chains and neck and waist bands used to confine prisoners can be seen in Hadrian's Tower and the branding iron that burned "M" (for malefactor) into the victims' hands is on view in the Crown Court.

Lancaster grew up around its castle and is notable for the fine Georgian buildings put up in the middle of the 18th century, when Lancaster's port, reached by vessels which had negotiated the treacherous Lune River, was the recipient of much of the tobacco, sugar and rum trade from the West Indies. Along St George's Quay, built between 1750 and 1755, are fine warehouses, but the jewel in the crown is the former Custom House, designed in 1765 by Richard Gillow, who was also famous as one of the family of fine cabinet-makers. His beautiful building is now the city's Maritime Museum. Many of the merchants who owned ships and stored goods on the quay lived on Castle Hill, where there are many fine houses. Queen's Square, Queen Street and Dalton Square, which was intended to resemble the new and elegant squares of London, are all worth exploring. If you descend Church Street from the Priory Church, other examples of fine buildings can be found; see especially Nos 78 and 80. At the head of Church Street is the Judge's Lodgings, built in 1620. It offered an early foretaste of the classical style that was soon to prevail and from 1826 on it accommodated judges visiting Lancaster for the assizes. The house is now a museum with a collection of dolls and fine furniture by the local firm of Gillow. The former Town Hall, circa 1783, in Market Square now houses the City Museum. Its ground floor was once open and unglazed and was used as a corn exchange. Tucked in behind Market Street is Sun Street, where the Music Room, for me Lancaster's most delightful building, can be seen. Dating from 1730, it was used as a sort of pavilion or summer house. There is gorgeous plasterwork on the ceiling.

The Priory and Parish Church of St Mary shares the castle's hilltop site, while the

Roman Catholic Cathedral was built in 1852. The Ashton Memorial (see Ephemera) was given to the town in the early part of the 20th century by Lord Ashton, who also gave the city its New Town hall (designed by E W Mountford, who was responsible for London's Old Bailey), the Queen Victoria Monument and the Luneside Gardens.

In St Leonardgate is the Grand Theatre, used by amateur drama companies in the city. It stands on the site of the old Athenaeum, where Mrs Siddons acted. Dickens stayed at the Royal King's Arms in Market Street, which was built in Victorian times on the site of an inn of 1625. It has a resident ghost, a murdered bride who walks the corridors at night. Luckily, most rooms have ensuite bathrooms! On his southward march in 1745, Bonnie Prince Charlie stayed in the house which is now the Conservative Club (he wasn't to know!) and Laurence Binyon, the poet and art historian best known for the famous line, "... they shall not grow old as we that are left grow old," used on Remembrance Sundays, was born in a simple house in the High Street.

WALK

Our **Lancaster Walk** begins at the car park in the Mitre Centre in Dameside Street off Bridge Street. Follow the pedestrian exit to the small square at the head of Church Street. The **Judge's Lodgings** occupy the whole of one side of the cobbled area. Go up the path and steps to **Lancaster Castle** and the **Priory Church of St Mary**. Go down the path at the rear of the church which is called Vicarage Lane and go through the first gap in the hedge, on the right, across the field where you can see the foundations of a **Roman Bath House**, perhaps once attached to an inn for official visitors. Return to Vicarage Lane and continue down to the cycle track at the bottom. Turn left along it and then right into Vicarage Terrace and down the steps to the river and **St George's Quay**. Turn left along the quay to the **Custom House Maritime Museum**. By the museum, turn right up Elm Street and then left, behind the warehouses back to the cycle track which is the track bed of the old railway line. Follow this along the curve of the river to Water Street where you turn right. Continue ahead through Chapel Street, past the elegantly proportioned **St John's Church**, built in the mid-18th century. The church's spire was added in 1784 by Thomas Harrison, who also added the cupola to the old Town Hall. The church is no longer used for worship but is lovingly cared for and occasionally opened for recitals and special tours. Go ahead through Stonewell and at the junction with Moor Lane on your left, fork right into Great John Street. In Moor Lane is the **Duke's Playhouse** and a little further on, the **Golden Lion** (see Ephemera). The **Ashton Memorial** is in the distance. At the top of Great John Street, cross into Dalton Square. Walk round the square, noting the **Town Hall** and **Victoria Memorial** and exit via Gage Street which is off Great John Street. Go through the arch at the bottom of the street and turn right into the pedestrianized Penny Street. Note the horse-shoe set in the pavement at Horseshoe Corner (see under John of Gaunt in Ephemera), and turn left into Market Street. Market Street is also pedestrianized and halfway along you will come into the Market Square dominated by the **Old Town Hall**, now the **City Museum**. A little farther along, through a low narrow archway by a bank is the **Music Room**, which stands in a little open square. Return to Market Street and go across the crossroads, past the Royal King's Arms and turn right up Castle Hill, noting the superb **John of Gaunt's Gateway** on your left. There are fine 18th-century merchants' houses to your right, while the Castle walls are on your left. No 15 Castle Hill houses the **Cottage Museum**. Continue till you see the Judge's Lodgings on your left and the car park is right ahead.

MUSEUMS AND PUBLIC BUILDINGS

Lancaster City Museum – Market Square, Tel 64637. Occupying the old Town Hall, the museum's collections illustrate the archaeology and history of the Lancaster area, including Roman artefacts and a wide range of industries such as cabinet-making, textiles, linoleum, pottery, clog-making, hand knitting and oatcake making. There is a splendid 18th-century fire engine and a 7th-century log coffin. Under the same roof is the museum of the **King's Own Lancaster Regiment**. Open daily April–Oct 11–5pm; Nov–May 2–5pm.

Lancaster Maritime Museum – Custom House, St George's Quay, Tel 64637. Built during the Golden Age of the town's overseas trade, the former Custom House, circa 1764, houses examples of the 18th- and 19th-century trade, especially with the West Indies, together with the development of shipbuilding and allied activities. Other displays show the former importance of the fishing and shellfish-gathering economy in Morecombe Bay and the Lune Estuary. There is an 18-foot salmon fishing boat and a reconstruction of an early 20th-century fisherman's cottage. There is a reconstruction of the room used by the Collector of Customs in 1880 and information about the Lancaster Canal, opened in 1797, which allowed coal to be brought cheaply to the textile mills which grew up along its banks. For a brief period between 1833 and 1846, travellers were provided with a fast packet boat service between Lancaster and Kendal and Preston. The boat travelled at the dizzy speed of 10 miles (16 km) per hour, meals were served on board and the Lancaster-to-Kendal fare was one penny. Opening hours as City Museum.

Judges' Lodgings – Church Street, Tel 32808. This distinguished and impressively sited town house contains two distinct museums – the Gillow and Town House Museum and the Museum of Childhood. The first has exhibits illustrating the history and products of the famous Lancaster cabinet-making firm of Gillow, together with period room settings containing Gillow furniture and other local makers. There is a parlour circa 1750, a dining room and servant's hall circa 1820 and a bedroom of 1850. In the Museum of Childhood one can see dolls from the Barry Elder Collection and reconstructions of a Victorian schoolroom and Edwardian day and night nurseries. Open April–Oct Mon–Fri 2–5pm; May–June also Sat 2–5pm; July–Sept also 10–1pm.

Cottage Museum – 15 Castle Hill, Tel 64637. The cottage forms half of a larger house, built in 1739, which was divided into two dwellings in 1820. It reconstructs the internal layout and furnishings of a better-off working-class home of the period when the house was divided. There is also a display of original documents illustrating the history of the property. Open as City Museum.

Cathedral Church of St Peter – East Road, Tel 61860. This is the Cathedral Church of the Catholic Diocese of Lancaster. It was designed as a parish church and completed in 1859, becoming a cathedral in 1924. It has an especially rich interior, a gilded roof in the chancel, vivid frescoes, stained glass, golden canopies over the reredos and decorated altars in all the lady chapels.

Priory Church of St Mary – Castle Hill, Tel 65338. A doorway in the west end of the church is probably Saxon in origin but little else of the period remains. The Benedictine Priory, built at the same time as the castle, about 1170, had a church attached to it and it was this church which formed the basis for St Mary's in 1430. Most of the buildings in the chancel stalls date from 1340 and have superbly carved oak canopies; there is further intricate woodcarving on the pulpit and font cover. The Vicarage of 1849 still stands, a monument to the power and wealth of the Victorian church, though the present incumbent is housed in a building begun in 1965.

Lancaster Castle – Castle Hill, Tel 64998. There is a full description of the castle in the introduction to this chapter. Part of the legal buildings in the castle surrounds is the Grand Jury Room, last used as such in 1933. Completely circular with furnishings mostly by Gillow. Castle open daily Easter–September.

Ashton Memorial – Williamson Park, Tel 33318. See Ephemera. Open Easter and May–Sept daily 10–5pm; Oct–April daily 11–4pm.

Friends Meeting House – Meeting House Lane. Lancaster was one of the places where the Quakers took root early. The present meeting house dates from 1708 and is an attractive plain building. Its burial ground, which perhaps gave the name of Golgotha to the neighbouring row of houses, is situated just opposite the Wyresdale Road Gate of Williamson Park.

THEATRE

The Duke's Playhouse – Moor Lane, Tel 66645. A lively and friendly regional theatre housed in a converted 18th-century building with two theatre auditoria, a film theatre, Theatre-in-Schools Company, Youth Theatre, workshops and restaurant. The theatre (307 seats), with its flexible staging, offers a good variety of quality drama in four-weekly rep. There is a real sense of this being a theatre for the community. Recent programming has included Alan Ayckbourn's *Intimate Exchanges,* Claire Luckham's *Trafford Tanzi* and Stephen MacDonald's *Not About Heroes,* an insightful examination of the relationship that existed between Wilfred Owen and Siegfried Sassoon. There is also a Christmas show for the family.

In the summer, the Duke's Theatre Company undertakes one of the most unusual and innovative theatre projects to be seen anywhere. Set in the grottos, glades and lakes of Williamson Park with the Ashton Memorial towering above and the sun sinking behind the lakeland hills, the Promenade Theatre Company moves its large audience from location to location as it presents plays such as Shakespeare's *The Tempest* or an adaptation of *Tales of King Arthur.* Playgoers come from all over England to see the unique productions and hardly ever is a performance cancelled due to bad weather. The season runs from early June to the first week in August. Call the box office for details.

Nuffield Theatre Studio – University of Lancaster, Tel 39026. Set in the campus of the University of Lancaster, the Nuffield Theatre Studio presents a year-round programme of small-scale touring companies together with work performed by the University Theatre Group and the Theatre Studies Department. Recent visitors have included some of the best professional experimental groups in the country including Compass Theatre in *Waiting for Godot,* Common Ground Dance Theatre and Theatre de Complicité. The University Companies have also produced a broad spectrum of work ranging from *Little Shop of Horrors* and *All's Well That Ends Well* to adaptations of Patrick Kavanagh, Anthony Burgess and Marianne Wiggins.
St Martin's College – Bowerham Road, Tel 770503. Small-scale touring companies such as Ludus Dance Company occasionally play in the theatre of this College of Further Education, and there are also occasional concerts and other art events. For details call 32878.
The **Grand Theatre** presents work by local and district amateur companies. The theatre itself was built in 1781 and has been used as a place of entertainment ever since. It has been beautifully restored and is worth a visit regardless of the quality of the current production. After all, you may see the ghost of Sarah Siddons who often appears to the cast members of modern plays.

MUSIC

Visiting orchestras can be heard in the **Ashton Hall**, a concert hall situated within the Town Hall in Dalton Square. Concerts are also given in the **Concert Hall at Lancaster University** where there is a flourishing music department. Recent visitors have included the BBC Philharmonic Orchestra, the European Community Chamber Orchestra and the Manchester Camerata. There are also concerts by University groups such as the Choral Society, the Symphony Orchestra and individual artists. For concerts in the Town Hall, call 841249. For University concerts, call 65201 Ext 3431.

In my experience, Lancaster has the most lively and enthusiastic Tourist Board in the United Kingdom. The city finds many occasions to celebrate Lancaster's heritage – perhaps it is because of the varied nature of Lancaster's past or perhaps it is due to the imagination of the Director of Tourism and his staff – but listed below are just some of the heritage celebrations which take place during the year.
Folklore Festival – A celebration of music, song and dance from all over the world. Usually held the third week of August.
Georgian Legacy Festival – A celebration based on a theme relevant to Georgian Lancaster (eg the election of 1796). The week's events included historical re-enactments of a Georgian wedding, a duel, lectures, an evening in the Highwayman's Den, a recital, election speeches, a country dance and actors intermingling with participants as contemporary characters in role. Held the last week of July/early August, each year the Festival explores a new theme.
Maritime Festival – A celebration of Lancaster's Maritime heritage focusing on the Golden Age of Maritime Trade and Commerce, circa 1850. Held Easter Thursday to Easter Monday.
Literary Festival "Litfest" – A celebration of the contemporary word through talking, singing, acting, dancing and the visual arts. Held the last week in October.

CINEMA

Commercial cinema at **Cannon Cinema**, King Street, Tel 64141 (2 screens).
The **Duke's Playhouse** – Moor Lane, Tel 66645, as well as offering a theatre programme, also offers excellent cinematic fare with a selection of foreign, classic and contemporary quality films. Recent offerings include work by Jean Vigo, Pier Paolo Pasolini, Louis Malle, David Lynch, John Boorman and Phillip Noyce.

BOOKSTORES

The best, almost inevitably, is **Waterstone's**, 2-6 King Street, Tel 61477, which is just below the Royal Kings Arms Hotel below the castle. The **City Bookshop**, 20 Common Garden Street, Tel 60491, is also worth a visit, as is the **Paperback Back Shop** (no, it's not a misprint), 33 North Road, Tel 382181, which has an excellent and wide ranging collection of sci-fi, fantasy and horror books and lots of comics. The **College Bookshop**, St Martin's College, Bowerham Road, Tel 60125, and **Lancaster University Bookshop** on the university campus at Bailrigg, Tel 32581, both have an excellent stock with popular and academic books. Bargain books can be found at **Book Clearance Centre**, 16 Market Entrance, Tel 844688, while religious books are at **Goodnews**, 3 Mary Street, Tel 841655.

ANTIQUARIAN AND SECONDHAND BOOKS

The best is **W B McCormack** with a good collection of antiquarian and secondhand books. They also have antique maps and prints. Well worth a visit, it's a charming shop. Secondhand books can also be found at **Atticus Books**, 26 King Street, Tel 381413, and **Books and Prints**, 26 Sun Street.

ART GALLERIES

Peter Scott Gallery at Lancaster University, Tel 65201, offers exhibitions of contemporary art work throughout the year. Paintings and prints are offered for sale and good-quality craft work and ceramics are sometimes available.

Paper Gallery – 66 Market Street, Tel 36636, has contemporary original prints as well as antique prints and watercolours.

Studio Arts Gallery – 6 Lower Church Street, Tel 68014, has 19th- and 20th-century paintings as well as limited edition prints. **Talbot Galleries**, 8 Cheapside, Tel 61216, has original oils, watercolours and fine art prints, while **Town House Gallery**, 50 Market Street, Tel 63436, also has fine art prints as well as original paintings and limited editions.

ANTIQUE DEALERS

Anne Tique – 73 North Road, Tel 65343. Antique and costume jewellery. Just around the corner from the bus station.

Article Antiques – 134/136 Greaves Road, Tel 67271 and High Street, Tel 39312, have 18th- to 20th-century furniture, porcelain, china and glass. On A6 off junction 34 of M6.

G W Antiques – 47 North Road and 4 St George's Quay, Tel 32050. 18th- to early 20th-century stripped pine and furniture of all periods.

Great British Antiques Wholesalers – 4 St George's Quay, close to Old Custom House Maritime Museum, Tel 841148. Large stock of pine.

Lancastrian Antiques – 66 Penny Street, Tel 843764. General antiques.

Sun Street Antique Centre – 26 Sun Street, Tel 37844. 19th-century stripped pine and related items, especially kitchen ware.

F W and A Smith – 20A Brock Street, Tel 65701. General antiques.

Vicary Antiques – 18A Brock Street, Tel 843322. Paintings, prints, art pottery and works of art 1850–1950, also arts and crafts, furniture and quilts.

The Warehouse – 49 North Road, Tel 39024. Antique and pre-war furniture, art nouveau and art deco.

RESTAURANTS

The best restaurant in the area is at Lock, which is 14 miles (22.4 km) north, just off the A683 and a mile south of Kirkby Lonsdale. **Cobwebs**, Tel 05242 72141, is a delight. Set in a country guest house at Cowan Bridge, the dining room commands views of the Lune Valley and the Pennines. The set evening meal could well start with a hot and cold soup served in a split dish and follow with the most beautifully herbed chicken or lamb with wonderfully fresh vegetables. Dessert is sinfully wonderful and there is a good wine list. There are gourmet evenings held once a month. Excellent value. Open Mon–Sat for dinner only, 7:30 for 8pm.

In the area, **Lupton Tower**, Lupton, Kirkby Lonsdale, Tel 04487 400, is also excellent. It is a serious vegetarian restaurant and if you are a meat eater and think you won't like vegetarian food, here is the place to come and have your mind changed. Very good cheese quenelles and wonderful soups. Creme brûlée is a delight as is tarte Tatin for dessert. Open all week, but check Mon and Tues in winter. Set dinner only, 7:30 for 8pm.

In Lancaster itself, I like **Pizza Margherita**, which is well above the normal run of pizza houses. It's at 2 Moor Lane, Tel 36333, and it's a very pleasant place to be with its tiled floors, marble-topped tables and flourishing plants. Plain or wholemeal pizzas are excellent. Open all week 11am–11pm. Just across the road at the Duke's Playhouse, the **Duke's**, Tel 843215, serves snack and light meals at lunchtime and then moves to pre-theatre supper and a full menu. Excellent tomato, orange and basil soup and the fish is beautifully prepared. Good value. Open Tues–Sat noon–2pm and 5:30–9pm.

Crows Restaurant – 10 King Street, Tel 382888, has excellent barbecued ribs and some interesting Cajun cooking. They also have vegetarian cooking. Open 12–2 and 6–9:30 daily.

Another place with a firm commitment to wholefood and vegetarian dishes is **Libra**, 19 Brock Street,

Tel 61551. This is one of the busiest and best value eating places in the city. Look for the daily specials on the blackboard. If you are lucky, they will have broccoli and cashew nut bake on the menu. Finish off with fresh fruit salad which comes with yoghurt and honey.

PUBS

Water Witch – Aldcliffe Road, Tel 63828. Pitch-pine panelling, flagstones, bare masonry and rafters give atmosphere to this canal-side pub. Summer barbecues on the terrace and hearty bar food all the year round.

Howe Ghyll – Green Lane, Tel 320211. (Head north on A6, last turn on right after leaving speed restrictions.) A spacious conversion of a former mansion, set in its own grounds on the edge of town. Efficient quick service lunchtime food counter with lots of variety.

Golden Lion – Moor Lane. (see Ephemera). Several small bars and even a no-smoking room (why don't all pubs provide one?). You can watch local teams playing Trivial Pursuit or even join in. Excellent pies at lunchtime and when I was last there they served a worker's lunch for £1.

John of Gaunt – 53 Market Street, Tel 65356. You can't come to Lancaster without drinking here and at the Golden Lion, come to that. Excellent bar meals and snack at lunchtimes, and in the evenings in an atmosphere which celebrates the myth of the original Duke of Lancaster. If this all wasn't enough, there is excellent jazz throughout the week with the host often getting in for a session or two.

White Cross – Quarry Road, White Cross, Tel 841048. The original building here dates back 120 years to a time when it was known as the Klondyke and you could travel from here to Preston by barge for a penny. This canal-side pub has a restaurant and also serves bar meals. Pleasant and friendly.

ARTISTIC ASSOCIATIONS

At No 1 High Street lived the poet and art historian Laurence Binyon. He was born here in 1869 and studied at Oxford. He then took a post in the British Museum and from 1913 to 1933 was in charge of Oriental prints and paintings. He wrote widely on Eastern art but other titles, such as *Botticelli* and *The Drawings and Engravings of William Blake,* testify to the wide range of his cultural interest. He is best known as a poet who is strongly in the tradition of Wordsworth and Matthew Arnold, but he wrote plays which were very successful in their day and his one-act pieces are still frequently performed by amateurs. He translated Dante into terza rima and in 1932 was created a Companion of Honour. He was made Norton Professor of Poetry at Harvard in 1933. He was a poet of affecting memory and imaginative reflection and he is himself forever commemorated in his poem "For the Fallen" (set to music by Elgar), extracts from which adorn war memorials throughout the British Commonwealth. Binyon's poem consists of seven verses, although, sadly, only the fourth verse is extensively quoted:

> They shall not grow old, as we that are left grow old:
> Age shall not weary them, nor the years condemn.
> At the going down of the sun and in the morning
> We will remember them.

EPHEMERA

John of Gaunt was born in Ghent in 1340. He was created Duke of Lancaster in 1362. His son became Henry IV, and ever since, the reigning monarch has always been Duke of Lancaster as well. John of Gaunt is much associated with Lancaster Castle and has entered Lancaster's mythology in a large way, in spite of the fact that he only spent a total of nine days in Lancaster. His statue presides over the great gatehouse, and a turret in the keep, named after him, was used as a beacon to signal the approach of the Armada. Until recent years a horseshoe, set in the roadway at the junction of Cheapside, Market Street and Penny Street, was renewed every seventh year. A local tradition tells that the original horseshoe was cast by John of Gaunt's horse as he rode through Lancaster (since these streets were pedestrianized, the horseshoe has worn less rapidly). Unfortunately for romantics, the more prosaic and likely reason for the horseshoe is that it marked the site of a horse fair. Shakespeare describes John of Gaunt as "Time-honoured Lancaster" and in *Richard II*, Act 2, Scene 1, gives him the speech beginning, "This royal throne of kings, this sceptered isle ...", one of the most stirring descriptions of England and perhaps the most famous "purple passage" in the whole canon.

Dominating Lancaster's eastern skyline are the great dome and shining white walls of the Ashton Memorial. This grandiose building, which has been likened to St Peter's in Rome, the Sacré-Coeur in Paris and even the Taj Mahal, was built between 1906 and 1909 by Lord Ashton as a tribute to his late wife (the likeness to the Taj is emotional rather than architectural). It stands at the highest point of Williamson Park, itself the creation of Lord Ashton's father who was a wealthy oilcloth and textile manufacturer. At one time, 70 percent of the homes in England had Ashton's linoleum on their floors. Lord Ashton, who sat as MP for Lancaster before being created Baron Ashton in 1895, inherited the family business after his father's death and it is estimated that at one time a quarter of the town's work force was employed by him. He also gave Lancaster its new town hall and the Victoria Memorial. The Memorial itself was described by Nikolaus Pevsner as being "...the grandest monument in England." Inside the Ashton Memorial, on the lower level, there is an exhibition of "The Life and Times of Lord Ashton," while in the chamber above there is an excellent multiscreen presentation on "The Edwardians." Adjacent is the Old Palm House, a splendid conservatory housing exotic butterflies which fly freely among a splendid plant collection. The Ashton Memorial cost £87,000 to build in 1909, the equivalent of £3 million today. It stands 105 feet (32 m) high and from its upper galleries there are panoramic views of Morecambe Bay, the Welsh mountains and even the Isle of Man.

Before the building of the railway, the usual route to and from the Lake District crossed Lancaster Sands at low tide. Although the graveyards around Morecombe Bay testify to the hazards of such a crossing, there were many occasions when the journey was so exhilarating that it lived in the memory of travellers for many years. Eminent writers such as William Wordsworth and Thomas Gray both celebrated the journey in the written word. Coach services, scheduled to accommodate the changing tides, ran between hotels in Lancaster and Ulverston. In 1820, one traveller relates, he was rudely awakened in his Lancaster hotel at five in the morning when the coach driver burst into his bedroom shouting, "For God's sake make haste! The tide is down ... if you delay we shall all be drowned." Lancaster Sands can still be crossed today, with a guide, although the train takes only 17 minutes to link Lancaster with the Lake District's main line station at Oxenholme. For a sense of what it was like in the early 19th century, J M Turner's superb *Crossing Lancaster Sands,* should be seen. The original is in the Birmingham Museum and Art Gallery, but the local tourist office has reproductions.

Tucked in behind the main streets of Lancaster are a number of alleys, some of them providing short cuts, others now forming cul-de-sacs. Until the 1920s and '30s, a large part of Lancaster's population lived in these. As new housing areas were developed outside the city centre, there was a rapid shift in population density – which accounts for the number of churches in the centre of Lancaster that are no longer used for worship. The best of the small houses in this area were clean and whitewashed and brightened by tubs of flowers. The worst were dark and damp and full of disease and misery, representing the worst aspects of the Industrial Revolution. Nearly all yards had communal wells or standpipes and rows of communal earth-closets. Names reflected nearby public houses such as the Golden Fall Yard or Railway Inn Yard. Others were named after landlords such as Wilson's or Barrow's Yard or Dickinson's Building. The entrances to the market are through old yards while others, such as Anchor Lane and Chancery Lane, provide a short cut between Market Street and Church Street. One of the most attractive links Market Street and King Street; it's called Bashful Alley (I have no idea why).

On Thursday, August 20, 1612, three generations of witches were marched through the crowded streets of Lancaster and hanged before large crowds on a gallows about a mile outside the town. The parson's prayer that God should show them mercy was cynical in the extreme, for little mercy had been shown to them in their trial. These "criminals" were a pitiable collection. Old Chattox was an 80-year-old, half-blind beggar woman, withered and spent by poverty. Mother Demdike, also 80 years old, blind and a beggar, would have gone to the gallows too, but she cheated the hangman by dying in Lancaster Castle gaol. Her daughter Bessie and two of her teenaged grandchildren were not so lucky.

The incident that started the witch hunt took place six months before in nearby Pendle. Alizon, one of Mother Demdike's grandchildren, met a pedlar, and begged for some pins. When he refused to undo his pack, she cursed him. A few minutes later the pedlar had a stroke and both he and Alizon believed it was because of her curse. The pedlar lived just long enough to accuse Alizon, who when questioned by the local magistrate, Roger Nowell, confessed her responsibility. Soon Mother Demdike and Old Chattox had also been accused and Mother Demdike's daughter, Bessie, was shown to have a supernumerary nipple for suckling the devil. Nowell seems to have had no trouble getting the women to admit their guilt. True, he had another of Mother Demdike's granddaughters, Gennet, as chief prosecution witness, but the confessions – to charges as various as desecration of graves, communing with imps and the Devil, plotting to blow up Lancaster Castle by magic, and at least 16 murders – were probably obtained by a mixture of astutely phrased questions and a naive simplicity on the part of the accused. It is possible that the two old women and their families did practise a form of black magic and that they were involved in a feud with one another. Mother Demdike believed that she had bewitched the child of a miller a year earlier and Alizon certainly thought she was responsible for the death of the pedlar. Alice Nutter, another of the hanged, was somewhat different. She lived in Roughlee Hall, a substantial residence, and by 17th-century standards was a rich woman. How she became so tragically involved is a mystery. Her tomb is often pointed out as being in St Mary's in nearby Newchurch-in-Pendle, but in fact the so-called Pendle witches were all buried in unconsecrated ground. The Pendle witch hunt, like those documented in Salem, Massachusetts, and Loudun, France, took place through a combination of fear, superstition, cunning questioning and false witness. In the view of many historians, the only crime the "witches" had committed was that of being poor.

The Golden Lion Inn, Moor Lane, stands directly on the route which was travelled by condemned prisoners between Lancaster prison and the gallows on Lancaster Moor. As the procession passed the Golden Lion, it was a tradition that the condemned were given an opportunity to quaff a final pint. It is reported that on one occasion a reprieve came through while the prisoner was drinking his farewell "jug," and if he had not done so the message would have arrived too late. By the same token, it is reported that one prisoner refused the penultimate stop and was hanged before his pardon could arrive. Many will no doubt see this as a vindication of their belief that being a teetotaller is bad for the health. The Golden Lion is also extensively haunted. Glasses often move, clocks go haywire, beer casks and pint pots explode and the central heating dials often spin around without visible cause. The publican and his customers seem to enjoy the goings-on immensely.

Among notable Lancastrians are Thomas Edmonson, who in 1836 invented the first machines for dating and printing railway tickets, and Sir Richard Owen, an anatomist, born in the city in 1804. Owen is credited with coining the word "dinosaur" and was entertained to dinner inside the skeleton of one at the Crystal Palace in 1855.

Lancaster specializes in excellent examples of the county's traditional fare. In its lively market can be found delicious Lancashire cheese in four strengths: mild, medium, tasty and tasty tasty. Also here are Morecambe Bay shrimps, while down Penny Street is Kinloch's, the traditional pork butchers. People come from miles around for home-made pies, sausages, ham, bacon and black pudding (must be tried). Lune smoke salmon is still smoked traditionally on St George's Quay and at Atkinson's, the tea and coffee importers in China Street, blends are concocted to order and can be returned if unsatisfactory. The old tea bins and coffee roasters here suggest that time has stood still since the turn of the century. Finally, back at the market, Grandad Daly's fish shop is locally famous for "fish from the Bay," with local salmon, shrimps, plaice and whitebait in abundance. The owner of Grandad's still wears clogs and a striped apron.

Lancaster is of course, the gateway to the Lake District and while I am not going into any detail with respect to this area of great natural beauty, the following may be of some use.

Keswick – Attractive small lakeside town. Of interest is the Cumberland Pencil Museum (the first pencils were made in Keswick following the discovery of graphite in Elizabethan times). The Blue Box Century Theatre is a unique touring complex on wheels (it is now permanently situated in Keswick) and runs a summer season of plays. (They were in deep financial difficulty the last time I spoke to them, so keep your fingers crossed.) There's the 16th-century Moot Hall, there is a railway museum, and in the Keswick Museum and Art Gallery is a world-famous collection of manuscripts of the English Romantic poets, especially the works of Wordsworth and Southey. The area is, of course, Wordsworth country. The great man was born at Cockermouth, lived at Dove Cottage in Grasmere and Rydal Mount in Ambleside and is buried in St Oswald's Church, Grasmere.

Bowness-on-Windermere – An ancient lakeside town. St Martin's Church dates from 1483. There is a steamboat museum, and a museum devoted to the life and work of the children's author Beatrix Potter is opening soon.

Kendal – My favourite Lakeland town. A thriving woollen town in the 18th century, it now has a good museum and art gallery, a healthy arts centre and the best shopping in the region. Kendal Castle was the home of Catherine Parr, the only one of Henry VIII's wives to outlive him. Levens Hall, a few miles away, is a lovely Elizabethan house with famous topiary gardens.

TOURIST INFORMATION BUREAUX: 7 Dalton Square, Lancaster, Lancs LA1 1PP. Tel (0524) 841098

Town Hall Highgate, Kendal Cumbria LA9 4DL. Tel (0539) 725758

Moot Hall Market Square,Keswick Cumbria CA12 4JR. Tel (07687) 72645

Glebe Road, Bowness Cumbria LA23 3HJ.Tel (09662) 2895

LEEDS

County of West Yorkshire
189 miles (302 km) by road from London by M1
One hour 45 minutes by rail from London (King's Cross)

Leeds was mentioned by the Venerable Bede (circa 700). He called it Loidis and recorded that King Edwin of Northumbria built a royal palace there. By Norman times the village was established and survived William the Conqueror's sacking of the north, probably because the place had been deeded to Ilbert de Lacy, of Pontefract Castle, to whom William gave huge tracts of land. It was de Lacy who caused Kirkstall Abbey to be built (4 miles/ 6.4 km north A65 West). This Cistercian Abbey, circa 1152, is the most impressive early monastic building in Britain. The self-contained brotherhood who founded the abbey, of necessity, had to be sheep farmers, spinners, weavers, coal miners, tanners, potters and the followers of many other occupations. They laid the foundations of Leeds as a city of numerous trades. The abbey gatehouse became a home and is now a museum. A bridge was built downstream of the abbey in the late 13th century and by the middle of the 14th century, cloth merchants were displaying their wares on its parapet. The street leading to the bridge became known as Briggate, Bridge Street, for Leeds called a street a gate, harking back to a much earlier Viking tradition, which we can also find in York. Briggate was to become the backbone of Leeds and around it the city grew up as a commercial centre. In 1619 the city's cloth trade was valued at the then staggering sum of £200,000 a year. Even today Leeds is the ready-to-wear clothing capital of Britain. Leeds had been granted municipal borough status by Charles I in 1626 and, perhaps in gratitude, the city stood by the King in the Civil War, characteristically taking the opposite line from its eternal rival, Bradford. After the Civil War, industrialization continued apace and even though Georgian Leeds must have been a gracious place, little remains today save for Holy Trinity Church in Boar Lane, circa 1720, and Park Square. The centre of Leeds represents perhaps the greatest expression of civic confidence in Victorian times. The Town Hall was built so as to be better (and bigger) than any of its competition. It was opened by Queen Victoria in 1858 and for that occasion the streets were lined with palm trees and triumphal arches and 18,000 Sunday School children sang the national anthem as the regal figure passed by. The immense building has become the symbol of Leeds. The Civic Theatre dates from this time, as does the Corn Exchange. The superb arcades – the Grand, Thorntons and the County – date from the last quarter of the 19th century, while the interior of the Grand Theatre is based on La Scala, Milan. The Victorian tradition in Leeds is as strong as anywhere in Britain and in spite of the up-to-date shops and traffic-free precincts, Leeds remains an amazing recreation of the great city it was in the years around 1900.

WALK

Leeds Walk – Leeds is a big city and limited space forces me to confine the walk to the city centre north of the river. The area around **Canal Wharf** and **Leeds Bridge** is also well worth exploring.

Begin from the car park at City Station (enter from Aire Street). Turn right along Aire Street into the monumental **City Square**. Leave the square by Wellington Street and turn right into King Street, opposite the Tourist Information Centre, and walk past the elaborate **Metropole Hotel**. Turn left along the 18th-century **Park Place**, and then right up Central Street to St Paul's Place; cross elegant **Park Square** making for the Town Hall tower. At the end of Park Square East, cross The Headrow to the **Town Hall**. Across Calverley Street from the Town Hall is the **City Museum and Art Gallery**. Turn right up Calverley Street after leaving the museum and then turn left along Great George Street to the Victorian Infirmary. Walk right along Portland Street, then over Calverley Street and across the gardens in front of the **Civic Hall**. Walk through the car park towards the **Civic Theatre**, past a modern mural, and turn right along Cookridge Street to **St Anne's Roman Catholic Cathedral**, then turn left up Great George Street. Continue into Merrion Street, past the St John's Centre, dominated by the spire ornaments of **St John's Church**. Turn right through the Centre, cross Dortmund Square (Dortmund is Leeds' twin town) and turn left along The Headrow and right into Lands Lane and right again into **Thornton's Arcade**. Walk through the arcade and turn left into Briggate. Walk back into The Headrow for the **City Varieties Music Hall Theatre** and then continue up New Briggate to the **Grand Theatre**. Turn right through the **Grand Arcade**, under the clock and out into Vicar Lane. Turn right past the **County Arcade**, re-cross The Headrow and fork right along Market Street. Opposite the **Corn Exchange** turn right down Duncan Street. Just down Briggate, to the left, is the **Time Ball Buildings**. This originated as John Dyson's clock and watch shop in 1865. There is a figure of Father Time and a time ball (no longer working) that gave the building its name. The façade of the shop, added at the end of the 19th century, is delightful, and the interior still wonderfully Victorian. Continue along Boar Lane, passing **Holy Trinity Church** to City Square and the car park.

MUSEUMS, GALLERIES AND PUBLIC BUILDINGS

Leeds City Museum – Calverley Street, Tel 462465. Yorkshire's finest collection of worldwide archaeology, ethnology, geology and natural history. Classical sculpture, mummies, costumes from every continent and an aquarium with live reptiles, amphibians and insects. Open Tues–Fri 9:30–5:30; Sat 9:30–4pm.

Abbey House Museum – Kirkstall Abbey, Tel 462465 (see Ephemera). A 12th-century abbey gatehouse, which now houses a lively folk museum, with three full-sized streets of shops and cottages. You can visit the 19th-century Hark the Rover Inn, and Victorian grocer's and ironmonger's shops. You can even try out early slot machines using old pennies. Open April–Sept Mon–Sat 10–6pm; Sun 2–6pm Oct–Mar Mon–Sat 10–5pm; Sun 2–5pm.

Lotherton Hall – Aberford, Tel 813259. Victorian country house, formerly the home of the Gascoine family. Fine collections of Oriental art and fashion, 19th-century decorative art and modern craft and design. Delightful Edwardian garden. Open May–Sept only Tues–Sun 10:30–6:15 (8:30 on Thursdays).

Temple Newsham House – Five miles (8 km) east of A63, Tel 647321. Large Tudor country house, the birthplace of Lord Darnley, the short-lived husband of Mary Queen of Scots. There is a world-famous collection of English decorative art, furniture and paintings. Large gardens and Rare Breeds farm. Called the Hampton Court of the north. Open Tues–Sun 10:30–6:15pm.

Leeds Industrial Museum – Armley Mill, Canal Road, Tel 637861. A woollen mill, built of stone, in an island site between the Leeds and Liverpool Canal and the River Aire. Displays on the local woollen tiles industry, including tailoring and cloth manufacturing. Engineering displays, machine tools, locomotive building, steam engines and a variety of heavy goods vehicles manufactured by local companies. Open April–Sept Tues–Sat 10–5:30pm; Sun 2–4pm. Oct–Mar Tues–Sat 10–4:30pm; Sun 2–4pm.

Museum of the History of Education – Parkinson Court, the University, Tel 334665. A small but fascinating collection relating to the history of education, from infant schools to teacher training. Textbooks, 17th to 20th century, displays of school furniture and 19th- and 20th-century science teaching equipment. Open Mon–Fri 9:30–12:30 and 1:30–3:30pm.

Leeds Art Gallery – Municipal Buildings, The Headrow, Tel 462493. Fine collections of British paintings of the 19th and 20th centuries, from Holman Hunt to the contemporary avant-garde. Modern sculpture is displayed in the Henry Moore Gallery (Moore began his career in Leeds). The piazza in front of the gallery is laid out with huge playable chess sets. Open Mon–Fri 10–6pm; Sat 10–4pm; Sun 2–5pm.

University Gallery – Parkinson Building, Woodhouse Lane, Tel 332777. One room contains changing displays from the Manton Bequest of 20th-century European prints and paintings and Oriental paintings and antiquities. Other rooms display aspects of the permanent collection of 19th- and 20th-century art together with changing temporary exhibitions. Open Mon–Fri 10–5pm.

Cathedral Church of St Anne – Cookridge Street. St Anne's Church, circa 1848, became the Cathedral in 1878. Between 1902 and 1904 the cathedral was largely rebuilt in a style known as "Arts and Crafts Gothic."

St John's – New Briggate. Founded in 1634 by John Harrison who, in 1647, is said to have offered a tankard containing not ale, but golden guineas to Charles I when he was imprisoned in Leeds. Harrison hoped the king could use the money to bribe his way to freedom. A bold ruse, but it failed. A memorial window recalls the incident. Caroline box pews and a fine Renaissance-style chancel screen are features of this splendid example of 17th-century Gothic architecture.

St Peter's Church – Kirkgate. The Gothic-style parish church of Leeds was built in 1841 on the site of a medieval predecessor. Its greatest treasure is the Leeds Cross, actually composed of the fragments of two or more crosses discovered when the medieval church was demolished. Probably dating from the 10th century, it is carved with figures that include the Norse god, Weland, strapped into his legendary flying machine.

Town Hall – Great George Street, Tel 462352. A celebration of Victorian civic accomplishment, the Town Hall with its tall tower, clock and elegant dome, is a major landmark of central Leeds. The building was opened by Queen Victoria and Prince Albert in 1848; their statues can be seen at the entrance, together with the busts of the Prince and Princess of Wales of the time. Beyond is the extravagantly ornate Victoria Hall, the setting for orchestral concerts and the prestigious Leeds International Piano Competition. Open by appointment.

THEATRE

Grand Theatre and Opera House – New Briggate, Tel 440971. This magnificent theatre, built in 1878, has a beautiful interior belied by its austere frontage. It is unquestionably one of the finest examples of a Victorian theatre and opera house in the country. It is the home of Opera North (Tel 445326), an excellent regional opera company. The Grand is a top class touring theatre with regular visits from Northern Ballet Theatre, D'Oyly Carte Opera Company, top class touring theatre companies and, of course, Opera North.

West Yorkshire Playhouse – Quarry Hill Mount, Tel 442111. An excellent repertory company operating two theatres at its location. A the larger Quarry Theatre there is a mixed programme of classic plays (*The Playboy of the Western World*), modern world theatre (*All My Sons*), and European and world drama (Dario Fo's *The Pope and the Witch*). The Courtyard Theatre focuses on more contemporary and experimental productions with recent work including plays by Charlotte Keatley, John Burrows and Kay Mellor. Not to be missed.

Leeds City Varieties – The Headrow, Tel 430808. The theatre has been famous for music hall for over a century. There are regular Old Time Musical Seasons (the BBC filmed its successful series of Old Time Music Hall here) plus one-night stands by such luminaries as Ken Dodd and Rory Bremner, evenings of stand-up comedy, jazz, pop and popular plays.

Civic Theatre – Cookridge Street. Built in 1865, the Civic is the home of amateur drama and operetta in the city. It also has a wide program::e of music and dance.

Yorkshire Dance Centre – St Peter's Square, Tel 426066. The centre offers performances, workshops, lectures and classes in every kind of dance. The centre is also the home of the Phoenix Dance Company, an exciting and innovative contemporary dance touring company.

MUSIC

The **Leeds International Concert Season** offers two dozen concerts throughout the year in the magnificent Victoria Hall at the Town Hall, Tel 462453. Besides the International Season there is a jazz season at the West Yorkshire Playhouse, lunchtime chamber music at the Leeds City Art Gallery, lunchtime organ music at the Town Hall and family concerts at the Civic Theatre. The **Harvey's Leeds International Piano Competition** is one of the most prestigious of its kind in the world. Tel 462121 for details. The **Leeds Festival** really dates from 1848 when the Leeds Triennial Festival and the Leeds Festival Chorus were founded to celebrate Queen Victoria's opening of the City Hall. There have been breaks in the sequence of festivals, notably in the '50s, but the Festival revived and in 1970 became a biennial event, but the presentation of large choral works, which had been a feature since the early days, remained. Almost every great orchestral/choral work has been performed here and many have had their premieres here. The Festival is normally held in early November. Tel 462121 for details. The **Leeds 20th Century Music Festival** should also be noted. Tel 462121 for details. The excellent **City of Leeds College of Music** offers a wide range of concerts throughout the year and a festival in the spring. Tel 452069 for programme details. A recent addition to the festival list has been the **Leeds International Conductors Competition**. Tel 462121.

FILM

Leeds International Film Festival has rapidly become established as a major event for both the city and the film world. The first moving image was created by Louis le Prince in 1888 as he filmed from his house over Leeds Bridge. The Festival is held in October. Tel 462121 for details. As I write there are hopes in Leeds for both a Regional Film Theatre and a Film School. A cinema showing "minority taste" features is indeed badly needed. Apart from the Civic Theatre and the University Film Society, commercial cinema reigns in Leeds.

They are listed below:

Cannon Cinema – Vicar Lane, Tel 451013 (3 screens)

Odeon Cinema – The Headrow, Tel 436230 (5 screens)

Lounge Picture House – North Lane, Tel 751061

Hyde Park Picture House – Brudenell Road, Tel 742045. The Hyde Park is the best bet for interesting films. Not only is it bravely independent but it's still lit by gaslight and has the most innovative programme in Leeds.

Leeds Summer Heritage Festival is held for two weeks in the middle of June and includes music in many locations, together with dance, film, talks and walks. Besides the usual venues, concerts are given in a dozen of Leed's top churches.

BOOKSTORES

There are a lot in Leeds but space constraints prevent me mentioning more than a few. The best are **Waterstone's**, Albion Street, Tel 420839, **Sherratt and Hughes**, 36 Albion Street, Tel 420839, and **Austicks** at 91 The Headrow, Tel 439607. Austicks is especially good, at 91 The Headrow. There they have books concerned with leisure, children, music, education and technical subjects; at 64 The Headrow, Tel 452326, they have maps and travel; at 44A Woodhouse Lane, Tel 342243, they have business and computing; at 21 Blenheim Terrace, Tel 432446, they have their university and academic department, and at 57 Great George Street, medical and legal and their branch of HMSO. They have other locations. Do check with them.

For children's books, the **Pink Banana Bookshop** at 51 Woodland Lane is excellent, Tel 696136, and religious and philosophical subjects are well served at **SPCK**, Holy Trinity Church, Boar Lane, Tel 442488. Fantasy and science fiction can be found at **Astonishing Books**, 1 The Crescent, Tel 607445, with many books on local subjects and **W H Stringer**, Tel 326611. **Lotus Multicultural Bookshop** at 10 The Crescent, Hyde Park Corner, Tel 742055, is interesting and both **Harvey's Bookshop**, 30 The Headrow, Tel 454285, and the **Bookcellar** at 38 Merrion Centre, Tel 45379, are worth a browse.

ANTIQUARIAN AND SECONDHAND BOOKS

Two very good shops with secondhand and antiquarian collections are **Bookside**, off Midland Road close to Hyde Park Corner, Tel 744021, and **Ken Spelman** at 70 Micklegate, Tel 624414. **Mr Miles of Leeds** at 12 Great George Street, Tel 455327, is wonderful, with some 35,000 books on display, while one of my favourites is **St Michaels Bookshop** at 69 St.Michaels Lane, Headingly, Tel 746067. They are close to the cricket ground and specialize in cricket books. Finally **Words and Music** at 3a Church Street, Wetherby, Tel 0937 586009, specializes in theatre, cinema, the arts, children's books and the 18th century.

ART GALLERIES

Parker Gallery, Oakwood Chambers, 450 Roundhay Road (opposite Safeways Supermarket) Tel 350384, has 19th- and early 20th-century oils and watercolours while **Oakwood Gallery**, 613 Roundhay Road, has a wide variety of contemporary and traditional oils and watercolours plus etchings and limited-edition prints. They are close to one another and worth a visit. **Headrow Gallery**, 588 Harrogate Road, Tel 694244, also has limited-edition prints and etchings and some quality oils and watercolours. The **Original Art Shop**, 7 Theatre Walk, Schofields Centre, Tel 341274, has limited-edition prints and some contemporary oils.

ANTIQUE DEALERS

Waterloo Antiques Centre – Crown Street, Tel 44187, is an antique market of 45 dealers which has been created within the ancient and famous White Cloth Hall in the centre of Leeds. Large and small furniture, clocks, prints and paintings, jewellery, art deco, porcelain, glass, period clothing, fireplaces, lamps and bric-à-brac are all on view and there's even a pleasant café. Well worth a visit.

To start with, the Arcades: **Aladdin's Cave**, 19 Queen's Arcade, Tel 45703, in the town centre, has jewellery and 19th- and 20th-century collectors' items. **William Goldsmith**, 23 County Arcade, Tel 441345, also has 19th- and 20th-century jewellery, 19th-century clocks and 18th- and 19th-century prints and samplers, while **Year Dot**, 15 Market Street Arcade, Tel 460860, has Oriental pottery and porcelain, paintings, clocks, barometers, glass, copper, brass, jewellery and watches. At 107/108 Briggate in the town centre, is **Roses the Jeweler**, Tel 439767. They have Victorian, antique and secondhand gold, silver, jewellery and diamonds. Continue north on Briggate through New Briggate and you will come to North Street. At No 56 you will find **Andrews Antique Shop**, Tel 445767, with general antiques and jewellery, and at No 116, **Ambassador Antiques**, Tel 420427, with general antiques. Continue north on North Street to Meanwood Road where at No 193 you will find **Originals**, Tel 431613, with a stock of fireplaces and furniture. Benson Street is off North Road to the right and at No 18/20 is **Windsor House Antiques**, Tel 444666, with 18th- and 19th-century English furniture, paintings and objets d'art. To the right at the point where New Briggate becomes North Street is Melbourne Street, where at No 1/2 you will find **Coins and Antiques International**, Tel 434230. They have coins, medals, silver, gold, jewellery and general antiques. South of Leeds City Station you'll find Holbeck Lane where at No 39 you'll find the **Piano Shop**, Tel 443685, specializing in just that. Far below the station, the River Aire rushes through cavernous brick tunnels. It is crossed by a dimly lit subterranean road, giving a view of murky darkness on one side and the canal basin on the other. The arched recesses flanking the road have been turned into workshops and shops with a craft market in the huge vaulted cave at the far end. This is the Dark Arches and together with nearby Granary Wharf, with more shops and an outdoor weekend market, they form one of the most unique browsing areas in the whole country. Another fascinating place to visit is the **Boston Pine Company**, Tel 441650, at Unit 10 with pine and furniture made from old timber. If you are going to Kirkstall Abbey you'll find **Kirkstall Antiques**, Tel 757367, at No 366 Kirkstall Road. They have stripped and painted pine and general small items while at No 400 is the **Antique Exchange**, Tel 743513, with 19th- and 20th-century furniture including satin walnut and ash. Likewise if you are on your way to Harrogate, and I recommend it, you'll find the **Antique Shop**, Tel 681785, at 226 Harrogate Road with general antiques and weapons. The suburb of Pudsey, to the northwest, is famous for producing excellent cricketers. Yorkshire County Cricket Club, whose ground at Headingly is famous as an English Test Match ground, still to this day will only allow Yorkshire-born players to play on its team, the only county side in England to maintain this rule. (It changed for the '92 season.) In Pudsey you'll find 18th- and 19th-century furniture at **M D Antiques**, 68A Lowtown, Tel 557544, **Memorabilia**, Tel 563653, with general antiques, ephemera, bric-à-brac, historical artefacts, Victorian prints, engravings and old photographs at Booth's Yard and **Brian Smith Antiques**, Tel 555815, with furniture, porcelain, pottery, glass, oils, watercolours and collectable items at 26/28 Chapeltown. Pudsey is between Leeds and Bradford. On the road to Stanningley, close to Pudsey, is **Balty's Antiques** at 3 Stanflingley Road, Tel 639011, with general antiques, while in Stanningley itself is **Geary Antiques**, Tel 564122, at 114 Richardshaw Lane with Georgian, Victorian and Edwardian furniture, copper and brass. Finally, the suburb of Morly, to the north, has **Serendipity**, Tel 424540, at 5 Fountain Street, with general antiques and in the same area **Bishop House Antiques** at 169 Town Street, Rodley, Tel 563071 and **Kingsway Antiques**, 223 New Rodd Side, Horsforth, Tel 587674.

RESTAURANTS

Grillade – Wellington Street, Tel 459707. Honest French cooking in a lively whitewashed basement. The set lunch and dinner are good value. Fish soup is excellent, which is rare, and the black pudding (boudin noir) very special. Desserts are the traditional – chocolate mousse, apple flan and sorbets. Open Mon–Sat 12–2:30 and 7:30–11pm. No Sat lunch.

Paris – 36A Town Street, Horsforth, Tel 581885. Well worth the journey out past Headingly to the north of Leeds. One of the best bistro-type restaurants in the north. Excellent value, with the "early bird" set price menu (served between 6 and 7:30) being exceptional – a sort of gourmet's happy hour. Excellent brasserie dishes like cassoulet and beef bourguignonne as well as really innovative things – scallops and Gruyere cheese sauce and avocado and elderflower sorbet and blackberry sauce. The fish is wonderful and the desserts out of this world. Highly recommended. Open all week, dinner only 6–10:30pm (11pm Fri and Sat).

Bryan's – 9 Westwood Lane, Headingly, Tel 785679. Close to the cricket ground is this Leeds institution of a fish-and-chip shop. Bryan's has been serving impeccable Yorkshire-style fish and chips for over 50 years. There's a seniors set lunch, which is wonderful value served from 2:30–4:30 and if you've never tasted a strong cup of Yorkshire tea, you'll get it here. Open Mon–Sat 11:30–11:30pm.

Close by is **Salvos**, 115 Otley Road, Headingly, Tel 755017. They are extremely popular and serve lively, imaginative food. Service is wonderful (they even provide menus in Braille). Excellent reports on the shark steak with tomato, citrus and basil, the liver with balsamic vinegar and red pepper sauce and the king prawns in coconut and tamarind curry. Excellent value. Open Mon–Sat noon–2pm and 5:30–11pm.

For a taste of Asia, **Jumbo**, 120 Vicar Lane, Tel 458547, is open all week from noon to 11:45pm and has good dim-sum, excellent chow mein and wonderful baked spare ribs with salted pepper.

Darbar – 16-17 Kirkgate, Tel 460381, with excellent lamb in various guises in a pleasantly decorated room with considerable ambience is open 11:30–2:30 and 6–11:30pm. Not open Sat/Sun lunch.

Hansa – 72-74 North Street, Tel 444408, has northern Indian and vegan food with crisp samosas and excellent vegetable curries. Open Tues–Sun noon–2pm and 7–10pm. (11:30pm Fri and Sat).

PUBS

Whitelock's – Turk's Head Yard, Tel 453950. A Yorkshire tradition this pub, rich with tiles and stained glass, is a must to visit. Inexpensive bar food with "bubble and squeak" especially good. The Dickensian bar is a nice venue for a business meeting.

Garden Gate – 37 Waterloo Road, Hunslet, Tel 700379. A beautifully preserved Victorian building with tiled floors, mahogany panelling and deep-cut glass, make up for the fact that the pub is about a mile and a half (2.5 km) from the town centre and not easy to find. Traditional bar food. Pizza only in the pm and on weekends.

Guildford Arms – The Headrow, Tel 423468. Busy city centre pub refurbished to look like a turn-of-the-century Paris brasserie with art nouveau theme. There are Monet prints and jasmine lamps, good sandwiches and freshly carved beef for lunch.

Victoria – Great George Street, Tel 451386 (just behind Town Hall). Beautifully preserved opulent bar with etched mirrors and plush seating. Interesting brass elephants' trunks support the bar rail. Friendly atmosphere. Good lunchtime bar food.

Duck and Drake – Kirkgate, Tel 465806 (by indoor market). Large and basic city centre pub with excellent beer. They have different beers from all over the country. Traditional, good value bar food. Friendly service.

ARTISTIC ASSOCIATIONS

Henry Moore, one of the most important 20th-century British sculptors, was born in nearby Castleford and his first commission came from the City Art Gallery. An equally important figure in British sculpting was Barbara Hepworth, who was born at nearby Wakefield. Both Moore and Hepworth trained at the Leeds School of Art. Louis Le Prince, a pioneer of cinematography, filmed the Leeds Bridge traffic from his house nearby, creating what is thought to be the world's first motion picture. To have something as artistic as the cardigan named after you must qualify one for artistic achievement. Lord Cardigan, who lived at Headingley Hall (circa 1663) led the disastrous charge of the Light Brigade against the Russians in the Crimean War. The woollen jacket is named after him. In St Peter's Parish Church there is a memorial to Ralph Thoresby, the famous Leeds traveller and historian who is sometimes called the Yorkshire Pepys. His accounts of contemporary events are vivid and lively, especially an account written in 1688 that Irish troops, disbanded by order of James I, were running riot in the land. William Congreve, the great Restoration dramatist and author of *Love for Love* and *The Way of the World* was born in Leeds in 1670.

EPHEMERA

Victorians delighted in shopping in the numerous arcades that, burrowing between the buildings from one street to the other, are a prominent feature of central Leeds. The most sumptuous of all the arcades is the County Arcade, completed in 1900. The pillars are of Sienna marble and light pours through the glass domes onto walls bright with mosaics. The Grand Arcade, a couple of years older than the County, complements the nearby Grand Theatre and is chiefly praised for its colourful glazed-tile decorations. It has an awesome clock, whose mobile figures include knights, a Grenadier guardsman and an Irishman with a shillelagh. Thornton's Arcade, built in 1877 between Lands Lane and Briggate, is the earliest of the Leeds arcades. Named after a former proprietor of the City Varieties Theatre, it is purely Gothic in style from its lofty, narrow proportions to its pointed glass vault. Like the Grand Arcade, Thornton's too possesses an entertaining clock on which the hours and the quarters are struck by four characters from Sir Walter Scott's *Ivanhoe* – Robin Hood, Friar Tuck, Richard Coeur de Lion and Gurth the swineherd.

In City Square there is a splendid equestrian statue of the Black Prince. Round him are grouped 12 smaller statues, of which four are men of local renown: the scientist Joseph Priestley, who discovered oxygen; James Watt, the inventor; John Harrison, the philanthropist; and Dean Hook, a prominent churchman. The remaining eight are scantily clad nymphs representing "Morn" and "Even." In the elegant 18th-century Park Square is a late-Victorian statue of the sorceress Circe, who in Homer's *Odyssey* turned the hero's men into pigs. Three of the pigs can be seen rooting around the statue's pedestal.

Early in the 19th century, John Marshall established a flax mill in Leeds, where flax was broken up into fibres for manufacturing linen – a mundane enough process. Marshall, however, was a man of vision and his vision was of the glories of the Nile. His mill was built in the style to be seen in such temples as that of the Great Ptolemaic Temple of Horus at Edfu. The façade of Marshall's building, circa 1843, has a huge doorway, six massive palm columns and looks for all the world like a setting for *Aida*. In order to ensure a constant temperature for the flax processing, the flat roof of the building was covered with insulating layers of plaster, tar, earth and grass. There is also historical evidence to support the legend that a flock of sheep grazed on the roof. The Marshall Mill is in Marshall Street, south of Leeds City Railway Station. Just down the road is another example of Victorian architectural fantasy. One of the chimneys at the Tower Works is based on the Campanile of Florence Cathedral, which was begun by Giotto in 1334 and completed by Andrea Pisano in 1359. Who said the Victorians were unimaginative and lacked humour?

Mary Bateman, the so-called Witch of Leeds, made a living by her skilful confidence tricks, the most famous of which was to show a hen apparently laying a magic egg on which were inscribed the words, "Christ is coming." In 1809, she was found guilty of poisoning Rebecca Perigo, one of her gullible clients. She was hanged at York and her body was later displayed at Leeds. It is said that souvenir hunters stripped the flesh off her bones for luck. Her skeleton was preserved and is now in Leeds Medical School.

The press-gang was the group of men who carried out the "impressment" of those liable for forced service in the navy. Although this vicious practice of taking any able-bodied man off the streets, beating him senseless and allowing him to wake up as a lowly member of the crew of one of His Majesty's ships was banned in 1641, the practice was widespread during the latter half of the 18th century and it was not only those living on the coast who were in danger. On Tuesday, July 13th, 1779, the *Leeds Mercury* published the following report – "Notwithstanding the fineness of the weather for some time past, our fair on Saturday and yesterday was remarkably thin, owing, as is supposed, to a report that was spread of 'the press having broken out here' but we can assure our readers, nothing of the kind has happened. It is imagined to have took its rise from a party of Marines parading around our streets, with colours flying, music playing and being dressed like sailors."

A month later, the Leeds *Intelligencer* issued the following assurance – "Notice to persons from West Yorkshire seeking Harvest Work in East Yorkshire, that they may safely pass as heretofore and not be liable to be pressed or molested in so doing. Signed, Richard Mawhood, Deputy Clerk of the Peace."

It must be remembered that sailors were badly needed to swell George III's naval crews, and conditions afloat were such that only the most desperate men would volunteer. The threat of Napoleon Bonaparte's aggression was very strong and the phrase "Boney will get you" passed into the language as a threat to small children and was still in use at the beginning of the 20th century.

On Cardigan Road in Headingly (once a village but now a suburb of northwest Leeds) is a quaint-looking structure consisting of two small battlemented towers with narrow apertures like arrow slits and between them a wall with an arched entrance in the centre flanked by what appear to be two low, square doors. This is the Bear Pits, the only relic of the old Leeds Zoological and Botanical Gardens which, in early Victorian days, was one of the places to visit during the hard-won leisure time of citizens of Leeds. When the construction of Cardigan Road was being planned, it was clear that the end was in sight for the zoo, which closed in 1858. But the path of the road was not impeded by the Bear Pits and so the structure remains, a pit in which "wild beasts" were viewed by onlookers, safe in the tops of the towers. The Pits had no provision whatever for the animals' comfort, but even this was an improvement on earlier "entertainments," when bears, sometimes blinded, would be set on by bulldogs and men with whips. Occasionally a bear would escape, causing havoc among the crowd, but such accidents were speedily terminated with the death of the tormented creature. Bear-baiting was a popular English sport from Norman times onwards and carvings depicting it are to be found in churches. It was banned by Parliament in 1835 but continued secretly for some time, discreetly ignored by the law enforcers. Even when it finally died out, there were still the dancing bears, whose performances continued into the 20th century.

Leeds University students, a great many of whom live in Headingly, felt a certain affection for the Bear Pits and undertook their restoration.

A collection which may be unique is housed in the Abbey House Museum at Kirkstall, north west of the city (see below). Its theme is the era of the "chimney boys," who used to be sent up chimneys to dislodge the accumulated soot. This collection of over 4000 models, prints, books and pamphlets is the work of Dr S A Henry and is called the Henry Collection. It was amassed while Henry was engaged in research into the causes of industrial cancer. Some exhibits show that far from being horrified by the sufferings of the chimney boys, the Victorians saw them as picturesque, sometimes cherubic figures, suitable as decorations for tiles, egg-timers and ornaments. The collection is often on tour but may be viewed on application.

In the churchyard of Otley (ten miles/16 km northwest of the city centre) is the large, elaborately carved memorial to the victims of a disaster which cost the lives of several navvies working on the construction of the Bramhope Tunnel of the Leeds and Thirsk Railway (built 1845 to 1849). The Memorial, which perfectly represents the entrance of the tunnel, with its mock castle design complete with battlements, was erected at the expense of the railway company, some of whom must have experienced a sense of guilt, since the disaster happened on Good Friday. It was seen locally as divine retribution upon the men for working on a holy day.

The ancient days of sanctuary are recalled by the great bronze ring on the door of St John the Baptist Church in the village of Adel, on the northern outskirts of Leeds. One of the most perfect Norman churches in Yorkshire, it is renowned for the south doorway, fantastically carved with zig-zag or chevron markings, beaked heads and the figure of Christ in majesty flanked by four beasts. The bronze sanctuary handle on the door is made up of a circular plaque on which the head of a beast is seen devouring a human head. According to the law of the medieval church, a fugitive from justice or a debtor was immune from arrest within the confines of a sacred place and holding onto the sanctuary ring conferred this immunity.

Southwest of Leeds in Kirklees Hall is a grave said to be that of Robin Hood, the most famous of the medieval outlaw heroes. Although it would be wise not to mention this in Nottingham, West Yorkshire seems to have been the likeliest home of the outlaw. The earliest ballads refer to "Robin of Barnsdale," and these predate any Nottingham reference. But as reminders of this legendary figure abound all over England, it is perhaps fitting that we shall probably never really know the true story of this most romantic and popular of medieval heroes.

TOURIST INFORMATION BUREAU: 19 Wellington Street, Leeds, West Yorkshire, LS1 4DG. Tel (0532) 421321

LIVERPOOL

County of Merseyside
202 miles (323 km) from London by M1, M6, M62
By train 2 hours 40 minutes from London (Euston)

Liverpool is a big city. The waterfront, dominated by the Royal Liver Building, Cunard Building and Port of Liverpool Building, forms a magnificent vista, particularly when viewed from the river, and supports Liverpool's claim to be Europe's greatest Atlantic seaport. (Take a "ferry cross the Mersey" from the Pier Head.) Seven miles (11.2 km) of docks are packed along this waterfront and here can be found the world's largest floating landing stage, about half a mile long and adjustable to move up and down with the tide. Liverpool began as a fishing village in the 13th century and its present comparatively modern form derives from its rapid growth during the 18th and 19th centuries. Today it concerns itself with many more industries than shipping, but in spite of its transformation the city retains distinctive landmarks, both historical and maritime, and has a flourishing musical and artistic life.

Liverpool may not be one of England's most beautiful cities but it is vigorous, tough and has a real sense of humour. Certainly its setting is magnificent with the mighty Mersey, lined by the finest Victorian dock buildings in the country, leading to the beckoning sea beyond. It is a call that pulled millions of emigrants, from all over Europe, seeking a new life in far-off lands. Many got no further than Liverpool itself and they produced in time one of the most cosmopolitan populations in the whole country.

Because of its size I have divided Liverpool into three walks. The first takes in the centre of the city, the museums, theatres, cathedrals, etc; the second focuses on the waterfront; and the third, more specialized still, looks at the old merchant quarter. You cannot do them all in one day so if your time is limited to say, a 72-hour period, Walks One and Two will show you most of the city's major attractions. But you will walk over five miles!

WALK

Walk One starts off in Lord Nelson Street which is behind **Lime Street Railway Station**. Walk down Lord Nelson Street emerging between the station and the **Liverpool Empire**. Ahead is St George's Plateau. Turn right along Lime Street, famed in seafaring yarns, then left down William Brown Street for the museums. **St George's Plateau** consists of a group of grave and imperial buildings that were designed not only to

THE WATERFRONT, LIVERPOOL

instruct and impress but also to announce that Liverpool had "arrived." They were all built at the high tide of Victorian architectural endeavour and their brilliant centrepiece is one of the first Neoclassical buildings in Europe, **St George's Hall**. Constructed in 1854 and designed for assemblies, concerts and court sessions, it has a Graeco-Roman front with a bank of columns and allegorical figures. Inside, the Great Hall is 151 feet (46 m) long and all chandeliers, pink marble and brilliant tiles. There is a superb organ, rebuilt in 1957 after its wartime destruction. The buildings in William Brown Street echo the Hall in their gravity and include the drum-shaped **Picton Reference Library**, the **Walker Art Gallery**, the **Liverpool Museum and Planetarium** and the **Museum of Labour History** (see below). At the bottom of the street is the entrance to the Queensway Tunnel, which crosses under the Mersey to Birkenhead. Turn left round the busy Haymarket to Victorian commercial Whitechapel. (To the right up Roe Street you will find the **Royal Court** and **Playhouse** Theatres.) Where this becomes a pedestrian precinct, turn right up Stanley Street and left in Matthew Street. At top of Matthew Street, turn left along North John Street, then left again down Lord Street, another pedestrian precinct. At the crossroads with Paradise Street, once famed among sailors the world over, turn right and then left into School Lane where you will find the **Bluecoat Arts Centre**. A Queen Anne building dating from 1717 and formerly the Bluecoat School, the building is now used as an Arts Centre. Turn left into Church Alley and then into Church Street. Turn right and continue up Church Street, noting its decorative upper storeys. Go across Waterloo Place in Ranelagh Street. At the point where Ranelagh Street becomes Ranelagh Place notice the Epstein statue above Lewis's Department Store, a salute to Liverpool's resurgence after the war. Go to the right of the monumental **Britannia Adelphi Hotel** and bear right up Mount Pleasant. Turn right along Rodney Street, the Harley Street of Liverpool; Prime Minister William Gladstone was born at No 62. Cross Upper Duke Street to the **Anglican Cathedral** (see below). Go right along Upper Duke Street and left along Hope Street with the Roman Catholic cathedral looming ever larger ahead. In Hope Street you will find the **Philharmonic Hall**, home of Liverpool's great orchestra, the Royal Philharmonic. The hall's acoustics are among the best in Britain and the hall is built on the site of the "Old Phil," which was destroyed by fire in 1933. Further along Hope Street is the **Everyman Theatre** and the wonderfully ornate **Philharmonic Pub** (see below). From the **Metropolitan Cathedral** (see below), turn left down Brownlow Hill, right into Lime Street and right again into Lord Nelson Street, where we began Walk One.

Walk Two starts at the car park to the left of Albert Dock (as you face the Mersey). To your right are the massive stone fronts of mid-18th-century warehouses. Inland, across busy Wapping, is the **Baltic Fleet** (see below), a famous dockland pub. Walk across Duke's Dock to the **Atlantic Pavilion**, one of the Albert Dock warehouses, now containing bakeries, antiques and craft shops and pleasant little cafés and restaurants. Albert Dock has the largest group of historically important, protected buildings in the country. Walk between Albert Dock and the warehouses past the Granada TV News headquarters to the tall-chimneyed **Pump House** which supplied hydraulic power to the docks – it's now a pub (see below). Turn left down the quay to the **Maritime Museum** (see below). From the museum, turn left and follow the railway across the swing bridge to the **Tate Gallery** (see below). Next door is the **Pier Master's House** and the **Cooperage**, where barrels for use in the docks were made. You will now go across the dock gates of the Canning Half Tide Dock to the **Pilotage Building**, the **Maritime Park** and the **Boat Hall**. Beyond Pier Head across St Nicholas Place and New Quay is **Our Lady of St Nicholas**, the Parish Church of Liverpool. It is known as the "Sailor's Church", and its lantern spire, circa 1815, is topped by a ship's weather vane. Carry on past the three great Merseyside buildings of the **Royal Liver Insurance Company**, the **Cunard Building** and the **Port of Liverpool Authority** and just as you pass the Royal Liver Insurance Company building turn left into Water Street. This is an impressive commercial street which slopes down to the Mersey. The ornate interiors of **Oriel Chambers**, **India Buildings** and **Barclay's Bank** should be seen. On your left is **Liverpool Town Hall**. It was designed by John Wood of Bath and completed in 1754. The interior was rebuilt between 1795 and 1802 after a fire, and it was at that time that the dome was added, together with the figure of Minerva. The building is open to the public for two weeks during August.

Walk back down Water Street and turn left into The Goree, which is named after a Cape Verde slaving port, and turn right down Mann Island. Continue to the waterfront and the **Merchant Navy Memorial**. Beside it is the **Podium**, the gift of the Transport and General Workers Union to the people of Liverpool. Turn left along Riverside Walk which offers one of the finest urban views in Britain, especially in the lamplit dusk when busy ferries, like miniature liners, plough through the dark waters taking their passengers to Birkenhead and Wallasey. By a tall mast turn left along Duke's Dock and repeat the first part of your walk back to the car park whence you came.

Walk Three – The 18th-century warehouses and terrace represent all that remains of the old merchant quarter and a tour around this fascinating area is most worthwhile. Make your way to the Bluecoat Arts Centre in School Lane off Paradise Street. Walk to the junction of Hanover Street and turn right. In earlier times this street was infamous for sailors' brawls and before that, for the press gang which operated here, thanks to which many a poor soul awoke to find he had been knocked senseless and forced into service aboard one of the navy's sailing ships. The brawling sailors in fact might have found themselves confined to the old **Bridewell Prison** in Argyle Street (off Duke Street) which was built in 1862. At the bottom of Hanover Street turn left onto Duke Street for the homes of a collection of Liverpool characters and eccentrics unlike any other street in the city. Sarah Biffen lived at **No 8**. She was born without arms and yet became a skillful needlewoman and a celebrated miniaturist. She painted with the brush held in her mouth and was patronized by numerous monarchs, including the King of the Netherlands. **No 84** was the birthplace in 1828 of Joseph Barber Lightfoot, who was regarded as an outstanding theologian. In 1889 he became Bishop of Durham. **No 105 Duke Street** became the first public library in the city in 1852 (it had previously been the Union Newsroom). At **No 116** lived Colonel Bolton. He was a bit of a Jekyll-and-Hyde figure. On the one hand he was a generous benefactor of the Bluecoat Charity School, and on the other took part in the last duel in Liverpool in 1805. He marked this occasion by shooting his opponent stone dead. He is probably best known for founding and financing the First Battalion of Liverpool Volunteers, which he mobilized to defend the city against possible French invasion during the Napoleonic Wars in 1797. "Bolton's Fencibles," as this merry band was named, were never called upon to fight. Next door to Colonel Bolton at **No 18** lived the poetess, Felicia Hemans. Her name is not exactly an artistic household word, but in her poem "Casabianca," appear the immortal lines

> The boy stood on the burning deck
> When all but he had fled

granting her lasting notoriety. The American author, Nathaniel Hawthorne, author of *The Scarlet Letter*, stayed at **No 133** when he was boarding with the jovial Mrs Blodget, the most welcoming and forthcoming boarding house manageress that one could wish for. Finally, the most notorious resident of Duke Street was John Bellingham, who in May 1812, in a fit of insanity, shot Prime Minister Spencer Percival. Bellingham was hanged within a month of committing his crime. Between 1714 and 1820 at least eight Lord Mayors had addresses in Duke Street for those connected with ocean commerce, the professions and financial success made a point of residing there.

At the bottom of Duke Street you will see Nelson Street to your right which is the location of Liverpool's Chinatown. Turn right onto Berry Street which has many fine Georgian properties, as does Sell Street to the left, where the **Blue Angel Club** is located. This is the place where the Beatles first got together in the early 1960s (see Ephemera). Turn left onto Bold Street, which is dominated by **St Luke's Church** in nearby Leece Street. St Luke's is Gothic in style and the bombed-out nave is a dramatic and elegant memorial to the suffering undergone by Liverpudlians in the Second World War. In the 1890s Bond Street was Liverpool's premier shopping street. Two famous photographic studios flourished here – Barrauds and Chambre Hardman – and among their clients were Thomas Hardy and the Shah of Persia.

Walk to the end of Bold Street, turn left in Hanover Street and at the junction of School Lane turn right and make your way to the Bluecoat Arts Centre, where you started your walk.

MUSEUMS AND GALLERIES

Liverpool Museum and Planetarium – William Brown Street, Tel 207001. In 1851 the 13th Earl of Derby bequeathed his extensive natural history collections to the City of Liverpool. To house the collection, the Liverpool businessman William Brown financed an impressive building, which was opened in 1861. In 1867, the basis of the museum was extended by the gift of a large collection of antiquities, historical relics and pottery from the wealthy Liverpool goldsmith, Joseph Mayer.

Since then the collections have expanded enormously to more than a million items, covering most aspects of natural and human history. The displays include a vivarium and aquarium and sections devoted to land transport, natural history, the social, industrial and maritime history of Merseyside, archaeology, ethnology, the decorative arts, the physical sciences and time-keeping. There is also a Space Gallery and Planetarium. Open Mon–Sat 10–5pm; Sun 2–5pm.

Museum of Labour History – William Brown Street, Tel 2070001. Opened in 1986 in the former County Sessions House erected in 1884, the museum tells the story of working-class life in Merseyside from

1840 to the present day. There is an introductory audio-visual programme ("Merseyside – The People's Story") and displays on employment, housing (including a reconstructed street and scullery), education (with a part-construction of an Edwardian classroom) leisure and trade unionism. A display of trade union banners can be seen in the main court room. Open Mon–Sat 10–5; Sun 2–5pm.

Merseyside Maritime Museum – Pier Head, Tel 2070001. The buildings of the dockside museum include the former headquarters (1883) of the Liverpool pilotage service, the 1765 dry docks with the original cast iron dock furniture, the Albert Dock Warehouse (1846) and the 1852 piermaster's house. There is a growing collection of full-size craft, including the pilot boat *Edmund Gardner* (1953), and important collections of models, paintings and marine equipment. Special exhibits illustrate the history of cargo handling in the Port of Liverpool and the development and operation of the enclosed dock system. A new section of the museum tells the story of the seven million emigrants who passed through Liverpool between 1830 and 1930. Open daily 10:30–5:30pm. Last ticket sold at 4:30pm.

Lark Lane Motor Museum – 1 Hesketh Street, Tel 727 7757. The museum is housed in a garage built in 1921 for the Crossville Bus Company. More recently it served as a repair garage for a removal firm and has been restored making use of cast ironwork from historic buildings recently demolished on Merseyside. The collection consists of cars, motorcycles and a wide range of mechanical devices. The museum is exceptional in having the facilities to carry out restoration projects for other museums and individuals, and in being in a position to manufacture one-off items required for restoration work or as replicas. Most vehicles on display are in roadworthy condition. Open Sundays and Bank Holidays 10–5pm.

Liverpool Scottish Regimental Museum – Forbes House, Score Lane, Childwall, Tel 772 7771. The collection of uniforms, weapons, equipment, photographs and documents illustrates the history of the Regiment from 1900 to the present day. Open Tuesday evenings 8–10pm and by appointment.

Museum of the School of Dental Surgery – University of Liverpool, Pembroke Place, Tel 709 0141. The museum, which is over a hundred years old, is primarily intended for members of the dental and allied professions and for medical historians, but members of the public are welcome, provided previous notice has been given. There are exhibits of dental pathology and a large number of artefacts relating to dentistry, including fine collections of early dentures and extracting instruments. Open by appointment.

Walker Art Gallery – William Brown Street, Tel 207 0001. To commemorate his year of office as mayor in 1873, tycoon Andrew Walker presented the city with an art gallery. It is now one of the most important in Britain with a massive collection of Italian masters, French Impressionists (*Woman Ironing* by Degas), works by Rubens, Rembrandt and Murillo and contemporary sculpture and paintings. The 19th century is dominated by Turner, Millais, Watts and the Pre-Raphaelites, with many narrative paintings including the celebrated *And When Did You Last See Your Father?* by W F Yeames. The 20th-century exhibits range from Sickert and Gilman to Hockney and famous British paintings in the permanent collection are Holbein's *Portrait of Henry the Eighth* (ascribed) and Gainsborough's *Countess of Sefton.* Open Mon–Sat 10–5pm; Sun 2–5pm.

Sudley Art Gallery – Mossley Hill Road, Tel 207 0001. Sudley is an early 19th-century neo-classical building with additions made in the 1880s by the Liverpool shipowner, George Holt, when he bought the property. It contains Holt's collection of paintings composed chiefly of 18th- and 19th-century works by British artists, including Gainsborough, Romney, Turner, Bonington and the Pre-Raphaelites. The important items are Gainsborough's *Viscountess Folkestone,* a sympathetic study of old age, and Turner's *Rosenau,* the German home of the Prince Consort. The gallery also has displays of late 19th-century "New Sculpture" and ship models and children's toys. Open Mon–Sat 10–5pm. Sun 2–5pm.

University of Liverpool Art Gallery – 3 Abercromby Square, Tel 709 6022. The building is a typical early 19th-century Liverpool merchant's house in a square of such houses. An effort has been made to retain the character of the house while adapting it as an art gallery. The gallery displays sculpture, paintings, drawings, prints, furniture, ceramics, silver and glass selected from the University's collection. The early English watercolours are outstanding, including works by Turner, Girting, Cozens and Cotman among others. There is some fine early English porcelain with examples from nearly all the main factories including Chelsea, Worcester, Derby and Bow. There are oil paintings by Turner, Audubon, Joseph Wright (of Derby) and Augustus John. Contemporary work includes sculptures by Elizabeth Frink, paintings by Lucien Freud and Bridget Riley and prints by Howard Hodgkin and David Hockney. Open Mon, Tues, Thurs 12–2pm; Wed, Fri 12–4pm.

Tate Gallery – Albert Dock, Tel 709 3223. A changing display from the National Collection of Modern Art of the Tate Gallery in London. Don't miss it if your forte is contemporary art. I suspect one of the reasons there is a provincial branch of the famous contemporary art gallery here is that the London Gallery was founded by Sir Henry Tate, the Liverpool sugar magnate.

Cathedral Church of Christ – St James' Street, Tel 709 6271. The great red sandstone Anglican cathedral dominates the city and was the life work of Sir Giles Gilbert Scott. The diocese was founded in 1880 and construction of the cathedral began in 1902. The building was completed in 1978. (Scott died in 1960 and was still supervising construction at his death.) It is a building in the grandest medieval manner and at 671 feet (204 m) long, is Britain's largest cathedral - in fact, only St Peter's in Rome is larger. The plan is unusual with the choir and the nave at opposite ends of a central space formed by the transept crossings and the huge area under the 331-foot (100.6 m) tower. The cathedral is spacious and theatrical, but I think the most charming corner is the Lady Chapel with a beautiful 14th-century Italian nativity group as its centrepiece. A lift (use it!) and steps ascend to the top of the tower, from which viewpoint the city and docks below are laid out like a relief map. On clear days, Blackpool and Llandudno can be seen.

Metropolitan Church of Christ the King – Mount Pleasant, Tel 709 9222. Its Anglican neighbour might have been built in the Middle Ages, but the Roman Catholic cathedral is entirely of our time. Its round nave, topped by a spiked lantern symbolizing the crown of thorns, has earned the cathedral the irreverent nickname of Paddy's Wigwam. Although the cathedral's exterior has evoked unkind criticism from some quarters, the overall effect is stunning and no one could fail to wonder at its interior. The entrance hall leads to a 193-foot (58.6 m) diameter circle from which radiate 13 chapels, each different in style, materials and symbolism. When the sun shines, everything, including the central white marble altar, is bathed in a shimmering light from the brilliant glass lantern high above. Designed by Sir Frederick Gibberd, the building was completed in 1967.

Speke Hall – The Walk, Tel 427 7231. Speke Hall is eight miles (12.8 m) southeast of the city centre, one mile off the A561 near Liverpool Airport. It is one of England's finest timber-framed manor houses, built piecemeal between the late 15th and early 17th centuries by members of the Norris family. In 1795, after a period of neglect, the house and estate were bought by Richard Watt, a Liverpool merchant, and remained in the same family until the death of Miss Adelaide Watt. After a period in the hands of trustees, the house and grounds were accepted by the National Trust in 1943. Visitors can see eight of the rooms, together with the remarkable Great Hall. The principal features of the interior are the panelling and the plasterwork. The "Elizabethan" and "Gothic" furnishings reflect the taste of the Watt family in the 19th century. There is a fine collection of clocks and Mortlake and Flemish tapestries. The kitchen and servants' hall are complete with the appropriate equipment. A spyhole in the Blue Bedroom and hiding places alongside the chimneys in the Green and Tapestry Bedrooms are reminders of the days when Catholic priests used the house as a refuge. Open April–Oct daily (not Monday) 1–5:30pm; Nov–mid-Dec, Sat and Sun 1–5:30pm.

Croxteth Hall – Croxteth Hall Lane, Tel 2285311. Croxteth, given to the city of Liverpool in 1974, was formerly the home of the Molyneux family, Earls of Sefton. Little remains of the original 1575 house, as major rebuilding took place in 1702, 1800, the 1870s and 1902. The Queen Anne Wing has the most attractive façade, but its finest roomswere destroyed by fire in 1952 and have not been fully restored. Suitable furnishings and paintings are being assembled on the ground floor, however, and an exhibition tells the story of the house and estate. The walled kitchen garden and glass houses have been carefully maintained and illustrate how the life of a great house used to be organized. Open early May to mid-Sept 11–5pm.

Besides the Tate, Walker, University of Liverpool and Liverpool Museum Galleries which have both permanent and changing exhibitions, the following often have interesting exhibitions:

Bluecoat Gallery in the Bluecoat Arts Centre (see above)

Merseyside Maritime Museum (see above)

Unity Theatre (see above)

Merseyside is of course, home to two of the greatest football clubs in the world. **Liverpool Football Club** has a visitor centre museum which is open Mon–Fri at 2 and 3pm. Phone 521 2631 for details. **Everton Football Club** has tours of the ground to see the club's trophies by special arrangement on Mondays only. Call 521 2020 for details.

Aintree Racecourse is the home of the Grand National, which is run the first week of April and it has much horseracing memorabilia.

THEATRE

Liverpool Empire – Lime Street, Tel 709 1555. Liverpool's largest theatre attracts all the major touring companies in the world of ballet, opera, plays, musicals and concerts. Recent visitors have included the Royal Shakespeare Company, the Welsh National Opera Company and Opera North. This huge theatre (2312 seats) may schedule a "safe" programme, but they always go for the best. There is a restaurant, and various bars.

Everyman Theatre – Hope Street, Tel 709 4776. Founded in 1964, the Everyman quickly established itself as an important community theatre presenting new and challenging work, much of it concerned with local Liverpool issues, in an innovative and daring way. Four well-known British playwrights were given their start at the Everyman – Alan Bleasdale, Chris Bond, Bill Morrison and Willy Russell of *Educating Rita* and *Shirley Valentine*. When classical theatre is presented it is given a fresh approach and music is a feature of many productions. The monthly programme and the pleasant 400-seat auditorium ensure that you mostly see excellent quality theatre at the Everyman. It is essentially lively, informal and welcoming, and having an Egon-Ronay-recommended bistro doesn't hurt – a nice bar too. Recent productions include a "participatory" *As You Like It* and a hard-hitting interpretation of Tony Harrison's adaptation of *The Nativity* drawn from the York, Wakefield, Chester and Coventry cycles.

Liverpool Playhouse and Studio – Williamson Square, Tel 709 8363. This is the oldest surviving repertory theatre in the country. Having started life in 1866 as the Star Music Hall, it became a rep theatre in 1911. The original stuccoed exterior still survives today, but in 1968 a drum-like extension, housing restaurant, bars and workshops, was added, offering a stark contrast to the Victorian elegance of the old Music Hall architecture. The main auditorium has a varied programme from popular theatre through to the classics. Recent productions include August Wilson's *Fences* (which was presented on Broadway and in the West End) and Anthony Shaffer's *Sleuth*.

The Playhouse Studio has a reputation for staging more avant-garde productions and has nurtured and presented both new writing and performing talent. The Studio recently started a programme designed to promote and present new theatre work from the Merseyside region. A good restaurant and bar.

Unity Theatre – 1 Hope Place, Tel 709 4988. The Liverpool venue for major national and international small-scale touring companies. Recently refurbished. Recent productions include plays by Arthur Miller and Steven Berkoff and visiting companies such as Hands On Theatre and Temba Theatre Company. The café/bar is open Mon–Sat noon–3pm for lunch and from 7pm when there is an evening performance.

Bluecoat Arts Centre – School Lane, Tel 708 8877 (noon–4pm). The Centre stages a varied programme of music, dance and theatre, as well as the Liverpool Festival of Indian Arts (October). There is also a film programme, a gallery and a café/bar.

Royal Court Theatre – Roe Street, Tel 709 4321. Mainly rock and pop groups with the occasional musical.

MUSIC

The jewel in Liverpool's crown is the **Royal Liverpool Philharmonic Orchestra**, which performs at the **Philharmonic Hall**, Hope Street, Tel 709 3789. The season includes concerts featuring the world's top performers and conductors. As the orchestra is essentially Liverpool's professional orchestra, it is heavily subsidized by the Corporation and gives about 75 public concerts in Liverpool each year. As well as this, the orchestra appears over 50 times outside of Liverpool and gives many concerts in schools. There are also a series of lunchtime concerts, which offer a recital by a chamber ensemble or soloist and a two-course lunch with a glass of wine for a very low price.

Concerts are also given in the **Liverpool University Theatre**, Tel 794 3096, and at other venues in the city (call 709 3631 for details). For details of music at **Liverpool Cathedral** (which sponsors a young-organist-of-the-year competition), phone 709 6271. The **Roman Catholic Metropolitan Cathedral of Christ the King** can be reached at 709 9222.

FILM

Commercial Cinema:

Cannon – Lime Street, Tel 709 6277. Three screens. City Centre.

Odeon – London Road, Tel 709 0717. Five screens. City Centre.

Cannon – Allerton Road, Tel 724 5095.

Showcase – Stonebridge Lane, Tel 549 2021. Twelve screens.

Of more interest to me is the **Merseyside Film Institute** which is based at the Bluecoat Arts Centre, School Lane, Tel 709 4260. They show interesting films about 23 or 24 evenings per month, usually at 6 and 8:15pm. Recent directors included Eric Rohmer, Peter Greenaway, Bertrand Tavernier and Woody Allen, and films such as *Jesus of Montreal* and *Les Enfants du Paradis* have been shown.

BOOKSTORES

The best are **Dillon's** at 14–16 Bold Street, Tel 708 6861, and **Waterstone's** at 52 Bold Street, Tel 709 0866. Dillon's incorporates Ryman the Stationer, the Athena Gallery, which has posters and prints and a very good classical music department. Waterstone's, as always, is excellent.

Of the local firms I would recommend **Charles Wilson** at 46 Renshaw Street. He has a children's Puffin Book Club at that address, Tel 709 4242 and 709 0994, and another branch at 17 Castle Street, Tel 236 3680. Two branches of the excellent Blackwell Bookshops are **Young's** at 15 North John Street, Tel 236 2048, and **Parry's** at Brownlow Hill, Tel 709 8146, which is the largest university bookshop in the north-west and is also an HMSO agency. If you are wandering in the Albert Docks then **Words Worth Books**, 12 The Colonnades, Tel 709 6799, is a pleasant experience, while in the middle of town **Atticus Bookshop** at 2A Hardman Street, Tel 708 9834, and **Brunswick Books** at 35 Pembroke Place, Tel 709 3704, are worth a look. Religious books are best obtained at **SPCK** at Christ's and Notre Dame College on Woolton Road, Tel 722 2784, but more centrally, try **Contact Christian Books** at 18 Slater Street, Tel 708 9550, or **Progressive Books** at 12 Berry Street, Tel 709 1905. Finally, horror, fantasy, science fiction comics *et al* are at **Chapter One**, 6 London Road, Tel 709 7011, and **Ogre Books** (aptly named) at 120 Picton Road, Tel 733 0149.

ANTIQUARIAN AND SECONDHAND BOOKS

Renshaw Street (just behind the Central Railway Station) and Mount Pleasant (just below the Roman Catholic Cathedral) are the two best places. Renshaw Street will give you **Hazeldine Bookshop** at No 61, Tel 708 8780, with a good extensive secondhand collection and **Antiquarian and Out of Print Bookshop** at No 97, Tel 708 9700, which specializes in local history but has antiquarian and secondhand books on all subjects.

In Mount Pleasant at No 105 you will find **Reid of Liverpool**, Tel 709 2312, with a very comprehensive stock covering antiquarian books, prints, pre-1920 illustrated books, science fiction, ordnance survey maps, modern paperback pre-1970 fashion magazines and other esoteric subjects. They are at No 105. **John D Rowles** is at No 55 and he is worth a visit – call him at 920 6801. Finally, I would recommend **Henry Bohn Books** at 32 Berry Street (see Walk Three). Besides a good book collection, they also stock classical music.

ART GALLERIES

One of my favourite galleries is **Acorn Gallery**, Newington, Tel 709 5423. They essentially represent Merseyside contemporary artists and there is always something of interest on view. Their Christmas show is an especially good time to visit, but you will find something interesting whenever you choose to drop in. The **Bluecoat Display Centre**, Tel 7094014, is part of the Bluecoat Arts Centre (see above) and always shows interesting work of a contemporary nature. The proprietors of **Davey Galleries**, 44 Duke Street (walk 3), Tel 7097560, besides being expert picture framers and restorers, have a good selection of modern prints and limited editions. **Frank Green's Liverpool Gallery** in Albert Dock, Tel 709 3330 is very different. Here you will find the changing face of Liverpool recorded by Frank Green with pen, pencil, watercolours and oils over the past quarter century. **Lyver and Boydell** on the other hand, has an ever changing collection of decorative and topographical prints and maps of Merseyside and the surrounding area. They also have some nice Victorian oils and watercolours. They are at 15 Castle Street, Tel 207 0001. **Merseyside Arts** is at Graphic House, Duke Street (Walk 3) and mostly deals in contemporary limited edition prints and graphics, Tel 709 0671, while **Open Eye** is a photographic gallery with, usually, some excellent work on display. Find them at 110 Bold Street (Walk 3) Tel 7092439.

ANTIQUE DEALERS

Because of its size I have only included those antique shops within reasonable walking distance of Liverpool city centre. Starting with the furthest away you will find Parliament Street on the other side of Chinatown (walk south on St George Street). There you can visit **P Cowan** at No 31, Tel 709 1217, with a general collection and **Theta Gallery** at the same address, Tel 708 6375. Further out, at Lorton Hall, 320 Upper Parliament Street is **H Swainbank** with a very nice collection, Tel 70897166. Closer to Chinatown you will find Renshaw Street with **Magpie Antiques** at No 65, Tel 7089260 – again a good general collection. If you turn left off Renshaw Street into Slater Street and then into Seel Street you will find yourself in Beatle country, but you'll also discover **Eldon Worrall** at 13–15 Seel Street, Tel 709 2950, with a very good stock of nice pieces and **Ryan Wood Maggs** Antiques at 26 Fleet Street, Tel 708 0221, and **Blason's Reproductions** at 37 Hanover Street, Tel 709 9529.

Right in the heart of the city you will find **Edward's Jewellers** at 45A Whitechapel, Tel 2362909. There is some fine antique and silver jewellery here. Very close by is **Buttonhook Antiques** at 24 Matthew Street, Tel 236 0036, which also has jewellery and silver as well as an interesting general selection. If you walk out on Lime Street, past Lime Street Station, you will intersect with London Road. At No 110 you will find the old established firm of **Edwin Pryor and Son**, Tel 709 1361, with an excellent general collection. If you walk on to where London Road becomes Prescott Street (just by the hospital) you will find Moss Street on your left. At number 12–14 you will see **Hartley and Company**, Tel 263 6472. They have weekly sales of antique furniture and effects and it's well worth trying to catch one. Finally, in Bridgewater Street (a continuation of Nelson Street in Chinatown), you will find **Pilgrim's Progress** at No 1A, with a good general collection, Tel 708 7515, and Belle Interiors at 3A (same telephone) which, besides antique furniture, have nice fabrics and wallcoverings. Not far away is **Richards of Liverpool** at 20 Newington, Tel 708 6845, with a good collection which is well worth a visit.

RESTAURANTS

Partly because of its name I am very fond of **La Grande Bouffe**, 48A Castle Street, Tel 236 3375, though it bears no resemblance to Marco Ferreri's 1974 film of the same name, in which Marcello Mastroianni, Ugo Tognazzi, Philippe Noiret and Michel Piccoli shut themselves up in a Parisian villa and gorge themselves to death. The helpings are ample in this basement bistro though, and both the cooking and service good. The cuisine is essentially French and there's an excellent cassoulet and good cheese. There's a guitarist on Tuesday and Saturday evenings and at lunch the restaurant moves down-market and functions as a self-service brasserie. Open Mon–Sat 12–2pm and 6–10:30pm. No Sat lunch.

Armadillo – 20–22 Matthew Street, Tel 236 4123. Another favourite of mine, mainly because the cooking is inventive and the setting friendly and informal. An excellent English/French menu with nods to Greece, Italy and even the Caribbean, so I guess you would call the menu international. In any case, unlike so many other restaurants, there is *always* something interesting to eat at Armadillo and a lot of people share my opinion. Open Tues–Sat 12–3 and 5–6:45pm (daytime menu) – very good value and 7:30–10:30 (evening menu) NB – Saturdays they serve straight through from 12–5pm.

Note that there are good restaurants at the **Liverpool Playhouse** and the **Liverpool Everyman** (see above) and the **Refectory of Liverpool Cathedral** serves a very good lunch and also cream teas. Open 10–4pm.

PUBS

Baltic Fleet – Wapping (just beyond Albert Dock) Tel 709 3116. Well known old Liverpool pub refurbished with maritime artefacts. Good bar food with separate restaurant upstairs.

Pump House – Albert Dock complex, Tel 709 2367. Recently converted from the Pump House that supplied hydraulic power to the docks. Lots of polished dark wood, a marble counter and a brass rail supported by elephants' heads. Very good bar food. The cheese ploughman's is especially good but there's hot food as well. Tables outside overlooking the dock, Museum of Shipping and Liver Building.

Philharmonic Hotel – 36 Hope Street, Tel 709 1163. A magnificent mosaic-fronted island bar with a mosaic floor, superb stained glass, mahogany and a fine fireplace. Beyond the Brahms and Liszt rooms is a grand lounge that acts as a food servery at lunchtime – good food too. In the evening there is often live music. A superb pub – not to be missed. The "gents" is a cathedral among washrooms.

Vines – 81 Lime Street, Tel 709 3977. Ornately carved wood, frescoes and a Viking mural over the fire-place with the famous ballroom at the rear. A classic city centre pub – not to be missed. Good hot bar food.

Ye Cracke – 13 Rice Street, Tel 709 4171. A fine traditional pub (Liverpool's best in many ways) with many separate drinking areas, good food and a garden. The Beatles used to drink here and there's a room named after them.

Central Commercial – Ranelagh Street (opposite Central Station). Mahogany woodwork, sumptous engraved glass, marble pillars and elaborately moulded Victorian domed ceiling. Good bar food and cold buffet.

Grapes – 25 Matthew Street. Friendly and lively city centre pub on atmospheric street close to the site of the old Cavern, of Beatles fame. Very good value lunchtime bar food and an unspoilt decor – at least at the time I write.

Pilgrim – 34 Pilgrim Street. Converted basement bistro, beamed ceiling, wooden floor and spiral staircase to art gallery. Very good food indeed especially if the sea bass or goulash is on the menu. You can even get breakfast here.

Globe – 17 Cases Street (opposite Central Station) Tel 709 5060. A one-hundred-year-old pub with a cozy snug off the main bar. Lots of atmosphere and a wonderful sloping floor.

Beehive – 7 Paradise Street, Tel 709 5875. Could be Liverpool's first licensed library! A long bar with bright lights and lots of people. Some very nice original "beehive" stained glass.

ARTISTIC ASSOCIATIONS

In 1724, Daniel Defoe, author of *Robinson Crusoe,* visited Liverpool and in his book *A Tour Through the Whole Island of Great Britain* (1724–27) comments most favourably on the fineness and beauty of Liverpool's streets and buildings. William Hazlitt, the critic and essayist, saw his first play in Liverpool at the age of 12 in 1790 and wrote his first piece of drama criticism in a letter to his father. Thomas De Quincey, the essayist, was fascinated by the city and called it "the many languaged town." He visited often, staying with his mother in Everton which was, in 1803, a pleasant little village. It was in that year that he wrote an enthusiastic letter to William Wordsworth praising the publication of *Lyrical Ballads,* which heralded the Romantic Movement in English literature.

Given its importance as a transatlantic port, Liverpool welcomed many visitors from the USA in the 19th century. Ralph Waldo Emerson, philosopher and poet, came here to lecture in 1848, while Herman Melville, author of *Moby Dick,* stayed in Liverpool on a number of occasions, the first in 1837, when he was 18 and a cabin boy on a sailing ship. Nathaniel Hawthorne, author of *The Scarlet Letter* and *Tanglewood Tales* was American Consul here from 1853 to 1857 and in his novel *Our Old Home* describes his dislike for the building in which the consulate was situated. Harriet Beecher Stowe, author of *Uncle Tom's Cabin* was a visitor in 1853. Perhaps the transatlantic arrival which caused the most consternation was that of the English journalist and political writer William Cobbett in 1819. He arrived with the bones of Tom Paine, the political philosopher and author of *The Rights of Man* and *The Age of Reason.* Cobbett had exhumed Paine's bones from a patch of unconsecrated ground near New York where he had been buried in 1809. He intended to build a mausoleum to house them in England. Paine's final resting place is still unknown.

Charles Dickens was a frequent visitor to the city, giving readings of his works on many occasions. In *Nicholas Nickleby* and *Martin Chuzzlewit* there are references to Sarah Biffin, the armless artist.

Another great English literary figure died in Liverpool in 1888. He was Matthew Arnold, author of one of the greatest poems in the language, "Dover Beach." He was here to meet his daughter on her return from the USA and it is reported that he suffered his fatal heart attack while running for a tram to take him to the landing stage of his daughter's ship. (There are other stories of his demise, but this is the one I think Arnold would have liked.)

John Masefield, the Poet Laureate from 1930 to 1967, was a sea cadet here in 1891 and wrote many poems about Liverpool. John Galsworthy's play *Style* in 1911 led to the formation of the Liverpool Playhouse – the oldest repertory theatre in the country. A C Bradley, the famous Shakespearean scholar, became the university's first Professor of Literature and History in 1882 and Sir James Frazer, author of *The Golden Bough,* was appointed Professor of Social Anthropology in 1907.

In 1901, Augustus John was invited to teach at the School of Applied Art which had been set up in the Architecture Department of University College. During his two years in Liverpool, he antagonized the older members of the city's art establishment by his unorthodox behaviour and his style of painting. He sowed the seeds of rebellion in a younger generation of artists and in 1905, the Sandon Studios Society was set up to challenge the School of Applied Art and to encourage a freer approach to draughtsmanship and painting. Two of the most important artists connected with the Sandon Studios were James Hamilton Hay, whose painting was much influenced by the American painter, James Whistler, and Maxwell Gordon Lightfoot, a painter who developed a very simplified style of painting but whose promising career ended in suicide in 1911 at the age of 25.

More recently, the painter and poet Adrian Henri has had a considerable impact on Liverpool's cultural life. Together with Brian Patten and Roger McGough, he founded a poetic movement entitled "Merseybeat," consisting of populist poetry with strong political and social overtones that was immensely popular in the 1960s.

EPHEMERA

Liverpool is inextricably linked with those four tousle-haired lads who created a revolution in popular music in the 1960s. One of Liverpool's newer tourist attractions is "The Beatles' Story – A Magical Experience," which can be seen at Britannia Vaults, Albert Dock, Tel 709 1963. Open all week 10–6pm. Matthew Street is Beatles country, however. If you come down Whitechapel moving towards the waterfront and turn right into Stanley Street, Matthew Street is the first on your left. Incidentally, "Eleanor Rigby," of the Beatles' song, sits in sculptured loneliness in Stanley Street. She was made by singer Tommy Steele who, taking a hint from the hit musical he was so successful in (*Half a Sixpence*), charged that small sum as a commission fee. At 31 Matthew Street is the Beatle Shop selling Beatles mementos, and opposite, Flanagan's Apple Pub is well known for its live music. The Cavern Club, where the legend began, has been rebuilt in its original location underneath a shopping arcade and contains statues of the famous four, as does the Abbey Road Pub. Above the door of the building opposite, confusingly named "Cavern" is a memorial to John Lennon. Though the surviving lads have all gone their separate ways, fans from all over the world still flock to see where the story started. If you call 709 3631, the Tourist Office will take you on a Magical History Tour which covers the homes and school plus the people and places that influenced the Beatles' music.

The Adelphi Hotel (now the Britannia Adelphi) is one of the most famous hotels in the country. In 1826 James Radley bought the end house of a terrace on Copperas Hill and opened it as the Adelphi Hotel. He gradually acquired every house in the terrace until the hotel occupied the entire block and became very successful. In the 1830s, after Radley's death, the hotel was sold to a company which altered and improved it, and in 1912 Arthur Towle, who was entrusted with the LMS (London Midland and Scottish Railway) group of hotels, decided to buy and rebuild it. It was the first hotel in Liverpool to have saunas, central heating in all rooms and an indoor heated swimming pool. The Adelphi became one of Europe's great hotels, where visitors enjoyed remarkable luxury. It flourished during the 1920s and '30s and became Liverpool's prestige arrival and departure point for passengers on the lines to America and other parts of the world. With the coming of transatlantic air travel and the fading of the passenger liner trade, the Adelphi declined until the 1980s when it was bought by the Britannia group, who renamed it and spent £6 million on bringing it back to its former glory.

One of the eye-opening facts contained within the Museum of Labour History concerns the harrowing conditions under which working-class men and women lived on Merseyside in the mid-19th century. In 1844 over 38,000 people lived in cellar dwellings. A contemporary account stated, "The cellars are 10 to 12 square feet, generally flagged, but frequently having only bare earth for a floor and sometimes less than 6 feet in height. There are frequently no windows, so light and air can gain access to the cellars only by the door, the top of which is often not higher than the level of the street."

No doubt these conditions influenced many people to decide to make new lives for themselves in the New World. Dioramas in the Maritime Museum tell us where they came from and how they fared in dockside lodgings and in the frequently squalid emigrant ships. Big shipping companies vied with each other for lucrative emigrant transportation to the USA. At the height of the exodus, in the second half of the 19th century, a single steerage passage from Liverpool to New York cost £4.

In Hale Church on the outskirts of Liverpool, in a peaceful grave marked by a flat grey stone, lies the body of John Middleton, the gigantic "Childe" of Hale. Middleton grew to a height of nine feet three inches (281 cm) and, after a visit to Lancashire in 1617 by James I, who was famous for his belief in witches, warlocks and indeed giants, Sir Gilbert Ireland, Middleton's benefactor and employer, took the young man to London where he became an instant celebrity. Sir Gilbert was a graduate of Brasenose College in Oxford and, as he was required to pass through the town on his way to London, he introduced the Childe to his professors and fellow students. John Middleton made an impression of his hand-print on one of the doorposts in the cellar under College Hall which remained at Brasenose until 1886. Samuel Pepys writes in his diary in 1668 of visiting the college to see this print. Even today two life-size paintings of the Childe's hands adorn the walls of Brasenose but they are of different sizes and are in all probability spurious. A life-size portrait of the giant does hang in the college library though, and Middleton occupies a prominent place amongst Brasenose traditions. Many undergraduates are more familiar with his name than they are with that of the founder of their college, and the college boats, which attempt to become Head of the River each summer, are invariably named after him.

At the beginning of the 1800s the spirit of scientific curiosity which animated the 19th-century investigators caused the Childe of Hale's bones to be exhumed. His height was confirmed at nine feet three inches and his palm, if you would like to compare, was 17 inches (43.1 cm) from the carpus to the end of his middle finger and eight and a half inches (21.5 cm) in breadth. By all contemporary reports, notoriety and fame did not change John Middleton who died peacefully in his bed at the age of 35. He now lies in Hale Churchyard and his gravestone is very easy to find – it's so much bigger than all its neighbours.

The Liver Birds, which top the twin towers of the Royal Liver Insurance Company building on Liverpool's waterfront, are thought to be cormorants and to have taken their name from the seaweed or laver on their beaks (see Cardiff). The city's symbol is a Liver Bird perched on a cupola and even as I write there is a furious debate going on in Liverpool over the suggestion that the bird should be replaced by a more appropriate symbol. Overnight, Save the Liver Bird campaigns sprang up and by the time you read this the matter may have been resolved – though knowing local government, I wouldn't bet on it.

Finally, in parts of the city, particularly around the predominantly Catholic dock area, children light bonfires on Good Friday and burn effigies of Judas Iscariot. Liverpool is the only city in Britain where this happens, though the custom is common in Spain, Portugal and Latin America, so it may have been introduced here by sailors from overseas.

TOURIST INFORMATION BUREAU: Merseyside Welcome Centre, Clayton Square Shopping Centre, Liverpool Merseyside, L1 1QR. Tel (051) 709 3631

MANCHESTER

County of Lancashire
200 miles (320 km) from London by road on M1 and M5
2 hours and 30 minutes by train from London (Euston Station)

When I look back on my working career as an actor in England, I find that in 15 years I never sought employment north of a line between Bristol and The Wash. Consequently, like so many other Southerners, I subscribed to the popular misconception of Manchester as a place comprising "dark satanic mills" and smoke-blackened buildings and little else. In recent years I have had reasons to spend a good deal of time in Manchester and discovered that, outside of London, there are more cultural events taking place in Manchester at any given time than anywhere else in the British Isles and although this is a region of England into which the tourist may not stray by chance, there is no doubt that Manchester is England's second city for exciting artistic activity.

Manchester is also England's second capital, a city and county in its own right, with a population of over 3 million. The opening in 1894 of the Manchester Ship Canal turned the city into a major inland port, and so it remains today, the trading centre of the British cotton industry (see Royal Exchange Theatre). The surrounding towns are the places of production, their towering brick-built mills standing proudly in the Pennine valleys. Even though many of the buildings in the centre of Manchester have been cleaned and now glisten in the sun, Manchester remains proud of being the world's first industrial city and continues to cherish her industrial heritage. Nowhere is this more vividly illustrated than in the Museum of Science and Industry (pamphlet at the Tourist Bureau in the Town Hall), located in the Castlefield Urban Heritage Park in the heart of Manchester. Here you can see exhibits which tell the story of power and industry from water wheels to turbines, an 1830s railway station, a history of Manchester (including a walk down a Victorian sewer) and the Air and Space Gallery which tells the story of flight, from the bi-plane to the Space Shuttle. I love the collection of steam engines and railway locomotives and for me, Europe's largest industrial museum is a must.

Walking around the city centre one finds many gems of Victorian architecture, among them the Town Hall, with murals by Ford Madox Brown, the Art Gallery with its fine collection of pre-Raphaelites, the Free Trade Hall, bombed and rebuilt in the Palladian style (home of the Hallé Orchestra), the Royal Exchange Theatre in St Ann's Square and St Ann's Church itself, a beautifully understated example of English ecclesiastical architecture and a haven of calm from the bustle of the centre of the city. Other worthwhile places to see are the restored Opera House, the John Rylands Library set in a superb mock-Gothic masterpiece and the old Shambles with its half-timbered buildings. When one considers the cultural richness of Britain's second city it's hard to understand why, in many ways, it remains so unjustly maligned. I discovered its exciting potential by accident – I advise you to make the discovery by design.

WALK

Manchester is divided into two walks as the city is too large to be contained in one:
Walk One begins in the car park at the rear of the great hooped, domed G-Mex Building, off Watson Street. Walk up Watson Street with this building on your right. On your left is an old warehouse of the Great Northern Railway and ahead, the **Free Trade Hall**. Turn left along Peter Street, which is crammed with Victorian and modern architecture, and go left again down Deansgate. At the junction with Liverpool Road is the **Castlefield Urban Heritage Park**. Turn right down Liverpool Road. Close by is the reconstructed gate of Manchester's Roman Fort and behind it, under a tangle of viaducts, the Castlefied Canal Basin, built in 1759 and now restored for leisure pursuits. Continue down Liverpool Road, passing the

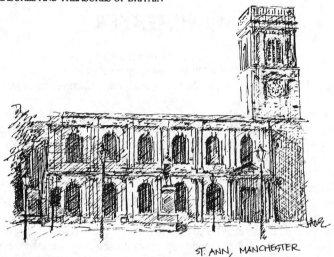

ST. ANN, MANCHESTER

Air and Space Gallery and the **Museum of Science and Industry** in Lower Byron Street to your right. Continue along Liverpool Road and turn right up Water Street for the **Granada Studio Tour**. Turn right on Quay Street and look out for the **Opera House** and opposite, the old **County Court**, once the home of political reformer Richard Cobden. Just before reaching the Free Trade Hall turn right down Watson Street and back to the car park.

Walk Two begins in the multistorey car park in Back South Parade, off King Street West. Turn left up King Street West, then right along Deansgate. Turn left into Brasenose Street and go past the statue of **Abraham Lincoln** which commemorates Manchester's support for the Union cause in the American Civil War. Walk into Albert Square, past a statue of Prime Minister **W E Gladstone**, to the **Town Hall**. Visit the Town Hall, built in 1877 and modelled on the medieval cloth halls of Flanders. Walk down Cross Street and just before you turn left into King Street there's a palatial **Lloyds Bank** and there's another worth looking at, the **Georgian Bank**, in King Street itself. Next to the bank is the entrance to St Ann's Court. Go through to **St Ann's Square** and **St Ann's Church**. Here you will find the **Royal Exchange Theatre** and a statue of **Richard Cobden**. Opposite the theatre is the **Barton Arcade**, a lovely Victorian creation of cast iron and glass. Continue straight ahead on Exchange Street and cross St Mary's Gate, bearing left through an alleyway to Shambles Square. Note the two very old pubs – **Sinclairs** and the **Old Wellington**, then cross Cateaton Street taking Hanging Bridge Alleyway to Manchester Cathedral. From the Cathedral, turn right up Victoria Street and then right again along Fennel Street and left up Long Millgate. Note the entrance to the former Chetham's Hospital School, founded in 1653, which is today a school for talented musicians. At the top of the street is **Victoria Station** which still has the roof that George Stephenson (inventor of the locomotive) designed for it in 1844. Turn right down Todd Street and right again on Corporation Street to the huge covered **Armdale Shopping Centre**. Leave Armdale by one of the exits into Market Street and turn left. Turn right along Spring Gardens. Cross Fountain Street to Mosley. Note the ornate pillared **Bank** pub which was formerly the Reading Room of a subscription library opened in 1806. Go down Charlotte Street into Chinatown. Turn right to Faulkner Street with its gold-and-crimson arch and Chinese garden and right again into Nicholas Street. You will find yourself now in Mosley Street, beside **Manchester Art Gallery**. The steps of the Art Gallery Cafe look onto the **Central Library** and **Town Hall** where you will find the Tourist Information Centre. Cross Princess Street and go between the two buildings. Then turn right, cross Albert Square into Brasenose Street, right onto Deansgate and left back to the car park.

MUSEUMS AND GALLERIES

Castlefield – Liverpool Road off Deansgate, City Centre. In this area, the heart of Manchester, you can experience all the history of the city. There are trails and walkways, fine Victorian buildings, canals, wharfs, viaducts, old pubs and the **Manchester Museum of Science and Industry** (see above). Open Mon–Sat 10–5pm, Sun 2–5pm.

Liverpool Road Station – The oldest railway station in the world and a reconstruction of part of Manchester's Roman Fort. Tel 832 4244 for full details.

Manchester Museum – The University, Oxford Road (1.5 miles/2.4 km from city centre). The museum is renowned for its selection of Egyptian mummies. They are shown, along with X-rays and information regarding diseases, dietary patterns and causes of death. The museum also has an impressive antiquary collection plus an aquarium and vivarium. Open Mon–Sat 10am–5pm. Admission free. Tel 275 2364 for special exhibition details.

Manchester Jewish Museum – 190 Cheetham Hill Road (1.5 miles/2.4 km from city centre). The museum houses a permanent exhibition of photographs, documents, objects and tape recordings tracing the history of Manchester's Jewish community. The spectacular stained-glass window depicting the seven-branched Menorah, and incorporating Psalm 67, is especially memorable. Open Mon–Thur 10:30–4pm; Sun 10:30–5pm. Tel 834 9870.

Museum of Transport – Boyle Street, Cheetham Hill (1.5 miles/2.4 km from city centre). Over 60 historic buses and goods vehicles. One of the largest collections of its kind in the country. Also a smaller collection of reminders of our transport heritage, all housed in a converted bus garage. Open Wed, Sat, Sun and Bank Hols. Tel 205 2122.

John Rylands Library – Deansgate (city centre). A magnificent neo-Gothic building (1890–99), it houses more than two million manuscripts and books ranging in date from the third millennium BC to the present day. Open Mon–Fri 10–5:30pm; Sat 10–1pm. Admission free. Tel 834 5343 for special exhibitions.

Chethams Library – Long Millgate, near the Cathedral, City Centre. Founded in 1653, Chethams is one of the oldest public libraries in England with a collection of circa 100,000 books. Open Mon–Fri 9:30–5:30. Admission free. Tel 834 7961.

City Art Gallery – Mosley Street (city centre). An outstanding collection of paintings, drawings and water-colours including work by Stubbs, Constable and Turner and a world-famous collection of pre-Raphaelites. There is a fascinating reconstruction of L S Lowry's living room and studio.

Next door, on the corner of Princess Street, is the smaller **Athenaeum Gallery** which houses major travelling and special exhibitions. Open weekdays 10–6, Sun 2–5:45pm. Admission free, Tel 236 9422.

Whitworth Art Gallery – Oxford Road (2 miles/3.2 km from city centre). The Whitworth houses collections of British watercolours and drawings, works by Blake, Lowry and Warhol as well as the largest collection of international textiles outside London. Open every day except Sunday 10–5pm. (Thurs till 9pm) Admission free. Tel 273 4865.

HALLS AND GARDENS

For lovers of how things used to be, Manchester has a wealth of historic houses and parks, all a short distance from the city centre.

Fletcher Moss Museum and Art Gallery – Stenner Lane, Pidsbury (5 miles/8 km from city centre). There is an excellent watercolour collection with works by Turner, David Cox and Paul Sandby and 19th-century silver and porcelain. Open April–end of Sept, weekdays (except Tues) 10–5:45pm; Sun 2–5:45pm. Admission free. Tel 445 1109.

Heaton Hall – Heaton Park, Prestwich (5 miles/8 km from city centre). The finest neo-classical house in the area, complete with 600 ares of parkland. Impressive period interiors, notably a unique Pompeiian room which has been newly restored. Note the fine organ built by Samuel Green in 1793 and still in use. Boating, golfing, fishing and a farm centre and pets corner in the park. On certain days, the Tramway and Vintage Bus Service goes into action. Tel 773 1231. Open April–end of Sept daily except Tues 10–5:45pm; Sun 2–5:45pm. Admission free.

Wythenshawe Hall - Wythenshawe Park, Northenden (10 miles/16 km from city centre). One of Manchester's oldest buildings, the hall dates partly from Tudor times. On show in the half-timbered hall are rare, recently discovered Tudor wall paintings and a collection of oak, walnut and inlaid furniture dating from the 17th century. Fine Staffordshire ware and English "Delft" pottery and a collection of English and European paintings. Open April–end of Sept except Tues 10–5:45pm; Sun 2–5:45pm. Admission free. Tel 998 2331.

Platt Hall – Platt Fields, Rusholme (2 miles/3.2 km from city centre). An elegant 18th-century family home housing one of the finest costume collections in the country. Displays show the ever changing world of fashion from the 1600s to the present day. Open throughout the year except Tuesdays, 10–5:45pm; Sun 2–5:45pm. Closes at 4pm Nov–Feb. Admission free. Tel 224 5217.

THEATRE

Opera House, Quay Street, Tel 831 7766, and **Palace Theatre**, Oxford Street, Tel 236 9922, are two theatres under the same management which are touring houses receiving distinguished visiting companies ranging from the Christmas pantomime through large scale musicals such as *42nd Street, My Fair Lady* and *South Pacific* to the London Festival Ballet and the Glyndebourne Opera Company. The Opera House especially, has been beautifully restored to its 19th-century splendour.

Library Theatre Company – Central Library, St Peter's Square, Tel 236 7110. The Library Theatre Company is unique in that it is the only provincial repertory theatre company in England that is 100-percent funded by the local authority. Artistic policy tends to encourage new writing and the theatre has an above average number of world and northern premieres. Proscenium stage with a seating capacity of 308. Productions have included *Torch Song Trilogy* by Harvey Fierstein, *Tom and Viv* by Michael Hastings and *Milk and Honey* by Jacqui Shapiro, which was commissioned as a contribution to Manchester's Jewish bicentennial and examined Jewish life in the city over the past hundred years. Visiting companies have included Hull Truck, Paine's Plough and the Black Theatre Co-op, who have presented original material as well as plays by Nick Dear and Brian Patten. Library Theatre Company also operate in a larger space, the **Forum Theatre**, Civic Centre, Simonsway, Wythenshawe. Proscenium stage with a seating capacity of 480. Productions at the Forum have included *Guys and Dolls, The Importance of Being Earnest, Ain't Misbehavin'* and not surprisingly, *A Funny Thing Happened on the Way to the Forum*. In fact, this company has been particularly noted for its staging of the musicals of Stephen Sondheim, with a production of *Pacific Overtures* especially remembered.

Contact Theatre Company – Oxford Road, Tel 274 4400. Contact Theatre Company is the professional theatre company based in the theatre of the University of Manchester. Formed in 1972 to provide "building-based" theatre for younger audiences, the company presents 8 to 10 productions a year which are relevant to young people. Contact has produced 60 world premieres since its formation in 1972 and writers such as Alan Bleasdale (*Boys from the Blackstuff*) and Willy Russell (*Educating Rita*) started their careers here. The Contact annual Christmas show, usually based on adaptations of children's novels, (*The Snowman, The Little Prince, The Red Balloon*) have been highly praised and have all been produced by other theatres across the country following their first production at Contact.

Productions have included *Feminine Singular* by Dario Fo and France Rame, *Meridian,* adapted from the book by Alice Walker (*The Colour Purple*), *The Duchess of Malfi* by John Webster, *Fool for Love* by Sam Shepard, *Master Harold and the Boys* by Athol Fugard and *Top Girls* by Caryl Churchill. One of the delights of seeing a play at Contact is that often 60 percent of the audience is between 16 and 21 and the immediacy and accessibility of the plays to their young audience create a stimulating evening.

Royal Exchange Theatre – St Ann's Square, Tel 833 9833. One of the finest provincial theatre companies in the British Isles, both for the quality of its work and the unique space in which it performs. The theatre is built in the heart of the old Cotton Exchange, a great hall that at the height of its power would see over 900 dealers packing the building twice a week to fix world prices. The 700-seat theatre is a modular shape suspended within the walls of the great hall, allowing theatre-in-the-round presentations to be given with the maximum of intimacy and contact. The first view of the spacecraft-like modern structure suspended inside the great hall of commerce offers the same kind of thrill as first seeing the Festival Theatre at Stratford, Ontario, Canada or first entering London's Albert Hall.

The Royal Exchange Company presents both modern and classical drama with very high production standards. Productions have included *Twelfth Night, A Midsummer Night's Dream, Macbeth* (a production set in a concentration camp), *All My Sons* by Arthur Miller, *Don Juan* by Moliere, *Arms and the Man* by Shaw, *She Stoops to Conquer* by Oliver Goldsmith and *American Bagpipes* by Ian Heggie.

The Green Room – 54-56 Whitworth Street West, Tel 236 1676. A lively arts centre presenting mostly avant-garde performances of theatre, dance, music and workshops. A recent programme sampling found a disabled theatre company performing in Aristophanes's *The Birds,* London Actors Theatre Company in *Frankenstein* and Gay Sweatshop, a lesbian and gay theatre troupe, performing a musical entitled *Paradise Then and Now.* If you add to this a contemporary Iranian theatre company performing in English and concerts of Cajun, rock, folk, jazz, Chilean and Ghanaian music, then you will understand why the Green Room is certainly a place to check out.

North West Arts – 12 Harter Street, Manchester, Tel 228 3062. The regional arts association of the North West is responsible for supporting and developing the whole spectrum of arts activity in the region. They distribute nearly £3 million in grant aid each year and support more than 1000 individuals and organizations. Their monthly arts magazine *The Artful Reporter,* has a wonderfully comprehensive listing of all arts events in the North West and interesting articles on current exhibitions and performers. A great deal of the theatre work supported by North West Arts is community oriented – much of it is performed in schools but the diversity of companies and work is staggering. Check with them for when public performances are offered.

MUSIC

The **Hallé Orchestra** is Britain's oldest professional symphony orchestra. It was founded by the German-born pianist and conductor Charles Hallé in 1858. A refugee from the 1848 revolution in Paris, Hallé was asked to form a professional orchestra to play throughout an international exhibition of art treasures held in Manchester. Rather than see his excellent orchestra disbanded when the exhibition closed, Halle launched his own series of concerts. The first Hallé concert was held in Manchester's Free Trade Hall on January 30th, 1858. After Hallé's death, the Hallé Concert Society was founded in 1898 and a series of distinguished conductors followed. Prominent among them was Sir John Barbirolli, who was largely responsible for establishing the international reputation enjoyed by the orchestra. There have only been seven permanent principal conductors through to Stanislaw Skrowaczewski, the eminent Polish-born American composer, who took up his appointment in 1984. The orchestra has undertaken overseas tours to Australia, Central and South America, West Indies, Hong Kong and Central Africa; it gives considerably more concerts than any comparable British orchestra and consequently performs a prodigious number of different works each year. Concerts are given in the **Free Trade Hall** and the season generally runs from early October to mid-May, with open air concerts in the summer and of course, the Hallé proms. Hallé Booking Office at 10-12 St Ann's Square, Tel 834 1712.

Camerata is Manchester's second orchestra. The orchestra performs at the Free Trade Hall and also at the Royal Northern College of Music, 124 Oxford Road, Tel 273 4504. Tickets and information regarding the orchestra's season can be obtained from Camerata Production Ltd, 30 Derby Road, Tel 248 6499.

Also performing at the Free Trade Hall and the Northern College of Music is the **BBC Philharmonic**, one of Europe's finest, and busiest, orchestras. The BBC Philharmonic's philosophy is quite simple – a varied and adventurous repertoire, with a strong commitment to 20th-century music and British composers. Tickets and programme from Manchester Ticket Shop, St Peter's Square, Tel 834 0943, or the Royal Northern College of Music, Tel 273 4504. There are also recitals at the **Royal Northern College of Music** with its fine student orchestra and an excellent midday concert series at the Royal Exchange, with individual tickets available at the Royal Exchange Box Office, Tel 833 9833.

The **Manchester Music Festival** in September (for details Tel 236 9422) began in 1978 as an organ jamboree – classical, theatre and fairground. Today, even though there is an international organ competition, the festival features jazz, classical music, drama, dance, exhibitions, light music, family events, films and open-air entertainments. Combining the talents of nationally known professionals with the best that Manchester's talented amateurs have to offer.

CINEMA

Commercial cinema performances can be seen at the following main locations:
Cano Cinema – Deansgate, Tel 832 2112.
Mayfair Cinema – Bury Old Road, Whitefield, Tel 766 2369.
Metro Centre – Old Street, Tel 330 1993.
New Curzon Theatre – Princess Road, Tel 748 2929.
Odeon Theatre – Oxford Street, Tel 236 8264.
Palace Cinema – 24 Middleton Garden, Tel 643 2852.
Roxy Cinema – Hollins Road, Tel 681 1441.
The Silver Screen – Regents Street, Tel 789 0651.
Theatre Royal – Corporation Street, Tel 368 2206.
Unit 4 Cinemas – Arndale Centre, Bolton Road, Tel 790 9432.

For me, the most exciting venue for cinema in Manchester is **Cornerhouse** on Oxford Street in the city centre. This lively centre for the visual arts presents a constantly changing programme of films in three cinemas. It also has television and video work, debates, courses and workshops. Its three galleries house changing exhibitions of photography, sculpture and painting. Cornerhouse also has bookshops, a video section, a bar and a popular cafe. Tel 228 2463. Open every day noon–8pm. Galleries not open on Monday. Admission free, except cinemas.

The films at Cornerhouse are constantly interesting. Besides films which are likely to get a commercial release, there are also thematic series, revivals of popular classics and experimental and "avant-garde" films. There are late-night showings on the weekends and even films for youngsters on Saturday afternoons.

BOOKSTORES

Waterstone's – 91 Deansgate (city centre). Tel 832 1992. Always reliable with a very comprehensive selection and knowledgeable assistants.

Dillons Bookshop – 1 Cross Street, Tel 832 1424. Good country-wide chain of bookstores that care about books. Often have good bargains on both new and remaindered stock.

Geoffrey Clifton's Performing Arts Bookstore – 44 Brasenose Street, Tel 831 718. For plays and books on drama, dance, film, media and music. Also has a mail order service.

Grass Roots Books – 1 Newton Street, Piccadilly (city centre), Tel 236 3112. Radical books – feminist, black, gay and left-wing.

Haigh and Hockland – The University booksellers. Branches within the University Precinct, Oxford Road and at 11 Whitworth Street, Tel 273 4156 and 236 9391.

HMSO Her Majesty's Stationery Office – 9-21 Princess Street, Albert Square, Tel 834 7201. A fascinating collection of over 40,000 government publications and related material. Far more interesting than it sounds.

W H Smith – Unit 5, Arndale Centre, Market Street (city centre) Tel 831 7441. Seems to focus more on stationery, gifts and tapes than on serious bookselling these days. Sometimes has good bargains.

ANTIQUARIAN AND SECONDHAND BOOKS

In the centre of Manchester try **Secondhand and Rare Books**, corner of Church Street and High Street with a good stock, Tel 834 5964, and **Frank's Bookshop** in the Royal Exchange Shopping Centre adjacent to the theatre in St Ann's Square, Tel 834 1427. Also centrally located is **Gibb's Bookshop Ltd**, 10 Charlotte Street, Tel 2367179, **Shaw's Bookshop** at 11 Police Street (close to John Dalton Street) Tel 834 7587, **Fennel Books** at 23 Fennel Street, Tel 835 3759, and **The Ginnel**, Lloyds House, Lloyds Street, Tel 833 9037. In Prestwick, **Browzers** at 14 Warwick Street, Tel 798 0626, has secondhand books, prints and maps, while off the Wilmslow Road in Didsbury is the excellent **Eric J Marten**, Warburton Street, Tel 445 7629 with an excellent antiquarian collection from the 16th to the 20th centuries. Finally, in Moss Side and well worth a visit is **McGill's Bookshop**, 115 Princess Road, Tel 232 9620. Here there is an extensive stock of rare and secondhand books with an excellent section on Irish interests in which they specialize.

ART GALLERIES

In the restored canal area in Whitworth Road there are two good galleries very close to one another. At Arch 63 you can find the **Amber Arch**, Tel 236 4181. They specialize in limited-edition prints, while at Arch 69, **Arts Intaglio**, Tel 236 9259, is mostly interested in original etchings and prints.

In the centre of town at 82 Portland Street is **Colin Jellicoe Gallery**, Tel 236 2716, with contemporary paintings and sculptures and original prints, a nice selection, while **Dixon Bate Ltd** at 283 Deansgate, Tel 834 0566, deals in contemporary paintings, prints and posters. **Shaw's Gallery**, 11 Police Street (off King Street), Tel 834 7587, has original oils and watercolours, limited-edition prints, maps and local topography, while **Garson Co Ltd** at 99 Port Street, Tel 236 9393, has old and modern masters, watercolours, gold carved mirrors, blackamoors, church altars and telescopes. In the Royal Exchange Shopping Centre adjacent to the theatre in St Ann's Square is the **Grenville Art Gallery**, Tel 832 6002, with some fine paintings, most of which are contemporary, while the **Ginnel Gallery** at 16 Lloyd Street has British arts and crafts and art pottery and metal work. Tel 833 9037. They also have antiquarian books.

Out of the city centre, **Fulda Gallery Ltd** is at 19 Vine Street, Salford (near Salford Police Station off Bury New Road), Tel 792 1962. They have a large selection of oils dating from 1500 to 1950 and watercolours from 1800 to 1930. They are open by appointment only. **Christopher James Fine Arts** is at 15 Alkrington Green, Alkringrton, Middleton, Tel 445 2504 (400 yards from Middleton town centre). Here you will find 19th- to early 20th-century oils and watercolours, art deco figures, bronzes and glass. They, too, are open only by appointment. In an area redolent with antique shops you will find **Donn Henry**

Galleries, 138-42 Bury New Road, Whitfield, Tel 766 8819. They have contemporary paintings and limited edition prints, while in Bramhall at 191B Moss Lane, Tel 440 0122, there is the **Village Gallery** with original prints as well as antiques.

ANTIQUE DEALERS

The Antiques Markets first:

Centrally located in the Royal Exchange Building, Exchange Street, St Ann's Square, is the **Royal Exchange Shopping Centre**, Tel 834 3731. Here you will find 25 dealers representing such interests as jewellery, ethnic art, books, paintings, stamps, coins, stripped pine, toys, dolls, lace, antiques and bric-à-brac. The **Manchester Antique Hypermarket** is set among a plethora of antique stores at 965 Stockport Road, Levenshulme, Tel 224 2410. The 50 dealers are housed in the old Levenshulme Town Hall and the market is well worth a visit. Start out at 643 Stockport Road where you will find **Albion Antiques**, Tel 225 4957. They have a large stock of antique furniture. Just up the road is **Britannia Antiques** at No 754, Tel 224 8350. They have furniture, clocks and architectural and decorative items. At No 973 is **Ross Antiques**, Tel 225 4666 with general antiques while at No 1034 is **Chestergate Antiques** with clocks and period and Victorian furniture, Tel 224 7795. Finally, at No 1090 Stockport Road is **Antique Fireplaces**, Tel 431 8075, with, not surprisingly, fireplaces and architectural items.

Bury New Road is essentially the A56 which leads out to the M62 motorway. This is a good browsing area and I suggest you begin at No 373 which is **The Baron Antiques**, Tel 773 9929. They have a large stock of 18th-century mahogany and early oak furniture, Victorian walnut, clocks, porcelain and objets d'art. Close by at No 393 is **Bulldog Antiques**. Here too there is a large stock of Georgian, Victorian and Edwardian furniture as well as clocks (especially longcase and wall clock sets). There are also swords, guns, pistols, shotguns, war medals and general militaria. There are some nice prints and pictures and pottery and general antiques. Practically adjacent are **Authentiques** at No 403, **Family Antiques** at 405/407 and **Village Antiques** at No 416. Authentiques, Tel 773 9601, has decorative items, silver, porcelain, glass, boxes, Staffordshire, watercolours and prints, small furniture, miniatures, brass and curios. Family Antiques, Tel 798 0036, has a stock of general antiques, while Village Antiques, Tel 773 3612, has 19th-century ornaments and pottery, 18th-century glass, 18th- to 19th-century porcelain and 18th- to early 20th-century furniture.

In Prestwick itself, close by, is **Acorn Antiques** at the Coach House, Blackburn Street, Tel 798 7117. They have clocks, scientific instruments and general antiques and are only open by appointment. Also in Prestwick and open by appointment only is **David Friend Antiques**, 23 Guest Road, Tel 773 1382. Here you will find porcelain and works of art.

Back in the centre of town you would be wise not to miss **David H Dickinson** at 17/19 John Dalton Street, Tel 834 1042. Here you will find 18th- and 19th-century English and Continental furniture, interior decorator items and objets d'art. Also not to be missed is **E and C T Koopman** at 4 John Dalton Street, Tel 832 9036, which has exquisite silver, objets d'art, jewellery and porcelain. Also centrally located are **Boodle and Dunthorne**, 1 King Street, Tel 833 9000. They have a large stock of 18th- and 19th-century silver, Victorian jewellery and mid-19th-century clocks and clock sets. Well worth a visit. Close by at 41 South King Street is **St James Antiques**, Tel 834 9632. They are just off Deansgate and have nice antique silver. Finally, **Cathedral Jewellers**, 26 Cathedral Street, Tel 832 3042, have antique jewellery.

If you are going towards Old Trafford for the cricket, nearby is Walley Range with **Didsbury Antiques**, Tel 227 9979 at 21 Range Road. They have 18th- and 19th-century furniture, pictures and ceramics. Just down the road in Didsbury is **Johnson Antiques** at 2 Warburton Street, Tel 434 6278, with general antiques and pine, and **Crown Antiques** at 123 Burton Road with jewellery, pottery and porcelain. Tel 445 7374. The **Village Furniture Company** is at 58 School Lane with 18th- and 19th-century pine, Tel 445 4747, and you can eat at the **Lime Tree** in Lapwing Lane, which is really nice (see Restaurants). Finally, to round off Manchester, visit **AS Antiques** at 26 Broad Street, Salford (on the A6 next to Salford Technical College), Tel 737 5938. They have excellent art nouveau and art deco, silver, bronzes and general antiques and **The Connoisseur** at 528 Wilmslow Road, Tel 445 2504 (four miles/6.4 km south down Oxford Road opposite Wilkington Fire Station). They have a good stock of 18th- and 19th-century English and French furniture and 19th- and 20th-century Sevres and Meissen porcelain. Good hunting.

RESTAURANTS

One of the best cuisines to sample in Manchester is Chinese, and where better to sample it than in one of the most vibrant and colourful areas of the city – Chinatown. The focus of Chinatown is the magnificent Chinese Archway – the first in Europe – on Faulkner Street. The Archway, designed by architects from China, is of classical design and has been decorated using ceramics, gold leaf, lacquer and paints, all of which came from China itself. There are two pavilions which provide seating for visitors to admire the jasmine, maples, junipers, cherries and bamboos in the ornamental garden. Chinatown is of course, packed with gift shops, herbalists, supermarkets and restaurants. The best Chinatown restaurants are listed below:

Quan Ju De – 44 Princess Street, Tel 236 5236. If I had to rate a number one, this would be it. The original Quan Ju De restaurant was founded in 1860 in Beijing and has an international reputation. This Manchester venue ranks with Mr Kuk's (see below) as the main gastronomic ambassador of Peking cuisine in the city. Elegantly designed, the menu has many challenging dishes. How about marinated sea crunchy (sea anemone) for starters? I had an excellent set dinner and there's even a separate one for vegetarians.

Pearl City – 33 George Street, Tel 228 7683. Truly authentic Cantonese cooking. Try the char sui with fresh pasta and the spare ribs with black beans and ginger. Swift, knowledgeable staff cope with rapid turnover with the minimum of fuss and maximum of efficiency. Open all week 12–4am.

Woo San – 19-21 George Street, Tel 236 3697. Situated on two floors over its own supermarket (walk around, it's fascinating). Good dim sum. Sample the wind-dried sausage wrapped in bread dough and my favourite, pork chops Shanghai style. Inexpensive.

Little Yang Sing – 17 George Street, Tel 228 7722. Good dim sum. Sample the honey and lemon chicken, or sea bass in black bean sauce. Dinner only 5:30–11:30pm.

Outside of Chinatown, but excellent, is **Yang Sing** at 34 Princess Street, Tel 236 2200. There has been high praise for their salt-baked chicken. Very good sizzling steaks and you know you are in Lancashire, as there are tripe dishes on the menu, and wonderful steamed pork pie with salted egg. Excellent dim sum. Open all week noon–11pm.

Siam Orchid – 54 Portland Street, Tel 236 1388, is just around the corner from Chinatown and was Manchester's first Thai restaurant. It has good inexpensive set lunches, orchids on the table, pictures of Thai boxers on the wall and fine Thai food. Excellent stir-fried dishes, good dim sum and wonderfully fiery curries. Exotic fruits for dessert and Thai Singha beer. Open all week 11:30–2:30 and 6:30–11:30pm. No Sat or Sun lunch.

Mr Kuk's – 55A Mosley Street, Tel 236 0659, is just a few blocks away from George Street and is Manchester's premier Peking restaurant. Fine hot and sour soup, deep fried crispy duck Szechuan style and crispy deep fried beef with carrot and ginger. Open Tues–Sat 12–2:30 and 6–11:15pm.

Mina Japan – 63 George Street. For a change try Japanese cooking on the edge of Chinatown. Good set meals for the inexperienced. Prime ingredients handled with skill and cooked to order.

Other Asiatic delights:

The Rusholme area of Wilmslow Road is Manchester's Little India, full of traders, sweet centres, cafés and restaurants. The best place to eat is **Sanam**, 145-151 Wilmslow Road, one of the best Indian restaurants in the North West. Authentic cooking and good value for money. Tandooris, shami kebab and palak gosht. If you are adventurous there are brains and quail cooked in potent chili sauce. Open all week 12–12pm.

Other Indian restaurants in the area are **Aladdin** at 529 Wilmslow Road, Tel 438 8588 (oddly it also serves Turkish food), **Al-Mamoor** at 704 Wilmslow Road, Tel 445 2446, **Al-Noor** at 71 Wilmslow Road, Tel 224 7760 and the **Ambala Sweet Centre and Restaurant** at 67 Wilmslow Road, Tel 224 4392. Closer to the centre of the city, and recommended, are the **Deansgate Indian Restaurant** at 244 Deansgate (entrance on Longworth Street) Tel 835 1888, **Gaylord's Restaurant**, Unit 4, Marriots Court, Spring Gardens, Tel 832 4866, and **Kathmandu Tandoori** 42-44 Sackville Street, Tel 236 4684.

Good Korean food at **Koreana Restaurant** 40A King Street West, Tel 832 4330. Their marinated beef cooked at the table on a metal shield is very special. Open Mon–Sat 12–2:30 and 6:30–11pm. No Sat lunch.

For those with tastes that are more mainstream and less exotic, a list of recommended restaurants grouped under national cuisines are listed below:

Dutch:
Dutch Pancake House – Elizabeth House, St Peter's Square. Tel 228 1851.

English:
Royal Exchange Theatre Café-Bar – Useful for pre-theatre suppers. Also lunch.

The Inn Plaice Fish Restaurant and Tavern – Dominion House, 48-50 Whitworth Street, Tel 236 5512.
Woodlands – 33 Shepley Road, Audenshaw, Tel 336 4241. Five miles (8 km) east of Manchester. Worth the trip for dinner. Filet of beef with port and Stilton sauce and lamb with tarragon are good. Open Tues–Sat 12–2 and 7–9:30pm. No Sat lunch.
Market Restaurant – Edge Street, Tel 834 3743. Opposite the old fruit market. Dinner only Tues–Sat 5:30–9:30pm. New English cuisine (creamed leeks in puff pastry and breast of chicken with honey) plus a range of English puddings. Good English cheese.
Woody and Dutch – 71 Church Road, Northenden, Tel 998 6336. British cooking with nods in the direction of France. Excellent bistro value.

French:
Blinkers French Restaurant – 16 Princess Street, Tel 228 2503. Good French cooking. Set lunch is good value. Service excellent. Open Mon–Sat 12–2:30 and 7:15–10:30pm. No Sat lunch.
Brasserie St Pierre – 57-63 Princess Street, Tel 228 0231. Touches of an authentic brasserie with good cooking to match.
Lime Tree – 8 Lapwing Lane, West Didsbury, Tel 445 1217. One of my favourites, especially for Sunday lunch. I recommend the black pudding with apple for a starter, followed by the duck in raspberry liqueur sauce or the calf's liver dijonnaise. Open dinner only 5:30–11:30pm, also Sun lunch.
Moss Nook Restaurant – Ringway Road, Tel 473 4778. Excellent French cooking. Try the four-course set menu or, if you are more adventurous, the "menu surprise," which is very special. Open Tues–Sat 12–2 and 7–9:30pm. No Sat lunch.

Greek:
Kosmos Taverna – 248 Wilmslow Road, Tel 225 9106. Dinner only except Sunday lunch, when it opens at 12:30pm. One of the best Greek restaurants in the north of England. Excellent value and atmosphere.

Italian:
Giulio's Terrazza – 14 Nicholas Street, Tel 236 0250. The tiled, whitewashed dining room has a Florentine ambience. The pasta is fresh and the dessert trolley very impressive.

Middle Eastern:
The Armenian Restaurant – Granada Hotel, 404 Wilmslow Road, Withington, Tel 434 3480. Some of the best Middle Eastern food in the city. Dinner only 6–10:30pm.
Cafe Istanbul – 79 Bridge Street, Tel 833 9942. Very inexpensive and good set lunch which is advertised on a blackboard outside. Genuine Turkish coffee to finish off your meal. Open Mon–Sat 12–3 and 6–11:30pm.

Vegetarian:
On the Eighth Day – 109 Oxford Road, All Saints, Tel 273 1850. Excellent value and inexpensive as one would expect from a worker's cooperative. Unlicensed – bring your own. No corkage. Open 10am–7pm.
Bullis' Vegetarian Restaurant – 115 Manchester Road, Chorlton, Tel 881 9338.

PUBS
Chester's Pie and Ale House – Cateaton Street (near Cathedral and Arndale Centre). Pastiche of Victorian ale house with good period feel. Good bar food; yes, pies as well.
Brewer's Arms – Great Ducie Street, next door to Boddington's Brewery, so the beer could hardly be better. Really interesting bar food.
Circus Tavern – Portland Street. Tiny character pub with two cosy panelled rooms. Weekend evenings they don't open till 8pm and they sometimes shut the door if it gets too full.
Britons Protection – 50 Great Bridgewater Street (corner of Lower Mosley Street). Fine tilework and solid woodwork in plush bar. Battle murals on wall. Good, well prepared food at lunchtime.
Tommy Ducks – East Street. This pretty black-and-white Victorian pub is convenient for the Exhibition Centre. There are theatre posters on the walls and an exuberant collection of women's knickers, donated by customers, pinned on the ceilings. Traditional bar food is good value.
Sinclairs – Shambles Square. Sinclairs has existed since 1738 and is one of the oldest oyster bars and chophouses in England. It occupies a building dating from 1700. Excellent food and atmosphere.
Old Wellington Inn – Shambles Square (behind Arndale Centre off Market Street). The only timber-framed building of its age to survive in the centre of Manchester. Flagstones and gnarled oak timbers.

Good bar food. Built around 1550, the inn was originally a shop and house and was the home of the Byrom family for 150 years. John Byrom (1692–1763) wrote the hymn "Christians Awake" here as a Christmas present for his daughter. He was also the inventor of phonetic shorthand.

ARTISTIC ASSOCIATIONS

The great English essayist Thomas De Quincey was born at the corner of Cross Street and John Dalton Street in 1785. He was baptized in St Ann's Church and attended Manchester Grammar School. He wrote "Vision of a Sudden Death" in a Manchester tavern.

Mrs Elizabeth Gaskell, the English novelist, lived in a house at 84 Plymouth Grove (now the University Overseas Centre) where she entertained such distinguished writers as Charlotte Brontë, Charles Dickens, Thomas Carlyle and Harriet Beecher Stowe. It was here that she wrote her controversial *Life of Charlotte Brontë*. She died in 1865.

Frances Hodgson Burnett, author of *Little Lord Fauntleroy* (1886), lived at 385 Cheetham Hill Road, while Howard Spring, author of *Fame is the Spur* (1940), was a journalist on the Manchester *Guardian* and lived at 26 Hesketh Avenue, Didsbury, until his death in 1955. Peter Mark Roget was a physician at the Manchester Infirmary and is best known as the author of *Roget's Thesaurus of English Words and Phrases* which was first published in 1832.

In the Town Hall and viewable by appointment (Tel 234 3157), are the superb murals of subjects from the history of Manchester, painted between 1879 and 1893 by Ford Madox Brown. The murals were his last important work as he died here in 1893. An interesting artist working in Manchester at the turn of the century was Adolphe Valette. He was the first artist to capture the spirit of industrial Manchester; his impressionistic canvases show lonely, stylized figures set against a foggy gloom. An excellent example of his work is *Under Windsor Bridge on the Irwell* which can be seen in the Manchester City Art Gallery. Ironically, the only one of Valette's pupils to achieve fame as an artist was the one who was most ridiculed at the Municipal School of Art where Valette taught for many years. L S Lowry was born at 8 Barrett Street near the Stretford Road in Old Trafford in 1887. He began attending Valette's evening classes at the Municipal School of Art and this constituted his only artistic training. In 1909 Lowry's father, finding he could no longer afford to live in the relatively prosperous residential district of Old Trafford, moved to 117 Station Road, Pendlebury, a poor industrial area. Lowry was initially depressed by his new home, but soon he began to like his surroundings; eventually he became obsessed with them and they became the major subject of his work. Lowry was a rent collector and clerk all his life, as well as an artist, and he retired in 1951. Changes in the urban environment have made it difficult to recognize the specific subjects of Lowry's paintings, but in any case his work was hardly ever faithful to an actual scene, as his imagination essentially transformed it. Lowry's influence continues to be felt in the work of many of Manchester's more recent artists such as Alan Lowndes and Helen Bradley. After he died in 1976, Lowry's living room and studio were reconstructed in the City Art Gallery. It's a fascinating reconstruction, and not to be missed.

The **Shakespeare Garden** in Platt Fields Park, Rusholme, near the Grangethorpe Road is an Elizabethan-style walled garden which reputedly contains all the plants mentioned in Shakespeare's works and nothing that is not mentioned.

EPHEMERA

Tatton Park, Tel 0244 320055, is within an easy half-hour drive of Manchester and is an 18th-century mansion, deer park, 14th-century Old Hall and Medieval Village. One of the National Trust's most popular historic properties. There are regular concerts from November through March, which are held in the Tenants' Hall. Built by the last Lord Egerton to house his collection of ethnic specimens and trophies gathered during 50 years of world travel, it has been described as the most extraordinary room in the kingdom. It has to be seen to be believed; it is a monument to a dying breed – the long line of British eccentrics. Tatton is open from April 1 to Oct 31. Park and garden are open all year round.

The Granada Studio Tour is great fun. Walk down Coronation Street to the Rover's Return and see sets of New York and Los Angeles. Visit Downing Street, the Baker Street of Sherlock Holmes, then go on to the make-up rooms, wardrobe and a chance to see yourself on TV. Granada Studios are located in Water Street, Tel 833 0880.

The Manchester Craft Centre and Design Studio, 17 Oak Street, Smithfield, Tel 832 4274, has ceramics, headwear, cloth heads, jewellery, enamel work, fashion and costume (theatrical and bridal) and even tacky T-shirts. Great fun and any teenagers with you will love it.

Belle Vue – Tel 226 0131 for information. A sort of northwest Coney Island with a zoo, concert and exhibition centre, boating lake, model village and a vast amusement park (midway). There's also a stadium that can hold 25,000 spectators, where you can see speedway (motorcycles racing round an oval track), which in spite of what the snobs say can be really exciting.

Manchester City Football Club, Maine Road, two miles (3.2 km) from city centre and Manchester United Football Club, three miles (4.8 km) from city centre, both offer tours of their grounds. City call 226 1191, United call 872 1661.

My fascination with the stories of theatrical ghosts focused on the Palace Theatre, Manchester, which opened in 1891 with the idea of bringing "culture" to the North. Within three years, after some financially disastrous highbrow programmes, it set out to successfully become the home of variety – attracting all the greatest stars. The Palace's Grey Lady, reputed to be the ghost of a cleaner who died on the premises, has been seen on a number of occasions. In 1981, during a period of renovation, a workman used one of the women's toilets as the new men's room wasn't ready. Sitting reflectively – the cubicle partitions were not yet in place, he was disconcerted to see an elderly woman sitting in the corner of the room looking at him. He averted his eyes and when he looked again she was sitting in another corner. When she finally vanished he was uncertain whether to be afraid or relieved. In other sightings, the ghost has appeared as a patch of grey smoke or as myriad pinheads of light. Admittedly an empty theatre is a mysterious place, but not eerie enough to explain positive identifications by a number of sober and sensible individuals.

SURROUNDING AREA

For theatre buffs, the **Octagon Theatre**, Bolton, is a beautifully designed theatre-in-the-round. If you are interested in the game of snooker, you'll be pleased to know it's the venue each year of the World Snooker Championships.

The **Coliseum Theatre**, Oldham, is a spawning ground for great talents. Comedienne Dora Bryan and Eric Sykes, Bernard Cribbins and Dame Eva Turner are all from here.

Wigan Pier (Wigan is not on the coast and the "pier" is a stop on the ship canal) was immortalized by George Orwell in his book *The Road to Wigan Pier* (1937), one of the most famous of all statements on socialism.

TOURIST INFORMATION BUREAU: Town Hall Extension, Lloyd Street, Manchester, Lancashire , M6O 2LA. Tel (061) 234 3157

NEWCASTLE-UPON-TYNE

County of Tyne and Wear
274 miles (438 km) from London by M1 and A1(M)
By rail, 3 hours from London (King's Cross)

Newcastle began as a minor fort and bridge on Hadrian's Wall, the famous defence line that started from neighbouring Wallsend and stretched 73 miles (117 km) west to Bowness on the Water in Westmoreland (see Ephemera). The Roman name for Newcastle was Pons Aelii, and relics of a Roman temple can be found in the residential area of Benwell, incongruously surrounded by tidy brick houses. After the Romans came an obscure religious colony known as Monkchester and then the Normans built a "new castle" on the Roman site in 1080. A stone castle replaced the wooden one in 1172 and of this, the very complete keep and a gate the 13th-century fortified Black Gate, survive as museums, now hemmed in by railway lines and the High Level Bridge. Note that the restored battlemented roof of the keep is a good place from which to view the Tyne.

Medieval Newcastle was a base for warfare with the Scots, which was (seemingly) continuous for many hundreds of years. The coalfield which surrounded Newcastle was one of the first to be worked in England, and the first to export coal. Because of this, Newcastle established itself as a market town and port. The 19th century and the Industrial Revolution brought the greatest growth, however, and established the city as a major heavy-engineering centre. Most of the city dates from this period of expansion and though the ship-building and repair that flourished in the first half of the century have been sharply reduced, the River Tyne still has its active shipyards and repair dry docks.

Five bridges span the Tyne at Newcastle. The oldest, the High Level Bridge for rail and road traffic, was designed by Robert Stephenson in 1849. The Swing Bridge, which can still swing but rarely does, was very innovative for its time, circa 1876. The King Edward Bridge, now the main railway bridge, opened in 1906, while the Redheugh and Tyne Road bridges were built in this century. The Tyne Bridge, perhaps Newcastle's most indigenous and recognizable feature, evokes memories of the Sydney Bridge in Australia. Close to the Swing Bridge is the 17th-century Guildhall, with a 1796 façade. It was the centre of local government until the 19th century and is still used as offices. Close by is the Merchant Adventurers' Hall and Bessie Surtees House (see Ephemera). A popular Sunday morning market is held on Quayside; an obelisk marks the spot where John Wesley first preached in 1742. Trinity House and the Trinity Maritime Centre are nearby in Broad Chare. St Nicholas Church is a 14th- and 15th-century parish church, which became the Church of England Cathedral in 1882. The Roman Catholic Cathedral, Church of St Mary, was designed by Pugin in 1844, while All Saints was designed in 1788 and is a beautiful example of a rare elliptical style. It contains the largest memorial brass in England to Roger Thornton, who died in 1429. Keelman's Hospital, built in 1701, was an important hospital for the old and impoverished.

The commercial centre of Newcastle is one of the finest and most imposing in the country. There is a sense of period, order and space which is missing in many other cities. Built between 1835 and 1840, the masterpiece is Grey Street, with its curve of gracious façades culminating in the stately Theatre Royal (circa 1837) and just beyond, Grey's Monument. Not to be missed is the Central Arcade with its wonderful brown ceramic tiling, while Grange Street leads into Neville Street and the impressively porticoed Central Railway Station. All this mid-19th-century elegance is in stark contrast with the sparkling new City Centre at Barras Bridge, with its 12-storey tower, carillon and 16-foot (4.8 m) sculpture of the River God Tyne.

TYNE BRIDGE, NEWCASTLE

The Town Moor is Newcastle's foremost park, which does much to give this highly industrialized city its breathing space. On its 972 acres (393.3 ha) citizens can, and indeed do, pasture cows. The country's biggest fair is held there in June each year.

WALK

The **Newcastle Walk** is a long one and I have planned it so that after one and a half miles (2.4 km) you pass your starting point before embarking in the second leg of two and a bit miles. You could therefore do the walk in two parts if you wish. Start out at the Manors multi-storey car park in City Road. Leave by the City Road exit, walk along the footpath and down the steps to the **Joicey Museum**. Turn left under the bridge and take the right fork along City Road, with **Corner Tower** across the road and terraced gardens below. At the junction opposite Sallyport Crescent follow the high level of City Road and continue past Sallyport steps and tower to **Keelman's Hospital**. Cross City Road and turn right and then left and right down Love Lane to Quayside; right again, bringing into view the tangled succession of bridges across the Tyne. Turn right into Broad Chare for the **Trinity Maritime Centre** and **Trinity House**, then retrace your steps back to Quayside, and pass under the arched **Tyne Bridge**. Go right, past the **Guildhall**, and along Sandhill passing **Bessie Surtees' House**. At the **Swing Bridge** walk out and look at the river. Return and cross the road to Castle Stairs and climb through the **Castle Gateway** to the **Keep**, then go under the railway arch to **Black Gate** and the **National Bagpipe Museum**. Continue up St Nicholas Street to **St Nicholas' Cathedral**. Turn right at Amen Corner and go round the churchyard, passing the site of engraver Thomas Bewick's workshop. A bust commemorates Thomas Bewick (1753–1828), who was recognized as the greatest of wood engravers. In his workshop he produced engravings for book illustrations (the two-volume *History of British Birds* is superb), banknotes and topographical prints using innovative techniques that gave new dimensions of light and shade to his work. Cross Mosley Street, in front of the cathedral, to the paved **Cloth Market**, passing the former **Balmbra's Music Hall**, which is now a pub. Balmbra's was named after a Newcastle licensee who owned the music hall in 1862 and was instrumental in engaging George Ridley, who first performed the famous Tyneside song "The Blaydon Races" there. Turn right along High Street, cross Grey Street with **Grey's Monument** and on to Pilgrim Street. Turn right down Pilgrim Street and, if you wish, return to the car park. If you intend to continue, go past the car park and turn right on to Mosley Street. Go ahead to Collingwood Street. At the junction with Westgate Road turn left for a few yards to see a plaque recalling the first demonstration of **George Stephenson's Miner's Safety Lamp** to the Literary and Philosophical Society in 1815. There is also an indication identifying the line of Hadrian's Wall. Turn left, back along Neville Street, past the Stephenson statue to the **Central Station**, circa 1850. Opposite the station turn right into Grainger Street and then left into Nun Street. **Grainger Market**, on the right, has colourful stalls with all kinds of merchandise. Turn left into Clayton Street and then right into Fenkle Street and left into Cross Street. The **Museum of**

Science and Engineering is about a quarter of a mile (400 m) away on West Blanford Street. Turn right at the end of the street and follow the line of the **West Walls**, passing **Durham Tower**. Turn right along Stowell Street, and right again on Friars Street to **Blackfriars**. Leaving Blackfriars, climb the cobbled slope below **Heber Tower** and turn right along the lane beneath the walls. At the end of the wall, turn right into St Andrew's Street, left along Newgate Street and right into Blackett Street and on past Eldon Square. Turn right down Grey Street and the Central Arcade. At the **Theatre Royal** turn left into Shakespeare Street, cross Pilgrim Street and turn right into Market Street. The **Laing Art Gallery** is on your left in John Dobson Street. Cross Market Street and continue ahead to Carliol Square. From the square return to the car park.

MUSEUMS, GALLERIES AND PUBLIC BUILDINGS

John George Joicey Museum – City Road, Tel 2324562. The museum occupies a three-storey building, dating from 1681. Originally an almshouse, it was later known as the Holy Jesus Hospital. The Austin Tower is at the east of the building. There are period rooms illustrating living styles from the early Stuart to the late Victorian periods. Much of this collection of local social history was endowed by a Gateshead coal-owner, John George Joicey. The displays include an audio-visual presentation of the Tyne Flood of 1771 and the Great Fire of 1854. Also to be seen are some old sporting guns and an exhibition of the craft of the German swordmakers who settled at Sholtey Bridge, Durham in the late 17th century. Part of the museum is devoted to the Northumberland Hussars and the 15th and 19th regiments of the King's Royal Hussars. Open Mon–Fri 10–5:30pm, Sat 10–4:30pm.

Trinity Maritime Centre – 29 Broad Chare, Tel 2614691. Housed in a former chandler's warehouse, the museum traces Newcastle's close association with the sea and includes a huge and finely detailed model of the great Cunarder *Mauritania*, built on Tyneside. Close by is **Trinity House**, built in the 15th century as the headquarters of Newcastle's Trinity Guild, dedicated to improving safety in the waters off the northeast coast. The chapel, completed in 1505, is designed on the lines of the "between-decks" of an old sailing ship. Open April–Oct Tues–Fri 10:30–4pm; Nov–March Tues–Fri 11–3pm.

Hancock Museum – Barras Bridge, Tel 2322359. Now part of the University of Newcastle, the museum began as a private collection in the 18th century. There is an extensive natural history collection, including animals, plants, fossils, minerals, rocks and insects. There is a section for young visitors and a room devoted to the great Newcastle wood engraver, Thomas Bewick. Open Mon–Sat 10–5pm, Sun 2–5pm.

Greek Museum – Department of Classics, the University, Claremont Road, Tel 2328511. The museum houses mainly Greek and Etruscan antiquities together with some items of Near Eastern, Celtic and Roman manufacture. There is an interesting range of Greek weapons and armour and a wonderful terracotta artefact in the shape of a Gorgon's head. Open Mon–Fri 10–4:30 or by appointment.

Museum of Antiquities – The Quadrangle, the University, Claremont Road, Tel 2328511. This is the principal museum for Hadrian's Wall. It contains scale models, life-size figures of Roman soldiers and a reconstruction of the Temple of Mithras. The collection of archaeological finds spans the prehistoric, Roman, Anglo-Saxon and Medieval periods. Open Mon–Sat 10–5pm.

Museum of Mining – The University, Queen Victoria Road, Tel 2328511. The museum forms part of the university's Department of Mining Engineering and contains an extensive collection of miner's lamps and other tools and items of equipment illustrating the history of the mining industry. Open Mon–Fri 9–5pm.

Museum of Science and Engineering – Blandford House, West Blandford Street, Tel 2326789. The magnificent 19th-century building which houses the museum was formerly the headquarters of the Co-operative Wholesale Society. It was built in 1895 and the scale and quality of the building indicates the prestige of the Co-operative movement in the area. The displays relate to mechanical and electrical engineering, mining, shipbuilding, science and a wide range of manufacturing industries with special ties to the North East. Some of the museum's larger exhibits, including a George Stephenson locomotive of 1826, are kept in Wallsend. Inquire for details. Open Mon–Fri 10–5:30; Sat 10–4:30pm.

National Bagpipe Museum – The Black Gate, St Nicholas Street, Tel 2615390. The museum is in the 13th-century gateway to the Castle Keep. Over a hundred sets of pipes are on display and, while the emphasis is on the Northumbria, small pipes and Lowland pipes, there are also good examples of Scottish, Irish and European bagpipes. There are some who claim that bagpipes should always be kept under lock and key in a case, but don't believe them. The sound is thrilling and atmospheric even if it does take some getting used to. Open Mon–Sat 9:30–5:30; Sun 10:30–5pm.

Laing Art Gallery – Higham Place, Tel 2327734. This lavishly baroque building has a notable collection of British watercolours and other British paintings including work by Edward Burne-Jones, Sir Edwin Landseer and Sir Joshua Reynolds. There is a fine collection of paintings by the Northumberland artist John Martin and impressive collections of Newcastle silver and enamelled glassware. Open Mon–Fri 10–5:30pm; Sat 10–4pm; Sun 2:30–5:30pm.

Hatton Gallery – The University, Claremont Road, Tel 2328511. The permanent collection includes Kurt Schwitters's last large relief, the *Elterwater Merzbarn* and the superb Uhlaman collection of African sculpture. There is a continuous programme of temporary exhibitions of contemporary and historical art. Open Mon–Fri 10:30–5:30; Sat 10:30–4:30pm.

Blackfriars – Blackfriars Tourist Centre, Monk Street, Tel 2615367. The museum building represents perhaps the most complete survival of a medieval friary in Britain. Exhibits show the development of Newcastle through trade and industry and information about the River Tyne. Open April–Sept daily 10–5pm; Oct–Mar Tues–Sat 10–4:30pm.

Cathedral Church of St Nicholas – St Nicholas Street, Tel 2321939. The mainly 14th- and 15th-century parish church, one of the great parish churches of England, became a cathedral in 1882. Its tower is crowned by a spire resting on flying arches, an architecturally daring scheme dating from 1450. The cathedral has fine 17th-century monuments and woodwork.

Cathedral Church of St Mary – Clayton Street West, Tel 2326953. The Cathedral Church of the Roman Catholic Diocese of Hexham and Newcastle was designed by A W Pugin in 1884. It reflects Newcastle's prosperity at that time. The 222-foot (67 m) spire, designed by Joseph Hansom, was added circa 1870.

Newcastle Station – Neville Street. The train shed is on a curve, which emphasizes the fine roof, the earliest in a station where round-arched ribs are used by themselves to form the framework which spans the main spaces of the building. Designed by Robert Stephenson and his associates, the station opened in 1849, the same year as the High Level Bridge.

Lloyds Bank – 102 Grey Street, Tel 2610271. The building was opened in 1839 for Lambton and Co, the private bankers, as part of the grand reconstruction of Grey Street. Lambtons were taken over by Lloyds in 1909. The original façade of the building is intact. Open normal banking hours .

The Castle – Castle Garth, Tel 2327938. The "new castle" began life as a wooden fort built by Robert Curthose, son of William the Conqueror, in 1080. Henry II added the stout-walled keep in 1172. In the 17th century a house was built over the gateway for one Patrick Black, thus the name Black Gate (now the National Bagpipe Museum). There is a Norman chapel on the ground floor and galleries overlook the Great Hall.

THEATRE

Theatre Royal – Grey Street, Tel 2322061. This is a grand, imposing theatre, built in 1837. Its interior was reconstructed in 1901 and recently it was again beautifully refurbished. The 1379-seat auditorium enhances the feeling that you are seeing something special – whatever the product. Large-scale, high-quality touring companies make up the programme, with visitors including the Royal Shakespeare Company, the Scottish and Northern Opera Companies, the English National Ballet Company and the Rambert Dance Company. There is a coffee bar, **Kinnear's**, for coffee and lunch, the **Grand Circle Bar** with one of the best views in town, for morning coffee, lunch or afternoon tea and **Matcham's Restaurant** which is more formal and has very good cuisine.

Newcastle Playhouse – Barras Bridge, Tel 2327079. Opened in 1970, the theatre is owned by the university and is based on the campus. As I write it is a receiving house for mid-scale touring companies such as the Cambridge Theatre Company and the Hull Truck Theatre. It offers an exciting and innovative programme. I remember the lively Tyne and Wear Theatre Company which used to work out of the theatre presenting a rep programme of new works, revivals and classics. University budget cuts and artistic belt-tightening unfortunately led to its demise. Perhaps by the time you read this, it or a successor will have reappeared. There is a bar and restaurant.

Gulbenkian Studio Theatre – Also on campus, Tel 2329974. It offers an exciting blend of experimental and small-scale touring companies such as Trestle Theatre Company and the Royal National Theatre Touring Company as well as dance, music, workshops and work by young people.

Northern Stage Company – The biggest and best company in the northeast. Does not at present have its own venue but tours in the area and at the Theatre Royal and Newcastle Playhouse. Watch for them, they're good.

Tyne Theatre and Opera House – Westgate Road, Tel 232 0899. The theatre has one of the best sets of Victorian stage machinery, in working order, in the country. Wonderful old stage lifts, devil traps and even gaslights. Owned by an amateur company, but with some touring companies visiting.

Two small companies producing good and mainly contemporary work are the **Live Theatre**, 27 Broad Chare, Tel 261 2694 and **Bruvvers Theatre Company**, Tel 2619230. Both are small-scale touring companies and are well worth a visit. They play at numerous venues around Newcastle and are certainly worth finding.

People's Theatre – Stephenson Road, Tel 2655020. Probably the best community theatre in the country, with an exciting programme of contemporary work such as *Habeas Corpus* by Alan Bennett and classics such as Chekhov's *Uncle Vanya*.

Newcastle Arts Centre – Westgate Road, Tel 2615618. Small performance space for small-scale touring theatre, dance, music and performance art. An annual crafts fair in November and an exhibition gallery for contemporary art.

MUSIC

The **Northern Sinfonia** is the region's orchestra, and a good one it is too. For details of concerts in the area call Freephone 0800 591 996.

The Northern Sinfonia and all major symphony orchestra generally play in the **City Hall**, Northumberland Road, Tel 261 2606. There is an excellent **International Season of Visiting Orchestras**, with ensembles like the Royal Philharmonic, the London Symphony and the Hallé. The **New Tyneside Orchestra** plays in various venues; it's a community orchestra but very good. Tel 0670 712203 for details. Newcastle Playhouse runs a **Chamber Series** throughout the year with groups like the Janacek Quartet and Heinrich Schiff, Tel 232 7079, while the **Bach Choir** is also active in the city. The **University Music Department** gives a series of lunchtime concerts in King's Hall in the Armstrong Building on campus, Tel 222 6000, and other musical venues include the **Literary and Philosophical Society**, Westgate Road, Tel 232 0192 and **All Saints Church**, Akenside Hill, Tel 232 9974.

CINEMA

Commercial cinema at:

Cannon Cinema – Westgate Road, Tel 232 32323. Two screens.

Odeon Cinema – Pilgrim Street, Tel 232 3248. Two screens.

Warner Cinema – Manors, Tel 221 0202. Nine screens.

Jesmond Picture House – Lyndhurst Avenue, Tel 281 0526. One screen.

Of more interest to me is the **Tyneside Cinema**, 10/12 Pilgrim Street, Tel 2321507, with a good selection of classic, foreign and contemporary films. There is a film festival, an excellent one, during the first two weeks in October. Finally, you might like to check the programme of the **Side Gallery and Cinema**, 9 Side, Tel 2321507.

BOOKSTORES

All the large national chains have good branches in Newcastle. **Waterstone's** is at 104 Grey Street, Tel 261 6140, **Dillon's** is on Blackett Street, Tel 261 7757 and **Sherratt and Hughes** at 6 Sidgate, Eldon Square, Tel 261 9921. **Thorne's Bookshops** are the best of the Newcastle-based bookshops and are very good indeed. They are agents for HMSO and have an excellent secondhand department and a "book bargains" section. They are at Grand Hotel Building, Haymarket, Tel 232 6421. Of the rest, I think the pick are: **The Book House**, 13 Ridley Place, Tel 261 6128 (they have a friendly coffee shop in the basement and are everything a bookshop should be), **Waugh's Books**, 4 Ridley Place, Tel 232 5927, and **Westend Books**, 241 Westgate Road, Tel 261 1489. Books on philosophy and religion are best found at **SPCK**, 8 Ridley Place, Tel 2323466 and **Bible House**, 14 Pilgrim Street, Tel 232 0335, while there's a large selection of comics, science fiction, horror, fantasy, cinema and collectables at **Forbidden Planet**, 5 Nun Street, Tel 261 9173.

ANTIQUARIAN AND SECONDHAND BOOKS

The best are **W Robinson**, 49-53 Grainger Market and **R D Steidman** 9 Grey Street, both with fine antiquarian collections. Of the rest, **Davis Books**, 140 Westgate Road, has a large secondhand collection and new book bargains, Tel 261 4580, **Newcastle Bookshop** 1 Side, Tel 261 5380, is great fun with antiquarian books and a large secondhand collection as well as postcards and printed ephemera. Finally,

Bookworms Paradise, 33 Green Market, Eldon Square, Tel 232 3196, has a large secondhand selection and Frank Smith, 100 Heaton Road, Tel 265 6333, has a good collection of maritime and aviation books.

ART GALLERIES

Dean Gallery – 42 Dean Street, Tel 232 1208, has oil and watercolours both local and national, 18th- to 20th-century.

Pot-Pourri – 6 Granby Terrace, Sunnyside, Tel 488 7901, has contemporary British oils and watercolours and limited-edition prints, while Corymella Scott, 5 Tankerville Terrace, Tel 2818284, specializes in 20th-century Scottish art, both oils and watercolours.

Chameleon Gallery – Milburn House, Dean Street, Tel 232 2819, has oils, watercolours and limited-edition prints, mostly contemporary.

The Side Gallery – 9 Side, Tel 232 1507, has photographic exhibits and also sells, while James Alder, 61 High Bridge, Tel 232 4075, has nice Victorian and Edwardian oils and watercolours, antique prints (mostly local) and selected contemporary oils and watercolours. Phone first, as last time I chatted he was thinking he might have to move to new premises.

ANTIQUE DEALERS

Firstly, the antique market, which in Newcastle is the Vine Lane Antique Market, 17 Vine Lane, Tel 261 2963. There are 18 dealers selling a wide range of general antiques including architectural items. You'll find the market in a cobbled lane just to the right at the top of Northumberland Street in the city centre. Close by, in the town centre, is the elegant Grey Street where at Nos 94 and 96 is Davidson's the Jewelers, Tel 232 2551, with a large stock of jewellery and silver. In Clayton Street at No 99 is Intercoin with a stock of coins and items of numismatic interest, jewellery and silver. In 75 Grainer Market (Alley #2), there is Spicker Jewelers with a good stock of antique, Victorian and secondhand jewellery. Finally, another jeweller at 14 Shields Road – Owen Jewelers, Tel 265 4332, has a large stock. The jewel in the crown of Newcastle antique shops is Shiners Architectural Reclamation, 123 Jesmond Road, Tel 281 6474, a real Aladdin's Cave of architectural items, Victorian and Edwardian fireplaces and wonderful odds and ends. Just in case you are travelling in the area, Tynemouth has Renaissance Antiques at 11 Front Street, Tel 259 5555, and David R Strain at 66 Front Street, Tel 259 2459. North Shields has Dixon Mitchell Antiques at 101 Howard Street, Tel 259 5552, Maggie Mays, 49 Kirton Park Terrace, Tel 257 0076, and Peter Coulson Antiques, Tel 257 9761, at 8-10 Queen Alexandria Road. Finally, in South Shields there's the Curiosity Shop at 16 Frederick Street, Tel 4565560, and William White at No 20 Frederick Street, Tel 256 8461.

RESTAURANTS

21 Queen Street – 21 Queen Street, Princess Wharf, Tel 222 0755. A very elegant restaurant in the developed quayside area. There's an excellent fixed-price lunch menu which offers good value and daily specials on the not too large à la carte menu. Fish is very well prepared with mullet, halibut, skate, turbot and lobster all being well received. This is as it should be, with the fish coming fresh from such places as the Fisherman's Wharf in North Shields, which is worth a visit. Last time I was in Newcastle I took 10 pounds of fish with me the 300 miles (480 km) back to the southwest and it was wonderful. The fish is not the only delight here though, and lamb, venison and veal have all been praised. The petits fours will make you wish you had skipped dinner. Open Mon–Sat 12–2pm and 7–11pm. No Sat lunch.

Fisherman's Lodge – Jesmond Dene, Tel 281 3281. Set in central park-like surroundings, the lodge is a bit like a Victorian set from Hansel and Gretel. Fish is the thing to eat here with lobster, turbot, sole or halibut the best bets. These are the fish that thrive in the chilly waters of the North Sea. Guinea fowl and duck have also been praised but the fish is the thing. They have wonderful petits-fours too. Open Mon–Sat 12–2 and 7–11pm. No Sat lunch.

Dragon House – 30-32 Stowell Street, Tel 232 0868. Newcastle must have the country's most northerly Chinatown and Dragon House is the centre of it. The cooking offers good Szechuan (my favorite) and Shanghai specialities and there is an interesting list of chef's recommendations. Vegetarian cooking is excellent with an extensive choice. The hot-and-sour soup is just that and the home-made spring rolls excellent. Try one of the "sizzling" dishes and don't miss the deep-fried oysters. Open all week 12–2 and 6–midnight. Sun noon–midnight.

Rupali – 6 Bigg Market, Tel 232 8629. The best Indian restaurant in town for my money. They care about their cooking and the menu even includes an explanation of the various dishes from the various regions.

I had a dhansak which comes from the west coast and is cooked in lentils, spices and pineapple. There is excellent vegetarian cooking and for once the pickles are complimentary. For especially good value try the lunchtime specials, the early eaters menu and the three-course set meal on Thursdays, which is Happy Night. Open all week 12–2:30 and 6–11:30pm. No Sun lunch.

Eastern Taste – 277 Stanhope Street, Fenham Tel 273 9406. Runs Rupali close for cuisine and value. It's more "down-market" but you can choose from a vast selection of tandooris, curries, tikkas and kormas. The chicken karahi gosht is highly recommended. Unlicensed but you can bring your own and there's no corkage. Open all week noon–midnight.

Mathers – 4 Old Eldon Square, Tel 232 4020. A basement bistro serving snacks or robust meals all day. Good soups and excellent spaghetti bolognese. There's always a vegetarian choice and the ratatouille is well spoken of. The cheesecake is excellent, if you have enough room. Open Mon–Sat 9:30am–10:30pm.

PUBS

Bridge Hotel – Castle Square. Tel 232 7780. A well-preserved Victorian bar with a carved mahogany fireplace, decorative mirrors and lots of atmosphere. Traditional simple bar food. The flagstoned back terrace is close to the remains of the city wall. The Thursday folk club is one of the oldest in the country.

Cooperage – 32 The Close, Quayside, Tel 232 8286. Set in a Tudor house, the pub has heavy Tudor beams and exposed stonework. Good bar food, especially the grilled kipper fillets and rabbit pie. The building is one of Newcastle's oldest and was indeed, once a cooperage.

Crown Posada – The Side, by Dean Street, Tel 232 1269. Right in the city centre, the pub has an imposing classical façade with big stained glass windows, authentic Victorian atmosphere with a long narrow bar, wood panelling, William Morris-type wallpaper and a long leather bench where the locals sit and read their daily papers. Friendly atmosphere but the bar food is confined to sandwiches.

Baltic Tavern – Broad Chare, close to the river. Tel 232 0214. A spacious and comfortably converted warehouse with lots of bare brick and flagstones as well as a carpeted area. Lots of separate sitting areas giving privacy and very good bar food.

Take a trip to **North Shields** on the metro and have lunch at the **Chain Locker** on New Quay, Tel 258 0147. There's a welcoming atmosphere here, an open fire when needed and a strongly nautical flavour. Their fish comes from the nearby Fish Quay so go for the cod, salmon, fish pie or the traditional fish and chips.

Tynemouth is worth a visit and it's easy on the metro. **Wooden Doll**, 103 Hudson Street, Tel 257 3747, overlooks the harbour. There's an open fire in winter and friendly service. Try their half pint of prawns and mackerel salad. The mackerel is smoked in smokehouses you can see from the pub's balcony, so any fish you eat here is pretty fresh.

ARTISTIC ASSOCIATIONS

Local coal has been exported from the Newcastle area since Tudor times, hence the proverbial saying for a useless activity has become "carrying coals to Newcastle." The poet and doctor Mark Akenside, who wrote *Pleasures of the Imagination*, was born in Newcastle in 1721. He studied at Edinburgh University. John Forster, the biographer of Charles Dickens and an eminent drama critic, was born in the town in 1812 and educated at the Royal Grammar School. His play, *Charles at Tunbridge*, was performed at the Newcastle Theatre in 1828; he also wrote lives of Oliver Goldsmith (1854) and Walter Savage Landor (1869). At nearby Jarrow, the Venerable Bede, the historian and scholar, lived in a monastery for much of his life, circa 730. He is buried in Durham Cathedral.

Thomas Bewick, the father of modern wood engraving, spent practically all his life in Newcastle. The site of his workshop near St Nicholas' Cathedral is marked by a statue and a room is devoted to his work in the Hancock Museum (see above). He lived in Gateshead, just across the river on the site of the present post office in West Street, and died there in 1828.

In the Laing Art Gallery (see above) there is a large collection of the work of John Martin, considered to be the greatest Northumbrian painter. He was apprenticed to a painter of heraldic devices but he abandoned this work to study under a Piedmontese teacher of fencing, perspective and enamel painting called Musso. In 1806 this bizarre character moved to London and persuaded his pupil to join him. Martin remained in London for the rest of his life but never forgot his early life. He was born in Haydon Bridge, east of Newcastle, on the road to Carlisle, in a single-roomed cottage. The wild scenery around Haydon Bridge, especially Allendale Gorge, undoubtedly helped foster his life-long fascination with the terrifying and the spectacular, which is a major focus of his work.

EPHEMERA

Hadrian's Wall, an amazing fortification that divided Britain from Caledonia, stretches 73 miles (117 km) from Wallsend to Bowness. The ruins of the wall constitute a unique monument to the Roman Empire and they are found among some of the most dramatic scenery in the country. The wall was built after a visit to Britain by the Emperor Hadrian. He decided a permanent barrier was required for defence against the unsubdued Caledonia tribes. Planned first as a series of signal stations, it consisted in the end of 17 forts, permanent quarters for garrisons, with "mile castles" every Roman mile for patrols, and turrets or signal towers between all, linked by a curtain wall. There was a ditch on the north side as an added protection and a flat-bottomed trench at the southern boundary of the military zone. The grand project was probably finished by AD138. Legionary soldiers were responsible for the building and the wall was garrisoned by some 5500 cavalry and 13,000 infantry. The wall stood perhaps 20 feet high (6 m) to the top of the parapet and 8 to 10 feet (2.5 m to 3 m) broad, but the highest remaining portion is about 9 feet (2.7 m). The work consumed one million cubic feet (28,000 cubic m) of stone.

The wall suffered destruction during three periods of civil disorder and in each case was rebuilt by the Romans. In the 4th century, uprisings in Continental Europe caused the reduction of Roman forces in Britain and by the 5th century the remaining token force of troops, or farmer-soldiers as many were by now, merged with the native tribes who had become allies of Rome. The wall became a vast quarry for building stone. The farmers built houses and outbuildings with it, but its greatest destruction occurred in 1751 when Parliament ordered a new road to be built between Newcastle and Carlisle. For much of the way, this was built on and with material from the Wall. Various pioneering scholars and antiquarians are to be thanked for enabling us to see what is left to see today; the Wall was described as early as 1599. The best place to appreciate the original conception is at such sites as Chollerford, Housesteads and Corbridge, and the A69 and B6318 going east from Newcastle towards Carlisle are the best roads for a drive.

The house on Quayside known as Bessie Surtees' House is a 17th-century structure and has retained its original timber-frame façade. It is a remarkable and rare example of Jacobean domestic architecture. Bessie Surtees was the daughter of a wealthy merchant, Aubone Surtees. She fell in love with the son of a coal merchant from nearby Love Lane, named John Scott, but her parents objected to the association. On November 18th, 1772, she eloped to Scotland with John Scott, where they were married. Scott, in time-honoured tradition, set a ladder against the first floor window and Bessie descended into his waiting arms. In due course all parties were reconciled and there was an English marriage ceremony in St Nicholas' Church. John Scott became a successful lawyer and later, as Lord Elton, was appointed Lord Chancellor of England.

The 147-foot (44.6 m) Grey's Monument marks the centre of Newcastle and commemorates the life of Charles, the 2nd Earl Grey, who was born at Fallodon, Northumberland, in 1764. In 1792 he helped to found the "Society of the Friends of the People," which he himself always was. As Foreign Secretary and leader of the House of Commons he carried through the act abolishing the African slave trade in 1806. He defended the right of public meeting and as Prime Minister his policy was peace, retrenchment and reform. His greatest triumph was the Reform Bill, which finally became law in 1832. It gave a much fairer representation of parliamentary seats across the country and got rid of many of the "Rotten Boroughs," so called because they were parliamentary seats whose constituencies had ceased to exist or were too small to need a member. The Reform Bill was the first great step to reform Parliament and led the way universal suffrage.

One of the fascinating aspects of the Tyneside region is the "Geordie" accent. It is perhaps the most distinctive accent in the whole of England and is notoriously difficult to capture. To try and demonstrate this I have taken a traditional song of Tyneside called "The Lambton Worm," and rendered it, as best I can, into colloquial Newcastle speech. I hope you will get some kind of idea of what many Tynesiders sound like.

Whisht lads, haad yer gobs
An' aa'll tell yer an awful story
Whisht lads haad yer gobs
An' aa'll tell yer boot the worm.
On Sunday morning Lambton went
A' fishing in the Wear,
And catched a fish upon his heuk,
He thowt leukt varry queer,
But whatnt kind of fish it was
Young Lambton couldn't tell
He waddnt fash to carry it hyem
So he hoyed it in a well.
Noo Lambton felt inclined to gann
An fight in foreign wars
He joined a group of knights that cared,
For nowther wounds nor scars,
An off he went to Palestine
Where queer things him befell,
An very seun forgot aboot
The queer worm in the well.
But the worm got fat and growed an'growed
An' growed an awful size
He'd greet big teeth, and a greet big gob
An' greet big goggly eyes.
An' when at neet he craaled aboot,
Ta pick up its a' news,
If he felt dry upon the road
He sucked a dozen coos.
This fearful worm wad often feed
On calves and lamb an sheep
An' swally little bairns alive
When they laid down to sleep.
An' when he'd eaten aa'll he could
An' he had hed his fill
He craaled away an lapped his tail
Curled many times 'round the hill
The nuws of this most aaful worm
An his queer gannins on
Seun crossed the seas an got the ears
Of brave and bold Sir John.

So hyem he came, and catched the beast
And cut him in two halves
And that seun stopped him eatin' bairns
An' sheep and lambs and calves.
So now ye knaa hoo aa'l thu folks
On byeth sides of the Wear
Lost lots o' sheep an' lots o' sleep
An' lived in mortal fear.
So lets have one to brave Sir John
That kept thu bairns frae harm,
Saved coos and calves by making halves
Of the famous Lambton Worm.

TOURIST INFORMATION BUREAU: Central Library, Princess Square, Newcastle, Tyne and Wear, NE99 1DX. Tel (091) 261 0691

SCARBOROUGH

North Yorkshire
233 miles (382 km) from London by M1 and A64
Three hours from London by train (King's Cross via York)

According to the Icelandic *Kormakssaga,* two Norwegian Viking brothers, Kormak and Thorgils, were the first men to set up the stronghold which was called Scarborough. For many years it was thought that the name of the town meant "the burg on the rocky hill," but more recent scholarship suggests the name comes from one of its founders. Thorgils was nicknamed Skarthi, "the hare-lipped," and the town's name deriving from Scarthiburg seems obvious. Skarthi's stronghold existed around 966 but in 1066 another Norseman, Harald Hardrada, burnt the settlement to the ground. Long before this, however, the Romans had built a signal station on the headland. The remains of the small square building with its tower can be seen between Scarborough Castle and the cliff edge. Built around 370, the station was erected to cope with piratical raiders but, although it was manned by a garrison, its prime purpose was not defence. The station was intended as a lookout post from which warning of enemy approach could be sent along the coast and to inland Roman garrisons. Scarborough Castle has been intermittently occupied since the Bronze Age. The Keep of the castle was built between 1157 and 1167 by Henry II, who incorporated the town in 1181. The castle looks down on the medieval red-roofed town. There is the Richard III House dating mainly from the 15th century and St Mary's Parish Church, which was built in the 12th century. The port, harbour and fishing industries are long established but since the 17th century the town has mainly been known first as a spa and second as a hugely popular seaside resort, which unlike so many others has an inherent elegance.

It was in the 1620s that Elizabeth Farrer, wife of a local merchant, discovered natural springs bubbling out beneath the cliff to the south of the town. The water, staining the rock and tasting slightly bitter, must be beneficial to the sick and suffering, she decided. The spring was high in magnesium sulphate and drinking it was really no more efficacious than taking a glass of Eno's salts, but Scarborough, its castle now a Cromwellian ruin, set about with a vengeance to develop its potential as a fashionable spa. In 1698 a sea wall was built, the natural spring water collected and a governor appointed to run things. The popularity and reputation of the resort continued to grow and in 1826 the ornate iron bridge across the valley was built, giving easier access from the cliff to the town where elegant hotels were being more and more heavily patronized. During the late 19th century the "taking of the waters" declined in popularity (the Pump Room finally closed in 1939) but Scarborough's reputation as a place of entertainment and relaxation continued to grow. The first orchestra appeared in the 1830s and the Spa Grand Hall, Theatre and Buffet came into use in 1879. Parallel with the discovery of the natural springs came the enthusiasm for sea bathing and the "sea cure" (documented under Brighton). Here the major advocate was a Doctor Wittie who seems to have insisted that both men and women take the cure while naked – a custom that continued until the end of the 18th century. As the spa developed it also offered facilities for the sea cure, and the attendant entertainments and amenities that grew up support Scarborough's claim of being one of the first seaside resorts developed to overcome the boredom of visitors not actually bathing or partaking of the spa waters.

The town has sands, terraced gardens, long wave-swept promenades, beautiful views, invigorating walks and bracing North Sea air. I like Scarborough immensely, perhaps because of its cricket festival, but mainly because it is a holiday town which has not completely lost its soul. Elements of the resort which attracted the rich and fashionable, and rivalled the sophistication of Bath, still remain; and while the more populist diversions of beach and sea have now taken precedence, elements of the past are much in evidence. This past of course is not only represented by the spa, but through memories of a much older Scarborough – the Scarborough of sailors and fishermen and of battles and kings whose symbol is the great castle on the headland.

WALK

Our **Scarborough Walk** begins at the Crescent Car Park. **The Crescent**, actually an oval, is composed of mid-19th-century brown sandstone terraces and houses reminiscent of Bath. Though it was built in early Victorian times, the inspiration here is entirely Georgian. Two of the larger houses are now the **Wood End Natural History Museum** and the **Scarborough Art Gallery**. Leave the Gallery and turn right. Note **Londesborough Lodge**, circa 1839. The most celebrated owner was Lord Londesborough who acquired the property in 1853. His son, grandfather of Sir Osbert Sitwell, was a 19th-century "jet setter," spending some £100,000 (a huge sum in those days) on his high society interests. Whenever the family visited the house, a mile of red carpet was laid to welcome them. The second Lord Londesborough helped to found Scarborough's Cricket Festival in 1876. At the roundabout, turn right along Falconers Road to St Nicholas Cliff and the yellow and red **Grand Hotel**. The hotel, with its four distinctive domes representing the four seasons, was considered the most luxurious in Europe when it opened in 1867. It had 365 rooms, 11 miles (17.6 km) of carpet and 32 speaking tubes to connect the manager with his underlings. One of the houses swept away to make room for the Grand was No 2, The Cliff, where the novelist and poet Anne Brontë died of tuberculosis on May 28, 1849. Take the path between the shops and the Grand Hotel and bear left up St Nicholas Street. Note the **Town Hall**, circa 1847, formerly the residence of a prominent banker, which is fronted by a statue of Queen Victoria, the only statue of a public figure to be found in the town. St Nicholas Street has some delightfully old-fashioned shops such as the **India and Colonial Outfitters** and the site of **Theakston's Bookshop**, now Marks and Spencers, whose present-day frontage is a faithful replica of the original. Cross the road and turn right onto St Helen Square. Go through the Victorian Market Hall and turn right along St Sepulchre Street, passing the handsome **Trinity House**. It is today retirement flats for seamen and indeed it has served a similar purpose since 1602. It is one of only four such establishments in the country, the others being London, Hull and Newcastle-upon-Tyne, and its foundation reflects the importance of Scarborough as a port in the early 17th century. As well as apartments for aged or maimed mariners, the house was the centre of Scarborough's maritime trade. It was rebuilt in 1832. At Princess Square turn left up St Mary's Steps to **St Mary's Church**. Leave the church, walk through the churchyard and turn right along Castle Road to **Scarborough Castle**. From the castle take the path down Castle Dykes to the **Old Harbour** – a mixture of fishing port, fairground and yacht basin. Pass the Coastguard Station and turn right along Sandgate to **Richard III House**. Continue along Foreshore Road, an attractive esplanade beside the beach, and bear right, up Valley Road, to the

Rotunda Museum. Leave the museum, turn left up the steps of Museum Terrace and then turn left again along Bridge Terrace. Cross the bridge over Vernon Road and climb up through Valley Park to Londesborough Lodge and the car park.

MUSEUMS, GALLERIES AND PUBLIC BUILDINGS

Wood End Museum of Natural History – The Crescent, Tel 367326. The museum has changing displays of the flora and fauna of the Scarborough district including a section on the geology of the area. A conservatory, built in the 1870s, contains tropical plants and a large aquarium. The west wing of the building gives an insight into the life of the literary Sitwell family who lived here from 1870 to the early 1930s. An almost complete library of their published works together with portraits and paintings relating to their writings can be seen here. Open Tues–Sat 10–1pm and 2–5pm, Sun 2–5pm (summers only).

The Rotunda – Vernon Road, Tel 374839. This delightful Georgian museum, dating from 1829, is associated with William Smith, the "father of British geology," who inspired the design. Originally only the central rotunda was constructed, the wings were added in 1860. It is the finest example of a purpose-built Georgian museum in existence and has many original showcases and fittings, all designed to illustrate Smith's geological principles. There is an extensive collection of archaeological material and also his exhibits illustrating local social history. Opening times as Wood End Museum.

The Art Gallery – The Crescent, Tel 374753. The admirable Italianate villa in which the collection is housed was built in 1845 and has a splendid entrance hall and marble fireplace. The nucleus of the collection is a series of local scenes painted over the last 200 years. On permanent display is a group of paintings given by Tom Laughton, once Scarborough's leading hotelier and brother of the actor Charles Laughton. These include work by Atkinson Grimshaw, who spent some years in the town, and Lord Leighton, the English painter who was born a short distance from the gallery.

Scarborough Castle – Castle Road, Tel 372451. The building of the castle was begun by William Le Gros, Earl of Aumale, in the early 12th century. What remains is the curtain wall and much of the massive rectangular keep. In the 13th-century King John spent £2000, a considerable fortune, on improving the Castle's defences. George Fox, the Quaker, was imprisoned here in 1665–66. The Castle was blasted by cannons during the Civil War and bombarded from the sea during the First World War.

St Mary's Church – Castle Road. A church probably occupied this commanding position even before the first castle was built. Due to severe damage in the Civil War, St Mary's is now only a fragment of the original cruciform church dating from 1450. During the Civil War the Parliamentarians used the church as a forward position to bombard the castle. Inevitably the castle batteries returned the fire, destroying the beautiful medieval choir and transept. The church steeple collapsed in 1659 but the nave, aisle and tower

SCARBOROUGH CASTLE

were quickly rebuilt. The north transept and choir have never been rebuilt, although the ruined sections are marked and visible, bearing silent witness to the terrible destruction that took place. Anne Brontë (Acton Bell) is buried in the east churchyard, beyond Church Lane.

St Martin's Church – Albion Road. A 19th-century church, circa 1863, St Martin's is built in Gothic style and contains a spectacular display of decoration by the architect G F Bodley, and many of his pre-Raphaelite friends. There is glass and mural painting by Edward Burne-Jones, the chancel roof is by Philip Webb and William Morris, and Dante Gabriel Rossetti, Ford Madox Brown and others worked on the walls, pulpit and stained glass.

King Richard III's House – Sandside. Richard III radically reorganized England's sea defences and is reputed to have stayed in this house when he was Lord High Admiral to his brother Edward IV. In front of the building there is a grotesque carving of a creature both caged and chained; doubled up though wearing a crown with a skull in one hand and with cloven feet. This caricature of Richard is probably Tudor and is thought to have originated in the Midlands. There was a shipyard and slipways in front of the house in the 18th century but all trace of that has disappeared. The house is now a restaurant.

THEATRE

The **Stephen Joseph Theatre in the Round** – Valley Bridge Parade, Tel 370451. A repertory theatre under the direction of Alan Ayckbourn, which serves as a tryout base for his work and that of aspiring playwrights. The season runs from May to January and features some touring during the winter. Stephen Joseph, who died in 1967, pioneered the idea of theatre-in-the-round in 1955 at the public library in Scarborough. The aim was to create a writers' theatre – a concept that was greeted with much suspicion by the die-hards, who firmly believed that writers should be kept at a good distance. It was as a result of this policy of encouraging bright young writers that Alan Ayckbourn, an erstwhile stage manager and actor, wrote and had his first play produced in 1959. Full seasons were not possible at the library in the early years, so Stephen Joseph took his company on tour, travelling the country with his theatre-in-the-round. Not until nine years after his death did the company find a permanent home in the municipal school. It is still a writers' theatre, and Ayckbourn's plays share the programme with new and "neglected" 20th-century playwrights. I hear whispers that a full-scale appeal will soon be launched to build a playhouse for this most exciting of theatre forms. Not to be missed.

Futurist Theatre – Foreshore, Tel 365789. Built on the site of the Arcadia Pierrot Theatre, the Futurist hosts variety and musical shows in the summer and cinema in the winter.

MUSIC

Scarborough Fayre was the longest and best-known of England's medieval fayres. It lasted for 45 days, was internationally famous and survived for 350 years, ending in 1788. The present Scarborough Fayre is held in the second two weeks of June each year and includes music (the Hallé Orchestra is a frequent visitor), art exhibitions, morris dancing, a film festival, lectures and processions. During the year musical visitors often use the Scarborough Spa Grand Hotel, Tel 3767744, while soloists and chamber groups use a variety of locations including the Town Hall and the Art Gallery. The Spa is also one of the best-known conference centres in Britain. Tel 373333 for details.

CINEMA

Futurist – Foreshore, Tel 365789 (winter).
Hollywood Plaza – North Marine Road, Tel 365119 (summer only).
Royal Opera House – St Thomas Street, Tel 369999.

BOOKSTORES

There's not a great deal of choice which perhaps is not surprising for a predominantly holiday resort. The best is probably **Harding's Bookshop**, 49 Westborough, Tel 360157, with **Bookstop**, 24 Bar Street, Tel 354975, also worth a look. Surprisingly, there are two outlets of a rather good bargain bookshop, the **Remainder Book Co** at 44 Sandside, Tel 500350 and 13 Westborough, Tel 500292.

ANTIQUARIAN AND SECONDHAND BOOKS

The best are **Scarborough Books**, 55 Castle Road, Tel 368813 with a good general collection, **L and M Mellor**, 2 Westover Road, Tel 371045, and **Bar Bookstore**, 4 Swanhill Road, Tel 500141.

ART GALLERIES

Harbour Gallery – 40 Eastborough, Tel 354261, has local artists' prints and also some limited-edition prints by contemporary British printmakers. **Hanover Arts**, 13A Hanover Road, Tel 371101, has similar stock but also has watercolours and some good books on art. **St John's Studio**, 112 Victoria Road, Tel 374689, has some nice antique prints of local scenes and also contemporary prints by local and national artists. Similar stock can be found at **Cockill's Prints**, 26 Bar Street, Tel 374474. Finally, **Marine Gallery** at 34 North Marine Road, Tel 354080, has watercolours and prints by the Yorkshire artist Allan Stuttle.

ANTIQUE DEALERS

Victoria Road is off Westonborough to the south of the station. At No 7 you will find **Shuttleworths**, Tel 366278, with a good stock of general antiques, while at No 119, **Grant Antiques**, Tel 367938, also has general antiques. Follow Victoria Street to its junction with Northway. Turn right and then left onto Westonborough. Walk up Westonborough and where it becomes Newborough turn right on to Bar Street. Here at No 14 you will find **Bar Antiques**, Tel 351487, with some fine silver, porcelain and glass, while at the same address is **Gerards**, with the same telephone number, but dealing in jewellery and bullion. Walk back down Westonborough and into Falsgrave Road. At the junction with Seamer Road you will find **Brown's Antiques**, Tel 377112, with furniture, pictures, porcelain, pottery and objets d'art. Finally, **Hanover Antiques** at 10 Hanover Road, Tel 374175, have militaria, medals, badges and general small items.

RESTAURANTS

Lanterna – 33 Queen Street, Tel 363616. I really like Lanterna. It's unpretentious, small, friendly and informal and the Italian cuisine is authentic and tasty. I thought the cannelloni was excellent and the mussels in wine and garlic superb. I have also heard good reports regarding the chicken cacciatore and the zabaglione was delightful. Open Tues–Sat 7–9:30 for dinner only.

Looking out across the North Sea, Scarborough is as good a place to eat fresh fish as anywhere I can think of in England. **Dilts**, 2 Princess Square, Tel 500146, is a remarkable little fish-and-chip restaurant tucked away in the old part of town close to the harbour. Inside there is dark oak panelling, fishing nets, storm lamps on the wall and excellent fresh fish ranging from cod and haddock to Dover sole and brill. The "Fisherman's Haul," with three kinds of fish, is strictly for large appetites. There's even an acceptable wine list. Open summers all week noon–midnight; winters 12–1:30 and 8–10:30, closed Sun–Tues.

While you are in Scarborough you should make the 16-mile (25.6 km) journey north to Whitby, a port and fishing town with the romantic ruins of an 11th-century abbey set on a headland dominating the town. There was a whaling fleet here in the 18th century and the great Captain Cook lived here for a time. It's a delightful place and there's a wonderful little fish restaurant called the **Magpie Café** at 14 Pier Road, Tel 602058, which serves the most wonderful fresh fish. In my experience you can get the cheapest lobster in Britain here and the special lunches are remarkable value. There's also fresh salmon from the River Esk. Not to be missed. Open all week 11:30–6:30pm. Closed late Nov to March.

Back in Scarborough, the **Square Cat Bistro** is part of the Stephen Joseph Theatre in the Round at Valley Bridge Parade, Tel 368463. It's convenient for a pre-theatre supper as they open at 6pm or 5pm if the performance starts at 6, as it does on Fridays and Saturdays. You can also eat after the show if you let them know. There is always a vegetarian choice and the value is excellent. They also serve lunch. Open Mon–Sat 11:30–2pm and 6–11pm (5pm when performance starts at 6).

PUBS

Leeds Arms – St Mary's Street, Tel 361699. Built in 1693 and sympathetically restored in 1900, this is perhaps Scarborough's most visually attractive public house. There is an elaborate woodwork finish to the upper storey and the inn sign is lettered in art nouveau style. There is a pronounced nautical feel to the pub and a nice atmosphere and it's set in one of the most interesting parts of Scarborough. Traditional bar food.

Hole in the Wall – Vernon Road, Tel 373746. A small pub with lots of atmosphere, some of it coming from the graffiti board in the gents! (I don't know if there's one in the ladies too.) In the early 20th century the Pierrots from Catlin's troupe (see Ephemera) used to gather in the pub to quench their thirst. It is close to the spa slipway where they used to perform, but can't be seen from the seafront, which was handy, as Will Catlin, the owner and director of the troupe, would not have approved. Traditional bar food.

Golden Ball – 31 Sandside, Tel 353899. Good bar food with a nice garden for the summer. The first-floor lounge overlooks the harbour and sea front. Friendly atmosphere and patronized by locals and tourists alike.

The Barn – Osgody Lane, Osgody, Tel 584372 (2 miles/3.2 km south of Scarborough on the A165, turn right into Osgody Lane and the pub is 400 yards/365 m on the right). Dating from the 10th century, this country inn is said to be haunted by the ghost of John Wyville who was executed in 1537. Excellent bar food and a restaurant serving more sophisticated cuisine. Full of atmosphere.

Blacksmith's Arms – Cayton, Tel 582272 (3 miles/5 km south on B1261). A traditional country style pub set in the heart of the village of Cayton. Very good bar food with an excellent carvery for trenchermen.

ARTISTIC ASSOCIATIONS

Richard Brinsley Sheridan, author of *The School for Scandal* and *The Rivals,* set his comedy, *A Trip to Scarborough* here in 1777 when the town was at the height of its elegance and popularity as a spa and social gathering place of the gentry and well-off. Anne Brontë, who wrote *The Tenant of Wildfell Hall, Agnes Grey,* and a small amount of beautiful poetry under the name Acton Bell, was especially fond of Scarborough. She arrived at The Cliff (in the then fashionable St Nicholas Cliff area on a site where the Grand Hotel now stands) on May 25, 1849, together with her sister Charlotte (author of *Jane Eyre*) and one of Charlotte's old school friends, Ellen Nussey. Anne was able to enjoy the incomparable views from The Cliff for just three days before she died, on May 28, and was buried in the detached part of St Mary's churchyard beyond the ruined part of the church.

The well-known Victorian painter Atkinson Grimshaw, famous for his moonlit scenes, lived in Scarborough from 1876 to his death in 1893, dividing his time between here and his house in Leeds. In Scarborough he lived in Castle-by-the-Sea, a curious castellated villa close by Scarborough Castle that is now a bed-and-breakfast cum tea-garden. One of the best examples of his work, *Scarborough Lights,* hangs in the Crescent Gallery.

Edith Sitwell, the poet and author, was born in the family's seaside home, "Wood End," now a museum, in 1887 and Osbert Sitwell's novel *Before the Bombardment* is set in the town. One of the legendary giants of Hollywood, Charles Laughton, was born in Scarborough in 1899. He was the eldest of three sons of a notable family of local hoteliers and lived in the Victoria Hotel, opposite the Railway Station. His younger brother Tom once suggested that a boyhood hero, Will Catlin of Pierrot fame (see Ephemera), probably first infected Charles with the theatre bug. His first successful stage performance was in an amateur production of *Hobson's Choice* in Catlin's old Arcadia Theatre, where the Futurist now stands. At the time he was helping his family to modernize the prestigious Pavilion Hotel which the Laughtons owned and which, sadly, was pulled down in 1973. The pull of the theatre was too strong and the young hotelier concentrated entirely on his acting. After success in Britain he married the dynamic actress Elsa Lanchester (perhaps best known for her portrayal of the bride of Frankenstein) and was drawn to Hollywood where he became a naturalized US citizen. Laughton died in Hollywood in 1962, but he often visited the town of his birth, even after his portrayal of such characters as Henry VIII, Rembrandt, Captain Bligh and Quasimodo had established his international reputation. He is still the subject of recollection and anecdote among the people of the town.

Also born in Scarborough, in 1906, was Eric Fenby, the amanuensis of the composer Frederick Delius. When Delius became blind, in the early 1920s, he dictated his last words to Fenby. Fenby went on to become a professor at the Royal Academy of Music.

Sixteen miles (25.6 km) north of Scarborough is Whitby, where Bram Stoker (who was born in Dublin in 1847 and became general manager of Sir Henry Irving's Company at the Lyceum Theatre in London) set his famous story, *Dracula.* The chapters in the book dealing with Whitby form a powerful evocation of this Victorian resort and there is now a Whitby Dracula Trail where you can follow in the footsteps of the characters in the book.

EPHEMERA

On Shrove Tuesday in Scarborough, practically the whole of the population makes its way down to the South Foreshore to skip. This is a custom which seems to have been carried on for at least 200 years and although no one can quite understand why the emphasis should be on skipping, there is no doubt that it has its origin in the fact that Shrove Tuesday was, in past times, one of the few public holidays when apprentices, in particular, could be sure of having at least a half day to themselves. Even as late as the end of last century the South Foreshore on Shrove Tuesday was like a fairground. Stalls of gingerbread, liquorice, coconuts and other delicacies were arranged along the sea front and, according to a contemporary account, "On this day grown up folk can skip and play without being thought childish." Everyone became something different from themselves on Shrove Tuesday. Today the road along the Foreshore is closed after lunch and thousands of people still enjoy themselves in this energetic fashion. The ringing of the Pancake Bell is also still observed. It is traditional to serve pancakes on Shrove Tuesday and a bell used to hang in St Thomas's Hospital which was then in North Street. It was used as a curfew signal at six o'clock, morning and evening, before the days of BBC time signals. On Shrove Tuesday, however, it was rung at noon as a signal to housewives to start frying the pancakes. With the demolition of the hospital the bell was removed to the Rotunda Museum where it is still faithfully rung each Shrove Tuesday morning.

When a member of the House of Commons wishes to resign as an MP, he applies for the Chiltern Hundred. The stewardship of the Chiltern Hundreds is a nominal office under the Chancellor of the Exchequer. Since 1751 the nomination to it has been the method of enabling an MP to relinquish his seat, on a plea that he holds an office of honour and profit under the crown. The holding of such an office has been a disqualification for Parliament since 1707. Few people know that when a Member of Parliament applies for the Chiltern Hundreds, the retiring MPs are appointed to the stewardship of, alternately, the Chiltern Hundreds and Northstead Manor. The Ancient Manor of Northstead lies under the waters of the lake in Peasholm Park, which is one of Scarborough's loveliest gardens.

John Paul Jones was a name that struck fear and hatred into the hearts of British seamen in the late 18th century. John Paul, as he was originally called, was born in Scotland in 1747 and went to sea when he was 13. By 21 he was master of a ship involved in the West Indies trade. In 1773 he was involved in a brawl with mutinous seamen in the port of Scarborough in Tobago, during the course of which he killed one of them with his sword. This and other scandalous acts made him so unpopular in the Indies that he fled to America where he offered his services to the government of the Colonies. He played a very active part in many naval engagements against the British during the War of Independence, which was then being bitterly fought. In 1779 John Paul Jones was in command of a squadron which for months had harried merchant ships in the North Sea and practically stopped Britain's trade with the Baltic ports. There was a furious battle with a British convoy off Scarborough, and although the British Royal Navy ships finally surrendered, John Paul Jones's flagship, the *Bonhomme Richard,* was sunk, and his virtual dominance in the North Sea ended. It is an ironic fact of history that in the eyes of the British, John Paul Jones was little better than a traitor, pirate and mercenary, but he remains one of the great American naval heroes.

One of the most popular seashore attractions in resorts all over England at the turn of the century was the Pierrot Show. This was an all-male show (by definition the cast were all bachelors) which consisted of comedy sketches and the singing of popular songs of the day. Pierrots were dressed in a traditional costume of white consisting of trousers and a long shirt with a ruffled collar. Black pompoms were attached to the shirt front and the costume was completed with a white conical hat. One of the most famous of the Pierrot troupes was that managed by Will Catlin, who was born in 1871 and who worked in Scarborough for many years. For sixpence (2 1/2p) you could sit in a front-row deckchair on the beach and watch the show performed from a portable stage. Those standing at the back behind the chairs were invited to put pennies in the cone-shaped Pierrot hats, a procedure known as "bottling." Catlin was charged a rent by the town corporation for performing his show on the sands, and as this increased he moved his pitch away from the central sands to the spa slipway. Finally he got fed up with what he saw as the avariciousness of the town council, and moved his show to the newly built Arcadia Theatre (the site now occupied by the Futurist). In the early years of the 20th century Catlin's Pierrot shows were to be seen all over the North of England and North Wales, and he was for 60 years the dominant figure in seaside entertainment. Pierrots were still performing on the sand until the early 1920s though they had no connection with the Catlin troupes. When Will Catlin died in 1953 he was on his way to the theatre. At his funeral the coffin bore a wreath in the shape of a Pierrot's hat.

Scarborough's annual Cricket Festival was launched in 1876 when Lord Londesborough sponsored one of the teams. The Festival celebrated its centenary in 1986 (a number of festivals had been cancelled due to two world wars). The event has attracted practically every first-class cricketer in the world since its inception, including W G Grace and Sir Donald Bradman. Yorkshire County Cricket Club also plays games at the Scarborough. Until recently the Club only used players actually born in the county. Although this has changed, even now the idea of having a non-Yorkshire-born player competing in the side is anathema to many supporters. The Scarborough Cricket Festival is held at the end of the English cricket season in late August and early September.

Although not as widely used as it was, the phrase "a Scarborough warning" meant essentially that a blow would be struck first and the warning given afterwards. There are two opinions as to the derivation of the saying. One is that in Scarborough robbers used to be dealt with in a very summary fashion – namely, they were quickly hanged by a sort of lynch law. In the early 17th century the dramatist and poet Thomas Heywood wrote,

> This term Scarborough warning, grew, some say,
> By hasty hanging for rank robbery here.
> Who that was met but suspect in that way,
> Straight he was trussed up, whatever he were.

Another origin of the phrase is that it came from Thomas Stafford's seizure of Scarborough Castle in 1557. It seemed Stafford occupied the castle so quickly that none of the townsfolk had any idea of what was happening.

TOURIST INFORMATION BUREAU: St Nicholas Cliff, Scarborough, North Yorkshire, YO11 2EP. Tel (0723) 376941

YORK

County of Yorkshire
By road, 191 miles (306 km) from London by M1 and A64
By rail, 2 hours from London (Kings Cross)

In the years before the Roman invasion of Britain in AD43, a powerful confederation of Celtic tribes known as the Brigantes ruled Northern England. These Iron Age people established a settlement at York called Eborakor. The Romans invaded Brigantia in AD71 and the Roman

Ninth Legion built a permanent fortress at York, calling it Eboracum. The town became one of the leading cities in the Roman Empire and the Emperor Severus made it the capital of Lower Britain. Severus had his court here (previously, Hadrian had used the city as a base for his northern campaign). In 306, Emperor Constantius Chlorus died here and was succeeded by his son Constantine. He was proclaimed Emperor while in York and went on to become the first Christian Emperor and founder of Constantinople. In 400, the Roman occupation ended when the legions were withdrawn to serve in Gaul.

Following the departure of the Romans, the Germanic tribes of the Anglo-Saxons began their long-term invasion of Britain and York became "Eoforwic," the capital of Northumbria. Legend has it that King Arthur recaptured York from the Anglo-Saxons during this period and it was about this time that Christianity was introduced here by a warlord named Edwin. He married a Christian princess from the south who brought a priest named Paulinius with her. Edwin and many of his subjects were baptized on Easter Day, 627, in a timber church – the first Cathedral of St Peter at York and the site of the present York Minster. The city became a great centre of learning, with renowned scholar Alcuin, who later was Master of Charlemagne's Palace School at Aachen, establishing a school here attended by students from all over Europe.

By the 8th century however, the power of Northumbria declined and the Danish King, Ivar the Boneless, captured York in 866. The Vikings ruled for nearly a hundred years. They called the city Jorvik, and by all accounts the rule was peaceful and prosperous. In 954, Eadred of Wessex united Northumbria with the south, but earls of both Anglo and Scandinavian blood ruled for another hundred years. In 1065, the Norwegians who had captured the city were defeated at Stamford Bridge by King Harold of England who in turn would fall to William of Normandy at the Battle of Hastings a year later.

The Normans ruthlessly subdued rebellion in the north. They built two wooden castles, on mounds on either side of the River Ouse. These survive today as Clifford's Tower and Baile Hill. The city prospered, the building of the Minster was begun and before long there were 45 parish churches, four monasteries and several religious hospitals in the city. The city became an important port and trading centre in the 12th century and merchants and craftsmen's guilds flourished – there were over 100 at one time, with many still existing today. York became the country's second largest and richest city.. The city walls were built and the Dukedom of York – held by the sovereign's second son, was established. Parliament was held here by Edward III and Richard III watched a performance of the Mystery Plays here in 1396. But the prosperity based on the woollen industry declined and the Wars of the Roses(1453–1487) disrupted normal life for 34 years. Afterwards, Edward IV never forgave the city for its Lancastrian sympathies and ruled the city harshly. Worse was to come though, when in 1533 Henry VIII renounced Rome, made himself the head of the Church of England and began the Dissolution of the Monasteries. York, as a major religious community, suffered terribly during this purge but fortunes revived when the Council of the North was established with York as its administrative capital. Under Elizabeth and James I, during the late 16th and early 17th centuries, York became a social capital for the gentry of the north, which perhaps explains the city's Royalist sympathies during the Civil War. The Parliamentarian forces laid siege to York, and the city fell on July 15, 1644. Luckily the Parliamentarian general, Sir Thomas Fairfax, was a local man. He respected the conditions of surrender and stopped his troops pillaging the town and York's magnificent churches and medieval stained glass were largely untouched.

During the Georgian era, York's role as a social and cultural centre rose while trade and manufacturing declined. Elegant new houses and buildings appeared, the York *Mercury*, the city's first newspaper, began in 1719 and the racecourse was built. Coffee houses became popular gathering places and by 1830 the journey to London, which before had taken four days, was cut to 20 hours. The coming of the railway was to make it much less. The railway came in 1839 and by the turn of the century York was a major railway centre. The chocolate factories of Rowntrees and Terry expanded and today they and the railway are still York's largest employees. Victorian prosperity brought a rapid rise in the building of schools, colleges, churches, banks and offices. Over the last 50 years the entire historic core of York has been designated a Conservation Area and a new university was established. King George VI said, "The history of York is the history of England" and as you walk through the streets steeped in tradition, the truth of that statement will be brought home to you again and again.

WALK

York Walks – There is so much to see in York that it would be easy to build an itinerary of five or six walks. The two outlined below cover much of the historic centre of the city and are each about two miles (3.2 km) in length.

Walk One – Start at the St John's Street car park, off Lord Mayor's Walk. Turn left into Lord Mayor's Walk and then turn right through Monk Bar. Walk ahead into Goodramgate and turn right into Ogleforth for the **Treasurer's House**. Leave the house and turn left into College Street, noting the 15th-century **St William's College**, which was built in 1453 for Minster Chantry priests and is now used for meetings of all kinds. Continue back into Goodramgate and turn right to the open space of King's Square. Cross the square and fork right into the **Shambles**. This is one of York's most interesting medieval streets, so called because it was the place where butchers slaughtered their animals and sold meat. The word has passed into the language and means a place where confusion and disorder reign. Note how the timber-framed upper storeys of the houses almost touch across the street. At the end turn right into The Pavement. On the left is the half-timbered **Herbert House**, home of Sir Thomas Herbert, who accompanied Charles I to the scaffold in 1649. Turn right at the junction into Parliament Street. At the junction is **All Saints Church**. There is a chained book here on the lectern, one of the few left in England, some beautiful 14th- and 15th-century stained glass, and a door knocker said to depict the devil swallowing a woman. At the end of Parliament Street, fork left into Davygate and right into Coney Street. Ahead is the **Mansion House** and behind it the **Guildhall**. Turn right into St Helen's Square and then into Stonegate. To your left are the **Assembly Rooms**. You will have walked, in Stonegate, along the Roman Via Praetoria, and now turn left into High Petergate and visit **York Minster**. After visiting the cathedral, turn right again along High Petergate and go through Bootham Bar, the city's 14th-century northern gateway, and cross Exhibition Square for the **City Art Gallery**. Return to Exhibition Square; on your left is **King's Manor**. Walk down the lane past the side of King's Manor into the Museum Gardens. The second pathway on the left will lead you to the **Anglian** and **Multiangular Towers**. The first was built between 600 and 700AD and the other by the Romans in the 4th century. Close by is **St Leonard's Hospital**, built just after the Norman Conquest. Also in the Museum

THE SHAMBLES, YORK

Gardens are the ruins of **St Mary's Abbey,** dissolved by Henry VIII in 1539. The famous York Mystery Plays are performed here every four years during the York Festival. Return to Bootham Bar and climb the steps to the top. Turn left and follow the walkway on top of the city walls with excellent views of the Minster. Go through Robin Hood Tower and descend the steps at Monk's Bar and back to the car park.

   Walk Two – Start from the Long Stay car park in Nunnery Lane. Turn left on Nunnery Lane. **Bar Convent Museum** is on your left. Turn right through Micklegate Bar into Micklegate. **Holy Trinity Church** on your right was where the Mystery Plays originally began their performances. Just before the bend in the road there are fine Georgian houses on your left, and just ahead on the same side of the road, **St John the Evangelist Church,** which now houses **York Arts Centre.** Cross the Ouse Bridge and continue ahead into Low and High Ousegate. High Ousegate was the home of many wealthy merchants and it is thought that, with The Pavement, it was the first street in York to be paved. Turn right into Fossegate. You will see an ornate arch between two antique shops on your left. This is the entrance to **Merchant Adventurers' Hall.** Continue along Fossegate, cross the bridge and turn right into Merchantgate and right again into Piccadilly. Walk ahead and turn left into Coppergate Centre for the **Jorvik Viking Centre** and **The York Story.** Leave the shopping centre by the Castlegate exit. Turn left, past **Fairfax House** with its fine collection of Georgian furniture, to **York Castle,** dominated by the 13th-century **Clifford's Tower.** To the south of the Castle is the **Castle Museum.** Turn left along the riverside walk of South Esplanade, go past St George's Gardens and cross the River Ouse by Skeldergate Bridge. Ascend the wall by **Baile Hill,** an artificial mound which William the Conqueror originally topped with a wooden castle, and passing **Bitchdaughter Tower** (the origins of the name are unknown) and the 19th-century **Victoria Bar,** arrive at **Micklegate Bar** where the severed heads of traitors were displayed. Ascend the walls here and return to the adjacent car park.

MUSEUMS, GALLERIES AND PUBLIC BUILDINGS

Bar Convent Museum – Blossom Street, Tel 29359. The theme of the displays is the history of Christianity in the north of England and of the Bar Convent in particular. The 18th-century building which houses the museum contains an interesting chapel of the period and there are early vestments, church silver and religious books on view. Open daily 10–5pm.

Fairfax House Museum – Castlegate, Tel 55543. The house dates from 1756 and contains a magnificent collection of Georgian furniture, paintings, porcelain and clocks. Open Mar–Jan Mon, Thurs, Sat 11–5pm; Sun 1:30–5pm.

Jorvik Viking Centre – Coppergate, Tel 643211. The centre is on the site of a Viking settlement and visitors are taken by electrically operated trains through a reconstruction of a Viking street, with a recorded commentary on the early history of the city and Viking life. There is a gallery with excavated artefacts. Open April–Oct daily 9–7pm; Nov–March daily 9–5:30pm.

National Railway Museum – Leeman Road, Tel 621261. The museum occupies a former steam locomotive maintenance depot and tells the story of railways and railway engineering in Britain. There is a large collection of locomotives, rolling stock (watch out for Queen Victoria's state railway carriage) signalling equipment and uniforms. There are also models, posters, paintings, photographs and a wide range of smaller railway memorabilia. Open Mon–Sat 10–6pm; Sun 2:30–6pm.

Regimental Museum of the Royal Dragoon Guards and the Prince of Wales' Own Regiment of Yorkshire – 3A Tower Street, Tel 642038. The museum illustrates the history of two regiments from the time they were formed in 1685. The exhibits include weapons, uniforms, medals and campaign relics. Open Mon–Sat 9:30–4pm.

Treasurer's House – Chapter House Street, Tel 624247. Treasurers of York Minster lived in a house on this site until the reign of Henry VIII when the office was abolished. The main part of the house was rebuilt in 1620. It was bequeathed to the National Trust in 1930 together with an exceptionally fine collection of 17th- and 18th-century furniture, china, pottery and glass. Look for the set of ivory chairs brought back from India by Warren Hastings, who was Governor-General in 1784. There is also a dressing table which belonged to Louis XVI. Open April–Oct daily 10:30–5:30pm.

York Castle Museum – Eye of York, Tel 653611. The museum is housed in two former prisons – the Debtors' Prison, circa 1705, and the Women's Prison, circa 1780. The collection is a folk museum of Yorkshire life with reconstructions of streets and shops and a huge array of domestic objects. There are also cars, hansom cabs and a stagecoach. You can also see the cell occupied by Dick Turpin, the famous highwayman hanged in 1939. Open April–Oct Mon–Sat 9:30–6:30; Sun 10–6:30pm. Nov–Mar Mon–Sat 9:30–5; Sun 10–5pm.

Yorkshire Museum – Museum Gardens, Tel 629745. There are important collections of archaeology, natural history, geology and pottery. Excellent Viking, medieval and Roman galleries. There is a fine display of mammals and birds which give a complete picture of Yorkshire wildlife, plus a large entomological collection. Open Mon–Sat 10–5pm; Sun 1–5pm.

York Racing Museum – York Racecourse, The Knavemire, Tel 620911. Located on the fifth floor of the Grandstand, the collection comprises a wide range of objects connected with the history of racing including memorabilia of racing personalities. Open on race days or by appointment.

The York Story – The Heritage Centre, Castlegate, Tel 28632. A museum interpreting the social and architectural history of York. Models, dioramas and audio-visual presentations are supplemented by artefacts by modern artists and craftspeople. Open Mon–Sat 10–5pm; Sun 1–5pm.

The York Dungeon – 12 Clifford Street, Tel 632599. Set in dark and musty cellars, the displays feature life-size scenes of medieval punishments and the persecution and torture of heretics. Grisly and gruesome – just the thing for the kids. Open daily 10–6pm.

Museum of Automata – Tower Street, Tel 628070. The largest collection of mechanical marvels in the world, from musical boxes to animated figures. Open daily 9:30–5:30pm

The ARC – St Saviourgate, Tel 654324. The first archaeological resource centre in Britain. It is possible to sort and date authentic finds and handle Roman tiles, medieval pottery and Viking bone fragments. Ancient crafts such as spinning, weaving and leatherwork can be tried. Excellent for youngsters.

The World of the Minster – St William's College, College Street, Tel 637134. A fascinating insight into the life and times of York Minster over a period of 800 years. Displays include the building and care of the Minster, the people who serve it, the saints, pilgrims and visitors and the church worldwide. Open Mon–Sat 10–5pm (4pm in winter) Sun 11–3pm.

Clifford's Tower – York Castle, Castle Street, Tel 646940. Built by Henry III to replace the wooden keep, which in turn had replaced William the Conqueror's wooden tower, burnt down by a mob attacking besieged Jews in 1190. Its name derives from Roger de Clifford, a Lancastrian leader, who was executed in 1322 and his body hung in chains from the tower. The Tower is really all that remains of the castle, although parts of the gatehouse and bailey can be seen behind the Castle Museum. Open April–Sept daily 10–6pm. Oct–March daily 10–4pm.

Mansion House – St Helen's Square, Tel 650011. Built in 1725–30 to be the official home of the Lord Mayor. The present Lord Mayor does in fact live there. A superb collection of Civic Plate on view. Open by appointment Mon–Fri.

Guildhall – St Helen's Square, Tel 613161. A restoration of the 15th-century Commonhall, the building was badly damaged by an air raid in 1942, but beautifully rebuilt (some rooms did escape damage). Open Mon–Fri 9–4pm. Weekends 2–5pm (not open weekends in winter).

Assembly Rooms – St Helen's Square, Tel 621756. Built between 1732 and 1736, the rooms were the fashionable centre of Georgian York with great balls and assemblies being held there. Open as Guildhall.

King's Manor – Exhibition Square, Tel 430000. The original building was the home of the abbot of St Mary's Abbey, and Henry VIII made it the official residence of the Council of the North. Charles I and James I both stayed here. Splendidly restored in 1964, now part of York University. Open Mon–Fri 10–5pm (subject to availability). Check at Porter's Lodge.

Merchant Adventurers' Hall – Fossegate, Tel 654818. Dating from the late 14th century, this is one of the few remaining medieval Guild Halls in the country. Its Great Hall is the largest timber-framed building in York. For nearly 600 years, the Merchant Adventurers' Company was the most powerful and wealthy trade guild in the city. Open Mar 21–Nov 6 daily 8:30–5pm. Nov 7–Mar 20 8:30–3pm. Not Sundays.

York Castle – Castle Street, Tel 646940. See Clifford's Tower above.

Cathedral Church of St Peter – (York Minster) Tel 624426. A west front of breathtaking grandeur is the curtain raiser to the largest medieval cathedral in England. The nave is 100 feet (30.4 m) high with an off-white, rib-vaulted roof with gold embossing. The Minster is nearly 500 feet (152 m) long, and the embossed roof, under the central tower, is 200 feet (60.8 m) high. The stained glass is nothing short of magnificent. There are 128 windows dating from the 12th century to the 20th. The east window, the size of a tennis court, is the world's largest area of stained glass and depicts the beginning and the end of creation. The rose window, restored after the 1984 fire, commemorates the 1486 marriage of Henry VII to Elizabeth of York, which ended the Wars of the Roses. The Minster museum displays Saxon tombs, part of the Roman Wall (the church stands on the site of the headquarters of the Roman legionary fortress) and the Minster's treasury. Open daily from 7am.

York City Art Gallery – Exhibition Square, Tel 623839. The collection dates from 1350 to the present day and covers most of the countries of western Europe. There is an impressive collection of Old Masters (the Lycett Green Collection) and an important collection of British paintings from the 16th to 20th centuries, including a substantial group of works by the York-born artist William Etty. There are special exhibitions, lectures, recitals and a shop. Open Mon–Sat 10–5pm; Sun 2:30–5pm.

Impressions Gallery of Photography – 17 Colliergate, Tel 654724. Impressions was the first photographic gallery to open outside of London, in 1972. There are three galleries showing a wide range of photographic exhibitions, both contemporary and historical and also darkrooms, courses and workshops. There is a good bookshop. Open Mon–Sat 10:30–5:30pm.

THEATRE

Theatre Royal – St Leonard's Place, Tel 23568. There has been a theatre on this site since 1765 although the building has often been reconstructed over the years. The auditorium and stage of the current theatre date from 1902, but in 1967 the stalls were reseated to accommodate a new cloakroom and exhibition space. At the same time an entrance foyer, restaurant and bars were added in the new glass-walled pavilion at the side of the theatre. The theatre offers a stock programme of classics and quality contemporary drama. It also hosts tours and concerts and produces an annual panto. There is a good restaurant open for lunch and pre-theatre dinner and a bar. Recent productions have included Noel Coward's *Private Lives*, Willy Russell's *One for the Road* and adaptations of *Pride and Prejudice*, *Wuthering Heights* and Catherine Cookson's *Fifteen Streets*.

Grand Opera House – Clifford Street, Tel 654654. This rather splendid building was refurbished at a cost of £2 million, opened as a touring house for ten months and then closed. As I write, the owners are looking for a buyer. Let's hope it will be someone who intends to use the building for a theatrical purpose. As York is one of the foremost tourist attractions in the country, it would seem logical that another theatre could be successful here.

York Arts Centre – St John the Evangelist Church, Micklegate, offers a varied programme of music, film, drama, poetry and dance in the intimate setting in this converted church. Restaurant and bar. Tel 627129.

The **York Festival and Mystery Plays** – The major cultural event in York is the **Quadrennial Festival** scheduled in 1992 and 1996 for three weeks in June. The York Festival embraces music, poetry, theatre, film and visual arts. Visitors have included the BBC Philharmonic Orchestra, the Royal Liverpool Philharmonic, Claudio Arrau, Janet Baker and Paul Tortelier. The Minster is the setting for most of the large-scale concerts, while chamber and solo recitals are presented in some of the city's many ancient halls and churches. There is a lively interest in new music at York and works by Richard Rodney Bennett, Virgil Thomson and Elizabeth Lutgens have premiered here.

The centrepiece of the Festival is the York cycle of **Mystery Plays**. These were originally written and performed by the city's ancient craft guilds, beginning in 1340. Each guild had its own play, performed from a wagon, and the cycle spanned the whole Bible, from Creation to the Last Judgement. There appears to have been some logical reasoning with respect to which guild played what story. The Shipwrights were responsible for the "Building of the Ark," while the story of Noah and the Flood was given to the Fishers and Mariners. The Armourers took responsibility for Adam and Eve driven from the Garden of Eden (cherubim with flaming swords, did after all, keep the apple-eating pair from returning) and the Visit of the Three Kings to the stable at Bethlehem was the responsibility of the Goldsmiths. The plays were presented every year on Corpus Christi in June. The wagons were pulled through the city streets, each stopping at a dozen points en route to perform. The performances went on from dawn to dusk. Today the Mystery Plays are staged at a specially created arena among the ruins of St Mary's Abbey. The original texts have been retained and the performers are almost entirely the people of York. The Mystery Plays are a compelling and moving experience and now attract thousands of people from around the world.

MUSIC

York Early Music Festival is held annually except during the Quadrennial Festival (see above). The Festival has earned a distinguished reputation in its few short years. The programme of concerts is designed to appeal to both specialist and general audiences alike. A recent festival has as its theme "Gods, Dreams and Fancies," and visitors have included the Consort of Musicke (Anthony Rooley, its director, is director of the Early Music Festival as I write), the Rose Consort of Viols and the Boston Camerata. There is an excellent children's programme. Throughout the year, concerts are held in a variety of venues around the city. The best place to get up-to-date musical information is from Ticket World, 6 Patrick Pool, Church Street, Tel 644194.

The University of York is situated on a lovely 190-acre (77 ha) campus at Heslington, just outside the city boundary. Its concerts, theatre performances and lecture series are open to the public. Tel 430000.
The Sir Jack Lyons Concert Hall, along with the Minster, hosts performances by large orchestras and there is also a large Central Hall. Look out for performances by the Yorkshire Bach Choir. They are excellent and they generally perform in St Michael-le-Bilfrey Church. Details from Ticket World, Tel 644194 or from YBC Monk Stray House, Stocton Lane.

CINEMA
Commercial cinema:
Warner Cinemas – Clifton Moor, Tel 691094 (multi screen).
Odeon – Blossom Street, Tel 623040.

Of more interest is the **York Film Theatre**, University of York, 1566 Haxby Road, Tel 612940, which presents a regular programme of quality films, including classic, contemporary and world cinema offerings. Also of interest is **City Screen** at the Yorkshire Museum, which also shows quality programmes. Tel 629745.

BOOKSTORES
York is well served for bookshops and for once the national chains do not overshadow the local dealers. **Waterstone's** at 28/29 High Ousegate, Tel 628740, is as good as always, as is **Dillon's** at 9/10 High Ousegate, Tel 610044. The locals are also excellent. **Pickering and Co** at 42 The Shambles, Tel 627888, was established in 1858 and has a wonderful aviation section, while **Godfreys** at 32 Stonegate, Tel 624531, opened for business in 1906. Having a long established business doesn't necessarily ensure excellence but in these two cases it does. If you are out at the University of York, you will find another **Godfreys** bookshop on campus. For the others, **Barbican Bookshop** at 24 Fossegate, Tel 653643, **John Bibby** at 1 Straylands Grove, **Blake Head Bookshop** at 104 Micklegate, Tel 623767, the **Bookcellar** at 10 Parliament Street, **Forum Books** at 45A Blossom Street, Tel 625495, and **Edwin Story**, 9 Minster Gates, Tel 622270, are all of interest. For religious books, **SPCK** at 20 Goodramgate, Tel 654176 is best, while for music and music books, **Philip Martin Music Books**, 22 Huntingdon, Tel 636111, is the best bet. For paperbacks, **Penguin Bookshop**, 21 Coppergate, Tel 654074, is excellent, and there is a good children's selection at **Puffin Bookshop**, 14 Coppergate, Tel 647174. There's a good selection of comics, science fiction and fantasy at NUEarth Comics, 4 Davygate Centre, Tel 611461, while for all leisure-time activities, try **Leisure Books** at 52 Gillygate, Tel 652410.

ANTIQUARIAN AND SECONDHAND BOOKS
Some excellent shops in York, among the best selection in the country. I've divided the shops geographically, into three areas:

Micklegate Area:
O'Flynn Antiquarian Books – 35 Micklegate, Tel 641404. General secondhand collection with some antiquarian books.
Ken Spelman – 70 Micklegate, Tel 624414. Very large stock of secondhand and antiquarian books on most subjects. Emphasis on fine arts, history and literature. Also has prints, maps and watercolours with occasional exhibitions.
Inch's Books – 54 Blossom Street, Tel 627082. Specialists in art and design subjects.

Fossegate Area:
Jack Duncan Books – 36 Fossegate, Tel 641389. Four booksellers on three floors in one shop. **John Hepworth** specializes in design and fine and applied art as well as sports, West Riding of Yorkshire, and some military and social history. **Mark Christodolou Books** has an excellent selection of books on medieval subjects. **Phillip Martin Music Books** has music books and scores while **Pandion Books** specializes in natural history and related subjects.
Barbican Bookshop – 24 Fossegate, Tel 653643. Twelve rooms of secondhand and antiquarian books. Specialities include a large theological department and also British topography. There are good selections of angling, architecture, history, literature and sport.
Passageway Book Room – 33C Fossegate, Tel 641389. (The passageway leading to the Book Room is on the left of Fossegate, just before the 18th-century bridge.) Wide-ranging secondhand and antiquarian selection. Literature and the arts are the main areas of specialization.

Minster Area:
Minster Gates Bookshop – 8 Minster Gates, Tel 621812. Good selection of secondhand and antiquarian books. Large stock of illustrated and children's books, history, literature, finely bound sets and folklore.
Taikoo Books Ltd – 29 High Petergate, Tel 641213. Good antiquarian and secondhand selection on Africa, the Orient and big game hunting.
The Chaucer Head – 41 Low Petergate, Tel 622000. Specializing in economics, economic and social history, science and medicine but good out-of-print books in all fields.
Rose Fine Art and Goodramgate Book Centre – Tel 641841. Antiquarian and secondhand books specializing in topography, sports and the arts.

ART GALLERIES

For antiquarian and decorative prints try **Thornburn Galleries**, 36 Fossgate, Tel 641389 and **Griffiths and Sharp** (at Past Times) 28 Castlegate, Tel 611608. **Rose Fine Art**, 58C Coodramgate, Tel 641841, also has prints as well as 19th-century watercolours and oils. **Walmgate Gallery**, 13 Walmgate, Tel 610345, also has original oil and watercolours as well as sculpture and some interesting stained glass. The **Stonegate Gallery**, 52A Stonegate, Tel 635141, has monthly exhibitions of pictures by both local and national artists in all media but not prints or photography. Close by is **Stonegate Fine Arts** at 47 Stonegate, Tel 643771, with fine oils and watercolours. Likewise, the **Grape Lane Gallery**, 17 Grape Lane, Tel 643825, has exhibitions of exclusively contemporary art by both nationally recognized and new artists. There is also a comprehensive stock of prints, ceramics and pottery. Ceramics too, at **Pyramid Craft and Design Gallery**, 10 Gillygatge, Tel 641187, plus glass, textiles, wood and jewellery. The **Japanese Print Shop**, 38 High Petergate, Tel 651080, has beautiful 19th-century Japanese woodblock prints. **Coulter Galleries**, 90 Tadcaster Road, Tel 706537, and **Robert Coulter**, 19 The Horseshoe, Tel 702101, both have pre-1900 watercolours and oils, while **French Fine Arts**, 1 Goodramgate, Tel 654266, has some fine oils. **Fettes Fine Art**, Meadow Court, Middlethorpe, Tel 641344, has early Victorian pictures and 18th-century oils and watercolours of the European School. Finally, two shops dealing mainly with watercolours and oils of local scenes. **Miniature Gallery**, 21 The Shambles, Tel 635187, and **A T Stuttle**, 50 Micklegate, who also has limited-edition prints.

ANTIQUE DEALERS

A good area to begin is around the Minster. **Barker Court Antiques and Bygones**, 44 Gillygate, Tel 622611, has pottery, porcelain, glass and plated items from the Victorian era to 1930. Walk up Gillygate with the city wall on your right and turn right into Lord Mayor's Walk. Here at No 26 is **St John's Antiques**, Tel 644263, with Victorian stripped pine and satinwood furniture. Turn left at the end of Lord Mayor's Walk and turn right into Goodramgate where at No 31/33 is **Bobbins**, Tel 653597, with small furniture, general antiques, art deco, clocks and oil lamps. Close by is **The Shambles** with **Inez Yates** at No 5: small furniture, porcelain, paintings, jewellery and collectors' items, Tel 654821, **R K Himsworth** at No 28 with Victorian jewellery and silver, Tel 629381, and close by, in the curiously named Whip-ma-Whop-ma-Gate, **Yon Antiques**, who have Georgian to art nouveau general antiques, Tel 627928. Just west of The Shambles is Stonegate where at No 45 can be found **Barbara Cattle**, Tel 623862, who has some nice jewellery and silver (Georgian to present day). Walk to the bottom of Stonegate, turn left onto Daygate Street, right onto Coppergate and then right again onto Fossegate where at No 42 is **Thacker's Antiques**, Tel 633077. They have a large stock of furniture and bric-à-brac and they're next to Merchant Adventurers' Hall. Continue down Fossegate and you will come to Walmgate where at No 11 you will find the fascinating **Clocks and Gramophones**. They have wind-up gramophones dating from 1905–1940 and clocks from 1800–1940, they also have 78 rpm records, Tel 611924. If you cross the Skeldergate Bridge by the Castle you will find yourself in Bishopgate Street with **Bishopgate Antiques**, Tel 623893, at No 23/24. They have a large stock of general antiques. Turn left into Nunnery Lane and follow the city walls until turning left into Blossom Street. Fork right into Holgate Road and **Holgate Antiques**, Tel 30005, with general antiques, furniture and bric-à-brac. Turn left off Holgate Street onto Dalton Terrace and you will find yourself in The Mount, not far from York Racecourse. At No 120 is **Aitken Antiques**, Tel 656211, with a large and excellent stock of English furniture 1700–1900, and general antiques. At No 131 is **Robert Morrison and Sons**, Tel 655394, with English furniture 1700–1900, porcelain and clocks. Neither of these should be missed. Nor should **Danby Antiques**, Tel 415280, at 61 Heworth Road, who stock 18th–19th-century boxes, writing accessories, small furniture and collectables. They are a mile from the city centre on the A1036. Turn right at Heyworth Green Road junction and the shop is 100 yards on your left. Well worth a visit. Finally, the **York Antiques Centre**, Tel 641582, is at 2 Lendal (just through the Museum Gardens). They have 20 dealers selling all manner of antiques and collectables.

RESTAURANTS

Kites – 13 Grape Lane, Tel 641750. I really like Kites, in spite of the stairs. It's unpretentious, fun and the food is excellent. The choice is huge. I can recommend the aubergine with pesto, the lamb and the banoffi pie (just one of a large number of superb desserts). Vegetarians are catered for in style, not just as an afterthought, and the cooking is full of ideas and excellent value. Sunday lunch is very good value indeed and the set dinner includes half a bottle of wine. Open Mon–Sat dinner only. Sun lunch 12–2 and 6:30–10:30pm.

19 Grape Lane – 19 Grape Lane, Tel 636366. Just down the road is this not too imaginatively named restaurant. Considering it was destroyed by fire and rebuilt in the late 1980s, it's recovered really well. The set menus are the best value – they nearly always are, with the salmon and lamb both highly recommended. The set lunch is especially good value.

Miller's Yard Café – Millers Yard, Gillygate, Tel 610676. The café is run as a worker's co-operative with the Gillygate Wholefood Bakery, which you should visit after your meal. The café is self-service and situated near the City Art Gallery. The bread and pastries here are very imaginative. Hot and cold dishes are equally good. I still remember the aubergine and potato curry and friends were wildly enthusiastic about the tofu cheesecake. Open Mon–Sat noon–2:30pm.

Betty's – 6-8 St Helen's Square, Tel 659142. A stylish, elegant tea room with a real pianist in the evenings. York is a wonderful place to have afternoon tea and there's no better place to have it than here. Excellent service. Fine tea with scones, muffins and a fine Yorkshire rarebit with ham. In the evening, the chicken provençale and the scrambled eggs with smoked salmon are well spoken of. They also do good breakfasts. Open all week 9am–9pm.

Taylors Tea Rooms – 46 Stonegate, Tel 622865. Owned by the same firm as Betty's, Taylors is located in a handsome 16th-century building and serves excellent tea and coffee. The sandwiches, omelettes and things on toast are all excellent, but in Taylors as well as Betty's you must expect to pay quite high prices which reflect the city's tremendous popularity with tourists. I should add that it's not just Taylors, but everywhere in York!

PUBS

Black Swan – Peasholme Green, Tel 625236. The Black Swan was a private house from the early 15th to the mid-18th century. It was once the home of Martin Bowes, goldsmith to Queen Elizabeth and twice Lord Mayor of London. Sir Martin, as he became, presented the Sword of State to the city, which is still borne before the Lord Mayor on special occasions. General James Wolfe, who defeated the French general Louis Montcalm at Quebec in 1759, spent his boyhood in the house. The pub is much what you would expect, given its claim to be York's oldest. There are heavy oak beams, wall panelling and a vast inglenook fireplace. There's even a period staircase leading upstairs. Traditional bar food. Oh yes, it's also haunted (see Ephemera) and a room on the first floor was used for illegal cock fighting in the 17th century and has a grille set in the wall where a guard could overlook the main staircase for signs of law enforcement officers.

King's Arms – Kings Straithe, Tel 659435. In a fine spot by the river, this ancient pub has picnic tables set on a cobbled riverside terrace. Unusually, the pub's "cellar" is above ground in a nearby building as the area is prone to flooding. There are bare brick and stone walls inside with a flagstoned floor and bowed black ceiling beams. Traditional bar food.

Olde Starre – Stonegate. The pub dates from 1644 but it has a Victorian layout with rambling beamed rooms, oak Victorian settles and cast-iron tables. There's an open fireplace and from the courtyard you can see the roofs of the Shambles with the Minster's tower looming beyond. Traditional bar food and a nice wine bar.

Angler's Arms – Goodramgate, Tel 656138. A nice town centre pub with imaginative bar food (fish pie is especially good). It has three ghosts; on the top floor, a spirit which announces itself by a whiff of lavender; on the middle floor, the ghost of a friendly Victorian child who was killed by a brewer's dray as she ran from the pub's door and in the cellar, a malevolent spirit which often turns off the gas taps which pump the beer from the cellar to the bar. Neither the pub cat nor the dog will ever venture into the cellar and the landlady won't go there alone.

Hole in the Wall – High Petergate, Tel 634468. Very friendly pub, cheerful and inviting with excellent bar food. Their roast beef sandwiches are a legend in the city. Just down the road is the **York Arms**, Tel 624508, which is another of York's haunted pubs. There is a dispute as to the exact nature of the pub's resident spirit. Some claim it is a child, but the more common belief is that it is the famous Grey Lady who inhabits the Theatre Royal (see Ephemera). In spite of the ghost's activities, which include moving objects and opening and shutting doors, this beautiful old pub continues to flourish, serving good bar food in a friendly atmosphere.

ARTISTIC ASSOCIATIONS

The famous scholar Alcuin, author of many philosophical works, was born in the city in 735 and became Master of the Cathedral School and later Archbishop. After meeting Charlemagne, he became Master of the great king's Palace School at Aachen.

The hero of Sir Walter Scott's *Ivanhoe*, home from the Crusades, is helped by Isaac the Jew, who lives in Castlegate, where Ivanhoe is nursed by Isaac's daughter Rebecca (Robert and Elizabeth Taylor in the film!).

Laurence Sterne, the novelist, was made a prebendary of York Minster in 1741. His great book, *Tristram Shandy*, was published in York but many in the city disapproved of it as its characters were based on real-life York residents. The city's unease about the book did not prevent it from becoming a huge popular success.

The 19th-century novelist, Harrison Ainsworth, in his book *Rookwood* (1834), greatly romanticized the life of the notorious poacher, thief and highwayman, Dick Turpin. As children, we were taught about his famous ride to York but it is pretty certain that it was not Turpin who made the journey but another equally celebrated robber, "Swift" John Nevinson, who in 1676 is said to have robbed a sailor in Gadshill at 4am and to have established an alibi by reaching York at 7:45pm the same day. Charles II, hearing of the feat, is said to have been amused and granted Nevinson a free pardon, christening him "Swift Nicks." Nevinson's luck did not last too long as he was hanged at York in 1685. Turpin, on the other hand, appeared to change his ways, for after riding north from Essex he changed his name and settled in the city as a gentleman. It didn't last, however. He was caught stealing a horse and a letter to his brother, demanding an alibi, was intercepted. He spent three months in the old Debtors' Prison, now part of the Castle Museum, and was hanged on the 7th of April, 1739. He had also been accused of murdering an Epping gamekeeper. Friends took his body to the Blue Boar Inn on Castlegate to cheat the grave robbers, and later buried him in St George's Church in Lead Mill Lane where his grave can be seen today. In York Castle Museum, the condemned cell where Dick Turpin spent his last hours has been preserved.

William Etty was a baker's son who became York's most famous painter, although at one time he was condemned for "impropriety and lasciviousness" for his many paintings of nudes. In 1822 he went to Italy, where he was greatly influenced by the Venetian masters. He depicted historical and classical subjects but was really at his best when working on a less ambitious scale. He was considered by many to be England's greatest figure painter, and his nudes, despite the reservations of some of the public, represent his best work!

The famous poet W H Auden, was born in York in 1907 into a family of physicians. Early in life he was interested in science and intended to become a mining engineer, but by the age of 15 he had discovered an abiding interest in poetry. In 1924 his first poem was published, and at Oxford Auden developed a formidable reputation as a poet and thinker. He later became an American citizen. His prodigious output includes several volumes of poetry, libretti for opera, travel books and criticism. He won a Pulitzer Prize for literature, gained the National Book Award and was Professor of Poetry at Oxford in 1956. He died in 1973.

EPHEMERA

York has the reputation of being Europe's most haunted city. I have already mentioned some instances of spirits inhabiting pubs, but the three very different psychic manifestations mentioned below deserve attention. Life was difficult and dangerous for Roman Catholics in the latter half of the 16th century. Margaret Clitherow, wife of a wealthy butcher who lived in The Shambles, converted to Catholicism and began to lead a brave and dangerous life by attending mass and offering refuge to priests at a time when both these activities were illegal. In 1586, she was caught and, refusing to testify at her trial, she was sentenced to die on the 25th of March. A door was placed on top of her prostrate body and piled with heavy stones until she was slowly crushed to death. She was canonized in 1970 and her home at No 35 The Shambles is now a shrine to her memory. Nearly everyone who enters her house comments on the uncanny peace and stillness that surrounds her home in spite of the front door opening onto one of the busiest streets in York.

Although Margaret Clitherow's presence is not marked by any visible manifestation, this is not the case with the Grey Lady of York's Theatre Royal. The theatre is built on the site of the medieval St Leonard's Hospital, which was one of the greatest hospitals of its day, and was served by a small order of nuns. One of them broke her holy orders by falling in love with a young man of noble descent. The lovers were discovered by the Mother Superior, and the youthful nun was made to pay for her indiscretion in a most horrible way. She was thrown into a windowless room which was then locked and sealed by a wall of bricks, leaving her to starve or suffocate. Today, a room behind the dress circle, infamous for its cold atmosphere, is thought to be the area where the nun ended her earthly life. More significantly, there have been numerous sightings of a whitish-grey apparition, misty yet clearly definable as a nun. Remarkably, the ghost always appears to be friendly and to take an active interest in what is going on in the theatre. A tradition has arisen that if this benign spirit is seen during rehearsals, the production is assured of success.

Finally, the Black Swan has perhaps the most famous ghost in York. She is a young woman with beautiful hair, wearing a long light dress glowing with an incandescent brightness. Despite her many appearances, no one has ever seen her face since she is always either staring down into the glowing coals of the pub fire or gazing thoughtfully out of the window with her back turned to the living inhabitants of the pub. She is infinitely preferable to the pub's second ghost, a small miserable man with a bowler hat who sits at a table waiting in an irritated way for someone who never arrives. After ten minutes he gives up and slowly dissolves into the air from whence he came.

Designed in the 19th century to be the hub of the North Eastern Railway, York was, and still is, the only really important railway capital apart from Derby. When it was built in 1873–77 to replace the old station within the city walls, York Station was the largest in the world. With its magnificent curved three-span train shed, it is one of the greatest buildings of Victorian England.

One of the principal treasures of York Minster is the great ivory drinking horn, over two feet (60 cm) in length, known as Ulph's Horn. Ulph was a Danish chieftain who held lands in western Yorkshire at the beginning of the 11th century. Legend relates how his eldest son, Adelbert, was killed in battle and Ulph attempted to bypass the claims of his other three sons and bequeath his lands to Adelbert's daughter, Adelwynne. She, however, persuaded him to bestow his lands on the church. Accordingly, Ulph rode to York, taking with him his largest drinking horn. Filling it with wine, he knelt at the high altar in York Minster and, drinking off the wine, laid the horn on the altar, to be held by the church for all time as title to the lands over which he held sway and to all his wealth.

Perhaps York's most infamous citizen is Guy Fawkes who, in the Gunpowder Plot of 1605, attempted to blow up King James I and the Houses of Parliament. Fawkes was born in 1570 in what is now Young's Hotel in Petergate and baptized at St Michael-le-Belfry, next to York Minster. The church's baptismal registry is now in the Minster Library. He attended St Peter's School on Bootham where he met many of his fellow conspirators. On November 4th, Fawkes and the gunpowder were discovered and he was hanged and quartered in

London on January 31st, 1606. The 5th of November, the day Parliament was supposed to explode, is still celebrated all over England as Guy Fawkes Day with bonfires, fireworks and the burning of Fawkes in effigy. Everywhere, that is, except St Peter's School in York.

Finally, the story of two rival saints. William Fitzherbert, nephew of King Stephen, was canonized in the 12th century. Thirty-six miracles were attributed to him, the most famous being his feat in saving hundreds of onlookers thrown into the River Ouse when a bridge collapsed in 1154. (The waters formed themselves into a bridge over which the good citizens reached dry land.) During the Middle Ages, St William's fame was rivalled by that of John of Beverley, his predecessor at York during the 8th century. A healthy rivalry grew up between the cults of these two Yorkshire saints, culminating in a miracle attributed to both of them. The devil caused a young student of Beverley to fall so much in love with a local girl that he lost all taste for his books. To make a young man fall out of love took all the powers of a saint but one of them – either William or John – intervened and the student was restored to his "right" mind. William's miracles are recorded in a beautiful stained-glass window, known as St William's window, in the north transept of York Minster.

More than most historic cities, York has a profusion of secret paths and alleys which are known locally as "snickle ways." Almost all evolved as the paths that people took to church, to market and to work. Following them is fun, giving a glimpse of hidden treasures between and behind the shop fronts and busy streets. Over 50 short snickle ways lie within a quarter of a mile (400 m) of York's most famous street, The Shambles; almost every one is a tiny oasis of quiet, more often in shadow than in sun. To see what I mean, seek out Lund's Court, Pope's Head Lane, Coffee Yard and Straker's Passage. Here perhaps, are the real ghosts of York.

TOURIST INFORMATION BUREAU: De Grey Rooms, Exhibition Square, York, North Yorkshire, Y01 2HB. Tel (0904) 621756

9

SCOTLAND

DUNDEE
EDINBURGH
GLASGOW
PERTH AND PITLOCHRY
ST ANDREWS

DUNDEE

County of Angus
434 miles (694.4 km) from London by road (M1,M6,A7,M90,A85)
By rail, 6 hours from London (King's Cross)

There was a Roman settlement in Dundee in 834. Kenneth MacAlpine used the town as his base when he set out to conquer the Picts and become first King of Scotland. The first settlement, however, was probably a small fishing community between Craig Pier and Castlehill, from which grew the seaport. Dundee was granted a royal charter in the late 12th century, and about that time the Church of St Mary was established. Today the handsome Parish Church with its famous old steeple stands on the site and acts as a focal point for the city. The original church had hardly been completed when, in 1296, Edward I of England sacked the city and burned the church in a foray from England, which resulted in the loss of the Stone of Destiny from Scone. The church was rebuilt, and in 1385 was burnt yet again by an English army. The next rebuilding was on a very ambitious scale, with the addition of the great bell tower, now known as the "Old Steeple." But the church's troubles were not over. In 1547 an English fleet sailed up the Firth of Tay, besieged the city and once again destroyed the church. The only consolation this time was that when the Reformers, spurred by the words of John Knox, descended on the city there was nothing left for them to tear down. In due course St Mary's rose again in splendour – and was burned again. All that now remains of the great 15th-century parish church is the "Old Steeple" (containing historical displays and open to the public), while on the main site, set among gardens in the very heart of the city, the City Churches have risen, housing three congregations under one cruciform roof.

In 1644 a Dundee regiment fought against the Royalist cause at the Battle of Marston Moor. A reprisal for this action was undertaken a year later when the Royalist Marquess of Montrose sacked and burned the town. Dundee was having no luck at all during this period because there were worse disasters to follow. In 1651 Oliver Cromwell sent General Monck to seek out Stuart sympathizers in Scotland. The city council removed all the valuables they owned to the Old Steeple, thinking it would be a safe sanctuary. Monck's men, however, sacked the city and, gathering all the old books and documents from the church library, stacked them round the tower and set them on fire. This time the city took nearly a century to recover.

The citizens of Dundee supported the 1715 Jacobite rebellion and James Stuart (the Old Pretender) was proclaimed as James VIII when he visited the town in 1716. In the period prior to the Jacobite rebellion led by Bonnie Prince Charlie (the Young Pretender) in 1745, Dundee had become prosperous through the flax and linen industry. When Lord Ogilvy of Airlie took the city for Charles Stuart in 1745, he found it necessary to lock up the Provost and City Council. Dundee, it seems, had decided that espousal of the Jacobite cause was a threat to economic progress. When news of Charles Stuart's crushing defeat was received in Dundee there was public rejoicing and a few months later the freedom of the city was conferred on the Duke of Cumberland who had been sent by King George II to put down the Scottish rebels. Considering that Cumberland's ruthlessness earned him the nickname of "Butcher," and taking into account the city's fervent support for Bonnie Prince Charlie's father, Cumberland's reception seems an odd display of changed loyalties.

The linen industry continued to flourish and in 1822 the East India Company sent samples of a new fibre, called jute, to England. To make it more workable it was necessary to add whale oil to the jute and since there was a long-established whaling industry in nearby Broughton Ferry, and an abundance of workers used to working in textiles, the boom in the spinning and weaving of flax began. Within 50 years the population of Dundee leapt from 35,000 to 130,000 and the prosperity lasted for more than 100 years until India herself developed the technology to manufacture the raw material. Jute is still vital to the the city's economy, but there has been considerable diversification among the old jute firms into new processes and new fabrics. A wealth of new industries, including engineering and bronze casting, have come to the city in the 20th century, and the harbour facilities and shipbuilding industry have been transformed in recent years by the advent of North Sea oil.

Because of numerous fires and destructive visitations, Dundee has little to show of its past. The city seems prone to pull down the old to make way for the new – in 1931 they demolished the beautiful town house built by William Adam in 1734. There are however, a number of plaques from which some history may be traced. One of these is in front of St Paul's Scottish Episcopal Cathedral (built by Sir Gilbert Scott in 1853) and it marks the site of Dundee Castle, which was razed to the ground in 1314 by Robert the Bruce because he considered it useless; another commemorates Mary Wollstonecraft Shelley, creator of *Frankenstein* (see Artistic Associations). There is really little of architectural interest in Dundee apart from the City Churches and the Old Steeple, the Victorian Museum and Library, and the Cowgate or East Port, which is all that remains of the town walls destroyed after the Battle of Culloden in 1746. On the outskirts of the city are Caird Park, in which can be seen the 16th-century Mains of Fintry Castle, and Camperdown Park, with Camperdown House, where there is an interesting museum of golfing relics. Finally, a walk or drive to The Law, the plug or core of an extinct volcano, once the site of a vitrified fort, affords a magnificent view of the city and surrounding area from its position 571 feet (173.5 m) above sea level.

WALK

The **Dundee Walk** – Start at the car park by the swimming pool and leisure centre off Riverside Drive by the Tay Road Bridge. Walk across to the riverside for a view of the **River Tay** and its bridges. Note the **Tay Bridge Monument**. Continue under the road bridge to Victoria Dock and **HMS Unicorn** and Captain Scott's **Discovery**. Close by is the **Custom House**. Follow Commercial Street to the junction with Meadowside for the **Museum and Art Gallery**. (Barrack Street Museum is a little further on to the left.) Follow Meadowside and turn left onto Reform Street to High Street for **Old Steeple** and the **Mercat Cross**. Turn left on High Street, go ahead to Nethergate, cross Market Gate and turn right onto South Tay Street for the **Dundee Repertory Theatre**. Retrace your steps to the junction of Nethergate and Marketgate and follow Marketgate towards the river until it meets Riverside Drive. Turn left and cross Riverside Drive back to the car park.

MUSEUMS AND GALLERIES

Barrack Street Museum – Barrack St, Ward Road, Tel 23141. Open Mon–Sat 10–5pm. Dundee's natural history museum. Displays illustrate the wildlife of the Dundee area, the geology and wildlife of the Lowlands and Highlands of Scotland and the Scottish coast. Exhibits include an observation beehive and the skeleton of the Great Tay Whale.

McManus Galleries – Albert Square, Tel 23141. Open Mon–Sat 12–5pm. Occupies a recently restored Victorian Gothic building designed by Gilbert Scott. The local history section has displays relating to the social and civic history of Dundee, to the trade and industry of the area and to archaeology. The art galleries contain collections of 19th- and 20th-century paintings, mainly by Scottish artists, as well as sculpture and ceramics.

Mills Observatory – Balgay Park, Glamis Road, Tel 67183/23141. Open April–Sept Mon–Fri 10–5, Sat 2–5; Oct–March Mon–Fri 3–10pm Sat.2–5pm. The Mills Observatory is Britain's only full-time public observatory. It is located in picturesque Balgay Park, two miles west of the city centre, and it houses a 10-inch (25.4 cm) Cooke refracting telescope. During the winter months viewing of the night sky is possible. There is a small planetarium, an audio-visual room and an exhibition of telescopes and scientific instruments.

Broughty Castle Museum – Broughty Ferry, Tel 76121. Open Mon–Thurs. 10–1 and 2–5pm, Sun 2–5pm (July–Sept) closed Fridays. Broughty Castle is a 15th-century estuary fort, six miles (9.6 km) from Dundee. Besieged by the English in the 16th century, and by Cromwell's army in the 17th century, it was left a ruin, but restored in 1861 as part of Britain's coastal defences. The museum has displays of local history, arms and armour and Dundee's whaling industry.

The Unicorn – Victoria Dock, Tel 23141. Open April–mid-Oct Wed–Mon 11–5pm. The *Unicorn*, a 46-gun frigate, was launched in 1824. It is the oldest British-built warship afloat and is now being restored to its original condition. Naval guns and other artefacts of the period help to tell the story of how 19th-century sailors lived, ate, slept and fought on board. **Captain Scott's Royal Research Ship Discovery** – Victoria Dock, Tel 201175. Open 21st March-31st of May Weekdays 1–5pm, Sats, Suns, Pub Hols. 11–5pm. 1st June–31st of Aug Daily 10–5pm. 1st Sept–7th Oct Weekdays 1–5pm, Sats, Suns, Pub Hols. 11–5pm. Across

H.M. FRIGATE UNICORN, DUNDEE

the dock from the *Unicorn* lies Captain Scott's *Discovery*. Built in Dundee with the lines of a whaler to withstand the ice of an Antarctic winter, the ship lies not far from where she was built in 1901. A guided tour gives an insight into the heroic story of Antarctic exploration and the character of the men who endured hardship in the pursuit of science and glory. A new heritage centre with shops, restaurants and leisure facilities is being built and will be open when this book comes to press.

Seagate Gallery – 38–40 Seagate, Tel 26331. Open Mon–Sat 10–5:30pm. Admission free. A gallery with visiting exhibitions of paintings, sculpture and photography.

The **Dundee Printmaker's Workshop** is at the same location and features the work of local artists. Open Mon–Fri 9:30–5pm, Sat 10–5pm, Sun. 12 noon–5pm. Mon–Thurs evening 6:30–9. Also worth taking a look at are the **Dundee Arts Centre**, St Mary Place, Tel 201035, and the **Windsor Gallery** at 61 Perth Road, Tel 202863.

THEATRE

Dundee Repertory Theatre – Tay Square, Tel 23530. Dundee Repertory Theatre was founded in 1939 (hardly an auspicious time for launching such an enterprise) and opened in a home in the Forresters Hall with a production of James Elroy Flecker's *Hassan*. Flecker's play is noted for its extreme length and the story goes that one gentleman, who had come alone, asked for a certificate when the curtain finally fell to prove to his wife that he really had spent all those hours in the theatre. In spite of the outbreak of the war the theatre prospered, even though it was forced to run a weekly season with a new show each Monday evening! In 1963 disaster struck when the theatre was completely destroyed by fire. The company struggled on, performing in a cinema and a marquee in the park, then finally finding temporary refuge in a converted church – temporary, that is, for 18 years! The building was woefully inadequate for the needs of the expanding and ambitious company and plans for a new theatre were developed. In 1982 the company moved into the attractive 450-seat "open stage" auditorium, which has a sense of intimacy unmatched by any theatre in Scotland. Productions have ranged from Shakespeare, Chekhov and Shaw, through Miller and Stoppard, to a policy of presenting the work of little-known Scottish playwrights. One exciting venture of the company is the establishment of the Dundee Rep Dance Company, which as well as providing classes for the community, has an extensive touring and in-house production schedule. There is also a Community Dance Team and a flourishing Youth Theatre Workshop.

The Theatre Restaurant is open from 10:30am to 10:45pm for coffee, lunch, snacks, afternoon tea, pre-theatre dinners or late suppers. There is an art gallery with visiting exhibitions and a bar open from 11am–2:30 and 5pm–11pm

Bonar Hall, Park Place and the **Whitehall Theatre** in Bellfield Street also have theatre performances. For programme details phone Dundee Central Booking office, Tel 202513. Events at Bonar Hall and Whitehall Theatre have included performances by Tayside Opera, Wildcat Theatre and the excellent Scottish Touring Theatre Company "7:84".

MUSIC

Although Dundee does not have its own symphony orchestra it does have regular concerts given by the Scottish National Orchestra which are performed in the **Caird Hall**. Tel 202513 for details. The Caird Hall also hosts a variety of musical events ranging from pop concerts to a wonderful fiddler's rally.

The **Dundee Chamber Music Club** sponsors regular concerts at the Music Centre, Bell Street. Tel 202513 for details. For both theatre and musical events at **Dundee University** call 202513 or 23181.

CINEMA

Commercial cinema at Cannon Theatre, Seagate. Tel 25247. Of more interest, I think, is the **Steps Film Theatre**, Wellgate Centre. Tel 23141 or 24983 (after 5pm and Sats), which presents a varied programme of classic, modern and foreign films throughout the year. Recent programmes included a double bill of *Jean de Florette* and *Manon des Sources*, Kenneth Branagh's *Henry V* and Woody Allen's *Crimes and Misdemeanors*.

BOOKSTORES

The best, as in St Andrews and Perth, is **James Thin** at 7 High Street, Tel 23999. **John Smith and Son** in Airlie Place is the Glasgow Smith and not "W H" and consequently worth a browse. The **University Bookshop** at 96 Nethergate also has a good selection of non-academic books. The excellence of Dundee

University's Medical Faculty is reflected in the **Medical Bookshop** at Ninewell's Hospital, Tel 66551 – well, everyone needs a copy of Gray's Anatomy. Finally, Christian literature can be found at **Christian Literature Crusade**, 23 Commercial St, Tel 26859, and **Church of Scotland Bookshop** at 112 Nethergate, Tel 200075.

ANTIQUARIAN, AND SECONDHAND BOOKS

The best antiquarian and secondhand book store in Dundee is across the Tay Bridge in Newport-on-Tay. This may seem a contradiction but Newport is essentially a suburb of Dundee. (Oh dear, lots of letters refuting this from the good folk of Newport.) Anyway, **Mair Wilkes Books** at 3 St Mary's Lane, Tel 542260, has a good stock of antiquarian and out of print books – far better than anything I could discover within the city limits of Dundee.

ART GALLERIES

The gallery with the largest selection, but not necessarily the best gallery, is **Picture Factory** at Jamaica Works, Jamaica Street, Tel 23800. A wide selection ranging from the very interesting to rubbish! For me personally, the **Eduardo Alessandro Studios** at 30 Gray Broughton Ferry is the most interesting. Tel 737011. They deal in Scottish contemporary art – paintings, lithographs, prints – and should not be missed. The same goes for **Dundee Printmakers Workshop** at the Seagate Gallery (see Galleries above). The **Dundee Art Society**, 17 Roseangle often has interesting work, Tel 22429, while **Fraser and Son**, at 38 Commercial Street, Tel 25284, has a wide stock of limited editions, contemporary prints and original paintings both traditional and modern. Finally, **McEwan and Ritchie** has some really interesting contemporary work from the students and staff of Dundee's fine art college – Duncan College of Jordanstone, which in some way accounts for the excellent visual art available in Dundee.

ANTIQUE DEALERS

If you are travelling to Perth, two shops on the Perth Road, just past Nethergate in the town centre, are of interest. **Past and Present** at 75 Perth Road, Tel 28370, has a general collection of collectables, while **Alan Beaton** at 140 Perth Road, Tel 24310, has some nice pieces in his showroom. Incidentally, if you are on your way to Perth, it's worth while stopping at Rait (halfway between Perth and Dundee) to call in at the **Rait Village Antiques Centre,** which has a large stock befitting their nine showrooms of furniture, Tel 08217 379. If you turn right into South Tay Street (Dundee Rep is here), just where Nethergate becomes Perth Road, and bear left at the top of the street into Westport, you'll find **Westport Gallery**, Tel 21751, at No 48, with all types of antiques, pictures and jewellery. If you turn into Brook Street and go right at the roundabout into West Henderson Wynd, you'll find **Croft's**, Tel 200097, at Ancho Mill. They have a large collection of furniture and bric-à-brac, plus things like gramophones and small decorative items.

Back in town make your way to the **McManus Galleries** in Albert Square. Just behind the galleries at 29 Albert Street, Tel 455000, is **Green's Antiques**, which has a good selection of jewellery and also old gold, silver and collectables. In the same part of town you'll find **Dundee Antiques** at Meadowmill, Tel 730447, with antique furniture, paintings, clocks and fire inserts and **Lorimer Antiques** at the Eagle Complex on Victoria Street, with a good general antique collection.

Rounding out this part of town are **Cornucopia Collectors** at 15 King St, who specialize in costume jewellery, old toys, old gold and silver. Tel 24946. You are bound to be in Seagate for the art and it's well worth calling into **Cooper of Dundee** at 131 Seagate who have fine furniture showrooms. Finally, at Broughton Ferry, there are **Town and Country Interiors** at 241 King St, Tel 480342, and the **Treasure Chest** at 109 Gray St, Tel 739777. They both have general collections and are in the town's centre

Although not strictly antiques, **Dens Market** at 39 Dens Rd has an amazing collection of bric-à-brac, junk, books and everything. Open Tues, Fri, Sat, Sun 9:30–mid-afternoon.

RESTAURANTS

Raffles – 18 Perth Road, Tel 26344. There's a wide range of food available here. I found their Italian cuisine very acceptable but friends swear by their vegetarian cuisine. It *is* certain, however, that their food is inexpensive and the helpings are generous. Open Tues, Wed, Thurs Noon to 2pm; Fri Noon to 2 and 6–10:30pm; Sat 10am–10:30pm.

Vulcan's – 189 Princess St, Tel 453295. It's unusual to find two good vegetarian restaurants in one town, but this is the case in Dundee. Vulcan's caters for vegetarian and vegan food and although they are not licensed, they are delighted if you bring your own bottle and they'll even chill it for you.

Deep Sea Restaurant – 81 Nethergate, Tel 24449. Good fish and chips though seekers of ambience should not foster too high expectations.

Gulistan Tandoori Restaurant – Queen St, Broughton Ferry, Tel 738844. About the best Indian and Asian cooking in the area. European food as well.

Royal Oak – 167 Brook St, Tel 29440. A rather superior bar and restaurant as well as excellent pub food.

PUBS

Sinatra's – King Street, Tel 29797. More of a wine bar than a pub, but the home cooked bar meals are good value and generous. Meals noon to 2:30 and 5–7:30pm.

Fisherman's Tavern – Broughton Ferry, Tel 75941. You get a nice view of two long, low Tay bridges as the tavern is on the seafront. There's a good choice of whiskies, hot dishes such as finnan pie and beef olives. The bars are pleasant, one with a Victorian fireplace and brass lamps.

Tally-ho – South Tay St. A popular pub which is fulsomely decorated with stuffed animals. The bar food is traditional, good and remarkably inexpensive. Very handy for Dundee Rep.

ARTISTIC ASSOCIATIONS

Mary Wollstonecraft Shelley, the English writer and the author of *Frankenstein* lived in a cottage near Peep-o'-Day Lane until she eloped with Percy Bysshe Shelley.

Thomas Hood, an English poet and journalist, spent two years in Dundee when he was in his teens. As he recuperated at his aunt's house from a serious illness, he wrote a novel, *The Bandit*, which is reminiscent of Sir Walter Scott.

The Scottish poet William Thom died here in poverty in 1848. William McGonagall lived for many years in Paton's Lane and worked as a carpet weaver (see Ephemera).

For a very brief period at the turn of the century, Dundee became an important centre of art nouveau in Scotland. At the head of the group of artists associated with this style were John Duncan and George Dutch Davidson. These two shared a studio at 31 Albert Square from the summer of 1898 until the autumn of 1899. By 1901, Duncan had emigrated to Chicago, and that same year Davidson died at the age of 24. Nearly all of Davidson's small collection of work is to be found in the Dundee Art Gallery. His art is full of morbid symbolism but it possesses a strange fascination. Would that there were more of it.

From more recent times, Dundee can boast an artist whose work is known to millions, though not, I suspect, his name: Dudley Watkins is the original illustrator of the famous children's comic, *The Beano*, which was first published in 1938 and is still going strong.

EPHEMERA

Many Scots must feel uneasy that Dundee conferred the Freedom of the City on William, Duke of Cumberland, in 1746, for there is no doubt that he committed atrocities upon those captured or wounded Highland soldiers whom his army pursued after their defeat at the Battle of Culloden in 1745. It was because of these vicious reprisals that the Duke has earned in history the name of "Butcher" Cumberland. Handel composed "See the Conquering Hero Comes" to welcome him back to England. As his Christian name was William, the English, as a compliment to him, named a flower sweet William. It seems an apt and just comment that the same flower was known in Scotland as stinking Willie.

The Tay, the Forth and the Severn rivers were the last barriers to direct railway communication in Britain and the problems involved in bridging them were not faced until late in the 19th century. The Tay was tackled first and in 1877 Queen Victoria opened the North British Railway's two-mile-long (3.2 km) lattice-girder bridge between Wormit and Dundee, and crossed it on her way to Balmoral. She knighted the designer, Thomas Pouch. Two years later the bridge collapsed, drowning 77 people. The principal cause of the disaster was Bouch's failure to allow for the high winds which were common in the area. The second and present Tay bridge, opened in 1887, was the first civil engineering project in Britain where an attempt was made to calculate the pressure of side winds as a factor in the design. Because of the previous disaster, the safety margin was very generous and the resulting structure is consequently not particularly elegant.

Dundee is one of those cities where sweet tastes are predominant. James Keiller's Dundee Marmalade is sought the world over, as are the famous Butterscotch Sweets made by the same firm. Marmalade was in fact invented here when, in the mid-18th century, James Keiller brought a cargo of bitter Spanish oranges to Dundee and gave them to his wife to boil in the same way as she prepared jam. At the top of the Hilltown there is a little shop which makes Dundee's famous Horehound Toffee, which has to be tasted to be believed. The original Dundee cake can be found in all its glory at **Goddfellow and Steven's Bakers**, 81 Gray Street, Broughton Ferry, Tel 730181. A visit to Derek Shaw's **Sweet Factory**, Fuller Road, Western Gourdie Industrial Estate, Tel 610369, will please those with a liking for candy. They have factory visits and tastings and there is an enormous selection of sweets including the delicious Dundee Fudge. On the other hand, **Braithwaite's Coffee**, 6 Castle St, Tel 22693 is as good as any thing coming out of Kenya or Colombia.

It is thought that William McGonagall, the best bad poet in the world, was born in Dundee in 1830. Son of an Irish weaver, he left Dundee for Edinburgh where he gave readings in public houses, published broadsheets of popular verse and was lionized by the legal and student fraternity. His poems are uniformly bad with bathos, irrelevant material and disjointed rhythms, but he does possess a disarming naiveté and a calypso-like disregard for metre which never fails to entertain. One of his finest (or worst) works is the poem he wrote on the opening of the first Tay Bridge. The first of five verses goes –

> Beautiful new railway bridge of the Silvery Tay
> With your strong brick piers and buttresses in so grand array
> And your thirteen central girders, which seem to my eye
> Strong enough all windy storms to defy.
> And as I gaze upon thee my heart feels gay,
> Because thou are the greatest railway bridge of the present day,
> And can be seen for miles away
> From north, south, east or west of the Tay
> On a beautiful and clear sunshiny day,
> And ought to make the hearts of the "Mars" boys feel gay,
> Because thine equal nowhere can be seen,
> Only near by Dundee and the bonnie Magdalen Green

Two years later when the bridge collapsed, the muse yet again descended on Willie and he wrote a new poem, "The Tay Bridge Disaster," Here is the first verse:

> Beautiful Railway Bridge of the Silv'ry Tay!
> Alas! I am very sorry to say
> That ninety lives have been taken away
> On the last Sabbath day of 1879
> Which will be remembered for a very long time.

Poetic Gems by William McGonagall (with a foreword by Billy Connolly) is published in paperback by Duckworth and is well worth the modest investment.

TOURIST INFORMATION BUREAU: 4 City Square, Dundee, Angus DD1 3BA.
Tel (0382) 27723

EDINBURGH

County of Lothian. Capital of Scotland.
378 miles from London by MI, M6, A7
Train 5 hours from London (King's Cross)

A well-known drama critic, upon seeing Edinburgh for the first time, exclaimed, "This is pure theatre." He was right. The capital of Scotland is highly dramatic in appearance. If you walk along the famous Princess Street thoroughfare, for example, and look up at the silhouette of the thousand-year-old Castle on its rock and the Old Town stretched against the southern sky, it is as if you were looking at a backcloth in a theatre. Built upon hills, Edinburgh produces many other dramatic effects. It has the sea at its feet in the shape of the Firth of Forth and a great rock hill – Arthur's Seat – which might pass as a mountain. From here you can see over half of southern Scotland and into the Highland hills. At the base of Arthur's Seat is the Royal Palace of Holyrood House, the stones of which are imbued with the shade of the beautiful, doomed Mary, Queen of Scots, who reigned in Scotland for a mere six years but who has left an indelible memory (see Ephemera). Couple this with the fact that Edinburgh has more buildings of architectural or historical importance than any other city in Great Britain outside of London, and you will begin to realize why it holds such a unique place in the hearts of all who visit and how it is a perpetual and very public reminder to all Scots of both their heritage and their roots.

Castle Rock had housed both Romans and Picts before the Angles, under Edwin, King of Northumbria (Edwin's burgh – hence Edinburgh) settled there in the 7th century, making this ancient volcanic peak the future heart of Scotland's capital. In the 11th century, Malcolm III built St Margaret's Chapel, which still stands within the castle precincts; in the following century, his son, David, gave the city its royal foundation a mile to the east, at Holyrood. It is hardly surprising that the thoroughfare between the Castle and Holyrood House is known as the Royal Mile. During the next four centuries the Old Town grew within these boundaries until, in the 16th century, the fear of English attacks led to the building of the Flodden wall, which effectively defined the area within which Edinburgh could grow. Until the 18th century, the city grew upwards instead of outwards, its busy commercial life hemmed in by the tall, narrow buildings, which still remain in the Old Town. A capital city could not, however, forever cling to its familiar shape and in 1767 the prosperous merchants

EDINBURGH CASTLE

of the Town Council commissioned an expansion programme which was to last 80 years and which was to make the New Town of Edinburgh the most stately example of classical architecture in Europe. In the 19th century the city turned its attention to commercial development and established the industries for which it has become known, such as printing, banking and brewing. The 20th century has seen some additions to the city skyline but for the most part the architecture that the visitor encounters today has its origins in the great building movements of the past. In fact, few cities have guarded their heritage as closely or as successfully as Edinburgh. The Old Town is still essentially medieval while the New Town belongs to the same noble Georgian order as Bath or Dublin. The Edinburgh walk explores these two very distinct manifestations of a magnificent city.

WALK

Old Town Walk (This is a long walk. I suggest you break your journey at Holyrood House and spread the walk over two days.) – Start from the Castle Terrace car park. Turn left over King's Bridge and walk up Johnstone Terrace. Near the top, turn left up the steps of Castle Wynd North to Esplanade and **Edinburgh Castle** (see below). Retrace your steps to Castlehill which is the start of the Royal Mile. On the left is Milne's Court, a restored Old Town "close." Farther on, Lady Stair's Close leads to **Lady Stair's House** (see below). Nearby is Gladstone's Land (see below). After the Royal Mile becomes the High Street, note on the left Robert Adam's fine **City Chambers**, which were originally the **Stock Exchange**. Opposite is **Parliament Square**; this contains the **Law Courts**, the **Signet Library**, St Giles Cathedral (see below) and **Parliament House** (see below). The shape of a heart set in the cobbles marks the site of the vanished Edinburgh Tolbooth – the Heart of Midlothian. Despite the fact that this is the name given to one of Sir Walter Scott's best novels, the area has a grim past. The Tolbooth was the town prison for some 400 years until it was demolished in 1817 and public executions were also held on the site. Continue down the Royal Mile. On the left, note the carvings on the houses and entrances to the closes. On **Paisley Close** note the inscription and bust (see Ephemera). On **Bible Land** a quotation from the Psalms adorns an elegant stone tablet. **John Knox's House** (see below) is close by as is **Huntley House Museum** (see below) and opposite, the **Canongate Tolbooth** which now houses **The People's Story** – one of the city's newest museums (see below). Adjacent is the **Canongate Kirkyard** which contains the graves of many famous Scots, including that of Adam Smith, the economist and author of *The Wealth of Nations*. Near the bottom of the Royal Mile is **White Horse Close** (on the left) a former coaching inn where Bonnie Prince Charlie's officers were once billeted (now converted to housing). **Queen Mary's Bath House** is a remnant of the boundary wall of Holyrood House. A Royal Bathhouse seems unlikely but it could well have been a royal garden pavilion or more prosaically a royal garden shed. One intriguing story is that during its restoration a dagger was found concealed in the roof: perhaps it was hurriedly thrust there by one of the murderers who assassinated David Rizzio on March 9th, 1566 (see Ephemera). A visit to Holyrood House is a must (see below). Leave Holyrood House and turn left along Horse Wynd and then turn left and right onto Queen's Drive. On the corner is a small Victorian lodge which houses the **Holyrood Park Visitor Centre** (see below). Follow Queen's Drive, turning right round the curve of Salisbury Crags where Queen's Drive passes James Clark School, bear right up the steps and through the gate and straight down St Leonard's Lane. At St Leonard's Lane turn right and then left into Rankeillor Street. Turn right and then left into Borough Loch Lane, leading to the Meadows. Turn right along North Meadow Walk, skirting the park. Archers' Hall, on the right, is the headquarters of the Royal Company of Archers, the Queen's Scottish Bodyguard. It is interesting that the famous Arthur's Seat is thought to be a corruption of Archer's Seat. Also on the right are the buildings of **Edinburgh University** (see below). Turn right up Middle Meadow Walk which passes between the University and the Royal Infirmary. At the top of the walk continue straight down Forrest Road. On the left, just beyond where this becomes George IV Bridge, is the entrance to **Greyfriars Kirkyard** with the statue of **Greyfriars Bobby** (see Ephemera) near the entrance. Walk across George IV and at the top of the street, on the right, is the **National Library of Scotland** (see below). Turn left down Victoria Street and West Bow to the Grassmarket where the gallows stood. Covenanters were hanged here in the 17th century and nearby stood the Edinburgh Maiden – an early guillotine and an unpleasant reminder of the "auld alliance" (with France). Turn right through Grassmarket and bear right into King's Stables Road. Follow this road as it passes under King's Bridge and you will be back at the Castle Terrace car park. The path you are on becomes Miller Row. Follow it to the bottom of Bell's Brae, then turn right to **King's Bridge**. Stand on the bridge and take in the view in both directions. For another view of the village, continue over the bridge and turn first left into Damside. This turns left again and leads down to the stream. Then retrace your steps back to the bridge. Walk up Bell's Brae until it merges with Queensferry Street. Follow Queensferry Street until it ends at the west end of Princess Street. Cross over Lothian Road and bear left into Castle Terrace car park.

MUSEUMS AND GALLERIES

Edinburgh Castle – Castle Hill, Tel 225 9846. The history of Edinburgh Castle is the history of Scotland and the jumble of buildings within the castle's walls bears witness to the variety of its functions as fortress, barracks, arsenal, palace, prison, museum and shrine. The oldest building, St Margaret's Chapel, is a tiny building named after Malcolm III's English Queen who brought Roman Catholicism to Scotland in the 11th century. The flowers in the chapel are arranged each week by girls named Margaret from all over Scotland. Other sights include the Scottish Crown Jewels and the **Scottish United Services Museum**, with displays relating to the armed forces for all periods of their history. There is a complete collection of Scottish military uniforms here, plus paintings, prints, weapons and equipment. The **Museum of the Scottish Royal Scots Regiment**, the oldest regular regiment in the British Army, is also in the Castle. The dignified **National War Memorial**, circa 1927, is also in the Castle. It pays tribute to the men and women who died in two world wars and 200 of the country's leading artists and craftspeople were engaged to work on it. It is essentially a gallery of fine and decorative arts with sculptures in stone and bronze, woodcarving, stained glass, heraldry and ironwork. The soldiers of the small garrison are dressed in the colorful garb of Scots Regiments and they fire a howitzer each day at 1pm. They vie in magnificence with the castle's official guides who wear tartan trousers. The celebrated Tattoo takes place here at Festival time and should not be missed. Open Mon–Sat 9:30–5:30, Sun 11–5:50 (closes earlier in winter).

Lady Stair's House – Ladystairs Close, Lawnmarket, Tel 225 2424. Built in 1622, Lady Stair's House was remodelled between 1893 and 1897 for the Earl of Roseberry, to be used as his town house. Now a museum, its displays relate to the life and work of Scotland's three greatest literary figures of the late 18th and 19th centuries, Robert Burns, Sir Walter Scott and Robert Louis Stevenson. The museum is the only place where the three are commemorated together. Open Mon–Sat 10–6pm (closes one hour earlier in winter).

Gladstone's Land – 477B Lawnmarket, Tel 226 5856. This twin-gabled six-storey tenement or "land" dates from the early 16th century and was modernized in 1617–1620. In the Old Town all classes lived cheek-by-jowl, in cramped conditions: on the ground floor there are wooden-fronted booths facing the Lawnmarket, which houses a reconstruction of a cloth merchant's shop. The interior two floors have been restored and furnished and there are fine fireplaces and painted walls and ceiling. This is a typical burgess's home of the period. Open Mon–Sat 10–5pm, Sun 2–5pm (closes 30 min earlier in winter).

St Giles' Cathedral – Parliament Square. Beneath its distinctive stone crown, the interior of St Giles' is medieval, with 19th-century overlay and a central altar. There are medieval carvings, military colours and a copy of the National Covenant, Scotland's religious "declaration of independence." There is a fine monument to the Marquess of Montrose, who raised the Highlands for Charles I in 1650 and was executed in the Grassmarket. There is a pretty chapel dedicated to the Knights of the Thistle and two very jolly angels playing bagpipes. Although Charles I elevated the church to cathedral status in the 17th century, its real name should be St Giles Kirk.

Parliament House – Parliament Square, Tel 226 5071. The Hall, built in 1632–39 by order of Charles I, is 122 feet (37 m) long and has one of the finest hammerbeam roofs in Britain. The Scottish Parliament met here until 1707 and so, ironically, did the Tables, the committee which organized the Protestant rebellion against Charles I. The neo-classical façade was added 1807–1810. Open Tues–Fri 9–4pm.

John Knox's House – 45 High Street, Tel 556 6961. This house would stand out anywhere with its gables, outside stairs and elaborate carvings. The oldest parts of the building date from the 15th century and it is believed to have been rented by the religious reformer John Knox, the Father of the Scottish Reformation, from about 1501 until his death in 1572. Inside there is a wealth of fine panelling and an impressive painted ceiling. Knox's small study contains a "preaching window" from which he is said to have addressed the crowds below. On display are a number of mementos not only of Knox himself but also of the social and religious life of his day. The house has been furnished to give an impression of how it might have looked in Knox's lifetime. Open Mon–Sat 10–4:30pm.

Museum of Childhood – 38 High Street, Tel 225 2424. This was the first museum in the world to be devoted solely to the history of childhood. There are displays relating to the health, upbringing, education and dress of children and important historical collections of toys, games, books and hobbies. The founder, Patrick Murray, who was a bachelor, always saw his museum as a source of social study and often alleged that he did not like children. He went so far as to suggest that the museum should feature a King Herod window. Open Mon–Sat 10–6pm (closes 1 hour earlier in winter) Sun 2–5pm during Festival.

Huntly House Museum – 142 Canongate, Tel 225 2424. Huntly House – actually three houses grouped around a picturesque close – is Edinburgh's principal museum of its own history. Visitors are welcomed by the charming sign of an 18th-century town crier and his drummer. There are exhibits detailing life in the city, interiors of shops, houses and workshops, Edinburgh silver and an exhibition devoted to Field Marshal Earl Haig that includes a reconstruction of his 1914–18 headquarters. Open Mon–Sat 10–6pm (closes 1 hour earlier in winter). Open Sun 2–5pm during Festival.

Canongate Tolbooth – 163 Canongate, Tel 225 2424. Built in 1591, the tolbooth has served as town hall, courthouse, prison and now museum. It houses **The People's Story**, an exhibition devoted to the lives of Edinburgh's citizens. Objects ranging from bus tickets to trade union banners give a vivid picture of the recent past. There is a restored prison cell and part of a "Steamie," or communal wash house. Open Mon–Sat 10–6pm (closes 1 hour earlier in winter) Sun 2–5pm during Festival.

Palace of Holyrood House – Royal Mile, Tel 556 1096. Over a period of five centuries, Holyrood House developed from an abbey into a palace. Founded by King David I in 1128, it became a wealthy and powerful Augustinian community, from whose guesthouse the present royal dwelling grew after James II was born there in 1430. However, once the Stuart kings moved to London, no reigning monarch slept at Holyrood until Queen Victoria. David Rizzio, secretary to Mary, Queen of Scots, was savagely murdered here in 1566 (see Ephemera) and Bonnie Prince Charlie held brief but dazzling court there in 1745. Incidentally, the spot in Holyrood where Rizzio was murdered used to be marked by a famous and annually renewed bloodstain. Alas, a brass tablet now marks the spot – such is progress. Holyrood is still a royal residence and the Queen stays here for two weeks each summer. Guides in tartan will show you the Royal apartments. In the great gallery is an extraordinary collection of 89 portraits depicting monarchs of Scotland. All were painted in the same year, 1684, by Jacob de Wet and most are highly imaginary and some in extreme bad taste.

Adjoining the palace is Holyrood Park, which brings rugged Highland scenery right into the heart of the city. It is rich in plant and animal life and its picturesque natural features have such colourful names as Lion's Haunch, Gutted Haddie and Arthur's Seat (the last named is the cone of an ancient volcano). Pathways too, have unusual names; Radical Road and Innocent Walkway. A visitor centre has exhibitions and details of a three-mile (4.8 km) nature trail through the park. Open Mon–Sat 9:30–5:15, Sun 10:30–4:30pm. Closed 14th–29th May and late June and early July when the Queen is in residence.

University of Edinburgh – South Bridge and Chambers Streets. Designed in 1789 by Robert Adam, the main building is in classic style with a large quadrangle in its centre. The large dome was added in 1883. One of Britain's largest universities, Edinburgh was founded in 1583 and has an especially famous medical school.

University Collection of Historic Musical Instruments – Reid Concert Hall, Bristo Square, Tel 667 1011. The Reid Concert Hall was built in 1860 and contains a fine Ahrends organ. The collection of instruments displayed ranges from the Renaissance to the present day. More than a thousand items are on display, including strings, woodwind, brass and, of course, bagpipes. Open Wed 3–5pm, Sat 10–1pm, also Mon–Fri 2–5pm during Festival.

Russell Collection of Harpsichords and Clavichords – Cecilia's Hall, Niddry Street, Cowgate, Tel 667 1011. Also administered by the University, the collection is housed in Scotland's oldest concert hall circa 1864 and the collection of early keyboard instruments is the most important in the country. Open Wed–Sat 2–5pm, Mon–Sat 10:30–12:30 during Festival.

The University Department of Geology administers the **Cockburn Museum of Geology**, West Mains Road, which is open from Mon–Fri 9–5pm, while the **University Department of Archaeology**, 16–20 George Square, also has an important collection which is normally only open by appointment, Tel 667 1011. See also Talbot Rice Art Centre below.

Greyfriars Kirk and Kirkyard – George IV Bridge. Dating from 1620, the Kirk achieved lasting fame when the National Covenant, rejecting Anglicanism, asserted Scotland's right to decide its own spiritual destiny. Today the Kirk is a centre for the city's Gaelic–speaking community and some services are held in that language. The Kirkyard contains the graves of the poet Alan Ramsay, the architect William Adam and the master of "Greyfriars Bobby," whose statue is outside the gate (see Ephemera). Over the Kirkyard back wall is George Heriot's School, opened in 1659. The founder, whose wealth earned him the nickname, "Jingling Geordie," was goldsmith to King James VI.

Royal Bank of Scotland – The Mound, Tel 226 6871. A neo-classical building designed between 1802 and 1806 by Robert Reid. It was believed that this particular architectural style gave banks an image of solidarity and reliability. The dome was added in 1865–70 and the interior sense of opulence is intensified by the panelled ceiling. Open Mon–Fri 9:30–3:30pm. (There is also a small museum.)

National Gallery of Scotland – The Mound, Tel 556 8921. The Gallery occupies an early 19th-century neo-classical building designed by William Playfair. Its collection of paintings includes works dating from the 14th century to 1900. Among the artists represented are Gainsborough, Constable, Van Dyck, Gauguin, El Greco, Monet, Rembrandt, Titian, Velasquez, Degas and Cézanne. Scottish painters are much in evidence. There are some excellent prints, watercolours and drawings by Dürer, Goya and Rembrandt and the Vaughn bequest of Turner watercolours. Open Mon–Sat 10–5pm, Sun 2–5pm. Extended hours during the Festival.

Scott Monument – East Princess Street Gardens. It says much about Scottish respect for the written word that the monument dominating Princess Street should commemorate not a monarch or a general but a novelist. Sir Walter Scott was born and brought up in the city and was an New Town resident for much of his life. His monument, completed in 1844, is a 200-foot (60.8 m) confection of Gothic spires, crockets, niches and gargoyles. Scott himself is not shown as a town-dweller but as a country gentleman in plaid with faithful dog. Spiral staircases lead to fine views of the city and the many statues depict both fictional and historical figures including John Knox, Ivanhoe, Rob Roy and George Heriot.

Nelson Monument – Calton Hill. Conceived in 1816, the year after the Battle of Waterloo, as a memorial to the fallen of the Napoleonic Wars, the monument was designed by Henry Playfair and is a truncated reproduction of the Parthenon at Athens (funding ran out before its completion). Its incompleteness has an appropriate symbolism. Also on Calton Hill is a small circular temple commemorating the philosopher Dugald Stewart (also by Playfair) and the **City and Old Observatories**. Although superseded by the Royal Observatory, the City Observatory is open to the public and presents a 3-D film presentation entitled *Edinburgh Experience*. Open May–Oct 2:30–5pm daily and 10:30–5pm weekends. Tel 6671081.

Royal Museum of Scotland – Chambers Street, Tel 227 7534. The museum contains a comprehensive collection of material relating to Scottish life from the earliest times. There are Celtic crosses and early Christian treasures – Bonnie Prince Charlie's canteen, said to be his favourite possession, and centuries-old costumes found in a peat bog. The notorious Edinburgh "Maiden," the guillotine mentioned above, can be seen here. Open Mon–Sat 10–5pm, Sun 2–5pm.

Scottish National Portrait Gallery – 1 Queen Street, Tel 5568921. Sharing the same ornate sandstone building as the Royal Museum is the Scottish National Portrait Gallery. Its 2000 works range from the time of James I to the present. As well as portraits of such historical figures as Mary, Queen of Scots, Robert Burns and Bonnie Prince Charlie, modern Scots such as the Queen Mother, Lord Home and poet Hugh MacDiarmid are represented. The mosaic depicting characters from Scottish history on the walls of the upper storey is great fun and popular with children. Open Mon–Sat 10–5pm, Sun 2–5pm. Extended hours during Festival.

Georgian House – 7 Charlotte Square, Tel 225 2160. The whole north side of Charlotte Square, which includes the Georgian House, represents Robert Adam's greatest achievement in the field of urban architecture. In 1796, John Lamont, a minor landowner, moved into the house and lived there for 19 years. The house has now been restored and furnished to represent, as nearly as possible, the home the Lamonts knew. It is a typical New Town house during Edinburgh's Golden Age and offers a perfect counterpart to the cramped intimacy of Gladstone's Land in the Old Town. Five recreated rooms on two floors include the parlour, kitchen and dining room and contrast with the Old Town is further emphasized by a magnificent mahogany and brass lavatory – very advanced when installed in 1810. The building contains, on its upper floors, the residence of the Moderator of the Church of Scotland. Neighbours include the National Trust for Scotland at No 5 Charlotte Square and the Secretary of State for Scotland at No 6. Open April–Oct Mon–Sat 10–4pm, Sun 2–4:30pm; Nov Sat 10–4pm, Sun 2–4pm.

Water of Leith – Edinburgh is unusual among British cities in not being built on a river. The Water of Leith flows through part of the city and emerges in Leith's Western Harbour. Moray Estate was laid out when the Earl of Moray sold his Edinburgh property as building plots. The householders still pay an annual fee for the key to the riverside as the banks of the river are common to all properties.

Dean Village – No more than five minutes' walk from Princess Street lies a rustic village set in a peaceful valley with picturesque buildings, some a century old. The ambience today is deceptive, as a century ago the village was a bustling industrial complex with many flour mills. The finest of these is the Baxter's Tolbooth at the bottom of Bell's Brae. The village owes its present-day seclusion to being bypassed when the new road to the Forth was built.

St Mary's Cathedral – Palmerston Place, Tel 225 2978. Dominating the New Town skyline is this Episcopal Cathedral with its three tall yet graceful towers. Built between 1874 and 1879, it was one of the largest Gothic churches to be built in Britain since the Reformation.

Braidwood and Rushbrook Fire Museum – McDonald Road, Tel 228 2401. The museum, in an old fire station, contains fire engines and fire-fighting equipment dating from the early 19th century to the present day.

Lauriston Castle – Cramond Road South, Tel 336 2060. A late 16th-century tower house, greatly extended in the 1820s in the Jacobean style. The Reid family bequeathed the house to the Scottish nation on the understanding that it should be maintained much as it was in their lifetime. Thus the rooms show the leisured lifestyle of the well-to-do middle classes in the years just prior to the First World War. Open April–Oct Sat–Thurs 11–1pm and 2–5pm; Nov–March Sun 2–4pm.

Museum of Communication – University of Edinburgh, Mayfield Road, Tel 667 1081. A collection of telephones, spark transmitters, crystal sets, early valve sets, communication receivers, transmitters, teleprinters, wire and tape recorders, television and radar. Open Mon–Fri 9–9pm, Sat 9–7pm.

Museum of Lighting – 59 Stephen Street, Tel 556 4503. The museum is in a restored Georgian house and the collection illustrates the progress made in domestic, transport and industrial lighting from the 18th to the early 20th century. The museum is small, a bit disorganized but fascinating. Open Sat 11–6pm or by appointment.

Museum of the Royal College of Surgeons of Edinburgh – Nicolson Street, Tel 556 6206. Installed in a William Playfair building of 1832, the museum illustrates the history of surgery in Edinburgh from 1505 to 1900. Surgical, dental, pathological and historical exhibits. Open Mon–Fri 9–5pm. (Closed during examinations, check dates.)

Scottish Agricultural Museum – Ingliston (on the A8 to the airport on the Royal Highland Society's Showground) Tel 556 8921. The museum illustrates the history of farming and rural life with particular attention being focused on the way in which tools and equipment were used.

Brass Rubbing Centre – Trinity Apse, Chalmers Close, High Street, Tel 556 4634. Display of replica brasses and Scottish carved stones. Facilities for making rubbings. Open Mon–Sat 10–5pm (one hour later in summer) and Sun 2–5pm during Festival.

Living Crafts Centre – 12 High Street, The Royal Mile (opposite John Knox's House) Tel 557 9350. An opportunity to see a weaver, silversmith, bagpipe maker, kiltmaker, stone painter and others working in their own workshops.

Edinburgh Wax Museum – 142 High Street, Tel 226 4445. Scottish history throughout the ages depicted in wax. Fantasy land for children.

Scottish Whisky Heritage Centre – 358 Castlehill, Royal Mile, Tel 220 0441. The centre provides an entertaining explanation of the making of Scotch whisky from the barley to the bottle. You can travel through 300 years of Scotch whisky history in a Barrelcar with accompanying commentary. Open daily 9–7pm (closes at 5pm in winter).

Scottish Telecommunications Museum – 4 Newbattle Terrace, Tel 228 2383. The collection contains items which illustrate the development of the telephone service from 1878 to the present day. Open by appointment.

City Arts Centre – 1–4 Market Street, Tel 225 2424. This late 19th-century building was erected as a warehouse for *The Scotsman* newspaper and was later used as a market. It now houses the city's large permanent collection of paintings, drawings, prints and sculptures, mostly by Scottish artists. Open June–Sept Mon–Sat 10–6pm; Oct–May Mon–Sat 10–5pm, also Sun 2–5pm during Festival.

Fruitmarket Gallery – 29 Market Street, Tel 225 2383. The Gallery with its extensive programme of video shows and lectures is one of the most important art centres in Scotland. It is concerned with international contemporary art and organizes a series of exhibitions throughout the year, each lasting for an average of six weeks. Open Tues–Sat 10–5:30pm.

Scottish National Gallery of Modern Art – Belford Road, Tel 556 8921. The Gallery occupies the building of the former John Watson's School, designed by William Burn in the neo-classical style in 1828. It contains the national collection of 20th-century paintings, sculptures and graphic art including works by Derain, Matisse, Braque, Picasso, Giacometti, Hockney and Hepworth. Artists of the Scottish School are also well represented. Open Mon–Sat 10–5pm, Sun 2–5pm. Extended opening during Festival.

Talbot Rice Art Centre – Old College, South Bridge, Tel 667 1011. The Centre is housed in the Old College of the University of Edinburgh, one of Robert Adam's most important public buildings, completed after Adam's death by William Playfair. The permanent display room is devoted to the collection of bronzes and paintings, especially Dutch, formed by Sir James Erskine of Torrie in the early 19th century. The large second gallery shows mainly contemporary Scottish art, but from time to time exhibitions are arranged which present works from earlier periods.

Camera Obscura – Royal Mile (next to the Castle) Tel 2263709. Old photographs and drawings plus a camera-obscura-eye's view of Edinburgh. Open daily 10–6pm (one hour earlier in summer).

THEATRE

King's Theatre – 2 Leven Street, Tel 229 1201. Built in 1905, the King's Theatre has a splendid auditorium with a surprising number of boxes – nine on each side. The entrance lobby is imposing with a wide marble staircase leading to the first floor foyer. It hosts the big touring companies offering ballet, opera and mainstream drama.

Royal Lyceum – Grindlay Street, Tel 229 9697. As I write, the Royal Lyceum is undergoing major renovations which will radically upgrade both the technical efficiency and the audience comfort of the theatre. By the time you read this, those renovations should he complete and this beautiful theatre, which celebrated its centenary in 1983, will be back in operation. The finest example of the work of the leading Victorian architect, C J Phipps, the theatre's most notable features are the impressive stuccoed façade and the richly decorated auditorium ceiling. The theatre is the home of the Royal Lyceum Theatre Company, one of the finest provincial theatre companies in the U.K.

Traverse Theatre – Grassmarket, Tel 226 2633. One of the mainstays of the annual Edinburgh Festival, the Traverse presents a year-round programme of progressive new work with the emphasis on Scottish playwrights. The Traverse stages up to nine productions a year, with the balance made up by touring companies, and it has long been hailed as one of the most original theatre companies in Britain. It was once a warehouse, but what it lacks in luxury it makes up for in creativity. There is music in the bar after the show and good vegetarian cooking in the restaurant.

Playhouse Theatre – Greenside Place, Tel 557 2590. The home of Scottish Opera in Edinburgh and the theatre also plays host to large-scale touring companies, mostly musicals, ballet, opera, etc.

Theatre Workshop – 34 Hamilton Place, Tel 225 7942. Dedicated to promoting theatre in its widest sense and particularly among the young, Theatre Workshop offers productions and workshops for young people and also an innovative and exciting programme of visiting companies such as TAG, 7:84 and Mandela Theatre Company. There are also art exhibitions in the Gallery and a café/bar.

Netherbow Arts Centre – 43–45 High Street, Tel 556 9579. Run by the Church of Scotland, Netherbow presents an imaginative arts programme for adults and children including a recent Festival of Scottish Storytelling.

MUSIC

Edinburgh is especially rich in music, with regular concerts from the Scottish National Orchestra, the Scottish Chamber Orchestra, the BBC Scottish Symphony Orchestra, Scottish Opera, the Scottish Early Music Consort, the Scottish Sinfonia, the Scottish Ensemble and Scottish Ballet.

Usher Hall – Lothian Road, Tel 228 1155. Edinburgh's largest concert hall, seating 2700, and the Edinburgh home of the Scottish National Orchestra and the BBC Scottish Symphony Orchestra.

Queen's Hall – Clerk Street, Tel 668 2019. The major home of the Scottish Chamber Orchestra and the smaller ensemble groups. Also hosts visiting chamber groups and soloists as well as jazz and ethnic music.

Recitals also take place in St Giles' Cathedral, the Reid Hall in Teviot Row, Bristo Square and many kirks throughout the city and there is an extensive University Music Department, Tel 667 1011.

Edinburgh Festival – For many people, Edinburgh is *the* Festival, the only reason they have come to know and love the city. For three weeks each year the city is packed to bursting point with actors, singers, musicians, comedians, bands, dancers, jugglers and poets, all gathered to perform at one of the most prestigious art festivals in the world. The Festival has been an annual August event since 1947 and now attracts the very top performers from all over the world. It is divided into different sections, the main attraction being the Festival proper, which features outstanding musical and dramatic performance in the city's finest concert halls and theatres. Then there is the ubiquitous Fringe, a tightly organized collection of 800 or so different performances from one-person shows to full-scale productions. Fringe events take place at venues all over the city and in the past have featured new talent that in later years has seen international success. The Military Tattoo features about 600 service personnel in a display of pomp and ceremony with the splendid backdrop of the floodlit Castle. There is also an International Film Festival and a very popular Jazz Festival which run concurrently.

CINEMA

Commercial Cinema:
Cannon – Lothian Road, Tel 229 3030 (3 screens).
Dominion – Newbattle Terrace, Tel 447 2660 (3 screens).
Odeon – Clerk Street, Tel 667 7331 (5 screens).
UCI – Craig Park, Kinnaird Road, Tel 669 0777 (12 screens).

Of particular interest is **Cameo**, Home Street, Tel 228 4141, which is a small and welcoming "art house" and **Edinburgh Filmhouse**, Lothian Road, Tel 228 2688, which together with the Glasgow Film Theatre offers the most exciting and imaginative film programming in Scotland. The **Edinburgh International Film Festival** is held concurrently with the Edinburgh International Festival in August and is one of the world's best.

BOOKSTORES

The best, and there are three, are **Waterstone's** at 114 George Street, Tel 225 3436 and 13-14 Princess Street, Tel 556 3034, **James Thin** at four locations, Waverley Market, Tel 557 1378, 57 George Street (the Edinburgh Bookshop) Tel 225 4495, 53-59 Southbridge, Tel 556 6743, and King's Building, Tel 667 0432, and **Bauermeister Booksellers** at 19 George IV Bridge, Tel 226 5561. Perhaps more than any place in Britain, Edinburgh has a proud tradition of the independent bookseller and the best and most central of these are **Alan Armstrong** at 45A George Street, Tel 226 4201, **Barbour B McCall** at 28 George IV Bridge, Tel 225 4816, **Bobbie's Bookshop** at 220 Morrison Street, Tel 229 2338, **Bookspeed** at 48A Hamilton Place, Tel 225 4950, **Harkins and Brothers** at 4 North Bank Street, Tel 225 6709, **Helios Fountain** at 7 Grassmarket, Tel 229 7884, **John McNaughton** at 3A Haddington Place, Tel 556 3695, **Portfolio Books** at 19 Merchants Street, Tel 225 3491, **Private Lines** at 60 Elm Row, Tel 557 6842, **ReadBooks** at 276 Raeburn Place, Tel 332 5299, **Reid and Reid** at 134 St Stephen Street, Tel 225 9660, **Stockbridge Bookshop**, 26 North West Circus Place, Tel 225 5355, **Henry Syme**, 32 South Clerk Street, Tel 667 1340 and **Til's Bookshop** at 1 Hope Park Crescent, Tel 667 0895. Religious books can be found at **Christian Bookshop**, 12 Forrest Road, Tel 225 6937, **Church of Scotland**, 117/119 George Street, Tel 225 2229 and SPCK at St John's Church, Princess Street, Tel 229 3776. Comics and science fiction at **Dead Head Comics**, 44 Victoria Street, Tel 2262774 and **Science Fiction Bookshop** at 40/42 West Crosscauseway, Tel 667 0426. New Age books are at **Body and Soul**, 52 Hamilton Place, Tel 226 3066, and bargain books are at **Discount Bookstore**, 7 Forrest Road, Tel 220 2178. **Her Majesty's Stationery Office** has a large outlet at 71 Lothian Road, Tel 228 4181.

ANTIQUARIAN AND SECONDHAND BOOKS

Dundas Street (off Queen Street, west of the Scottish National Portrait Gallery) is a good place to start. **Andrew Pringle**, who specializes in Scottish history and literature and has a good selection of secondhand and antiquarian books is at No 7, Tel 556 9698. Just up the road is the **Dundas Book Shop** at No 23A, Tel 556 4591, and **Iain Ramsay** with a good collection at No 29A, Tel 557 4485. If you walk up Queen Street past the Royal Museum you will come to Broughton Place with **Broughton Books** at No 2A, Tel 557 8010. Close to Usher Hall and the Lyceum Theatre is Spittal Street where at No 3 you will find **Old Grindles Bookshop**, Tel 229 7252. Close by is West Port with **West Port Books** at No 151, **Peter Bell** at No 68, Tel 229 0562 (a good antiquarian selection), and **Grant and Shaw** at No 62, Tel 229 8399. Go up Grassmarket to the Traverse Theatre and close by is **Bookfare** at 8 Victoria Street, Tel 225 9237. Down behind the University you will find George Square with Buccleuch Street leading off it. Just where the street meets Melville Drive you will find Hope Park Crescent with **Til's Bookshop**, Tel 667 0895. Besides secondhand books they have some excellent original old movie posters. The other side of the University, close to the Royal Museum of Scotland, is Forrest Street with **James A Dickson** (antiquarian and second-hand theology) at No 12, Tel 225 6937. Walk up Forest Street, across George III Bridge and turn right onto High Street. High Street becomes Canongate and at No 204 you will find **Castle Books** with a large selection of rare and secondhand volumes, Tel 556 0624. On the other side of Waverley Station you will find **John McNaughton** at 3A Haddington Place, Leith Walk, Tel 556 3695 – a good secondhand and antiquarian stock. Finally, **Donald MacCormick** at 19 Braid Crescent, Tel 447 2889, **John Updike** at 7 St Bernard's Row, Tel 332 1650 (some excellent modern first editions), **Second Edition**, 9 Howard Street, Tel 556 9403, and **Jay Books**, 1 Roull Grove, Tel 316 4034, are all worth a browse.

ART GALLERIES

There are a great many galleries, so my selection is influenced by the nature of their stock and specialization and their geographical location. I have also tried to separate the galleries into traditional and contemporary, but it is a difficult task. (I would start off in Dundas Street.)

Traditional Galleries:

Carlyle's Gallery – North Bridge Tel 557 5068. 19th- and 20th-century Scottish decorative painting, lithographs and engravings.

Bourne Fine Art – 4 Dundas Street, Tel 557 4050. British paintings 1800–1950, together with decorative arts 1860–1930.

Calton Gallery – 10 Royal Terrace, Tel 556 1010. British and Continental paintings and watercolours from 1800. A large stock with some justifiably high prices. The accent is on quality here.

Carson Clark Gallery – 173 Canongate, The Royal Mile, Tel 556 4710. Maps, atlases and topographical prints.

Tom Fidelo – 49 Cumberland Street, Tel 557 2444. Paintings and works of art from the 18th to the 20th century.

Fine Art Gallery – 41 Dundas Street, Tel 557 4569. Scottish, British and Continental oils, watercolours, drawings and etchings from the 18th to the 20th centuries.

Fine Art Society – 137 George Street, Tel 220 6370. Paintings, watercolours, drawings and sculpture from 1770 to the present day.

Malcolm Innes Gallery – 67 George Street, Tel 226 4151. Scottish landscape, sporting and natural history pictures. Also Scottish contemporary art.

John Mathieson and Company – 5–5A Johnston Terrace (top of Royal Mile) Tel 225 6798. Paintings, watercolours and prints – 19th and 20th centuries.

Alan Rankin – 72 Dundas Street, Tel 556 3705 (open by appointment). Prints and maps from the earliest times to 1860, also antiquarian books.

Waverley Gallery – 9 Jeffrey Street, Tel 553 4536. 18th–20th-century oil paintings.

Contemporary Galleries:

Scottish Gallery – 94 George Street, Tel 225 5955. 20th-century and contemporary Scottish art, crafts, studio ceramics and jewellery.

Backroom – 42 London Street (underneath the arches) Tel 556 8329. Often has first-time exhibitors. The place to see new work and new artists.

Collective Gallery – 166 High Street, Tel 220 1260. Lively contemporary gallery.

Richard Demario Gallery – 17–21 Blackfriars Street (off The Royal Mile) Tel 557 0707. One of the liveliest and most interesting contemporary galleries in the British Isles. Many young artists have been given their first showing here.

Fruitmarket Gallery – 29 Market Street, Tel 225 2383. Has both national and international contemporary art. One, two, group and thematic shows. The gallery is a converted warehouse.

Gateway Gallery – 2–4 Abbeymount, Tel 661 0982. Paintings by local artists.

George Street Gallery – 38 George Street.

Kingfisher Gallery – Northumberland Street, North West Lane, Tel 557 5454. Exclusively contemporary Scottish, British and foreign art. Works by established and new artists.

Graeme Murray Gallery – 15 Scotland Street, Tel 556 6020. Top-notch Scottish contemporary art.

The Open Eye Gallery – 57–59 Cumberland Street, Tel 557 1020. Contemporary and fine arts, studio ceramics, 20th-century etchings and seventeen mainly contemporary exhibitions per year.

Prescote Gallery – 5 Northumberland Street, Tel 557 0800. Newly renovated space. Shows contemporary art.

Photography Workshop – 43 Candlemaker Row, Tel 556 1230. Offers photographers the chance to show and sell their work with monthly exhibitions throughout the year.
Printmakers Workshop Gallery – 23 Union Street, Tel 557 2479. The gallery acts as an outlet for prints made in its workshops and for work produced by other printmakers in Scotland.
The Scottish Gallery – 94 George Street, Tel 225 5955. Quality contemporary painting, original prints, crafts and jewellery.
The Scottish Craft Centre – 140 Canongate, Tel 556 8136. The best of Scottish craftsmanship by professional craftsmen and women.
Stills Gallery – 105 High Street, Tel 557 1140. Ten exhibitions a year and the only major gallery dedicated exclusively to photography.
369 Gallery – 233 Cowgate, Tel 225 3013. Regular exhibitions of contemporary Scottish art. Very lively shows by relatively young, established, colourful artists.
Torrance Gallery – 29B Dundas Street, Tel 556 6366. Two gallery spaces. One shows contemporary prints and the other contemporary art.
Wasps Gallery – Patriothall, Hamilton Place, Stockbridge, Tel 225 1289. Lively contemporary art, mostly by artists working out of Wasps studios but not always.
Other dealers and galleries worth a view:
Ash Gallery – 156 Canongate, The Royal Mile, Tel 556 2160.
Barnes and Fitzgerald – 47B George Street, Tel 220 1305.
Tom Fidelo – 49 Cumberland Street, Tel 557 2444. Paintings and works of art – 18th to 20th centuries.
Flying Colours Gallery – 35 William Street, Tel 225 6776.
Fraser and Sons – Waverley Market, Tel 557 3875.
Gallery Mirages – The Lane, 46A Raeburn Place, Tel 315 2603.
Grayfield Gallery– 77A Broughton Street, Tel 546 2553.
Hanover Fine Arts – 22A Dundas Street, Tel 556 2181.
Miller and Shackleton – 23 Dundas Street, Tel 556 0234.
Hillsed Gallery – 6 Hillside Street, Tel 556 6440.
Innes Art – 219 Bruntsfield Place, Tel 447 8929.
Forrest McKay Gallery – 38 Howe Street, Tel 226 2589.
La Belle Angele – 11 Hasties Close, Cowgate, Tel 225 2774.
Moving Pictures – 24 Avondale Place, Tel 332 9886.
Daniel Shackleton – 17 Dundas Street, Tel 557 1115. Paintings, watercolours, prints.
Quercus – 16 Howe Street, Tel 220 0147.
Solstice Gallery – 18A Dundas Street, Tel 557 5227.
Step Gallery – 39 Howe Street, Tel 556 1613.
Huw Vaughan – 73 Dublin Street, Tel 557 5259.
Waverley Taylor Gallery – 54 Constitution Street, Tel 553 4536.

ANTIQUE DEALERS

I have divided the antique shops in Edinburgh into three sections. Section One is the area north of Princess Street bordered by Queensferry Street in the west and Leith Street in the east. Section Two is the area south of Princess Street bordered by Lothian Road in the west and Canongate Tolbooth in Canongate on the east. Section Three is essentially specialist shops.

Section One:
A good place to start is Dundas Street, which is the continuation of Hanover Street to the north of Queen Street just before the National Portrait Gallery. Here you will find **Bourne Fine Arts** at No 4 (see under art galleries), **Alan Day Antiques**, Tel 557 5220, at No 13C (19th-century furniture and general antiques), **Daniel Shackleton Fine Arts** at No 17 (see Art Galleries), **Letham Antiques** at No 20, Tel 556 6565 (furniture, late 18th-century to art deco, glass, pottery, porcelain, silver, 18th to 20th century), **Fine Art Gallery** at No 41 (see Art Galleries), **James Scott** at No 43, Tel 556 8260 (curiosities, unusual items, silver, jewellery, small furniture), **The Thrie Estaits** at No 49, Tel 556 78084 (pottery, porcelain, glass, unusual decorative items and some furniture), **Unicorn Antiques** at No 65, Tel 556 7176 (glass, china, curios, prints, paintings, metalware and bric-à-brac), **Artisan** at 65A, Tel 556 4253 (stripped pine furniture, antiques, curios, and prints), and **Alan Rankin** at No 72 (see Art Galleries). Continue to the bottom of Dundas

Street and turn left on Cumberland Street. Here you will see **Tom Fidelo** at No 49 and **Open Eye Gallery** at 75/79 (see Art Galleries). Turn right at the junction of Cumberland and Howe and then left into St Stephen Street. There are many riches here. **Margaret Brown** is at Nos 14–16, Tel 225 9357 (general antiques), **Avarice Antiques** is at No 24, Tel 225 7237 (furniture from 18th to early 20th centuries, silver and ceramics), **Michael Hart** is at No 30, Tel 220 1036 (general antiques), **Cinders** is at No 51, Tel 225 3793 (period fireplaces), and **R B Garriock** is at No 58 at the Edinburgh Antique Market, Tel 669 4836 (furniture, porcelain, Victoriana, curios). Walk to the end of St Stephen Street and turn left on to North West Circus. **Hand in Hand** is at No 3 (Victorian linen, embroidery, furnishings, lace, shawls and period costumes), **Dunedin Antiques**, Tel 220 1574 is at No 4 (furniture, period items, chimney pieces, architectural fittings from the 18th and 19th century), **Quadrant Antiques**, at No 5, Tel 226 7282 (nautical items, furniture, brass beds and clocks), and **A F Drysdale** Tel 225 4686, is at Nos 20 and 35 (small antiques, lamps, decorative items and furniture). Close by are **Galloways**, corner of St Stephen's Street and Stockbridge, Tel 225 3221, and **Goodwins Antiques** at 15/16 Queensferry Road, Tel 225 4717 (jewellery and silver). Walk south from North West Circus into Howe Street, passing **Behar Carpets** at No 12A, Tel 225 1069 (Oriental carpets and rugs, 19th century mostly), and continue into Fredericks Street. **John Mathieson** (see Art Galleries) is here at No 48, but you will have turned left onto Thistle Street. Thistle Street has **Fyfe's Antiques** at No 41, Tel 225 4287 (18th- and 19th-century furniture, oil paintings, silver and porcelain), **Aldric Young** at No 49, Tel 226 4101 (general antiques, English and Continental furniture and painting, mostly 18th and 19th century), **Kenneth Jackson** at No 66, Tel 225 9634 (English and Continental furniture – 17th to early 19th centuries), and **Joseph H Bonner** at No 72, Tel 226 2811 (antique and period jewellery). Turn onto Hanover Street and then onto Rose Street where there is another excellent jeweller at 116B. **John Wyte**, Tel 225 2140, has jewellery, watches and silver. Walk east along Rose Street and turn right on Castle Street, you will pass George Street with the **Malcolm Innes Gallery** (see Art Galleries) and then turn right onto Queen Street where **Herald Antiques** is at No 38, Tel 225 5939 (furniture and Persian rugs). Walk the length of Queen Street and opposite the National Portrait Gallery turn left onto Dublin Street and right onto Abany Street where at No 13 is the **Old Golf Shop**, Tel 663 7647. A fascinating place, even if you don't play, with pre-1910 woodshaft clubs, oil painting, art work, bronzes, pottery, silver and medals all related to golf. Last time I was there they seemed to be moving into tennis.

Section Two:
South of Princess Street, bounded by Lothian Road in the west and the Canongate Tolbooth in the east. Start at the Usher Hall and walk down Grindley Street to Spittal Street, turn left and then right across King's Stables Road into Grassmarket. If you turn right here and take the second on the right, High Riggs will take you, via Home Street and Leven Street, into Bruntsfield Place where **Donald Ellis Antiques** is at No 9, Tel 229 1819 (18th- and 19th-century furniture, silver, porcelain, brass and copper), and **Young Antiques** at No 36, Tel 229 1361 (Victorian and Edwardian furniture, ceramics, Persian rugs, oils and watercolours). If you turn left in Grassmarket you will have **Eric Davidson Antiques** at No 83, Tel 667 4119 (furniture, 18th century to Regency, Oriental carpets and rugs and decorative objects to art deco). Grassmarket leads into Candlemakers Row where at No 25 you will find **Another World**, Tel 225 1988 (Netsuke and Oriental art). Due south of Candlemakers Row, across The Meadows, is **This and That Antiques and Bric-à-Brac** at 22 Argyle Place, Tel 229 6069 (porcelain, silver, small furniture, Scottish pottery and bric-à-brac). At the junction of Grassmarket and Candlemakers Row turn left into Victoria Street. Victoria Street is known locally as West Bow, which is a bit confusing, but at 22–24 Victoria Street is **John O Nelson**, Tel 225 4413 (maps, prints and watercolours – a beautiful selection and included here because of some fine antiquarian maps), while at No 38 is **Antiques**, Tel 226 3625 (paintings, glass, china, curios and postcards). Under its more familiar designation of West Bow you will find **Greg Linton Antiques** at No 95, Tel 226 6946 (pictures, glass, bronzes, art nouveau, prints and ephemera), **West Bow Antiques** at No 102, Tel 226 2852 (furniture, pottery, porcelain, glass, brass and decorative items) and **Serendipity** at No 118 (small silver, plate, bijouterie, china, glass and prints). At the end of Victoria Street turn left onto George IV Bridge. In a few yards this intersects with Lawnmarket. Turning left on Lawnmarket will take you to Johnston Terrace and **William Mackintosh and Company** at No 5–5A, Tel 225 6113. They have a large stock of brass architectural and light fittings, fenders, pine panelling and mantelpieces and furniture – mostly Victorian. In Lawnmarket itself you will find **H Parry** at No 330, Tel 225 7615 (silver, porcelain, clocks, English and Continental furniture), and **Court Curio Shop** at No 519, Tel 225 3972.

Lawnmarket, to the east, leads into High Street with **Royal Mile Curios** at No 363, Tel 226 4050 (jewellery and silver). Finally, just past the City Chambers, you will find Cockburn Street on your left with the **Collectors Shop** at No 49, Tel 226 3391. They have coins, medals, militaria, cigarette cards and post-cards, jewellery, silver and plate.

Section Three – Specialist Shops:
Laurence Black at 45 Cumberland Street, Tel 557 4545, specializes in Scottish furniture and decorative items, pottery, porcelain, paintings and prints mostly from north of the border. The **Edinburgh Coin Shop** deals in bullion but also has coins, medals, badges, militaria, postcards, cigarette cards, stamps, jewellery, clocks and watches. They are at 2 Polwarth Crescent, Tel 229 3007. If you are in Leith, three miles (4.8 km) north on the Firth of Forth, you should see **Georgian Antiques** at Poplar Lane, Pattison Street, Tel 553 7286. They specialize in Georgian, Victorian, inlaid and Edwardian furniture, and have a large and excellent stock. Finally, **William MacAdam** at 86 Pilrig Street, Tel 553 1364, is only open by appointment. He specializes in 17th–19th-century collectors of glasses, 18th–19th century coloured glass and usable and pressed glass. If I tell you that some items have sold for £5000 you will realize the exquisite nature of his collection. Serious buyers only.

RESTAURANTS

I used to love to eat in **Pierre Victoire**, 10 Victoria Street, Tel 225 1721, before it was as hugely popular as it is today. I shouldn't resent the restaurant's popularity, but I feel a twinge of regret for how things used to be. What is most important is that the food is still excellent and the prices are still remarkably low. The cooking has real style; mussels with coriander and pink peppercorn, pork with crayfish and salmon with raspberries and champagne. I defy you to find a better set lunch for the price anywhere in the British Isles. The tremendous popularity of the place does cause cramped tables and noise but it's still worth the effort of booking. There is now a branch in Leith (opposite the theatre), which is a bit less crowded, and a new one opposite the castle in Inverness if you are bound for the Highlands. Open all week 12–3pm; 6–11pm.

While we are on the subject of value, **Chinese Home Cooking** at 21 Argyle Place, Tel 229 4404, is excellent. The name says it all. The food is honest, no-frills home cooking produced with care and the meals have none of the "mono-plasticity" of the average take-away. Especially good are the spare ribs, sweet-and-sour prawns and red-cooked char siu pork. Vegetables, as you would expect, are excellent. It's unlicensed, but they do not charge corkage if you bring your own. Open all week, dinner only 5:30–11pm.

The **Indian Cavalry Club** at 3 Atholl Place is ethnicity of a very different kind. The staff are in para-military uniforms and there's a Tiffin Room for snacks. The cooking is traditionally Indian and the lamb is especially good. For vegetarian Indian food I wholeheartedly recommend **Kalpna** at 2–3 Patrick Square, Tel 667 9890. For those who have not sampled the vegetarian cuisine of Gujerat, the place will be an eye-opener. I think the most attractive thing about Indian vegetarian food is its range of flavours. I recommend the set meals which are available at lunch or dinner. Do try the kulfi – you reduce boiling milk for three hours, flavour with saffron, pistachio and sugar and freeze – delicious.

Kelly's – 46 West Richmond Street, Tel 668 3847. A delightfully cosy neighbourhood restaurant, open for dinner only, with a short set menu whose cuisine is French with a nod to Nouvelle Anglaise. The fish soup is especially good as are the puddings. Open Tues–Sat 6:45–9:45pm.

Finally, for something special, I suggest **Martins** at 70 Rose Street, Tel 225 3106. The set lunch is excellent value as is the "carte" dinner. Pheasant, rabbit, salmon have all been commented on favourably and wonderfully. There is no music. Open Tues–Sat 12–2 and 7–10pm. No Sat lunch.

For that very special evening, the **Vintner's Room** at 87 Giles Street, Leith, Tel 554 6767, is housed in the oldest commercial building in Scotland. It's a 17th-century auction room complete with an alcove for the auctioneer and the plasterwork ceiling is superb. The restaurant provides some of the best cooking in the area with seafood especially strong and wonderful desserts. A beautiful place to eat.

PUBS

Deacon Brodie's – 435 Lawnmarket, Tel 225 6531 (see Ephemera for explanation of Deacon Brodie). Period lounge with leather armchairs, lots of woodwork and an open fire. Good traditional bar food.
Abbotsford – Rose Street (beside south St David Street) Tel 225 5276. A pleasantly formal place with a

lovely heavily panelled Victorian island bar. Good bar food with especially good haggis and neeps. Crowded at lunchtime.

Also in Rose Street at No 55 is the **Rose Street Brewery**, Tel 220 1227, which brews its own ale and has good traditional bar food – especially the Ploughman's. Rose Street is rich in pubs, for at the corner with Hanover Street. you will find **Daddy Milnes**, Tel 225 6738, which used to be the focus of Edinburgh literary life in an earlier time. Photographs of the literati who used the pub decorate the walls and it's comfortable and friendly.

Bannerman's Bar – 212 Cowgate, Tel 556 3254. A cellar-like bar in the Old Town, deep under some of its oldest and tallest buildings. Brightly lit rooms with brick barrel-vaulted ceilings, massive stone walls and flagstones. It's furnished with old settles, pews and settees around barrels and red-painted tables. Very good salads at lunchtime and rolls and baps in the evening.

Bennet's Bar – 8 Leven Street (near the King's Theatre) Tel 229 5143. There are art nouveau stained-glass windows, arched and mahogany-pillared mirrors, tilework, cherubs, Florentine-looking damsels and Roman warriors – what more could you want? Red leather seats and marble tables. There's an excellent seafood pie and also very inexpensive curries and casseroles.

ARTISTIC ASSOCIATIONS

There are many ... Allan Ramsay, the great Scottish poet, came to Edinburgh in 1701 as a wig-maker's apprentice. In 1718 he opened a bookshop and by 1720 he was publishing books. He made a collection of new Scots songs set to old melodies, which was extremely popular and *The Gentle Shepherd*, his best-known work, was written in 1725. In 1728 he began the first circulating library in Scotland, which was looked at askance by certain sober-minded people as a potential source of lewd and profane reading for the young. Ramsay retired to a house of his own design on Castle Hill, nicknamed the "Goose Pie" on account of its curious octagonal shape. The first major Edinburgh artist was the portraitist Allan Ramsay, son of the poet, who began his visual art studies at the short-lived Academy of St Luke in Edinburgh (founded in 1729 and dissolved in 1731). Although much of his subsequent career was spent in London where he made his reputation as portrait painter to George III, he continued to visit Edinburgh throughout his life, staying in the unusual octagonal house his father had built. (Now called Ramsay Gardens, the house is marked with a plaque and is much altered.) In 1759 he founded the Select Society of Edinburgh which, in 1760, gave birth to the city's first important art school, the Trustees Academy. John Gay, author of *The Beggar's Opera*, was a friend of Ramsay Senior and they shared many a drink when Gay was employed as a secretary to the eccentric Duchess of Queensberry.

Dr Johnson knew Edinburgh and visited it often with his amanuensis, James Boswell. David Hume, the great historian and philosopher, was born and educated in Edinburgh and lived here most of his life. He is buried in the Calton Old Burial Ground. Tobias Smollett, the author of *Humphrey Clinker*, knew the city well too, and describes it and its notable authors in his best known work. Robert Burns came to Edinburgh in 1786 after the success of the first edition of his poems. He published a second Edinburgh edition in 1787 which was extremely popular and Burns was a hit in Edinburgh society as he played up his role of "ploughman poet." In fact he charmed society with his conversation and vitality and managed to fall in love with a Mrs Maclehose, whose husband was abroad. The relationship inspired Burns's poetry and was a meaningful one for him.

Sir Walter Scott was born in Edinburgh on the 15th of August, 1771. He attended Edinburgh High School and passed his university exams as an advocate in 1792. He married Charlotte Carpenter in 1797 and the couple moved to 39 Castle Street where they lived for 28 years and where Scott wrote the Waverley novels. He retired from the court in 1830 and spent the final two years of his life at his house in Abbotsford in the Borders. The poet Thomas Campbell studied law in Edinburgh in 1796 and was a friend of Scott's. Campbell's most famous line, supposedly written on Calton Hill, is "'Tis distance lends enchantment to the view." The great historian and essayist, Thomas Carlyle, lived in Edinburgh and was elected Lord Rector of the University in 1865. Robert Louis Stevenson grew up in Edinburgh and scenes of his childhood are contained in *A Child's Garden of Verses*. His famous *Treasure Island* began as a story told to his stepson and was first published as a serial. Like Scott, he was an advocate, but ill health took him to America and finally to Samoa, where he died. The commemorative tablet in St Giles' Cathedral bears the lines from his grave in Samoa.

> Under the wide and starry sky
> Dig the grave and let me lie.

Other Edinburgh natives were Kenneth Grahame, author of *The Wind in The Willows* and Sir Arthur Conan Doyle, creator of Sherlock Holmes, J M Barrie, author of *Peter Pan* and Sir Compton Mackenzie, author of *Whisky Galore*, also spent much time in the city.

More recently, the great sculptor, Sir Eduardo Paolozzi, was born and trained in Edinburgh, while Sir Harry Lauder, the popular singer and entertainer was born in a cottage in the city. Sean Connery used to deliver milk in the city in a horse-drawn cart. He delivered milk to Fettes College, which was the school that Ian Fleming chose to be attended by his fictional secret agent, James Bond, a character Connery will always be associated with. Connery donated £1,000,000 from one of his Bond films to found the Scottish International Education Trust. The novelist, Muriel Spark *(The Prime of Miss Jean Brodie)* was born here and educated in the city where, no doubt, some of the ideas for "Jean Brodie" had their genesis.

Two celebrated figures in the early history of Scottish painting were exceptional in remaining largely in Edinburgh during their careers. The landscapist, Alexander Nasmyth, was also responsible for designing and building a classical temple on the banks of the Water of Leith at Stockbridge (see above). Henry Raeburn was a portraitist and a very good one at that! He was born in the Saunders Bridge area of the city in 1756 and in 1780 he married Anne Edgar, a well-off widow 12 years his senior. No doubt with her financial help he built one of the first of Edinburgh's suburbs, on land he acquired at Stockbridge; the splendid Ann Street was reputed to have been built by him as a present to his wife. Raeburn's reputation as a painter was excellent and he was very successful in obtaining patrons; in all, he produced about a thousand portraits in his lifetime. In spite of this he suffered a severe financial setback around 1810 and was forced to sell a large studio he had built at 32 York Place (there is a plaque). He even considered moving to London, which would undoubtedly have been more lucrative, but he decided finally to remain in Edinburgh and did so for the rest of his life. He died in 1823.

George IV visited Edinburgh in 1822 and four years later the Scottish Academy was founded. The Academy improved exhibiting facilities for local artists and offered encouragement and support to all. In 1838 it was granted a royal charter and from then on Edinburgh became an important art centre in its own right. In the early 1900s the Edinburgh College of Art was founded and the flow of excellent Scottish painters graduating from its halls has continued to this day.

EPHEMERA

In the Grassmarket in 1736, an Edinburgh mob lynched Captain Porteous, the commander of the town guard. Porteous had ordered the guard to fire upon a crowd, with fatal results, and was convicted of murder, but then received a reprieve from London. Incensed, the mob dragged Porteous from the Tolbooth prison which stood in the Royal Miles near St Giles' Cathedral, purchased a rope in the West Bow (Victoria Street) and hanged him in the Grassmarket from a dyer's pole. There are elements of mystery in the affair. It is said that the abduction and hanging of Captain Porteous was carried out with orderliness and some evidence of organization (a guinea was left on the shop counter in payment for the rope) and the crowd dispersed immediately after the fatal deed. In London, Queen Caroline, the wife of George II, was acting as Regent during the King's absence in Hanover. The news of the death of Porteous infuriated the Queen, who made all sorts of dire threats including the abolition of the city charter. Finally a fine was levied against the city, which was paid without demur.

Mary, Queen of Scots, reigned in Scotland for a mere six years, but she has left an indelible memory. Married at 15 to the Dauphin of France, widowed at 19, she returned to her native Scotland and ascended the throne in a great wave of popularity. She married her weak and debauched cousin, Lord Darnley, who was then a leading conspirator in the murder of her Italian secretary, David Rizzio, who was dragged from her presence and stabbed to death. Darnley himself was murdered in a mysterious explosion and the Queen was suspected of being involved. Within weeks she married the Earl of Bothwell. Mary, a devout Roman Catholic, found her throne assailed by the father of the Protestant Reformation, John Knox. She was humiliated by the mob on the streets of Edinburgh, and imprisoned; then, having been persuaded to abdicate, she escaped in disguise, was defeated in battle, and fled to England. There she threw herself on the mercy of the English Queen, Elizabeth, and was kept under house arrest in England for the next 19 years. In 1587 she was accused of plotting against the English throne and beheaded in Fotheringay Castle. She was still only 44 years of age.

Contemporary accounts inform us she was the most beautiful woman of her time. Her native sweetness and graciousness was heightened by the polish of manner she had gained at the French court. She was warm, affectionate, graceful and generous and this was combined with a loveliness which almost everyone who approached her felt to be irresistible. It is said that at her death her face retained its exquisite form but that her hair was as white as snow.

One more mystery that still surrounds Mary is that of the "Casket Letters." These were eight letters and a series of poems written by Mary to James, Earl of Bothwell, whom she married after the mysterious death of her husband Henry, Lord Darnley, in 1567. At least one of the letters was held to prove Mary's complicity with Bothwell in Darnley's death. The letters were found in a casket that fell into the hands of the Earl of Morton four months after Darnley's death and a few days after Mary's surrender to the rebelling Scottish lords. The following year, the letters were used as evidence in the investigation of the charges brought against Mary by the rebels. All trace of the original letters disappeared after 1584 and their authenticity is still a matter of dispute.

Most holy wells in Britain were healing wells, the greatest number of them being sought for eye troubles. One of the Scottish eye wells (now dry) was St Triduana's Well, Restalrig, on the outskirts of the city, which was housed in a chapel adjoining the parish church. St Triduana was invoked for curing diseases of the eye because of the tale that when a local prince became enamoured of her beautiful eyes, she had them cut out and given to him – she is probably a Scottish version of St Lucy. It is thought St Triduana came to Scotland in the 4th century with St Rule (see St Andrew's).

Whether it was simply the bathing of the eyes in cold water that was efficacious, or whether it was a matter of faith, eye wells were visited up and down the country. Just two of them are the Eye Well at Llandrindod Wells in Powys and St Mary the Virgin's Well at Dunsfold in Surrey (just south of Guildford).

Immediately outside the entrance to Greyfriars Kirkyard, at the crest of Candlemaker Row, stands the celebrated bronze likeness of Greyfriars Bobby. This is perhaps the most famous memorial to a dog to be found anywhere. For more than a century now, this true story has had an extraordinary hold on the public imagination; moreover, the story now seems to be as well known abroad as it is in Scotland, to judge by the number of foreign tourists being photographed beside the monument.

In 1858 the faithful Skye terrier followed the remains of his master, John Gray, to Greyfriars Kirkyard. After the interment, the dog refused to leave the graveside. For the next 14 years, until his own death, Bobby was never far from the kirkyard. A shelter was constructed there for him and he was given his food regularly in the kitchens of dining rooms nearby. When the awkward question of his licence arose, the Lord Provost of the day paid it personally. The story of Bobby's fidelity spread throughout the land and people came from all over the country to see the dog. One of these, the philanthropist Baroness Burdett Coutts, was so impressed that she caused the statue to be erected. Bobby's collar is on display at the Huntly House Museum in the Canongate.

Close to the junction of South Bridge and High Street is Paisley Close. It was near here in 1861 that one of the tenement buildings collapsed, burying a number of residents in the ruins. As rescuers toiled amid the debris, they were encouraged by a cry, "Heave awa' chaps, I'm no' dead yet." The entrance to the close now bears a sculpted head of the spirited young man who survived the calamity.

On the south side of the Lawnmarket is Brodie's Close. It is named after a respectable craftsman, Francis Brodie, but it is his son, William Brodie, whose name and deeds everyone remembers. William Brodie was, ostensibly, a respectable member of the Town Council but he was also a professional burglar on the grand scale. He was unmasked as the result of an unsuccessful armed raid on the Excise Office at Chessels Court, off the Canongate. Brodie managed to escape to Holland, but he was arrested there, brought back for trial, convicted and hanged in public in the High Street in 1788. The final irony was that Brodie was executed with an improved version of the gallows invented by himself. His nefarious career certainly made a lasting impression. The largest public house in the Lawnmarket is named after him and his double life inspired Robert Louis Stevenson to write "The Strange Case of Dr Jekyll and Mr Hyde."

Very close to where an Edinburgh mob lynched Captain Porteous in the Grassmarket is West Port where, between 1827 and 1828, there lived in Tanner's Close the infamous murderers Burke and Hare. The University's anatomists at that time had difficulty in finding cadavers, and Burke and Hare hit on the idea of digging up recently buried bodies and selling them to the University, where not too many questions were asked. Soon it struck the evil pair that they could supplement their grisly income even further if they found derelict street people and encouraged them to meet their maker. In this way they suffocated close to a score of men and women in less than a year and sold their bodies for profit. When they were finally discovered, Hare turned King's evidence and escaped the rope but Burke was hanged in the Lawnmarket.

I've just realized that the majority of the stories above have some macabre or brutal aspect to them, and if this is to your liking you should take an Edinburgh Ghost Walking Tour, which visits many of the places mentioned above and will introduce you to the haunted aspects of Edinburgh. Tours last about 90 minutes and details can be obtained from either Mercat Tours at 661 4541 or Robin's Tours at 661 0125.

There has often been friction between the essentially conservative nature of Edinburgh and the avant-garde nature of some of the Edinburgh Festival offerings. In 1949, T S Eliot's *The Cocktail Party* was premiered and it created the same kind of bemused antagonism as Harold Pinter's plays created a decade later.

The eminent critic, Ivor Browne, writing in *The Observer*, comments, "What was it all about? Well, there at a party is Alec Guinness as a Mystery Guest, who might be devil or saint and turns out to be a psychotherapist remarkable for taking no fees and keeping Lady Sneerwell (Catherine Nesbit) as an eavesdropper in his anteroom. His business seems to be mending other people's marriages or lack of them. He tells a quarrelsome couple some stinging home truths, which apparently reconciles them and sends a sad young woman to a death worse than fate in a way which struck me as purely sadistic. I have rarely disliked someone so much as this icy healer of Mr Eliot's." Not very flattering you might think, but certainly better than Alan Dent, who wrote in the *News Chronicle*, "The week after – as well as the morning after – I take it to be a finely acted piece of flapdoodle."

Perhaps it's time to put the critics in their place. Even one of the 20th century's finest critics, Kenneth Tynan, described the critic as "a man who knows the way but can't drive the car." Others have been less kind. Christopher Hampton, British playwright, once said, "Asking a working actor what he thinks about critics is like asking a lamp-post how it feels about dogs." But, as in so many other things, it would be wise to leave the last word to the Irish. The author of *The Hostage*, Brendan Behan, was one of the most flamboyant theatrical figures of this century. His views require just a pinch of salt – "Critics are like eunuchs in a harem. They're there every night, they see it done every night, they see how it should be done every night, but they can't do it themselves."

TOURIST INFORMATION BUREAU: Waverley Market, Princes Street, Edinburgh, EH2 2QP. Tel (031) 557 1700

GLASGOW

County of Strathclyde
Five hours by train from London (Euston or King's Cross)
397 miles (635 km) from London by M1, M6 and A74

St Kentigern, more familiarly known as St Mungo, founded Glasgow in the 6th century. He is the city's patron saint and the 12th-century cathedral is dedicated to him. Kentigern was a missionary and the first buildings he constructed on the site were of wood and wattles, but there is reason to believe that his chapel was of stone and about 20 feet (7 m) long and six feet (1.8 m) wide, with a cell attached to it, in which he lived. Kentigern was visited at his little church by St Columba of Iona. When one is in the Glasgow of today it is hard to realize that the original meaning of the name Glagu, Glesgu, Gleschow or Glasgow was "beloved green place" – truer in Kentigern's time than now.

After Kentigern there were dark centuries, and although the saintly influence of Queen Margaret spread to St Andrew's it does not appear to have reached Glasgow. As far as we know the Cathedral was built between 1238 and 1438 and is now occupied as the parish Church of Glasgow by the Church of Scotland (see below). This great building escaped the wrath of the Reformation because the tradesmen and craftsmen of Glasgow would not allow its destruction. The "idolatrous" statues of the saints were removed from their niches but the overall fabric was saved. There is an excellent account of this event in Sir Walter Scott's novel *Rob Roy*. Virtually nothing remains of pre-Reformation Glasgow except the Cathedral and the Provand's Lordship House in Cathedral Square (see below). Glasgow University was founded in 1451, the second in Scotland, and only 40 years behind St Andrew's. Classes were held in the Cathedral Crypt until the 17th century. Of the original buildings in the High Street, nothing remains (they were knocked down to accommodate a railway goods yard) and the University is now housed in Victorian Gothic buildings in Kelvingrove Park.

During the Border Wars, Glasgow was a rallying point for Scottish armies engaged in feuds and battles with England, in particular with the city of Carlisle. It remained a small

ART GALLERY AND MUSEUM, KELVINGROVE   GLASGOW

port, market and university city until the 18th century. It was a noted salmon port and, hard as it may be to imagine today, the Clyde was a noted salmon river. Glasgow began as a salmon fishing village and fishing rights were eagerly sought after and are mentioned in 12th-century charters. In 1748 the Glasgow *Journal* announced that salmon could be bought in the market for one penny per pound. Much of this salmon was smoked and exported and large quantities of herring were also caught. Gradually the Clyde was allowed to silt up and the herring disappeared, but as late as the middle of the 19th century fishing remained an industry. In the early part of the 18th century, Glasgow became an important centre for the tobacco trade. With the American Revolution in 1775, this trade diminished and shipbuilding and publishing industries became the city's foremost employers. The wide Clyde, with its docks and quays stretching right to the heart of the city, became a great centre for shipbuilding and many great liners and warships bore the word "Clydebuilt" which, in itself, was a sign of excellence in craftsmanship. The shipbuilding has declined of late but the printing industry, headed by the House of Collins, still remains a major Glasgow industry. Much of Glasgow has been rebuilt, rejuvenated and restored in recent years, and the city has undergone both a transformation and a renaissance, culminating in its award as Cultural Capital of Europe in 1990. Given this remarkable progress, it would be no surprise if, very soon, salmon will once again make their way up the Clyde to their ancient spawning grounds far up the hills of what used to be Lanarkshire.

Glasgow is a big city, the largest in Scotland; if you attempt these two walks on the same day make sure you are fit, for at the end you will have walked seven miles (11.2 km).

WALKS

Walk One – Start out at the parking lot just behind Strathclyde University in George Street. Turn right along George Street into **George Square**. This is the oldest of Glasgow's public squares and is a popular lunchtime rendezvous. Sir Walter Scott's statue looks over the square from an 80-foot (24.3 m) pillar. Less elevated is the statue of Lord Clyde, formerly Sir Colin Campbell, who was born nearby and commanded the 93rd Highlanders at Balaclava. The east side of the square is looked upon by the **City Chambers**, a massive Renaissance-style building of 1888, with opulent interiors. At the opposite corner, a gilded sailing ship on a globe marks the **Merchants' House** founded in 1605 and still administering many charitable trusts. Leave George Square at its northwest corner, along West George Street. Just beyond the Merchants' House, turn left along Anchor Lane and then right into **St Vincent Place**. A rich variety of late-Victorian architecture graces the north side of this short street, named after the British naval victory over the Spanish at Cape St Vincent in 1797. White-glazed Doulton tiling covers the façades of Nos 12–16, whose anchor decorations recall that the buildings were once the shipping offices of the Anchor Line.

Next door the colour changes to sandstone, with fine window arrangements and decorated pillars rising to a Dutch-gabled roof. Carved medallions spell out the words, "Citizen Office" reminding us that the building was formerly the home of the now defunct *Citizen* newspaper. The row is completed by the pillars, carvings and balustrades of the frontage of the **Clydesdale Bank**. Continue ahead along St Vincent Street and the Victorian splendours continue. Here, among the monumental banking and insurance houses, the classical frontage of the **Bank of Scotland** should be noticed and, beyond Hope Street, No 142, known as the Hatrack from its ten sandstone storeys on a narrow base. Turn right up Blythswood Street into Blythswood Square. Built around wooded gardens, the square is one of the most sought-after business addresses in Glasgow. The **Royal Scottish Automobile Club** headquarters occupies the Square's east side and this used to be the British starting-point for the Monte Carlo Rally. A resident of No 7 was Madeline Smith, who in 1857 figured in the most notorious of all Glasgow's murder cases. She was accused of poisoning her lover, Emile L'Angelier. Feelings for and against her ran so high in Glasgow that the trial was held in Edinburgh where the jury reached the uniquely Scottish verdict of "not proven." Come back into Blythswood Street and at the crossroads turn left and then right down Douglas Street. Go into Sauchiehall Street and turn left. Beyond the **Royal Highland Fusiliers Museum** (see below) follow the pavement round to the right. Immediately before a high footbridge over the main road, turn right up Renfrew Street, then bear left across the street and take the shrub-lined path below the steps. Bear right into Buccleuch Street. Pass **Tenement House** (see below) and turn right up Garnet Street, across Hill Street, then left into Renfrew Street to **Glasgow School of Art** (see below) on the right. Turn right down Dalhousie Street, then left onto Sauchiehall Street (which becomes a pedestrian precinct) to the **Willow Tearoom** at No 217. This was the last and finest of a series designed by architect Charles Rennie Mackintosh (see Ephemera) for a turn-of-the-century caterer, Miss Kate Cranston. Disused for several years, the first-floor "Room de Luxe" is again a tearoom, with replica Mackintosh chairs and tables and art nouveau decorations restored to the original designs. Turn right down West Nile Street, then left on West George Street. Here the **Clydesdale Bank Headquarters** is a striking example of modern commercial architecture while the Venetian-Gothic **Stock Exchange** and the red sandstone extravaganza of **No 34** (the sculpted heads are of Glasgow industrialists and shipowners) should not be missed. Keep St George's Church on your left and continue along George Street back to the car park.

Walk Two – Walk down George Street, then turn left into John Street, through archways decorated with carvings of ships' prows. Continue along Hutcheson Street. Turn right into Garth Street and cross to **Trades House**. This building is the only major building in Glasgow designed by Robert Adam. It is occupied by a federation of 14 of the city's trade guilds from Hammermen to Bonnetmakers. The finest room, completed in 1794, is the banqueting hall which has a silk frieze showing the work of all the historic trades. Leaving Trades House, turn right on Glassford Street. Take the first turning to the right into Wilson Street, then turn left into Virginia Street to **No 33**. This building, built in 1819, is today a warren of antique and collector's shops but it was once the tobacco exchange and later the sugar exchange. High on an inner wall is the "pulpit" from which the auctioneer called for bids. Retrace your steps on Virginia Street and then go left and right along Virginia Place. Keep left onto Ingram Street towards the Corinthian columns of **Stirling's Library**. Originally the pillared mansion of a tobacco lord, the house is now the city's largest lending library. It is named after Walter Stirling, whose gift in 1791 of an 804-volume collection formed the basis of Glasgow's public library service. Follow the south side of Royal Exchange Square through the archway and go left into Buchanan Street. This pedestrian precinct's mix of old and new includes the charming **Clydesdale Bank**, built in 1891 of multi-coloured sandstone and a five-level atrium of shops, restaurants and cafés. A constantly swinging pendulum suspended from the roof of the atrium is a replica of one designed in 1851 by the French physicist, Foucault, to prove the rotation of the earth on its axis. The glass-roofed **Argyll Arcade** was built in 1827, modelled on arcades in Paris. Continue straight on across Argyll Street, keeping right of the underground station. Continue along Clyde Street, then turn left to cross the river by the Suspension Bridge. The River Clyde that divides Glasgow and gives it its character provides an atmospheric view when seen from the 1853 Suspension Bridge, which pedestrians used to pay a halfpenny to cross. Turn left along Carlton Place. Here the Georgian buildings of Glasgow's finest riverside terrace look out across gardens to the River Clyde. Moored on the north bank, the sailing ship *Carrick*, originally the fast wool clipper *City of Adelaide*, now serves the Royal Naval Volunteer Reserve. On the skyline behind it, the **Merchants' Steeple** of 1665 retains the high-level balconies from which traders used to scan the river to see if their ships were safely on the incoming tide. Continue left along the river, noting the mosque towers. At the second main road bridge, Albert Bridge, turn left back over the Clyde and turn right into Glasgow Green. Glasgow people have had free use of the green since the 12th century. The two great Glasgow football teams, Rangers and Celtics, played their early matches here. A Doulton earthenware fountain depicts Queen Victoria, while a 144-foot (43.7 m) obelisk is Glasgow's memorial to **Lord Nelson**. Nearby, another memorial celebrates James Watts's sudden inspiration for a new steam engine as he strolled through the green in 1767. Pass the fountain and the obelisk and bear left through gates into the **People's Palace** (see below). Leave by the front entrance, turn left and follow the path left and then right out of the avenue of trees. Cross Greendyke Street and turn left over the crossing, then right into Saltmarket (recalling that for centuries the Clyde was a great salmon river). Turn left into Trongate; close by is **Glasgow Cross**, topped by a heraldic unicorn. This is a 1929 replica of a cross removed in 1659. Across the road is the 17th-century **Tolbooth Steeple**, and nearby the arched **Tron Steeple** is all that remains of a 17th-century church burned down in 1793 by the Hellfire Club. Now turn right into Albion Street, left into Bell Street and right into Candleriggs. On the wall of **City Hall** note the plaque to John Maclean, Lenin's Soviet consul in Scotland. Facing **Ramshorn Kirk** and its secluded graveyard, turn left into Ingram Street, then right into Montrose Street back to the car park.

MUSEUMS, GALLERIES AND PUBLIC BUILDINGS

Glasgow Art Gallery and Museum – Kelvingrove, Argyle Street, Tel 357 3929. Home of Britain's finest civic collection of British and European paintings, including a fine display of Impressionist work. Also displays of natural history, archaeology, history and ethnography and collections of silver, pottery, porcelain and arms and armour. Open Mon–Sat 10–5pm, Sun 2–5pm.

Burrell Collection – Pollok Country Park, 2060 Pollokshaws Road, Tel 649 7151. The Burrell Collection was given to Glasgow in 1944 by Sir William and Lady Burrell. The unique collection has more that 8000 items and includes exhibits from the ancient world, Oriental art, paintings (especially 19th-century French) furniture, carpets, ceramics, tapestries and stained glass. Open Mon–Sat 10–5pm, Sun 2–5pm.

Haggs Castle – 100 St Andrew's Drive, Tel 427 2725. Over four centuries old, originally built in 1585, the house is now a children's museum and features a reconstructed kitchen, Victorian nursery and 18th-century cottage. Activities for children are available throughout the year. Open Mon–Sat 10–5pm, Sun 2–5pm.

Hunterian Museum – Glasgow University, University Avenue, Tel 330 4421. Glasgow's oldest museum features displays of geology, archaeology and ethnography. Also the history of Glasgow University, and William Hunter's world-famous corn cabinet. Open Mon–Fri 9:30–5pm, Sat 9:30–1pm.

Thomas Muir Museum – Crowhill Road, Bishopbriggs, Tel 775 8592. Once the Muir family home, Huntershill House is now a recreation centre and has a room devoted to the life and work of Thomas Muir, the radical reformer. Open by appointment only.

People's Palace – Glasgow Green, Tel 554-0223. A fascinating museum devoted to the history of Glasgow. Items related to trades and industry, trade unions, labour movement, women's suffrage, entertainment and sport. Open Mon–Sat 10–5pm, Sun 2–5pm.

Pollok House – Pollok Country Park, 2060 Pollokshaws Road, Tel 632 0274. In 1966 Mrs Anne Maxwell MacDonald and her family gifted Glasgow with this ancestral home, which stands in 361 acres (146 ha) of parkland and gardens. The house's centre block dates from 1750 and is Glasgow's most important example of 19th-century architecture. One of the finest collections of Spanish paintings in Britain is housed here and there are also works by other European masters including William Blake. There is furniture dating 1750–1820 and displays of silver, ceramics and glass. Open Mon–Sat 10–5pm, Sun 2–5pm.

Provand's Lordship – 3 Castle Street, Tel 552 8819. Built in 1471, this is the oldest house in Glasgow. It has displays, including the 16th-century room of the chaplain of the Hospital of St Nicholas, and a fine collection of 17th-century furniture. Open Mon–Sat 10–5pm, Sun 2–5pm.

Regimental Museum of the Royal Highland Fusiliers – 518 Sauchiehall Street, Tel 332 0961. Uniforms, pictures, medals, mementos and militaria relating to the regiment's fascinating 300-year history. Open Mon–Thurs 9–4:30pm, Fri 9–4pm.

Springburn Museum – Ayr Street, Tel 557 1405. A recent museum devoting itself to the social history of Springburn, once the largest locomotive manufacturing centres in Europe. Open Mon–Fri 10:30–5pm, Sat 1–5pm, Sun 2–5pm.

Tenement House – 145 Buccleuch Street, Tel 333 0183. Built in 1892, the Tenement House captures the living conditions of the Victorian era for the working class and presents a picture of great social significance. Open daily 2–4pm (April–Oct) Sat, Sun 2–4pm (Nov–Mar)

Museum of Transport – Kelvin Hall, Bunhouse Road, Tel 357 3929. A new and considerably enlarged museum of the history of transport including a reproduction of a typical 1938 Glasgow Street. The museum also features a comprehensive display of model ships and a walk-in motor car showroom, with cars from the 1930s to modern times. Other displays include Glasgow trams and buses, Scottish-built cars, fire engines, horse-drawn vehicles, commercial vehicles, cycles and motorcycles, railway locomotives and a Glasgow subway station. Open Mon–Sat 10–5pm, Sun 2–5pm.

Museum of the 602 (City of Glasgow) Squadron – Queen Elizabeth Avenue, Hillingdon, Tel 882 6201. Evocative tribute to a famous squadron with many photographs and pieces of memorabilia on display, including the Battle of Britain necktie and the book containing the names of those who took part in this famous battle.

The Dome of Discovery – South Rotunda, Govan Road, Tel 427 1792. "Hands on" exhibits make science a lot of fun for all the family. Special events during the school holidays.

Crookston Castle – Brockburn Road. The 15th-century tower house has links with Mary, Queen of Scots, and Lord Darnley. Although the castle is a ruin, the remains of the tower can still be seen. Open Mon–Sat 9:30–4pm, Sun 2–4pm.

Glasgow Cathedral – Castle Street. Established by Saint Mungo, Patron Saint of Glasgow, in 543. The present building dates in part to the 12th century and is a fine example of pre-Reformation Gothic architecture. It contains the tomb of St Mungo. Open April–Sept Mon–Sat 9:30–7pm, Sun 2–5pm; Oct–Mar Mon–Sat 9:30–4pm, Sun 2–4pm.

The Necropolis – John Knox Street (close to Glasgow Cathedral). Laid out in 1833, with paths leading up a sugar-loaf hill, the Necropolis is one of Britain's great cemeteries. Based on the Père Lachaise burial ground in Paris, the hill is dominated by Thomas Hamilton's monument to John Knox, which was erected in 1825 and is consequently earlier than the Necropolis itself.

St Mary's Cathedral – Great Western Road. St Mary's is the Cathedral Church of the Diocese of Glasgow and Galloway in the Episcopal Church of Scotland. It was built in 1870–71. Its 205-foot (62.3 m) spire, a notable Glasgow landmark, was added in 1892. It should be noted that St Mungo's Cathedral (above) is no longer really a cathedral, but a parish kirk of Glasgow where services are conducted according to the Presbyterian rites of the Church of Scotland.

Collins Gallery – University of Strathclyde, 22 Richmond Street, Tel 552 4400. A lively gallery presenting an annual programme of 12 exhibitions from home and abroad. Most exhibitions are supplemented by workshops, talks, demonstrations, dance, drama and music. Open Mon–Fri 10–5pm, Wed 10–7pm, Sat 12–4pm.

Glasgow Arts Centre – 12 Washington Street, Tel 221 4526. Two large gallery spaces maintain a varied programme of events, exhibitions, courses and workshops. Operated by Strathclyde Council's Community Education Service. Open Mon–Fri 10–8pm, Sat 10–3pm.

Glasgow Print Studio – 22 King Street, Tel 552 0704. A contemporary gallery in Glasgow's Merchant City with a monthly exhibition programme of original prints, paintings and sculpture by local, national and international artists. Open Mon–Sat 10–5:30pm.

Glasgow School of Art – 167 Renfrew Street, Tel 332 9797 (see also Ephemera). GSA has two exhibition spaces, the Mackintosh Building and the Newberry Gallery. The changing exhibition programme ranges from contemporary visual art through to design and architecture. There are also tours of the school. Term time – Mon–Thurs 9:30–8pm, Fri 9:30–5pm, Sat 10–noon; Non term time – Mon–Fri 9:30–4:30, Sat 10–noon.

McLellan Galleries – 270 Sauchiehall Street, Tel 331 1854. The purpose-built 1854 exhibition galleries, completely refurbished for Glasgow's celebrations as Cultural Capital of Europe, provide a major exhibition venue. Open Mon–Sat 10–5pm, Thurs 10–10pm, Sun 12–6pm.

Glasgow Sculpture Studios – 82 Hanson Street, Tel 551 0562. The studios bring together sculptors, the community, public bodies and private business to develop an understanding of how sculpture can improve our environment. The studios initiate commissions, exhibitions and exchange programmes. Open Mon–Fri 10–5pm.

Hunterian Art Gallery – University of Glasgow, Hillhead Street, Tel 330 5431. Major collections of work by J M Whistler and C R Mackintosh, including the Mackintosh House (see Ephemera), also works by Rembrandt, Stubbs, Reynolds, Pissarro and Rodin, and Scottish painting from the 18th century to the present. Varied exhibitions. Open Mon–Fri 9:30–5pm, Sat 9:30–1pm; May–Oct Mon–Sat 9:30–5pm, Sun 2–5pm.

Open Circle – Hillhead Library, 348 Byres Road, Tel 339 9492. A group of writers, artists and composers whose policy is to take art to the public through a continuous programme of exhibitions. Mostly contemporary and international. Open Mon–Fri 10:30–8pm (closed Wed) Sat 9:30–1 and 2–5pm.

Kelly Gallery – Douglas Street, Tel 248 6386. The Kelly Gallery, owned by the Royal Glasgow Institute of Fine Arts, hosts a wide variety of paintings and sculpture. The emphasis is on encouraging younger artists to exhibit. A good place to see contemporary Scottish art. Open Mon–Fri 10:30–2 and 2:30–5:30pm, Sat 10–12:30pm.

Third Eye Centre – 346–354 Sauchiehall Street, Tel 332 7521. Glasgow's major centre for new developments in the visual and performing arts. Up to 24 exhibitions a year by Scottish, English and international artists. Three exhibition spaces, two theatres, bookshop and wholefood café. Open Tue–Sat 10–5:30pm, Sun 12–5:30pm.

Glasgow Group Gallery – 17 Queen's Crescent, St George's Cross, Tel 332 4924. Run by artists and housed in a listed building, the Glasgow Group has provided a focus for contemporary work in the West of Scotland since 1957. There are continually changing exhibitions. Open Mon–Fri 11–6pm.

Transmission – 28 Kings Street, Trongate, Tel 552 4813. A non-profit organization run voluntarily by practising local artists. The gallery supports a diversity of working methods, which would not otherwise be represented through commercially oriented or established art institutions. Open Mon–Sat 11–5:30pm.

Note – **Tramway** (see Theatre) often has exciting visual art on show.

THEATRE

Arches Theatre – The Arches, off Jamaica Street, Tel 204 3993. Essentially an arts centre presenting mostly avant-garde productions of theatre, performance art and music. This is a good place to see new Scottish drama.

Citizens Theatre – Gorbals Street, Tel 429 0022. An internationally renowned theatre with low seat prices and an excellent, hard-hitting repertoire of unusual, high-quality plays. Contemporary drama, little-known classics and European works make up the rich and varied programme. The theatre also plays host to some visiting companies.

Glasgow Arts Centre – 12 Washington Street, Tel 221 4526. Mainly avant-garde small-scale theatre, with other arts activity.

Kings Theatre – Bath Street, Tel 227 5511. A splendidly grand and ornate theatre, built in 1904, offering top touring theatre attractions and also ballet, music, opera and one-night stands. Seating 1792.

Mitchell Theatre – Granville Street, Tel 227 5511. Opened in 1981, the Mitchell, like the Kings, is run by Glasgow City Council. Besides acting as an overspill venue for touring companies, it also plays host to amateur drama productions, lectures and meetings.

Theatre Royal – Hope Street, Tel 331 1234. Rescued in 1975 from its fate as a TV station, this fine theatre has been restored to its original Victorian splendour. It is Scotland's only opera house and acts as a home to Scottish Opera and as a regular host to Scottish Ballet, the Royal National Theatre, Glyndebourne Touring Opera, the Rambert Ballet Company and other international performances. Seating 1500.

Tron Theatre – 38 Parnie Street, Tel 552 4267. Housed in an 'A' listed church building, the Tron has an impressive record of innovative theatre in a club atmosphere. Mostly contemporary drama with some musical events.

The Tramway – 25 Albert Drive, Tel 227 5511. Glasgow's old Museum of Transport has been transformed into an exciting venue for opera, drama and dance performance.

Old Athenaeum Theatre – 179 Buchanan Street, Tel 332 2333. Small-scale touring venue, with related arts activities.

Pavilion Theatre – Renfield Street, Tel 332 1846. Variety, rock and pop concert venue with a popular pantomime season.

Third Eye Centre – 350 Sauchiehall Street, Tel 332 1846. One of Glasgow's most exciting theatre spaces. Small scale, mostly avant-garde touring.

Royal Scottish Academy of Music and Drama – 100 Renfrew Street, Tel 332 5057. Presents a varied programme of international performances. Festival Theatre and School of Drama productions.

It's well worth phoning the **Glasgow University Visitors' Centre** to see if the University Drama Department has a play in production. Tel 330 5511. **Glasgow's Grand Ole Opry** operates Friday, Saturday and Sunday evenings at 2/4 Govan Road, Paisley Road Toll, Tel 429 5396, for country music devotees.

For the arts, the best time to visit Glasgow is for **Mayfest**, the year's major arts festival held over three weeks every May. Tel 552 8000. Touring out of Glasgow and well worth looking for are the 7:84 Scottish People's Theatre, Tel 331 2219, Wildcat Stage Productions, Tel 951 1200 and TAG Theatre out of The Citizens, Tel 429 2877.

MUSIC

City Hall – Candleriggs, Tel 227 5511. An impressive venue with performances from the Scottish National Orchestra to folk music.

Glasgow International Concert Hall – Killermont Street, Tel 227 5511. The city's superb new 2500-seat concert venue. The new permanent home of the Scottish National Orchestra. The SNO give weekly concerts in the winter season and promenade concerts in June.

Henry Wood Hall – Claremont Street, Tel 332 7244. The former Trinity Church, converted into a concert hall with excellent acoustics.

Royal Scottish Academy of Music and Drama – 100 Renfrew Street, Tel 332 5057. Varied programme of visiting orchestras, chamber groups and soloists in the Chandler Studio and Stevenson Hall.

Note that information and tickets for all events, both theatrical and musical, can be obtained at the **Ticket Centre**, Candleriggs, Tel 227 551. For specialized musical information, the following may be of help;

BBC Scottish Symphony Orchestra – Tel 330 2353.
National Youth Orchestra of Scotland – Tel 332 8311.
Scottish Ballet – Tel 331 2931 (They perform regularly at the Theatre Royal).
Scottish Early Music Consort – Tel 334 9229.
Scottish National Orchestra – Tel 332 7244.
Scottish Opera – Tel 332 9000 (Resident at Theatre Royal from Sept–June.)
Scottish Music Information Service – Tel 334 6393.

CINEMA

Commercial cinema;
Cannon – Clarkson Road, Muirhead (2 screens) Tel 637 2641.
Cannon – The Forge, Parkhead (7 screens) Tel 556 4282.
Cannon – Sauchiehall Street (5 screens) Tel 332 1592.
City Centre Odeon – Renfield Street (6 screens) Tel 332 8701.
Grosvenor – Ashton Lane, Hillhead (2 screens) Tel 339 4298.
Salon – Vinicombe Street, Tel 339 4256.

Of great interest is the **Glasgow Film Theatre** which, together with the **Edinburgh Filmhouse**, offers the most exciting and innovative programming in Scotland. A blend of contemporary, foreign, classic and British films not likely to be shown in the commercial cinema and consequently those films in which readers of the book will be interested. The GFT is on Rose Street (at the corner of Rose and Renfrew Streets) close to the School of Art and the McLennan Galleries. Tel 332 6535.

BOOKSTORES

Glasgow has some excellent bookstores. Of the major chains, the best, predictably enough, are **Hatchard's** at 50 Gordon Street, Tel 204 4109, **Sherratt and Hughes** at 45/50 Princess Square, Buchanan Street, Tel 221 9650, and **Waterstone's** at 132 Union Street, Tel 221 0890. But there are some excellent local independent bookstores as well. **William Porteous**, 9 Royal Exchange Place, Tel 221 8623, is an old established Glasgow bookseller and **John Smith and Sons** at 57 Vincent Street, Tel 221 7472, is not only one of a number of outlets in a well respected Scottish chain of bookstores, but is also the university bookseller and the agent for HMSO publications. Other central Glasgow bookshops well worth a browse are **Pickering and Inglis** at 26 Bothwell Street, Tel 221 8913, **Parks Bookshop**, 83 St Vincent Street, Tel 221 1369, **Robert Gibson and Sons**, 17 Fitzroy Place, Tel 248 5674, **Albany Bookshop** at Units 1 and 2, level 4, Union Building, 90 John Street, Tel 553 2300, **Volumes Bookstore**, 63–65 Queen Street, Tel 226 5762, and **Clyde Books** at 15 Parnie Street, Tel 552 4699, have a good Scottish collection. Religious books can be found at the **Church of Scotland Bookshop**, 160 Buchanan Street, Tel 332 9431, and the **Christian Book Centre** at 455 Great Western Road, Tel 334 6908. Science fiction and comics are best at **AKA Books and Comics**, 33 Virginia Street, Tel 552 8731, and **Forbidden Planet**, 168 Buchanan Street, Tel 331 1215. There is an excellent selection of film books at **Filmworld Cinema Bookshop**, De Courcey's Arcade, Cresswell Lane, Tel 339 5373 and a good selection of educational and children's books at **ABC Educational Co**, Telfer House, 74 Miller Street, Tel 204 3445.

ANTIQUARIAN AND SECONDHAND BOOKS

Not as wide a selection as you might have thought, given Glasgow's reputation as a place of learning. **Caledonia Books** at 483 Great Western Road, Tel 334 9663, has a large stock of both antiquarian and secondhand volumes, as does **Gilmorehill Books** at 43 Bank Street, Tel 339 7504. I'm inclined to think the aptly named **Voltaire and Rousseau** at 12 Otago Lane, Hillhead, Tel 339 1811, is the best, but **Cooper Hay Rare Books** in the Bath Street Antique Galleries is strong on antiquarian volumes, Tel 226 3074, and I'm also fond of **John Smith and Son** in the city centre at 57–61 St Vincent Street, Tel 221 7472. They also have nice prints. Overall, a disappointing selection. In this *one* respect Edinburgh is much better.

ART GALLERIES

Barbizon Gallery – 40 High Street, Tel 553 1990. The gallery specializes in contemporary and modern British painting with a strong emphasis on Scottish artists. Monthly exhibitions, an art bookshop and fully licensed café/restaurant.

Compass Gallery – 178 West Regent Street, Tel 221 6370. Glasgow's longest-established contemporary gallery. Paintings, prints and sculptures by young and mid-career Scottish contemporary artists and major British artists.

Cyril Greber Fine Art – 148 West Regent Street, Tel 221 3095. Large stocks and changing exhibitions of British paintings and drawings. These include the Glasgow School artists, the Scottish Colourists and modern Scottish masters.

Barclay Lennie Fine Art – 203 Bath Street, Tel 226 5413. A gallery featuring 19th- and 20th-century Scottish oil and watercolour paintings along with sculpture and local topographical etchings. The "Glasgow Boys" and the Scottish Colourists are also represented.

Main Fine Art – 16 and 34 Gibson Street, Tel 334 8858. The gallery concentrates on the work of recent Fine Art graduates and is now run in tandem with the Michael Main Gallery which specializes in the work of the Scottish painter Lesley Main.

Ewan Mundy Fine Art – 48 West George Street (1st floor) Tel 331 2406. The gallery specializes in modern Scottish painting, the "Glasgow Boys", the Scottish Colourists, contemporary Scottish artists and English and French art of the late 19th and early 20th centuries.

90s Gallery – 12 Otago Street, Tel 339 3158 (West End). The gallery specializes in Scottish contemporary art and design, mostly from Glasgow and the West of Scotland. Monthly exhibitions. A separate craft area has contemporary jewellery, ceramics, stained glass and metalwork.

Street Level Gallery and Workshop – 279–281 High Street, Tel 552 2151. The gallery is devoted entirely to photography. A wide variety of work on contemporary and historical themes is shown in two galleries. The exhibition programme is accompanied by talks and events and the darkrooms are used by members and as a teaching resource.

The Fine Art Society – 134 Blythswood Street, Tel 332 4027. One of the city's largest commercial galleries with an extensive stock of both historical and contemporary works covering two centuries of British art. The "Glasgow Boys," Mackintosh and his contemporaries and the Colourists are among the artists whose work is normally held in stock.

Gatehouse Gallery – Rouken Glen Road, Giffnock, Tel 620 1235. The gallery shows painting and sculpture by recent graduates and established artists with exhibitions changing monthly. A wide selection of drawings, lithographs and etchings are always on display.

The Original Print Shop – 25 King Street, Tel 552 0704. The gallery has a vast display of original limited prints and is Scotland's premier outlet. Specializing in contemporary work, the gallery stocks prints by many of Scotland's leading artists.

William Hardie Ltd – 141 West Regent Street, Tel 221 6780. The gallery sells Scottish art of all periods. Recent exhibitions have included the Stanley Cursiter Centenary and a one-man-show by Peter Howson.

ANTIQUE DEALERS

There are a great many antique shops in Glasgow. A full geographical listing is not possible but I have done my best. Perhaps more important, I have listed each shop's speciality as best I can. First, the antique markets:

Bath Street Antique Galleries – 203 Bath Street, Tel 248 4229. There are ten dealers covering a wide range of antiques and collectables. There are two good general dealers, two fine art dealers, **John Green** specializing in 19th- and 20th-century oils, watercolours and etchings and **Barclay Lennie** in Scottish oils, watercolours and sculptures, two fine stores selling antique jewellery, a very good clock specialist, two dealers selling pottery, ceramics and porcelain, a specialist weapons dealer and **Cooper Hay Rare Books** – not to be missed. While you're in the Bath Street area, **Behar Carpets** – mainly Oriental and very lovely – are at No 15, Tel 332 2858, and **Tim Wright Antiques**, with an excellent stock, is at No 147, Tel 221 0364.

The **Victorian Village** is at 53 and 57 West Regent Street, Tel 332 0808. There are 30 dealers here covering a wide range of interests including jewellery, silver, militaria, china, Victorian lace, '20s clothing and general collections. While you are in this area, check out **Muirhead Moffat and Co** at 182 West Regent Street, Tel 226 4683. They have an excellent stock of period furniture, jewellery, barometers, clocks, silver, weapons, porcelain, tapestries and pictures. There's also **Hamilton Wright Antiques** at Nos 172/174, Tel 248 4570. They have 18th- and 19th-century furniture and decorative and architectural items. **Virginia Antique Galleries** are at 31/33 Virginia Street (off Argyle Street) Tel 552 2573. There are 20 dealers here selling furniture, glass, silver, jewellery, porcelain and brass. The **Glasgow Antiques Centre** is at Unit 6A Yorkhill Quay, Tel 334 4924. There are ten dealers here selling a wide range of general antiques, furnishings and fine arts.

The **West of Scotland Antique Centre** is at Langside Lane, 539 Victoria Road, Queen's Park, Tel 422 1717. Eight dealers sell pine – Georgian to Edwardian – an excellent stock.

Individual dealers and their interests are listed below;

Albany Antiques – 1345–1351 Argyle Street, Tel 339 4267. Chinese and Japanese porcelain and Victorian and Edwardian furniture.

Butler's Furniture Galleries – 24–26 Millbrae Road, Tel 632 9853. Georgian, Victorian and Edwardian furniture plus small decorative items.

The Den of Antiquity – 61 Dixon Avenue, Crosshill, Tel 637 4434. General antiques.

James Forrest and Co – 105 West Nile Street (city centre) Tel 332 2332. General antiques.

Hour Hand Furniture and Antiques – 287 High Street, Tel 552 2332. General antiques.

Keep Sakes – 27 Gibson Street, Tel 334 2264. General antiques and jewellery.

Caroline Kerr Antiques – 103 Niddrie Road, Queen's Park, Tel 424 0444. General antiques.

I E Lovatt Antiques – 100 Torrisdale Street (adjacent to Queen's Park Railway Station) Large stock of general antiques and Victoriana.

Jean Megahy – 481 Great Western Road, Tel 334 1315. Furniture, brass, silver and Oriental items.

Yesteryear – 158 Albert Drive, Tel 429 3966. General antiques.

Mercat Antiques – 1 Royal Exchange Court, Tel 204 0851. Furniture, brass, glass, porcelain, clocks, watches and antique jewellery.

Nice Things Old and New – 1010 Pollokshaws Road, Tel 649 3826. General antiques with some interesting and unusual pieces.

R L Rose and Co – 19 Waterloo Street, Tel 248 3313. Oriental carpets.

Frank Russell and Son Antiques – 1 Rutherglen Road, Tel 647 9608. Georgian, Victorian and Edwardian furniture. Art deco and bric-à-brac. Large stock. (Near Exhibition Centre).

Saratoga Trunk – 1st floor, 136 Renfield Street, Tel 331 2707 (opposite STV studios). Linen and textiles – Victorian to 1940s. Costumes and jewellery.

K Stanley and Son – 86 Maryhill Road, Tel 332 3462. General antiques.

Stenlake and McCourt – 1 Overdale Street, Langside, Tel 632 2304 (Close to Battlefield Monument.) Edwardian postcards, cigarette cards, ephemera 1700–1930.

Temptations Unlimited – 127 Douglas Street, Tel 332 4403 (second right after Christie's). Jewellery, glass and pictures.

There are two excellent auction houses in Glasgow: **Christie's Scotland** at 164–166 Bath Street, Tel 332 8134, has regular specialist sales of jewellery, silver, ceramics , works of art, glass, pictures, clocks, mirrors, carpets, pianos, et al.

Phillips Scotland – Just down the road at 207 Bath Street, Tel 221 8377, is equally good with fortnightly sales and specialist sales throughout the year.

RESTAURANTS

Café Gandolfi – 64 Albion Street, Tel 552 6813. Excellent value, and what's more, it's open all day. I always have the daily hot dish but there are Scottish treats such as Cumbrian ham with pease pudding, Finnian haddock or smoked venison that should be sampled. A small but inexpensive wine list. Open Mon–Sat 9:30am–11:30pm.

Colonial India – 25 High Street, Tel 552 1923. This is the British Raj in the middle of Glasgow. Lots of military prints, tiger murals and ceiling fans. Unlike a large number of Indian restaurants, this one has good fish dishes. Indeed, all the cooking is well above average and portions are very generous. I really recommend the set lunch served from noon–2pm. Open all week noon to 11:30pm (midnight Fri and Sat) No Sat lunch.

Rogans – 11 Exchange Place, Tel 248 4055. Housed in a fine art deco building which alone is worth the visit, the emphasis is on fresh fish which is beautifully cooked. Friends tell me the restaurant recently underwent a change of chef, but by the time you read this things should have settled down. I'm told the Cafe Rogano is pleasanter than the main restaurant. Open Mon–Sat 12–2:30pm and 7–10:30pm.

Triangle – 37 Queen Street, Tel 221 8758. Located above a "magic" shop, there was a suggestion that the premises were once a snooker hall, but the present decor completely masks any seaminess. There is a bar/brasserie and a more formal dining room and the cooking – nouvelle Anglaise and French traditional – is excellent. The fish is good and, rather oddly, I had an excellent home-made ravioli for lunch. Lunch is good value and the brasserie is less expensive than the dining room, but with cooking as good as this one must not cavil about price. Open Mon–Sat 12–3pm and 7–11pm.

Ubiquitous Chef – 12 Ashton Lane. A converted warehouse with lots of plants and a commitment to reviving the glories of Scottish cooking. It all starts with the ingredients of course. Fresh fish, venison, pigeon and salmon to name a few. The kipper pâté is excellent, as are the haddies, and there's even a venison haggis. As we are in Glasgow, there's a long and impressive list of malt whiskies if that's your tipple. Open all week 12–2:30pm and 5:30–11pm. (Open 6:30 on Sun.)

October – 128 Drymen Road, Tel 942 7272. There is a wide range of eclectic dishes to choose from in this stylish and interesting restaurant. Teriyaki, fish soup, polenta, seafood tourte and the vegetarian food have all been praised. The restaurant seems really committed to quality. The short lunch menu is a real bargain. Open all week 12–2pm and 7–10pm. (No Sun dinner.)

Rab Ha's – 83 Hutcheson Street, Tel 553 1545. Excellent fish, especially the mussels.

Jimmys – 1–7 Victoria Road, Tel 423 4820. The best fish and chips in Scotland.

PUBS

Babbity Bowster – 16–18 Blackfriars Street, Tel 552 5055. The name comes from "Bab at the Bowster," a Scottish folk song and there's a big ceramic illustrating it. Set in a beautiful Robert Adam town house, there are big windows, stripped floorboards and open fires. Very good bar food. Try the haggis, neeps and tatties or the stovies. There's even a Scottish traditional breakfast.

Bon Accord – 153 North Street. There's one of the best beer selections in Glasgow here – served from real ale founts. The food is good too, with the beef stew in Belgian beer guaranteed by me to keep you going for 24 hours. Nice atmosphere, but crowded on weekend evenings.

Horseshoe – 17–19 Drury Street, Tel 221 3051. The horseshoe motif here runs from the large bar to the fireplace and even the wall clocks. Lots of mahogany, mosaic tiles and photographs of old Glasgow and her people. There's a good and very inexpensive three-course lunch and hot bar food too.

Pot Still – 154 Hope Street, Tel 333 0980. This is the place for malt whiskies with several hundred available. In fact, there is only malt whisky – no grain – and they sell by the bottle as well as the glass. Good bar food – nothing fancy.

Baby Grand – India Street, Charing Cross, Tel 248 4942. Continental style café/bar, chattery and noisy with terazzo floor and long grey marble counter. Excellent and imaginative food, with herb mackerel and salt beef hash leading the way. Live jazz on Saturday evenings.

Monty's (formerly the Outside Inn) – 1256 Argyle Street. A very pleasant bar furnished with lots of dark wood. Traditional bar food. Entertainment in the evening includes live jazz and quizzes.

ARTISTIC ASSOCIATIONS

Bret Harte was appointed American Consul in Glasgow in 1880, after his exciting days on the gold fields were over. He is best known for *The Luck of Roaring Camp* and after his appointment was over he settled in London. William Sharp wrote many mystical novels and Celtic tales under the name of Fiona Macleod (a secret kept until after his death in Sicily in 1905). He attended Glasgow Academy and the University but was forced to go abroad for health reasons. His work could not be more Scottish though, and *The Mountain Lovers* and *The Sin Eater* still read well today. The poet Gerard Manley Hopkins was a priest at St Joseph's Church in 1881. He visited Loch Lomond in September of that year and wrote the poem *Inversnaid* as an expression of his delight in the wildness of nature. A C Bradley, the Shakespearean scholar, was Professor of English at Glasgow from 1890 to 1900. John Buchan, author of *The Thirty-nine Steps*, went to school and university in Glasgow. His first novel, *Sir Quixote of the Moors*, was begun while he was still attending college here. Many characters in his book are based on people be met in Glasgow. Neil Munro, who wrote many historical novels about the Highlands (especially *The Vital Spark*) was editor of the Glasgow *Evening Times*. James Bridie, one of Scotland's best-known playwrights, was really called O H Mavor, taking his pseudonym from his grandparents. He qualified as a doctor from Glasgow University, and practised here. His plays, especially *The Anatomist, Tobias and the Angel, Mr Bolfry* and *Daphne Laureola*, written in the '30s and '40s are much loved and still widely performed.

Until the second half of the 19th century, Glasgow was much less of a cultural centre than Edinburgh. In 1752 Robert Foulis tried to rectify this situation by founding an academy, to which he contributed his extensive collection of Old Master paintings. The Foulis Academy ceased to function after its founder's death in 1775 and apart from the artist, John Knox, one of the first to portray Glasgow's cityscape, not a lot happened until the second half of the 19th century. At that time there was an extraordinary burst of cultural activity, coupled with Glasgow's rapid commercial development.

The painters who formed the main part of this movement were known as the "Glasgow Boys." The group took a keen interest in the latest artistic developments in Europe and many studied in France. The group greatly admired the work of the expatriate American painter, James Whistler, and they supported the adventurous Glasgow City Corporation in buying the artist's *Arrangement in Grey and Black, No 2: Thomas Carlyle* (Glasgow Art Gallery). The "Glasgow Boys" were concerned with realism, but many of them took little interest in the visual aspects of urban Glasgow. They escaped to the intimacy of an interior, or to quiet country surroundings, and their work is essentially sunny and carefree, far removed from the realities of industrial life. Their overall style initially raised controversy but subsequent success by many of the group members led to a style which depended more on the merely slick than the cosmopolitan or avant-garde.

An isolated and eccentric painter working in Glasgow at the turn of the century was J Q Pringle. Pringle, a practising optician for most of his life, evolved a technique that bore an uncanny though entirely fortuitous resemblance to the pointillism of Seurat and his followers. In contrast to the "Glasgow Boys," Pringle found the subjects for many of his best-known works in the city's urban landscape.

My own favourite Glaswegian artistic figures are Joan Eardley and Charles Rennie Mackintosh. Working in Glasgow since the Second World War, Eardley painted innumerable scenes of Glaswegian slum life and moved in 1952 to the now largely demolished Townhead, where her studio was a ramshackle photographer's shop at 204 St James Road. Charles Rennie Mackintosh, born in 1868, was undoubtedly one of Europe's leading architects and designers. As a leader of the Glasgow School, he and his contemporaries developed a unique style combining art nouveau and the modern movement. Most of Mackintosh's working life was spent in Glasgow and the city boasts a large number of his finest achievements from the famous Glasgow School of Art to the Willow Tearoom. Mackintosh's unrealized "House for an Art Lover," originally designed in 1901, was built as a major contribution to the Cultural Capital of Europe celebrations in 1990. The major Mackintosh buildings are listed below:

Queen's Cross Church – 870 Garscube Road, Tel 946 6600. This former church is the headquarters of the Charles Rennie Mackintosh Society. This was the only church to be designed by Mackintosh and today contains an information centre, reference library and shop relating to Mackintosh and his work.
Glasgow School of Art – 167 Renfrew Street, Tel 332 9797. Designed by Mackintosh in 1896, each façade of this exceptional building reflects a totally different facet of the architect's renowned imagination. Guided tours available Mon–Fri 10–noon and 2–4pm.
Scotland Street School – Scotland Street, Tel 429 1202. This Mackintosh building, now a museum of education, has a fascinating display of furniture, equipment and materials from Glasgow schools.
The Willow Tearoom – 217 Sauchiehall Street, Tel 332 0521. Of all the tearooms commissioned by Miss Kate Cranston, this is the last one still in operation.
Glasgow Art Gallery and Museum – Kelvingrove, Argyle Street, Tel 357 3929. There is a permanent exhibition room at the Gallery consisting of the interior designs of Mackintosh and many of his contemporaries (see Museums above).
Mackintosh House – Hunterian Gallery, Hillhead Street, Tel 330 5431. Reconstructed principal interiors of Mackintosh's house in Glasgow using original furniture, prints and designs. Open Mon–Fri 9:30–12:30 and 1:30–5pm, Sat 9:30–12:30pm.
Daily Record Building – Renfield Lane. View from outside only.
Glasgow Herald Building – 70 Mitchell Street. View from outside only.
Martyrs' Public School – Parson Street near Castle Street. View from outside only.
Ruchill Church Hall – 24 Ruchill Street, Tel 946 0466. Contact caretaker for viewing.
House for an Art Lover – (Haus Eines Kunstfreunds) – Bellahouston Park, Tel 427 6844. Designed in 1901 for an international competition, the suite of rooms, faithfully created, is open to visitors.

EPHEMERA

It was once said of Glasgow's coat of arms that it depicted:

> The bell that never rang
> The fish that never swam
> The tree that never grew
> The bird that never flew.

Perhaps surprisingly, there is some truth behind this piece of schoolboy doggerel. Enough at any case to rate an explanation, for each object in the crest is related to St Kentigern (or Mungo) Glasgow's patron saint.

The bell in the crest was probably given to St Kentigern by another bishop at his ordination. Originally it is thought to have been quadrangular, made of bronze and less than four inches (10 cm) high and three inches (7.6 cm) broad at the mouth. The fish is, of course, a salmon, for that fish was still being caught in the Clyde until the river was commercialized in the last century. The legend of the fish tells that the King of Cadzow suspected his Queen of having an affair with a certain knight. She had given a ring to the knight, which the King himself had given her. While the knight slept, the King took the ring from his purse and threw it into the Clyde, then demanded its return by the Queen on pain of death. The distraught Queen told Kentigern everything and promised abject penance if he would help. Kentigern, noted for his compassion, sent one of his men to the river with rod and line and instructed him to bring back, alive, the first fish he caught. The saint was given the fish and he reached into the fish's mouth, took out the ring that had been lost and returned it to the Queen. The tree on the crest is again concerned with St Kentigern. As a boy, Kentigern was told by his master, Servanus, to tend the ever-burning holy fire. One night, while he was asleep, some envious boys extinguished the fire. When Kentigern awoke to find the fire out, he broke off a frozen branch from a nearby hazel and breathed on it in the name of the Holy Trinity – it immediately burst into flames. It's interesting to note that until 1647 a branch was correctly shown as part of the crest – since then, it has grown into a tree. Finally, the bird. It is suggested that this is a robin which was accidentally killed by a disciple of Saint Serf who blamed Kentigern. The youthful future saint took the bird in his hands and made over it the sign of the cross, whereupon the bird was restored to life and flew away.

In 1976 Scotland, and Glasgow in particular, acquired a new saint. John Ogilvie, who was canonized in October, was born in 1579 and was received into the Roman Catholic Church as a convert in 1596. Although the Roman Church was then proscribed in Scotland, Ogilvie returned from France in disguise to work as a missionary in Glasgow. In 1614 he was betrayed and after suffering grievous captivity and torture, was hanged at Glasgow Cross on March 10, 1615. Before his death he declared his loyalty to the Sovereign; he was executed, he said, "for religion alone." He was buried in ground set aside for malefactors but re-interred at a castle in Ayrshire when friends removed his body from its original grave. The miracle attributed to Saint John Ogilvie through the prayers of the congregation of John Ogilvie Parish (the only one named after him) concerns the miraculous recovery from terminal cancer of a John Fagan, who was on the edge of death. John Ogilvie is the first native-born Scot to be canonized. Kentigern and other early saints became saints through usage, without formal canonization, and St Margaret, canonized in 1250, was Scots only by marriage and adoption.

In 1858 a scandal, which is still remembered by some who were told the story by their parents or grandparents, broke over the city. Madeline Smith was the daughter of wealthy architect, James Smith, designer of the McLellan Galleries. The family lived in Blythswood Square. Madeline, by all accounts an attractive girl and too intelligent to be readily confined within the semi-literate female conventions of the age, took herself a lover. He was Pierre Emile L'Angelier, a clerk from the Channel Islands who found himself working in Glasgow. Three years later an eligible suitor for Madeline appeared but L'Angelier was unwilling to give up his mistress. When he died in mysterious circumstances, Madeline was accused of his murder. L'Angelier was thought to have died of arsenic poisoning after drinking a cup of cocoa prepared by Madeline. She was shown by the prosecution to have purchased arsenic and because she admitted that L'Angelier had been her lover, the public at large prejudged her guilty of his murder. At her trial, Madeline was deserted by all her family except for one brother. Much against public opinion, the jury returned the Scots verdict, "not proven." This verdict has been said by some to mean, "We know you did it but we can't prove you did." Madeline was unperturbed by all the fuss, although shortly after she emigrated to America and a new life. She lived into her 90s. Her story has continued to exert a fascination on writers and playwrights, possibly because she was the first Victorian "London-finished" woman to rebel, in however an unorthodox manner, against social beliefs which refused to admit that the female of the species had the right to possess either intelligence or the capacity for physical passion.

In 1918, a Royal Commission on housing found that 45 percent of the people in Scotland were living in overcrowded conditions, by which was meant more than two people to a room. In Glasgow itself the percentage was undoubtedly higher. A controversial pamphlet, *Cancer of Empire*, reporting upon Glasgow's housing conditions, was published in 1924. It said, in part: "On each landing opens the water closet which the municipality installed thirty years ago. This is clean, the municipal inspectors are vigilant, but on an average, 25 people share its use. In some houses the number is nearer 50. On the other side of the tiny landing opens a long, impenetrably black gulf; the central corridor of five homes. We feel our way, knock at a door and enter. A small room, one side taken up by a Scots fireplace with two hobs and an ever boiling teapot. An enormous drabbled woman, dressed in the same dish clothes which do not show the dirt so plainly as her face, explains the arrangements. She has five children. There is one bed set in an evil smelling niche strewed with heaps of clothes. Bed, hearth and chair – humanity's minimum. Under the window is the 'jaw box,' the boarded greasy sink. On the mantelpiece are two china dogs."

A year after this pamphlet was published, Glasgow Corporation began to build houses for letting – "council houses," as they were called – for the most part semi-detached cottage-type dwellings, each with its own garden. The rents were low, subsidized by the tenant and rate-payer at large. In ten years, 20 percent of Glasgow's population was living in decent subsidized housing.

Amongst the grand and historic monuments in Glasgow Cathedral is a canopied chair with a story. During the Second World War a motor torpedo boat crew found a lucky lady-bird on board. It turned out to be lucky indeed, because when their boat was sunk, every single member of the crew survived. The canopied chair was presented in gratitude for their escape and if you look carefully you will see, resting permanently on the underside of the canopy, a full colour ladybird delicately carved in the wood.

The handloom weavers of Paisley, to the southwest of Glasgow, are remembered for the distinctive Paisley pattern shawls they wove to a colourful design brought back from Kashmir by the East India Company. The shawls were internationally popular in the 19th century and a collection of over 700 can be seen in the local museum.

In their own time, however, the weavers were also highly skilled as "florists" – flower growers who aimed at producing blooms of perfect size and shape. The skill of growing flowers had come to Britain in the 17th century with the French and Flemish refugees, and by the end of the 18th century there were many florists' societies and eight official flowers that could be grown. The Paisley florists specialized in cultivating the laced pink or Dranthus flower. Florists' societies flourished particularly around the manufacturing towns because for weavers and other cottage workers, growing flowers for show proved an ideal recreation. The florist's art required little space but intense cultivation. The weaver was on hand all day to give the plants attention, ". . . and this" said William Hanbury in 1770, "was an ease and pleasure to him in his repetitive work."

TOURIST INFORMATION BUREAU: 35 St Vincent Place, Glasgow G1 2ER. Tel (041) 4400

PERTH AND PITLOCHRY

PERTH

County of Perthshire
By MI, M6, A7 and M90, 418 miles (668.8 km) from London
6 hours 30 minutes by train from London (King's Cross); 38 (60.8 km) miles from Edinburgh

Perth is thought to have originated around a 1st-century Roman camp. This theory is supported by the plan of the old town, which was set within a city wall, remnants of which remain. There are many places around Perth which have great significance for the Scots. Abernethy, Forteviot and especially Scone, are all mentioned in records going back before the 9th century, but Perth receives no mention until the 12th century by which time it appears to have been firmly established. It has been claimed that for centuries Perth was essentially Scotland's national capital. Kings and their courts were peripatetic in feudal times and Perth was frequently the royal residence. Scone, nearby, was the place of many coronations, and parliament and general councils are known to have been held there.

Perth itself is referred to in records as the Royal City and "the principal seat of our kingdom" and the case made for the city as being the governing centre of Scotland is too well documented to be ignored. James II established Edinburgh as Scotland's capital city in the 1450s, but many inhabitants of Perth are firm in their belief that if James I had not been murdered, and if his six-year-old son, James II, had not been brought up in Edinburgh Castle, then Perth would have been established as the permanent capital of Scotland.

Perth has had a turbulent history. The city has been besieged seven times. John Knox preached here in 1559 and his message, as father of the Reformation in Scotland, was directly responsible for the destruction of four monasteries and the altars in the Kirk. In 1600 John, Earl of Rutheven, was killed at his home in Perth for purportedly attempting to murder or kidnap King James VI (who became James I of England in 1603). This so-called Gowrie Conspiracy is surrounded with mystery even today. Oliver Cromwell invaded the city in 1651 and in 1745 Charles Edward Stuart known more familiarly as "Bonnie Prince Charlie," stopped in Perth on his way to London. He lodged at the Salutation Hotel in South Street, drilled his troops at the edge of the town and proclaimed his father, James Stuart – known as the "Old Pretender" – King from his headquarters there.

Perhaps it is the nature of Perth's past or perhaps its unenviable reputation for iconoclasm, but few substantial historical buildings have survived. One magnificent exception to this rule is St John's Kirk in the city centre, which was founded in 1126. It was here that John Knox preached his inflammatory sermons. There are many examples of excellent modern stained glass and the congregation's collection of old pewter and silver-gilt sacramental vessels is priceless. There is a fine 16th-century baptismal basin, while the carillon of 35 bells was hung in 1936.

The memorials of Perth's vanished buildings, activities and conditions of life are in the names of the streets and lanes of the city – Charterhouse, Blackfriars, Whitefriars, Greyfriars, Clover Street, Skinnergate, Ropemaker's Close, Cow, Vennel and the rest. In the courtyard of the Salutation Hotel (said to be the oldest in Scotland) is a stone bearing the motto and arms of the Earls of Moray and dated 1619; more than likely it marks the site of a house of nobility. In North Ports once stood the Castle of Perth, while the present waterworks marks the place of Cromwell's Citadel. Tokens in the paving of the High Street commemorate the old stone cross and pillory, the remains of which can be seen in the museum.

The centre of Perth is bordered by the North and South Inches, two large areas of open land running along the banks of the River Tay. Today these spaces are preserved as parks and are used for events such as the Perth Highland Games, but in 1396 the North Inch was the scene of the infamous Battle of the Clans. Hundreds of men from the Chattan and Kay Clans were slaughtered when King Robert III attempted unsuccessfully to put an end to the feuding between Highlanders. This battle forms the backdrop to Sir Walter Scott's novel *The Fair Maid of Perth*, which in turn inspired Bizet's opera of the same name. In North Port is "The Fair Maid's House," in which, legend has decreed, lived the Fair Maid herself. It is worth a visit, if not for its historical accuracy, then for the very pleasant craft shop it now houses. St Ninian's Cathedral in Methven Street was built between 1850 and 1890. Whereas St John's Kirk houses the congregation of the Church of Scotland, St Ninian's serves the Episcopal Church of Scotland.

Three miles (4.8 km) north of Perth on the A93 is Scone Palace. The present Gothic Palace was built between 1803 and 1808 on the site of a house of 1580, which in turn was based on a monastery of 1120. This monastery was one of those sacked after John Knox's sermon of 1559. Scone is one of the most historic places in Scotland. All 42 of Scotland's kings were crowned at Scone, many atop the mystical Stone of Destiny (see Ephemera). Abernethy, seven miles (11.2 km) south on A 913/913, was a place of some importance in the Iron Age and a fort was established here. The Romans built a legionary fortress at

FAIR MAID'S HOUSE, PERTH

Carpow, then a port, and the town was a bishopric as early as the 11th century. There is an impressive Round Tower from the 11th century which is 74 feet (22.4 m) high and one of only two on mainland Scotland. (Tower open daily Mon–Sat 10–5pm, Sun 12–5pm.) Finally, there's Forteviot, five miles (8 km) southwest just off the A9, a village which was once the capital of the Pictish kingdom of Fortrenn. Kenneth MacAlpine, who in AD 843 united the Picts and Scots into a single kingdom, established his capital and died here in 860. There was a Celtic church here as early as the 8th century and Invermay House is associated with *Redgauntlet* by Sir Walter Scott. It is difficult to associate a town so far from the open sea as Perth with maritime trade, but built as it is on the navigable River Tay, the town was an important harbour in earlier times. Salmon, wool and other agricultural products were exported and there was a thriving import trade of claret from Bordeaux. Agriculture still plays a very important part in the life of the city and the traditional industries of whisky distilling and blending, and the dyeing and cleaning of wool, still flourish. In the 20th century tourism has flourished and the city is regarded as the "Gateway to the Highlands" both northwards and westwards.

WALK

The **Perth Walk** starts from the large car park beside the South Inch at the corner of Shore Road and Marshall Place. Take the riverside pavement along Tay Street, past the column on the parapet which recalls the **Monk's Tower** corner of the 14th-century city wall, and cross Queen's Bay Bridge which spans the River Tay. Before the A85 traffic lights, turn left into Riverside Walk and continue through the landscaped gardens. At the end of the gardens, which afford beautiful views of the city, recross the river by the **Perth Bridge**. At the town end of the bridge you will see the domed **Museum and Art Gallery**. Turn right onto Charlotte Street, which is mainly Georgian, then left down the cobbled Charlotte Place to the **Fair Maid's House** (now a gift shop). Beyond the house continue on the pedestrianized Union Street until you can turn right up Kennoull Street. Turn left onto Union Lane and left again on North Methven Street. On your left is **St Ninian's Cathedral**, the first cathedral to be built in Scotland after the Reformation. A short way down North Methven Street turn right on West Mill Street (the signpost says Lower City Mills) and continue on the cobbles around the mill buildings and past the house of **Hal o' the Wynd** (husband of the Fair Maid in Scott's novel) to the junction with High Street. The **Theatre** is in High Street but turn left, cross at the traffic lights and continue along High Street to King Edward Street on your right. Follow this street, and St John's Place around **St John's Kirk** into St John Street. Turn right on St John Street and continue to the T-junction which is opposite the richly decorated **Salutation Inn**. Turn left on to South

Street, and continue past the entrance to Fountain Close and on to the town end of Queen's Bridge. Return along Tay Street to the car park.

MUSEUMS AND GALLERIES

Perth Museum and Art Gallery – George Street, Tel 32488. Open Mon–Sat 10–1 and 2–5pm. The Marshall Monument, which dates from 1824, was extended in 1935 to house the collections of earlier museums of antiquities and the natural sciences, and to include an art gallery. On the side of the visual arts, most of the paintings and drawings in the gallery are Scottish with the main strength being in 19th- and 20th-century works. The print collection has examples of the "etching revival" period and fine work by Legros, Whistler and Sir D Y Cameron. The sculpture collection comprises portrait busts and small bronzes by Sir Alfred Gilbert. There are also good collections of long-case clocks, Perth art glass and silver. The Human History section of the museum holds collections of archaeology, social history, costumes, photographs, maps, documents, costumes, ethnography, weapons and armour. The natural history collection, which is large, houses exhibits mostly collected by local naturalists.
Black Watch Museum – Balhousie Castle, Hay St, Tel 21281. Open Easter–Sept Mon–Fri 10–4:30 Sun and public hols 2–4:30; Sept–Easter Mon–Fri 10–3:30. Other times by appointment The museum is in a 12th-century tower house with Victorian wings added. The collections illustrate the history of the Black Watch Regiment over a period of 250 years, and include uniforms, colours, paintings and regimental silver.
Scone Palace – Perth Tel 52300. Open Easter to mid-Oct Mon–Sat 10–5:30, Sun 12–5:30. The Gothic modelling, circa 1802, effectively disguises the old palace. There are remarkable collections of French furniture, European carved ivory, clocks, silk wall hangings and bed hangings made by Mary, Queen of Scots. A complete room is devoted to Chelsea, Sevres, Meissen and other porcelain and there is a fine collection of Vernis Martin objets d'art.
Fairways Heavy Horse Centre – Walnut Grove, Kinfauns, Perth Tel 25931. Open daily April–Sept 10–6pm. Clydesdale horses, dray rides, vintage horse instruments and a blacksmith, with video shows and a tearoom/shop. Chiefly though, the chance to see the impressive Clydesdales and other heavy horses, which have a magnificence all their own.
Lower City Mills – West Mill St, Perth Tel 30572. Open all year, Mon–Sat 10–5:30, Sun 12–5:30. This fine example of a Victorian town watermill is in full working order and visitors can watch Scotland's largest working waterwheel powering the machinery, which produces flour and oatmeal in the traditional manner. An exhibition room tells the story of the Perth Mills, which have been on this site for 900 years. There is also a tearoom, a gift shop and several craft workshops.
Caithness Glass – Inveralmond, Perth (on A9 Bypass North) Tel 37373. Open Mon–Sun 9–5 (Oct–mid-April Sunday opening 1 pm). A chance to watch glass blowers at work as they make the intricate paperweights for which the factory is famous. There is a paperweight collector's gallery and a well-stocked factory shop with bargains in crystal and glass. Restaurant for snacks and meals.
Whisky Tasting – Perth is the home of such successful whisky companies as Bell's, Dewar's and Famous Grouse. To fail to visit one of the many distilleries and bottling plants would be a mistake. In Perth itself, **Dewar's**, just by the A9/A912 roundabout gives you the chance to visit their bottling plant which fills over 300,000 bottles of whisky each day for world markets. Conducted tours take place Mon–Fri all year at 10, 11:15, 2, and 3:15. At peak periods it's best to book in advance at 21231. Note only morning tours on Fridays. Further afield, near Pitlochry you can visit the **Blair Atholl Distillery**, Tel Pitlochry 2234, which is open all year 9:30–5 pm, and **Eradour Distillery** by Moulins which is two and a half miles (4 km) east of Pitlochry, Tel Pitlochry 2095. Eradour is open daily 9:30–5pm March–Oct and Nov–Feb Mon–Sat 10–6pm. It's the smallest distillery in Scotland and a tour and tasting is free. Finally, if it's the oldest you're interested in, you'll have to find the **Glenturret Distillery**, Tel Crieff 2424. It's Scotland's oldest distillery. Open for tours and tasting Mar–Dec Mon–Sat 9:30–5:30pm.

THEATRE

Perth Theatre – 185 High Street, Tel 21031. One of the most successful repertory theatres in Scotland and one of the oldest, the Perth rep plays in a delightfully renovated old theatre, which in recent years has had a completely redecorated and restored auditorium as well as extensive rebuilding backstage. Beginning in 1935, the Perth Repertory company has built up an enviable reputation for the excellent production of quality plays. Recent productions have included works by Alan Ayckbourn, Robert Bolt, Stephen Poliakoff, Brian Friel, Louise Page, Tom Stoppard and Noel Coward. The theatre is known for its commitment to new Scottish drama. In this respect, Joy Hendry's new play *Gang Down Wi' A Sang*, dealt with the life of local poet William Sontar and *Weemen Stratagem* was a Scots adaptation, set in Edinburgh, of a Carlo Goldoni comedy. There is a small studio theatre dedicated to providing the kind of drama best suited to a small, intimate audience. There are excellent restaurant and bar facilities with dinner served from 6pm and after the curtain has fallen. The restaurant, bar and coffee bar are open at lunchtime and in the evenings.

MUSIC

Perth Symphony Orchestra, a community organization, gives concerts throughout the year. Tel 21031. **Perth Chamber Music Society** organizes concerts in the Art Gallery and Museum. Recent visitors have included the Vanbrugh and the New Budapest String Quartets. Tel Perth 29716.

One of the most artistically active times of the year is during the **Perth Festival of Arts** which is held for two weeks in the middle of May. There are performances of ballet and opera and symphony concerts at this time. Among recent participants have been Yehudi Menuhin, the Moscow Radio Symphony Orchestra and the Polish State Symphony Orchestra. Tel 24168 for details.

CINEMA

The Playhouse – Murray Street. Tel 23126, has three separate screens.

BOOKSTORES

The best is **James Thin**, 176 High St Perth, Tel 35222. It's a real pleasure to find an independent bookstore still in operation. In spite of the huge stock and undoubted efficiency of Waterstone's and Sherratt and Hughes and the like, there is a different atmosphere to be found in a shop such as this. There's a real sense of personal service and concern, which the big chains, good as they are, can't match. Somehow it's especially true in Scotland. Don't ask me to explain all this, just take my word for it.

ANTIQUARIAN AND SECOND HAND BOOKS

Perth Bookshop – 3A Abbot St, Tel 33970, is the best. A large and comprehensive stock with a nice antiquarian section as well, and some maps and prints.
Collector's Booksearch – 4 King Edward St, Tel 43706, also has a good general secondhand selection. They also advertise for any book which you have difficulty in finding. I've used this service on numerous occasions in other parts of the country and it's excellent at tracking down hard-to-find volumes.

ART GALLERIES

George Street Gallery – (Michael Hardie), 38 George St, Tel 38953. Specializes in late 19th-century and early 20th-century Scottish paintings. A good collection. **Robertson and Cox** at 60 George St, Tel 26300, is a well-established gallery, with some very attractive 18th- and 19th-century paintings and prints. Their contemporary acquisitions tend to be Scottish, but there is an international quality about their collection which is most pleasing. Finally the **Ronan Gallery** at 1/3 South Methven St, Tel 26402, specializes in hunting, shooting and fishing prints and pictures. There were some superb prints of game birds the last time I was there and they also have a general collection of paintings and prints.

ANTIQUE DEALERS

The best area for antiques in central Perth is George Street and its essential extension into St John Street and Princess Street. This area runs parallel to Tay Street, which borders the River Tay. Close to the Perth Bridge and the Museum is **Robertson and Cox** at 60 George Street, Tel 26300. They have antiques, furniture, oil paintings, watercolours and Oriental rugs. A good showroom. Just down the road, at the junction of George and High Streets is **Whispers of the Past** (Christine Wilson). They specialize in stripped pine but they also have good linen and lace, jewellery, silver, paintings, glass and decorative items. Close to City Hall at 25 St John Street you will find **Timothy Hardie**, Tel 33127. They focus on antique jewellery and generally have some very nice pieces. Just across the junction at 12 South Street is **A S Deucher**, Tel 26297. They have a large stock of general antiques and Victorian furniture. They also have a warehouse at the rear of the shop which is ideal for browsing.

At the bottom of Princess Street at the junction with Marshall Place is **Atholl Antiques** at 80 Princess Street. Tel 20054. They have a large collection of antique and Victorian furniture, while just round the corner at 70 Tay Street, facing the river, is the **Tay Street Gallery**, Tel 20604, which, besides period furniture, collector's items and decorative objects, usually has some nice pictures. Running parallel to George Street but two blocks away from the river is Kinnoull Street. At the top, the junction of Kinnoull and Charlotte Streets, you'll find **Coach House Antiques** (John Walker) at 77-79 Kinnoull Street, Tel 29835. They are well worth a visit as they have a comprehensive collection of period furniture, metalware, decorative items and pictures. If you carry on another two blocks away from the river you' ll come to North Methven Street. Turn left onto Methven and at No 5 you'll find **W T G Henderson**, Tel 24836, who has good collections of antique jewellery, stamps, coins and militaria. Continue down Methven Street and where it is intersected by High Street you'll find St Paul Square on your right. At No 8 is **Forsyth Antiques**, Tel 22173, specializing in Scottish provincial silver, and very beautiful some of it is, too. They also have Monart glass and general antiques. Still going down Methven you'll come to Canal Street which has **John Wilman**, Tel 38007, at No 95. He has Victorian furniture aplenty and will also ship for you. The biggest selection in Perth is at **Ian Murray's Antique Warehouse**, 21 Glasgow Road, Tel 37222. Glasgow Road is essentially a continuation of South Street away from the river. There are nine dealers and 20,000 square feet (1857 m²) of antiques at Ian Murray's, so if you only have time for one visit, this should probably be it. Close to Ian Murray's is **Leslie's Antiques**, Unit 3, Gray Street, Tel 36825. They have easy parking and a large collection of general antiques. Finally, if you are on your way to Scone, pop into **Robert Ainslie Antiques** at 80 Perth Road, Tel 52438. He's on the other side of the river just after you turn left off the Perth Bridge. He has a good and varied antique collection.

RESTAURANTS

Timothy's – 24 St John Street, Perth, Tel 26641. It's slightly incongruous to find this Danish-style restaurant in the middle of Perthshire, especially as I think it's the best place to eat in town. Partly that's due to the warn welcome given by the owners – they not only welcome children, they provide toys for them – but of course it's the cooking that counts. The menu is built around 20 snitter (appetizers) and the same number of smorrebrod, adapted to include all kinds of interesting ingredients, which are given names such a "Roaming Dave" and "Red Dragon" and includes some un-Danish delights such as curried banana and sweet and sour chicken. Friends raved about the fondue bourguignonne (six sauces, salad and half a pound of beef), so maybe you'll have an event to celebrate as you pass through. Timothy's loves birthday celebrations. Good desserts. Good French house wine. Open Tues–Sat 12–2:30 and 7–10:15.

Murrayshall Hotel – Scone, Tel 51171. Follow the road to Coupar Angus out of Perth and after two miles (3.2 km) you come to Murrayshall which is surrounded by 300 acres (121.4 ha) of parkland, some of which is devoted to a golf course. (There are lunchtime snacks in the club house.) If you are on a budget it's best to eat here at lunch-time; but, although the prix fixe dinner is not cheap, it is good value. Expect delicacies such as pigeon salad, curried pea and lettuce soup, grilled goat's cheese, guinea fowl with madeira or veal with langoustines and brandy sauce. Wines are good but there are few bargains. Open all week 12–1:45 and 7–9:30.

Just as a footnote, I find the food at the **Perth Theatre Restaurant** to be good and inexpensive. As you will no doubt be going to the theatre it's well worth a try. Tel 21031. Open 6pm and after fall of curtain for dinners. (Also lunch)

PUBS

Granary – Canal Crescent, Tel 36705. Lovely building with lots of old farm equipment, stone walls, etc. Good pub food (especially pies and fish). Friendly service and a comfortable restaurant upstairs.

Ewe and Lamb – South Street. Small with restaurant upstairs and good value pub food. Friendly with a nice atmosphere.

At Scone . . . . **Scone Arms**, Tel 51341. Pleasant comfortable surroundings and friendly service. Good, well-presented bar food.

Salutation Hotel – 34 South Street, Tel 30066. Reputed to be Scotland's oldest, the Salutation has good bar food plus a comfortable dining room.

ARTISTIC ASSOCIATIONS

The house of the heroine of Scott's *The Fair Maid of Perth*, is mentioned above and the City Hall contains stained-glass windows of scenes from the novel. The fair maid of Perth was in fact Catherine or Kate Glover, who was much sought after by the gallants of Perth and also by the son of Robert III of Scotland, the Duke of Rothesay. The Duke tried to abduct her from her bedroom but was thwarted by Harry Gow, alias Hal o' the Wynd, who arrived just as the ladder was put against the wall. In the ensuing skirmish, Hal cut off the hand of the Duke's Master of Horse, Sir John Ramorny. After the abductors had fled, Hal carried the hand indoors and presented it to Simon Glover, Kate's father. What he did with it has not been recorded.

At Blackfriars Monastery (destroyed), James I of Scotland was assassinated. His poem, "The King's Book," is a beautiful account of his courtship of his wife, written in 1424 while he was a prisoner in England.

John Ruskin, the English author and art critic, spent many childhood holidays in Perth. He married a Perth lass. The greatest 19th-century dramatic critic, William Archer, was born in Perth, as was John Buchan, the author and statesman. Buchan wrote *Prester John* and *The Thirty-nine Steps* and became the first Baron Tweedsmuir in 1935. He was a very popular Governor General of Canada. William Sontar, probably the best Scottish poet of his generation, was born in Perth. He lived with his parents at 27 Wilson Street. His collected poems were published in 1948. He kept diaries from 1930 until his death and these were published posthumously in 1954 as *Diaries of a Dying Man*. In spite of their title they are sensitively and beautifully written with no sense whatever of self-pity.

Perth was the home of Euphemia (Effie) Gray, who married John Ruskin, the art critic and social theorist, in 1848. The marriage was not a success and it was annulled in 1854. Ruskin had been a good friend of Sir John Everett Millais, the leading Victorian artist and founder of the pre-Raphaelite movement. The friendship ended in 1855, however, when Millais married the ex-Mrs Ruskin. Effie Gray was the daughter of a wealthy solicitor living at Bowerswell, a large house on the hill of Kinnoull (now a rest home for the elderly). After their marriage, Effie and Millais lived for several years in Annat Lodge, a short distance above Bowerswell, where Millais painted some of his best-known pictures, including *Autumn Leaves*, which is now in the Manchester City Art Gallery, and *The Vale of Rest*, which is in the Tate Gallery in London. Even after settling in London, Millais continued to visit Perth regularly and the first of a series of large Scottish landscapes he produced from 1870 onwards was painted just on the other side of Kinnoull Hill beside the River Tay. This was *Chill October*, a view downstream from opposite Sleepless Inch, looking across a backwater that has now become the river's main course. *Chill October* can be seen in the Perth Art Gallery. The 19th-century Kinnoull Parish church contains a window with 14 designs in stained glass based on Millais's illustrations to the Parables.

EPHEMERA

The Stone of Destiny, or the Stone of Scone (pronounced *skoon*), was brought to Scone during the reign of Kenneth MacAlpine, who in 843 united the Picts and Scots into a single kingdom. The stone was stolen by Edward I of England in 1296 and has never been returned to Scotland. It became part of the Coronation Chair in Westminster Abbey. It should be said that many Scots regard the stone's being kept at Westminster Abbey in much the same way as the Greeks regard the Elgin Marbles from the Parthenon in Athens being kept in London's British Museum. The stone itself is an oblong block of red sandstone and may originally have been a portable altar stone belonging to some Celtic ecclesiastic or missionary. The Scots may very well have the last laugh over this one though. There are persistent rumours that the monks of Scone Abbey hid the original Stone of Destiny at the top of Dunsinane Hill, and allowed Edward to take away a replica made of local stone. If this story is apocryphal, then there is another concerning Arbroath Abbey. In 1951 some young Scots removed the Stone of Destiny from Westminster Abbey and, after three and a half months, placed it on Arbroath's high altar. There is some belief in Scotland that the stone, later taken ignominiously back to Westminster, is a copy and that the real Stone of Scone is safe in Scottish hands and still in Scotland. That is the story I like to believe, anyhow.

The world-famous Perth Bull Sales are generally held in mid-October at the Perth Agricultural Centre. The sales are still probably the best-known such occasions held anywhere in the world. Dealers from across the world fly in and the bidding is often fast and furious with record prices regularly set. While in recent years it has been breeds like the Charolais that have captured much attention, it will always be for the noble Aberdeen Angus that the Perth sales are renowned. In fact, you can attend the Perth Agricultural Centre at any time, where regardless of what is at auction, an authentically Scottish agricultural atmosphere can be enjoyed.

The area around Perth might be considered Macbeth country. Dunsinane Hill is traditionally the site of Macbeth's castle and even though it lies 12 miles (19 km) east-south-east of Birnam Wood it is certainly possible to see the wood from Dunsinane's summit. (15 miles/24 km north by Dunkeld). Glamis Castle is 24 miles (38.4 km) to the northeast. As well as its historically vague connections with the play, it is in fact the place where Queen Elizabeth, the Queen Mother, spent much of her childhood.

TOURIST INFORMATION BUREAU: 45 High Street, Perth PH2 8NU,Perthshire
Tel (0738) 38353

PITLOCHRY

This famous holiday resort lies 36 miles (57.6 km) to the northwest of Perth, almost at the centre of Scotland, and in the beautifully wooded valley of the Tummel. Golf, tennis, pony-trekking, fishing, skiing, climbing and walking can all be enjoyed here as well as the two whisky distilleries mentioned above, and a famous tweed mill. At **Faskally House** there is a brown trout research station and observation chambers at the Pitlochry dam enable visitors to watch the passage of salmon upriver to their spawning grounds. Nearby is **Blair Castle** (open daily April–mid-October Mon–Sat 10–6, Sun 2–6), a white-turreted baronial castle, seat of the Duke of Athol. Notable collections of furniture, pictures, embroidery, arms, porcelain and Jacobite relics.

The festival of drama, music and art runs from May through September at the **Pitlochry Festival Theatre**. Unbelievably, it is possible to stay six days and see six plays. The repertoire of plays is varied with recent productions ranging from Terence Rattigan and Somerset Maugham to Chekhov. The programme also includes puppet shows, foyer recitals and touring events. The first festival in 1951 was held in a makeshift tent, but in 1981 a brand-new state-of-the-art theatre was opened by Prince Charles. The theatre has fine views overlooking the river, and has gained the reputation of being Scotland's most delightful venue for drama.

BOOKSTORES

There is a branch of **Book Sale Today** at 8 West Moulin Road, which has publishers' remainders at bargain prices, Tel (0796)3812, and there is a branch of **Menzies** at 83 Atholl Road, Tel 2929.

ANTIQUE DEALERS

Blair Antiques at 14 Bonnethill Road, Tel 2624, has a general collection with some very nice pieces, as does **Pitlochry Antiques**, just down the road at 26 Bone-ill Road, Tel 2710.

RESTAURANTS

Whenever I am in Pitlochry I eat at the **Luggie Restaurant and Carvery** on Rie-Achen Road, Tel 2085. Once a dairy, this long-beamed barn now houses an enormously popular self-service restaurant.

At lunchtime there are good salads with cold meat and salmon, plus a daily hot pie. The evening menu is more elaborate and usually includes venison. Open 9:30–5 and 6–9:30pm. Closed mid-Nov to early March.

PUBS

The **Killicrankie Hotel**, just north of the town on the A9, is hardly a pub but its bar, which opens into a front sun-lounge extension, has excellent light meals and snacks ranging from crab and avocado sandwiches to a Highland game casserole. In the evening you can sample fresh trout in oatmeal and excellent Angus sirloin steak – and their "smokies" are sensational.

EPHEMERA

Fifteen miles (24 km) west of Pitlochry lies the attractive village of Fortingall. One of the strangest and most persistent of Scottish legends has grown up around this area. Many believe that Pontius Pilate was born in Fortingall. It is suggested that Pilate's father may have been an ambassador in North Britain during the Roman occupation and that he married a Menzies or a MacLaren from Balquhidder. It is oddly appropriate that Mrs Pilate could have come from Balquhidder as it is the birthplace of perhaps the greatest legendary hero of all Scotland – Rob Roy MacGregor. To lend plausibility to the Fortingall legend, a rectangular site defended by ditches southwest of the village is referred to as the "Praetorium." It makes a nice story, even though the Praetorium is probably an early medieval fortified homestead.

If you really want a taste of Scotland, call in at Macdonald Brothers, butchers on Bonnethill Road, and try their venison sausages. Of course you'll have to find somewhere to cook them – a campfire by a rushing Scottish stream perhaps (how romantic).

While we are on the subject of romance, one of the most romantic figures in Scottish history is Robert the Bruce, who took up arms against Edward I of England, uniting Highlands and Lowlands in a single fierce desire for liberty, and against overwhelming odds defeated the English at the Battle of Bannockburn in 1314. The story is told that Bruce sat in a cave, dispirited at odds that gave him a 4-to-1 chance of defeating the English. As he sat, he noticed the persistence of a spider attempting to weave its web in a draughty corner. That persistence and determination inspired Bruce and the Battle of Bannockburn was a foregone conclusion.

As a matter of fact, Scotland's greatest hero was of French descent. His father was Robert de Bruis, who lived near Cherbourg and who accompanied William of Normandy to England in 1066. While we are gently debunking tradition, I suspect that Robert the Bruce went into battle with the skirl of bagpipes encouraging his troops, but this most Scottish of institutions did not in fact originate in Scotland. Its origin was most likely in Persia. From there it spread to ancient Rome and Greece, arriving here thanks to the Roman invasion. Some say, and I can hear claymores rasping in their scabbards even now, that the haggis came through the same door, the Romans having devised it as marching rations with a usefully long "shelf life." Finally, the word should be bagpipe (in the singular). There may be several drones but there is only one chanter or pipe.

TOURIST INFORMATION BUREAU: 22 Athol Road, Pitlochry PH16 5BX, Perthshire. Tel (0796) 2215/2751

ST ANDREWS

County of Fife
477 miles (763.2 km) from London by MI
By train, 5 hours 30 minutes from London

For me, St Andrews is the most beautiful small town in Scotland. It's also a charming seaside resort with an abundance of fresh air straight from the North Sea, blessedly unpolluted by factories or through traffic, and in term time its fine, quiet streets are enlivened by the traditional scarlet gowns of the students of Scotland's oldest university (circa 1411). As if all that weren't enough, the town was for several centuries the ecclesiastical centre of the country, it also served as a pulpit for John Knox's denunciations of Roman Catholicism, and, perhaps best known of all, it houses the Royal and Ancient Golf Club – the ruling body of the game. In short, St Andrews is a delight.

The Celtic Church had a settlement in St Andrews from the earliest times, but the town became known as the result of a shipwreck. A monk, later canonized as St Regulus (or St Rule), was taking some relics of St Andrew the Apostle from Patras in Greece to an unknown destination when his ship foundered in St Andrews Bay. It was these relics that gave the town her religious supremacy and Scotland her patron saint. St Rule's arrival is thought to have been around the middle of the 8th century and he is believed to have converted the Pictish King Fergus, who gave him some land. There, St Rule continued his missionary work. The earliest buildings are gone but in 1144 the fine small Church of St Rule was built. Little remains but the massive square bell tower, 108 feet (32.8 m) high, with each of its sides at the base measuring 20 feet (7 m). It is adjacent to the cathedral ruins at the top of South Street and can be visited. The relics of St Andrew were kept in St Rule's church while the great cathedral was being built. The Cathedral was the largest church in Scotland. Three hundred and ninety-one feet (119 m) long, it was begun in 1161 and not completed until 1318 when its dedication was attended by King Robert the Bruce. The Cathedral and Priory occupied some 30 acres (74 ha) and were enclosed by a huge wall, 4 feet (1.2 m) thick and 20 feet (6 m) high with 13 projecting defensive towers. Substantial parts of the cathedral survive, enough to give one an idea of the magnificent structure it must have been. Thousands of pilgrims visited the cathedral during its heyday, but in 1559 a mob of reformers, inflamed by John Knox's teaching, and watched by him, set about "casting it doon." Their main targets were the idols and ornaments, but the building, uncared for, quickly became a ruin and in 1649 Parliament (under Cromwell's influence) took the extraordinary step of authorizing the people of St Andrews to use the ruined cathedral as a quarry for building stone. Many of these stones may now be seen built into local houses. At this time too, the relics of St Andrew brought to the cathedral by St Rule were "lost'," but it is interesting to note that there are still several relics of the Apostle in churches in Scotland, albeit from different sources.

St Andrews Castle (at the seaward end of Castle St) was built at the end of the 12th century as an Episcopal residence. It was built on a rocky promontory jutting into the sea and was separated from the land by a deep moat. It was dismantled in the 1320s and a new castle was built in 1390. The castle was notorious for its deep Bottle Dungeon cut out of solid rock. Seven feet (2 m) in diameter at the top and 16 feet (4.8 m) at its bottom, it was a prison no one ever left alive.

St Andrews Castle, the Cathedral and Priory, Blackfriars Monastery and St Rule's Tower are all in the care of the Department of the Environment and are open all year Mon–Sat and Sun pm. Tel 72021 for details.

The buildings of the University are spread throughout St Andrews. St Salvator's College

HOME OF GOLF, ST. ANDREWS

(between North Street and The Scores) was founded in 1450 by Bishop James Kennedy and its chapel is of that date. Each April the Bishop's beautiful niece is honoured in a colourful student parade called the "Kate Kennedy Pageant," while the Bishop's mace is carried on ceremonial occasions. Dean's Court (at the junction of North and South Streets) was built in the 12th century and is now a postgraduate hall of residence. St Mary's College (close to the Information Centre on South Street) has housed the Faculty of Divinity since the mid-16th century. Its Foundation Charter was confirmed by James V and this is commemorated by the Royal Arms of Scotland on the street frontage. In the quadrangle is a thorn tree, planted in 1563 by Mary, Queen of Scots. The building containing Parliament Hall (between South Street and Queen's Terrace by the Town Hall) stands on a site where the Faculty of Arts began to meet in 1416. The present building was completed in 1643. Its lower room has been known as Parliament Hall since Charles I, fleeing from the plague in Edinburgh, met his parliament in it in 1645 and 1646. Until the end of the 19th century university activities were concentrated on this site, with the university library in an upper room. It is now used as a student reading room although the principal governing bodies of the university still meet here. The University has been considerably extended during the present century, partly by the acquisition of historic buildings in the town and partly by new construction. This university still has, as its greatest treasures, the three 15th-century silver maces of the Faculty of Arts, the Faculty of Canon Law and St Salvator's College. During July and August guided tours of the University are given by student guides. Tel 76161.

Holy Trinity Church (South Street) was built in 1410 as the Town Kirk. The tower is the main remnant of the earlier structure, but restorations have preserved much of its former glory. There is some fine stained glass and silver plate and some interesting old parish registers. There is a Stool of Repentance and the Bishop's Branks – a sort of helmet with a metal piece inserted in the mouth to hold down the tongue – used to silence scolding wives. There is a handsome memorial to the renegade Archbishop Shairp (see Ephemera). Holy Trinity, housing the congregation of the Church of Scotland, is one of the handsomest and most interesting parish churches in Scotland. The Episcopal Church in Scotland makes its home, ironically, in the only church in St Andrews to bear the name of the patron saint. St Andrew's Church, built in 1868, flourishes partly because about a third of St Andrews students are from England.

The Royal and Ancient Golf Club at St Andrews was founded in 1754 and is, by common consent, the world's leading golf club.

Golf is wholly indigenous to Scotland and is traditionally a classless pastime there. James I (James VI of Scotland) introduced the game to England in 1603, although it did not become popular until the 19th century. The origin of the game is clouded in mystery. It is perhaps related to medieval cross-country ball games such as the Dutch kolven or the Irish shinty, but unlike them it is a test of individual skill, not a team game. Wherever it began, it was flourishing in Scotland by the 15th century. Like other ballgames, it was frowned upon because it took people away from archery practice and in 1457 it was banned. James IV banned it again in 1491. Although he was the first Scottish king to figure in the historical record as a golfer, he still found the game "unprofitabill" for his subjects. The Stuart kings were ardent golfers and so, it may be, were the queens, for it was alleged by Mary Stuart's enemies that she "was seen playing golf and pallmall in the fields" a few days after the death of her husband, Henry, Lord Darnley in 1567. Pallmall was a game in which a boxwood ball was driven by a mallet through an iron ring suspended in a long alley. If anything, the game sounds even more difficult than golf, but perhaps not as frustrating. Modern golf began with the formation of gentlemen's societies or clubs in the mid-18th century. The Honourable Company of Edinburgh Golfers originated in the setting up of an annual prize match on the links at Leith in 1744, followed in 1754 by a similar scheme at St Andrews. The St Andrews Society of Golfers became the Royal and Ancient in 1834 when William IV authorized it to change its name. It was not however until 1897 that the club accepted authority with respect to the rules of the game. There are four courses at St Andrews – the Old, the New, the Eden and the Jubilee. Until 1913 anyone could play the hallowed Old Course without charge, and although the state of affairs was changed (by an act of Parliament no less), until comparatively recently any resident of the town could play as often as he or she wished on these courses for 50 pence a year! Even now the courses are open to the public and anyone may play on them subject only to a ballot for places in busy times and certain privileges for "R-and-A" members in May, August and September. The Old Course, over which golf has been played continuously for five centuries, originally consisted of 22 holes – 11 out and 11 back. In 1764 it was converted to 18 holes which, quite accidentally, became the accepted number for a round of golf. The club's neo-classical Clubhouse was built in 1854 and is not open to the public. The "guttie" – a ball made of gutta-percha and forerunner of the present golf ball – was invented by a St Andrews clergyman in the mid-19th century. The British Golf Museum is located opposite the Royal and Ancient Club (see below).

The Town Hall (next to the Information Centre in South Street) has recently been reno-vated and has on display the town charter granted by Malcolm Canmore in the 11th century and the executioner's axe which ended many lives on the market square, including that of a would-be lover of Mary, Queen of Scots. Also on display is a striking mosaic panel given to the town for its hospitality by Polish troops garrisoned here during the First World War.

The Martyrs' Monument on The Scores, overlooking the sea, commemorates those who met their death by being burnt at the stake in St Andrews during the Reformation. The Pends, on Pends Road, was originally a magnificent vaulted gatehouse, forming the prin-cipal entrance to the Priory Precinct. It dates from the 14th century, and the Precinct Wall from the early 16th century. It is said that the Pends will collapse when the wisest man in Christendom walks through the archway. It hasn't collapsed yet! The West Port, at the west end of South Street, was the principal entrance to the old city and was built in 1589. It is the finest surviving example of a "burgh" gate or "port" in Scotland. Finally, the Harbour is one of the most picturesque features of the town. The main pier was rebuilt in the 17th century using – you guessed it – stones from the Cathedral and Castle ruins.

Savouring the beauty and charm of St Andrews today, it is difficult to believe that, at the end of the 17th century, the town was in such a state of decline that there was a proposal to move the university to Perth. Dr Johnson and his biographer visited here in 1773. Dr Johnson's description of the town at that time gives one some inkling of the problem. "In the morning we arose to perambulate the city, which only history shows to have once flourished, and surveyed the ruins of ancient magnificence, of which even the ruins cannot long be visible, unless some care be taken to preserve them; where is the pleasure of preserving such mournful memorials? One of its streets is now lost, and in those that remain there is the silence and solitude of inactive indigence and gloomy depopulation." Things are certainly not like that today and it's a pity Dr Johnson could not come back and see how the negative picture he paints of the town has changed.

WALK

The **St Andrews Walk** begins at the car park between Doubledykes Road and Argyle Street, west of West Port. Turn left onto Argyle Street and cross the road. Pass through West Gate into South Street. Pass the remains of **Blackfriar Chapel**, remnant of the 13th-century Dominican monastery. Past the **Town Hall** and **Tourist Information Office** is **St Mary's College** on the right. Just past St Mary's turn right into an alley marked **Byre Theatre**. Walk through a pleasant 17th-century courtyard with the theatre on your left. Just past the theatre, which was converted from a cowshed (hence the name), turn left and left again into Abbey Street. At the junction turn right on South Street to the **Cathedral**. Walk through "The Pends," the ruined entrance to the cathedral precinct, and turn right down Pends Road and left to the **Harbour** and **Pier**. Turn left up the steps by the cathedral grounds. Fork right along a footpath to the cliff edge and continue ahead to the ruins of **St Andrew's Castle**. From the castle turn right into North Castle Street and right again into North Street. Opposite **St Salvator's College** (on the right) turn left into College Street and right into Market Street, with its cobbled **Market Square**. Turn right into Greyfriars Gardens, cross North Street and turn left into Murray Park. At the end turn left into The Scores, walk past the **Martyrs' Monument** and the **British Golf Museum** to the **Royal and Ancient Golf Club**. Turn left along Golf Place, right into Links Crescent and left into City Road. At the crossroads turn right into Doubledykes Road and left into the car park.

MUSEUMS AND GALLERIES

St Andrews Cathedral Museum and St Rule's Tower – Tel 72021. Open daily, the museum houses many fascinating relics including an unusual sarcophagus. St Rule's is a square tower and one of the most remarkable buildings of its kind in Britain. From the top (158 steps) it affords the visitor a panoramic view of the town and adjacent coastline.

British Golf Museum – (opposite R and A Golf Club) Tel 73423. The museum tells the fascinating history of golf. Highly visual displays and Compac Disc Interactive touch screens give video accounts of famous matches, personalities and events. Comprehensive collection of clubs, balls and memorabilia. Displays of golf fashion trends and a shop selling a wide range of apparel, golfing items and reproductions of historic memorabilia. Open June–Oct 10–5:30 pm daily, Nov from Tues–Sun 10–5 pm and Dec Tues–Sat 10–4 pm. Opening times may vary during major St Andrews golf events.

Sea Life Centre – The Scores, Tel 72950. You can come face to face with hundreds of exciting sea creatures from the octopus to 11 varieties of shark found in British waters. Excellent viewing facilities and a wonderful seal observatory which will ultimately become Europe's premier Common Seal breeding facility. Open mid-Feb to Dec daily, 9–6 pm (until 7pm July and Aug).

THEATRE

It is appropriate that St Andrews should be a centre of professional theatre in Scotland. In 1538 Mary of Guise, mother of Mary, Queen of Scots, was married in St Andrews Cathedral to King James V. Before her wedding she watched a performance of Sir David Lindsay's *Satire of the Thrie Estaits*. Lindsay's play, which had received its first performance in the open air at Cupar (10 miles/16 km west) three years earlier, was reported to have lasted nine hours. As Cupar was Lindsay's home maybe the audience didn't mind, but the play itself, which satirizes the state of the Catholic Church in Scotland as well as that of the nobility and the burgesses, seems a strange choice for the strongly Catholic Mary to make. The play was only known among academics for centuries, until Sir Tyrone Guthrie revived it and produced it at the Edinburgh Festival in 1947 using a cast of only Scottish actors. (The play is in the old Scots tongue.) The play did much to awaken interest in ancient and indeed contemporary Scottish theatre.

The **Byre Theatre** – Abbey Street, Tel 76288. The Byre is so called because it was originally housed in the Abbey Street dairy farm. In 1933 the St Andrews Play Club converted the barn into a small, intimate theatre with 74 seats. During the war it was taken over by a small professional company, and in 1969 the old Byre was demolished and the present theatre established. Even today the intimacy remains as the theatre seats under 200 people. There is a professional summer company but the theatre is open all year and plays host to visiting and local community companies. The summer season is a mix of popular and more serious theatre and there is a strong commitment to work by Scottish playwrights. The Byre is one of Scotland's five recognized repertory theatres. Recent productions have included a comedy about the Open Golf Championship and *Holiday Snaps* by Michael Pertwee and John Chapman and more seriously, *Blood and Ice*, by Scottish playwright Liz Locheah which was a mixed-media examination of the romance and tragedy surrounding Mary Shelley's creation of her fictitious creature, Frankenstein's monster.

The **Crawford Arts Centre**, Tel 74610, presents major art exhibitions and performance events throughout the year and there are also young people's arts workshops. The **Studio Theatre** plays host to a number of local and visiting theatre companies. The **Buchanan Arts Building** of the University also plays host to a number of cultural events during the year. Tel 72021.

MUSIC

The major musical events in St Andrews are the regular visits of the Scottish Chamber Orchestra to the **Younger Hall**. For details of these regular concerts call 74610. The Younger Hall also hosts chamber groups and visiting individual artists. The **St Andrews Festival** was created in 1971 upon student initiative and has continued as a biennial event (odd years). It is unique throughout Europe in that it is run entirely by students, yet it has gained a national reputation for its professionalism and earned the title "Scotland's Winter Festival." Held in mid-February. The 1991 festival included the Compass Theatre Company, the Tuckwell Wind Quintet and the Scottish Chamber Orchestra. Previous festivals have seen appearances by Julian Lloyd-Webber, the Cambridge Footlights Revue and the Moscow String Quartet. There is a Festival Café which is a social focus and the setting for fringe events. The Festival's climax is the Festival Ball. Tel 77878

CINEMA

Commercial cinema at the **New Picture House**, Tel 74902 (two screens).

BOOKSTORES

The best is **James Thin**, Students' Union, St Mary's Place, Tel 76367. An old established bookseller (1848). Thin's also has branches in Perth and Dundee.

J and G Innes Ltd are a local firm at 107 South Street, Tel 72174. As well as books they have an extensive selection of stationery and office supplies. One advantage of the **Ladyhead Bookshop** at 33/35 North St, Tel 77886, is that it also has a coffee shop which allows you to sip and browse, while **John Smith and Son**, Glasgow-based bookseller, is not related to the English W H Smith chain. There is a branch of **Menzies** at 90 South Street, Tel 72621, which will serve you if you are interested in pulp fiction or newspapers. Finally, there's a good remainder shop with excellent bargains at **Book Sale Today**, 15 Church St, Tel 77433.

ANTIQUARIAN AND SECONDHAND BOOKS

The best in my view is **A and F McIlreavy**, 57 South St, Tel 72487. They are just up from the Tourist Information Office on the other side of the road. They have a good selection of antiquarian books and a wide range of secondhand volumes on all subjects. They are especially strong on art, voyages and travel, military history, literature and Scottish books of all kinds.

Quarto Bookshop – 8 Golf Place, Tel 74616, also has a good general secondhand stock and some nice antiquarian volumes. They are especially strong on the subjects of Scottish literature and golf.

Billson of St Andrews – 15 Greyfriars Gardens, Tel 75063, is a good and well-established store which is charmingly old-fashioned, while **Bouquiniste** at 31 Market St, Tel 76724, has an interesting and varied selection of secondhand and antiquarian books with new stock added almost daily.

ART GALLERIES

Dorothy Quinn Interiors – 121 South St, Tel 73551, modern paintings, prints, sculptures; **St Andrews Fine Art**, 84 Market St, Tel 74080, is worth a look; but St Andrews is not a mecca for the visual arts.

ANTIQUE DEALERS

The antique dealers in St Andrews are usefully clustered in the vicinity of South Street. At No 68 South Street, close to the Tourist Information Office is **Bygones**, Tel 75849. They have a good general collection of antiques and collectables. Just down the street on the other side of the road is **Claire's Country Store** at 149 South Street, Tel 72927. They specialize in Scottish country furniture and they also have decorative items and gifts. Just past Claire's, turn right onto Bell Street and at No 28 you will find **Magpie**, Tel 78391. They have real quality collectables together with furniture, porcelain and silver. They have a good jewellery collection ranging from Georgian to present-day. Come back on to South Street and turn right and you'll find **West Port Books and Antiques** at 205 South St, Tel 73586. They specialize in Edwardiana and have linen, lace, period costumes and good quality bric-à-brac. They also have good-quality publishers' remainders at half price. Close by at 211 South Street is **Circa Antiques**, Tel 76798, with a general collection of antiques and bric-à-brac. Go past Circa and turn right on City Road. Follow it until the intersection of Albany Place. Go right and then left into Golf Place and at No 10 you will find **Old St Andrews Gallery**, Tel 78712. This is a fascinating shop with a large collection of golf memorabilia, which is only to be expected as Golf Place skirts the 18th hole of the Old Course. The Gallery also has reproduction golf art. Come back into Albany Place and turn left, and at No 9 you will find another **Old St Andrews Gallery** which also has golf memorabilia, plus collectables and the largest selection of Scottish jewellery and silver in Fife. Tel 77840.

Finally, if you are in St Andrews on a Friday, check if **Macgregor Auctions**, Tel 72431, are having an auction sale. They operate fortnightly sales and it's well worth trying to catch one. They also have a quarterly specialist antique sale. You can find Macgregor's by going through the West Port on South Street and turning left onto Bridge Street. This becomes Largo Road and Macgregor's is at 56A.

RESTAURANTS

Each year the **St Andrews and NE Fife International Festival of Food and Wine** is held in mid-March. There are theme dinners, cookery competitions, wine and spirit tastings and a plethora of gourmet cooking. Tel 72021. This is the best time to eat in St Andrews but there is a wide selection of interesting cuisines at all times, befitting the town's status as a popular resort.

The **Vine Leaf Restaurant** – 131 South St, Tel 77497. The Vine Leaf offers local game, fresh seafood and vegetarian dishes. Best value is the fixed-price menu. I advise you to reserve as the dining room is not huge.

Brambles Restaurant – 5 College St, Tel 75380. Excellent for lunch. Brambles has home cooked food using fresh local produce, and good vegetarian cookery. They are open for a traditional Scottish breakfast at 7:30 but note the early closing time of 4:30.

The Merchant's House – 49 South St, Tel 72595. Informal eating which is great fun, especially in term time. They do morning coffee, snack lunches and suppers. They bake their own bread and their soup and pot suppers in the evening are excellent. They also have fondues, quiches and a salad table. Inexpensive.

For a really special night out make the 15-minute drive to **Cupar** (west on B939/940). There you will find **Ostler's Close** at 25 Bonnygate, Tel 55574. The cooking emphasizes fish and game. You can try crab in a dill mayonnaise or, if you are in a non-fishy mood, they do wood pigeon with sloe gin and blackcurrants, which is worth a drive to Edinburgh, let alone Cupar. The desserts are sinful and very good and the wine list is reasonable and imaginative. Open Tues–Sat 12:15 to 2pm and 7–9:30pm (also Monday dinner). I applaud them on their no smoking rule. Finally, if you are fond of fish, it's well worth the nine-mile (14.4 km) drive to Anstruther (B9131) to eat at the **Cellar**, 24 East Green, Tel 0333310378. For me this is one of the best fish restaurants anywhere. The fish is absolutely fresh and in true Scottish style they don't mess about with it. Do not miss the crayfish and mussel bisque to start with. There is excellent halibut, turbot, sole and monkfish and of course, lamb and local beef for carnivores. The wine list is remarkable for a place of this size. The restaurant is low profile yet has a rich atmosphere. This is a real "insider's" eating place, populated mainly by locals and those who know, who drive miles to eat here, so keep it to yourself. By the way, if your taste for fresh fish becomes sated the **New Balaka** at Alexandra Place, Market Street, is the best Indian Restaurant for miles around. Their tandoori dishes are excellent, which is hardly surprising as the spices they use are either homegrown or especially imported from India.

PUBS

Victoria Café – 1 St Mary's Place (corner of Bell St) Tel 76964. Great fun in term time as it's a real university hang-out. Stripped panelling, fans, bentwood chairs and an oak floor. Lots of brass lamps and potted palms. Bar food from noon–7pm. Table service with Bistro 7pm–9pm (July&Aug). Interesting food too – carrot and dill soup, broccoli and Brie quiche, and tortellini. On a different level, they have great bacon rolls. Open to midnight at weekends.

Ma Bells – 40 The Scores. Another lively student pub overlooking the sea by the golf course. They have 75 different bottled beers and lots of different malt whiskies. The bar food is reasonable, with the hot pies especially recommended. But they only serve from lunch to 6 pm. Ten miles (16 km) south on the A917 is **Crail**, a delightful fishing village with probably the most photographed harbour in Scotland. At 4 High Street is the **Golf**, a comfortable village inn with a neat and cosy bar. Their bar food is excellent with Scotch broth and local fish at the top of the list. They also have clean and comfortable bedrooms and they serve a very good breakfast.

Lower Largo is 13 miles (20.8 km) south on A915. Largo Bay has some of best beaches in the area. Lower Largo's main claim to fame is that in 1676 Alexander Selkirk was born there. Selkirk was the castaway who provided Daniel Defoe with his model for *Robinson Crusoe*. Just inland at Upper Largo is the **Largo**. I mention it mainly because the helpings of bar food are as large as any I have encountered anywhere and who knows what the keen Fife coastal air might have done to your appetite. The Largo also has inexpensive accommodation.

Finally, on Grange Road back in St Andrews is the **Grange**. It's about a mile (1.6 km) south of the town centre but there's an excellent atmosphere in the bar and it's housed in a fine old building. The bar food is particularly good and the restaurant has changing set-price meals at lunchtime and in the evening, with interesting dishes such as avocado with raspberry vinaigrette and baked halibut with lobster and brandy sauce.

ARTISTIC ASSOCIATIONS

William Dunbar, one of the greatest of the early Scottish poets, studied at St Andrews University before joining the court of James IV at the end of the 15th century. Dunbar has been said to be as rich in poetic fancy as Edmund Spenser in *The Faerie Queene*, but his work is much less known. Sir David Lindsay was also a student at the University about the same time. He was involved in the education of King James V and many of his poems contain advice for the young king (see Theatre above). John Major, the early Scottish philosopher, spent much of his life at the University here. He wrote in Latin and one of his works is said to be an account of the making of black pudding – the mind boggles. He died in 1550.

Andrew Lang, the Scottish poet, was educated here before going to Balliol, Oxford. He returned to live at 8 Gibson Place until his death in 1912.

Edwin Muir, the excellent Scottish poet who was born in the Orkneys, moved here in 1953. He lived at Castlelea in The Scores and was a reviewer for *The Scotsman*. Both *Scottish Journey* and *The Story of the Fable* were written in St Andrews.

EPHEMERA

Scotland's ecclesiastical ways are extremely strange and often very violent. In 1528 the Lutheran preacher Patrick Hamilton was burned at the stake for heresy just at the foot of the Old Tower by St Salvator's College. At the foot of the Tower in North Street you can see the initials "P H" on the cobbles. High above on the archway there is a weathered stone which appears to have a face etched upon it. Legend has it that this is the face of Hamilton burned into the stone by the psychic power of his martyrdom.

In 1546 Cardinal Beaton had caused the reformer George Wishart to be burnt at the stake. Beaton had sentenced many reformers to death, but in Wishart's case he gloated over his victim's fate from the castle battlements. Before he died, however, Wishart prophesied from the stake that the Cardinal would soon be seen on the same spot "in as much shame as he now shows pomp and vanity." This statement did not unduly worry Cardinal Beaton as he thought the castle was impregnable, having prepared it for an expected attack by the forces of Henry VIII. But a party of Fife lairds gained access to the castle and stabbed the Cardinal to death. They then, in fulfilment of George Wishart's prophecy, hung Beaton's body from the battlements in the exact spot from which he had gloated over the reformer's death.

Just south of St Andrews is Magus Muir, famous as the place where Archbishop Shairp was murdered. Shairp had become a respected minister of the Presbyterian faith and, at the Restoration of Charles II (1660), went to plead with him for the church's freedom. Charles had signed the "Declaration of Dumferline" in 1650, yielding to the demands of the Presbyterian church, and it might have been thought that he would be sympathetic to Shairp's pleas. We can only guess at the conversation that took place between Shairp and his sovereign, but when he returned to St Andrews it was as Archbishop, and he set about, with great zeal, persecuting all those who resisted him. To call the good cleric a turncoat is probably a gross understatement. On May 3, 1679, a party of Covenanters led by two Fife lairds, Haxton of Rathillet and Balfour of Kinloch, were searching for William Carmichael, Sheriff of Fife. Carmichael had been appointed by Archbishop Shairp to persecute those who sought to betray the Catholic faith and he had carried out this task with "terror and cruel oppression." Lying in wait by the roadside the band of men stopped a coach travelling with its escort thinking it to be the Sheriff. Instead, it turned out to be carrying Archbishop Shairp. Dragging the luckless priest from his coach, Balfour, as leader, then denounced Shairp as "a murderer, betrayer of the Kirk, an open enemy and persecutor of Jesus Christ and His Members." Balfour and his men then brutally murdered their captive. Although Shairp had been greatly hated the affair shocked all Scotland. The nature of the religious turmoil of Scotland's past can be summed up by the fact that in Holy Trinity Church in St Andrews, a Presbyterian church, there is a handsome memorial to this Roman Catholic Archbishop.

TOURIST INFORMATION BUREAU: 78 South Street, St Andrews, Fife KY16 9TE. Tel (0334) 72021

10

NORTHERN IRELAND

BELFAST

BELFAST

County of Antrim. Capital of Northern Ireland
By sea from Stranraer to Larne (2 hours), then by train to Belfast (1 hour)
By air from many English provincial airports (1 hour flying time)

Belfast, capital of Northern Ireland since 1920, is an important port and industrial city. It is beautifully situated on Belfast Lough at the mouth of the River Lagan, and the coastal scenery is some of the most beautiful in the British Isles. There are numerous fine buildings and churches, and the Belfast shipyards are among the largest in Europe.

Belfast (Beal Feirste – the ford on the coast) possessed a fort in the early Middle Ages, circa 1177. A castle was built soon after, which like Belfast itself, remained a bone of contention between the native Irish and the English conquerors. In 1613 the town that had grown up around the castle was granted a charter by James I, but in 1657 the population was only 500. Within 30 years it had quadrupled. The manufacture of linen had long been an important industry in Belfast, and it received additional impetus in the latter part of the 17th century when Huguenots fleeing from France introduced improved industrial methods. By this time the British Crown had expropriated the nine counties of Ulster and the great Plantation of Ulster brought new settlers, mostly Scots, to swell the population. The Scots were good farmers and craftsmen; it was they who built neat towns and gave the northern countryside much of the character it has today. The Huguenots gave Belfast a French atmosphere and contributed to its intellectual life so that it became known as the Athens of the North. The settlers from the British mainland and elsewhere built their own churches, giving Belfast its present multiplicity of religious denominations and sects. The industry of shipbuilding grew alongside that of linen manufacture and by 1800 the population of Belfast had grown to 20,000. This had grown to 200,000 when the Treaty of 1921 reduced Ulster to six counties – Cavan, Monaghan and Donegal joining the Republic of Eire. The great industrial expansion of the 19th century, the golden age of Belfast's development, can be seen in the great Victorian buildings that are today Belfast's pride. Many guide books do not mention the religious and sectarian troubles with which Belfast is plagued. I think it is important to visitors to know that the streets of Belfast are patrolled by armed soldiers and police in full body armour and that there is considerable evidence of the armed struggle which has been going on, seemingly forever, and has severely limited the development of the tourist industry. On the other hand I found that, like the people of the city themselves, I soon forgot these external signs of conflict and immersed myself in the delights of a city that triumphantly refuses to be intimidated by terrorist activity.

WALK

Our **Belfast Walk** starts from the multi-storey car park in High Street opposite the Tourist Information Centre. Walk out onto High Street. Two doors from the tourist office is the old **National Bank** with its copper pinnacles. Another fine bank building is one block north of the High Street at **No 2 Waring Street**. This is Belfast's oldest surviving public building. Built in 1769 as a market house, it was the venue in 1792 for a famous assembly of Irish harpers. At No 5 Waring Street is the **Royal Ulster Rifles Museum**, and at No 35, the **Ulster Bank**. Walk east down Waring Street to the junction with Victoria Street. Here you will find the **Albert Memorial Clock Tower** (a kind of mini Big Ben) which subsidence has made lean more than three feet (.9 m) from the vertical. Directly across from the Clock Tower is the **Custom House**, a mellow building in golden-coloured stone representing the best in Belfast architecture. Walk back along Queen's Square to the Clock Tower and turn left down Victoria Street, cross Chichester Street and soon on your left you will see the massive building of the **Royal Court of Justice**. At the back of the courts is the **Cattle Market** and close by the **Variety Market** which has much of interest for shoppers. Continue down Victoria Street until it forks right to become Cromac Street. Just at the fork turn right down Sussex Hamilton Street and then left on Alfred Street to **St Malachy's Catholic Church**. Directly across from St Malachy's, take Clarence Street and turn right on Linenhall Street. You will go past the side of the **Ulster Hall** and soon come into Donegal Square and **City Hall** and the massive stone decorated **Scottish Provident Building**. On the northwest corner of the Square you can find the **Linenhall Library**. Leave the square at the southwest corner by Howard Street, and turn left on Great Victoria Street for the **Opera House** on your right and the **Crown Liquor Saloon** on your left. Go back down Great Victoria Street and on your left you will see two bastions of education, the **College of Technology** and the **Royal Belfast Academical Institution**. The street has now become College Square and where it forks left, go straight onto King Street. Turn left onto Berry Street and then Rosemary Street with the **First Presbyterian Church** on your left. The church was praised for its admirable elliptical interior by John Wesley. At the end of Rosemary Street turn left onto Donegal Street and **St Anne's Cathedral**. Close by are the **Central Library** and the offices of the **Belfast Telegraph** and the **Irish News**. Walk back down Donegal Street, turn left on Waring Street to Victoria Street and turn right to the Clock Tower. At the Clock Tower turn onto High Street and the car park. South of City Hall by Bedford Street, Dublin Road and University Road (3/4 of a mile/1.2 km) are **Queen's University** and the **Ulster Museum**.

MUSEUMS, GALLERIES AND PUBLIC BUILDINGS

Ulster Museum – Botanic Gardens (off Stranmillis Road), Tel 668251. The Ulster is one of Britain's national museums. The displays are divided into five sections – antiquities, art, botany and zoology, geology, and technology (including flax and linen). In the antiquities section there are important collections of Irish archaeological material and artefacts recovered from two ships wrecked in the Spanish Armada. There is a significant collection of modern art, with some old masters and Irish art and in the Local History Gallery there is a fascinating historical survey of Ulster, which focuses on political and military events. Open Mon–Sat 10–5pm.

Belfast Transport Museum – Witham Street, Newtonards Road, Tel 515129. The museum contains part of the Ulster Folk and Transport Museum's comprehensive collection of all types of transport. (The Ulster Folk Museum itself, which has rebuilt urban and rural houses, is at Cultra, seven miles/11.2 km east of Belfast.) There are railway, horse -hauled and electric trams, cars, cycles and an example from the Giant's Causeway Tramway. Especially notable is "Maeve," the largest railway engine ever built in Northern Ireland. Open Mon–Sat 10–5pm.

Royal Ulster Rifles Regiment – Regimental Headquarters, 5 Waring Street, Tel 232086. A large collection of uniforms, badges and medals together with the histories of units of the Regiment, war diaries, photo albums and scrapbooks.

Linenhall Library – 17 Donegal Square, Tel 321707. The library was founded in 1788 and the first librarian was Thomas Russell. He was an active member of the United Irishmen and was hanged in 1803 for trying to obtain support for Robert Emmet's Dublin uprising. Open Mon–Fri 10–5pm, Sat 10–12:30pm.

Ulster Bank – 35 Waring Street, Tel 235232. Built in 1845, the building is an imitation of Sir Charles Barry's Reform Club, which was completed ten years earlier in London, and was itself an imitation of the Farnese Palace in Rome.

St Malachy's Catholic Church – Alfred Street. The richest interior of any church in the city. A fine fan-vaulted ceiling with an altar framed by an open-work screen and tracery which is echoed in the pulpit. The altar paintings are by one of the Tyrolean Piccioni family.

First Presbyterian Church – Rosemary Street. An elliptical church, completed in 1783. The exterior was crudely remodelled in 1833 but the elegant interior survives with nearly all its fittings.

St Anne's Cathedral – Donegal Street, Tel 328332. The basic design is "Hiberno-Romanesque" and the mosaic on the roof of the baptistry depicting the Creation is impressive, as is the 85-foot (53.2 m) nave paved with Irish marble and Canadian maple.

Sinclair Seamen's Church – Corporation Square, Tel 232081. Like a maritime museum with a "Moby Dick" corner pulpit, a binnacle as a lectern, ships' bells, a steering wheel and port and starboard lights on the organ. Open only on Sundays for services at 11:30am and 7pm.

City Hall – Donegal Square, Tel 220202. This Renaissance-style building dominates the centre of the city. It is massive with four corner towers and a 175-foot (53.2 m) copper dome. It has a lavishly decorated marble interior and a large mural of Belfast's industrial history. A fine sculpture commemorates those who lost their lives on the Titanic disaster; the ship was built in Belfast's yards. Free tour on Wednesday morning.

Crown Liquor Saloon – Great Victoria Street, Tel 249476. For me the most fascinating pub in the British Isles. Late 19th-century in design, it shows the High Victorian hostelry at its flamboyant best with elaborate ornamentation and fine quality joinery, tiles and engraved glass. Mercifully, it has resisted all modernizing tendencies and is managed for the National Trust by Bass Breweries. Not to be missed (see Pubs).

Belfast Castle – Cave Hill, Tel 370133. Built in 1870 in the Scottish Baronial style and presented to the city by the Earl of Shaftesbury in 1934, the building has a square six-storey tower and a baroque staircase snaking up from flowerbeds and lawns. Now a restaurant.

THEATRE

Grand Opera House – Great Victoria Street, Tel 241919. Designed by the celebrated theatre architect, Frank Matcham, the theatre is a splendid example of Victoriana and was beautifully restored in 1980. It is Northern Ireland's only large venue for touring opera, drama and ballet and it hosts such companies as the Abbey Theatre, Dublin, the Royal Flanders and Moscow Festival Ballet Companies, the Royal Shakespeare Company and Opera Northern Ireland.

Lyric Player's Theatre – Ridgeway Street, Tel 660081. The place to see new Irish drama in Belfast. Recent work has included plays by Sam Thompson (*Over the Bridge*) and Seamus Heaney (*The Cure at Troy*). Also presented are modern classics such as *The Importance of Being Earnest* and *The Playboy of the Western World*.

Group Theatre – Bedford Street, Tel 229685. Primarily a venue for amateur theatre but there is also some professional drama. Local playwrights get a chance to showcase work here and the quality of the amateur offerings is well above normal. This is a quirky little theatre with a long tradition of producing excellent actors and is worth a visit.

The Belfast Festival at Queen's University – Has been running for 28 years and many people, including myself, think it is second only to the Edinburgh Festival for quality and choice. It is held for two to three weeks beginning in the first week of November each year and includes folk and classical music, drama, film, poetry, workshops, lectures and art exhibitions. The Festival is packed with international names and is the most significant cultural event of the year in Northern Ireland. Any visitor would be wise to plan a stay in Belfast during Festival time. Tel 667687 for information.

During the Festival other theatrical venues are brought into operation which sometimes offer programmes during the rest of the year. The most significant of these are:

Belfast Civic Arts Theatre – 41 Botanic Avenue, Tel 324936 (amateur and professional theatre).

Whitla Hall – Queen's University, University Road, Tel 245133 (university events).

Harty Room – Queen's University, University Square, Tel 245133 (university events).

Elmwood Hall – Queen's University, Elmwood Avenue, Tel 2452133 (university events).

Crescent Arts Centre – 2–4 University Road, Tel 242338 (arts activities).

Old Museum Arts Centre – 7 College Square North, Tel 235053 (arts activities).

Stranmillis College Theatre – Stranmillis Road, Tel 38127 (college events).

MUSIC

The main venue for music is the **Ulster Hall** on Linenhall Street, Tel 323900. It is the home of the excellent **Ulster Orchestra** whose recent conductors include Vernon Handley and Yan Pascal Tortelier. They give concerts throughout the year, and there are visiting orchestras, such as the Scottish National, the Montreal Symphony and the Leipzig Gewandhaus. At Festival time many of the venues mentioned above are also used for musical events, especially Whitla, Elmwood Hall and the Harty Room.

There is a Jazz and Blues Festival in June, a Folk Festival and an Opera Festival in September and the Belfast Civic Festival in May. Tel 246609 for details.

CINEMA

Commercial cinemas are:

Cannon Film Centre – 1/11 Fisherwick Place, Tel 322484 (4 screens).

The Strand – 156 Holywood Road, Tel 673500 (4 screens).

Curzon Film Centre – 300 Ormean Road, Tel 641373 (4 screens).

Movie House – 13 Glenwell Road, Newtonabbey, Tel 833424 (5 screens).

Of great interest is the **Queen's Film Theatre**, University Square Mews, Tel 244857, which is attached to the university and situated on Queen's campus. It shows an excellent mixture of classic, modern, foreign and art films and recent programmes have shown directors such as David Lynch, Costa-Gavras, Martin Scorsese and a Woody Allen season.

BOOKSTORES

The best are **Dillon's** at 44/46 Fountain Street, Tel 240159 and **Waterstone's** at 8 Royal Avenue, Tel 247355. There is also a very good selection (general as well as academic) at the **University Bookshop**, 91 University Road, Tel 662552. Local bookshops worth a browse are **Stewart Miller Ltd**, 97 High Street, Holywood, Tel 428725, **Harry Hall**, 39 Gresham Street, Tel 241923, **Grahams** at 573 Antrim Road, Tel 776632 and **Gavin Smyth**, 245 Lisburn Road, Tel 668033. Children's books can be found at **Familybooks**, Fisherwick Place, Tel 321323, and **EDCO**, 47–49 Queen Street, Tel 324687. Books on religion are best at **APCK Book Centre**, Belfast Cathedral, Donegal Street, Tel 244825, **Bethel Bookshop** close by at 3 Donegal Square East, Tel 439525, **Christian Book Room**, 49 Belmont Road, Tel 653718, **Christian Bookshop**, 40 Gregagh Road, Tel 450335, **Methodist Book Room**, Aldersgate House, University Road, Tel 320078 and **Scripture Union**, 157 Albenbridge Road, Tel 454806. There is an **HMSO** branch at 80 Chichester Street, Tel 238451. For comics, fantasy, science fiction et al, try **Talisman** at 36/37 Smithfield Market, Tel 438744 and **Dark Horizon**, 30A Chichester Street, Tel 233808. Finally, good bargain books at (not surprisingly) **Bargain Books**, 15 North Street and 19 Royal Avenue, Tel 325425 and 247320.

ANTIQUARIAN AND SECONDHAND BOOKS

The best antiquarian selections are at **J A Gamble**, 539 Antrim Road, Tel 370798, **P and B Rowan**, 92 Malone Road, Tel 666448, **Ryan Roma Books and Prints**, 92 Malone Road, Tel 242777 and **Antiquarian Booksellers**, 93 Dulin Road, Shaftesbury Square, Tel 245787. Secondhand collections can be found at **Bookfinders**, 47 University Road, Tel 328269, **Volume One**, 45 Winetavern Street, **Leaves Bookshop**, 84A Stranmillis Road, Tel 664600, **World of Books**, 329 Woodstock Road, Tel 454272, and **Emerald Isle Books**, 539 Antrim Road, Tel 370798 (by appointment). There's even a Christian secondhand bookshop called the **Evangelical Book Shop** at 15 College Square East, Tel 320529, which is perhaps not indirectly related to the fact that Belfast has more religious bookshops for its size than any town I've come across.

ART GALLERIES

Arts Council Gallery – 16 Bedford Street, Tel 321402, has continuing exhibitions of contemporary art as well as a good bookshop. The **Bell Gallery**, 13 Adelaide Park, Tel 662998, specializes in the work of Irish artists and also has a good selection of contemporary graphics as well as engravings, sculptures and bronzes.

Tom Caldwell Gallery – 40–42 Bradbury Place, Tel 3233226, has one of the best collections of work by living Irish artists in the city, while the **Cavehill Gallery**, 18 Old Cavehill Road, Tel 776784, has a good collection on the same subject, as does the **Eakin Gallery** at 237 Lisburn Road, Tel 668522, although the artists displayed here are more likely to be established rather than unknown. The **Kerlin Gallery**, 199 Botanic Avenue, has a good collection of the work of contemporary artists, and also an accessory shop, while **John Magee** at 455 Ormeau Road, Tel 693830, deals in the work of established painters. **Roma** at 73 Dublin Road, Tel 242777, has an interesting collection of antique prints and maps while the **Ormonde Gallery** at 193 Upper Lisburn Road, Tel 301613, has contemporary original art and prints. **Sheldon Galleries** at 43 Great Victoria Street, Tel 330077, has a wide selection of contemporary and general prints as befits a business with four outlets in the city and **Scenes** also has modern prints with some limited-edition lithographs. They are at 2 North Street Arcade, Tel 247878. Finally, **Arches Art Gallery**, 2 Holywood Road, Tel 459031 (oils and watercolours), the **Eimear Gallery**, 110 Donegal Pass, Tel 231377 (Irish art) and Laganside Galleries, 35/37 Queen Square, Tel 439851, round off one of the better collections of art galleries of any city.

ANTIQUE DEALERS

There are antique markets at **St George's Variety Market**, 119 May Street, Tel 324712 (Tues and Fri 7am–2pm), and **Grate Expectations Antique Market**, 145 Donegal Pass, Tel 223244. The best place to start is, in fact, in Donegal Pass which is off Shaftesbury Square just to the south of the city centre. Here you will find a large collection of interesting shops. **Past and Present** at No 58, Tel 333137, has furniture, porcelain and prints; at No 64, **Country House Antiques**, Tel 244568, has Irish pine and French Provincial furniture. At No 126 is **Alexander the Grate**, Tel 232041, with, not surprisingly, fireplaces and architectural fittings. At the same location and telephone is **Belfast Antique Market** with stamps, coins, porcelain and clocks. At No 135 is **Dara Antiques**, Tel 248144 with furniture, silver, clocks and porcelain, while at No 137 is **Oakland Antiques**, Tel 230176, with furniture, silver, bric-à-brac, clothes, jewellery and, of course, fireplaces at **Grate Expectations**, Tel 230088. There is also an auction the first Thursday in the month at 7:30pm (viewing Tues, Wed, Thurs 10am–7pm). A Belfast auction is something you certainly shouldn't miss. The most likely locations are as follows: **Anderson's Auction Rooms** – 28 Linenhall Street, Tel 321401. Auctions generally Wednesdays at 1am. Viewing on Tuesdays. They also have fine art, furniture, furnishings and jewellery for sale Monday to Friday.

Grays Antiques and Fine Art Auction Rooms – Owen O'Cork Mills, 288 Beersbridge Road, Tel 456404. Auctions every two weeks on Tuesdays. Viewing Sunday 2–5pm, Monday 10am–9pm and 10am on day of sale. They also have special quarterly picture sales.

Kennedy Wolfenden – 218 Lisburn Road, Tel 381775. Several fine art auctions yearly. Furniture, paintings, silver, glass, porcelain and jewellery in showroom.

Morgan's Auctions – Suite 6, Duncrue Crescent, Tel 771552. Weekly auctions of fine art and furniture Tuesdays at 11am. Viewing Monday 9am–6pm.

John Ross – 37 Montgomery Street, Tel 325448. Fine art auctions every month on the third Thursday. Viewing Wednesday 9am–9pm.

Alexander Spence Ltd – 79 Great Victoria Street, Tel 322734. Auctions of furniture, furnishings and paintings every week on Fridays at 11am. Viewing Thursday 9:30am–5:30pm. Also **Antiques and Collectables Fairs**, Mayfield Leisure Centre, East Bridge Street. Inquiries Tel 0238 528428. They have showings of jewellery, silver, postcards, porcelain, glass, linen, bric-à-brac and general collectables the first Saturday of each month from 10:30–4pm.

Stamps and coins can be found at **Antiquarian**, 30 Smithfield Market, Winetavern Street, Tel 327301. They also have swords, guns, jewellery and first editions. More stamps and coins at **William Rodman**, 83 Dublin road, Tel 240052, and **The Stamp Shop**, 11 Victoria Street, Tel 231954. The rest of the recommended antique shops are listed below together with their specializations:

Munns – 531 Lisburn Road, Tel 381057. Antique pine furniture, bric-à-brac, baskets and rugs.

Balmoral Antiques – 661 Lisburn Road, Tel 665221. Linen, jewellery and general items.

Janet Clarke – 338 Woodstock Road, Tel 738577. Paintings, Victorian dishes, oil lamps, china and second-hand books.

Fortwilliam Antiques – 270 Antrim Road, Tel 743551. Furniture, paintings, silver and jewellery. By appointment.

John and Charlotte Lambe – 41 Shore Road, Tel 370761. Furniture.

Fred J Malcolm – at 18 Chichester Street, Tel 321491, and 74 Botanic Avenue, Tel 226793 – good collections of jewellery.

Mews Antiques – 38A Newington Street, Tel 751319. Fireplaces and books.

Sinclairs Antique Gallery – 19 Arthur Street, Tel 322335. Silver plate and jewellery.

RESTAURANTS

Nick's Warehouse – 35–39 Hill Street, Tel 439690. A wine bar downstairs and a restaurant upstairs works well in this conversion of an old warehouse and the eccentric opening hours make it good for a pre-theatre supper. The cooking is lively and the service good with fillets of sole with chili and ginger sauce, and lamb cutlets with port and redcurrants being especially well-spoken of. Interesting food too in the wine bar section, especially the Turkish almond dip with pitta bread. Inexpensive wine list. Open Mon–Fri 12–3pm and 5–6:30pm.

The Strand – 12 Stranmillis Road, Tel 682266. A friendly bistro style restaurant, which can get very full so booking is a good idea. Good honest cooking with lots of imagination – plaice in a peanut and breadcrumb coating for example. Food and wine remarkably reasonable and good value. Open all week noon–11pm.

La Belle Epoque – 103 Great Victoria Street, Tel 323244. A popular French restaurant with a pleasing ambience and excellent service. Local ingredients are extensively used and I have had good reports about the lobster and the pheasant. Not expensive for the quality of the cooking. Open Mon–Sat 6pm–midnight.

Manor House – 47 Donegal Pass, Tel 238755. Friendly atmosphere and excellent Cantonese cooking. There are the usual spare ribs and king prawns but the stuffed scallops are delightfully different and there are sizzling steaks and hot pots. The dim sum is a must for daytime eating. Open all week noon–11:30pm.

Ashoka – 363/365 Lisburn Road, Tel 660362. Traditional Indian cooking with rogans, tikkas and masalas especially good. Vegetarian food is always available and there is an excellent business set lunch. According to the restaurant's advertising, the pianist Peter Donohue and Derek Bell of the Chieftains loved the food.

CROWN BAR, BELFAST

PUBS

The Crown Liquor Saloon – 46 Great Victoria Street, Tel 249976. Beloved of that great lover of things Victorian, John Betjeman, the Crown is one place in Belfast that is *not* to be missed. It is quite simply one of the finest examples of High Victorian Art left intact in the world. Built in the late 1800s by Michael Flannagan, its design was influenced by Flannagan's travels in Spain and Italy, which prompted him to build the ultimate architectural fantasy of the day, complete with walled-off "snugs" where "serious drinkers can hoist their pints in contented privacy." If you are there at lunch or supper, try the Irish champ – it's a wondrous mix of mashed potatoes and scallions served with pork or savoury sausages. The Irish stew is also very good.

Lavery's – 12 Bradbury Place, Tel 327159. A one time "gin palace" which has considerable atmosphere and a range of clientele you'll find it hard to believe. Some have called the pub a dim atmospheric dungeon but I assure you you won't forget your visit in a hurry. Traditional bar food. Open 12–5pm and 12:30–2pm Sundays.

White's Tavern – Winecellar Entry, Tel 243080. The city's oldest pub, full of atmosphere and "characters." All kinds of food from steaks through lasagne to salads. They have excellent jazz on Wednesdays.

Kelly's Cellars – 30 Bank Street, Tel 324835. This was a haunt of the United Irishmen who rebelled in 1798. You can get grills, *et al*, upstairs and pub grub and oysters in the bar. They have live traditional music most nights.

Atmospheric dock pubs are: **Rotterdam Bar**, 54 Pilot Street, Tel 746102, which does sandwiches and very filling stews, and has live traditional music; and **Sunflower Bar**, 60 Corporation Street, which has a wonderful Ulster fry (a variation of Irish champ) and often has folk music. Finally, other musical pubs in the city centre are **Duke of York**, 1 Commercial Court, Tel 241062 and **Front Page**, 106 Donegal Street which has excellent prawns in garlic, haddock mornay and a not-to-be-missed oyster pie. Both pubs have live traditional music.

ARTISTIC ASSOCIATIONS

Dr William Drennan founded the Belfast Academical Institution and was also the first president of the United Irishmen. As a poet he is best remembered as the first to call Ireland the "Emerald Isle" in a poem of 1795. Novelist Anthony Trollope was a surveyor for the Post Office and was sent to Belfast in 1853 to take postal charge of the northern counties. While in Belfast he completed *The Warden*, the first of the Barsetshire novels, and the first of his novels to meet with success. Poets Louis MacNeice and Seamus Heaney were both born in Belfast, as was C S Lewis, perhaps best known for *The Screwtape Letters* and *Out of the Silent Planet* as well as his wonderful books for children, *The Chronicles of Narnia*.

In Hillsborough, a village on the southern outskirts of Belfast, Sir Hamilton Harty, the composer, was born in 1880. He conducted the Hallé Orchestra in Manchester and his music is at present undergoing a well-deserved revival. On the northeastern outskirts of Belfast is the ancient small port of Carrickfergus. There is a splendid Norman castle, and in 1678 the future Restoration dramatist, William Congreve, who was eight, came to live in the castle as his father was a soldier posted there. Even at this early age, Congreve was storing up impressions for the future. Sailor Ben, a character in *Love for Love* is thought to be based on one of the "rough and jovial sailors" Congreve met while in the town. Jonathan Swift, author of *Gulliver's Travels*, was granted the living of nearby Kilroot in 1695. He wrote his celebrated poem *A Tale of a Tub* while a resident of the village.

In 1856, John Lavery (later Sir John Lavery) was born at 47 North Queen Street where his father owned a spirits store. His parents died when he was three and he unhappily spent his boyhood with various relatives before entering the Glasgow School of Art in 1876 and becoming a leading member of the group of painters known as the "Glasgow Boys" (see Glasgow). Although a Catholic, Lavery's attitude towards politics was always a conciliatory one. In 1917 he presented a triptych of the Madonna and Child with St Brigid (a work for which members of his family posed) to St Patrick's Catholic Church in Donegal Street, where he was baptized. At the same time he presented the city's Protestant community with the original study for his Royal Portrait Group of four years earlier. Nor did his Catholic upbringing prevent him from painting the *Orangemen's Parade*, one of his finest works. In 1935, he was made an honorary LLD of Queen's University, Belfast and was given the freedom of the city.

The landscape painter, Paul Henry, born the son of the Baptist minister of Great Victoria Street Church, was less able to reconcile the sectarian conflict in the city. As a young man he fell in love with a fellow art student, Mary McCracken, at the Government School of Design. Mary was a passionate nationalist, and Henry, who had little interest in politics, involved himself in the nationalist movement for Mary's sake. In 1896 there was a militant nationalist procession, which ended in violence. Shaken and deeply depressed, Paul Henry left the city almost immediately for Paris and never again lived in Ulster.

The present troubles in Ulster have of course found expression in its art. Deborah Brown, who specializes in delicate fibreglass constructions, uses barbed wire in some of her studies, and T P Flanagan, known for his freely painted landscapes, makes repeated use of glacial imagery. The most powerful images of violence inspired by the Ulster situation are F E McWilliam's sculptures, entitled *Women of Belfast*. These works, portraying single figures caught either in cross-fire or bomb blasts, can be seen in the Ulster Museum.

My own favourite Belfast painter is one whose work and career seem most closely tied to the city, William Conor, who lived most of his life in Belfast. Born in 1881, he trained at the Belfast School of Art and then sought to make a living by painting portraits, but he was never very successful in obtaining commissions. The son of a gas fitter, he had a special sympathy for the Belfast working class whose lives provided him with the subjects of his best and most characteristic works. The Ulster Folk and Transport Museum has excellent examples of his work.

EPHEMERA

The pretty flax plant, from which linen is made, may soon be seen again in Northern Ireland after a gap of more than 30 years. Linen exports have been on the increase recently, mainly to Japan and Italy for high-fashion garments, but all flax has had to be imported for processing. A hundred years ago, 240,000 acres (97,000 ha) were given over to flax growing and as early as 1787 the province had nearly 400 bleach greens, where the woven linen was spread on the grass to bleach in the weather. When the agriculturalist Arthur Young visited in the 1770s he was dismayed by the size of the linen industry. He thought it had destroyed the country's agriculture. "A whole province peopled by weavers," he said in dismay. While agriculturalists today do not expect the growing of flax to be anything like that of 1787, the flax plant on the reverse of the Northern Ireland £1 coin may become more than just nostalgia.

Curiosity about their ancestry brings many people to Northern Ireland. The North American connection is especially strong. However you look at it, the Ulster contribution to the foundation and development of early America seems to have been disproportionately great for such a small country. About 250,000 emigrants took a one-way ticket to America in the 18th century. Five of them signed the Declaration of Independence in 1776. At least a dozen US presidents have had Ulster ancestry. They include Andrew Jackson, hero of the Battle of New Orleans, Ulysses S Grant, commander of the Union Army, and Woodrow Wilson. Other Americans with Ulster roots include Davy Crockett, Sam Houston, who avenged the Alamo, the writer Mark Twain, and Neil Armstrong, the first man on the moon. Genealogy is one of Northern Ireland's growth industries and although most people's ancestors were neither famous nor especially brave, thousands come to trace their roots in libraries or in dusty parish offices. The American connection is still strong today and outside City Hall there is an obelisk commemorating the arrival of the first US troops in Europe – in Northern Ireland in January 1942.

It is hard to pinpoint when the dreadful schism between the Protestants and Roman

Catholics of Northern Ireland first started. The roots of the problem are so deeply embedded in history that it is hard for anyone outside of the province to understand the difficulties and perhaps not many within do so either.

Had it not been for the Reformation it is possible that there might have been a united Ireland today. In 1601, after the Battle of Kinsale, the Irish chiefs left the north and it was handed over to settlers, mostly from Protestant Scotland. Matters were not helped during the Civil War when Cromwell massacred the best part of the populations of Drogheda and Wexford. In 1690, James II made a last stand for Catholic Ireland but he lost at the Battle of the Boyne to William of Orange, a victory still celebrated in some areas today, and soon Roman Catholics were deprived of most of their political and educational rights. Throughout the 18th century repercussions from the American War of Independence and the French Revolution fed the idea of Irish independence. In spite of the fact that Irish Catholics could not sit in the English Parliament if elected, changes were on the way – but any sense that these more liberal ideas would be implemented without violence were put an end to by the great famine in the middle of the 19th century. The suffering was exacerbated by the mismanagement of absent landlords and the famine caused a wave of emigration that reduced the population by 25 percent. The republican movements, strongly supported by Irish emigrants in America, culminated in the Easter Rising of 1916. The repercussions of this event, and a stubborn policy of guerrilla warfare, so harassed the forces of the English Crown that in 1921 the English Prime Minister, David Lloyd George, negotiated a truce conceding dominion status to the Irish Free State, which in 1949 became the Republic of Eire. The agreement also stated that the six counties of Northern Ireland should not be forced to join and could remain under the protection of the British Crown.

The violence, bloodshed and misery caused by the schism between Roman Catholics and Protestants in Northern Ireland continue to this day. A complete book would be needed to give any sense of the reasons for the conflict. Without being simplistic however, I think there are five categories of people who make up the conflict in Northern Ireland.

First, and central to the problem, are the Northern Protestants of the six counties. Internal differences apart, they are generally united in not wanting to share an Irish nationality with the rest of Ireland.

Secondly, there are the inhabitants of the rest of Ireland, predominantly Catholic, who live in their own sovereign state but without the northern six counties.

Thirdly, there are the Catholic inhabitants of Northern Ireland, who do not live in that sovereign state but among Northern Protestants in a province ruled by Britain. They not only live in a society dominated by a Protestant majority but there are good reasons to believe that they have been treated in an inequitable fashion over the past 70 years.

Fourthly, there are those, both in Eire and in Northern Ireland, who wish to merge the Protestant-dominated north with the Irish sovereign state by any means up to and including violence: the Irish Republican Army.

Finally, caught in the middle by a strange leftover of history, there is the British government.

At present the situation seems to be insoluble. Even as I write, the latest round of talks between the various parties is on the verge of collapse. Not because of any difference of opinion but because various factions cannot agree where to meet for the first time! Perhaps these or future talks will bring a political solution. The impact of the EEC, together with the affluence that could ultimately come with the fuller European union ratified by Ireland and France in 1992 but rejected in Denmark and now in doubt, would probably encourage mutual tolerance. But it will not be easy.

Meanwhile the much-publicized violence remains localized and visitors to Northern Ireland, while seeing evidence of it, need not be affected by it. There still remains a countryside of tranquil lakes and mountains, of ancient castles and quiet villages and of soft-spoken friendly people whose droll sense of humour indicates that the present crisis must somehow be overcome by common sense in the end.

To end on a happier note; while you are visiting the Ulster Museum in the Botanic Gardens, take time to see the Palm House and Tropical Ravine which are close by. The Palm House, begun in 1839, is older than the Great Palm House at Kew Gardens in London. Coffee, bananas and cotton plants grow in this splendid curvilinear glass-and-cast-iron conservatory. The Tropical Ravine, or Fernery, completed in 1886, is a fine example of horticultural Victoriana. The plants grow in a sunken glen overlooked by a balcony.

TOURIST INFORMATION BUREAU: River House, High Street, Belfast, County Antrim, N Ireland BT1 2DS. Tel (0232) 246609

SOURCES

BOOKS

Note: An asterisk indicates books of special interest.

TOPOGRAPHY

Great Britain
A.A. Town Tours in Britain. Reader's Digest Press.*
Birnbaum's Great Britain (Birnbaum). Houghton Mifflin.
Blue Guide: Victorian Architecture in Britain. A and C Black.
Book of British Villages, The. Automobile Association Publications.
Cambridge Illustrated History of British Heritage, The (Isaac and Mont, eds.).
    Cambridge University Press.
Exploring British Cities (Braithwaite). A and C Black.
500 Mile Walkies (Wallington). Arrow.
Historic Houses, Castles and Gardens of Great Britain and Ireland (Alcock, ed.).
    British Leisure Publications.
Journey Through Britain (Hillaby). Paladin.
Kingdom by the Sea (Theroux). Penguin.*
Michelin Red Guide: Great Britain. Michelin Publications.
Ordnance Survey Leisure Guides (by County or Region). Jarrold.*
Places to Visit in Britain. Automobile Association Publications.
Reader's Digest Discovering Britain. Reader's Digest Press.
Secret Britain (Wood). Cassell.*
Treasures of Britain. Automobile Association Publications.*

England and Wales
Blue Guide: Churches and Chapels of Northern England. A and C Black.*
Blue Guide: Churches and Chapels of Southern England. A and C Black.*
Blue Guide: Gardens of England. A and C Black.
Blue Guide: Wales. A and C Black.
Buildings of England and Wales (by Country) (Pevsner). Penguin.*
Everybody's Historic England (Kiek). Quiller Press.
Guide to the Abbeys of England and Wales. Constable Press.
Guide to the Castles of England and Wales. Constable Press.
Historic Cities of England. Pevensey Press.
Short Walks in English Towns (Frank). Weidenfeld.
Traveller's Guide to Medieval England, The (Platt). Secker and Warburg.

Scotland
Blue Guide: Scotland. A and C Black.*
Guide to the Abbeys of Scotland. Constable Press.
John Prebble's Scotland (Prebble). Secker and Warburg.
Michelin Green Guide: Scotland. Michelin Publications.
Ordnance Survey Leisure Guides (by Region). Jarrold.*
A Traveller's Guide to Historic Scotland. Phillip Crowl Contemporary Books.
Wainwright in Scotland (Wainwright). Michael Joseph.*

Northern Ireland
Intelligent Traveller's Guide to Historic Ireland, The. Phillip Crowl Contemporary Books.*
Ireland, a History (Kee). Weidenfeld and Nicolson.*
Ireland. Fodor's Travel Publications.
Ireland Revisited (Uris). Doubleday.
Ordnance Survey Leisure Guides; Ireland. Jarrold.*

London
Best of London, The (Evans). Prentice Hall.
Companion Guide to London, The (Piper). Collins.*
Fodor's London Companion (Nicholson). Fodor Travel Publications.
London; A Definitive Guide (Nicholson). The Bodley Head.*
London Dossier (Deighton). Cape.
London; Places and Pleasures (Simon). Putnam.
London Walks (Powell). Holt, Reinhart and Winston.

HISTORICAL TOPOGRAPHY
A Tour through the Whole Island of Great Britain (Defoe). Penguin.*
Illustrated Journeys of Celia Fiennes 1685–1712. Webb and Bower.*

ACCOMMODATIONS
British Selection, The (Eperon). Pan Books/A.A. Publications.*
Charming Small Hotels in Britain and Ireland (Gill, ed.). Duncan Peterson.
Egon Ronay's Guide to Hotels and Restaurants. A.A. Publications.
England on $50 a Day. Porter Prentice–Hall.
Good Bed and Breakfast Guide, The. Hodder and Stoughton (Consumers' Assoc.).*
Johansen's Recommended Country Inns and Restaurants. Johansen's Publishing.
Johansen's Recommended Hotels. Johansen's Publishing.
Recommended Country Hotels of Britain (Williams, ed.). F.H.G. Publications.
Recommended Wayside Inns of Great Britain (Williams, ed.). F.H.G. Publications.
The 'Which' Hotel Guide. Hodder and Stoughton (Consumers' Assoc.).*

RESTAURANTS
Ackermen-Martel Guide, The. A.A Publications (also hotels).
A Guide to Eating, Drinking and Sleeping on the Waterfront (Hart-Davis, ed.). Fontana.
Best of Vegetarian Britain, The (Brown). Thorson's Publishing.
Eat, Drink and Sleep Smoke-Free (Mooney, ed.). Headway Books.*
Good Food Guide, The (Jaine, ed.). Hodder and Stoughton (Consumers' Assoc. – published yearly).*
Out to Eat (Carter, ed.). Hodder and Stoughton (Consumers' Assoc.).*
Vegetarian Good Food Guide, The (Whittet, ed.). Hodder and Stoughton (Consumers' Assoc.).*

PUBS
Classic Town Pubs (Hanson). Pavilion.
Good Beer Guide, The (Daniels, ed.). A.A. Publications.
Good Pub Guide, The (Aird, ed.). Ebury Press.*
Historic English Inns (Coysh). David and Charles.

MUSEUMS
Times Museums and Galleries Guide, The (Tate, ed.). Times Publishing.*

THEATRES
Contacts; Theatres and Arts Centres in Britain. The Spotlight (publishers).

ART GALLERIES
The Artist's Directory (Waddell and Layzell, eds.). A and C Black.

TAPES AND CDs
Good C.D. Guide, The. Gramophone Publications.

ANTIQUES
Guide to the Antique Shops of Britain (Adams, ed.). Antique Collectors Club.*

EPHEMERA AND ARTISTIC ASSOCIATIONS
Astonishing Britain (Burton). David and Charles.
Atlas of Magical Britain (Bord and Bord). Sidgwick and Jackson.
Britain's Haunted Heritage (Brookes). Jarrold.
English Eccentrics (Sitwell). Vanguard.
Folk Heroes of Britain (Kighly). Thames and Hudson.
Insider's England (Timpson). Jarrold.*
Literary Britain (Brandt). Aperture Foundation.
Timpson's Towns (Timpson). Jarrold.*
Undiscovered Britain and Ireland (Burton). David and Charles.

CLASSICAL MUSIC STORES

Note: I was to have included in this book a section on the best places to buy recorded classical music (CDs, cassettes and records). Space considerations made this impossible to do in detail, but below is a list of recommended retailers throughout the country.

South West

Bath	Bath Compact Discs, 6 Broad Street, Tel 464766
Bristol	Pastoral Music, 11 Christmas Steps, Tel 273936
Exeter	Opus Classical Music, 14A Guildhall Shopping Centre, Tel 214044
Plymouth	Amadeus Classical Records, 17 Frankford Gate, Tel 671992
Salisbury	The Collector's Room (at Sutton Music Centre), 3 Endless Street, Tel 326153

South

Brighton	The Classical Longplayer, 31 Duke Street, Tel 29534
Canterbury	The Classical Longplayer, 6 Street Peter's Street, Tel 768888
Cheltenham	Good Music, 26 Winchcombe Street, Tel 239793
Chichester	Bastow's Classics, 50 North Street, Tel 533264
Guildford	Sound Barrier Compact Disc Centre, 24 Tunsgate Shopping Centre, Tel 300947
Oxford	Record House, 217 Banbury Road, Tel 513350

Portsmouth	Orpheus, 27 Marmion Road, Tel 812397
Winchester	Caruso's, St. George Street, Tel 842383
London	Farringdon Records, 52/54 High Holborn, Tel 071 2482816

The East

Cambridge	Cambridge Classical Records, 6A King's Parade, Tel 350565
Colchester	Howard Leach Classical Records, 49 Crouch Street, Tel 574189
Ipswich	Amberstone Bookshop, 49 Upper Orwell Street, Tel 250675
Norwich	Prelude Records, 9 St. Giles Street, Tel 628319

Wales

Cardiff	Cardiff City Radio, 27A Morgan Arcade, Tel 228169

West Midlands

Birmingham	Dillons, 116 New Street, Tel 6314333
Coventry/	
Warwick	University Bookshop (Warwick University Arts Centre – see Coventry Theatre), Tel 524524

East Midlands

Leicester	St. Martin's Records, Unit 2, 23 Hotel Street, Tel 539292
Northampton	Spinadisc Records, 75A Abington Street, Tel 31144
Nottingham	Classical CD, 27 Heathcote, Tel 483832

The North

Chester	Chester Compact Disc Centre, 18 Paddock Row, Tel 311991
Harrogate	Adagio Classical Records, 6 Westminster Arcade Parliament Street, Tel 506507
Lancaster	Kenneth Gardner Ltd, 28 New Street, Tel 64328
Leeds	The Classical Record Shop, 2 Merrion Centre, Tel 452059
Liverpool	Circle Records, 33–35 Victoria Street, Tel 2361000
Manchester	HMV, 21 Market Street, Arndale Centre, Tel 8349920
Newcastle	Windows of the Arcade, 1–7 Central Arcade, Tel 2328765
York	Banks and Son, 18 Lendal, Tel 658836

Scotland

Edinburgh	James Thin, 53/59 South Bridge, Tel 5566743
Glasgow	James Kerr and Co, 98–110 Woodlands Road, Tel 8848439
Perth	Concorde, 15 Scott Street, Tel 21818

Northern Ireland

Belfast	Classical Tracks, 15A Castle Arcade, Tel 333868

ABOUT THE AUTHOR

David Kemp was born in England and trained as an actor at the Central School of Speech and Drama, where two of his classmates were Julie Christie and Lynn Redgrave. At the tender age of 36, he emigrated to Canada to teach at Queen's University in Kingston, Ontario. He is now head of the Drama Department at Queen's and divides his time between his home in Kingston and a rambling 18th-century house just outside Bath in England.

David Kemp continues to work as an actor on both sides of the Atlantic. Recent roles include Alfred P. Doolittle in *My Fair Lady,* Tevye in *Fiddler on the Roof,* the King of France in *All's Well That Ends Well* (for the Nanaimo Festival) and Harry in *Sleuth*. He is probably best known as the writer and director of *Have Some Madeira M'Dear,* an entertainment based on the songs of Michael Flanders and Donald Swann, which he performed in seasons at the Thousand Islands Playhouse, the Morrisburg Festival and at Shakespeare Plus in British Columbia.

Internationally, his one-man show, *A Child Growing Up,* has been performed in 36 countries around the world, ranging from Nepal to El Salvador and including Australia, Egypt, France, Colombia and Israel as well as across Canada, the USA and in the United Kingdom. He has directed plays in Denmark, Sri Lanka, Bermuda, England and Egypt. His books have been translated into Swedish, Sinhalla and Arabic.

As an actor, lecturer and traveller, David Kemp has visited more than 50 countries around the world, so there can be hardly anyone more qualified to write a book that could be read by people of many different nationalities. He has also had an interesting career in journalism. Besides being a regular book reviewer for a number of journals and newspapers, he has served as a drama critic for the *Bath Chronicle* in England and for 10 years has been film critic for a Kingston, Ontario, newspaper. He has written articles on such wide-ranging subjects as travel, cricket and food. Perhaps the term "Renaissance man" has been devalued in recent times, but it is hard not to apply it to David Kemp in its best sense.

The Pleasures and Treasures of Britain is an insider's view of the artistic mosaic of the United Kingdom. Quirky, eclectic and entertaining, the book is written by a man who has lived fully and long on both sides of the Atlantic . Although his dual citizenship may suggest that David Kemp is a citizen of Great Britain and Canada, it could quite easily be argued that he is indeed a citizen of the world.

READER'S RECOMMENDATION FORM

Town:
Recommendations:

Town:
Recommendations:

Town:
Recommendations:

Town:
Recommendations:

Town:
Recommendations:

Sender's Name:
Sender's Address:

Send to: David Kemp
                Dundurn Press Limited
                2181 Queen Street East, Suite 301
                Toronto, Ontario, Canada
                M4E 1E5

READER'S RECOMMENDATION FORM

Town:
Recommendations:

Town:
Recommendations:

Town:
Recommendations:

Town:
Recommendations:

Town:
Recommendations:

Sender's Name:
Sender's Address:

Send to: David Kemp
                    Dundurn Press Limited
                    2181 Queen Street East, Suite 301
                    Toronto, Ontario, Canada
                    M4E 1E5

READER'S RECOMMENDATION FORM

Town:
Recommendations:

Town:
Recommendations:

Town:
Recommendations:

Town:
Recommendations:

Town:
Recommendations:

Sender's Name:
Sender's Address:

Send to: David Kemp
                  Dundurn Press Limited
                  2181 Queen Street East, Suite 301
                  Toronto, Ontario, Canada
                  M4E 1E5